American Literary Scholarship

An Annual / 1973

Edited by James Woodress

Essays by Walter Harding, Nina Baym, G. R. Thompson, Hershel Parker, Bernice Slote, Hamlin Hill, William T. Stafford, James B. Meriwether, Jackson R. Bryer, J. A. Leo Lemay, M. Thomas Inge, Warren French, James H. Justus, Richard Crowder, Linda W. Wagner, Walter J. Meserve, John T. Flanagan, Michael J. Hoffman, Jean Rivière, Hans Galinsky, Rolando Anzilotti, Akiko Miyake, Rolf Lundén

Duke University Press, Durham, North Carolina, 1975

 Library of Congress Catalogue Card number 65–19450. I.S.B.N. 0–8223–0338–8. Printed in the United States of America by Heritage Printers, Inc.

Foreword

This volume begins the second decade of *American Literary Scholarship*, and with this volume there is a changing of the guard in editors. J. Albert Robbins, who has edited *ALS* ably for the past five years, has turned the project back to the original editor. Among contributors there has been a loyal continuity, as 14 of the writers for *ALS 1972* have supplied essays for the current volume. The new editor wishes to thank both Professor Robbins and the 14 continuing contributors for helping make the transition in editors painless. He also thanks the four new contributors for their part in the joint effort.

The first volume of *ALS* was 224 pages in length. The volume for 1972, which appeared one year ago, ran to 448 pages. This volume is even larger, and it seems clear that the economics of publishing will not allow *ALS* to grow much larger. The clear inference of these figures is that the amount of scholarly activity during the past decade has increased steadily. There are more places to publish, and more material finds its way into print. Beginning with the next volume of *ALS* it will be necessary to demand more rigorous selectivity by the contributors and the omission of material that makes minimal contributions to scholarship. The complaints that Professor Robbins listed in his foreword last year of careless, inept, tasteless, and repetitive scholarship still are valid.

There are some changes and innovations in the present volume. Poe has been moved to a separate chapter instead of being lumped with other minor nineteenth-century poets, and this will continue as long as the minor poets fail to attract much academic attention. T. S. Eliot appears for the first time in the chapter on American poetry from 1900 to the 1930s, and next year there will be a separate chapter on Eliot and Pound. Finally, in an effort to take note of the considerable amount of American literary scholarship done outside the United States, a final chapter on foreign contributions to American literary scholarship has been added.

For next year, in addition to the Eliot-Pound chapter mentioned above, there will be other changes. The time has come to divide twentieth-century into three segments to lighten the load on the two contributors who have until now covered between them fiction from 1900 to the present. Thus there will be three chapters on twentieth-century fiction next year divided roughly as follows: 1900 to the 1930s, from the 1930s to the 1950s, from the 1950s to the present. In addition, a chapter on black writers will be added, and this innovation will eliminate the fragmentation that this growing topic has undergone in *ALS* in recent years.

The contributors to the 1974 volume are as follows, and books and offprints should be sent directly to the appropriate person—not to the general editor.

In all cases addresses in care of the Department of English:

1. Emerson, Thoreau, and Transcendentalism: Lawrence Buell, Oberlin College, Oberlin, Ohio 44074

2. Hawthorne: Nina Baym, Univ. of Illinois, Urbana, Ill. 61801

3. Poe: G. R. Thompson, Purdue Univ., Lafayette, Ind. 47907

4. Melville: Hershel Parker, Univ. of Southern California, Los Angeles, Calif. 90007

5. Whitman and Dickinson: Bernice Slote, Univ. of Nebraska, Lincoln, Nebr. 68508

6. Mark Twain: Hamlin Hill, Univ. of Chicago, Chicago, Ill. 60637

7. Henry James: William T. Stafford, Purdue Univ., Lafayette, Ind. 47907

8. Faulkner: James B. Meriwether, Univ. of South Carolina, Columbia, S.C. 29208

9. Fitzgerald-Hemingway: Jackson R. Bryer, Univ. of Maryland, College Park, Md. 20742

10. Literature to 1800: Robert D. Arner, Univ. of Cincinnati, Cincinnati, Ohio 45221

11. Nineteenth-Century Fiction: Warren French, Cornish Flat, N.H. 03746

12. Fiction—1900 to the 1930s: David Stouck, Simon Fraser Univ., Burnaby, B.C., Canada V5A 1S6

13. Fiction—1930s to the 1950s: Margaret O'Connor, Univ. of North Carolina, Chapel Hill, N.C. 27514

14. Fiction—1950s to the present: James H. Justus, Indiana Univ., Bloomington, Ind. 47401

15. Eliot and Pound: Richard M. Ludwig, Princeton Univ., Princeton, N.J. 08540

16. Poetry—1900 to the 1930s: Richard Crowder, Purdue Univ., Lafayette, Ind. 47907

17. Poetry—1930s to the Present: Linda Wagner, Michigan State Univ., East Lansing, Mich. 48823

18. Folklore: John T. Flanagan, Univ. of Illinois, Urbana, Ill. 61801

19. Drama: Jordan Y. Miller, Univ. of Rhode Island, Kingston, R.I. 02881

20. Black Literature: Charles Nilon, Univ. of Colorado, Boulder, Colo. 80302

21. Themes, Topics, and Criticism: Michael J. Hoffman, Univ. of California, Davis, Calif. 95616

James Woodress

University of California, Davis

Table of Contents

Part I

Part II

Key to Abbreviations

ABC / *American Book Collector*
A Dangerous Crossing / Richard Lehan, *A Dangerous Crossing: French Literary Existentialism and the Modern American Novel* (Carbondale, So. Ill. Univ. Press)
Aegis
AFF / *Annali Facoltà di Lingue e Letterature Straniere di Feltre*
AFS / *Abstracts of Folklore Studies*
Agora / *Agora: A Journal of the Humanities and Social Sciences*
AJ / *Appalachian Journal*
AL / *American Literature*
AlaR / *Alabama Review*
ALitASH / *Acta Litteraria Academiae Hungaricae* (Budapest)
ALR / *American Literary Realism, 1870–1910*
ALS / *American Literary Scholarship*
Althanor
American Free Verse / Walter Sutton, *American Free Verse: The Modern Revolution in Poetry* (Norfolk, Conn., New Directions)
American Short Story / Arthur Voss, *The American Short Story: A Critical Survey* (Norman, Okla., Univ. of Okla. Press)
Americana Norvegica / Brita Seyerstedt, ed., *Americana Norvegica: Norwegian Contributions to American Studies 4* (Oslo, Universitetsforloget)
AmerS / *American Studies*
AN&Q / *American Notes and Queries*
Anxiety of Influence / Harold Bloom, *The Anxiety of Influence: A Theory of Poetry* (New York, Oxford Univ. Press)
Apollo
Approaches to Poetics / Seymour Chatman, ed., *Approaches to Poetics: Selected Papers from the English Institute* (New York, Columbia Univ. Press)
Approdo / *L'Approdo Letterario* (Roma)
APR / *American Poetry Review*
AQ / *American Quarterly*
Arcadia
Archiv / *Archiv für das Studium der Neueren Sprachen und Literaturen*
Ariel / *Ariel: A Quarterly Review of the Arts and Sciences in Israel*
Arion (Univ. of Tex.)
ArQ / *Arizona Quarterly*
ASAIN / *American Studies: An International Newsletter*
ASch / *American Scholar*
ASLHM / *American Society of Legion of Honor Magazine*
ATQ / *American Transcendental Quarterly*
AW / *American West*
BA / *Books Abroad*
BB / *Bulletin of Bibliography*
BCCQN / *Book Club of California Quarterly Newsletter*
BI / *Books at Iowa*
BlackW / *Black World*
BNYPL / *Bulletin of the New York Public Library*
Boundary 2 (State Univ. of New York, Binghamton)
Bright Book of Life / Alfred Kazin, *Bright Book of Life: American Novelists and Storytellers from Hemingway to Mailer* (Boston, Atlantic-Little Brown)

BRMMLA / *Bulletin of the Rocky Mountain Modern Language Assn.*
BSUF / *Ball State University Forum*
BUJ / *Boston University Journal*
BuR / *Bucknell Review*
Caliban (Toulouse)
CALM / Calendars of American Literary Manuscripts
CE / *College English*
CEA / *CEA Critic* (College English Assn.)
CEAA / Center for Editions of American Authors
CentR / *The Centennial Review*
ChiR / *Chicago Review*
CimR / *Cimarron Review* (Okla. State Univ.)
Cithara (St. Bonaventure University
CL / *Comparative Literature*
CLAJ / *College Language Assn. Journal*
ClioW / *Clio: An Interdisciplinary Journal of Literature, History, and the Philosophy of History* (Univ. of Wisc.)
CLJ / *Cornell Library Journal*
CLQ / *Colby Library Quarterly*
CLS / *Comparative Literature Studies*
CM / *Carleton Miscellany*
ColQ / *Colorado Quarterly*
Comic Imagination / Louis D. Rubin, Jr., ed., *The Comic Imagination in American Literature* (New Brunswick, N.J., Rutgers Univ. Press)
Commentary
Commonweal
CompD / *Comparative Drama*
ConL / *Contemporary Literature*
ConP / *Contemporary Poetry* (Fairleigh Dickinson Univ.)
Costerus /*Costerus: Essays in English and American Language and Literature* (Amsterdam)
CP / *Concerning Poetry* (Western Wash. State College)
CQ / *The Cambridge Quarterly*
CR / *Critical Review* (Melbourne)
CRevAS / *Canadian Review of American Studies*
Crit / *Critique: Studies in Modern Fiction*
Criticism (Wayne State Univ.)
DAI / *Dissertation Abstracts International*
D&T / *Drama and Theatre*
Directions / Stanley Weintraub and Philip Young, eds., *Directions in Literary Criticism: Contemporary Approaches to Literature* (University Park, Pa. State Univ. Press)
DN / *Dreiser Newsletter*
DQR / *Dutch Quarterly Review of Anglo-American Letters*
DR / *Dalhousie Review*
DSI / *Doshisha Studies in English* (Japan)
EA / *Etudes Anglaises*
EAL / *Early American Literature*
ECr / *L'Esprit Créateur* (Lawrence, Kan.)
ECS / *Eighteenth-Century Studies*
EDB / *Emily Dickinson Bulletin*
Edda (Oslo)
EIC / *Essays in Criticism*
EIHC / *Essex Institute Historical Collections*
ELH / *ELH: Journal of English Literary History*
ELN / *English Language Notes*
Encounter (London)
EnlE / *Enlightenment Essays*
Epoch
ES / *English Studies*
ESQ / *Emerson Society Quarterly: A Journal of the American Renaissance* (Wash. State Univ.)
EST / Sencer Tonguç, ed., *English Studies Today*, 5th Ser. Acta of the 8th Conference of the International Association of University Professors of English (Istanbul, Matbaasi)
ETJ / *Educational Theatre Journal*
Expl / *Explicator*
Fabula / *Fabula: Zeitschrift für Erzählforschung* (Berlin)
Falcon (Mansfield, Pa. State College)
FCN / *Faulkner Concordance Newsletter*
FForum / *Folklore Forum*
FHA / *Fitzgerald-Hemingway Annual*
FHQ / *Florida Historical Quarterly*

FMLS / *Forum for Modern Language Studies* (St. Andrews Univ., Scotland)
FMod / *Filología Moderna* (Madrid)
FOB / *Flannery O'Connor Bulletin* (Ga. College, Milledgeville)
Folklore (London)
ForumH / *Forum* (Houston)
FQ / *Florida Quarterly*
GaR / *Georgia Review*
Genre
GHQ / *Georgia Historical Quarterly*
Gohdes Festschrift / James Woodress, ed., *Essays Mostly on Periodical Publishing in America: A Collection in Honor of Clarence Gohdes* (Durham, N.C., Duke Univ. Press)
HAB / *Humanities Assn. Bulletin* (Univ. of New Brunswick, Canada)
HC / *Hollins Critic*
HLB / *Harvard Library Bulletin*
HLQ / *Huntington Library Quarterly*
HMPEC / *Historical Magazine of the Protestant Episcopal Church*
HN / *Hemingway Notes*
HUS / *Hebrew University Studies* (Jerusalem)
ICarbS
IF / *Indiana Folklore*
IJSym / *International Journal on Symbolism*
IllQ / *Illinois Quarterly*
IMH / *Indiana Magazine of History*
IN / *Indiana Names*
InR / *Intercollegiate Review*
IowaR / *Iowa Review*
JA / *Jahrbuch für Amerikastudien*
JAAC / *Journal of Aesthetics and Art Criticism*
JAF / *Journal of American Folklore*
JAH / *Journal of American History*
JAmS / *Journal of American Studies*
JEGP / *Journal of English and Germanic Philology*
JEMFQ / *John Edwards Memorial Foundation Quarterly*
JFI / *Journal of the Folklore Institute*
JHBS / *Journal of the History of the Behaviour Sciences*
JHI / *Journal of the History of Ideas*
JMH / *Journal of Mississippi History*
JML / *Journal of Modern Literature*
JNT / *Journal of Narrative Technique*
JOFS / *Journal of the Ohio Folklore Society*
JPC / *Journal of Popular Culture*
JPF / *Journal of Popular Film*
JPH / *Journal of Presbyterian History*
JPsy / *Journal of Psychology*
Judaism
KanQ / *Kansas Quarterly*
KFQ / *Keystone Folklore Quarterly*
KFR / *Kentucky Folklore Record*
Knave, Fool and Genius / Susan Kuhlman, *Knave, Fool, and Genius: The Confidence Man as He Appears in Nineteenth-Century American Fiction* (Chapel Hill, Univ. of N.C. Press)
L&I / *Language and Ideology*
L&P / *Literature and Psychology*
Lang&S / *Language and Style*
LaS / *Louisiana Studies*
L/FQ / *Literature/Film Quarterly* (Salisbury, Md., State Coll.)
LHUS / R. E. Spiller, et al., eds., *The Literary History of the United States* (New York, Macmillan, 1948)
LHY / *Literary Half-Yearly*
Libri (Copenhagen)
Literary Theory and Structure / Frank Brady, John Palmer, and Martin Price, eds., *Literary Theory and Structure: Essays in Honor of William K. Wimsatt* (New Haven, Yale Univ. Press)
Lucifer in Harness / Edwin Fussell, *Lucifer in Harness: American Meter, Metaphor, and Diction* (Princeton, N.J., Princeton Univ. Press)
LWU / *Literatur in Wissenschaft und Unterricht* (Kiel)
MAQR / *Michigan Alumnus Quarterly Review*
MarkhamR / *Markham Review*
MD / *Modern Drama*
MDAC / *Mystery and Detection Annual*

MFS / Modern Fiction Studies
MHQ / Maine Historical Quarterly
MHR / Missouri Historical Quarterly
MichA / Michigan Academician
MinnR NRP / Minnesota Review (New Rivers Press)
MissQ / Mississippi Quarterly
MLQ / Modern Language Quarterly
ModSp / Moderne Sprachen
Montana: The Magazine of Western History
Mosaic
MP / Modern Philology
MPS / Modern Poetry Studies
MQ / Midwest Quarterly
MQR / Michigan Quarterly Review
MR / Massachusetts Review
MSE / Massachusetts Studies in English
MSF / Mid-South Folklore
MSS / Manuscripts
MTJ / Mark Twain Journal
MuK / Maske und Kothurn
NA / Nuova Antologia
NALF / Negro American Literature Forum
Names: Journal of the American Name Society
NAmR / North American Review
N&Q / Notes and Queries
Nation
NCarFJ / North Carolina Folklore Journal
NCF / Nineteenth-Century Fiction
NCHR / North Carolina Historical Review
NConL / Notes on Contemporary Literature
NDEJ / Notre Dame English Journal
NEF / Northeast Folklore
NEQ / New England Quarterly
NewL / New Letters
NewRep / New Republic
NHJ / Nathaniel Hawthorne Journal
NLauR / New Laurel Review
NM / Neuphilologische Mitteilungen
NMW / Notes on Mississippi Writers
Novel: A Forum on Fiction
NS / Die Neueren Sprachen
NYFQ / New York Folklore Quarterly
NYRB / New York Review of Books
NYTM / New York Times Magazine
OhR / Ohio Review
OQ / Ohioana Quarterly
OSP / Oxford Slavonic Papers
OyezR / Oyez Review (Roosevelt Univ.)
PAAS / Proceedings of the American Antiquarian Society
Paideuma: A Journal Devoted to Ezra Pound Scholarship (Orono, Maine)
Parnassus: Poetry in Review (New York)
Paunch (Buffalo, N. Y.)
PBSA / Papers of the Bibliographical Society of America
PCP / Pacific Coast Philology
PCSM / Publications of the Colonial Society of America
PH / Pennsylvania History
Phylon
Players
PLL / Papers on Language and Literature
PMHB / Pennsylvania Magazine of History and Biography
PMHS / Proceedings of the Massachusetts Historical Society
PMLA / PMLA: Publications of the Modern Language Assn.
PoeS / Poe Studies
Poetica
PQ / Philological Quarterly
PR / Partisan Review
Proof / Proof: The Yearbook of American Bibliographical and Textual Studies
Prose
PrS / Prairie Schooner
PUBR / Punjab University Research Bulletin
QJLC / Quarterly Journal of the Library of Congress
QJS / Quarterly Journal of Speech
RALS / Resources for American Literary Studies
RANAM / Recherches Anglaises et Américaines (Strasbourg)
Regeneration through Violence / Richard Slotkin, *Regeneration through Violence: The Mythology of the American Frontier, 1600–1860*

(Middletown, Conn., Wesleyan Univ. Press)
REH / Revista de Estudios Hispánicos
Renaissance 2 / Renaissance 2: A Journal of Afro-American Studies (Yale)
Renascence
Rendezvous: Journal of Arts and Letters
Response / Response: A Contemporary Jewish Review (Brandeis Univ.)
RHL / Revue d'Histoire Littéraire de la France
RJN / Robinson Jeffers Newsletter
RLC / Revue de Littérature Comparée
RLMC / Rivista di Letterature Moderne e Comparate (Firenze)
RLV / Revue des Langues Vivantes (Bruxelles)
RomN / Romance Notes
RS / Research Studies (Wash. State Univ.)
RusR / Russian Review
SAB / South Atlantic Bulletin
SAF / Studies in American Fiction
SAP / Studia Anglica Posnaniensia: An International Review of English Studies
SB / Studies in Bibliography: Papers of the Bibliographic Society of Virginia
SBL / Studies in Black Literature
SCN / Seventeenth-Century News
SCR / South Carolina Review
SDR / South Dakota Review
SELit / Studies in English Literature (Univ. of Tokyo)
Semiotica
Serif / The Serif (Kent State Univ.)
SFQ / Southern Folklore Quarterly
Shenandoah
SHR / Southern Humanities Review
SIR / Studies in Romanticism
SLitI / Studies in the Literary Imagination
SLJ / Southern Literary Journal
SNL / Satire Newsletter
Smithsonian (Washington, D. C.)
SN / Studia Neophilologica
SNNT / Studies in the Novel (North Tex. State Univ.)
SocR / Social Research
SoR / Southern Review
SoRA / Southern Review: An Australian Journal of Literary Studies (Univ. of Adelaide)
Sprachkunst
SR / Sewanee Review
SRAZ / Studia Romanica et Anglica Zagrabiensia
SSF / Studies in Short Fiction
SSL / Studies in Scottish Literature (Univ. of S.C.)
StH / Studies in the Humanities (Indiana Univ. of Pa.)
StQ / Steinbeck Quarterly
Style
Subversive Vision / Michael J. Hoffman, *The Subversive Vision: American Romanticism in Literature* (Port Washington, N.Y., Kennikat Press)
SwAL / Southwestern American Literature
SWR / Southwest Review
TCL / Twentieth-Century Literature
TFSB / Tennessee Folklore Society Bulletin
Thoth (Syracuse Univ.)
Thought
THQ / Tennessee Historical Quarterly
ThR / Theatre Research
TJQ / Thoreau Journal Quarterly
TLS / Times (London) *Literary Supplement*
TriQ / Tri-Quarterly
TS / Theatre Survey
TSB / Thoreau Society Bulletin
TSE / Tulane Studies in English
TSL / Tennessee Studies in Literature
TSLL / Texas Studies in Literature and Language
TUSAS / Twayne United States Authors Series
UWR / University of Windsor Review
VQR / Virginia Quarterly Review
WAL / Western American Literature
WCR / West Coast Review
WF / Western Folklore
WHQ / Western History Quarterly

WHR / *Western Humanities Review*
WMQ /*William and Mary Quarterly*
Words (Emerson College)
WP / *Winthur Portfolio*
WVUPP / *West Virginia University Philological Papers*
WWR / *Walt Whitman Review*
WWS / Western Writers Series (Boise State College)
XUS / *Xavier University Studies*
YAM / *Yale Alumni Magazine*
YES / *Yearbook of English Studies*
y/t / *Yale Theatre*
YR / *Yale Review*
YULG / *Yale University Library Gazette*

Part I

1. Emerson, Thoreau, and Transcendentalism

Walter Harding

Once again as one surveys the year's scholarship on Emerson, Thoreau, and Transcendentalism the most obvious fact is its quantity. It is veritably a full-time job to keep up with the flood of books, articles, and dissertations in this one comparatively narrow field. I would that all of it were good, but sadly—and perhaps inevitably—it is not. So much of it is obviously the result of the publish-or-perish syndrome; so much of it is simply a rehash of what has already been said and often been said better. When there is so much that needs to be done in the field one can but lament the unstinted flow of trivia. When is someone going to produce a good solid history of the American Transcendentalist movement? The only book-length approach to the subject is Frothingham's volume that is now a century old and unsatisfactory even when it was first written. When are we going to have an authoritative account of Brook Farm? As it is now, pertinent information remains ungathered in a hundred places. When is someone going to update Arthur Christy's pioneer study of Oriental influence on the Transcendentalists? When are we going to have a biography of Frank Sanborn who although a "minor" figure nonetheless had a significant contribution to make to Transcendentalism? When are we going to have an up-to-date biography of John Sullivan Dwight delineating, among other things, his massive contributions to American music? When are we going to have a definitive edition of the writings of Margaret Fuller, which have never been properly edited? Or of Jones Very? When is there going to be a comprehensive study of the impact of the Transcendentalists on American education? All these and so many other significant studies need to be made and yet we find so much time and space wasted on trivia.

But pardon the blast. Perhaps I should not be so dyspeptic. All is by no means bad. There has been some decidedly good work done in the year 1973, and now that I have vented my spleen, I shall turn to some of that.

i. Books

The major book of the year, it seems to me, is Lawrence Buell's *Literary Transcendentalism* (Ithaca, Cornell Univ. Press), perhaps the most significant volume in the field since Matthiessen's monumental *American Renaissance* of more than 30 years ago. Buell's is a solid book based obviously on a tremendously wide reading in and about the field, but it is much more than a rehash of things already said. It is a breath of fresh air in the scholarship of the period, a book that does not hesitate to demolish accepted theories and evaluations and propose new ones. Not all of Buell's ideas may win acceptance, but they should result in a much-needed rethinking about the achievements of the Transcendentalists.

Another sturdy volume is Stanley Cavell's *The Senses of Walden* (New York, Viking, 1972). It is not a book for the simple-minded. It was only on the third reading that I began to appreciate what he had to say. But he asks the pertinent (and impertinent, as Thoreau would say) questions that get at the heart of Thoreau's masterpiece. In comparison, I must confess I find James McIntosh's *Thoreau as Romantic Naturalist* (Ithaca, Cornell Univ. Press) disappointing. It is described as "an attempt to read certain of Thoreau's writings by calling attention to his divided attitudes toward nature."

Robert Hudspeth in *Ellery Channing* (New York, Twayne) wisely makes no attempt to duplicate McGill's 1967 biography of Channing, but rather supplements it by concentrating on evaluating his works and discussing his relationships with his more famous friends. Channing is best described as a "transcendental brat," but Hudspeth, through his insights, makes us at least begin to understand what Emerson and Alcott saw of value in him.

There are two new volumes on Emerson's thought. Jeffrey L. Duncan, in *The Power and Form of Emerson's Thought* (Charlottesville, Univ. Press of Va.) challenges Stephen Whicher's well-known thesis that Emerson in his later years turned his back on much of his earlier thinking. Duncan argues that Emerson's concept of polarity has led many to think him inconsistent when he is not. Although the book is a well-organized synthesis of Emerson's ideas (and valuable as such), I still find Whicher more convincing. Warren Staebler's *Ralph Waldo Emerson* in "The Great American Thinkers" series (New York, Twayne) is "an introduction to the character and thought" of Emerson. Unfortunately the book is so filled with errors of fact—confusing William Ellery Channing with William Henry Channing and identifying Samuel Sewall as the minister of the Second Unitarian Church of Boston, for example—that I cannot recommend it.

From the textual standpoint, the two most important books of the year are the new Emerson and Thoreau volumes in the CEAA series. Volume 9 of *The Journals and Miscellaneous Notebooks of Ralph Waldo Emerson* (Cambridge, Harvard Univ. Press) is edited by Merton M. Sealts, Jr., and covers 1847–48. It has been produced with all the care and scrupulousness of the earlier volumes in the series. A large part of this volume is devoted to financial and engagement records and will be of little interest to a general reader, but will be enlightening to the biographer. Although I have admired the scholarship of this whole series as it has appeared volume after volume over the years, I must admit to a growing question in my mind—is their meticulous endeavour to reproduce in type all the minute details of the manuscript really worth the effort and the cost? The researcher who needs this type of information is still going to insist upon going back to the manuscript itself to make certain and the general scholar as well as the general reader is often annoyed or even turned off by the two pages of symbols he must memorize if he is going to comprehend what is going on. A clear text edition with all the apparatus and explanations of scholarly minutia relegated to the appendices—or even better to a separate microfiche printing—seems not only more practical from the standpoint of cost to both the publisher and the reader, but also far more appealing to all but the extreme specialist.

The Thoreau volume, *Reform Papers*, edited by Wendell Glick (Princeton, Princeton Univ. Press), gives us for the first time accurate texts of many of Thoreau's political essays and as an added bonus the first printing of "Reform and the Reformers," an essay he left in rough draft. The clear text with all apparatus confined to the appendices serves to enforce my caveats against the Emerson edition, though even with it I wish the more pedantic appendices were relegated to a microfiche printing. The P. J. Conkright typography and design make this edition the only one in the CEAA series that is an aesthetic triumph. But here too I have a caveat. I seriously question the choice of copy text in at least two cases: "Herald of Freedom" and "Resistance to Civil Government." I know I am not alone in believing that there are better copy-texts available for each of these than the one used, though I do not have the space to present the arguments here. (In fairness to Mr. Glick I must point out that he very honestly summarizes my arguments against his choice.)

Coleridge's American Disciples: The Selected Correspondence of James Marsh, ed. John J. Duffy (Amherst, Univ. of Mass. Press) fills an important gap in the early history of Transcendentalism, for it for the first time makes available to us primary material on the man who through his editing of Coleridge's *Aid to Reflection* became an intellectual catalyst for Emerson and his friends. It includes correspondence with Coleridge himself, George Ripley, and Charles Follen among others. Brian M. Barbour, in *American Transcendentalism: An Anthology of Criticism* (Notre Dame, Notre Dame Univ. Press) provides a helpful volume in gathering together 17 pertinent essays on the movement by critics as varied as Perry Miller, H. C. Goddard, Yvor Winters and Tony Tanner. Kenneth Walter Cameron, in *Transcendental Log* (Hartford, Transcendental Books) offers another of his invaluable omnibuses of facsimiles of forgotten newspaper and magazine articles of the 19th century on the Transcendentalists, a gold mine of research material for the advanced scholar.

Two bibliographical items should be noted. Richard Ludwig, in *Literary History of the United States: Bibliography: Supplement II* (New York, Macmillan, 1972) updates his earlier bibliographies on Transcendentalism and the major figures. L. D. Geller, in *Between Concord and Plymouth: The Transcendentalists and the Watsons* (Concord, Thoreau Lyceum) catalogs the little known Transcendentalist manuscript treasures of the Pilgrim Hall in Plymouth, Massachusetts.

Chapters that pertain to our subject in several books should be mentioned. In the early portions of *The Man of Letters in New England and the South* (Baton Rouge, Louisiana State University Press), Lewis P. Simpson discusses some of the early phases in the development of Transcendentalism, a work which I hope he will eventually expand to a full book in itself. So rare is it to find a scholarly book that is beautifully written that I must particularly commend Mr.

Simpson on this point. In *The Subversive Vision,* Michael J. Hoffman in part discusses Emerson's *Nature* and Thoreau's "Civil Disobedience" as documents subversive to the "official faith" of the establishment, and has some pertinent things to say. Todd M. Lieber, in *Endless Experiments* (Columbus, Ohio State Univ. Press) devotes chapters to discussing dualism in the works of Emerson and Thoreau, but I find little new there. Charles Anderson, in "Thoreau and *The Dial*: The Apprentice Years" in the *Gohdes Festschrift,* extends his study of Thoreau as a literary artist to these early works. Raymond Gozzi's 1957 New York University doctoral dissertation, "Tropes and Figures: A Psychological Study of Henry David Thoreau" has had a significant influence on recent biographical studies of Thoreau, but it has not been widely read because it has been available only on microfilm. Now his two most important chapters, "Some Aspects of Thoreau's Personality" and "Mother-Nature" are available in Walter Harding's *Henry David Thoreau: A Profile* (New York, Hill & Wang, pp. 150–72, 172–87), as is James Armstrong's perceptive new study "Thoreau as Philosopher of Love" (pp. 222–43).

ii. Periodicals

A preliminary MLA checklist of periodical articles published in the field runs to more than fifty items and yet is by no means complete. It is obviously impossible to discuss each one of them. I have made a concerted effort to read each (though four or five proved too elusive for me to obtain) and have tried to select the more significant ones to comment on.

So far as Emerson is concerned, Sheldon Liebman, in "The Origins of Emerson's Early Poetics" (*AL* 45:23–33), emphasizes the influence the Scottish "Common Sense Critics" had on Emerson's poetic theory before he turned to the writings of Coleridge. Despite its title, Leonard Neufeldt's "Emerson and the Civil War" (*JEGP* 71 [1972]:502–13) deals much more broadly with the question of Emerson's attitudes towards slavery and abolition as well as towards the war itself, tracing his changing attitudes over the years. One should also note Mario D'Avanzo's "Seeing and Hearing in 'Each and All,' " (*ESQ* 19:231–35). Charles W. Mignon, in "Emerson to Chapman: Four Letters About Publishing" (*ESQ* 19:224–30), gives us the text of four hitherto unpublished letters concerned with the English publication of his *Essays: Second Series* and *Poems*. William Gavin, in comparing "[Peter Yakovlevich] Chaadayev and Emerson" (*RusR* 32:119–30), asserts that both the Russian and the American, who were contemporaries, were "mystic pragmatists," who influenced their respective countrymen to take new stances "on the relationship of man to the cosmos." Leonard J. Deutsch, in "Ralph Waldo Ellison and Ralph Waldo Emerson: A Shared Moral Vision" (*CLAJ* 16 [1972]:159–78), points out that despite an early aversion towards the man he was named for, Ellison in *Invisible Man* evinces a deep philosophical indebtedness to him.

The entire issue of *ESQ* 19, iii, is devoted to a "Thoreau Symposium," edited by Joseph R. McElrath, which contains seven articles, chiefly by well-known scholars in the field. Among the most interesting are Lewis Leary's " 'Now I adventured': 1851 as a Watershed Year in Thoreau's Career" (pp. 141–48); Wendell Glick's "Go Tell It on the Mountain: Thoreau's Vocation as a Writer" (pp. 161–69); Robert C. Albrecht's "Conflict and Resolution: 'Slavery in Massachusetts' " (pp. 179–88), a thoughtful analysis of one of Thoreau's most neglected essays; and Paul O. Williams's "Thoreau's Growth as a Transcendental Poet" (pp. 189–98). Michael West's erudite "Charles Kraitsir's Influence upon Thoreau's Theory of Language" in the following issue of *ESQ* (19:262–74) documents a little-known impact on Thoreau by one of Elizabeth Peabody's proteges.

Despite its title, Richard Hocks's "Thoreau, Coleridge, and Barfield" (*CR* 17:175–98) is primarily an analysis of the structure of *Walden*—and a very good one at that. I found Gordon E. Bigelow's "Thoreau's Melting Sandbank: Birth of a Symbol" (*IJSym* 2,iii[1971]: 7–13) the most detailed analysis yet of the symbolism in Thoreau's much-discussed sandbank passage in *Walden*. Gordon Boudreau, in "H. D. Thoreau, William Gilpin, and the Metaphysical Ground of the Picturesque" (*AL* 45:357–69), expands somewhat on the well-known Templeman article on the subject of some forty years ago. James Devlin contrasts "Henry Thoreau and Gilbert White: Concord and Selborne" (*XUS* 2[1972]:6–15) and concludes that White was perhaps the more scientific naturalist of the two. William Nichols ("Individualism and Autobiographical Art: Frederick Douglass and Henry Thoreau," *CLAJ* 16[1972]:145–58), in comparing Douglass's *My Bondage* (1855) and Thoreau's *Walden* (1854), asserts that the two volumes shed a good deal of light and understanding on each other because of the varying backgrounds and differing viewpoints of the authors. After examining Heinz Eulau's oft-quoted condemnation of Thoreau's "Civil Disobedience," Robert Saalback, in "Thoreau and Civil Disobedience" (*BSUF* 13,iv:18–24) concludes that Thoreau theories are still valid and proved useful in the protests against the war in Vietnam.

Thoreau scholars should at least be aware of the publication of three different journals, the *Concord Saunterer*, the *Thoreau Journal Quarterly*, and the *Thoreau Society Bulletin*, published respectively by the Thoreau Lyceum, the Thoreau Fellowship, and the Thoreau Society, even though a great deal of their material is aimed at the enthusiast rather than the scholar. The *TSB* publishes regularly an "Additions to the Thoreau Bibliography," which not only lists all new material, both primary and secondary, as it appears, but also fills in gaps in earlier bibliographies. Both it and the *Saunterer* frequently publish significant primary and documentary material. The *TJQ* is generally devoted to poetry and appreciative essays on Thoreau. In the *TJQ* for 1973, attention should be particularly called to Joel Myerson's "Thoreau and the *Dial*" (5,i:4–7) which cites a number of forgotten newspaper comments on Thoreau's early writings; Sidney Poger's "Yeats as Azad: A Possible Source in Thoreau" (5,iii:13–15); Laraine Fergenson's "Was Thoreau Re-reading Wordsworth in 1851?" (5,iii: 20–23); Bette S. Weidman's "Thoreau and Indians" (5,iv:4–10); Elliott S. Allison's "Thoreau of Monadnock" (5,iv:15–21); and Edward C. Peple, Jr.'s "Thoreau and Donatello" (5,iv:22–25) on Hawthorne's character. In the *Saunterer* for 1973, note in particular Thomas Blanding's "Daniel Ricketson's Reminiscences of Thoreau" (March, pp. 7–11); Blanding's "Of New Bedford 'Feelosofers' and Concord Real Estate" (June, pp. 2–8), which includes an unpublished Thoreau letter; and Jeanne M. Zimmer's "A History of Thoreau's Hut and Hut Site" (December, Supplement). In the *TSB* for 1973, articles worth mentioning are B. F. Skinner's "*Walden* (One) and *Walden Two*" (122:1–2); Roger Cummins's "Thoreau and Isaac Newton Goodhue" (123:2–3), a forgotten reminiscence; Robert Sattelmeyer's "David A. Wasson's Elegy on Thoreau" (123:3–4); Victor Friesen's "Alexander Henry and Thoreau's Climb of Mount Katahdin" (123:5–6); and Mary Gail Fenn's "Thoreau's Rivers" (*Thoreau Society Booklet, No. 27*).

As for the lesser Transcendentalists, the most significant article is

Charles Strickland's "A Transcendentalist Father: The Child-Rearing Practices of Bronson Alcott" (*Hist. of Childhood Quart.* 1:4–61), a very moving account of Alcott's role as a parent. The article is followed by commentary by three child-psychologists: Henry Ebel, J. Louise Despert, and John Walzer. George Carter, in "Theodore Parker and John P. Hale" (*Dartmouth College Lib. Bul.* 13[1972]: 13–33), publishes for the first time the text of 41 letters of Parker and his wife to the Abolitionist politician John P. Hale, many on anti-slavery topics. Margaret V. Allen, in "The Political and Social Criticism of Margaret Fuller" (*SAQ* 72:560–73) traces her development "from political innocent to dedicated activist." Miss Allen, in " 'This Impassioned Yankee': Margaret Fuller's Writing Revisited" (*SWR* 58:162–71) laments the long neglect of Fuller's work and predicts that a well-deserved recognition awaits the publication of a scholarly edition of her writings.

Special recognition must be given to that indefatigable researcher of Transcendental archives Joel Myerson. He has in this one year contributed five noteworthy articles: "An Annotated List of Contributions to the Boston *Dial*" (*SB* 26:133–66), which corrects and supplements greatly George W. Cooke's long outdated list; "More Apropos of John Thoreau" (*AL* 45:104–16), which gives us new details of Thoreau's brother's tragic death; "Transcendentalism and Unitarianism in 1840" (*CLAJ* 16:366–68) which centers on a letter of Christopher Cranch complaining about his lack of success in finding a Unitarian pastorate because he has been branded a Transcendentalist; a delightful and enlightening account of home life at the Emersons—"Margaret Fuller's 1842 Journal: At Concord with the Emersons" (*HLB* 21:320–40); as well as the *TJQ* article listed above. I do hope, incidentally, that Mr. Myerson's doctoral dissertation on the *Dial* soon gets into print. It is a tool we cannot spare.

I must also add a word of commendation for Kenneth Walter Cameron. I miss greatly his hand in *ESQ*, which has turned into quite a different journal since it transferred to the West Coast, but thankfully he still continues to edit *ATQ*, which in its 1973 issues contains the usual "god's plenty" of miscellaneous materials on Transcendentalism; among the more significant are Arthur Biddle's "Bronson and Chatfield Alcott in Virginia—New Evidence" (17:3–9); Vivian Hopkins's "Margaret Fuller: Pioneer Women's Liberationist" (18:29–35); Gay Wilson Allen's "Emerson and the Unconscious"

(19:26–30); Madeleine B. Stern's invaluable "Elizabeth Peabody's Foreign Library (1840)" (20:5–12); and Cameron's own "Some Alcott Conversations in 1863" (17:3–9), "Emerson, Transcendentalism, and Literary Notes in the Stearns Wheeler Papers" (20:69–98), and his continuing "Literary News in American Renaissance Newspapers" (20:13–36; 195–97).

iii. Dissertations

The flow of doctoral dissertations on our subject continues unabated. Its quality this year, I am happy to say, seems appreciably higher than usual. Fewer dissertations seem to be *pro forma* exercises in graduate research. Several seem to me to make genuine contributions to our knowledge of the field. Unfortunately in most cases the complete dissertation was not available to me, and I have had to base my judgments on the abstracts. It is thus entirely possible that I am inadvertently unfair in denigrating or dismissing some of them.

On Emerson, I find Sharon Stuart Cobbs Olds's "Emerson's Innovations in Prosody: *Poems* (1847)" (*DAI* 34[1972]:330A, Columbia) most rewarding. She finds an interesting correlation between subject matter and form in his poems. Poems conventional in subject matter tend to be conventional and regular in form; those unorthodox in subject matter tend to be unconventional in form. In this latter group are included most of Emerson's best poems and the ones through which he makes his special contributions to American prosody. By analyzing Emerson's use of certain word clusters—*beauty*, *culture*, *fate*, *genius*, *greatness-heroism*, *nature*, and *soul-spirit*—Mary Alice Ihrig, in "Emerson's Transcendental Vocabulary: An Expositional Analysis and Concordance to Seven Word-clusters in His Prose" (*DAI* 34:2565A, N.C.), concludes that "the period of 1836–1844 did indeed represent Emerson's prime and transcendental peak." William Michael Ross, in "The Shifting Viewpoint: A Key to the Thought and Art of Emerson's Essays" (*DAI* 34:285A, Fordham) asserts that Emerson regularly shifts his viewpoint between Reason and Understanding in his essays and a realization of this fact is vital to an appreciation of the artistry of his essays. Jerome Francis Keating, in "Personal Identity in Jonathan Edwards, Ralph Waldo Emerson, and Alfred North Whitehead" (*DAI* 33[1972]:5682A, Syracuse) not surprisingly concludes that Emerson stands mid-way between Edwards's belief that God controls man's existence and Whitehead's belief that man determines his own fate. In considering "Form and Process in American Literature" (*DAI* 34: 1291A, Rice), Carolyn Jane Porter, in a chapter on Emerson asserts that his journals reveal "A persistent conflict between the urge to reject social, intellectual and religious forms in the service of private growth and personal freedom, and the recognition that such growth and freedom presuppose a formlessness inimical to human needs." There are three studies of Emerson's influence. George Sebouhian in "The Emersonian Idealism of Henry James" (*DAI* 34:739A, Ohio State) concludes that "James is a part of the idealist tradition that informs the work of Emerson and . . . James dramatizes that tradition in his work.'" Maurice Yaofu Lin, in "Children of Adam: Ginsburg, Ferlinghetti and Snyder in the Emerson-Whitman Tradition" (*DAI* 34: 781A, Minn.), endorses the frequently observed parallel between the Transcendental revolt of the 19th century and the "Beat" revolt of the 1950s. And Richard Welke Cass, in "The Implications of Ralph Waldo Emerson's Statements on Knowing for Revising Curriculum Concepts" (*DAI* 33[1972]:3251A, Wis.; Milwaukee, Education) offers suggestions for modern educational reform based on Emerson's philosophy.

The most interesting of the new dissertations on Thoreau is Annette Matthews Woodlief's "Style and Rhetoric in the Sentences of *Walden*" (*DAI* 33[1972]: 4372A–73A, N. Car.), which makes a very enlightening statistical study of Thoreau's use of grammatical form in the first thousand sentences of *Walden*. Brian Christopher Bond, in "Thoreau's *A Week on the Concord and Merrimack Rivers*: A Generic Study" (*DAI* 33[1972]: 3574A, Bowling Green) investigates the influence of the classical epic and the pastoral tradition on Thoreau's first book and concludes that Thoreau was not attempting to carry on specific literary traditions but rather was adapting classical techniques to his own purposes. In "'Thoreau's Development as an Observer and Critic of American Society" (*DAI* 34:[1972] 282A–83A, Miami) Douglas Arthur Noverr discusses the tensions created when Thoreau in his writings attempted to fulfill his obligations both to Transcendental idealism and practical society. Rhoda B. Nathan, in "'The Soul at White Heat: Metaphysical Tradition in Thoreau's *Journal* and Dickinson's Poetry" (*DAI* 33: 6925A, City Univ. of N.Y.) wisely concludes that while there is hard evidence that Thoreau was impressed by the metaphysical poets, his work was not an imitation of theirs but rather a "'resurgence of an equivalent ironic temperament." Robert Glen Deamer, in a chapter on Thoreau in "The American Dream: A Study in the Beliefs, Possibilities, and Problems in the American Dream as Dramatized in the Lives and Writings of Major American Authors" (*DAI* 33[1972]: 5717A–18A, N. M., 1972), comes to the rather interesting conclusion that "the ideal frontiersman which [Thoreau] dramatized in his life and writings was actually—and most ironically—embodied in the Old World social ideal of the English gentleman"!

Dissertations on the more general topic of Transcendentalism include Elizabeth Ann Meese's "Transcendental Vision: A History of the Doctrine of Correspondence and Its Role in American Transcendentalism" (*DAI* 33[1972]: 6319A–20A, Wayne State), which surprisingly chooses Thoreau rather than Emerson as its chief example for discussion, and Robert Emerson Ireland's "The Concept of Providence in the Thought of William Ellery Channing, Ralph Waldo Emerson, Theodore Parker, and Orestes A. Brownson: A Study in Mid-Nineteenth Century American Intellectual History" (*DAI* 34[1972]: 703A, Maine), which finds "a distinct transformation" of the meaning of *providence* from 1830 to 1860, from the "Puritan concept of a providence which controlled the thoughts and actions of man . . . to a view which stressed the active, conscious agency of man." Attention is particularly focused on the "Higher Law" issue. Charles T. Summerlin, in "The Possible Oracle: Three Transcendentalist Poets" (*DAI* 34: 3435A–36A, Yale), suggests that Emerson saw the poet "as a dissolver of the empirical distinctions which imprison man's imagination and a perceiver of the infinite soul of the universe," while for Thoreau "Poetizing involved absorption into nature rather than dissolution of it," and Jones Very "believed that the conscious ability of man to perceive and do his duty was the key to" poetry.

iv. Conclusion

I complete this survey with feelings of both frustration and humility. So voluminous is the scholarly literature in our field today that it is impossible to examine the better works with the depth they deserve or even to mention some of the lesser but nonetheless worthwhile pieces. I have, for space's sake, arbitrarily ruled out virtually all reprints of either articles or books and have likewise eliminated effusions and popularizations even though they serve their purpose. I am even more aware than the reader is that judgments I have made herein are inevitably deeply colored by my own predilections and prejudices. For that fact I beg the forgiveness and understanding of both authors and readers.

State University College, Geneseo, N.Y.

2. Hawthorne

Nina Baym

In 1973 there were no new Centenary texts published and—for the first time in years—no book-length studies. *ESQ*, in its pleasing new format, brought out a two-issue symposium on the mature romances edited by Buford Jones; the annual *Nathaniel Hawthorne Journal* (now in its third year of publication) presented some important new primary material as well as several interpretive articles. These two journals between them accounted for about half of the items I discuss this year (the total number is just under 70, down almost 20 from last year). Despite the smaller quantity of Hawthorne publication this year, the listing of 19 new Hawthorne dissertations in *DAI* does not augur for any long-term slackening of the flood of criticism on this author. But austerity may be imposed on the profession by the tighter budgets of university presses and scholarly journals. Should the result of economic hard times be that trivial and redundant publications vanished, and lardy books reduced to meaty articles, the crisis would be a blessing.

i. Texts, Life, Reputation, Bibliography

Although there were no additions to the Centenary Texts of Hawthorne's works this year, Claude M. Simpson, Jr., did contribute to textual discussion in his "'Correction or Corruption: Nathaniel Hawthorne and Two Friendly Improvers," *HLQ* 36:367–86. This essay derives from a talk delivered to the Friends of the Huntington Library, and focusses on Sophia Hawthorne's changes in the American Notebooks and Franklin Pierce's changes in the manuscript of the campaign biography. The material on Pierce is new (it had not been previously recognized that some of the manuscript revisions were in his hand) and fascinating, although more pertinent to Pierce, of course, than to Hawthorne. As for Sophia, not a year goes by without her being taken to task for her handling of Hawthorne's papers. It is unquestionably imperative that we restore the original readings where she made alterations; but I wonder very much about the restoration in *The Blithedale Romance* (Simpson devotes some space in his talk to this issue) of two passages cancelled by Hawthorne himself. The excised material is the sort that Sophia cut out in the notebooks and therefore, it is reasoned, Hawthorne probably made these changes under her influence.

I think the editors are wholly unjustified in their practice here. Assuming it were true—and there is no direct evidence—that Sophia advised Hawthorne to make these cuts, we still must hold Hawthorne responsible for following her advice. Otherwise, we would have to maintain that he was "out of his mind" in some definable sense when he accepted her suggestions. Moreover, we would be setting a precedent for discounting all revisions made at the suggestions of others—a precedent which would virtually force us to present rough drafts as containing an author's final intentions regarding a text. And a different issue is raised by the fact that we know no more about Sophia's influence on the *Blithedale* excisions than that they are consistent with her later practice. This issue, of course, is the critics' use of Sophia as a means of excusing Hawthorne's mistakes. Perhaps Sophia and Hawthorne were of a mind about the type of revisions she carried out. Perhaps, even, Sophia worked on the manuscripts not (as cliché has it) to sanctify the image of her husband, but simply to present them to the world as she believed Hawthorne himself would have done. Like the Centenary editor, I find the restored passages very nice, and *Blithedale* is indeed better for their inclusion. But personal preference is not supposed to be an editorial principle.

Most of the primary material published this year appeared in the *Nathaniel Hawthorne Journal*, which has rapidly established itself as a focal point for ongoing Hawthorne scholarship. "Hawthorne's 'Moonlight,'" by Arthur Monke and C. E. Frazer Clark, Jr. (*NHJ* 3: 27–35) discusses the textual circumstances of Hawthorne's first printed writings, the poems "The Ocean" and "Moonlight" published in the *Salem Gazette* on August 26 and September 2, 1825, respectively. The article also proposes a third poem ("The Battle Ground," *Salem Gazette*: August 30, 1825) for inclusion in the canon. This same suggestion is put forward by Allen Flint in his unfavorable review of *Nathaniel Hawthorne: Poems* edited by Richard Peck and published in 1967 by the Bibliographical Society of the University of Virginia (*NHJ* 3:255–60). Flint's review, which gives the texts of "Moonlight" and "The Battle Ground," also reprints a poem called "The Marriage Ring," which Flint thinks Hawthorne wrote. The poetry, in Flint's view (and that of everyone else who has read it) is banal and without craft. *NHJ* 3 printed Joel Myerson's transcription with introduction, of "Sarah Clarke's Reminiscences of the Peabodys and Hawthorne" (pp. 130–33) and a letter in the Clark collection dated September 2, 1851, from Hawthorne to his friend William B. Pike (pp. 3–8). Kenneth Walter Cameron reproduced some "Hawthorne Memorabilia in the National Records," *ATQ* 20(sup.):144–53, a pot-pourri of official documents dating from his service in the Salem custom-house including some material relating to his appointment and removal. Daniel R. Barnes reprinted "Two Reviews of *The Scarlet Letter* in Holden's Dollar Magazine," *AL* 44:648–52, and Arlin Turner contributed "Hawthorne's Final Illness and Death: Additional Reports" (*ESQ* 19:124–27), reprinting letters about Hawthorne's death written to Horace Mann, Jr., by Una, Sophia, George C. Mann (his brother) and Mary Peabody Mann (his mother).

"Hawthorne and the London *Athenaeum* 1834–1864" by Seymour L. Gross is an intensive study of the reviews of Hawthorne's work written by Henry Fothergill Chorley which appeared in the influential English periodical and which contributed substantially to Hawthorne's prestige (*NHJ* 3:35–72). The most interesting material in the essay concerns *The Marble Faun*, because Chorley's mixed review of the romance seems to have been directly responsible for Hawthorn's decision to add the postscript. Anne Henry Ehrenpreis' "Elizabeth Gaskell and Nathaniel Hawthorne" (*NHJ* 3:89–119) adroitly meshes two careers with distant but definite points of contact. *The Scarlet Letter* certainly influenced *Ruth*, and Gaskell had a roundabout influence on *The Marble Faun.* Both authors wrote about witchcraft and their treatments show similarities because both used the same source, Charles W. Upham's *Lectures on Witchcraft* (Boston, 1831). It is astonishing, as Ehrenpreis comments, that Hawthorne scholarship has completely overlooked the basic importance to Hawthorne's development of Upham's work. Upham is hardly an unknown figure. His later work, *Salem Witchcraft* (Boston, 1867), became the standard history of the subject, and is still influential. Upham himself figures as the great villain in Hawthorne's life, the leader of the Whig faction that ousted him from the custom-house and the model for Judge Pyncheon. Perhaps it is just because they have seen him as a villain of melodrama that critics have been unable even to imagine him as a scholarly source. Yet Ehrenpreis demonstrates his influence on the revision of "Alice Doane." This work might be carried much further; and it would be especially interesting to examine *The House of the Seven Gables* for influences. For, ironically, if Upham was the model for Pyncheon, his views on witchcraft constitute a defense of the Maules. He interpreted the Salem trials in the light of preexisting political factions in Salem town and village, and Hawthorne's explanation of the Pyncheon-Maule feud as originating in a quarrel over land is precisely the sort of idea he might have drawn from Upham. It is a further irony that Hawthorne the author plays the role of Upham-Pyncheon's accuser in *The House of the Seven Gables* while Upham the historian was extremely harsh on Hawthorne's magistrate ancestors.

C. E. Frazer Clark, Jr., published a "Census of Nathaniel Hawthorne Letters 1850–1864," thus completing the work he had carried through 1849 in *NHJ* 1 (*NHJ* 3:202–52). The census totals 1,233 letters, and while there will surely be additions made to it, it is an indispensable starting point, a basic research tool for Hawthorne scholars. But how distressing it is that there is still no edition, and none in sight, of the letters themselves, and that we have only partial and incorrect copies of but a fraction of those on Clark's list available to us in print! Another bibliographical first is Raymona E. Hull's "British Periodical Printings of Hawthorne's Works, 1835–1900: A Partial Bibliography" (*NHJ* 3:73–88). Having examined the files of almost 300 British periodicals in the British Museum (along with those of a few American Universities as well), Hull was able to discover only 48 reprintings of Hawthorne's works—a very small number considering Hawthorne's high English reputation. In a bibliographical note, C. E. Frazer Clark, Jr., points out a basis for distinguishing between the first and second printings of *The Blithedale Romance* (*NHJ* 3:172–75). Gloria A. Francis compiled a bibliography of "Recent Scholarship 1971–1972" (*NHJ* 3:269–77) which includes several 1973 items.

ii. General Studies

The year's best general article is Leo B. Levy's "The Notebook Source and the 18th Century Context of Hawthorne's Theory of Romance," *NHJ* 3:120–29. Levy observes that the moonlight passage from "The Custom-House," when it first appeared as an entry in Hawthorne's notebooks, lacked the crucial terms "Actual," "Imaginary," and "neutral ground" and offered a psychological rather than a symbolic description of the imaginative process. Levy links this psychology to then-current concepts which had been originally articulated by Allison and Kames: the concepts of association and of ideal distance. The process of imagination, which a romance records, is that of free association of ideas and images. Distance from immediate experience is necessary to free the memory for its function of supplying associations. Distance from events is also required for aesthetic effect; hence the romancer positions himself toward his subject as a spectator. Levy suggests that we can see here 18th rather than 19th century influences on Hawthorne's work; it can be maintained, however, that association psychology underlies the entire romantic movement. Robert Penn Warren's general overview of Hawthorne's work, "Hawthorne Revisited: Some Remarks on Hellfiredness," *SR* 81:75–111, takes up a selection of tales and concentrates on *The Scarlet Letter*. Warren points out tensions basic to Hawthorne's writing, and emphasizes in particular how the works are at once self-disclosing and self-concealing. He thinks that the major tension in *The Scarlet Letter* is between flesh and spirit. In this essay Warren modifies some of his earlier views of Hawthorne and integrates into his critical perceptions some more recent interpretations; it is a beautifully written piece, but probably more interesting to a student of Warren than of Hawthorne.

Buford Jones introduced his *ESQ* symposium with "After Long Apprenticeship: Hawthorne's Mature Romances," *ESQ* 19:1–7. He argues that Hawthorne considered the decades before *The Scarlet Letter* as a long, necessary, but frustrating apprentice period. The long romances represented, in Hawthorne's own view, his perfected craft and his literary maturity. A probing but rather desultory article by John McElroy, probably mistitled, is "The Hawthorne Style of American Fiction," *ESQ* 19:117–23, which relates authorial self-consciousness and self-effacement—the persona's "way of barely asserting anything"—to Hawthorne's ambivalent feelings about being a "writer of story books." David W. Pancost looks at "Hawthorne's Epistemology and Ontology" (*ESQ* 19:8–13) and finds a metaphysical mixture of the conservative and radical. Hawthorne accepts any human experience as real; therefore reality consists in an interaction of the mind and the external, natural world. Since the external world is common to all, the "key" to reality is the individual mind. Pancost thus places Hawthorne as a forerunner of existentialism and phenomenology. I am struck with a connection that Pancost does not make—Hawthorne comes through as an incipient interaction psychologist or sociologist. Hennig Cohen in Louis Rubin's collection, *Comic Imagination*, contributes a chapter called "A Comic Mode of the Romantic Imagination: Poe, Hawthorne, Melville" (pp. 85–99). Cohen holds that these mainly grim authors employ two kinds of humor: first, humor within a tragic or pathetic context intended to bring a saving balance to romantic extremism; second, overtly comic writing characterized by topicality and affinities with folklore and popular culture. Some lines from "The Hollow of the Three Hills" serve as an example of the former type of humor in Hawthorne, while "Mrs. Bullfrog" and "Feathertop" exemplify the latter.

In "Hawthorne's Houses and Hidden Treasures," *ESQ* 19:61–73, Samuel Scoville reminds us of the regular presence of "visionary structures" built upon "dreams of hidden treasure" or "an inheritance left by previous generations of a family," and of Hawthorne's employment of houses and their parts as props, emblems, symbols, and as structural and thematic devices. Allen Flint in "The Saving Grace of Marriage in Hawthorne's Fiction," *ESQ* 19:112–16, says that marriage in Hawthorne's works is given as the only remedy for isolation, since the ideal of community is unworkable. But marriage requires absolute content in her traditional sphere from the woman, the sacrifice of his "calling, be it art, social reform, or the pursuit of knowledge," from the man. This is to say that the price of happiness is dullness and mediocrity. Like most readings of Hawthorne, Flint's article makes no discriminations among different periods in Hawthorne's career, assuming that he felt the same on all issues throughout his long literary life.

Of less interest, Katharine M. Morseberger in "Hawthorne's 'Borderline': The Locale of the Romance," *Costerus* 7:93–112, analyses the ambience of a Hawthorne romance as a blend of locale and manner, neither in itself sufficient. Charles Eugene Mounts capitulates some of "Hawthorne's Echoes of Spenser and Milton," (*NHJ* 3:162–71) while Hazel M. Koskenlinna's "Setting, Image, and Symbol in Scott and Hawthorne," (*ESQ* 19:50–59) sets out some of the well-known similarities of these two authors. A comparative article by Elaine Gottlieb, "Singer and Hawthorne: A Prevalence of Satan," *SoR* 8[1972]:359–70, draws the two writers together for no purpose other than to produce an article. Harold Schecter, "The Unpardonable Sin in *Washington Square*," *SSF* 10:137–41, compares James's Dr. Sloper to Hawthorne's scientific or medical "'unpardonable sinners," from whom he thinks the character is probably derived.

iii. Long Romances

A good general article by Arne I. Axelsson, "Isolation and Interdependence as Structure in Hawthorne's Four Major Romances," *SN* 45:392–402, studies the design of the works as movements between isolation and integration. In *The Scarlet Letter*, for example, four familiar types of "isolatoes"—the passionate idealist (Hester), the shy, sensitive man (Dimmesdale), the innocent victim (Pearl), and the villain (Chillingworth)—begin in states of total separation from society and move toward whatever integration is consistent with their characters. *The House of the Seven Gables* demonstrates a decisive movement from isolation to integration; *The Blithedale Romance* reverses its movement a quarter of the way through; *The Marble Faun* moves one couple to integration and the other to isolation. The relation of the individual to his fellows, then, is not only a theme in Hawthorne. It provides a principle of structure.

Nina Baym's article, "The Romantic *Malgré Lui*: Hawthorne in the Custom-House," *ESQ* 19:14–25, considers "The Custom-House" as an "autobiographical romance" about Hawthorne's final commitment—or recommitment—to authorship, about which he felt so ambivalently. The plot of this romance is as follows: by working in the custom-house Hawthorne attempts to take his place in the real world and also to placate the internal demons who, in the shape of his ancestors, continue to castigate him for his literary inclinations. However, in the custom-house Hawthorne discovers that the price of peace is the loss of his imaginative powers, and having made that discovery, he loses the very peace he had hoped to find. Therefore he rebounds to the romance, and presents *The Scarlet Letter* as an example of his art. This article contributes to a way of looking at "The Custom-House" proposed in earlier articles by McCall (*ALS 1968*, p. 22), Stouck (*ALS 1971*, p. 30) and Eakin (ibid.). An article by Clifford Chalmers Huffman compares "The Custom-House" with Book II of *The Faerie Queene* in order to understand Hawthorne's awareness of history or his view of the role of history in human life ("History in Hawthorne's Custom-House," *ClioW* 2:161–69). We cannot deny Spenser a place among influences on Hawthorne; but the numerous source studies which cumulatively attribute virtually everything in Hawthorne's writings to him have quite overemphasized his importance. Although Hawthorne was influenced by Spenser, Milton and Shakespeare, he was so to a much smaller degree than by his own time and the literary era immediately preceding his own. That is, he is a product of the late 18th and early 19th centuries, and not of some magical literary kingdom peopled only by the Great English Writers.

Surprisingly, there was no work on *The Scarlet Letter* dated 1973. Michael J. Hoffman's essay on the novel, "Illusion and Role in *The Scarlet Letter*," in *The Subversive Vision*, pp. 70–86, is copyrighted 1972, although it was published in 1973. It presents a reading of *The Scarlet Letter* designed to show how the romance, and Hawthorne's work in general, is a response to the excesses of Transcendentalism. I overlooked a very important article, however, on the romance which appeared in 1972. Michael J. Colacurcio's "Footsteps of Ann Hutchinson: The Context of *The Scarlet Letter*," *ELH* 39:459–94, is one of the more substantial articles on the work to have appeared in recent years. Taking his cue from the famous phrase in the first chapter of *The Scarlet Letter*, Colacurcio pursues the question of "what *The Scarlet Letter* may mean if it does indeed call up a fairly exclusive set of associations from Puritanism's most crucial theological controversy." Colarcurcio accepts to considerable degree the recently revived idea that Hawthorne is basically a romantic—and not a neo-orthodox—writer, but he argues with great skill and considerable detail that his "romantic" themes can be discerned in earlier times, and were in fact "first formulated [in America] in the theological context of Puritan heresy." Colacurcio also believes that the sexual implications which Hawthorne develops in his story were basic in the Hutchinson business, and he draws a parallel, which he believes Hawthorne intended, between John Cotton and Arthur Dimmesdale. The essay demonstrates a link between Puritan thinking and Hawthorne's 19th-century world that does not distort either.

In contrast to the absence of work on *The Scarlet Letter*, a good deal was published on *The House of the Seven Gables*. I begin with an overlooked 1972 piece, Robert Moore's "Hawthorne's Folk-Motifs and *The House of the Seven Gables*," *NYFQ* 28:221–33, which studies a cluster of folkloristic elements in the romance centered on the motif of the curse. This is one of several good recent articles by folklore scholars documenting Hawthorne's familiarity with and use of extra-literary tradition. This approach expands our knowledge of Hawthorne's frame of reference and counteracts the unrealistic tendency of much source criticism to place him in narrowly defined abstract literary and religious traditions. Sheldon W. Liebman's "Point of View in *The House of the Seven Gables*," *ESQ* 19:203–12, argues that the romance's legends and traditions are not merely decorative but establish thematic concerns as well. There is, he contends, a "historical" interpretation for all events in the romance, and a "legendary" interpretation, reflecting different modes of understanding; these different modes of understanding are, in part, the subject of Hawthorne's story. Anne Farnham wrote an excellent history of the Salem workhouse, "Uncle Venner's Farm: Refuge or Workhouse for Salem's Poor?" *EIHC* 109:60–86, showing how from the beginning the institution was supposed to fulfill opposing functions: to serve as an asylum for the virtuous poor and workhouse for the vicious and idle poor. The article provides no specific aid in interpreting the romance but is good background for the contemporary arena.

In "Hawthorne's Sense of an Ending," *ESQ* 19:43–39, Jerome Klinkowitz compares the ending of *The House of the Seven Gables* with the endings of the other romances. He says that the happy finale is not really anomalous because in fact love does not solve any problems or transform the world of the romance. Rather, the world has already been transformed, and therefore love is made possible. Thus this romance gives the obverse of, rather than a contradiction to, the conclusions of the others. A more ambitious article defending the novel's conclusion is Barton Levi St. Armand's "The Golden Stain of Time: Ruskinian Aesthetics and the Ending of *The House of the*

Seven Gables," *NHJ* 3:143–53. St. Armand's argument appears to be that because Holgrave converts to an organic theory of architecture very close to that articulated by Ruskin in *The Seven Lamps of Architecture* (1849), his conversion is intended as a good thing, involving a more mature acceptance of the past in its good as well as bad aspects. The influence of Ruskin on the statements about architecture in *The House of the Seven Gables* seems to me well demonstrated, but the thematic argument I find a non-sequitur.

Carol Schoen's "The House of the Seven Deadly Sins," *ESQ* 19:26–33, diagrams a structure of seven chapter groupings, each concerned with one of the deadly sins. This is ingenious but utterly unconvincing, bearing no relation either to the experience of reading the romance or (I am told by my colleagues in the Medieval period) to any traditional scheme for the seven deadly sins. Wayne Troy Caldwell's "The Emblem Tradition and the Symbolic Mode: Clothing Imagery in *The House of the Seven Gables*," *ESQ* 19:32–42, considers some items of clothing (the Puritan ruff, Clifford's dressing gown, Hepzibah's turban) as emblems, or "restricted symbols," in the romance. Charles N. Watson, Jr., "The Estrangement of Hawthorne and Melville," *NEQ* 46:380–402, suggests provocatively that Holgrave is a portrait of Melville, embodying Hawthorne's attraction to and reservations about his volatile friend. On the other hand, Daniel R. Barnes argues in "Orestes Brownson and Hawthorne's Holgrave," *AL* 45:271–78, that Holgrave is a satiric portrait of Brownson.

Carl Dennis in "*The Blithedale Romance* and the Problem of Self-Integration" (*TSLL* 15:93–110) proposes a full new reading of the romance. He sees its psychological meaning as emerging from each character's need to integrate the qualities of an opposite character type; the social meaning lies in the need to integrate a realism focussed on externalities and associated with the town, with a contrasting internal idealism associated with the country. Zenobia and Coverdale are "town" characters while Hollingsworth and Priscilla are associated with "country" values. On the psychological level, Zenobia and Hollingsworth are strongly self-assertive characters with firm senses of their identities, contrasted to Coverdale and Priscilla, weakly-defined characters with little sense of self. Yet again, the women are contrasted to the men as emotional and rational types, respectively. Each character would be a psychological whole if he/she could incorporate some of the qualities lacking within but possessed by the others. Dennis's article is extremely interesting and many of its points are illuminating. On the whole, though, it seems to me too schematic, too divorced from the articulated dilemmas of the characters and from the actual plot of the romance.

There were three slighter articles on this novel. Rita K. Gollin discussed "'Dreamwork' in *The Blithedale Romance*," *ESQ* 19:74–83, saying that *Blithedale* is about daydreams and dreaming, but failing to develop an argument. John O. Rees, Jr., points out echoes of, or at least resemblences to, *Antony and Cleopatra*, *The Tempest*, and *As You Like It* in his "Shakespeare in *The Blithedale Romance*," *ESQ* 19:84–93. The theatricality of the romance is enhanced by these overtones. Harold D. Pearce proposes an analog rather than a source in Shakespeare. His "Hawthorne's Old Moodie: *The Blithedale Romance* and *Measure for Measure*" (*SAB* 38,iv:11–15) presents Moodie as the "absent father-god," a magistrate like Shakespeare's Duke of Vienna retiring from society to see how his surrogates perform.

Richard Harter Fogle added "Coleridge, Hilda, and *The Marble Faun*," *ESQ* 19:105–11, to his series of articles linking Coleridge and Hawthorne through characters in the latter's work said to represent the former's principle of imagination. I thought his 1972 essay was wrong in equating the anemic Priscilla with Coleridge's vigorous principle (and he compounded the error by labelling Priscilla the "fancy" and discussing her as though fancy and imagination were the same in Coleridge's terminology). This year I feel that he is wrong in identifying the fresh and convention-shattering power posited by Coleridge with the bowdlerizing talents of Hilda. Fogle says that when Hilda copies the great masters she catches the spirit rather than the letter of their works; but Hawthorne shows that the spirit she reproduces is not that of the great masters whose paintings struggled with lust, evil, and complex passions, but rather the spirit of her own pietistic morality. "Her art," Fogle writes, "achieves Coleridge's as well as Hawthorne's ideal of imaginative truth" because she goes "beyond surfaces." But we can accept this reading of Hawthorne only if we grant that Hawthorne saw imaginative truth as deliberately inadequate to human experience. The shortcomings of Hilda's view are demonstrated again and again in *The Marble Faun*.

At the close of the romance, Kenyon gives in to Hilda's view, but not because he believes it. He is worn out and wants peace at any price, and he hopes to find escape from the issues he cannot resolve precisely in the evasions of Hilda's outlook. I think that Fogle does justice neither to Hawthorne nor Coleridge in his very special interpretations; he has forced his thesis.

David B. Kesterson, "Journey to Perugia: Dantean Parallels in *The Marble Faun*," *ESQ* 19:94–104, focusses on chapters 24–35 and demonstrates the resemblences between Donatello and Dante, Kenyon and Virgil, Miriam and Beatrice. The whole episode follows Dante's journey to the Mount of Purgatory. Donald G. Darnell, "'Doctrine by Ensample': The Emblem and *The Marble Faun*," *TSLL* 15:301–10, characterizes the romance as a sequence of emblems—first a picture, then an interpretation. He uses a different and more traditional definition of emblem than does Caldwell in his essay on *The House of the Seven Gables*. In general, discussions of Hawthorne as allegorist, symbolist, and emblemist are confused by the unfortunate fluidity in the meanings of the major critical terms.

iv. Short Works

Two articles published this year consider collections of short stories as entities in themselves. J. Donald Crowley in "The Unity of Hawthorne's *Twice-Told Tales*," *SAF* 1:35–61, investigates "totality of effect" and the "unifying principle or device" in the 1837 and 1842 volumes. He does not find unity in the diverse materials, but in the rhetorical considerations that bind them together—the presence of a storyteller, the running interplay of fiction and actuality, of an imagined world and an audience. Crowley considers the order and positioning of the tales, and discusses differences between the first and second collections. His analysis is rich and fascinating, and represents an important new direction in Hawthorne criticism. Nina Baym in "Hawthorne's Myths for Children: The Author Versus his Audience," *SSF* 10:35–46, examines the two books of classical myths retold for children (*A Wonder-Book for Boys and Girls* and *Tanglewood Tales*, published in 1852 and 1853 respectively), considering the framing strategies by which each collection is unified, the ideas of myth and of childhood according to which the stories are developed, and finally the persona of the author as a smiling public man. The entire project of writing children's stories is viewed in the light of Hawthorne's continuing wish to be a popular author—not merely to achieve a popular success, but actually to be the sort of person who naturally wrote books with mass appeal.

Although it should not necessarily be so, it does seem that the type of essay which takes a theme or aspect of Hawthorne's writing and traces it in a sequence of stories is almost always competent but somewhat mechanical. Perhaps this is because the genre represents Hawthorne as a static rather than changing mind, and there is always something tedious in fixed ideas. There are four such articles this year. Claudia D. Johnson, in "Hawthorne and Nineteenth-Century Perfectionism," *AL* 44:585–95, outlines the doctrine and links it to Hawthorne through his Bowdoin Professor Thomas C. Upham, one of its exponents. Hawthorne used the doctrine's contention that the convert, after having descended into his heart for meditation and purification, must return to loving community with his fellows if his regeneration is to be complete. Several characters represent a failure to go beyond the first stage of inwardness, especially Goodman Brown, Rev. Hooper, Wakefield, Digby, Adam Coburn, and Roderick Elliston. Perfectionism may have been an influence; but the narrative pattern has been often noted before, and Hawthorne's characters held up to censure for the same human defects from various other points of view. Mary Allen discusses "Smiles and Laughter in Hawthorne," *PQ* 52:119–28. She observes that these seldom represent humor but are at best benign, more often grotesque and bitter. This too is not a new observation.

In "The Forsaken Maiden in Hawthorne's Stories," *ATQ* 19:13–19, Sheldon W. Liebman groups Beatrice Rappaccini, Lady Eleonore, and Georgiana under this rubric and considers them as symbols of the idea that "death and evil are inherent in human life and that these are the very qualities that make immortality possible." Again, this conclusion is not exactly news. Finally, Dennis Brown uses two stories to demonstrate the resemblance of Hawthorne to R. D. Laing, in "Literature and Existential Psychoanalysis: 'My Kinsman, Major Molineux' and 'Young Goodman Brown'" (*CRevAS* 4:65–73). The focus is on Laing's concept of "disorientation," the ontological insecurity generated by an encounter with experience that cannot be explained, as a way of explaining the adventures of Hawthorne's protagonists. The concept works better for Robin Molineux than for Young Goodman Brown.

Taking up the stories in alphabetical order, I begin with James E. Devlin's proposal of "A German Analogue for 'The Ambitious Guest,'" *ATQ* 17:171–74, an 1829 ballad "Das Gewitter" ("The Thunderstorm") by the Swabian poet Gustav Schwab. There is no evidence that Hawthorne read it, but there is a probability, and the similarities between the poem and the tale are considerable. George Monteiro adds to all the other sources of serpent imagery in "Egotism; or, the Bosom Serpent" that of the medieval emblem tradition in which Envy is figured as a person whose heart is being gnawed by a snake ("Hawthorne's Emblematic Serpent," *NHJ* 3:134–42). Robert E. Morsberger tries to draw a parallel between the spiritual tension in Jonathan Edwards's works and the spiritual tension of Reverend Hooper in an unoriginal and unfootnoted article titled "'The Minister's Black Veil': Shrouded in a Blackness, Ten Times Black," *NEQ* 46:454–63. B. R. Brubaker studies "Hawthorne's Experiment in Popular Form: 'Mr. Higginbotham's catastrophe,'" *SHR* 7:155–66. The tale is more characteristic of popular humor than anything else Hawthorne wrote, containing such conventional elements as the frame, the figure of the shrewd Yankee, the use of vernacular, and so on. Brubaker feels that the story is a successful experiment with the genre, and regrets that Hawthorne found the mode uncongenial to his temperament. He incorrectly places it in the early projected collection *Seven Tales of My Native Land* when in fact it was part of a later project, *The Story Teller.*

Mario D'Avanzo purports to study "The Literary Sources of 'My Kinsman, Major Molineaux' [sic]: Shakespeare, Coleridge, Milton," *SSF* 10:121–36, but in fact discusses tonal echoes and reinforcements that can be felt if one puts the story in relation to *Midsummer Night's Dream*, *Biographia Literaria*, and *Paradise Lost*. Far too many articles that masquerade as source or analog studies are like this one, arbitrary yokings of various literary works for the sake of exercising one's critical perceptiveness. The genre is excellent for term-papers, but probably should not be published. John C. Willoughby's fine "'The Old Manse' Revisited: Some Analogues for Art," *NEQ* 46:45–61, studies the tone of the preface and the metaphors involving the author's relation to his audience and to his work. He points out how the reader is always approached, with "strangely remote intimacy," as a guest, and how Hawthorne takes a "graciously Janus-like stance upon the threshold of his works." The works are sometimes figured, then, as the author's house; they are also described in botanic metaphors where the author is the gardener. These metaphors, Willoughby states, stress the transciency of the work of art.

Robert Daly, in "Fideism and the Allusive Mode in 'Rappaccini's Daughter'" (*NCF* 28:25–37) interprets the story according to a doctrine with which Hawthorne can be connected only remotely, if at all. If we apply this doctrine to "Rappaccini's Daughter" we get this reading of the story: Giovanni lacks faith, and killing Beatrice doesn't solve his dilemma. This, however, we ought to get directly from reading the story itself. What, then, is the point of cluttering up the field with interpretative apparatus that is unnecessary and quite possibly unjustified? Jack Scherting suggests that the description of the Upas tree in Erasmus Darwin's *The Botanical Garden* is a source for "Rappaccini's Daughter." Possibly, too, the original account of the tree by a Dr. N. P. Foersch in the *London Magazine*, 1783, was another source. If Hawthorne read Foersch, he might have used the doctor himself as a model for Dr. Rappaccini ("The Upas Tree in Dr. Rappaccini's Garden: New Light on Hawthorne's Tale," *SAF* 1:203–07).

Robert J. Daly has written a good article in "History and Chivalric Myth in 'Roger Malvin's Burial,'" *EIHC* 109:99–115. He traces the transformation of the sordid historical event that was Lovells's fight into the chivalric myth that it became; he suggests that Hawthorne knew just how the real facts had been heroicised; and finally he argues that Reuben Bourne's story is a commentary on the events and the mythologising process. For Reuben, too, tries to transform the events of his life into a chivalric lie, and the lie destroys him. The attempt to embody a chivalric fantasy leads to a total entrapment. Thus by extension Hawthorne would conclude that a writer of New England history must set himself to rewrite it truthfully in order that the current generation might establish a right relation to the past. This is a sophisticated discussion of Hawthorne's sense of history and of himself as a historian, a welcome relief from the generally platitudinous discussions of the past in Hawthorne's work. Dieter Schulz contributes to the psychological reading of this story in "Imagination and Self-Improvement: The Ending of 'Roger Malvin's Burial,'" *SSF* 10:183–86. Schulz says more plainly what other critics have recently hinted: that Reuben progresses into madness, and that his final act coupled with his sense of absolution signifies a total withdrawal into subjectivity, i.e., into insanity.

Edward J. Gallagher looks at "Hawthorne's 'Sir William Phipps,'" *ESQ* 19:213–18, and finds even in this early piece an author "already exercising considerable latitude with his historical material," departing radically from the favorable treatment given Phipps in the source he used. Mark L. Asquino's "Hawthorne's 'Village Uncle' and Melville's *Moby-Dick*" (*SSF* 10:413–14) takes its cue from the fact that Melville included a passage from the sketch in his "Extracts," and reads the piece as though Melville had written it. A much better article on this sketch is "The Technique of Counterstatement: Theme and Meaning in Hawthorne's 'The Village Uncle,'" *NHJ* 3:154–61. R. K. Gupta argues that an under-layer in the sketch modifies its surface meaning. The sketch is not simply an assertion of the preferability of a quiet, warm, domestic life over the difficult, isolated life of the artist. Since the story does not recapitulate actual experience but is rather a reverie of the uncle, in effect it only pretends to reject the artist's life while in fact it nostalgically or yearningly imagines it.

Two articles on "Young Goodman Brown" this year propose virtually the same reading of the story, and that reading—"Young Goodman Brown" as a critique of American innocence—is an interpretive commonplace. Robert E. Morsberger in "The Woe that is Madness: Goodman Brown and the Face of the Fire," *NHJ* 3:177–82, says that "Brown's tragedy is not the loss of his simple faith; rather it is that his faith is too simple to begin with." Barton Levi St. Armand takes his reading beyond the psychological to the historical, as many critics have done before him, claiming that Hawthorne intended his tale to represent a particularly American dilemma—naive idealism giving way before the stress of the real to equally naive apocalyptic pessimism ("'Young Goodman Brown' as Historical Allegory," *NHJ* 3:183–97). St. Armand's historicism is faulty, however; if it were true (and it can only be a supposition, given the available evidence) that "Young Goodman Brown" was originally one of the *Provincial Tales*, then it is unlikely that it was intended as a criticism of the nation; for *Provincial Tales* was conceived under the influence of the critical doctrine of literary nationalism. Hawthorne's historical purposes in "Young Goodman Brown,"—if the story was intended to have any—would have had to be different. Actually, I do not think that American writers became consciously preoccupied with the theme of innocence as a dangerous national trait until after the Civil War. And, on the psychological level, I doubt that it is so much Brown's innocence that interests Hawthorne—indeed, I doubt that he thinks him "innocent," given his behavior on that fateful night—as his hypocrisy.

University of Illinois

3. Poe

G. R. Thompson

Since the Poe bibliography has been resumed (see below) and the MLA International Bibliography has become more nearly current, it is apparent that a number of works, especially foreign ones which characteristically show up late in bibliographies, have been omitted from review in these pages; accordingly, I have made an effort to go back and pick up major items since 1970. As observed some years ago, Poe, like it or not, seems to be our most widely read 19th-century author abroad; and this year's section on literary relations and foreign views of Poe is large, including nearly a dozen books and 40 articles. Four recent books attest to the special interest that Poe holds for the Japanese; two books in Spanish have appeared; and three books have been published on Poe's reputation and influence in Scandinavia, Russia, and Hungary. In addition to a small anthology of criticism, a catalogue of manuscripts, and two editions, four critical books on Poe appeared in 1973. The number of articles of all kinds treated here exceeds one hundred.

i. Manuscripts, Texts, Sources and Allusions, Bibliography

Joseph J. Moldenhauer, in "Poe Manuscripts in Austin" (*LCUT* n.s. 3[1971]:82–87) summarized the holdings of the Koester collection at the University of Texas. Now his *Descriptive Catalog of Edgar Allan Poe Manuscripts in The Humanities Research Center Library* (Austin, Univ. of Tex.) has been published. The Koester collection contains among other items, 63 letters and epistolary fragments, six drafts and copies of poems, two long tales, 14 whole and partial

Editor's Note: Usually Poe is treated in Chapter 11 ("Poe and Nineteenth-Century Poetry"), but this year the work on minor poets has been inconsequential and the chapter has been moved into the single-author section. Next year it may resume its usual place.

critical essays, five printed volumes marked or annotated by Poe, and seven documents bearing his signature. Added to the ten items from the Miriam Lutcher Stark Library, the University of Texas now has 107 separate Poe manuscripts. In addition, the Koester collection includes first editions of all but one of Poe's books, contemporary magazine and newspaper printings, collected editions, daguerreotypes, portraits, sculptures, original illustrations, music written for the poems, an extensive body of material by Poe's relatives, friends, admirers, and so on. The importance for Poe studies is considerable. The collection contains three previously unpublished letters, allows for corrections to letters published from transcribed copies, enlarges and refines the corpus of Poe's critical writings, makes available unpublished fragments, and reveals extreme variations between manuscript material and published essays. For example, the collection contains five manuscripts of late revisions to the *Literati* papers, enough new material for the reconstruction of one or more unpublished *Marginalia* installments, a new manuscript of "The Spectacles," and a text of *Eureka* that reveals the progress of Poe's revisions. Except for the lack of an exhaustive index, Moldenhauer's *Descriptive Catalog* is a model for other Poe repositories to emulate.

Other new manuscript and holograph material is scarce. "Three New Poe Letters" (*ATQ* 14:89–91) reprints catalogue descriptions of three letters offered for sale in 1971, along with photostats: Poe to John Kirk Townsend (March 9, 1843), Poe to Edgar S. Van Winkle (Nov. 12, 1836), Poe to Van Winkle (Nov. 26, 1836). The Poe-Townsend letter, however, is not precisely "new"; it is instead a relocated original, a version of which has already been published in John Ward Ostrom's edition of the *Letters* (Cambridge, Mass., Harvard Univ. Press [1948], pp. 226–27) transcribed from a copy. Burton R. Pollin, in "A Spurious Letter to A. N. Howard" (*PoeS* 6:27–28) identifies a letter in the New York State Library at Albany as a forgery.

A definitive edition of Poe's tales and critical writings is the single most urgent need in Poe studies. Kevin M. McCarthy, for example, in "'Sameness' Versus 'Saneness' in Poe's 'Morella'" (*AN&Q* 11:149–50) demonstrates that Poe was accurate in his quotation from Locke's *Essay Concerning Human Understanding* (II,27,ix), whereas R. W. Griswold and T. O. Mabbott among others, allowed the word "sameness" to become "saneness," thereby distorting Poe's meaning into a slightly more psychological one than he apparently intended. Two recent textual items not previously noticed in these pages further illustrate the problems. James B. Reece's "An Error in Some Recent Reprintings of Poe's 1847 Critique of Hawthorne" (*PoeS* 4[1971]:47) shows in the standard Harrison edition of 1902 and in a selected edition by Mabbott in 1954 (as well as in other recent editions) that Poe's original word "unpopular" becomes the reverse, inverting his denial of the incompatibility of popularity and originality. George Egon Hatvary in "The Whereabouts of Poe's 'Fifty Suggestions'" (*PoeS* 4[1971]:47) notes that the Harrison edition erroneously gives *Graham's Magazine* for May and June 1845 as the first appearance of "Fifty Suggestions," confuses the publication data of "A Chapter of Suggestions," and includes other errors that suggest that Harrison did not go back to the originals, as he implied, but instead based his editing of these items on Griswold, whom he had disparaged. Benjamin Franklin Fisher's "To 'The Assignation' from 'The Visionary' and Poe's Decade of Revising" (*LC* 39:89–105) reprints the earliest version of the tale from *Godey's Lady's Book* of January 1834, which contains significant variations from the 1845 text; Fisher comments on the romantic qualities of the style and narration of this early version. Richard P. Benton's *"Eureka: A Prose Poem" by Edgar Allan Poe: New Edition with Line Numbers, Exploratory Essay, and Bibliographical Guide* (Hartford, Conn., Transcendental Books) fills an important need by reprinting a facsimile of the 1848 Putnam edition; Benton includes a critical survey of the scholarship on *Eureka* and a four-part bibliographical guide.

With Poe's critical essays and reviews, the problem of accurate texts is compounded. In a useful note, "Thomas Ollive Mabbott on the Canon of Poe's Reviews" (*PoeS* 5[1972]:56–57), J. Lasley Dameron lists 15 reviews in the Harrison edition that Mabbott felt should be rejected, along with two that he thought questionable. Mabbott's rejections of the Harrison reviews, however, are unaccompanied by argument or supporting data and seem in some instances to be purely arbitrary. One thing Poe scholarship does not need are reviews either added to the Poe canon or rejected on the basis of vague stylistic nuances or indirect allusions. Mabbott's edition of the *Poems* (see *ALS 1969*, pp. 182–83) is a monument to the late scholar's life's work, and the continuation of his edition by Burton Pollin through the tales and sketches will doubtless render Poe scholarship an immeasurable service. But a thorough, accurate, and conservative edition of Poe's critical essays and reviews needs to be undertaken by a team of qualified textual editors acting in accordance with the CEAA's highest standards.

In a densely packed note, "Another Look at Poe's Dr. Ollapod" (*PoeS* 6:28), A. John Roche challenges the conclusions of Burton Pollin's "Poe's Dr. Ollapod" (*AL* 42[1970]:80–82). Pollin pointed out that the continued use of the name of a comic character from George Coleman's *The Poor Gentleman* in succeeding versions of "A Predicament" would have been indiscreet during the time Poe worked for William E. Burton, for Burton had played the role of Dr. Ollapod on the stage. Roche believes the matter more complicated. In the 1830s, Willis Gaylord Clark's "Ollapod" papers were appearing in his twin brother's journal, the *Knickerbocker.* Poe and Willis Gaylord Clark had quarreled over Poe's mocking review of *Norman Leslie*, and later Poe and Lewis Gaylord Clark quarreled. Poe then satirized the posthumous publication of *The Literary Remains of Willis Gaylord Clark* (edited by Lewis Gaylord Clark) in his tale "The Literary Life of Thingum-Bob, Esq." Roche feels the original jab in the 1838 version of "A Predicament" was at the Clarks and the 1845 jab aimed at both Burton and the surviving Clark brother. The reader is also referred to Pollin's "Poe's Literary Use of 'Oppodeldoc' and Other Patent Medicines" (*PoeS* 4[1971]:30–32) for a contrary view, though that essay is primarily a study of Poe's playful uses of the names of patent medicines.

In "Dean Swift in the Works of Poe" (*N&Q* 218:244–46), Pollin also provides a chronological survey of about a dozen references Poe made to Jonathan Swift or his works; but about half of these have already been noted by other scholars, and several of the new allusions Pollin adduces derive from what seem to me rather tenuous inferences. In "Poe as Edward S. T. Grey" (*BSUF* 14:44–46), Pollin suggests that the provenance of the pseudonym may be discovered in Poe's review of Henry Hirst's *The Coming of the Mammoth*, where he praises the poem "Everard Grey"; but this review and a resemblance to Poe's line about Emily Gray has already been noticed by Mabbott (*Poems*, pp. 395, 462); Pollin then suggests that the "S. T." part of the name came from Coleridge's full name, but Coleridge has no connection with any of the previous argument. In "Poe's Illustration for 'The Island of Fay': A Hoax Detected" (*MDAC* 1[1972]:33–

45), Pollin reprints the John Martin plates that John Sartain adapted to illustrate Poe's story. Another illustrated story, "Morning on the Wissahiccon," along with "The Oblong Box," bears vague resemblances to two 1827 pieces published in a New York periodical, according to Gerald E. Gerber in "Poe and *The Manuscript*" (*PoeS* 6:27); specific resemblances between "The Angel of the Odd" and two pieces published in the same journal in 1828 are also suggested. In a posthumously published note, "The Books in the House of Usher" (*BI* 19:3–7), Mabbott discusses Poe's "peculiar knowledge in a field where one would little expect to find him expert–bibliography." All of the exotic books in Roderick Usher's library are real, and Mabbott discusses their publication history and contents.

Two works deal with "Oriental" sources, Athar M. Murtuza's "An Arabian Source for Poe's 'The Pit and the Pendulum'" (*PoeS* 5[1972]:52) and Mukhtar A. Isani's "Some Sources for Poe's 'Tale of the Ragged Mountains'" (*PoeS* 5[1972]:38–40). Murtuza, noting previous commentary on Poe's use of George Sale's translation of the Koran in "Al Aaraaf," draws attention to two relevant Koranic passages that occur within an apocalyptic framework underscoring the theme of retribution eventually overtaking the oppressors. Isani regards the Orientalism of "Ragged Mountains" as legitimate use of historical matter, rather than plagiarism. It is clear from an error in the account in C. R. Gleig's *Memoirs* that the *Memoirs* themselves are the source for Poe's version of Oldeb's fatal sortie rather than Macaulay's review. Warren Hasting's *Narrative of the Insurrection* (1782) and Richard Brinsley Sheridan's impeachment speeches also contributed.

The "Current Poe Bibliography" that had been exhaustively compiled and brilliantly annotated by Richard P. Benton for several years (1965–1971) has now been resumed after nearly a two-year lapse by J. Lasley Dameron, Thomas C. Carlson, Judy Osowski, and John E. Reilly (*PoeS* 6:36–42). Following the form of Dameron's *Edgar Allan Poe: A Bibliography of Criticism, 1827–1967* (forthcoming from the Univ. Press of Va. in 1974), the annotations are a good deal briefer than Benton's. They are also objectively nonjudgmental, whereas Benton did not hesitate to express an opinion, so that perhaps the losses and gains balance out. One could wish, however, for an inclusive round-up of reviews, consistent annotation of foreign items, and continuation of the "fugitive" bibliography (see *ALS*

1971, pp. 190–91). The Poe section in Harry Hayden Clark's Goldentree Bibliography, *American Literature: Poe through Garland* (New York, Appleton-Century-Crofts [1971], pp. 76–82), is a somewhat eccentric selection of 132 items, and there are errors of dates and the like. Another selected bibliography, covering the years 1958–70, is the updating of the Poe section in the *Bibliography Supplement II: LHUS*, ed. Richard M. Ludwig (New York, Macmillan [1972]), pp. 237–39, which is concise and accurate. A highly specialized bibliography is Pollin's "More Music to Poe" (*Music and Letters* 54:391–403), a listing of more than 200 compositions based on Poe's works, supplementing May Garrettson Evan's 1939 study, *Music and Edgar Allan Poe*, and two additions to the bibliography by R. C. Archibald (1940) and I. B. Cauthen (1949), but Pollin fails to cite the holdings in the Stark Library announced in 1971 (see above). Pollin has also contributed a specialized index, "Place Names in Poe's Creative Writings" (*PoeS* 6:43–48), which supplements his *Dictionary of Names and Titles in Poe's Collected* [*sic*] *Works* (see *ALS 1968*, p. 158).

ii. Biography

Two works on Poe's army years have appeared. Kenneth W. Cameron, in "Young Poe and the Army—Victorian Editing" (*ATQ* 20[Sup.]: 154–82), presents a number of facsimiles supplied by the National Archives, Washington, D.C., relevant to Poe's time in the army, pointing out that in the days before photostats and xerography scholars like George Woodberry had to rely on badly transcribed or edited papers prepared by army clerks. Disputing previous assumptions that Poe's life at West Point contributed little to his literary and intellectual development, Karl E. Oelke's "Poe at West Point—A Revaluation" (*PoeS* 6:1–6) is a carefully detailed consideration of the military and academic regimen of the academy during Poe's time.

Two more contemporary responses to Poe have been presented recently, along with the text of a reminiscence of Poe not readily available. Burton Pollin, in "An 1839 Review of Poe's *Tales* in Willis' *The Corsair*" (*PoeS* 5[1972]:56), presents a previously unnoticed review of Poe, sketches the probable circumstances leading to the review. John E. Reilly discusses the connections between a fragmentary version of a contemporary satire on Poe, Bryant, Longfellow, Whittier, and Willis, called *A Mirror for Authors* (1848), and an expanded version, *Parnassus in Pillory* (1851) in his "Poe in Pillory: An Early Version of a Satire by A. J. H. Duganne" (*PoeS* 6:9–12). Poe is portrayed as a "literary Mohawk" and "mad on analytics." Reilly reproduces five F. O. C. Darley cartoons illustrating the text.

In "Reminiscences of Poe by an Employee of the *Broadway Journal*" (*PoeS* 6:33–34), Mukhtar Ali Isani presents the complete text of one version of Alexander Crane's account of Poe's kindnesses to him when he was an office boy for the *Broadway Journal*, published in the Omaha *Sunday World Herald*, July 13, 1902. Isani renders a service by publishing the entire account, but he is in error in assuming that the article is unknown, for references to other versions occur in Mabbott's 1969 "Annals" and Edward Wagenknecht's 1963 biography. Emilio De Grazia, in "Poe's Devoted Democrat, George Lippard" (*PoeS* 6:6–8), discusses Lippard's attacks on George Graham and his group; Lippard repeatedly came to Poe's defense, and Poe in turn defended Lippard. Ottavio M. Casale, in "The Battle of Boston: A Revaluation of Poe's Lyceum Appearance" (*AL* 45:423–28), argues that Poe's reading of "Al Aaraaf" to the Boston Lyceum was not, as he afterwards claimed, a hoax," or, as his biographers have claimed, a characteristic act of perversity; it was instead a sincere attempt to impress his audience with an appropriate "philosophical" and "weighty" work, and Poe's ironic defense was an overreaction to negative criticism. As presented, however, the evidence for this not implausible thesis is thin.

iii. General Studies

Haldeen Braddy's slim *Three Dimensional Poe* (El Paso, Texas Western Press) is a somewhat romantically conceived "guidebook" for the general reader and the undergraduate student, whom he wishes to introduce to Poe's "brilliance in three dimensions, as a poet, a storyteller, and an essayist"; primarily biographical in approach, it turns on Poe's "life and loves" and the pattern of his "brief, tragic career." Also apparently aimed at the undergraduate is David B. Kesterson's *Critics on Poe* (Coral Gables, Univ. of Miami Press), a brief anthology of snippets of criticism from Margaret Fuller to Floyd Stovall. Eric W. Carlson's 23-page *Poe on the Soul of Man* (Baltimore, Edgar Allan Poe Society and the Enoch Pratt Free Library) is an attempt to extend and refine his recent interpretations of Poe's central theme as the "rediscovery of the psychal power of man" (see *ALS 1972*, pp. 212–13). As before, Carlson divides Poe's writings into early, middle, and late "phases" in his career. He also draws parallels between Poe and several recent "counterculture" books, the Women's Liberation Movement, and the like.

Noriko Mizuta Lippet's "The Grotesque and Arabesque in Poe" (*Jōsai Jinbun Kenkyu* [Studies in the Humanities] 1:132–70) presents a highly interesting approach to Poe through the terms "grotesque" and "arabesque," which Lippit regards not as separable categories but contiguous and complementary. Lippit argues that Poe believed in the power of the imagination to "transcend" the phenomenal world. But since this world is in a degenerated state and man alienated from it by his own divided consciousness, the destructive imagination (the grotesque) must be pushed to its logical extreme: the Poe hero retreats from phenomenal reality into a solipsistic dream world; here, in the final act of inwardly "creative" thinking (the arabesque), he subjectively destroys the outside world for himself and thus "transcends" it. This pattern is the central narrative myth in Poe's writings: the hero loses the paradisaical valley of idyllic nature in which he once dwelt with an ideal woman and retreats to the city (grotesque symbol of sterility and meaninglessness); but instead of trying to regain the former idyllic state of nature, he tries to recover his equilibrium by retreating even further, into a Gothic mansion or a closed room (arabesque symbol of his inner consciousness), where he prepares himself for an inward spiralling transcendence of the alienated state through death and reunion with nothingness. Lippit's argument, however, suffers from a failure to define firmly and precisely the historical root meanings of the two terms, so that the definitions assigned seem increasingly arbitrary.

Two essays address themselves to Poe's "duality," in different terms and in differing degrees of clarity, by positing a crisis in intellectual history in Poe's time: the shifting away from one world order to an incomplete assumption of a new one (Allen Tate's "perfect literary situation," Peckham's "negative romanticism"). Terrence Hipolito, in "On the Two Poe's" (*MDAC* 1[1972]:15–20) asserts that Poe "lived simultaneously in two worlds." One of these is the "grotesque and arabesque world" (the terms are left undefined), in which truth is symbolic and apprehended intuitively; the other is the "ratiocinative" world, in which truth is knowable through the physical senses and the rational mind. "Poe's heroes, thus, tend to be either mystical lunatics or detectives." The other essay is by Erich W. Sippel. Quoting Daniel Hoffman on Poe's "obsession" with "unity" and the contradictory "particularity" of Poe's work as a whole, Sippel chooses a breezy title, "Bolting the Whole Shebang Together: Poe's Predicament" (*Criticism* 15:289–308) for an essay on Poe's metaphysical concerns. Poe's career, Sippel argues, is a series of incomplete attempts to reconcile two opposing world views: one which sees the universe as an orderly, logical, mechanical, closed system of cause and effect; and one which sees the universe as a disorderly, irrational, capricious, open-ended affair. The longest and most interesting of the discussions is that of "The Murders in the Rue Morgue," a tale Sippel sees as posited on a system of cause and effect, in which the ourangutan—then thought by some an intermediate link in the Chain of Being between man and animal and thus between rationality and irrationality—simultaneously affirms order and threatens it. Dupin's logic becomes a "last-ditch defense" against the encroachment of the chaotic world of chance. Roger Forclaz, in "Edgar Poe et les Animaux" (*RLV* 39:483–96), observes that Poe's characteristic duality may be seen in his attitude toward animals: affection and appreciation of them opposed to the mystery and terror they inspire. Animals are frequently used for comparison to human beings, as grotesque metaphors for human beings, and as symbols of the human condition itself (as in "The Conqueror Worm").

Sharon Furrow, in "Psyche and Setting: Poe's Picturesque Landscapes" (*Criticism* 15:16–27), deals with Poe's exterior settings as symbols of the "interior world of the artist." Going beyond previous critics, she argues that Poe specifically conceived his works in terms of conventional styles of pictorialism in landscape painting: the sublime and the picturesque. She cites the recurrence of these aesthetic terms in Poe's writings, along with allusions to Claude and Salvator Rosa. The sublime depicts nature at its most impressive and threatening; the picturesque depicts nature more gently, evoking a somewhat pleasing gloom or nostalgia. She argues that the picturesque, with its indefiniteness and its distortion of the natural world to heighten emotion and to evoke a sense of mystery, was generally more suitable for Poe's psychological themes.

Why one should go to the trouble of writing a book on a writer he does not like is puzzling. Yet here is such a book, apparently—Richard M. Fletcher's *The Stylistic Development of Edgar Allan Poe* (The Hague, Mouton). Fletcher discusses the "seeming incoherence and lack of sustained momentum" in Poe's poetic career, his tendency to "toy with punctuation" rather than to experiment with real meaning, his sacrifice of sense to sound to produce "bathetic gibberish," his intellectual shallowness, his charlatanism in prose as well as in poetry, his inability to create an effective "persona," his limited vocabulary, the frivolousness of such works as "The Fall of the House of Usher," the "junk heap" quality of *Pym*, and so on. Fletcher's thesis is that Poe's method is neither that of the "allegorist" nor the "symbolist," but that of the "synonymist." What this label means, however, is that Poe is a "word painter," a "manipulator of vocabulary," whose main concern it is to give the *illusion* that his work is more "dense and dramatically rendered" than it actually is.

To attack Poe is not reprehensible, but to do so while pretending to study his "development" suggests some uncertainty or disingenuousness of purpose. In a real attack, on the other hand, would not a major stratagem be a detailed engagement of those critics who have seen something of value in Poe? Yet one is not at all sure that Fletcher knows who such critics are. A single example will suffice: some of the specific analyses of Poe's levels of vocabulary and stylistic devices in individual stories are not without merit, and yet Fletcher gives us an extended analysis of the apocalyptic language of "The Pit and the Pendulum" without a single reference to David Hirsch's excellent study of the very same matter (see *ALS 1968*, p. 168). Similarly, the "most helpful" modern selected bibliography, according to Fletcher, is to be found in Vincent Buranelli's TUSAS study, an introductory guide more than a decade out of date.

Once one works through the frequently cumbersome jargon that seems overlaid upon the basic argument, he finds that the thesis of David Halliburton's *Edgar Allan Poe: A Phenomenological View* (Princeton, N.J., Princeton Univ. Press) is simply that Poe's imaginative writings reveal a unified pattern of experience. This statement, however, does some injustice to Halliburton's study, which, despite a methodology that leads to frequent elaboration of the obvious, is still an important contribution to Poe criticism, for it contains provocative discussions of Poe's major works.

"This book is, I believe," Halliburton writes, "the first general interpretation of an American author from a phenomenological point of view." Halliburton's chapter on methodology, however, only sketches the critical theory he seeks to employ, and he is careful to point out that he is more interested in the readings of Poe's texts than in the illustration of a critical method. Nevertheless, the "phenomenological" element is constantly present, and some further clarification is in order. According to phenomenological philosophy, since the very act of perceiving objective reality is complicated by filtering that reality through the mind, we should attempt to describe "phenomena" with a cautionary awareness that the mind is prone to impose meanings on objects external to it. We should approach the description of any phenomenon with a mind empty of preconceptions and reduce the object under scrutiny to basic forms (geometric shapes, numbers, fundamental elements of space and time, and so on). By this reduction, we may begin to reconcile the subjective structure (the mind) and the objective structure (external reality). In literary criticism, a first step is the analysis of language by naming and classifying sounds, sentences, and concatenations of sentences. A second step is to look at this language as "gestural," as expressive of the shaping consciousness behind the reported phenomena. The critic must look at the presented objects in an author's fictive world with an awareness of the special "perspective" in which they are presented; the *manner* of perception by the author becomes the major concern of the phenomenological critic. His task is somehow to get inside the subjective world of any individual work, to discover its "latent essence," which connects it as a structure of "intentionality" to all other writings by the same consciousness. The critic recreates the world of the literary work and its creator by empathetic alignment of his unprejudiced mind with the reported phenomena in such a way as to perceive the structuring patterns of the author's habitual way of seeing.[1]

For Halliburton, the collective consciousness of Poe's narrators become Poe's consciousness. Separate chronological examinations of the poetry, the gothic fiction, the philosophical colloquies, and

1. For a fuller discussion of current "structuralist" criticism, to which phenomenological criticism is related, see *ALS 1969*, pp. 332–43, *ALS 1971*, pp. 369–76. A lucid survey of phenomenology is Robert Magliola's "The Phenomenological Approach to Literature: Its Theory and Methodology" (*Lang&S* 5 [1972]:79–99. Halliburton's is a rather loosely applied mode.

Eureka reveal patterns of psychological and material phenomena that embody tensions between existential states of power and powerlessness, aggression and victimization, dehumanization and transcendence, man and God, despair and affirmation. But, Halliburton argues, Poe's total corpus of writing reveals gradual ascension toward transcendence and affirmation, to becoming one with the "other," to bridging the gulf between man and God. Shifting from poetry to prose, Poe's writings demonstrate an expanded consciousness ceaselessly seeking to complete his full aesthetic design. The unfolding process of intentionality in Poe's body of work illustrates a cosmogony, contained within that microcosm of Poe's total consciousness that each work presents. With his final cosmological work, Poe "transcends" the earlier problems of annihilation and separation plaguing his vision of unity, and he achieves a supernal vision of beneficence, beauty, plenitude, and oneness with the Godhead. (See also chapter 18 ["Themes, Topics, and Criticism"] pp. 411–438.

This sort of reading of Poe's entire body of work has been argued before, notably by Joseph J. Moldenhauer (see *ALS 1968*, pp. 159–60), but there are fundamental problems with it, as I tried to point out in a reply to Moldenhauer (see *ALS 1970*, p. 208). This is not the place to make those arguments again, but surely it is clear that both the affirmative and the negative impulses coexist throughout Poe's writings. To call Poe's vision of death and annihilation blissful, as Moldenhauer does, is to read the gothic tales in a most peculiar way. To call, as Halliburton does, "Ligeia" his strongest testimonial to the "indestructibility of life" is to ignore many of its "phenomena." Nothing in Halliburton (or Eakin, below) demonstrates that we as readers are supposed to share the final "ecstatic" vision of the narrator (an equivocal point in itself). Moreover, even if we do surmise that the narrator is pleased rather than awestricken or horrified at the end, what about the now dead Rowena? The theory that Poe's consciousness may be arrived at by the total consciousness of Poe's narrators is plausible insofar as the consciousness of Poe's characters bears a steady relationship to Poe's. But Poe habitually places his narrators in "perspectives," and Halliburton repeatedly overlooks the psychological complexities of these narrators as fictional characters.

More importantly, phenomenology is insistent on dealing with the total corpus of the writings of an author; and yet Halliburton selects only a few of Poe's many comic pieces for discussion. In fact, he even tells us that the pursuit of irony and satire leads us away from the serious intentionality of Poe's cosmogony. In other words, in a study—avowedly undertaken without preconceptions—of an author's consciousness as it is revealed in the various patterns of perception from work to work, the critic has arbitrarily decided to dismiss nearly half of his subject's work because it apparently does not fit his preconceived pattern.

A more reasonable attitude is that of Hennig Cohen, who, in "A Comic Mode of the Romantic Imagination: Poe, Hawthorne, Melville," (a chapter in Louis Rubin's valuable collection, *Comic Imagination*, pp. 85–99), observes that the comic writings of these three authors stems from a "dark knowledge" that generally blurs the line between comedy and tragedy; the reader must always be alert to the sardonic joke. Overtly and covertly, both Poe and Melville are deliberately playful with their readers, "toying with them and pushing them about . . . often making them the butt of their jokes." Especially with Poe it is hard to tell when his intention is serious or comic. In "The Cask of Amontillado" and "Hop-Frog," for example, the revenge theme paradoxically embodies a ritual that is potentially restorative of order in the traditional high comic sense; but Poe pushes it to an excess that approaches the parodic; thus Montresor is in one sense a grim practical joker and Hop-Frog a parodic exaggeration of him. Bruce K. Martin, in "Poe's 'Hop-Frog' and the Retreat from Comedy" (*SSF* 10:288–90), argues that "Hop-Frog" by means of steadily increasing narrative distance effects a "moral reversal" wherein the comically negative presentation of the king and his court becomes "relative and highly qualified," so much so that the comic element is "exhausted and Hop-Frog's final deeds . . . horrify the reader." These studies may be supplemented by J. Marshall Trieber's brief but provocative "The Scornful Grin: A Study of Poesque Humor" (*PoeS* 4[1971]:32–34).

iv. Fiction

The technique of Poe's fiction as it developed from the early gothic tales to the detective story is the subject of Benjamin Franklin Fisher's "Blackwood Articles á la Poe: How to Make a False Start Pay" (*RLV* 39:418–32). Many of Poe's stories begin, Fisher argues, as the "traditional thriller" but alter into something comic or hoaxical.

The false-start technique, in conjunction with that of the "explai gothic" of Mrs. Radcliffe, leads logically to the detective story, which false starts are initially given the reader as he tries to pick c clues and solve the mystery. Conversely, do we find techniques simil to that of the comic tale and the detective story in the "serious" gothi stories? Fisher is not specific on this point, and it is well to note that he has on occasion argued the reverse (see above, and *ALS 1971*, p. 198). But apparently we are to see "a strong vein of conscious irony underlying" much of Poe's fiction: Poe is often simultaneously winking at an elite core of "aware readers" while hoodwinking the "lumpish masses." This thesis is perhaps not without merit.

In *Poe's Fiction: Romantic Irony in the Gothic Tales* (Madison, Univ. of Wis. Press), I attempt to show by application of theories of irony "in the air" in Poe's time and by close readings of Poe's works that the comic, the parodic, and the absurd are structural as well as thematic elements in Poe's gothic stories. The book attempts systematically to reconcile the comic and gothic sides of Poe's writing. In an earlier work (see *ALS 1972*, pp. 213–14), I offered a brief discussion of the concept of romantic irony as the simultaneous entertainment of belief in and seriocomic detachment from any subject. At the heart of romantic irony is simultaneity of contrastive structures of meanings in an interpenetrating system of structures held in harmonious tension. Poe, I argue, early perfected the "ambiguously explained" mode of the gothic tale, which became the dominant form of 19th-century American romantic fiction. In the ambiguous gothic tale, although the occult element is undercut by insinuated natural and psychological explanations, the events rarely can be distinguished as either actual or mental but are instead an ambivalent combination of both. This ambivalence of meaning in the tales is a structural parallel to Poe's awareness of the incomprehensibility of human existence, so that Poe's ironic vision has as its philosophical basis the question of epistemology: the ambiguity of human experience suggests a meaningless universe, but this apprehension is itself ambiguous. One of Poe's major strategies of irony is to combine a ubiquitous undercurrent of mockery of the human mind with parodic elements directed at the very form embodying the nightside vision that obsessed him—the gothic tale itself as a literary convention. Poe's romantic skepticism joins the polar opposites of neoplatonic faith and nightside vision into a unified world view wherein the ironic yet

…cognizing and re-creating absurdity and contra-…" them.[2] (Further discussion of this approach …ALS 1968, p. 169, ALS 1969, p. 192, ALS 1970, pp. …2, pp. 217, 220).

…with a work that intends to discover the "latent semi-…" of Poe's fiction by combining the rigor of symbolic …guistic science with structuralist methodology, it is dis-…to find that the first "syntactic" narrative structure formu-…Poe's fiction begins with an error. And yet that is precisely …lin Martindale sets out in "Transformation and Transfusion …ality in the Narratives of Poe" (*Semiotica* 8:46–59). The first …rn–illustrated by triangles, squares, circles, arrows up, arrows …wn, superscript and subscript numbers within horizontally se-…uential and vertically parallel boxes–is supposed to describe the …ypical Poe story, exemplified by "The Black Cat" and "The Tell-Tale Heart." "Each story begins with a 'conjunction' or relationship between the characters, progresses through the murder and burial of one by the hero and a macabre 'reunion' of the main characters." In this pattern, Martindale writes, "too much" is characteristically buried with the victim, the cat in the one tale and a watch in the other. "The Tell-Tale Heart" contains several metaphoric references

2. *Editor's note*: The following evaluation of Prof. Thompson's book has been supplied by the former editor of *ALS*, J. Albert Robbins.

In the "old" days of Poe scholarship many an admirer winced that the author of "Ligeia" could write *and* publish so silly a thing as "Why the Little Frenchman Wears His Hand in a Sling"; failed to grasp why, in the *Prose Romances* pamphlet, the master paired the splendid "Murders in the Rue Morgue" with such a trashy piece as "The Man That Was Used Up"; and offered no convincing explanation of why Poe wrote so many more comic-satiric-burlesque-hoax pieces than solid, "serious" gothic and ratiocinative tales. Within the past two decades many scholars have usefully examined the comic fiction and proposed reasons for its relationship to the "serious." In *Poe's Fiction: Romantic Irony in the Gothic Tales* G. R. Thompson provides a useful synthesis of such criticism, argues and demonstrates that there is unity of purpose and vision in all of the fiction, details Poe's affinity for the theory and practice of German ironists, and provides close readings of several key stories. The result is a carefully documented, closely reasoned study of Poe which, in my judgment, is the most important work on Poe in recent years.

In successive chapters, Thompson discusses the basic premises of romantic irony (chiefly Germanic) and Poe's familiarity therewith; examines the first five tales and other Folio Club stories as examples of "flawed Gothic" and as "the touchstone for all his subsequent fiction"; considers such later stories as "Ligeia" and "Usher" as examples of "explained Gothic"–tales which are "supernatural on one level, psychological on another, satiric and ironic on

to timepieces, but there is no conclusive evidence that a watch, the ticking of which then impells the protagonist to confess, is buried with the corpse. In "Never Bet the Devil Your Head," Martindale designs a "negative transformation" from "too little" being buried (Toby Dammit is buried without his head). This inversion in part gives rise to Martindale's theory of an "energy interchange" element in the pattern, as illustrated by Roderick Usher's "gain" in vitality as Madeline sinks (another imprecision). The problem of thematic interpretation also blurs the paradigm, as demonstrated by "The Cask of Amontillado" where Fortunato *stays* buried. This phenomenon Martindale explains by an "essential difference" of a "distinctive feature"; the relationship between the major characters is "pure" rather than "ambivalent" as in the other tales (another debatable point). After a discussion of "Eleonora" and the mesmeric stories, he formulates the "general diachronic structure" of the tales: by a process of "double negation" Poe's narratives always return to the starting point. In achieving this pattern, the tales always mediate opposites, and this latent semiotic structure of Poe's fictive universe parallels Poe's conscious articulation in *Eureka* of the binary structure of the universe in the mediated forces of repulsion and attraction. *Eureka*

---

another" (p. 77); argues that *grotesque* and *arabesque* are not antithetical terms but "a continuum . . . indicating closely proximate areas of feeling or impact, as that point between laughter and tears, calmness and frenzy, seriousness and mockery" (p. 105); under the term "nightside" treats Poe's use of the subconscious, the occult, and pseudoscientific; and in the final chapter, "Romantic Skepticism," discusses a range of well-known tales, *Arthur Gordon Pym*, and *Eureka* as emblematic of a universe "not so much malevolent as mocking or 'perverse'" (p. 165)—justifying a skeptical, philosophical despair.

As to the basic term, Thompson says that the Romantic Ironist "strove, in his contrariness, deceptiveness, satire, and even self-mockery, to attain a penetrating view of existence from a subliminally idealistic height of aesthetic perception—but always with an eye on the terrors of an ultimately incomprehensible, disconnected, absurd, or at best probably decaying and possibly malevolent universe" (p. 12). In so unstable and uncertain a universe, not even the artistry by which the writer expresses his vision and his doubts is reliable. In the ambiguous gothic tale, for which Poe is best known, the occult—itself shadowy and uncertain—is undercut by insinuated natural and psychological explanations; and events frequently can be taken as neither actual nor mental but must be seen as an ambivalent combination of both. It is apt, then, that some "serious" tales turn out to be disguised hoaxes and some "comic" tales have serious purport. All we can be certain of—aside from the powers of the imagination—is an awareness of the dark paradox of human existence.

Thompson's book is richly perceptive and does indeed support Poe's contention that there *is* book-unity in his fiction.

presents the "exact diachronic structure" of the tales: original union, repulsion, maximal separation, attraction, union. In a final bold leap, Martindale relates this pattern to the traditional alchemical quest of "separating and synthesizing opposites" and to the analysis and refinement of this philosophy by Carl Jung (see Martindale's discussion of "Usher," *ALS 1972*, p. 219).

Some parallel formulations emerge in the discussion of one tale. Christina J. Murphy, in "The Philosophical Pattern of 'A Descent into the Maelström'" (*PoeS* 6:25–26), notes that *Eureka* provides a significant commentary upon the nature of Poe's "fictive universe," especially in the concepts of attraction and repulsion, constitutive elements in the "Heart Divine" created by the volition of God. These principles of attraction and repulsion operate on two levels in "Maelström." On the physical level, the maelström is composed of opposite forces held in balance. On a symbolic level, the sailor's fears and hopes parallel attraction and repulsion, leading to an overwhelming sense of awe, an epiphany in which he experiences an "intuitive and metaphysical realization of the ultimate." Richard D. Finholt's "The Vision at the Brink of the Abyss: 'A Descent into the Maelstrom' in the Light of Poe's Cosmology" (*GaR* 27:256–66) discusses parallels with *Eureka* in more detail, though making essentially the same point. A "moment of lucidity" is vouchsafed the sailor as he hangs in the maelström suspended between the forces of attraction and repulsion: he senses his own relation to the total design of the universe.

Such a view is complemented and modified by a more critically astute analysis of the tale as a fictional structure, Gerard M. Sweeney's "Beauty and Truth: Poe's 'A Descent into the Maelström'" (*PoeS* 6:22–25), which examines both the themes and the "double narrative" of the story. The sailor saves himself not merely by rational comprehension of nature but by poetic appreciation of its awesome beauty. A rational element of the aesthetic—the perception of symmetry—is what saves him, and yet the sailor has forgotten his schoolmaster's scientific "explanation" of the maelström and only borrows his scientific terms; the sailor's own narrative style is a flood of poetic tropes. The first narrator, Sweeney argues, is a "capsule double" of the sailor, and he too reacts aesthetically. Despite his initial scientific descriptions, his language becomes highly metaphoric; moreover, his retrospective account incorporates the sailor's metaphors, confirming the impress of the sailor's subjective and aesthetic experience on him, in contrast to the disbelief of the other fishermen of Lofoden.

Several studies relating the detective stories to some larger concern have appeared. Leon Howard's "Poe's *Eureka*: The Detective Story That Failed" (*MDAC* 1[1972]:1–14) is hardly about *Eureka* at all; it is an attempt to draw (rather vague) parallels with the Dupin stories, concluding that *Eureka* reveals an unsuccessful mixture of the "detective descending from . . . rarified intellectuality" and the detective "rising into the even more rarified atmosphere of the poetic imagination." S. K. Wertz and Linda L. Wertz in "On Poe's Use of Mystery" (*PoeS* 4[1971]:7–10) argue that the plot structure of Poe's stories is frequently determined by the concept of "mystery" employed, which is of three kinds: *puzzle* (a question that can be answered without extra knowledge); *problem* (a question that has a solution but which may require going beyond the immediate data); *genuine mystery* (a question defined by contemporary theologians as one the answer to which may be incomprehensible to the human mind). The particular sense of mystery or mystification involved is a key to the meaning of Poe's stories.

One of the finest explications of recent years is Liahna Klenman Babener's "The Shadow's Shadow: The Motif of the Double in Edgar Allan Poe's 'The Purloined Letter' " (*MDAC* 1[1972]:21–32). Gracefully written and cogently argued, the essay presents an analysis of the "insistent uses of the double pattern in the story" that goes well beyond any previous commentary. Babener details an incredible number of verbal doublings and a complicated system of duplicative plot structures. Among the highlights of the argument are the following. Dupin and D—— (the Minister) are moral doubles, each having a talent for duplicity and malice. Dupin's interest in the case is "morally dubious," based on a desire for revenge, a love of game, financial profit, and acquisition of power: all traits duplicated in D——. The strategies of sizing up one's opponent and of deception, especially as seen in the method used to steal the letter, are exactly the same in both. Dupin and D—— may even be literal twin brothers, as a series of details suggests, especially the concluding reference to Crebillon's *Atrée*, a play about the fatal opposition between two brothers with a marked capacity for malice. Yet the evidence for literal fraternity has enough ambiguity that a further, more symbolic meaning emerges. Dupin and D—— may constitute a single composite being, each the rival doppelgänger of the other. One goes out only at night, the other only by day; D—— is never presented directly; his actions are reported by Dupin. In its total ambiguity of multiple structures, the double element of the tale comes to symbolize basic oppositions in the human mind itself.

Raymond Paul's *Who Murdered Mary Rogers?* (Englewood Cliffs, N.J., Prentice-Hall [1971]) followed John Walsh's *Poe the Detective* (see *ALS 1968*, p. 168) by three years, even though according to Paul, his book was "composed prior to the publication of Walsh's." Both of them have covered much the same ground while reaching different conclusions, as is suggested in Paul's remark that "Walsh fails to understand that Poe intended only his original story as a hoax. He took his revised version, and his claims for it, quite seriously."

Jack D. Wages in "Isaac Asimov's Debt to Edgar Allan Poe" (*PoeS* 6:29) claims that Asimov "with numerous backward glances to Poe's work . . . amalgamated the detective story with science fiction." Poe and science-fiction is also discussed in Sam Moskovitz's introduction to *The Crystal Man: Stories by Edward Page Mitchell* (Garden City, N.Y., Doubleday), and in Brian W. Aldiss's *Billion Year Spree: The True History of Science Fiction* (New York, Doubleday).

David E. E. Sloane, in an interesting but curiously blurred essay, "Gothic Romanticism and Rational Empiricism in Poe's 'Berenice'" (*ATQ* 19:19–26), suggests that "Berenice" embodies a grotesque rejection of American empirical science at the same time that it burlesques the "violation of the female principle of beauty in the European Gothic novel." The rhetoric of the narrator bears similarities to Dr. Benjamin Rush's account of how extractions of diseased teeth (some showing no visible sign of decay) from several young women (including one who suffered from epilepsy) cured them of symptoms of other seemingly more serious diseases. The narrator's insane reliance on an already "discredited" physical means to cure his own spiritual and mental malady constitutes a basic irony in the tale and represents a paradoxical paradigm in American culture. Donald B. Koster's "Poe, Romance and Reality" (*ATQ* 19:8–13) is an attempt to defend Roy P. Basler's psychological interpretation of "Ligeia" from the strictures of Edward Wagenknecht, James Schroeter, and other "supernaturalist" critics. In fact, Basler did not go far enough, according to Koster, whose "own hypothesis is that the narrator murdered not only Rowena but Ligeia as well." Gracefully written, the article is flawed by insufficient marshalling of evidence on this point and by Koster's apparent ignorance of recent studies already exploring that and other more sophisticated hypotheses (some defending Basler in the very terms he does). When John B. Humma, in "Poe's 'Ligeia': Glanvill's Will or Blake's Will?" (*MissQ* 26:55–62), begins by asserting that criticism has failed to consider the moral or psychological implications of the epigraph to the tale, he blithely consigns to scholarly oblivion several recent critical speculations by Jay L. Halio, Walter Garrett, Kenneth T. Reed, and others. Pointing out that William Blake sometimes conceived of the "will" as mean egotism (though establishing no connection with Poe), Humma tries, not totally without success, to read "Ligeia" as an allegory of the murder of selflessness (Rowena) by the selfish will (Ligeia) under the influence of the intellect (the narrator).

In "Poe's 'Usher' Tarred & Fethered" (*PoeS* 6:49), Benjamin Franklin Fisher IV extends the parodic potential of "The System of Dr. Tarr and Professor Fether" beyond the speculations of William Whipple, Ada Nisbet, and Richard P. Benton by pointing out a number of parallels between that story and "The Fall of the House of Usher" which suggest that Poe was indulging in self-parody. Herbert F. Smith, in "Is Roderick Usher a Caricature?" (*PoeS* 6:49–50), suggests that a comic element may be found in Usher himself; the protagonist may be a burlesque of James Gates Percival, "poetaster, lexicographer, geologist, and neurotic," whose wan countenance, large eye, high forehead, pale hair, musical and artistic sensitivity, suicidal temperament, and taste in sepulchral houses are suspiciously like Roderick Usher's. " 'The Masque of the Red Death': An Interpretation" (*SAB* 38:101–05) by H. H. Bell, Jr., is a brief, somewhat arbitrary, discussion of the color symbolism of Prospero's seven chambers as an allegory of life. Most of the valid points that Bell makes have already been made by Walter Blair and Kermit Vanderbilt, but Bell's schematic drawing of the rooms at the end of the article is interesting.

The Narrative of Arthur Gordon Pym has attracted attention from a number of French critics. A new bilingual edition has been published, *Les aventures d'Arthur Gordon Pym* (Paris, Aubier-

Montaigne), which reprints Baudelaire's translation and contains an introduction surveying the criticism by Roger Asselineau. Noting that Poe's influence on French poets is well known, J. M. Santraud, in "Dans le sillage de la baleiniere d'Arthur Gordon Pym: *Le Sphinx des glaces, Dan Yack*" (*EA* 25[1972]:353–66), sets out to show Poe's influence on French novelists as well, especially on Jules Verne's *Le Sphinx des glaces* and Blaise Cendrar's *Dan Yack.* Verne's novel is actually a sequel to *Pym*; he was dissatisfied with the ending, for his own novels do not end until the enigma is *explained.* All three novels embody a denial of the world of contingency, a turning away from rational imperatives; but in Cendrars and Poe the search for the South Pole represents metaphysical obsession with the abyss of ultimate knowledge rather than mere entertainment. The initial purpose of André Gendre's "Gaston Bachelard et *les Aventures d'Arthur Gordon Pym* d'Edgar Poe" (*LR* 26[1972]:169–80) seems to be to defend Bachelard against the frequent criticism that he is unable to see a work whole. Bachelard's work on reveries concerning water led logically to his two studies of Poe's ocean adventure, for as the surface story develops, the "oneiric world deepens: 'the voyage reveals the voyager.'" What distinguishes *Pym* from 18th-century fantastic voyages is that the latter describe social utopias, whereas Poe reveals the drama of the solitude of man in the face of the elements; but before external solitude is realized, it is internal; Pym is "shipwrecked before the shipwreck."

Todd M. Lieber's "The Apocalyptic Imagination of A. Gordon Pym," in his *Endless Experiments: Essays on the Heroic Experience in American Literature* (Columbus, Ohio State Univ. Press), pp. 165–89, modifies Edward H. Davidson's reading of the story as a progressive retreat from social and natural reality, from a world of flux to that of the fixed and eternal, by suggesting that Pym creates a new world constituted purely of the expanded imagination, existing "out of space—out of time," a process we may call "apocalyptic" since it destroys the old reality. *Pym* thus narrates a retreat into solipsism. (For a more penetrating discussion, see N. M. Lippet above.) Cordelia Candelaria's "On the Whiteness at Tsalal: A Note on *Arthur Gordon Pym*" (*PoeS* 6:26) suggests that the sensations of drowsiness, numbness, and heat that Pym and Peters experience at the Pole are the natural results of "freezing snow and its hallucinatory effects." J. Gerald Kennedy briefly examines "The Preface as a Key to the Satire in *Pym*"(*SNNTS* 5:191–96). After surveying critical approaches to *Pym*, Kennedy calls attention to possible satiric thrusts aimed at the general reading public; the preface, flowing in two directions at once (thus creating an ironic effect), sets the opening tone for the narrative itself (see also *ALS 1972*, p. 233).

Discussion of criticism on the fiction may be concluded with an essay that, though focused on *Pym*, seeks to identify a shaping pattern in the body of Poe's fiction that bears direct relationship with his characters' recurrent motion toward "visionary experience." This is Paul Eakin's "Poe's Sense of an Ending" (*AL* 45:1–22), an original and important article that yet somewhat avoids the critical issues it raises. Criticism of the "incompleteness" of *Pym*, Eakin asserts, stems from "a failure to recognize . . . the familiar concluding strategies of [Poe's] major fictions." Richard Wilbur's formulation of movement toward the "hypnagogic state" in Poe's "dream voyages" suggests movement in one direction only, whereas Eakin argues that it is the voyage out and back—what he calls the "Lazarus plot"—that is the pattern of Poe's fiction. In the colloquies, the novel sensations of life after death are directly reported by angels. But these angelic dialogues fail to offer a "human solution to the pursuit of final knowledge"; the mesmeric tales, however, offer a means to cross the barrier between the angelic and the mortal realms. "Mesmeric Revelation," for example, "constitutes an anticipation of angelic experience." But with regard to "Valdemar," Eakin can only assert that it is "surely the most grisly avatar of the Lazarus figure in all Poe," and his failure to deal fully with the utter loathsomeness of the conclusion constitutes a major critical equivocation, evident also in his subsequent argument. After discussion of patterns of inconclusiveness in "A Descent into the Maelström" and "Ligeia," Eakin turns to *Pym*, which he calls "an elaborate sleight-of-hand, designed to establish . . . [it] as a genuine Lazarus fiction." Why *Pym* is not as "genuine" as any of the other stories is not made clear, but Eakin claims that the protagonist "inhabits a significance he fails to comprehend." Moreover, the "equivocation" of the "double ending" calls into question man's capacity to apprehend the meaning of existence. Then, having repeatedly set up an argument that brings Poe's epistemological views into question, Eakin dismisses as mistaken "the recent tendency to identify [*Pym*] as an existentialist or absurdist work." In what way this criticism is wrong is not specified, for the essay abruptly ends.

v. Poetry

As usual, the poetry received comparatively little attention. James H. Sims's "Death in Poe's Poetry: Variations on a Theme" (*Costerus* 9:159–80) is a cursory catalogue of "six variations on the death theme: death as a Being, as ultimate privacy, as emotional release, as spiritual release, as an unpleasant end, and as static Beauty." Gerald F. Amyot, in "Contrasting Visions of Death in the Poetry of Poe and Whitman" (*WWR* 19:103–11), argues the not very startling thesis that death for Whitman is "somehow a new beginning, a new life" whereas for Poe it is "not the principle by which life is renewed but the unmerciful, grim conqueror of all men." Julienne H. Empric, in a concise "Note on 'Annabel Lee'" (*PoeS* 6:26), observes that the simple ballad form of the poem reinforces the "frozen perspective" from which it is narrated; the narrator creates a child's explanation for his feelings of loss: the "vision of the angel-murderers." His present "distraught consciousness" regresses to "the child mind" and tries by "nightly ceremonial act" to freeze time. Mario L. D'Avanzo, in " 'Like Those Nicéan Barks': Helen's Beauty" (*PoeS* 6:26–27), comments on Thomas Ollive Mabbott's explanation of the word "Nicéan" as a reference to a traditional figure in Grecian art, the "Nike," a beautiful woman symbolic of victory; Mabbott neglected to mention the inseparable counterpart to the figure, the prow of the boat or bark on which she stands, a fact which clarifies the meaning of Poe's full simile.

In a highly original if not totally convincing essay, " 'Quaint and curious' Backgrounds for Poe's 'Raven' " (*SHR* 7:411–19), John J. Teunissen and Evelyn J. Hinz draw upon Ovid and the Bible to suggest a new dimension to the symbolism of the raven; they argue that the bird is simultaneously the projection of Lenore's character and her lover's guilty conscience. Like Browning's "Porphyria's Lover," Poe's poem is a "dramatic monologue in which the speaker attempts to convince his implied audience of the innocence of both himself and his lover but in the process reveals quite an opposite picture—that he is impelled by guilt and that she has been sexually unfaithful." S. Gerald Sandler, in "Thomas Holley Chivers, M.D. (1809–1858) and the Origin of Edgar Allan Poe's 'The Raven' " (*New Eng. Jour. of Medicine* 289:351–54), briefly reviews the Poe-Chivers controversy, arguing unconvincingly that the principal source of Poe's poem was the earlier innovative poetry of Chivers. Howell J. Heaney's "'The Raven' Revisited" (*MSS* 25:87–95), although it touches on a possible connection between "Grip," Charles Dickens's favorite raven, and Poe's poem, is principally a brief history of the Poe collection of Colonel Richard Gimbel, now in the Free Library of Philadelphia.

In a brief, evocative discussion of the steady change in metaphors and images from music and harmony to noise and thence to soundlessness during the 18th and 19th centuries, "The Music of Silence" (*Prose* 7:79–91), John Hollander comments on Poe's "paradoxical formulation . . . of the phonic silence in its fully mythological form" in "Al Aaraaf," the tale "Silence," and "Sonnet—Silence." "Al Aaraaf" is a "repository of romantic sound imagery," and "its spirit, Ligeia, is a . . . form of English romantic musical myth." One of Poe's phrases in that poem, "a sound of silence," suggests the "object of transcendent listening" and points up the lack of "an auditory equivalent for the word 'visionary.'" But the phrase also suggests something else, listening to "nothing." Silence in Poe "suggests an emblem of the poetic mind's awareness of its own listening, and a reciprocal picture of the uncommunicativeness of nature, her blank pages."

vi. Literary Relations, Foreign Views

Poe's influence and literary reputation is an area of continuing interest. For convenience I have also included here foreign interpretations of Poe that do not readily fit elsewhere. Mildred K. Travis, in a not completely convincing "Note on 'The Bell-Tower': Melville's 'Blackwood Article'" (*PoeS* 6:28–29), asserts that there is a comic element in Melville's story corresponding to Poe's burlesque instructions for employing "the tone elevated," "the tone didactic," and "the tone heterogeneous." Another study of Melville and Poe is H.-J. Lang's "Poe in Melville's 'Benito Cereno'" (*EST* 5:405–29). Associating Negro slavery, color symbolism, contemporary allusions to baboons, Henry Hudson on Shakespeare, Melville's reference to "St. Iago's monkey," Poe's apparent attacks on Hudson as a "baboon" in the *Broadway Journal*, "Murders in the Rue Morgue," "The System of Dr. Tarr and Professor Fether," and so on, Lang writes what is simultaneously one of the most interesting and one of the most inconclusive essays of recent memory. Gerald M. Garmon's "Emerson's 'Moral Sentiment' and Poe's 'Poetic Sentiment': A Reconsideration"

(*PoeS* 6:19–21) is a somewhat casual comparison of the two writers' concepts of the relation of art and divine being. Both agree, according to Garmon, that the imagination is the faculty that creates poetry through the contemplation of beauty, generating an elevation of soul; but while Emerson sought it in nature Poe sought it out of nature. Pollin in "Poe and Henry James: A Changing Relationship" (*YES* 3:233–42) argues unconvincingly that James "rediscovered" Poe after 1890. As is often the case in studies of this sort, many of the parallels are repeated from earlier studies and the "new" ones forced. For example, Pollin points out an echo of "The Raven" in *The Sacred Fount*, an allusion already treated by Jean Frantz Blackall (cited by Pollin). Pollin also convinces himself that *The Golden Bowl* is an allusion to Poe's "Lenore" ("Ah, broken is the golden bowl") primarily because R. P. Blackmur remarks that "James could not use religion because he knew nothing of the Christian Church"! The inference is that James would thus not be alluding to Ecclesiastes but to something more contemporary; similarly, Psalms is not the immediate source for the title of *The Wings of the Dove* but instead a contemporary song-book. J. Gerald Kennedy, in "Jeffrey Aspern and Edgar Allan Poe: A Speculation" (*PoeS* 6:17–18), argues that Poe rather than Byron is the literary prototype of James's novella, and he raises questions about whether Aspern is really the literary giant the narrator imagines him to be. Kennedy details James's condescending attitude toward Poe, and offers a source for the basic situation of *The Aspern Papers* (1888) in Thomas Wentworth Higginson's *Short Studies of American Authors* (1880). Higginson's book not only contains an unfavorable essay on James, which James seems to have read, but also a sketch of Poe in which the aged Sarah Helen Whitman, as Poe's "betrothed," is pictured in terms strongly reminiscent of James's depiction of Juliana Bordereau.

Wendy Stallard Flory, in "Rehearsals for Dying in Poe and Emily Dickinson" (*ATQ* 18:13–18), suggests that Poe sought to study and "experience" death and dying in much the same way as Emily Dickinson, especially as seen in their consistent recurrence to states of paralysis and vertigo. A comparative analysis on these very terms would, in fact, be useful, but Flory's discussion is thin. Jack Scherting, in "Poe's 'The Cask of Amontillado': A Source for Twain's 'The Man That Corrupted Hadleyburg' " (*MTJ* 26,ii[1972]:18–19), asserts that Poe's tale was a "prototype" for Mark Twain's because of the "structural" similarities: both tales involve men seeking revenge for an unspecified insult, who defer their revenge for a long period of time, and who exploit human vanity. Of course, the absence of any specific parallels and the differences in methods of narration, focus, theme, and tone run counter to the argument; but these objections disappear in the face of the final evidence: *both* tales use the device of a motto. Lloyd N. Dendinger's "The Ghoul-Haunted Woodland of Robert Frost" (*SAB* 38:87–94) is a badly conceived discussion of the "applicability of Poe's theories to much of Frost's poetry" and of the "similarities in the allegorical use the two poets make of the natural world." Richard Tuerk reprints a 1929 essay in "Sadakichi Hartmann's 'How Poe Wrote the Raven' [sic]: A Biochemical Explanation" (*MarkhamR* 3:81–85) and gives a brief introduction to the eccentric Hartmann's "psycho-physiology" of genius and talent. Much more useful are two studies of Poe and Richard Wright, Michel Fabre's "Black Cat and White Cat: Richard Wright's Debt to Edgar Allan Poe" (*PoeS* 4[1971]:17–19) and Linda T. Prior's "A Further Word on Richard Wright's Use of Poe in *Native Son*" (*PoeS* 5[1972]:52–53).

Only a handful of essays on the reciprocal influences between Poe and British writers has appeared in recent years. In "Dickens and Poe: *Pickwick* and 'Ligeia'" (*PoeS* 6:14–16), Benjamin Franklin Fisher IV explores in detail the similarities between Dickens's "A Madman's MS." and Poe's tale, a relationship only tangentially noted by Mabbott and others. Sometimes editors of learned journals make mistakes; one such mistake would seem to be another article on Poe and Dickens, Laurence Senelick's "Charles Dickens and 'The Tell-Tale Heart'" (*PoeS* 6:12–14), which repeats Edith Smith Krappe's discovery of close parallels between Poe's tale and Dickens's "Confession Found in a Prison in the Time of Charles the Second" (*AL* 12[1940]:84–88). Florid, yet graceful and lucid, is Joseph J. Gerhard's "Poe and Tennyson" (*PMLA* 88:418–28), a discussion of a poetic and thematic relationship little analyzed by scholars, despite the fact that the two writers repeatedly announced their admiration for each other's work. The major parallels Gerhard suggests are as follows. Both writers took extraordinary delight in sound for its own sake; in pursuit of an ethereal and pure beauty, both sought spiritual escape from the gross materiality of the world; both valued a "suggestive indefinitiveness" and were alert to the symbolic potential of setting, especially in the employment of oppressive imagery of the dream-shrouded entrapment of the poetic soul. Moreover, the recurrent heroes of both writers, in pursuing divine essence, self-destructively etherealize their women; yet both writers continue to believe in the absolute primacy of the spirit and in that beauty that is the spirit's clearest, although ineffable, expression. A. I. Grieve, in "Rossetti's Illustrations to Poe" (*Apollo* 97:142–45), reproduces illustrations to works by Poe and pictures influenced by him. Richard Swigg's "Waste and Idealism in the Tales of Edgar Allan Poe" in *Lawrence, Hardy, and American Literature* (London, Oxford Univ. Press [1972]), pp. 189–200, is a discussion of D. H. Lawrence's "novelistic" understanding of American culture and the problem of the American artist in bondage to the public but constantly asserting his spiritual individualism in an effort to rise above the demands of the mass audience. Dupin and the landscape artist embody this paradox of the superior will in bondage to the grovelling masses; eventually the imagination becomes self-destructive.

Scandinavian interest in Poe is lucidly surveyed by Carl L. Anderson in *Poe in Northlight: The Scandinavian Response to His Life and Work* (Durham, N.C., Duke Univ. Press). Anderson finds that this interest in Poe accompanies the development of Symbolism in European literature. Although before 1890 Scandinavian critics were heavily dependent upon French criticism of Poe and hampered by inadequate biographical facts, they nonetheless produced a number of perceptive appraisals. Like the French, they admired Poe's genius for rational analysis of the irrational. Anderson observes that in part Scandinavian interest in Poe was a reaction to literary naturalism and social realism. Although a certain enthusiasm for Poe continued after 1890, he seems, according to Anderson, not deeply to have influenced any major Scandinavian author. A Danish article discusses Poe's continuing importance for 20th-century European writers. Av Sissel Lie Haggen, in "Grunntrekk i Edgar Allan Poes literaturteori og estetikk" (*Edda* 71[1971]:25–36), surveys Poe's critical theories, which, though diverse and even occasionally contradictory, nevertheless form a coherent system. Haggen discusses the pervasive influence of Baudelaire and Poe and notes two tendencies in Poe's writings that are also evident in the two main camps of French Symbolists—the visionary writers ("les voyants") and the devotees of the internal power of the word as an absolute ("les artistes")—whose attitudes still persist in Europe today.

Related are studies of Poe in Russia and Hungary. Joan Delaney Grossman in *Edgar Allan Poe in Russia: A Study in Legend and Influence* (Wurzburg, Jal-Verlag), a volume in the Colloquium Slavicum Beitrage zur Slavistik, goes about the two purposes announced in the title with clarity and dispatch. First, she traces the legend of Poe ("Mad Edgar"), which had both a positive and a negative aspect. Distinguishing between the legend, specific influence on other writers, and general popularity and wide recognition, Grossman discusses the important role played by Baudelaire in establishing Poe's European reputation and notes the underground associations of the name Poe in Russia. Poe had a "slow penetration" into the Russian consciousness; there were "just enough" occasional translations and critical notices so that when Poe finally did come into real prominence—coinciding, as in Scandinavia, with the growth of the Symbolist movement—his work was thought of as "underground stream." Before the Symbolists apotheosized him, however, Dostoevski and Turgenev had produced imitations of Poe that can be called "romantic realism," and later Poe's name figured pervasively in the war between the Realists and the Symbolists. He was then "demythologized" into a human being, possessed of great talent but also possessed of great moral weaknesses. Finally, his overall influence was more as a literary figure than as a direct model to emulate. Ivan Elagin, in "Poe's in Blok's Literary Heritage" (*RusR* 32:403–12), concludes that "even though it is impossible to establish the existence of a consistent and firm bond between Blok and Poe . . . there can be no doubt about the sporadic fascination that Poe held for Blok." André Karatson's *Edgar Allan Poe et le groupe des ecrivains du 'Nyugat" en Hongrie* (Paris, Presses Universitaires de France [1971]) discusses Poe's reception in Hungary by those writers associated with the journal, *Occident* ("Nyugat"). Poe was a major influence on Hungarian poetry and on the emergence of Hungarian literature in general in the 20th century. Karatson reviews Poe's image as the "poète maudit" who was yet the "incarnation of the ideal of the civilization and culture" of "the West." Karatson then discusses the problems of translation that Poe's writings present and details Poe's specific influence on a variety of specific writers.

Poe's indebtedness to and affinities with German writers has long been a subject of debate. A detailed but highly repetitive consideration of the various translations and reviews of Ludwig Tieck available to Poe in the 1830s and 1840s is Eberhard Alsen's "Poe's Theory of Hawthorne's Indebtedness to Tieck" (*Anglia* 91:342–56). Alsen argues that Poe's charging Hawthorne with lack of originality (because he was simply imitating Tieck) in his second review of *Twice Told Tales* (in 1847) derived primarily from a review by Evert Duyckinck in 1842 which specifically links Hawthorne and Tieck. One may object, however, that while Duyckinck's review and several others prior to 1847 may have influenced Poe to tone down his first enthusiastic praise of Hawthorne, the conclusion does not necessarily follow that Poe "discovered" Tieck after 1842, especially since Poe made one of his characters a cousin of Tieck as early as 1837. For an essay that argues that Poe's knowledge of Tieck was largely second-hand, but which yet suggests Poe's familiarity with the writings and career of Tieck, see Edwin H. Zeydel, "Edgar Allan Poe's Contacts with German as Seen in His Relations with Ludwig Tieck," in *Studies in German Literature of the Nineteenth and Twentieth Centuries: Festschrift for Frederic E. Coenen*, edited by Siegfried Mews (Chapel Hill, Univ. of N.C. Press [1971], pp. 47–54). Manfred Smuda, in "Variation und Innovation: Modelle literarischer Möglichkeiten der Prosa in der Nachfolge Edgar Allan Poes" (*Poetica* 3[1970]:165–87), uses Abraham Moles's formulation that every communication falls between two poles—perfect originality and perfect banality—to suggest that Poe founded a "tradition" in both modes. He is the source of "innovation," in the "true art" of the short story, and of "variation," in the "trivial art" of the detective story. Josefine Nettesheim, in "Kriminelles, Kriminalistisches und Okkultes in der Dichtung der Droste und Edgar Allan Poes" (*Jahrbuch des Wiener Goethe-Vereins* 74[1970]:136–46), argues that although Annette von Droste-Hülshoff seems not to have known Poe's work, the two writers share many traits in common in their handling of the criminal and the occult. Hans-Bernhard Moeller, in "Perception, Word-Play, and the Printed Page: Arno Schmidt and his Poe Novel" (*BA* 45[1971]: 25–30), discusses *Zettels Traum*, which is about a quartet of people who review their friendship while working on a German-language edition of Poe. The pages are printed in three columns: the first is a quotation-loaded discussion of the life and works of Poe, the second is the interior monologue of the first-person narrator, the third is composed of marginal comments on the first two, including footnotes, source references, and comments on the basic questions of life.

Interpretationen zu Irving, Melville, und Poe, edited by Hans Finger (Frankfurt, Diesterweg [1971]) is a collection of introductory essays and exercises for students. Herwig Friedl, in "Die Bedeutung der Perspektiv in den Landschaftsskizzen von Edgar Allan Poe" (*Archiv* 210:86–93), deals with "perspective" in Poe's landscape tales as a means of presenting "truth." For Poe, a split between nature and art—the one an unordered mirror of the macrocosm, the other an ordered reflection of the microcosm—exists, and this "unceasing" complexity in the universe is revealed in the landscapes. (See also Sharon Furrow above.) Setting is also the subject of Gerhard Hoffmann's "Raum und Symbol in den Kurzgeschichten Edgar Allan Poes" (*JA* 16 [1971]:102–27). Hoffmann offers an analysis of the settings of "The Fall of the House of Usher" and "The Masque of the Red Death" as complex spatial symbols involving external fusion of detail with overall pattern and internal fusion of the emotional responses and mental processes of Poe's spectator-narrators. Hoffmann discusses several different symbolic modes (associative symbols, rational-allegory, milieu symbols, analogical symbols, and so on), concluding with observations on Poe's "expressive ambiguity."

Aside from the Symbolist movement in general, Baudelaire still remains the focal point for much French interest in Poe. In 1971, W. T. Bandy brought out an English-French edition of *Seven Tales by Edgar Allan Poe* (New York, Schocken) translated by Baudelaire so that his French version could be compared page-by-page with Poe's original English. Now Bandy's edition of Baudelaire's *Edgar Allan Poe: sa vie et ses ouvrages* (Toronto, Univ. of Toronto Press) attempts "for the first time" to present a "complete and accurate account of the genesis of Baudelaire's essay, with supporting documents showing his indebtedness to American, British, and French sources. It provides the reader an opportunity to distinguish clearly between what Baudelaire himself knew or thought about Poe and what he borrowed from other writers." In addition to presenting the complete essay with line-by-line textual notes, Bandy provides a detailed introduction and includes in appendices John M. Daniel's 1850 review of Poe's works, John R. Thompson's 1849 obituary of Poe, Baudelaire's 1856 preface to Poe's *Histoires extraordinaires*, and an annotated bibliography of studies of Baudelaire and Poe. Baudelaire figures also in Thomas H. Goetz's "Taine on Poe: A Neglected French Critic" (*PoeS* 6:35–36), which translates the correspondence concerning Poe between Baudelaire and Hippolyte Taine; Taine associated Poe with the melancholy "Germanic-English" tradition of "profound intuition" combined with an "overactive nervous system" and expressed dislike for *Eureka* as "too akin to philosophy." David J. Kelley, in "Delacroix, Ingres et Poe: Valeurs picturales et valeurs littéraires dans l'oeuvre critique de Baudelaire" (*RHL* 71[1971]: 606–14), examines the apparent contradictions in Baudelaire's thought, noting that while Baudelaire saw similarities between Poe and Delacroix at one point, elsewhere he uses the same language to characterize Ingres whom he opposes to Delacroix. Hartmut Brie, in "Die Theorie des poetischen Effekts bei Poe und Mallarmé" (*NS* 21[1972]:473–81), asserts that the fundamental difference between the two writers is that Poe worked on a "traditional" level of language, concerned with technical matters of versification, aimed at "novelty" and "effect," not finally recognized as legitimate by Mallarmé despite his strong reliance on Poe's theories. John Erickson's "Valéry on Leonardo, Poe and Mallarmé" (*ECr* 13:252–59) comments on the several related essays comprising the 470-page eighth volume of the Bollingen *Collected Works of Paul Valéry*. Each of the three writers represented for Valéry a unique "resistence," a "consciousness" that was an "absolute system" within itself, one of many "solutions" among an infinitude of solutions of "universal problems." Poe especially represented "disciplined effort" of "conscious *elimination*" as he created a "language within a language," mirroring a universe the "profound symmetry of which is present, to some degree, in the inner structure of our minds." Hélène Cixous, in "Poe Relu: Une Poétique du Revenir" (*Critique* 28[1972]:299–327), in a "re-reading" of Poe's "poetics of return from the dead" discusses the theme of love and death in "Morella," "Berenice," "The Oval Portrait," "Ligeia," and other such works in evocative rather than precise prose.

Two booklength works in Spanish have recently appeared. Armando Ocano's *Edgar Allan Poe* (Madrid: Ediciones y Publicaciones Españolas, S. A. [1971]) is a volume in a series of introductory biographies on such writers as Machado, Dostoevski, T. S. Eliot, Proust, Unamuno, Neruda, Fitzgerald, Byron, Borges, and the like, done on a fairly serious level for the general reader, with a selection of translated excerpts from Poe's writings. *Edgar A. Poe* (Verona: Editorial Prensa Española [1971]), No. 7 of a series entitled "Los Gigantes," is a volume similar to the Thames & Hudson author-and-his-world series, generously illustrated, with brief introductory essays for the general reader and a sampling of Poe's poetry and tales in translation. Robert Lima in "A Borges Poem on Poe" (*PoeS* 6:29–30) offers a translation of the Argentine author's poem ("The pomp of marble, black anatomy . . .") along with brief commentary on the deep impact Poe has had on Borges. In an article in Portuguese, "Edgar Allan Poe: Una engenharia de avessos" (*Colóquio/Letras* 3[1971]: 5–16), Haraldo de Campos discusses Roman Jakobson's analysis of Poe's careful use of various kinds of sound effects in "The Raven" and assesses the merits of various Portuguese (including Brazilian) versions of the poem.

We may conclude with a brief survey of recent Japanese interest in Poe. James Roy King's "Richmond in Tokyo: The Fortunes of Edgar Allan Poe in Contemporary Japan" (*Papers on Poe*, pp. 194–205; see *ALS 1972*, p. 208) is really a brief survey of the modern Japanese horror story with little specific reference to Poe, though King does point out generalized "Poesque" effects in the writings of Akutagawa Ryunosuke, Junichiro Tanizaki, and Harai Taro (who took the name Edogawa Rampo, a Japanese form of Edgar Allan Poe). But Japanese interest specifically in Poe is amply demonstrated by no less than four recent books and several articles. In *Edoga Aran Po: Geijutsu to Byori* (Tokyo: Kongosha, 1969, 1973), the title of which translates as "Edgar Allan Poe: Art and Pathology," Akichika Nomura gives in his first section a brief life of Poe and in his second section deals with Poe's poems and tales, with specific reference to the mesmeric works and the "medical" aspect of "Tarr and Fether." Of more interest to English-speaking readers is the third section on Poe's influence on Japanese authors, including the aforementioned Edogawa, Akutagawa, and Junichiro Tanizaki, along with Seiji Tanizaki, Ito Haruo, and Nakagawa Yoichi.

Yuko Eguchi's *Edoga Po Ronko: Akutagawa Ryunosuke to Edoga Po* (Tokyo: Sobunsha, 1968) deals with Poe's changing literary reputation in the 20th century, his social environment as a Southerner, and his general literary environment; Eguchi compares Poe and Akutagawa in terms of their philosophy of art and composition, their technique of tale writing, and their concept of the weird. Gibun (Yoshifumi) Oyamada, in *Edoga Po no Sekai: Shi Kara Uchu e* (Tokyo: Schichosha, 1969), the title of which translates as "Poe's World: from Poetry to the Universe," deals with six aspects of Poe's world: the poetry as microcosm, *Eureka* as macrocosm, the combination in Poe of the prodigy and the madman, the problem of "mystification," the "genealogy" of the grotesque, and the problem of Poe and women. Seiji Tanizaki's *Edoga Po: Hito to Sakuhin* (Tokyo: Kenkyosha, 1968, 1971), in English "Edgar Poe: The Man and His Work," has eleven sections: Poe's life, an anatomy of his works, discussion of his involvement in the literary warfare of his times, his relationship to Baudelaire, *The Raven and Other Poems*, his concept of plot, principles of criticism, theory of poetry, the grotesque, and a concluding biographical commentary on Poe's last hours.

The purpose of Ichigoro Uchida's "Edoga Aran Po no Shuzuga Oyobi Shuzu Shashin ni Tsuite" [A Study of the Portraits and Daguerreotypes of Edgar Allan Poe] *Collected Essays by the Members of the Faculty*, No. 14 (Tokyo: Kyoritsu Women's Junior College, 1971), pp. 19–38, is to estimate the "real" face and physique of Poe by comparing biographical accounts with more than 20 19th-century likenesses, reproduced at the end of the article. Uchida selects eight of these as best representing the young Poe, the adult Poe, and the tired and aging Poe. It is useful to have the gallery of portraits collected together, but Uchida's choice of the most "accurate" of these is questionable, the names of some of the artists seem to have been scrambled, and some famous likenesses are omitted, including an exceptionally fine daguerreotype at the Lilly Library (the only known three-quarter length picture of Poe), which gives a better sense of Poe's physique and bearing than any other portrait.

Purdue University

The Department of English at Washington State University provided a summer's grant-in-aid for this project. I am indebted to Athar Murtuza, Frederick H. Newberry, Robert C. McLean for help with various aspects of this review; for help with the large number of foreign language works, I am indebted to David P. Benseler, Aloysius Chang, Robert Knox, Arne Lindberg, Frank M. Towne.

4. Melville

Hershel Parker

Writing on Melville in 1973 abounds with the same old faults—casual use of inferior texts when better ones are in print, careless inaccuracies about his life and works, breezy ignorance of earlier commentary, free-and-easy distortion of scholarly opinion, and the like. Heroic reforms are long overdue. In *ALS 1972* scholars suggested that graduate schools reconsider the way they train students and that editors of journals adopt more rigorous standards. Great benefits would come if departmental committees began assessing scholarly and critical writing more stringently, daring to penalize for superficial publications while rewarding for substantial ones. Ultimately, the best hope is that writers on Melville will determine for themselves that they will not send off hasty and ill-informed articles, however strong the pressures for publication are. Yet Mortmain yields to Derwent: reading the year's writing on Melville is not without its ameliorating effects. My conclusion is downright cheery: people are wrong who declare that too many are writing on Melville and that too much has been written already. Back in 1938 Willard Thorp wrote of the "good fortune" his generation had in coming upon "hitherto unpublished writing" by Melville and "new records of episodes in his life." Perhaps none will experience that particular fortune in the next years, but many might realize that their own fortunes are equally good if they will only begin by making conscientious use of the best that other scholars and critics have said. Despite the annual hosts of unneeded writings, substantial and even classic essays on many aspects of Melville's life and works cry out to be written.

i. Editions and Bibliographies

Editions published in 1973 were routine reprints of reprints, not worth mentioning, except for a pamphlet of *Herman Melville's Au-*

thentic Anecdotes of Old Zack with the original illustrations (New Brighton, Minn., Starosciak). The editor-publisher, Kenneth Starosciak, contributes an appropriately blithe introduction.

A full-scale bibliography was published, Beatrice's Ricks's and Joseph D. Adams's *Herman Melville: A Reference Bibliography, 1900–1972, With Selected Nineteenth Century Materials* (Boston, G. K. Hall). Nina Baym's rueful comments about the companion volume on Hawthorne (*ALS 1972*, p. 23) apply almost full-strength to the Melville book: "[It] is meant to answer a clear research need, but is so ineptly done that it serves no purpose whatever, and one hopes that if other, more qualified persons have planned to produce such a work they will not now be deterred. Trying to understand the vast number of mistakes and inconsistencies in the handling of material, in the annotating, and in the subject index, I finally had to conclude that article titles were almost the sole source of information utilized by the compilers, and hence that this bibliography was put together by people who had read almost none of the material they indexed." Many dozens of the errors in the Melville volume (such as crediting Samuel O. Egbert with Egbert S. Oliver's dissertation) could have been noticed and corrected by almost anyone working regularly with the scholarship and criticism. The publisher ought to have hired genuine scholars to make the bibliography; failing that, they might have submitted the manuscript to two or three scholars for inspection, offering suitable remuneration. *Anyone* who regularly uses such bibliographies could have warned the compilers to put the entries for works by Melville at the beginning or the end instead of making an ugly clot of them in the middle of the book. G. K. Hall has lately gone honest, we are assured, with the hiring of Joseph Katz to supervise its bibliographical and textual series; but of this pre-Katz Melville bibliography little good can be said, except that many entries are correct and that not every user will be misled every time he consults it.

David H. Bowman and Ruth L. Bohan's "Herman Melville's *Mardi, and a Voyage Thither*: An Annotated Checklist of Criticism" (*RALS* 3:27–72) "attempts to be a nearly inclusive record of all published criticism" on *Mardi* from 1849 through 1971. The bibliography is divided into "Contemporary Reviews: British, 1849," "Contemporary Reviews: American, 1849," "Criticism Appearing in Books, 1849–1971," "Criticism Appearing in Periodicals, 1849–1971," "Criticism Appearing in Books and Periodicals in Other Languages, 1849–1971" (though the first foreign language item is dated 1937), and "Index to Authors." The succinct annotations contrast very favorably with annotations in *Herman Melville: A Reference Bibliography*, and my checking indicates a high degree of inclusiveness.

ii. General

The reproachful Melville essay in *The Chief Glory*, "Herman Melville, 1972," is by Jay Leyda, that inspired biographical researcher and sensitive critic. Leyda has read up on recent criticism without being edified:

> There are brilliant analysts who have won the right to interpretation, but their imitators are too often motivated by their schools' and their ambitions' demand to show "more in print"—and if this can be done without leaving your study, all the better. Another academic merit that has done harm to Melville studies: the importance of being the *first* to reveal a find, and to keep it locked up as the finder's property. The quantity of publications produced by the Melville industry (at one time second only to the Shakespeare industry in the United States) is not a measure of its usefulness—or use. We cannot expect second-rate scholars to acknowledge or consider the harm they are doing, to writer and reader, both.

Leyda is deeply chagrined to realize that little has been done to supplement the researches of the 1940s which culminated in the first edition of *The Melville Log*: "How many family papers and attic archives must have vanished while the people equipped for biographical research played, instead, the game of interpretation."

Leyda may exaggerate the number of people equipped for biographical research; in any case, pat comes an illustration of our general failure to unite sound scholarship with responsible criticism in Charles N. Watson, Jr.'s "The Estrangement of Hawthorne and Melville" (*NEQ* 46:380–402). Once again (see *ALS 1972*, p. 44) Watson sets out to reassert a version of a 1920s theory, this time justifying his study by distorting the prevailing state of scholarly opinion, which holds that no dramatic estrangement occurred, not that no estrangement occurred at all; an obvious contrast is the truly dramatic (though imperfectly understood) estrangement of Melville and Evert Duyckinck. Throughout, Watson's essay is flawed by forced interpretations and flimsy biographical guesses (especially about dates of composition of particular passages in Hawthorne's and Melville's works). The upshot is that Watson compounds earlier confusion on this major topic which demands literary sensitivity and a comprehensive knowledge of the lives and works of both men. An illustration of misguided spot-job biographical work is Kenneth Walter Cameron's "Melville and National Matters" (*ATQ* 20:183–92), which purports to list and transcribe all the Melville items in the National Archives. The transcriptions are reasonably accurate, but still more documents should be in the files: have sub-sub-librarians been feeding Melville fodder to the paper shredders since my photocopies were made? Cameron presents his transcriptions without commentary, and apparently without knowing that the documents in the National Archives (including some of those he does not mention) were used by Harrison Hayford and Merrell Davis in their immensely detailed two-part history of "Herman Melville as Office-Seeker" (*MLQ* 10[1949]:168–83, 377–88). The only value of Cameron's transcriptions is as a supplement to this still indispensable study.

Articles dealing with literary criticism, aesthetics, and literary history may be surveyed together. Two significant essays on literary criticism make incidental use of Melville. Max Westbrook in "The Ontological Critic" (*Rendezvous* 7[1972]:49–66) argues that "New Criticism and Archetypal Criticism can get off their dead centers and become ontological only when we see that New Criticism must take its Platonic-Kantian tradition into the archetypal world that rationalists have long flirted with but always feared." Convincing in his exposure of weaknesses in earlier critical studies of Melville, Westbrook fails to advance cogent readings of his own. Taking *Typee* as "a story about the struggle to birth from out of the universal state of unconsciousness of an ego that can shape and not just obey the unconscious," he says not a word about the exigencies of Melville's own struggle to stretch his brief impressions into a suspenseful, informative, and saleable narrative. A more comprehensive theoretical article—required reading for anyone interested in the history of literary criticism—is Wystan Curnow's "Romanticism and Modern American Criticism" (*SR* 12:777–99), which briefly uses Melville to show how New Critics (represented by R. P. Blackmur, Charles Feidelson, Jr., and Robert Penn Warren) have failed to deal astutely and faithfully with American literature. One of the most disappointing pieces of the year is the essayette by Max I. Baym in his *A History of Literary Aesthetics in America* (New York, Ungar), pp. 68–70, which draws its meager evidence only from *Moby-Dick*. Sentences like this one hardly show an incisive, richly informed understanding of Melville's aesthetics: "For Melville, beauty was the product of the collisions of man with the elements and of man with himself—the classic tragic conflict." A minor contribution to the history of literary history is Eddy Dow's "Van Wyck Brooks and Lewis Mumford: A Confluence in the 'Twenties" (*AL* 45:407–22). Although Dow says Mumford's book on Melville is "very much on the model of Brooks's books on Twain and James," he traces only casual connections between Brooks's and Mumford's ways of regarding Melville.

Six articles deal in one way or another with Melville's debts and affinities. Both the contributions to a symposium on Romanticism are thin. In "Melville's Problem of Detachment and Engagement" (*ATQ* 19:30–37), Vincent Kenny does not work from a sound philosophical framework in surveying the major question of whether "Melville's early judgments on man, society, nature, God, the universe and art" are Romantic; misreadings and misquotations further weaken this superficial essay. Joyce Adler's "The Imagination and Melville's Endless Probe for Relation" (*ATQ* 19:37–42) glides over many of Melville's writings to refute the generalization "that the Romantic Imagination rejects the contemporary world." (On p. 42, following Adler's article, the editor of *ATQ* reproduces the broadside of "Billy in the Darbies" printed and sold by the Melville collector B. Mosher, co-author of "The Mobled Dick," which was excerpted in *"Moby-Dick" as Doubloon.*) Robert J. Schwendinger's "The Language of the Sea: Relationships between the Language of Herman Melville and Sea Shanties of the Nineteenth Century (*SFQ* 37:53–73) is a refreshing if casual reminder of some of Melville's nautical contexts. Schwendinger, who has concertina and will travel with his "lecture-concert of songs, readings, and slides" on Melville and other sea-writers, may be sought at 2729 Prince Street, Berkeley, California, 94705. A major topic is inadequately treated in D. Nathan Sumner's "The Function of Historical Sources in Hawthorne, Melville, and R. P. Warren" (*RS* 40[1972]:103–14). The Melville section (pp. 105–

08) is a casual survey of commonplaces about Melville's use of sources, with some glaring gaps in information and some outright misinformation (such as the assertion that *Billy Budd* was based on the *Somers* case). Sharon Furrow's "The Terrible Made Visible: Melville, Salvator Rosa, and Piranesi" (*ESQ* 19:237–53) is awkwardly ordered and marred by insensitivity to subtler literary functions of the picturesque in Melville, but full of good comments on Melville and artists, especially the two in the title. (Lest anyone be misled, Melville did not live out his last years in a New York apartment house; what Frank Jewett Mather, Jr., visited was Bessie Melville's apartment at the Florence.) Mary Allen in "Melville and Conrad Confront Stillness" (*RS* 40[1972]:122–30) makes only very simple comparisons (e.g., both writers "depict exotic land settings where stillness is awesome"); she nowhere mentions Jesse D. Green's much more significant treatment of affinities between these writers (*MFS* 8:287–305).

The remaining discussions of general topics resist further classification. A disappointing article, vague and curiously overlong, is Thomas Edward Lucas's "Herman Melville: The Purpose of the Novel" (*TSLL* 13[1972]:641–61). Initial focus is soon lost as Lucas expatiates on a variety of related subjects without rigorously analyzing any of them. Jay B. Hubbell's chatty survey of Melville's reputation in *Who Are the Major American Writers?* (Durham, Duke Univ. Press [1972]), pp. 57–63, offers a little that is new (an 1868 quotation from the Cincinnati *Times* by way of the Richmond *Southern Opinion*) and a little that is erroneous (the assertion that the first Harper's reprinting of *Moby-Dick* after that firm's fire was in 1863), but almost no serious exploration of the reasons for the vicissitudes which he traces. Still, these pages and many other comments on Melville scattered throughout the book have the fascination of good gossip. Hennig Cohen's "A Comic Mode of the Romantic Imagination: Poe, Hawthorne, Melville," a chapter of *Comic Imagination*, takes on a momentous topic but makes only a few flaccid comments about Melville's humor. Alfred Kazin's "Melville the New Yorker" (*NYRB* 20:3–8), a printing of an address to the Melville Society, is evocative though not strenuously analytical and not always precise in its biographical information.

iii. **Redburn** **and** ***White-Jacket***

In "Melville's *Redburn*: Initiation and Authority" (*NEQ* 46:558–72), Michael Davitt Bell offers a rigorously somber reading of *Redburn* as dealing with "only the most incomplete sort of social initiation." Bell's sobriety is often misplaced, especially in passages where Melville is pretty clearly having satirical fun at the expense of his mature but still orthodox and sentimental narrator (sometimes while that older Redburn is having his own joke at his younger self). Bell does not replace James Schroeter's "*Redburn* and the Failure of Mythic Criticism" (*AL* 39:279–97) as a starting place for new discussion of initiation in *Redburn.* Curiously, Bell gets through the whole article without once mentioning an older critical topic, that of point of view, which might have complicated his thesis.

Robert C. Albrecht's "White Jacket's Intentional Fall" (*SNNTS* 4[1972]:17–26), an unsuccessful attempt to relate the narrator's behavior to "certain patterns of the archetypal hero as described by [Joseph] Campbell," is particularly weak in its failure to demonstrate (rather than assert) that White Jacket regards the man-of-war as a utopia. Indeed, Albrecht's reading seems 1950s-like in its rebuking of individuality. Still, the middle paragraph on p. 19 suggests what good evidence can be adduced in showing the unity of *White-Jacket.* A note, Hennig Cohen's "Melville's Surgeon Cuticle and Surgeon Cutbush" (*SNNTS* 5:251–53), merely records the slight similarity between the names of the surgeon on the *Neversink* and that of a real naval surgeon, Edward Cutbush (1772–1843). The first half of Priscilla Allen's "*White-Jacket*: Melville and the Man-of-War Microcosm" (*AQ* 25:32–47), an abstract of her dissertation on the world-ship metaphor in nautical writings of Melville's time, contrasts the attitudes of officers (represented by Enoch Cobb Wine's *Two Years and a Half in the Navy*) and men (represented by Samuel Leech's *Thirty Years from Home; or a Voice from the Main Deck*—one of Melville's sources). The second half attempts to show how Melville brought "the isolated and disparate tendencies of the ship world metaphor together" and welded them "into a literary tool of some force." Despite some initial awkwardness in structure and a few strained arguments (in Melville's "conscious synecdoche" the name of the *Neversink* alludes to the Neversink Highlands of New Jersey and therefore stands for America), this is an interesting article, a valuable reminder of how richly *White-Jacket* may yet reward readers who give it the attention it deserves.

iv. *Moby-Dick*

Robert Zoellner's ultimately unsatisfying *The Salt Sea Mastodon: A Reading of "Moby-Dick"* (Berkeley, Univ. of Calif. Press) is a major study, with perhaps more mind-stuff in it than the rest of the year's work on Melville put together. The initial pity is that there can be little aesthetic exhilaration in reading it. Anyone who loves the prose of *Moby-Dick* will be distressed by the grotesque jargon Zoellner employs (one mild sample: a critic "correctly perceives Ishmael's transcendental tendencies, but not their concomitant metanaturalistic truncation"). Sometimes the writing is not even that of a particular ugly jargon but simply bad writing by any standards (see the last full sentence on p. 11). Vulgarities poison many pages: Henry Adams lies "in the great hall of the dynamos at the Paris Exposition with his historical back broken," the humped old bull of chapter 81 is "the Medicare Whale," Jehovah is a megaton God. Yet the book is good enough to make every Melvillean suppress his revulsion at the style while he struggles with the arguments.

The best arguments, one must say, are seldom wholly original. Indeed, there is a 1950s air throughout the twelve chapters, for all the overlay of a 1970s sense of ecological disaster. In the first two chapters, Zoellner distinguishes between "the Ahabian and Ishmaelian epistemologies," saying that Ahab conceives "of a total dissociation between his perception and the outer world" while Ishmael "suggests that the mind illuminates reality so that an organic relationship between inner imaginative construct and outer empirical datum occurs." Ishmael's "lamp-mind" (chap. 3) "stamps the world with the features" of his unique self. Melville is preoccupied "with the physical and metaphysical 'hits' and 'punches' of life," which make up "the protodynamic" of the novel, that of "*thumper: thumpee*" (chap. 4). "Queen Mab" proves through Stubb ("a serious figure of consummate realism," Zoellner uncompellingly argues) that ultimately "*there is no thumper*, though there are indeed thumps, the inexorable consequence of blind process" (chap. 5). Ahab, "the central expression of the protodynamic of *thumper: thumpee*," is not a tragic hero (chap. 6). Ishmael's own hypos (chap. 7) are gradually dispersed in the course of the voyage. The redemption of Ishmael is possible partly because he comes to see a naturalistic whale while Ahab sees only a transcendental, conceptual one (chap. 8); his further study of real whales leads him away from Ahab (chap. 9). Ahab sees death as an "entropically terminal entity," while Ishmael, cheered by perceiving the cyclical nature of life, alters his despairing view of cosmic reality (chap. 10). Queequeg plays the major role in finally resolving Ishmael's hypos (chap. 11). During the three days' chase the conception of a "Presumptive Moby Dick" (the murderous monster Ahab may have led the reader to expect) is replaced by the perception of the Veritable Moby Dick, a powerful, instinctive, real whale (chap. 12). Ahab "forgot, or never understood, that the image he saw in the world was in part an image of himself. But Ishmael knows the meaning of Narcissus, and never forgets it. Consequently, Ishmael never—despite his Christian background and Ahab's temporary influence—really sees either the whale or the world as *antagonist.* He is part of the world, at one with it, and so cannot conceive of it as adversary."

The deep flaw in all this is that Zoellner writes as if the first chapter of *Moby-Dick* began "In those times long ago I used to have the hypos so bad that you might almost have called me an Ishmael then." As Zoellner traces the process, Ishmael is gradually redeemed from his hypos by a successive series of insights, each one arrived at once for all, during the voyage of the *Pequod,* without relapses. Thus what Ishmael "learns" in "The Try-Works" is of a stage subsequent to what he "learns" in "A Squeeze of the Hand" (even in literal terms this particular reading is wrong, since by the chronology of the voyage the later chapter occurs earlier, the night the first whale is killed). Zoellner's misapprehension about the way Ishmael learns leads him to fumble over many passages where Ishmael playfully ends an essayistic chapter with a rhetorical flourish which may imply a philosophical or metaphysical certainty which he does not feel. It also leads Zoellner to slight what drives Ishmael to tell the story and what he realizes in the course of telling it. Throughout, Zoellner badly underestimates the nature and power of Ahab's sway in Ishmael's memory, ignoring the ways in which Ahab is like Ishmael and the degree to which he may be a projection of Ishmael precisely because he shares some of Ishmael's own most obsessive patterns of perception. Zoellner's simple, quick-study Ishmael may be a nice person, but hardly one to be haunted by the story of Ahab and Moby Dick; his Ahab is a distinctly bad and limited person, hardly one the Ishmael of *Moby-Dick* would be powerfully and permanently drawn toward. Just as some critics of the Eisenhower years were anxious to show that Ahab was bad because he was antisocial and Ishmael was good because he retained his capacity for making friendships and conforming, Zoellner is too eager to make *Moby-Dick* a hopeful book for our dark times, a potent cure in a technological world "sick unto death."

Yet this book will be of enduring value just because, unlike most of what gets published, it is a genuine "reading," never merely an exercise in rehashing other critical opinions or engaging factitious issues in the text. Zoellner ranges widely over *Moby-Dick*, citing both familiar passages and many which most critics never refer to; sometimes he strains at a self-consciously "new" interpretation, but more often he is fresh and cogent. His uses of Melville's other writings to bolster arguments about *Moby-Dick* are often apt (one of the apparent exceptions is on p. 77, where he sees pyramids in *Typee* which I cannot find). Happiest of all, this book will require its best readers to re-read *Moby-Dick*, if only to determine precisely where Zoellner went wrong in some of his own prolonged grapplings with Leviathan.

None of the articles on *Moby-Dick* this year has anything like the significance of Warwick Wadlington's "Ishmael's Godly Gamesomeness: Selftaste and Rhetoric in *Moby-Dick*" (*ELH* 39:309–31; see *ALS 1972*, pp. 45–46); that study bears up bravely in rereadings.

Two articles deal with textual problems. The first, Hershel Parker's "Regularizing Accidentals: The Latest Form of Infidelity" (*Proof* 3:1–20) draws examples from *Moby-Dick* in arguing that "any thoroughgoing regularizing of the accidentals of a writer like Melville would prove ludicrous," since he "was making a virtue—actually, a structural principle—out of the lack of 'finishing touches.'" The implications of the evidence is that to regularize 19th-century American texts, particularly those from early in the century, is in fact to modernize them. The second is Parker's "Practical Editions: Herman Melville's *Moby-Dick*" (*Proof* 3:371–78), one of a series of reports on classroom editions of standard American novels. Perhaps not surprisingly, Parker finds that the Norton Critical Edition is the most responsible modern text (the only one besides the Mansfield-Vincent edition to be set from the first edition), but he also analyzes the ways in which it "falls short of being definitive." (The survey of respectable ways a scholar might once again proceed to edit *Moby-Dick* was written before Harold Beaver showed that the simplest way of all was to reprint the Norton lists, slightly condensed and rearranged, as if textual discoveries once printed were in the public domain; see *ALS* 1972, p. 41).

Three pieces deal with Melville's relationships with other writers. A note by Mark L. Asquino on "Hawthorne's Village Uncle and Melville's *Moby-Dick*" (*SSF* 10:413–14) draws only forced parallels (masked by words like "exactly," "very similar," and "very same"), though Melville's acquaintance with "The Village Uncle" in *Twice-Told Tales* is not in doubt. Felix S. A. Rysten's chapter on "Melville's *Moby-Dick*" in his *False Prophets in the Fiction of Camus, Dostoevsky, Melville, and Others* (Coral Gables, Fla., Univ. of Miami Press, 1972) is superficial and unoriginal; the few comparisons of Melville to Dostoevsky and Camus are too hasty to be meaningful. Frederick Busch's "The Whale as Shaggy Dog: Melville and 'The Man Who Studied Yoga'" (*MFS* 19:193–206) contains dubious readings and some outright errors but is a good step toward a full evaluation of Mailer's enduring interest in Melville. Busch should often provoke further investigation and reflection even though his breathlessly offered similarities between the writers may not always seem as obvious to others as they do to him.

Three articles and a note deal with general matters. Joseph Lawrence Basile's "The Meridians of Melville's Wicked World" (*SDR* 11:62–76) smoothly and without much intensity discusses familiar topics (what Melville meant by calling the book wicked, why Ishmael survives), leaving the state of knowledge about where it was before. David S. Berkeley's "*Figurae Futurarum* in *Moby-Dick*" (*BuR* 21:108–23) is a typological reading of the book as "predicting the shipwreck of modern civilization for its having entrusted to science in place of the truths of the church the conquest of moral and spiritual evil in a world that God designed and still governs." This may be the most rigidly straitjacketing reading since William Gleim's book appeared in 1938, but it is at least informative about typology, though not about Melville. "The Shape of *Moby-Dick*" (*SNNTS* 5:197–210) by Henry L. Golemba grimly imposes a "geometric regularity" upon the book, dividing it into sixths, "the typical formal structure of the classical epic which the novel in many ways resembles." The main argument is implausible and minor awkwardnesses and misreadings are strewn throughout. Scott Donaldson's note, "Damned Dollars and a Blessed Company: Financial Imagery in *Moby-Dick*" (*NEQ* 46:279–83), is an otherwise pedestrian survey marred by inexcusable sloppiness at a crucial point. Donaldson condemns Stubb for already knowing that Captain Gardiner's son is in the lost whaleboat when he offers to wager Flask " 'that some one in that missing boat wore off that Captain's best coat; mayhap, his watch—he's so cursed anxious to get it back.' " (Last year I suggested half in jest what I now propose in all seriousness: scholarly journals should begin listing names of readers who recommend articles for publication. Maybe then editors and readers would begin to take their responsibilities seriously, even if writers like Donaldson do not.)

The most narrowly focused article is John Stark's " 'The Cassock' Chapter in *Moby-Dick* and the Theme of Literary Creativity" (*SAF* 1:105–11), an implausible reading which claims the whale phallus performs the important function "of symbolizing a potentially [*sic*] creative personality type" and that a three-chapter sequence (ninety-four through ninety-six) "recapitulates Ishmael's development into an artist."

v. Pierre

Michael Davitt Bell in "The Glendinning Heritage: Melville's Literary Borrowings in *Pierre*" (*SIR* 12:741–62) rehashes what has been written about Melville's sources but makes almost no sustained new analysis. Bell says that "for all the attention given the 'sources' of *Pierre*, relatively little attention has been paid to the *function* of the literary allusions and parallels in the novel; little has been said about the relation of Melville's extensive literary borrowings to the form and themes of *Pierre* as a whole." True: true before Bell wrote and still true, except for Brian Higgins's unpublished 1972 dissertation on "The English Background of Melville's *Pierre*" (*DAI* 33:1726–A). (Like Wadlington's article on *Moby-Dick*, Higgins's article on the Pamphlet in *Pierre* promises to be of permanent value; see "Plinlimmon and the Pamphlet Again" [*SNNTS* 4:27–38; *ALS 1972*, p. 49].) The only other article this year is Maxine Moore's "Melville's *Pierre* and Wordsworth: Intimations of Immorality" (*NewL* 39:89–

107). Curiously, both Bell and Moore cite Wordsworth's French love affair and his *The Prelude* and other writings as sources for characters and events in *Pierre*, though only Moore makes that "discovery" the central point. Even more curiously, the Wordsworthian influence is assumed in a section of an article not otherwise worth mentioning here next year, James D. Wilson's "Incest and American Romantic Fiction" (*SLitI* 7[1974]:31–50). These simultaneous arguments provide fascinating if demoralizing variations in the use (and more often abuse) of evidence as to just how notorious Wordsworth's affair with Annette Vallon was in 1849–52 and precisely when (if ever) Melville read *The Prelude*. Two of these writers appear to think that the story of Vaudracour and Julia was in the 1850 edition of *The Prelude* and none of them appears to know where Melville might have had access to that story before 1850. A scrupulous scholar well acquainted with the history of Wordsworth's reputation and with the French connections of Melville's family (his uncle Thomas as well as his father) ought to review the subject: as it is, the various misuses of evidence by Bell, Moore, and Wilson may make one too hastily dismiss the whole case for any Wordsworthian influence on *Pierre*.

vi. The Stories

Two half-hearted attempts to demonstrate the unity of "The Encantadas" are Margaret Yarina's "The Dualistic Vision of Herman Melville's 'The Encantadas'" (*JNT* 3:141–48) and Arlene M. Jackson's "Technique and Discovery in Melville's *Encantadas*" (*SAF* 1: 133–40). In a variation on William Bysshe Stein's charitable notion (see *The Poetry of Melville's Late Years*) that Melville's worst poetry must be purposefully, strategically awful, Yarina argues that "Melville's seemingly erratic writing technique in 'The Encantadas' deliberately exploits his subject matter to outwit the expectation of his readers and to displace trite anticipations with startling revelations." (She does not realize that the middle initial of "Salvator R. Tarnmoor" stands for "Rosa," and she much too confidently identifies the first sketches of "The Encantadas" with the book on tortoises Melville had promised the Harpers: could the sample he submitted to them have been identical to sketches of "The Encantadas" already published in *Putnam's*?) Jackson says the "basic philosophical meaning" reveals itself "through the general arrangement of the sketches, through Melville's use of myth, through certain key symbols, and through the most overlooked feature of *The Encantadas*, the unnamed narrator." Neither Yarina nor Jackson seems aware that cautious study of the way the sketches were composed and published must precede any meaningful discussion of their unity. Neither mentions Warner Berthoff, whose couple of pages in *The Example of Melville* strike me as among the most fruitful yet written on "The Encantadas." A substantial essay is long overdue, but when it comes it will not deal with the work in isolation from Melville's other writings of the period. Richard Haber's "Patience and Charity in *The Encantadas*' 'Chola Widow' Sketch and in 'Cock-A-Doodle-Doo!' " (*MSE* 3 [1972]:100–07) routinely reviews the story of Hunilla as exploring "the nature of patience and endurance" and that of Merrymusk as exploring "the nature of true and false charity." Comparisons between the two pieces are perfunctory.

In "Grace Church and Melville's Story of 'The Two Temples' " (*NCF* 28:339–46) Beryl Rowland makes a good case for thinking that in "Temple First" Melville drew some architectural details from New York's Trinity Church even while portraying the sexton from Grace Church, Isaac Brown. Syntactical similarities in the parts of another diptych are very briefly traced in James K. Bowen's "England's 'Bachelors' and America's 'Maids': Melville on Withdrawal and Sublimation" (*RLV* 38[1972]:631–34). Ruth B. Mandel's "The Two Mystery Stories in 'Benito Cereno' " (*TSLL* 14:631–42) moves from simple summary into routine, unoriginal interpretation. Her article seems all the more unneeded since, unlike "The Encantadas," this story has had its small share of complex, vigorous analyses. I mention Guy A. Cardwell's "A Surprising World: Amasa Delano in Kentucky" (*MTJ* 16:12–13) only to say it has nothing to do with "Benito Cereno." Shoh Yamamoto's "The Source and the Structure of 'Benito Cereno' " (*SELit* 49[1972]:43–54) is very sensible and well-informed, judging from a translation of the conclusion made by one of my students, but not of value to English-speaking critics. H.-J. Lang read reams of criticism before writing "Poe in Melville's 'Benito Cereno' " for *EST* 5:405–29, but he never conclusively demonstrates any Poesque (as distinguished from garden-variety gothic) influence. "Robert Lowell's *Benito Cereno*" (*MD* 15:411–26) by Mark W. Estrin is an attempt to define Lowell's purposes by detailed contrasts to Melville's story, about which Estrin makes many unexceptionable though not original comments.

A reasonable note is Gerard M. Sweeney's "Melville's Hawthornian Bell-Tower: A Fairy-Tale Source" (*AL* 45:279–85), which points out that Melville's Talus may owe a good deal to Hawthorne's "The Minotaur" in *Tanglewood Tales.* Following the example of J. A. Leo Lemay (*ALS 1972*, p. 170), I single out Jacqueline A. Costello's and Robert J. Kloss's "The Psychological Depths of Melville's 'The Bell-Tower' " (*ESQ* 19:254–61) as the article with the year's silliest thesis: "Bannadonna's true ambitions and his real crime become clear; he is enacting those forbidden fantasies common to all men but taboo to all societies. He seeks to supplant his father as his mother's lover and, ultimately, to subjugate and even eliminate his mother in his quest to create 'life' on his own. Retribution for this sin can only be castration; it is not merely appropriate, it is necessary." Mildred K. Travis in "A Note on 'The Bell-Tower': Melville's 'Blackwood Article' " (*PoeS* 6:28–29) makes some suggestive but tenuous comparisons, none of which proves that Melville was specifically indebted to Poe.

vii. The Confidence-Man

Writing on *The Confidence-Man* was as erratic as usual. Donald Yannella's "Source for the Diddling of William Cream in *The Confidence-Man*?" (*ATQ* 17:22–23) is offered with proper tentativeness; what Yannella has found in a sketch by Denis Corcoran (1846) is indeed most likely "a rough-hewn analogue," not a true source. Elizabeth Keyser's " 'Quite an Original': The Cosmopolitan in *The Confidence-Man*" (*TSLL* 15:279–300) starts off as a routine review of commonplaces, then goes on to argue unconvincingly, with inadequate reference to earlier scholarship, that the Cosmopolitan is not the last disguise of the Confidence Man but an embodiment of "a healthy balance between the deaf-mute's Christlike meekness and the barber's churlish misanthropy." When earlier writers are cited they are not always cited accurately; for the record, in "The Metaphysics of Indian-hating" (*NCF* 18:165–73), Hershel Parker did not contend that "the allegorical episode shows the failure of Christians (Indian-haters) to be Christlike in their attitudes towards pagans (Indians)."

Susan Kuhlmann's chapter "And Back to Melville" in her *Knave, Fool, and Genius*, pp. 104–22, is often superficial, simplistic, and derivative, but it does one of the neater and more elaborate jobs of categorizing some of the American shibboleths Melville was satirizing. Much weaker is David Ketterer's chapter on "Melville's *The Confidence-Man* and the Fiction of Science," pp. 267–95 in his *New Worlds for Old: The Apocalyptic Imagination, Science Fiction, and American Literature* (Bloomington, Ind. Univ. Press). Here is Ketterer's thesis: "In the spirit of confidence and uncertainty, then, I propose the argument that, in *The Confidence-Man*, Melville is singling out and attacking Christianity as a particularly inhumane and impractical fiction because of the immense gap it establishes between material appearances and the supposed spiritual reality." Haltingly written, the chapter is erroneous in regard to facts of Melville's life and works as well as in its interpretations, and makes inadequately acknowledged use of studies by Elizabeth S. Foster and others. Ketterer nowhere reveals any strenuous grip on either the techniques or the meanings of *The Confidence-Man.*

The most ambitious article on the book this year is Watson G. Branch's "The Genesis, Composition, and Structure of *The Confidence-Man*"(*NCF* 7:424–48). As Branch says, the "dearth of manuscript and of extra-textual evidence relating to *The Confidence-Man* makes it difficult to determine exactly how Melville composed a book out of the materials he had at hand: ideas about society, human nature, philosophy, aesthetics, and religion; knowledge of the lives of actual people; works of literature, in particular the Bible, Shakespeare's plays, Milton's poetry, Hawthorne's tales, and the stories of the West by Judge James Hall." Branch's own arguments do a good deal to advance our knowledge of that process of composition, particularly the passage which convincingly refutes Foster's notion that manuscript evidence shows Melville began the book as an attack on Emerson. My immediate doubts about other passages are conveyed in "*The Confidence-Man* and the Use of Evidence in Compositional Studies: A Rejoinder" (*NCF* 28:119–24). As I said there, "I hope the cogency of much of Branch's study will not lead others to take all his hypotheses about *The Confidence-Man* for fact—to assume that he has conclusively proved (rather than provocatively speculated) that the mute was a very late addition, that the long tales were interpolations into completed parts of the manuscript, and that the chapters on the art of fiction were late insertions." Remembering glib, contradictory guesses about the composition of *Moby-Dick*, I was concerned to voice a general warning against "hypotheses based too exclusively on insufficiently complex assessments of the evidence or based primarily on critical rather than physical evidence." But Branch's tightly-argued essay deserves to be pondered by everyone interested in *The Confidence-Man.*

viii. The Poetry

Joyce Sparer Adler's "Melville and the Civil War" (*NewL* 40:99–117) could use fuller refutation than it will receive here. The first part, "Melville's Tragic Drama of the Civil War," is an attempt to read *Battle-Pieces* as a three-act tragic drama. It consists of unsubtle summaries of randomly chosen poems, with running commentary but with almost no close analysis of technique or meaning. The basic problem with the second part, "Melville's Flawed Vision in the 'Supplement,'" is that Adler once again (see *ALS 1972*, p. 53) writes more as a political zealot than a literary historian or critic. She idealizes Melville for his political attitudes as revealed in everything from *Typee* through the poems of *Battle-Pieces*—this at the high cost of distorting those attitudes, especially as expressed in *Mardi.* Then she self-righteously condemns Melville for his alleged moral failings in the "Supplement," falsely claiming that his dominant motivation for the essay was fear the South might renew the war and totally ignoring the genuine evils being planned and perpetrated by Radical Republicans just as he was writing. In 1973 we could do without the spirit of Thaddeus Stevens in our literary criticism.

An object-lesson in the evils of trying to dress up a dissertation for publication is Vincent Kenny's *Herman Melville's "Clarel," A Spiritual Autobiography* (Hamden, Conn., Archon). The dissertation will typically contain a long, needless biographical review, not without error; a needless plot summary of the literary work at hand; a needless and indiscriminate summary of previous criticism; many dutiful footnotes that piously cite previous scholarship and criticism, treating each item with equal respect and never genuinely engaging the issues raised therein; and some lengthy sections of uncompelling commentary. After the passage of a decade, the study will be published as a "book," with only the most perfunctory attempts to take any account of work done after the dissertation committee approved it and the India ink began to encrust the pen that made the last corrections. It is inconceivable that anyone could profit at all from Kenny's study who could not profit infinitely more from Walter E. Bezanson's splendid edition of *Clarel*. Slapping a price tag of $12.50 on a dissertation does not make it a book.

The Mystery of Iniquity: Melville as Poet, 1857–1891 (Lexington, Univ. Press of Ky.) by William H. Shurr, the first full survey of Melville's poetry and related prose, is altogether more responsible than Kenny's study, except when Shurr indulges in guesses about dates of composition on the basis of emotional qualities of poems rather than tangibles like ink and paper. Shurr's thesis is that in his poetry Melville "expands his metaphysics of an evil universe and explores the problems of discriminating various levels of reality": "Much of Melville's poetry lies in that area of theology where it comes close to psychology and to metaphysics in the broadest sense of that term. Its greatest affinity is with those writers who create a symbolism for ultimate realities, as those realities impinge most disturbingly upon the author's own consciousness." But what Shurr provides is less a grand and well-illustrated thesis than a series of New Critical readings, usually careful and intelligent, though never brilliant; he is most often disappointing just where the most grasping imagination is called for. No one who has read Bezanson on *Clarel* will learn much more about that work from Shurr, but many undergraduates and some graduate students and teachers may find him a faithful guide to the surfaces, if not the lower depths, of the other poems and related prose, especially the neglected Burgundy Club sketches. Pending publication of the Northwestern-Newberry *Poems*, readers will be interested in passages where Shurr profits responsibly from Robert C. Ryan's dissertation and other textual information Ryan conveyed about many poems and groups of poems.

In "Textual Criticism and Error" (*AN&Q* 11:102) Theodore Johnson points to the passage in *The Poetry of Melville's Late Years* where William Bysshe Stein's fit of "inventive criticism" led him to explicate nine lines of "To Ned" as if they formed the "coda" of "The Maldive Shark." Two essay-reviews which had already pointed out Stein's amazing analysis of the non-Melvillean version of "The Maldive Shark" should be consulted, since they relate the blunder to pervasive errors in the book: Ryan's in *SIR* 10:230–40 and Parker's in

MLQ 33:54–66. (With any luck Johnson's reference to "the 'soiled serpent' affair" will not confuse readers: he means "the 'soiled fish' affair.")

ix. Billy Budd

Robert Merrill's "The Narrative Voice in *Billy Budd*" (*MLQ* 34:283–91) is a seemingly reasonable effort that goes wholly to waste because the author does not take into account Hayford's and Sealts's evidence about the composition of the book, especially the effects of the late pencil revisions, and does not make any use of their Genetic Text in studying the emergence of the narrative voice. After Hayford and Sealts have elaborately demonstrated that F. Barron Freeman's theory of dramatic scenes preceding analysis "is just about the reverse of the actual case," it is distressing to have Merrill innocently say that in the first half of *Billy Budd* "a very few incidents are made to yield a great deal of authorial analysis." As I said in *ALS 1972*, "critics refuse to recognize that the Hayford-Sealts textual discoveries, now a decade old, have interpretative implications"; maybe the only hope is to persuade editorial boards to reject articles on *Billy Budd* which do not take account of relevant information about its composition.

William H. Shurr (see the previous section) promisingly stresses "the importance of the poetry as immediate background for this masterpiece," but he too dissipates his efforts by treating *Billy Budd* as a finished work of art.

x. Miscellaneous

New biographical information about Melville seldom turns up these days, but Patricia Barber's "Melville's House in Brooklyn" (*AL* 45:433–34) describes a significant item in the Shaw Papers (overlooked by earlier scholars), a property contract which shows that in July, 1857, Melville agreed to purchase a three-story brownstone in Brooklyn (price: $4250) but cancelled the agreement the next month. Scholars have a new little bone—one that fits into the skeleton otherwise well-articulated by Hayford and Davis in their 1949 article (see section ***ii***).

Although *American Literature* and other bibliographies are now picking up items from *Extracts: An Occasional Newsletter of the Mel-*

ville Society, I prefer not to mention them here, lest the newsletter cease to be a place where scraps of information can be disseminated informally and questions asked tentatively. Let us take it for granted that anyone writing on Melville knows what's in *Extracts* by virtue of having paid the $5 dues for Melville Society membership to Donald Yannella, Department of English, Glassboro State College, Glassboro, N.J., 08028. I also prefer not to notice articles on Melville in the well-meaning new journals which accept papers only from graduate students. Preparing articles for avowedly second-class outlets is time wasted; the best papers by graduate students are always welcome in the established scholarly journals.

Two reviews deserve mention. Kingsley Widmer's "The Learned Try-Works: A Review of Recent Scholarly Criticism of Melville" (*SNNTS* 5:117–24) is a slightly belated companion to the several essay-reviews which appeared on the 1970 flotilla of Melville craft (see *ALS 1972*, p. 58). Widmer's analyses are witty, vigorous, and feisty. Robert R. Allen's "The First Six volumes of the Northwestern-Newberry Melville: A Review Article" (*Proof* 3:441–53) is the fullest assessment of the edition to date, notable for the amount of attention given to the design and the historical essays as well as the textual principles and procedures.

University of Southern California

5. Whitman and Dickinson

Bernice Slote

Work on Whitman this year was primarily critical, a good deal of it attempting to "place" Whitman as personality and persona, or in relation to other writers. It included three new books, several special editions, and a number of chapters or sections dealing with Whitman in other book-length studies. For once, no new theories about the structure of "Song of Myself" were advanced. Dickinson scholarship leaned heavily to organization and explication, and there were no new books.

i. Whitman

***a.* Bibliography, collections.** One salutary thing for scholars to observe is that most bibliographies remain unfinished. In the Whitman record, for instance, corrections and additions continue to appear. A clarifying note by William White, "Editions of *Leaves of Grass*: How Many?" (*WWR* 19:111–14), shows that if an edition is defined as a complete resetting of type, then there are six, not nine, editions of Whitman's book: 1855, 1856, 1860, 1867, 1871, and 1881. Other volumes must be counted as reissues, for new plates were not used. Artem Lozynsky, in "Whitman's *Complete Poems & Prose*: 'Bible' or 'Volume'" (*WWR* 19:28–30), examines the variations in three printings of Richard Maurice Bucke's "An impromptu criticism." Changes in terminology reveal something of the relationship of Bucke and Whitman.

Re-examinations of source material have resulted in some new information. G. R. Thompson has found an early printing (the third chronologically) of Whitman's short story, "Death in the School-Room: A Fact," in the *New York Mirror: A Weekly Gazette of Literature and the Fine Arts*, August 21, 1841. There are a few variations in text ("An Early Unrecorded Printing of Walt Whitman's 'Death in the School-Room,'" *WWR* 19:64–65). Kenneth P. Neilson notes that Whitman's "Ode to the Prison Ship Martyrs" was sung to the tune of the "Star Spangled Banner" at the 4th of July celebration at Fort Greene in 1846. His article, "A Discovery Rediscovered in the Search for Walt Whitman Music" (*WWR* 19:114–18) tells about the event.

Additional letters continue to be recorded. The earliest known Whitman letter, dated March 30, [1841], a recommendation of a fellow teacher, Miss Clarissa Lyvere, has been acquired by the Library of Congress. John C. Broderick adds an informative biographical account of Whitman's association with the Whitestone School in "Walt Whitman's Earliest Letter" (*QJLC* 30:44–47). Artem Lozynsky points out a transcript of a previously unnoted postcard from Whitman in a letter written by R. M. Bucke, October 19, 1879 ("A Lost Whitman Letter to Bucke," *WWR* 19:168–69). Two new Whitman letters in the Feinberg Collection are described by William White in "Unknown Letter to W. S. Huntington" (*WWR* 19:73) and "A New Whitman Letter to *The Century*" (*WWR* 19:118).

More anthologies and special editions appear than can be noted here. Two, however, have special interest. Walter Teller has selected and arranged (under topics such as "Censorship," "Love & Friendship," "Writing") excerpts from Traubel's *With Walt Whitman in Camden*, with illustrations and an introduction, in *Walt Whitman's Camden Conversations* (New Brunswick, N.J., Rutgers Univ. Press). The volume is readable, but without contexts the brief statements by Whitman are bodiless, even remote from his voice. Robert Creeley's "Introduction" to his selection of poems in *Whitman* (Baltimore, Penguin Books Ltd.) is a revealing account of how a modern poet came to know Whitman through Allen Ginsberg, Robert Duncan, and Louis Zukofsky; Creeley found in Whitman's prosody and diction something he could use. A review of recent facsimile editions is in William White's "Whitman Reprints from Haskell House & Others" (*WWR* 19:30–32). White's Whitman bibliography in each issue of the *Walt Whitman Review* continues to be indispensable.

***b.* Biography.** Although Whitman lore is full of anecdotes and brief glimpses behind the poet's veil to the human being and his everyday affairs, we have not had so complete a story of Whitman's life before 1855 as Joseph Jay Rubin presents in *The Historic Whit-*

man (University Park and London, Penn. State Univ. Press). In great and careful detail, taken largely from newspaper accounts, Rubin recreates the world of Whitman's youth and the life of the young journalist, teacher, wanderer, and political activist. One fault of the book is that it may be too detailed, too dense for good reading. Nevertheless the material is there, and we can come closer to the live Whitman of those years before *Leaves of Grass*. Included in the book is Rubin's valuable find—the previously uncollected "Letters from a Travelling Bachelor," eleven articles on Long Island, New York, and environs first published in the New York Sunday *Dispatch*, October 14, 1849, through January 6, 1850. These pieces, signed "Paumanok," are, like many of Whitman's journalistic articles, filled with perceptive comment—the exact sound of the bell of the Long Island Railroad, for example, or the catchers of blue-fish in their "swallow-like boats."

We have other views of Whitman as he appeared in person. William White presents an account of a reception given for the poet in parlors of New York's Westminster Hotel, April 15, 1887, after Whitman had lectured in the afternoon on Lincoln ("An Unknown Report of a Whitman Social," *ABC* 23,iii:22–25). Another newspaper account of an interview with Whitman during his visit with Richard Maurice Bucke in London, Ontario, is contributed by Artem Lozynsky in "Walt Whitman in Canada" (*ABC* 23,vi:21–23). Particularly interesting are Whitman's comments on other writers.

Whitman's attitude toward slavery, especially as it is expressed in his journalism, is examined by Mary-Emma Graham in "Politics in Black and White: A View of Whitman's Career as a Political Journalist" (*CLAJ* 17:263–70). She concludes that he was not a true reformer, a champion of the black man's cause; that he "never accepted the free Black man." His attacks on abolitionists combine, however, with his feeling that slavery had to go because it clouded the ideal of the American dream.

***c.* Criticism: general.** Several publications this year turn our attention to criticism in history—early statements on Whitman which at least give us a more complete sense of the response he drew from his readers. A major contribution is Jan Christian Smuts's *Walt Whitman: A Study in the Evolution of Personality*, edited by Alan L. McLeod (Detroit, Wayne Univ. Press). This book, written in 1894–95, while Smuts was a student at Cambridge, has been used by some scholars in manuscript, but is only now made generally available as primary material. The man who later became South Africa's chief political and military leader was also a perceptive reader of Whitman, interpreting *Leaves of Grass* in ways that seem to us now quite modern. His central concern was psychological, and his study was of Whitman as a prime example of the evolution of a great personality. He stresses wholeness (of both poet and book), but he also traces the changing stages in the development of Whitman's themes and personality, concluding that the full "wholeness" had not been reached. Part of Whitman's effectiveness is his ongoing force: "The last word in Whitman is not attainment but rather unattainment." Another unusual document is a translation (with notes) by R. K. Dasgupta of Kshitindranath Tagore's essay "Walt Whitman," written in Bengali in 1891 (*WWR* 19:3–11). Tagore notes the universality of Whitman's works (again, his "wholeness"): "every work and every feeling of a man is celebrated in this great and triumphant poet of democracy." The critical reception of Whitman in his own time was unquestionably mixed. In Paul J. Ferlazzo's "Anne Gilchrist, Critic of Walt Whitman" (*SDR* 10,iv[1972]:63–79) the relationship between Mrs. Gilchrist and Whitman is summarized, but emphasis is placed on her as "the first great critic of *Leaves of Grass*." And Paul P. Reuben in "Whitman in B. O. Flower's *Arena*" (*WWR* 19:11–19) reviews articles on Whitman which appeared in Benjamin Orange Flower's Boston monthly magazine, 1889–1909. A transcendentalist and reformer, Flower seemed to stress Whitman's "message of equality, comradeship and freedom of religious beliefs" rather than his literary qualities.

Wholeness and personality are also the themes of a book by E. Fred Carlisle, *The Uncertain Self: Whitman's Drama of Identity* ([East Lansing], Mich. State Univ. Press), in which the writer applies principally the "I-Thou" concept of Martin Buber to his exploration of Whitman's form and meaning. "For me," he says, "the drama [of Whitman's poetry] involves an interaction between the self and the external world in which that world plays an essential role and in which the major tensions occur between self and other" (p. 4, note). Only in this dialogue with the world and others does Whitman discover his essential self. In his analysis, then, Carlisle emphasizes the dialogical nature of poetry: the poem is "a spoken word that engages the reader and calls on him to respond" (p. xv). This is a serious book, and there are many helpful analyses throughout; yet, to me, two restrictions which the writer places on himself are damaging to a full realization of the poet's identity. No account is taken of the chronological order of the poems or the development of the poet, and only the final versions of the poems—the 1891–92 edition of *Leaves of Grass*—are considered. It seems to me that a concept of identity is without dimensions if one sees it as fixed in time; even "dialogue" implies the motion of going and returning.

Roland Hagenbüchle's "Whitman's Unfinished Quest for an American Identity" (*ELH* 40:428–78) is another serious exploration of the nature of the poet, his forms, and his themes. Though perhaps overlong and too thoroughly annotated (110 footnotes), it is an impressive piece and worth attention. In general, Whitman's "mode of thinking in terms of bipolar unity" is analyzed, particularly in the way stylistic elements support this central characteristic. For example, changes of identities in the poetry are paralleled by the syntax, and thought is represented organically in rhythmic or measured movement, balanced by free patterns—by "the erratic motion of eddies or vapours, by the irregular growth of trees and the free flight of birds." The circular movement in Whitman "may symbolize Whitman's quest for identity as an endless process of individuation within the human psyche." There is more on Whitman's emblematic, not symbolic, mode of thinking; on sex as a reconciliation of the Apollonian and Dionysian elements in the poetry; and on American identity as "a bipolar unity of pride and love." Whitman's fault, here, according to the writer, is that finite man was sacrificed to the vision of the cosmic man. His success was his challenging belief in man's possibility.

Three substantial essays appear as parts of new books. Floyd Stovall's "Whitman and the Poet in *Leaves of Grass*," which opens the *Gohdes Festschrift*, pp. 3–21, is a fine statement on the development of Whitman's persona in his poems, the relationship between it and his private self, and Whitman's own concept of the "Poet" he had created. Though Whitman knew the difference between the two, says Stovall, he and his Poet "were more nearly a single identity after 1860 than they had been before," particularly in the poems of the Civil War. A similar point on the importance of the war is made by Daniel Aaron in "Whitman: The 'Parturition Years,'" a chapter of

The Unwritten War (New York, Knopf), pp. 56–74: "If the War killed Hawthorne, it completed Walt Whitman." The chapter is a good survey of Whitman's attitude toward slavery, his insights gained through his hospital experiences, his *Drum-Taps*, and his feeling for Lincoln. A judicious review of problems and conclusions about Whitman's sexuality is "Walt Whitman's Omnisexual Vision," by James E. Miller, Jr., in *The Chief Glory of Every People: Essays on Classic American Writers*, edited by Matthew J. Bruccoli (Carbondale and Edwardsville, Southern Ill. Univ. Press, pp. 231–59, 283–85). Miller argues against literal biographical interpretations of Whitman's sexual terminology and references, but says that whatever Whitman's own personal sexual makeup and experience, "his imagination and vision were omnisexual. He had the artist's capacity to imagine and recreate many sexual roles, and he showed understanding of them and sympathy for them, and flung out his lines in celebration of them all," as sexuality "bestowed being and identity on individuals and helped to form, mold, and shape relationships, societies, nations."

Michael J. Hoffman in a section of *The Subversive Vision*, pp. 58–68, called "Whitman's Preface: Every Man His Own Priest" views Whitman as a kind of "Transcendental activist," a liberating force in Romantic poetry in his role as the visionary heroic redeemer. Two articles deal with Whitman's attitudes toward women, especially as revealed in his poetry. One is Judy Womack's "The American Woman in 'Song of Myself' " (*WWR* 19:67–72). The other, and more complete, discussion is by Kay F. Reinartz, also in the *Walt Whitman Review* (19:127–37). The title, "Walt Whitman and Feminism," appears in the table of contents but not with the article. Several pieces treat stylistic and rhetorical characteristics. The most detailed is by P. Z. Rosenthal, "The Language of Measurement in Whitman's Early Writing" (*TSLL* 15:461–70); more general is Galway Kinnell's "Indicative Words" (*APR* 2,ii:9–11). "Meaning in Whitman's Use of 'Electric' " (*WWR* 19:151–53) by Cynthia Sulfrudge is a useful note.

***d.* Criticism: individual works.** Five articles are the best of the explications this year. Although much has been written about Whitman's use of the catalogue as a technique, John B. Mason has a particularly lucid discussion in "Walt Whitman's Catalogues: Rhetorical Means for Two Journeys in 'Song of Myself' " (*AL* 45:34–49). The catalogues in "Song of Myself," he says, are not merely evidences of the poet as the "passive absorber" of experience, but they are the means for both poet and reader to move "from the 'I' to the cosmos," from "inactive observation to active participation." Moreover, rhetorical details suggest that the arrangement of a catalogue is not haphazard. The catalogue may also affect the narrative technique. By the end of Section 33 of "Song of Myself" the poet has completed his journey, the expansion of the self. He is then free of boundaries of space and time, and the subsequent narratives illustrate this release. Arthur Golden in "Passage to Less than India: Structure and Meaning in Whitman's 'Passage to India'" (*PMLA* 88:1095–1103) uses two manuscripts, especially that in the Oscar Lion Collection in the New York Public Library, to show that "Passage to India" developed as a kind of patchwork, with the incorporation of other poems in its body. Although Whitman's aim was high—to present a cosmic poem, one fusing traditional philosophies and visions—Golden feels that the poet was not in control of his material; the separate parts do not fuse, and some necessary development is omitted. "Whitman simply had not fully realized the potentialities of his theme."

Various critical views of "Out of the Cradle Endlessly Rocking" are summarized and then unified in Tracey R. Miller's "The Boy, the Bird, and the Sea: An Archetypal Reading of 'Out of the Cradle'" (*WWR* 19:93–103). This emphasis on the unity of recurring primordial images in Whitman's poem, whatever they are named, helps to reassert the complexity of art by a reading that is inclusive, not restrictive. An interesting view of another poem is in Lois A. Cuddy's "Exploration of Whitman's 'Eidólons'" (*WWR* 19:153–57): the strict form or structure of the poem is the "stable linear framework" for the ever-changing definitions of "eidólons" as the term is used throughout. Thus "Eidólons" becomes "the symbol of the undefinable in metaphysics and semantics"; the ideal of illusiveness is conveyed by indirection. One poem not often explicated is discussed by Harold Aspiz in "A Reading of Whitman's 'Faces'" (*WWR* 19:37–48), in which he gives helpful notes on phrenology and physiognomy for the understanding of details in the work. Whitman uses the countenance "as a dial plate of the human condition," and ends "Faces" with a vision of a new breed, a splendid progeny, of mankind.

Other briefer articles include Judge M. Schonfeld, "No Exit in 'Passage to India': Existence Precedes Essence in Section 5" (*WWR* 19:147–51); Stephen L. Tanner, "Star-Gazing in Whitman's *Specimen*

Days" (*WWR* 19:158–61); and Norbert Krapf, "Whitman's 'Calamus': Adam from the Garden to the City" (*WWR* 9:162–64).

e. **Relationships.** More than usual attention has been given this year to placing Whitman in a tradition, comparing him with his contemporaries, or showing possible influences on later writers. A general article by Arnold Mersch, "Cosmic Contrast: Whitman and the Hindu Philosophy" (*WWR* 19:49–63) says that Whitman "unintentionally" reflects some elements of Hindu philosophy on "the unity of life, the nature of reality, man's place in the universe, the idea of caste and duty, and man's goals." Contrasts (though views of the poets are not entirely convincing) are suggested by Jeanne Bugliari in "Whitman and Wordsworth: The Janus of Nineteenth Century Idealism" (*WWR* 19:63–67). A misinterpretation, though admiration, of Whitman is described in "Whitman and the Harvard Poets: The Case of George Cabot Lodge" (*WWR* 19:165–68), by John W. Crowley.

Whitman and Jules Michelet are linked in two articles. Arthur Geffen sees these writers as "the two classic messianic democrats of the nineteenth century" and argues that Michelet's *Woman* was a source and influence ("pervasive and continuous") for "Passage to India" ("Walt Whitman and Jules Michelet—One More Time," *AL* 45:107–14). Similarities between Michelet's *The Bird* and Whitman's mocking-bird in "Out of the Cradle Endlessly Rocking" are described in Gay Wilson Allen's "Whitman and Michelet—Continued" (*AL* 45:428–32). Charles M. Lombard, in "Whitman and Hugo" (*WWR* 19:19–25) notes that there are similarities in themes used by both writers, that both were innovative rebels, and that Whitman may well have been directly influenced by Hugo's work.

Melville's and Whitman's poems of the Civil War have often been viewed together; Vaughan Hudson offers another good, detailed account in "Melville's *Battle-Pieces* and Whitman's *Drum-Taps*: A Comparison" (*WWR* 19:81–92). He concludes that Melville seems "more complex, detached, almost fatalistic"; Whitman is more immediately involved, personal, reflective, and anguished. Instead of Melville's detachment, Whitman suggests "sincere dedication, an almost religious devotion to a cause"—the difference, perhaps, between "the composition of a good poet and a great poet." Contrasts between Whitman and Poe and their attitudes toward death are illustrated in Gerald F. Amyot, "Contrasting Visions of Death in the Poetry of Poe and Whitman" (*WWR* 19:103–11). Whitman saw death as positive, as healing, as a form of life; Poe saw death as tragic loss and the realm of the "Conqueror Worm."

Among other studies of influence, J. R. LeMaster places Jesse Stuart's poetry in the Whitman tradition ("Jesse Stuart's 'Album of Destiny'—In Whitman's Eternal Flow," *IllQ* 36,i.38–48), and Lois Hughson observes that John Dos Passos's revolutionary "ideas about political action and the exercise of power" come from Whitman ("In Search of the True America: Dos Passos' Debt to Whitman in *U.S.A.*" *MFS* 19:179–92). Rimbaud is also linked to Whitman by David J. Wells ("Whitman and Rimbaud," *WWR* 19:25–28)—"a thirst for new experiences of an unanalyzed, mystical nature with an energetic, primitive, sexual approach to these experiences dominates their poetry." Kjelal Kadir makes some clear distinctions in "Neruda and Whitman: Short-Circuiting the Body Electric" (*PCP* 8:16–22). Although the two poets used similar techniques (illustrated here by their enumerative style), their visions were different. Whitman's enumerations convey "a secular religiosity, a mystical exuberance," a sense of flight. Neruda's objects "assume the countenance of walls which hem in their perceiver and enumerator. They achieve unity in their oppressive solidarity." And, finally, we are reminded again that there is little of the generation gap between Whitman and youth of the 1960s and 1970s. As Arnold Mersch shows in "Whitman and the Age of Aquarius: A Message for the 'Woodstock Generation'" (*WWR* 19:138–46), the transmuted voice of Whitman—one of the roughs, a Kosmos—is still heard in the land.

ii. Dickinson

***a.* Bibliography.** A useful addition to Dickinson studies is a yearly bibliography now contributed by Sheila Taylor Clendenning ("Emily Dickinson: Annual Bibliography for 1972," *EDB* 23:187–90). Not much else was done this year for the Dickinson record. Frederick L. Morey has at times suggested new ways of arranging the poems for an "inclusive edition"; in "The Reader's Edition" (*EDB* 23:144–55) he reviews the problems and possibilities. And further information seems to remove entirely from the Dickinson canon the 1895 *Chap-Book* poems once attributed to her by Charles Gullans and John Espey (see *ALS 1972*, p. 66). William White writes that he had long ago discussed (but not attributed) the same poems (*EDB* 23:168); and in two letters Jay Leyda and George Monteiro comment further on the misattribution (*EDB* 24:207–09). Leyda gives some evidence that the two poems were parodies by Bliss Carman.

***b.* Biography.** To find another portrait of Emily Dickinson would be an event. Coming at it slantly, F. Dewolfe Miller in "Emily Dickinson: Self-Portrait in the Third Person" (*NEQ* 46:119–24) calls our attention especially to the poem beginning "A Mien to move a Queen—Half Child—Half—Heroine—" for the poet's "objective appraisal of the effect that her physical, psychic, and intellectual self has on other people." The playfulness of her mind, especially in the kind of "naughtiness" she uses in some of her comments on Christianity, is discussed by James A. Hijiya in "The Rascal Emily Dickinson" (*EDB* 24:224–26). In an impressive review-article, "Emily and the Psychobiographer" (*L&P* 23:68–81), Simon Grolnick discusses rather fully the implications of and what he judges to be errors in the approach used by John Cody in *After Great Pain* (see *ALS 1971*, p. 71; *ALS 1972*, pp. 67–68). He considers Cody's book to be "studious" but "one which seems depersonalized and tangential"; it is "often reductionistic." Dr. Grolnick disagrees not only with the particular psychological approach in the book, but points out numerous omissions of fact and context and the general ignoring of more complex interpretations. All who have worried about *After Great Pain* should read this article.

***c.* Criticism: general.** Critical writing on Emily Dickinson has not been heavy this year, but there are a half dozen or so substantial articles that deserve reading. Two of the most interesting, partly because they present opposing arguments, attempt to define Dickinson as a metaphysical or a romantic poet. B. J. Rogers in "The Truth Told Slant: Emily Dickinson's Poetic Mode" (*TSLL* 14:329–36) sees her as like the metaphysical poets in her separation of subject and object: she "makes a circuit around her central point by a series of analogous restatements, arriving at a vision of the center from every point of view except the inside." There are some good examples of this technique in poems such as "To hear an Oriole sing" or "I heard a Fly buzz—when I died." Her "characteristic digressive movement" shows "the knower's separation from the known and his power over it. The aim is not to see the object steadily and see it whole, but to see its eternal aspect broken down prismatically." Perhaps even more persuasively argued is Michael G. Yetman's "Emily Dickinson and the English Romantic Tradition" (*TSLL* 15:129–48), in which he shows her work as a blend of new and old—Keats and Wordsworth as well as Emerson. Yetman finds that the poems have an "Inner/Outer antithesis" (and here he seems to agree with B. J. Rogers that Dickinson's technique, at least, is similar to that of the metaphysicals) and by intuitional perception and creation. The author relates Dickinson in specific ways to certain Romantics—Keats, Shelley, Hopkins, Wordsworth, Blake. She was like them, too, in creating a personal heaven, and in believing in "the absolute importance of the self and its truths as discoverable through poetry."

In "A Circumference of Emily Dickinson" (*NEQ* 46:250–71) Robert Gillespie calls her word "circumference" and certain related symbolic words and images her "special vocabulary of awe"; they can best be understood in relation to the journey, which to Dickinson is the image of both change and "the separation between the self and what the self desires." The journey is often inward, sometimes an expansion of consciousness and a return. Certain symbols in nature (sun, noon) are discussed, and there is an extended explication of the poem "Our journey had advanced." Less precise, but still helpful because it includes comments on a number of poems not widely interpreted ("Bloom upon the Mountain—stated—"; "The Mountain stood in Haze"; "A lane of Yellow led the eye") is Kenneth R. Ball's "Emily Dickinson and the Beautiful" (*SHR* 7:287–94). Beauty is discussed as including the picturesque.

Rebecca Patterson's extensive discussion of "The Cardinal Points Symbolism of Emily Dickinson" was published in two parts (*MQ* 14:293–317; 15:31–48). In this work she supports with great detail her argument that Dickinson organized a vast body of imagery according to the four directions, associating north, east, south, and west with day, season, color, element, and emotional significance. And on a double axis of north-south and east-west divisions "she has suspended literally hundreds of poems, many of them interlocking with scores of other symbol clusters." Thus Dickinson achieves an economy of allusion, an organization of her emotional experience, and a unified body of poetry. The north-south axis is presented in part I of the article, the east-west axis in part II; both discussions have detailed examples and illustrations and need to be read rather than summarized. The author says in conclusion that "this web of symbolism would suggest treating the work of her major period not as a series of tiny, fragmented lyrics but as one total poem." Another well-developed discussion is Vivian R. Pollak's " 'That Fine Prosperity': Economic Metaphors in Emily Dickinson's Poetry" (*MLQ* 34:161–79). These are metaphors drawn from public life (commerce, labor, contracts, and the like) in vocabulary common to any educated person of her day. The three basic uses of these metaphors are "to satirize the social and religious values of Amherst" (a microcosm of the United States); to describe feelings of fullness and deprivation; and "to work out a notion of subjective valuation and to delineate an intangible estate." The value of this use of economic metaphor, says the author, is primarily "to anchor the romantic extravagance of Dickinson's sensibility and the abstraction of her poetic method to the material facts of everyday life."

Several other slighter articles also attempt to organize and relate Dickinson's types of imagery and metaphor. Their topics are apparent in the titles: Frederick L. Morey, "The Four Fundamental Archetypes in Mythology, as Exemplified in Emily Dickinson's Poems" (*EDB* 24:196–206); Maurice Hungiville, "Creation and Salvation: a study of pain images in the major themes" (*EDB* 24:231–34); Douglas A. Noverr, "Emily Dickinson and the Art of Despair" (*EDB* 3:161–67).

Various special topics are touched on, though none is explored deeply. James E. Mulqueen argues that Emerson was not a major influence on Dickinson: She does not have his concept of the Over-soul, his sense of the unity of all being, nor his idea of correspondences between object and thought ("Is Emerson's Work Central to the Poetry of Emily Dickinson?" *EDB* 24:211–20). With "Emily Dickinson's 'Private Campaign' " in *The Unwritten War* (New York, Knopf), pp. 355–56, Daniel Aaron recognizes that the Civil War did affect Dickinson, with isolation but not indifference: "The War inflamed her imagination, illuminated old enigmas, touched her deeper sympathies." She used martial imagery because "the national conflict coincided with her private anguish . . . the wars of the Heart and Mind." Emily Dickinson is viewed as a woman writer and related to some of those who went before and who came after in "Sappho to Sexton: Woman Uncontained," by Linda Mizjewski (*CE* 35:340–45). The tradition is that of escape, of breaking out, in tension with "woman contained."

***d.* Criticism: individual poems.** Several explications look at less familiar Dickinson poems. Laurence Perrine notes that in "There Are Two Ripenings" the contrast between the ripening of a fruit and a nut suggests a parallel with the growth of the body and the mind ("Dickinson's 'There Are Two Ripenings,'" *Expl* 31:item 65). Jo C. Searles in "The Art of Dickinson's 'Household Thought'" (*CP* 6,i:46–51) sees "Of Bronze—and Blaze—" as different from Emerson's idea of man in nature, that is, man identifying with the powers of an immense universe. It is, rather, "a poetic picture of man as center of his individually perceived universe." Nat Henry's "Dickinson's 'As by the Dead We Love to Sit'" (*Expl* 31:item 35) is a note on the syntax of that poem. The "we" in the first line is "not editorial, but representative of all," and we sit to remember our "dear dead," our kin and comrades. "The sharpened remembrance of what is gone triggers fretful joy in what we still have to lose." In "Dickinson's '*Death is a Dialogue*'" (*EDB* 23:171) Lee J. Richmond notes that the metaphor of the body as "overcoat of clay" has sources in Carlyle, the German philosophers, the Bhagavad Gita, Emerson, and the book of Revelation. Constance Rooke in "'The first Day's Night had come—' An Explication of J.410" (*EDB* 24:221–23) sees that poem as "a lyric projected as drama." Characters (small, like dolls) are born within the speaker; they are confined within that frame.

René Rapin in "Dickinson's 'I Never Lost as Much but Twice'" (*Expl* 31:item 52) disagrees with George Monteiro's interpretation of the poem, in which he suggested a Jobean "three-personed God" as Father, Burglar, and Banker (see *ALS 1972*, pp. 69–70). The order in the poem, however, progresses through the mood of the speaker—from the protesting term "Burglar" to the more helpful "Banker" and finally to the protecting "Father," who is needed once more. Stephen Axelrod discusses "I Years had been from Home" in "Terror in the Everyday" (*CP* 6,i:53–56). By the second stanza, he says, "what might have been a nostalgic going-home has become . . . a crucial confrontation with self." The house the speaker refuses to enter is "in some way her own soul and the universal soul." She becomes aware "of her own inability to know the whole truth of self and the universe." Yet in recognizing hell, she also perceives the outlines of heaven.

As a concluding note, let me say that it is becoming an increasing distraction to read so much criticism of Emily Dickinson in which she is persistently called "Emily." This seems to me a symptomatic habit; it gives a patronizing air even to the most serious criticism. I hope this will not happen to Edgar and Ernest, to Nathaniel, Herman, and Ralph.

University of Nebraska–Lincoln

6. Mark Twain

Hamlin Hill

Probably the most surprising aspect of Mark Twain scholarship and criticism in 1973 was the silence surrounding *Huckleberry Finn. Tom Sawyer, A Connecticut Yankee*, and *Pudd'nhead Wilson* each received more attention than the central work; and the later years after 1885 enjoyed the notoriety of a new volume in the Iowa/California Edition (*What Is Man? and Other Philosophical Writings*), a collection of "radical" writings, and a biography, in addition to a flowering of scholarly articles. Given the recent availability of later writings in the Mark Twain Papers, the direction seems a salutary one, and Huck must be enjoying the brief vacation.

i. Textual and Bibliographical

H. Jack Lang in "Mark Twain A.L.S. More Valuable Than Lincoln" (*MSS* 25:187–91) reprints an eleven-line bread-and-butter letter to Thomas Nast dated December 4, 1884, and then, in the accepted ritual for inflating trivia to give it the appearance of significance, provides a thumbnail biography of Nast and quotes extensively from *Mark Twain's Autobiography*. Two other equally unimportant notes, one of January 2, 1891, declining an invitation and the other dated May 8, 1894, saying goodbye to copublisher Fred Hall, provide the substance of Karl Kiralis's "Two More Recently Discovered Letters by S. L. Clemens" (*MTJ* 16,iv:18–20).

"Mark Twain's Last Manuscript" (*Bancroftiana* [Berkeley] 55 [June]:9) briefly describes the "Ashcroft-Lyon Manuscript," a 400-page segment of the Autobiography written as a letter to W. D. Howells and cataloging in meticulous detail the suspicions Clemens held against Ralph Ashcroft and Isabel Lyon (his business manager and personal secretary), which was given to the Mark Twain Papers in 1973. Thomas H. Pauley's "The Contents Tables in *Adventures of Huckleberry Finn*" (*Proof* 3:63–68) focuses upon two sets of extraneous matter—the table of contents and running heads that Charles L. Webster supplied for the first American edition, and the table of contents prepared, presumably by Albert Bigelow Paine, for issues of the novel in the Author's National Edition published after 1912. Each of the tables is, according to Pauley, in effect an interpretation of the novel: Webster's concentrated on plot and physical journey while Paine added "moral consequences" and structural linkings in his titles. And even though neither had Mark Twain's authority, Pauley believes that the Paine table of contents "seems to have had great effect on contemporary critics of the novel." Such chapter titles as "I Have a New Name," "They're After Us," and "You Can't Pray a Lie" foreshadow current interest in Huck's identity crisis, his bond with Jim, and his struggles with his sound heart and deformed conscience. It is possible, of course, that Paine had a unique moment of critical insight when he composed his titles, but it seems equally possible that, because he used Huck's own language for over a fourth of his headings, he could not avoid capturing some of the significance and importance of the novel.

Maxwell Geismar's anthology *Mark Twain and the Three R's* (Indianapolis, Bobbs-Merrill) provides a comprehensive collection of writings on Race, Religion, and Revolution—93 selections of "radical social commentary." Even Geismar's introduction does not dull the edge of Twain's satire and invective against bigotry, imperialism, and "patriotism." But Geismar continues in his own commentary to ride the same hobby horses which distorted *Mark Twain: An American Prophet*. There is, he claims, "more than a hint of censorship and suppression about this vein of Twain's work," even though the bulk of his selections come from *Following the Equator*, *A Connecticut Yankee*, *The Mysterious Stranger*, *Europe and Elsewhere*, and other works published by major presses and sold widely or stocked on all library shelves for many years. Geismar sets up the same academic strawmen he assaulted in the earlier book—Brooks, Kaplan, Neider—and implies his own unique resistance to the psychological hordes. He misses the date of Olivia Clemens's death by a month, calls Jean Clemens "Jeanne," and proposes that Mark Twain was "one of the most openly sexual writers of the Victorian period (and in American letters)." But, as Geismar says, "it is hard to . . . keep a great artist silent, or, more subtly, to transmute his values"; and this is an admirable collection of a significant—and usually familiar—facet of Mark Twain's literature, which does not require its editor's pose of iconoclasm and martyrdom to justify its importance.

Paul Baender's edition of *What Is Man? and Other Philosophical Writings* (Berkeley, Univ. of Calif. Press for the Iowa Center for Textual Studies) is a major editorial achievement. This superb volume, the second published in the Iowa/California Edition, prints philosophical writings from the 1866 "Sabbath Reflections" to the 1909 essay "The Turning Point of My Life." All but one of the 24 texts—"Things a Scotsman Wants to Know"—have been previously published, but important deleted segments from *Christian Science, What Is Man?* and "The Turning Point of My Life" add to the significance of the book. Baender's introduction moves crisply through the major outlines and evolutions in Twain's philosophical thought to a detailed historical discussion of the three major texts—*Christian Science* and "Letters from the Earth" in addition to *What Is Man?* Editorial apparatus is lucid and unlike last year's *Roughing It* (see *ALS 1972*, pp. 76–77, and Hershel Parker, "Three Mark Twain Editions" [*NCF* 28:225–29]) conservative; in this volume Baender affirms that Mark Twain "commonly insisted that printers follow his idiosyncratic punctuation" and normalizes sparingly.

Baender's introduction traces a slow growth by Mark Twain to the mature expression of his pessimism between 1897 and 1909 and a corresponding development of "devices of indirection" which mute or mask the ideas he was attempting to express: "rhetorical occasion," in which "he would often assume the pose that only the stimulus of recent events and current topics made him reveal his beliefs"; and the use of disguised "spokesmen to deliver his arguments," Negroes, supernatural beings, and animals. A single minor—indeed, microscopic—quibble: a note written by Isabel Lyon in 1933 claimed that Mark Twain despised the Warner family because "Susy became so interested in this new religion [Christian Science] that in the early stages of her tragic illness she refused to see a doctor, & then it was too late." While Miss Lyon was not totally reliable in her memories, it seems plausible that Susy's death might have been a major submerged catalyst for the lengthy attack on Mrs. Eddy. But this is an infinitesimal point of historical background for a volume of the first importance.

ii. Biographical

Curtis Dahl, "Mark Twain and Ben Ely: Two Missouri Boyhoods" (*MHR* 66[1972]:549–66), compares the childhood of Clemens and Ben Ezra Stiles Ely, a Marion County resident at roughly the same time. Ely's description of Hannibal and his recounting of a camp-meeting (notably more theological than the scene in *Huckleberry Finn*; Ely was a minister's son and later a minister himself) occupy the bulk of Dahl's article.

William C. Miller, "Samuel L. and Orion Clemens vs. Mark Twain and His Biographers (1861–1862)" (*MTJ* 16,iv:1–9) relies upon much unpublished material of Orion's now in the National Archives, and Miller brings to light some startling corrections of "facts" from *Roughing It.* Sam Clemens was not hired by Orion as his secretary, but went to Washoe only on the possibility of being hired as "messenger or porter" or "additional help." In fact, Sam drew $480 for sixty days of clerking in the autumn of 1861, and in that year probably used his influence to gain passage through the territorial legislature of a recording-fee bill which was profitable to Orion. Further, it seems possible that the offer to Sam to work for the *Territorial Enterprise* in 1862 was prompted by that paper's interest in securing the contracts to publish the territorial laws and legislative journals (awards solely under Orion's control), rather than by Clemens's own earlier burlesque writings.

AW chose Mark Twain as the subject for two articles in 1973 which are as biographical as they are anything else. In "Mark Twain: Senatorial Secretary" (*AW* 10,i:16–17,60–62), William Hedges Robinson, Jr., assembles from the two men's reminiscences a brief description of Clemens's secretaryship to Senator William M. Stewart in Washington during the last months of 1867. And T. H. Watkins's "Mark Twain and His Mississippi" (*AW* 10,vi:12–19) is an adaptation of broad historical material, with several nice illustrations, from a book to be published in 1974. Neither article makes any contribution to Mark Twain biography or scholarship.

Ernest J. Moyne, "Mark Twain and Baroness Alexandria Gripenberg" (*AL* 45:370–78), notes that the Baroness visited Hartford in 1888, met Mark Twain for dinner, and engaged in a brief correspondence. Of substantial interest is Twain's reply to a charge of plagiarizing an anecdote which the Baroness reported to a European newspaper. His December 27, 1888, letter (reprinted from the holograph in the Manuscript Archives of the Finnish Literature Society) defends and elaborates upon the idea that "there is no merit in ninety-nine stories out of a hundred except the merit put into them by the teller's *art*." Kenton J. Clymer's "John Hay and Mark Twain" (*MHR* 67:397–406) is a superficial account of the lifelong friendship culled from the obvious sources.

Hamlin Hill's *Mark Twain: God's Fool* (New York, Harper and Row) is an intimate biography of the last decade (1900–10) which concentrates on the domestic events of that period, with some discussion of the literary and financial aspects of the twilight years. Using the recently discovered "Ashcroft-Lyon Manuscript" and the hitherto-restricted diaries of Isabel Lyon, it attempts to trace the disintegration of "the King," the vicious quarrels of his family and entourage, and the effects of isolation and vanity upon his literary work—especially the autobiographical dictations. Hill hoped to pierce through the Mark Twain legend manufactured by Albert Bigelow Paine and Clara Clemens in order to find the mortal Samuel Clemens; the man he discovered, obsessed by his own image and insulated from the world by a coterie of fawning sycophants, was unpleasant enough to produce an enormous range of commentary.

"The rantings of Lear on the heath, the chaos of Robert Frost's last years . . . seem no more than mild interludes of discomfort when contrasted with Twain's last decade," John J. McAleer said in a review in *Best Sellers*. Justin Kaplan found the book "moralistic and even hostile" (*Book World*); but Robert Evett (in the Washington *Star-News*) called it "the most important contribution to the field since Justin Kaplan's great biography." Gene Baro (in *The Smithsonian*) believed that the author "sometimes works the material unnecessarily for effect" and Malcolm Muggeridge suspected that he "made the picture rather darker than it really was to correct the previous hands which strove to make it lighter" (*Esquire*). But *Publishers Weekly* called it "an important milestone in the literature on Twain" and Robert E. Spiller (Philadelphia *Bulletin*) and Henry J. Lindborg (*Library Journal*) both used the adjective "definitive." William Harrington (in the Columbus *Dispatch*) thought it "tasteless" and Doris Grumbach in *The New Republic* labeled it "notable, graceful, convincing." Leslie Hanscom in *Newsday* thought it "feeble," and *Choice* said it was "splendidly, grippingly written." Finally, *The Book-of-the-Month-Club News*, making the book sound like a Hollywood column, said that it was "of great gossipy appeal." The truth probably lurks in there, somewhere.

Finally, Narbert Blei, in "Marking Twain in Hannibal" (*American Libraries* 5:128–34), records his recent visit to Hannibal—a trip which apparently consisted of asking everyone in town if he had ever read a Mark Twain book. Most hadn't, and didn't plan to.

iii. General Criticism

David B. Kesterson has edited *Critics on Mark Twain* (Coral Gables, Univ. of Miami Press) in four sections—"Critics on Mark Twain: 1882–1940," "Critics on Twain Since 1940," "General Critical Evaluations," and "Critics on Specific Works." Forty-four critics appear in selections ranging from a single paragraph to a dozen pages. One might prefer a dash of Leslie Fiedler or James M. Cox or Leo Marx to some of the contributors Kesterson included; and any specialist will feel frustrated by the brevity of most of the excerpts. All the same, the volume succeeds, in limited space, to suggest the range and scope of Twain criticism and ought to be a useful introduction for undergraduates.

Robert L. Gale's two hefty volumes—a total of 1300 pages—of *Plots and Characters in the Works of Mark Twain* (Hamden, Conn., Archon Books) will become an indispensible reference work for Twainians. There are plot summaries of all the published works (including nonfiction except for letters, notebooks, and the *Autobiography*) and over a hundred unpublished items in the Mark Twain Papers. There is an index of all the characters' names and nicknames in the second volume, including twenty-six epithets for Joan of Arc. Clearly a labor of love, and exhaustion, *Plots and Characters* even makes for entertaining browsing (who knows where a political candidate named Nixon appears in Twain's works, for instance?).

In "Episodic Analysis of Novels" (*JPsy* 85:267–76), Robert R. Sears and Deborah Lapidus have reported their pioneering attempt to utilize Mark Twain's literature quantitatively to evaluate his personality. Basic is Sears's and Lapidus's assumption that "an author's novels (or stories, or plays) are successive fantasy-behavior outputs; their motivational contents are subject to the changing experiences of his life and of his own personality development." The present exercise is in fact a record of the authors' success in tabulating thematic episodes in *Tom Sawyer, Huckleberry Finn, A Connecticut Yankee, Pudd'nhead Wilson, The Mysterious Stranger, Innocents Abroad, The Prince and the Pauper,* and "Extract from Captain Stormfield's Visit to Heaven" (with a chart showing the reporters' effectiveness); but ultimately they will report their "analyses of aggression, exhibitionism, and attachment behaviors" in Mark Twain's novels.

Paul A. Eschholz, "Mark Twain and the Language of Gesture" (*MTJ* 17,i:5–8) catalogs some samples of nonverbal communication in a few selected works: Huck's trials with Mrs. Judith Loftus in *Huckleberry Finn,* Hank's description of peasant body language in *A Connecticut Yankee,* and Tom Driscoll's various facial contortions during the trial scene in *Pudd'nhead Wilson.* But I am not sure why. Sholom J. Kahn in "Mark Twain as American Rabelais" (*HUSL* 1:47–75) expands traditional definitions of *Rabelaisian* from "smutty" or "artificial" to include a broad range of literary techniques: "largeness of soul and themes," "quixotic satire," "a blend of fantasy and realism," gigantic or microscopic dimensions, and such stylistic devices as mock-erudition, slang, exuberant experimentation, and irony, and then suggests Mark Twain's affinity to these techniques throughout his literary career.

Similarly, Andrea Goudie in " 'What Fools These Mortals Be!' A Puckish Interpretation of Mark Twain's Narrative Stance" (*KanQ* 5,iv:19–31) suggests that "the absence of poise" is the key to Mark Twain's humor; and among the various stances which he chose, the comic pose resembles Puck's role in *A Midsummer Night's Dream.* Common characteristics include a willingness to be both auditor of and actor in the events, an impish and irreverent criticism of the foolishness of mortal life, and a "Puckish superiority" to human society. Explications of the narrative poses in *Innocents Abroad, Roughing It, Life on the Mississippi,* and *Huckleberry Finn* show the injection of increasingly bitter satire into the Puckish stance. While Goudie acknowledges that Huck is not an American Puck, she points out that both characters are alike in "the nature of their alienation from the world of men." Huck blends the auditor and actor roles, but because he is human, his Puckishness is limited by his sympathy. And in the later works, sardonic irony and sarcasm replace Twain's irreverent and lighthearted humor, when, "in the life-long process of fixing the ass's head on humanity as a rollicking good joke, he eventually discovers a perfect fit."

Robert Rowlette notes parallel passages from Twain and Artemus Ward (mostly from the Mormon chapters of *Roughing It*) in " 'Mark Ward on Artemus Twain': Twain's Literary Debt to Ward" (*ALR* 6:13–25). He suggests Twain's strong dependence on Ward's humor until the early 1870s when, as Rowlette puts it, "Twain's strong resentment at being unfavorably compared with Ward" produced antagonism and silence. Daniel J. Fuller, "Mark Twain and Hamlin Garland: Contrarieties in Regionalism" (*MTJ* 17,i:14–18) is mostly about *Main-Travelled Roads*; but the influence of Taine, the significance of setting (both as beneficent and as destructive), and a basically autobiographical source for their fiction unite Twain and Garland.

Equally inane are J. M. Gogol, "Nikolai Aseev and Mark Twain" (*MTJ* 16,iv:15–16) and D. L. Emblem, "Mark Twain Alive and Well—Very Well Indeed—in Sweden" (*MTJ* 16,iv:16–18). The former tells us that the Russian poet liked Mark Twain, the latter lists the Swedish translations of Mark Twain's works. Neither of these bits of information seems particularly worth recording.

Sydney J. Krause, "Steinbeck and Mark Twain" (*StQ* 6:104–11), notices a number of parallel affinities between the two writers: the Western background, "the same natural feeling for footloose comic extravagance," a predilection for the travel narrative and the fable, and most significantly the "interest in history and the Middle Ages." Steinbeck's *Cup of Gold* has important overtones of *A Connecticut Yankee* as a parody of *Morte D'Arthur*, as does "Saint Katy the Virgin." More elemental than these resemblances, however, Krause argues "a deep and pervasive similarity of philosophic outlook," which includes a misanthropic view of humanity, ironic skepticism, and a pessimism ameliorated by comic escape from social responsibility or tragic confrontation with the implacability of reality. A sequel will consider the specific relationships between *The Pearl* and "The Man That Corrupted Hadleyburg."

iv. Earlier Works

More specific than Rowlette's general study of Ward's influence on Twain (above) is Paul C. Rodgers, Jr., "Artemus Ward and Mark Twain's 'Jumping Frog' " (*NCF* 28:273–86). Rodgers provides an extensive and helpful summary of critical interpretations of the story and then offers a lengthy analysis of Ward's probable influence upon the techniques of its humor. Twain's decisions to use the frame technique, to employ two deadpan narrators (both perpetrating hoaxes on their listeners), and to address the earliest version as a letter to "Mr. A. Ward" rest upon Browne's "decisive, albeit indirect and quite unconscious influence upon Twain's determinations regarding characterization, point of view, style, pace, tone, structure, and so on."

Herman Nibbelink's mistitled "Mark Twain and the Mormons" (*MTJ* 17,i:1–5) is actually about the humor in *Roughing It* with almost the entire emphasis on comedy about polygamy, with gentle humor backfiring upon Twain's presumably monogamous readers "to help men recognize their bond with one another." And Yorimasa Nasu's "A Study of Mark Twain's *Roughing It*—the Horseshoe Pattern" (*DSI* 5:1–47) is a positively delirious examination of the "T-A-A′-T′ (T = travel record of the innocent; A = autobiographical narrative as a tenderfoot miner; A′ = autobiographical narrative as a news-reporter; T′ = travel record as a special correspondent and a lecturer") pattern in the book. A final incomprehensible conclusion tells us that we have learned "that the duality in Mark Twain is a mask of one of the *personae* the writer uses in this book; it shows two contrasting points on the curving line of the horseshoe pattern. Between these two contrasting points, can be found Mark Twain's position." Well, *I* did not learn that, not a bit of it.

Wayne Mixon's "Mark Twain, The Gilded Age, and the New South Movement" (*SHR* 7:403–09) convincingly parallels the platform of various spokesmen for the New South—"economic regeneration, sectional reconciliation and adjustment of the race question"—with portions of *The Gilded Age*. The railroad speculation, the gathering of Southerners in Washington (usually in the area of the Treasury), and the Knobs University Bill represent fictional applications of the doctrines of Henry Grady and Richard Edmonds, with the additional element of Mark Twain's satiric assault on "a culture which placed so high a premium on material success." John W. Crowley's "A Note on *The Gilded Age*" (*ELN* 10[1972]:116–18) prints Warner's June 8, 1874, letter to the editor of *Appleton's*, affirming the novel's satiric intent and giving two months as the span of composition.

Substantial examinations of *Tom Sawyer* in 1973 include Lyall Powers, "The Sweet Success of Twain's Tom" (*DR* 53:310–24). The "Edenic" atmosphere of St. Petersburg, the happy resolution of all Tom's escapades, and the sense of timelessness and agelessness which contribute to the novel's appeal disguise more ornate configurations, according to Powers. Three sections of the novel (chapters 1–11, 13–20, and 29–32) move to strict chronology from the vague and nebulous, "heightening the realism and making the story more convincing." Powers discusses three narrative themes—the romantic story involving Becky, the escapades involving Injun Joe, and Tom's relationship to Huck (the obverse of which is Tom's relationship to society). There are three motifs: death, the quest for hidden treasure, and romantic heroic adventure. These various elements move to predictable resolutions: "playful action matures into earnest action; the romantic hardens into reality; rebellion is regularized into respectability."

Steven Karpowitz offers a psychological interpretation of *Tom* in "Tom Sawyer and Mark Twain: Fictional Women and Real in the Play of Conscience with the Imagination" (*L&P* 23:5–12). Both Mark Twain and Tom "frequently combined thoughts of fame and death with a woman's suffering. Behind the writer's Victorian image of a pure woman was the vindictive wish to see her in pain." Tom constantly daydreams fantasies of death and near-death in order to enjoy the thought of Aunt Polly's or Becky's remorse. These useful parallels become murky, however, when Karpowitz says that the River assumes a "birthgiving rush" as Tom "pushed his head and shoulders through a small hole" in the cave and was thus reborn to mediocrity.

Building on the "counterpoint" method of alternating comic and serious scenes, which Walter Blair, Richard P. Adams, and others have discussed as a unifying structure for *Huckleberry Finn*, Virginia Wexman imposes the same process on *Tom* in "The Role of Structure in *Tom Sawyer* and *Huckleberry Finn*" (*ALR* 6:1–11). Tom's and Joe Harper's mock quarrel and murder immediately precede Injun

Joe's murder of Dr. Robinson in chapter nine; a fantasy treasure-hunt immediately precedes the scene in the haunted house when real treasure is uncovered; and that part of the picnic scene in which the children explore the cave precedes Huck's wandering through a maze of dark streets following Injun Joe. It is important, Wexman argues, that the ominous echoes always follow the childish or comic action, for, "while the presence of serious episodes saves the novel from a complete moral naivete, the fact that the make-believe event *precedes* the real one means that the more somber incidents are, to some degree, invested with the childish whimsy of the earlier ones." About a third of the way through *Huck* (in chapter 17), Mark Twain reversed the ordering of the counterpointed pairs: "now, rather than preceding the serious event with an imaginary one . . . the real action is now *followed* by a scene of make-believe that mirrors it." Such a twist makes the comic variant (Bilgewater's "deef and dumb" act after Jim's story of his daughter, for instance) grotesque and depraved. Tom's reappearance and the evasion do not restore comedy at the conclusion but, instead, emphasize the ironic seriousness of the last two-thirds of the novel.

Arthur C. Cloutier's decision to write a letter to John Seelye in the language of Tom, protesting Tom's absence from *The True Adventures of Huckleberry Finn*, was an unfortunate one. "Dear Mr. Seelye . . . Yours Truly, Tom Sawyer" (*CE* 34:849–53) takes too long to say nothing and, because its language is Huck's rather than Tom's, becomes merely inept and cute.

R. Galen Hanson has discovered what he apparently believes is a startling and original truth: in the Bluejay Yarn from *A Tramp Abroad* Mark Twain "is using the description of the behavior of a lower animal, the bluejay, to shed light on the ways of that most complex creature, man." For readers who have survived this initial revelation in "Bluejays and Man: Twain's Exercise in Understanding" (*MTJ* 17,i:18–19), there is another: the wise owl at the conclusion is the Kierkegaardian individualist "who sees things clearly, and it is no coincidence that the owl stands alone." For sheer nonsense, so does this article.

Guy A. Cardwell has published two extensive articles on *Life on the Mississippi*: "Mark Twain, James R. Osgood, and Those 'Suppressed' Passages" (*NEQ* 46:163–88) and "*Life on the Mississippi*: Vulgar Facts and Learned Errors" (*ESQ* 19:283–93). The former study, utilizing some Osgood-Twain notes at Harvard College Library, questions the generalization that it was Osgood who insisted on the suppression of 10,000 to 15,000 words of the travel book (especially chapter 48) because he feared that they would offend potential Southern purchasers; to the contrary, Cardwell believes that Osgood made only recommendations rather than demands and suggests that there is no extant evidence which would label Osgood a censor. In the latter essay, Cardwell catalogs factual errors which persist in the scholarship on *Life on the Mississippi.* It was conceived, in some form, in 1866 rather than 1874. Howells' recollections about the *Atlantic* series were faulty; and Osgood was less catalytic for the completion of the book than usually supposed. Accurate dates for the river trip itself are included and some of the details of composition and publication are corrected.

Robert F. Stowell, "River Guide Books and Mark Twain's Life on the Mississippi" (*MTJ* 16,iv:21), incidentally, is a brief catalog of guide books for pilots and rivermen which were published during the early part of the 19th century and may or may not have been familiar to Sam Clemens.

v. Huckleberry Finn

It is worth celebration that the University of California Press has decided to reissue Walter Blair's out-of-print *Mark Twain & Huck Finn* in its California Library Reprint Series, but the unconscionable price of $15 will unfortunately keep the primary study of the novel from the hands of students or the booklists of courses.

A few brief notes were all the new attention that *Huck* received in 1973. John R. Byers, Jr., "Mark Twain's Miss Mary Jane Wilks: Shamed or Shammed?" (*MTJ* 17,i:13–14) suggests that when Huck says that the Duke and Dolphin were "right under her own roof, shaming her and robbing her," Mark Twain really intended to write *shamming* (tricking or cheating) even though the manuscript supports the published reading. Norton D. Kinghorn, "E. W. Kemble's Misplaced Modifier: A Note on the Illustrations for Huckleberry Finn" (*MTJ* 16,iv:9–11) notices that when Kemble illustrated the phrase "Uncle Silas he had a noble brass warming-pan which he thought considerable of, because it belonged to one of his ancestors with a long wooden handle," he provided both the pan and the Pilgrim with handles by drawing a wooden leg on the ancestor. David M. Wells, "More on the Geography of 'Huckleberry Finn'" (*SAB* 38, iv:82–86) pinpoints some fictional locations in the novel: the wreck of the *Walter Scott* (fifty miles above Cairo); the Grangerford farm (on the Tennessee-Kentucky state-line); Bricksville (a few miles above Memphis on the Arkansas side); and the Wilks' village (in northern Mississippi). Finally, Jürgen Schäfer, "Huckleberry, U.S.," (*ES* 54:334–35) proves that a sixteenth-century English usage of *huckleberry* shows that the lexicographical attribution of the word as an Americanism is false.

vi. Later Works

Kenneth M. Roemer has uncovered an 1898 novel, Franklin H. North's *The Awakening of Noahville*, with such striking parallels to *A Connecticut Yankee* that he nominates it as a conscious "rewriting" of Twain's book (in "The Yankee(s) in Noahville," *AL* 45:434–37). Illustrations containing contemporary portraits, the plot based on a pair of Yankees who modernize a feudal kingdom, and the destruction of the kingdom when its inhabitants revolt against the outsiders, as well as a confusion of satiric targets, mark the similarities.

Judith Fetterley continues her examination of the major characters in Twain's fiction with "Yankee Showman and Reformer: The Character of Mark Twain's Hank Morgan" (*TSLL* 14:667–79). She notices perceptively that "Hank repeatedly pictures himself with his hand hovering over a switch, his fingers resting lightly on a button, which, if thrown or pushed, will flood the world with light or blow it to bits." This image blossoms as its ambiguous connotations become the central tension in *A Connecticut Yankee.* Power (both destructive and creative) is converted to theatricality ("effects") and is used to humiliate others—Dowley and Sir Sagramour—and to inflate Hank's own ego. Underlying and monitoring Hank's showman instinct is his violence; and although he attempts to sublimate his aggression with humor, philosophizing, and claims of reform, he ultimately fails, destroying himself as well as Arthurian knighthood.

Similarly, Chadwick Hansen emphasizes Hank's despotic qualities in "The Once and Future Boss: Mark Twain's Yankee" (*NCF* 28:62–73). "Society to the Yankee is a competitive race in which the prize is holding power over the losers—being boss. To this view of society he is consistently faithful," Hansen suggests, "and it is this view which explains his otherwise ambiguous behavior throughout the novel." Hansen's is a devastating critique of Hank's totalitarian and dictatorial personality, which uses fraud and farce to obtain his ends. Contradictions in Hank's actions merely underscore his simple-mindedness; and his "humanitarianism" is only Victorian melodramatic bathos.

David Ketterer, "Epoch-Eclipse and Apocalypse: Special 'Effects' in *A Connecticut Yankee*" (*PMLA* 88:1104–14) catalogues the startling number of instances in the novel when the sun (and fire or light) contrast with darkness (and night or shadow) to indicate the apocalyptic shift from the sixth to the 19th century. As a consistent set of images initiated with the eclipse and continuing through to the Battle of the Sand-Belt, these "effects" are in fact a product of Hank's own self-inflated rhetoric. For, underlying Hank's attempts at apocalyptic transformation, is the truth that the two centuries are essentially identical and, indeed, that both are dream worlds.

Rodney O. Rogers compares a passage deleted from *A Tramp Abroad* with its appearance in *A Yankee* in "Twain, Taine, and Lecky, The Genesis of a Passage in *A Connecticut Yankee*" (*MLQ* 34:436–47). The passage, largely borrowed from Taine's *The Ancient Regime*, deals with the various monstrous "rights" of French feudal lords over peasants; and, although the details remain essentially the same in the two passages, the "bias and perspective" of Lecky are apparent in the latter use of the material. Outrage replaces sarcasm, the rhetoric becomes indicting rather than merely descriptive, and the Roman Catholic Church is introduced as a symbol of feudal oppression.

James D. Wilson's "Hank Morgan, Philip Traum and Milton's Satan" (*MTJ* 16,iv:20–21) offers a few specious parallels between Satan's speech in Book VI of *Paradise Lost* and the diabolical perversity of Mark Twain's characters.

Paul A. Eschholz's "Twain's The Tragedy of Pudd'nhead Wilson" (*Expl* 31:item 67) suggests that Wilson's acceptance by the town at the conclusion of the novel shows him finally "trapped and trained into being a true 'pudd'nhead,' " and the book's "most tragic example of man in the deterministic grips of *circumstance*." Stanley Brodwin explicates *Pudd'nhead* as "a theological study of man's nature whose intrinsic pattern is modeled on the myth of the fall of man" in "Blackness and the Adamic Myth in Mark Twain's *Pudd'nhead Wilson*" (*TSLL* 15:167–76). In the novel itself the focus is upon the fall of the victims who are the characters; but, through the implications of the chapter mottoes, the fall of America (through slavery) is also implied. Roxy—who plays God by switching the babies—falls and is beyond salvation: "In the end, there is only the realization that man is tricked by God or Providence and his own sinful nature into thinking that . . . he could change destiny and reform the world and himself." Michael L. Ross, too, is interested in the relevance of chapter mottoes to the novel in "Mark Twain's Pudd'nhead Wilson: Dawson's Landing and the Ladder of Nobility" (*Novel* 6:244–56). Ross says that *Pudd'nhead* "presents from first to last a corrosive exposé of those flaws in American society that turn Columbus Day into a national day of mourning." The "central target . . . is the inescapable propensity of any society—even of one that claims officially to be classless—to accept and abide by a rigidly hierarchical caste system." By drawing identical behavior patterns in Judge Driscoll and Roxy (obedience to the "unwritten" Southern code, affirmation of the controlling influence of "blood," and vacillating attitudes toward Tom), Twain ironically shows the cultural entrapment which exists on both levels of Dawson's Landing society. Tom, a variant of a confidence man with his many disguises, underscores "the ultimate insanity of the townspeople's criteria of moral judgment."

Stanley Brodwin continues (see *ALS 1972*, p. 90) his trenchant examination of the later works in "Mark Twain's Masks of Satan: The Final Phase" (*AL* 45:206–27). Brodwin enumerates four roles for Satan in the later works: (1) the "conventional tempter and 'Father of Lies,'" the "quietly sinister, embittered manipulator of human souls" who appears in "The Man That Corrupted Hadleyburg"; (2) "a sympathetic commentator on the tragedy of man's fall, but one who fails to make Adam and Eve understand the concepts which would have saved them," the figure of "That Day in Eden," "Eve's Dairy," and "Sold to Satan"; (3) "a mischievous, sarcastic questioner of God's ways," the "questioning, intellectual Archangel, unafraid to voice his opinions about God," who appears in *Letters from the Earth*; and (4) "a force of spiritual though amoral 'innocence' charged with divine-like creative power." This fourth Satan, the one of *The Mysterious Stranger Manuscripts*, attracts Brodwin's attention for half the article.

While it is impossible to summarize briefly the complex patterns of the fourth Satan, Brodwin suggests that the essential dichotomy of "earthly" man and "divine" artist, which Twain saw as components of his own personality, became objectified in the character of Theodor/August and Satan/Philip Traum in the three *Stranger* fragments. "The kind of determinism that characterizes fallen man . . . is a fixed, mechanical process well suited to man's nature. . . . Yet, as we shall see, that determinism is itself, when examined, intrinsically absurd in its workings and results." By contrast, "the determinism that characterizes unfallen Satan is really a species of idealism; that is, it describes the nature of the universe and its manifestations as dream—as unreal ontologically speaking, though 'real' enough in appearance." But, for man at any rate, the solipsistic dream alternative is no solution, because the dreams that man dreams are insane; and the ultimate "picture is that of a fallen world that cannot be redeemed, deterministically structured yet at the same time chaotic and a 'sham' through which man wanders in a kind of schizoid dream-state, never knowing quite who and what he is." Brodwin proposes that "a god can create out of a thought-stuff which is pure essence; man can only create by associating external realities received through the senses into set forms as a machine does. Man does not enjoy *true* creativity. Only unfallen Satan can experience this. Ultimate salvation is to be set free from the consequences of the fall and to become a god." As first-rate criticism should, Brodwin's article raises many provocative questions: Did August dream Satan as well as his world, and does that fact impugn Satan's testimony earlier in the fragments? In view of the "Dream other dreams, and better!" injunction which Satan makes at the conclusion, would it be profitable to pursue those brief glimpses of Theodor/August's world *after* Satan's revelation?

Richard Cary prints two communications from Clemens to Elizabeth Akers Allen in "In Further Defense of Harriet Shelley: Two Unpublished Letters by Mark Twain" (*MTJ* 16,iv:13–15). In the letters (dated July 17, 30, 1901), Twain defends his assault on Shelley as unprincipled and immoral; unfortunately, Cary does not bother to locate the originals of his texts or to include the legally mandatory copyright notice in the name of the Mark Twain Company for previously unpublished materials.

Martha M. Park offers some Biblical allusions beyond those of

Henry B. Rule (see *ALS 1969*, p. 87) for "Mark Twain's Hadleyburg: A House Built on Sand" (*CLAJ* 16:508–13). Her attention centers on Matt. 7:24–27 and Luke 6:48–49 and the parable of the houses built on rock and sand. Hadleyburg, with sandy foundations, collapses after the climactic town-hall sequence—a scene with an astonishing complexity of storm imagery.

Henry J. Lindborg, "A Cosmic Tramp: Samuel Clemens's *Three Thousand Years Among the Microbes*" (*AL* 44:652–57), offers a cogent study of the scientific sources for the 1905 "novel" which focuses on two central themes that the book debates: the "attribution of life to all matter and the existence of a God whose body is the universe." C. W. Saleeby's *The Cycle of Life* and W. H. Conn's *The Life of the Germ* were important sources for some of these notions, but Clemens was unable to find solace or credibility in them; he could not "resign himself to being a part of an eternal process, because he could not believe that that process was conceived in love." And, finally, Edward Mendelsohn suggests in "Mark Twain Confronts the Shakespeareans" (*MTJ* 17,i:20–21) that *Is Shakespeare Dead?* served a significant function as "a shattering delineation of the complacency and superficiality of the contemporary arbiters of taste" in 1909.

University of Chicago

7. Henry James

William T. Stafford

My speculation in *ALS 1972* that the completion of Edel's life and the radically reduced number of explications of individual works might hopefully mark some meaningful shifts in the criticism of Henry James appears to have been, on the evidence of 1973, woefully inaccurate. Jamesian criticism during 1973 is in many ways unfortunately similar to what it has been during the last two decades: four book-length studies of uneven quality (all formerly, I believe, dissertations), narrowly focused on highly limited specialized topics; still another collection of reprinted essays readily available in other forms; repetitious attention to already overly analyzed individual tales and novels; source studies by the bucketful that rarely go beyond informed speculation and many of which appear to be totally uninformed about what others have done with their topics; and humorless, witless, and graceless pedantry everywhere rampant and rife. Still, some signs are encouraging: additional critical mileage in all sorts of unexpected ways through delayed reaction to Edel's Life; a new variant edition of the complete tales; an amazingly good overview (by John Paterson) of James's conception of the novel as an act of faith; intricately informed reconsiderations of the novelist by established scholars as varied as Mark Spilka, Dorothea Krook, and Christof Wegelin; and two or three studies of individual works that still "shock" with their illumination and verve (such as those by Vanderbilt, Veeder, and Rowe). That over half of the more than seventy items surveyed this year fall into the categories of general criticism and source studies is probably a mixed blessing, the reduction in repetitious explications a clear plus, the proliferation of nit-picking source studies perhaps a minus. *Plus ça change, plus c'est* . . . ? —Perhaps.

i. The Edel "Life": Reaction Continued

Among the many belated reactions certain to appear in response to the completion of Leon Edel's monumental life in early 1972, three appeared in 1973 that are worthy of notice, Millicent Bell's thoughtful and knowledgeable "Henry James: The Man Who Lived" (*MR* 14:391–414), Thelma J. Shinn's imaginative adaptation of the subject matter of Edel's fourth volume in her "A Question of Survival: An Analysis of 'The Treacherous Years' of Henry James" (*L&P* 23:135–48), and Mark L. Krupnick's cantankerous "polemic," "Henry James: The Artist as Emperor—On *Henry James, The Master, 1901–1916*" (*Novel* 6:257–65). Millicent Bell's is among the most important of the overviews of Edel's biography, biographer as she herself is and one, unlike so many of Edel's detractors, who considers the kind of tribute Edel's five volumes purports to make not inappropriate to its subject. "Edel's monument is no taller than it should be." She nevertheless views Edel's life of James a failure, however good it is with details of people and places, however "thorough and precise," however readable and (at least initially) engaging through its technique of brief, dramatic chapters. But the method wears, she continues, because substance is everywhere superficial, with practically no attention to "the intellectual roots of . . . [James's] style and aesthetics," with far too little attention to "the political events and movements of his time," and with a psychoanalytic method that is much too reductive about life itself, about Henry James in particular. In her volume-by-volume survey of the biography she raises striking objections about Edel's view of James's relation to his family, to Constance Fenimore Woolson, to his circle of purported homosexual friends, and, of course, to Edith Wharton. Her provocative conclusion is that Edel himself has been done a disservice by having had the exclusive right to material on James for far too long a period and thus denied the "public correction" that might well have come had others been able to read that material and reach different judgments. It is an important assessment.

Thelma J. Shinn's totally different reaction to a part of the biography, that provocative body of fiction produced by James between the *Guy Domville* debacle of 1895 through *The Sacred Fount* of 1901 and called by Edel "The Treacherous Years," is not so much disagreement as supplementation. For her, the Jamesian novels of those years reflect in a variety of experimental forms the conflict between concepts of "passive" and "passionate" love, concepts that are ultimately reconciled only in *The Golden Bowl.* But the importance here is Edel as model, however different his aims or his conclusions; for Shinn his was obviously a subject and a method she found extremely useful for her own illuminating deliberations.

So too, in a quite still different way, did Mark Krupnick—although his ostensible purpose is to attack Edel, his biography, and, to a lesser extent, James himself. What he more obviously wants to do is put forth his own psychological view of James as one whose personal life was dismally bare, especially in the areas of love and sexuality, and consequently one whose embrace of "the religion of art" is interpreted as an attempt "to redeem this failure," "emotional impotence," at it were, "accompanied by imaginative omnipotence." For Krupnick this is obviously inadequate recompense, as indeed, even Krupnick contends, it was for James—but never, he says, for Edel, whose "biography is an American romance, in which the scholar has merged himself with the artist and taken on his omnipotence." There is more —including his psychological profile of James as playing out "the role of mother to his own infant self," including also a much too simplistic view of the conflict between Maggie and Charlotte (in *The Golden Bowl*) as one in which "consciousness, forms, art" is said to triumph over "sexuality, gross life"—but nevertheless provocatively concluding that we should view James with at least some of the irony with which he was capable of viewing himself.

ii. A New Edition of the Tales

The first volume of Maqbool Aziz's variant edition *The Tales of Henry James* (London, Oxford Univ. Press) is an impressive performance, more useful (I think) than Leon Edel's 12-volume edition (*The Complete Tales of Henry James*, 1961–64), although the need for two separate complete collections might well be raised. The great plus is in Aziz's reprinting the original serial versions of the tales as his basic texts (in contrast to Edel's uses of the first book versions, for those published in book form) and of course in providing also the "substantive variants" of subsequent reprintings. Less desirable, I think, was Aziz's decision silently to correct misprints, missing punctuation marks, and to normalize spelling, as was his decision to ignore accidentals, although he promises an essay on the differences between James's early system of punctuation and that of the New York Edition for the final volume of the collection. But generally the volume is impressive, with a knowledgeable introduction that gives its major attention, after an elaborate explanation of the editorial rationale, to a "history"of each story's publication history, not how it came to be written, but how it came to be published, where it was sent, editorial reaction (when it can be determined), and so on—all extremely useful information. Its attention to the publishing rationale of the two collections in which some of these tales are later to be collected and to the subject matter and techniques of these first 14 tales (those written between 1864–69) is also useful. Additional apparatus includes a prefatory chronological listing of the complete tales, with place and date of initial publication, and with asterisks indicating those to be collected in the New York Edition; prefaces to each tale with complete accounts of its publishing history; and, following the variants at the end of the volume, a note by James on the text of *Stories Revised* and a brief compilation of some early public and private notices about these tales. It is an ambitious and extremely useful collection, especially in its list of variants, mere "substantive" ones though they are, and Aziz's treatment of accidentals notwithstanding. The edition is to be completed in eight volumes—a publishing event of major importance to all James scholars.

iii. Criticism, Essays, Autobiography, Drama

Although there is not a great deal in Mark Spilka's "Henry James and Walter Besant: 'The Art of Fiction' Controversy" (*Novel* 6:100–19) that has not been seen before, I know of nowhere else a fuller, rounder, more clearly rendered account of the cultural setting in which James's famous essay took shape, the issues and personalities involved, before and after the fact, the way we are convinced, as we read it, that this is indeed how it *must* have all happened. Spilka's view that James's "definition of experience speaks to the modern predicament, . . . of alienation and isolation, in a way he did not fully understand" raises occasional questions, as does his view of James as perhaps excessively open to "the vitality of ideas, . . . the value of discussion, experiment, exchange of views." But few would argue that with "The Art of Fiction" was begun "an adventure of immense importance to the novel's history." Also good is David A. Cook's "James and Flaubert: The Evolution of Perception" (*CL* 25:289–307), a survey of James's evolving sensibility as revealed through his four essays on Flaubert, especially in terms of *Madame Bovary*, seeing James's last essay on the novel (1902) as "classic," as "prophetic."

James Kraft, in his "On Reading *The American Scene*" (*Prose* 6:115–36), sees the book indelibly "American," charged as it is by "the country's wholesale rejection of the past . . . [as] a manifestation of its weakness and insecurity as a new nation, but also of its basic experimental sense, its belief in change, that is part of its freedom from the restrictive past of Europe." Possibility lost is its great power, what "magnificently might have been over against what pitifully is."

Of the two articles to appear during the year on James's autobiographies, Jane P. Tompkins's "The Redemption of Time in *Notes of a Son and Brother*" (*TSLL* 14:681–90) makes the more telling point in her view of how James's sense of his own mortality at the time of writing the volume gave a special urgency to his sense of making the remembered characters of his youth "live." David K. Kirby's "Henry James: Art and Autobiography" (*DR* 52[1972–73]: 637–44) makes the less speculative point of demonstrating various techniques of his fiction, shaping . . . [his material] by form or getting at its essence through literary analogue," at work in his memoirs.

Judy Larson's "The Drama Criticism of Henry James" (*y/t* 4,ii:103–09), the single study of James as dramatist during the year, is an unimportant recasting of some well-known Jamesian attitudes toward the theater, its audience, French vs. British examples of both, and the actors Tomasso Salvini, Coquelin, and Edmund Got.

iv. Sources, Influences, Parallels

It does not instill a great deal of confidence in the author to read in the second sentence of Philip Grover's *Henry James and the French Novel: A Study in Inspiration* (London, Elek Books, Ltd.) that "no one has hitherto undertaken a serious examination of the abiding interest that James had in French literature and examined the important effect his constant reading and rereading of French novelists had on his own development as a writer." Two books on James's relation to France and to French writers have appeared during the last few years (see, for example, *ALS 1971*, 89–91), not to mention many, many articles on the subject. Grover's book, to be sure, has its particularized focus—on the lesson of Balzac, on the stylistic influences of Flaubert on James, and on affinities and differences between James's fiction and that of "*L'Art pour l'Art*" movement. Although Grover is "sound" enough in seeing the Balzacian gift to James in terms of technique, structure, composition—the way James felt that "Balzac had solved problems that he [that is, James] had failed to solve in some of his early works," an example to provoke analogous solutions rather than one to be directly imitated—the more suggestive section, for me, is on James's relation to Flaubert. Although I am not quite convinced that it *was* Flaubert from whom James learned to create what Grover calls "a unified language—one in which there is no distinctive break between narration, description, dialogue and interior monologue"—I *am* convinced that James's language works pretty much as Grover describes it. The influence of "*L'Art pour l'Art*" movement, especially as represented by Daudet and the Goncourts, are said to make their finest mark in *The Ambassadors*. And the culmination of the whole is then said to be found in *The Golden Bowl*, where Balzacian "intensity of presentation is everywhere present" and where the "intense artificiality of the formalized and patterned human relationships," it is maintained, derive from Gautier and "*L'Art pour l'Art*" via Flaubert. Perhaps. One is convinced that James and these French novelists were often doing some of the same things, but that the sources of James's practice were precisely the ones Grover specifies is perhaps another question. That James was throughout his life interested in French fiction is indisputable—indeed, Grover appends to his study a specialized 18-page chronology of his life that details James's active attention to aspects of French literature—but the nebulous field of parallelism cannot so easily be transformed into the less-nebulous one of sources, even when sources are carefully qualified as assimilation or "inspiration" rather than as sources per se.

Other studies of James and French literature include Adeline R. Tintner's "Balzac's 'Madame Firmiani' and James's *The Ambassadors*" (*CL* 25:128–35), Mildred S. Greene's "*Les Liaisons dangereuses* and *The Golden Bowl*: Maggie's 'Loving Reasons'" (*MFS* 19 [1973–74]: 531–40), and Jeremiah J. Sullivan's "Henry James and Hippolyte Taine: The Historical and Scientific Method in Literature" (*CLS*

10:25–50). Adeline Tintner's is another of her persuasive examples of the ubiquitous influence of Balzac on James's fiction, in this instance by citing a remarkable series of parallels between the French story and the American's novel—"closeness of plot, the technique of presentation through a 'point of view,' the anatomy of a civilizing liaison, and evocation of an Arcadian mood." Mildred Greene points to many parallels and differences between Laclos's Mme. de Merteuil and Maggie in order to give emphasis to what may have been for James an obverse lesson, "that manipulation of others need not always lead to evil consequences." And Jeremiah Sullivan, although perfectly aware that James was often reacting against Taine, nevertheless makes a strong case for the French critic's impact on Jamesian works as disparate as his 1875 essay on Balzac, his *Hawthorne*, and his *The American Scene*, not to mention such works of fiction as "A Bundle of Letters," *The American*, and *The Bostonians.*

Studies of English sources for James's fiction proliferated during the year. It is Adeline Tintner again and her phenomenal store of information about James's fiction, his reading, his life, and his friends that are brought to play in her "Keats and James and *The Princess Casamassima*" (*NCF* 28:179–93) to display the variety of ways "allusions to Keats's poetry and to the legend of Keats's life underline Hyacinth's conflict between the aesthetic and the socially dedicated life." And although I do not think I agree that "the Keatsian strain" is absolutely essential to an understanding of the novel, as Tintner suggests without quite stating, it provides one way of reading the novel that is rich and rewarding enough. (The material in her "The Elgin Marbles and Titian's 'Bacchus and Ariadne': A Cluster of Keatsian Associations in Henry James" [*N&Q* 20:250–52] is all repeated in her *NCF* study of *The Princess.*)

Two studies of *The Tragic Muse* trace idealogical contributions to aspects of James's conception of Gabriel Nash. Ronald Wallace, in "Gabriel Nash: Henry James's Comic Spirit" (*NCF* 28:220–24), sees ties with Meredith's conception of comedy and Bergson's classic essay on laughter. Robert S. Baker's more important "Gabriel Nash's 'House of Strange Idols': Aestheticism in *The Tragic Muse*" (*TSLL* 15:149–66), "places" Nash's role in the development of James's views toward aestheticism, seeing the conception of Nash tied to Roderick Hudson, to Pater, even to "Arnoldian social criticism." But, says Baker, the mere aesthetic is finally rejected, for attractive and witty and beautifully persuasive as Nash is, he finally is made to disappear, fade away as does his portrait, representing ultimately "a peculiarly Jamesian vision of narcissism."

Another fine free-ranging source study is Samuel F. Pickering's "The Sources of 'The Author of Beltraffio'" (*ArQ* 29:177–90), which demonstrates that, in addition to the well-known "germ" of *The Notebooks*, also at play in the tale are the issues between James and Walter Besant that resulted in "The Art of Fiction," memory of James's youthful enthusiasm for Pre-Raphaelite art, an 1869 visit to the William Morrises, and the later, then more recent familiarity with the art of Sir Joshua Reynolds. And David K. Kirby's "A Possible Source for James's 'The Death of the Lion'" (*CLQ* 10:39–40) is persuasive enough in its case for the painter William Powell Frith in *A Victorian Canvas* as *donné* of the story.

Three studies of *The Golden Bowl* point to disparate sources for that complex novel. Ronald Wallace's "Maggie Verver: Comic Heroine" (*Genre* 6:404–14) strikes me as somewhat fanciful in asserting that the shape of the novel "closely resembles the shape of . . . *A Midsummer Night's Dream*," especially in light of the concomitant view that Maggie's final "inward vision remains relatively small," however fresh it is to have the "comic" aspects of the novel thus emphasized. Scott Byrd's "The Fractured Crystal in *Middlemarch* and *The Golden Bowl*" (*MFS* 18[1972–73]:551–54) exhibits common-sensical restraint in suggesting this small tie between George Eliot and James. Equally brief is Adeline R. Tintner's "Maggie's Pagoda: Architectural Follies in *The Golden Bowl*" (*MarkhamR* 3:113–15) and its small central point that the Pagoda Fountain, Alton Towers, in Staffordshire is remarkably similar to the famous pagoda metaphor with which the second volume of the novel begins.

Among the several studies of American sources, both Robert Emmet Long, in "James's *Washington Square*: The Hawthorne Relation" (*NEQ* 46: 573–90), and Harold Schechter, in "The Unpardonable Sin in 'Washington Square'" (*SSF* 10:137–41), make approximately the same point about the same novel, as even their titles indicate. Long's is the more elaborate study in its view of the variety of ways the novel is tied to Hawthorne, but especially, he maintains, in the parallels between "Rappaccini's Daughter" and the novel, "romance" though one is, and "a comedy of manners" the other. Schechter's focus is primarily on Doctor Sloper, as one whose intellect is separated from his heart. J. Gerald Kennedy's admitted speculation, "Jeffrey Aspern and Edgar Allan Poe: A Speculation" (*PoeS* 6,i:17–18), is built on the initial assumption that Aspern is meant to represent a bad poet. And John H. Randall's long, long "Romeo and Juliet in the New World: A Study in James, Wharton, and Fitzgerald: 'Fay ce que vouldras'" (*Costerus* 8:109–75) views *Daisy Miller, The House of Mirth,* and *The Great Gatsby* as cultural documents "establishing and defining American attitudes toward politics and sex," embodying both the idealistic hope and the restrictive realities of American life.

Remaining studies appropriate to this grouping are varied. John A. Cook's "The Fool Show in *Roderick Hudson*" (*CRevAS* 4:74–86) gets finally to Shakespeare's *King Lear* via Turgenev's *A King Lear of the Steppe* as a way of attempting to support a view of the novel as "a similarly ironic tragedy" built around "the issues of irresponsibility, rashness, and lack of trust." Equally slight is Anthony D. Briggs's speculation, in his "Someone Else's Sledge: Further Notes on Turgenev's *Virgin Soil* and Henry James's *The Princess Casamassima*" (*OSP* 5[1972]:52–60), that some sort of intentional obscuration must have been at work in James's omission of references to the Russian in his Preface to the novel in the light of the many parallels reviewers saw between the two when the novel was first published. Shirley Rose's "Waymarsh's 'Sombre Glow' and der Fliegende Holländer" (*AL* 45:438–41) sees ties between Waymarsh and the legend of the Flying Dutchman, the Waymarsh-Sarah alliance at the end of the novel as conscious parody of that legend. Viris Cromer's "James and Ibsen" (*CL* 25:114–27) is still another (and somewhat needless) account of the novelist's attitude toward the dramatist, without benefit, apparently, of Michael Egan's previously published book on the subject (*ALS 1972*, 100–01), even though Cromer finally views James as much more critical of Ibsen than does Egan. Like Egan, however, Cromer also reprints some letters from James to Edmond Gosse about Ibsen, one of Oct. 17, 1890, another of April 28, 1891.

My final item for this grouping is John Tytell's "The Jamesian Legacy in *The Good Soldier*" (*SNNTS* 3[1971]:365–72), one of the best cases I know for the variety of ways that James, his fiction, his characters, and his techniques (especially after 1895) are transformed by Ford into his own fictional lines, especially in *The Good Soldier.*

v. Criticism: General

Of the three book-length studies to be surveyed here, Donald Mull's *Henry James's 'Sublime Economy': Money as Symbolic Center in the Fiction* (Middletown, Conn., Wesleyan Univ. Press) reveals by far the richest critical intelligence. Although mostly about *The Portrait of a Lady* and *The Golden Bowl*, the ostensible thesis of the role of money in the fiction is in some senses a mere convenience, yet the book is valuable enough for its analyses of these two important novels. Money as a possibility for freedom and as restrictive fact, as symbol for "the ideal and the actual, the potential and the mutable . . . both the voice of the nightingale and the cry forlorn" (as Mull describes its uses in *The Portrait*), is of course one central way of viewing the Jamesian dialectic of "the relation of the self to that which is 'other.'" And the frame Mull uses to make this application to the two great novels—a brief biographical sketch of Jamesian attitudes toward money, its uses in some early tales, four early novels, and the unfinished *The Ivory Tower*—works persuasively and illuminatingly enough. But the core of the work is his 67-page analysis of *The Portrait*, a careful re-examination of the role of each of the major characters, especially as they collectively contribute to our understanding of Isabel within the terms of Mull's thematic concern. It is a fine analysis of that much-analyzed novel, finally viewed as it is, as "less a symbolic novel than a novel about the symbolic imagination—about the mind's coming to terms with itself and the world, imposing categories upon or discovering them in the welter of the world's detail, finding meaning in particularity and extending it to generality." I was otherwise especially impressed with Mull's illustration of Isabel's adoption (late in the novel) of Madame Merle's tactics as, among other things, a way of looking forward to Maggie's adoption of Charlotte's in *The Golden Bowl*, about which Mull's analysis is also good. His treatment there of the ambivalent conception of Adam Verver and his wealth, of the theme of inversion in the novel, and especially his articulated awareness of Amerigo's limited "incomprehension" of Maggie's "emphatic imaginative inclusion" all make his analysis of this novel (and of *The Portrait*) well worth, even in these inflated times, the price of the whole.

John P. O'Neill's *Workable Design: Action and Situation in the*

Fiction of Henry James (Port Washington, N.Y., Kennikat Press), although also a provocative book, is generally reductive in effect, his "method" in some ways more promising than his results. To be sure, one of his intentions *is* reductivism, convinced as he apparently is that analysis of characterization, attention to psychological or moral issues, meaning as derived from social content are all less important than the highly stylized and rigid "design" that he sees basic to all the fiction: "the way the novel's action moves character from one situation or condition through successive stages to a final resting point that is discovered to be in virtual polar opposition to the point of origin." Hence, the polar structure is absolute, "the terms of the conflict . . . stark and irreconcilable," with "reversals . . . complete." The intervening details, details of realistic representativeness, techniques of suspense, illusions of free choice, are all mere affective manipulation of reader response *within* the rigid schematization. James's major interest, it is contended, was in the design itself. The five novels he examines under this rubric reveal, perhaps predictably, uneven results—*The Portrait of a Lady, The Princess Casamassima, The Spoils of Poynton, The Awkward Age*, and *The Wings of the Dove*. The similarity of design is certainly there, but the meaning he works out therefrom is grossly ill-balanced. The polarities in *The Wings of the Dove*, for example, are neatly delineated between Milly's "limitless possibility for life and certain death," the polarity irrevocably followed in a variety of ways, the accruing action of the book all contributing to a concept of "life" intensified by an act of death. O'Neill also sees clearly the polar concepts of sexuality, the transcendent benevolence of Milly in constant contrast to the vitality of Kate. O'Neill can nevertheless blithely assume that Milly is the unequivocal victor, that Densher's ultimate rejection of Kate is also James's rejection of her, never once considering the sense in which Densher's act is also Kate's (and thus, in these terms, also James's) rejection of him. It is, in short, much too simple, the design of *The Wings* much more open (or more compactly or complexly involuted) than O'Neill appears to admit. The concept of the design is exciting (and potentially productive); its application, disappointing.

In *Sensuous Pessimism: Italy in the Works of Henry James* (Bloomington, Ind. Univ. Press) Carl Maves is at his best in his final insight that James's long and obsessive love affair with Italy had at its center "the underlying polarity of his creative urge, which on the one hand moved him to imagine, idealize, and romanticize, and at the other extreme to notate, specify, and depict social and ethical realities." Italy for James, he also remarks, meant "romance, and the dangers of romance and the sensual realities beneath romance, alternately and also simultaneously." And still elsewhere, he says, James had always "been less stimulated by the 'idea' of Italy than by the 'fusion' Italy comprises. Behind the romance he had always sought the reality; what has interested him . . . most is not Italy's tendency to inspire irresponsible imaginings but its capacity to reconcile diverse experience." This complex gaggle of rewarding observations, however, is arrived at in a very simple and direct and perhaps too predictable manner: a chronological tracing of James's visits to Italy, an account of his personal and professional responses to those visits (the latter in travel essays), and an examination of the uses of Italy in his fiction (both those set there and those, such as *The Golden Bowl*, which have Italian characters in them). We are hardly surprised therefore to discover that James's attitudes toward Italy were continuous and coherent, that they are chronologically identifiable (although mixed and mingled) by the motifs of "romance, of treachery, and of sensuousness," that the older James got the more complex his treatment of the subject became, and that consequently the most mature and complex vision of Italy is embodied in Prince Amerigo of *The Golden Bowl*. But in many ways perhaps his best chapter is the penultimate one, entitled "Deaths in Venice," covering the years 1882–1902, tying together as it does the felt Italian presence in scene and in characterization in the works, the visits and the momentuous meetings there (including significantly both Hendrik Anderson and Constance Fenimore Woolson) between *The Princess Casamassima* and *The Wings of the Dove*. *Sensuous Pessimism* is thus a useful book, even if finally not as useful as it might have been had it more carefully utilized and summarized for the reader the not inconsiderable earlier scholarship on the subject by both Italian and American scholars. The volume contains a brief foreword by Ian Watt.

The single other book on James during the year is Lyall H. Powers's collection, *Henry James's Major Novels: Essays in Criticism* (East Lansing, Mich. State Univ. Press). The editor's "Introduction" (xiii–xxxix) is a knowledgeable overview of James's work, its characteristic themes, its experimental methods, some sources, some influences—but hardly news, cast as it is for the nonspecialist. The collected essays, moreover, are all well-known and readily available elsewhere.

Quite important, on the other hand, is John Paterson's chapter, "Henry James: The Romance of the Real," in his *The Novel as Faith: The Gospel According to James, Hardy, Conrad, Joyce, Lawrence and Virginia Woolf* (Boston, Gambit), pp. 3–39. Paterson's final description of these six novelists as ones who believed that "to be true-to-life in the representational sense was to be true to it in the moral sense . . ." is a statement certainly true enough in so far as his fine treatment of James is concerned as his lead-off figure. In beautifully lucid prose, Paterson eloquently recounts how "special" for James the distinctions between realistic and romantic, particular and universal, the nearly-viewed and the far visioned, and how, "since life [for James] was by definition life reflected, life appreciated, life appraised, to evaluate it wasn't really distinct from representing it."

The brief chapter devoted to James in Susan Kuhlmann's study of the confidence man, *Knave, Fool, and Genius*, promises more than it delivers. The examples are predictable, the victimized Caroline Spencer of "Four Meetings," Isabel of *The Portrait*, and Milly of *The Wings*. Only with the latter is there a move toward new insight, in her view of James's esthetic attraction to Kate through their mutual "love of design." Kuhlmann is far less interesting in her subsequent equation of Milly with heart, Kate with head, and the far too simplistic notion of the novel's resolution as one of how "goodness defeats sin by pardoning the sinner."

Among the best articles of general criticism of the year is Dorothea Krook's "The Madness of Art: Further Reflections on the Ambiguity of Henry James" (*HUSL* 1,i:25–38), her reconsideration of some esthetic and ethical ramifications of how James's intentional ambiguity in *The Turn of the Screw* reflects the truth that "human knowledge is irremediably uncertain" and how that "irremediable uncertainty" is generally most profound in James through his knowledge of the complex of forces which determine our apparent "choices." Only one's own "experience" finally determines his choices, but experience as James reflects it for Krook is a rich and problematic concept, involving among other forces "intuition," and thus making an act of choice also an act of faith. Finally, the extent to which that "faith corrects or redeems or destroys has to be decided by each man himself," this process becoming James's method.

James is central exemplum in both Roy Fuller's "The Two Sides of the Street" (*SoR* 9:579–94) and in Mark Spilka's "Ian Watt on Intrusive Authors, or the Future of an Illusion" (*HUSL* 1,i:1–24). Fuller's long essay is on the subject of how with and since James the modern novel has "annexed the 'poetic' areas of life as well as those more mundane traits which were initially its special preserves." And Spilka gives central attention to the novelist as first giving focus to the problem of the intrusive narrator and thus opening the door to the modern development of "'an immanent rather than an omniscient narrator,' one who works "through techniques rather than with them."

Christof Wegelin's "Henry James and the Treasure of Consciousness" (*NS* 9:484–91) and Ross LaBrie's "The Power of Consciousness in Henry James" (*ArQ* 29:101–14) are radically different approaches to a single subject. Wegelin's is a beautifully lucid little statement of the centrality of human consciousness in James as "the most real thing we know"—as illustrated in the fiction from the early "The Romance of Certain Old Clothes" to "The Turn of the Screw," from *Daisy Miller* to *The Wings of the Dove*, and from questions of whether there is a life after death to the psychological aspects of transcendental experience to questions of scientific determinism vs. freedom of the will. LaBrie's far less lucid account is of Jamesian concepts of consciousness that are sometimes satirized, sometimes admired, or sometimes damned, with illustrations from *The Bostonians*, *The Sacred Fount*, and *The Sense of the Past*, among others.

Evelyn J. Hinz's "Henry James's Names: Tradition, Theory, and Method" (*CLQ* 9[1972]:558–78) is an onomastic overview of the fiction, with such hardly surprising demonstrations as how names both distinguish and particularize, how some appeal to the eye, some to the ear, some embody historic allusiveness, some are metaphors, and so on. William F. Smith, Jr.'s "Sentence Structure in the Tales of Henry James" (*Style* 7:157–72) accomplishes little more with its selection of "The Madonna of the Future," "The Death of the Lion," and "The Jolly Corner" as representative examples of early, middle, and late tales whose predominant sentence patterns respectively change from the simple to the complex to the compound-complex.

vi. Criticism: Individual Tales

Studies of individual tales may be said to get off with a rousing start through Kermit Vanderbilt's beautiful explication, in his "Notes Largely Musical on Henry James's 'Four Meetings'" (*SR* 81:739–52), of the variety of ways this story coheres, expands, compresses—through "structure, movement, concision, and texture." The analogue of music through which the analysis is made, Vanderbilt's plea for James's sense of music as still another way his fiction remains to be studied, although valid enough, I suppose, is really not necessary to the achieved revelation here made of the story's elaborate structure.

Studies of three subsequent tales are not so rewarding, although Maqbool Aziz's "Revisiting 'The Pension Beaurepas': The Tale and Its Texts" (*EIC* 23:268–82) is solid enough in its view of how the revisions of the tale recharge and reinforce its satire. But Ian Kenney's Freudian view, in his "Frederick Winterbourne: the Good Bad Boy in *Daisy Miller*" (*ArQ* 29:139–50)—his analysis of how underneath Winterbourne's surface of Puritan respectability "hides the fires of a repressed libido which seeks to devour the object of its sexual attention"—is hardly meaningful even if true. And James W. Gargano's "'The Aspern Papers': The Untold Story" (*SSF* 10:1–10) is merely another analysis of the narrator's obtuseness, the ways in which he stultifies as Tina grows young and beautiful and knowledgeable.

Edward Recchia's "James's 'The Figure in the Carpet': The Quality of Fictional Experience" (*SSF* 10:357–65) and Shlomith Rimmon's "Barthe's 'Hermeneutic Code' and Henry James's Literary Detective: Plot-Composition in 'The Figure in the Carpet'" (*HUSL* 1,ii:183–207) both appear to be primarily concerned with the tale's structure. For Recchia, the reader himself, in coming to share the narrator's perspective, himself becomes part of the subject of the tale, the structure thus demanding a special kind of distancing by the reader in order to see his own part in it. For Rimmon, as I no doubt imperfectly understand him, hermeneutics reveals the tale to be one which "goes far beyond a 'classical,' 'readable' text both in its consistent evasion of a solution and in its violation of the law of non-contradiction by creation of a fully sustained ambiguity," whatever that means.

William B. Stone's "On the Background of James's 'In the Cage'"

(*ALR* 6:243–47) is a little note demonstrating that James's "facts" regarding the profession of his young telegraphist are historically correct ones. Joseph Kau's "Henry James and the Garden: A Symbolic Setting for 'The Beast in the Jungle'" (*SSF* 10:187–98) and Randall H. Waldron's "Prefiguration in 'The Beast in the Jungle'" (*SAF* 1:101–04), on the other hand, are neat explications of how meaning is intrinsically ordered in the tale of their mutual concern. For Kau, whose analysis is somewhat more elaborate than his title indicates, the garden symbol is alternately a potential for fruitful growth and atavistic regression. For Waldron, whose concern is limited to the function of the tale's opening at Weatherend, James is more than justified in prefiguring the action and meaning of the tale through his opening conversation.

Finally, in Sara S. Chapman's "The 'Obsession of Egotism' in Henry James's 'A Round of Visits'" (*ArQ* 29:130–38), we have a fine analysis of this last of James's tales through an examination of how each of Montieth's visits mirrors for him a dimension of his own personality, thus prefiguring his "embryonic recognition of common humanity with Newton Winch," for whose ultimate suicide the protagonist accepts responsibility.

vii. Criticism: Individual Novels

Because all of the book-length studies and many of the articles already discussed have extensive analyses of individual novels, students of individual works should refer to them in addition to what follows. In fact, many of the better discussions of individual works are more likely to be found there than here.

Lee Ann Johnson's "'A Dog in the Manger': James's Depiction of Roger Lawrence in *Watch and Ward*" (*ArQ* 29:169–76) is a simple but forceful analysis of the "imprecise distinction between good and evil" embedded in James's characterization of Roger Lawrence, one who "can be seen as a comic, well-intentioned hero," but also one who is "a meddler in disguise who . . . imposes his designs upon another."

Robert Secor's "Christopher Newman: How Innocent is James's American?" (*SAF* 1:141–53) is much too blind to the novel's humor and melodrama, however correct, if hardly original, in its long, tedious tracing of the various ways Newman's "own potential for evil" reveals itself by the end of the novel. Somewhat, but only somewhat, more provocative is Mutlu Blasing's "Double Focus in *The American*" (*NCF* 28:74–84) in seeing the novel reflecting "James's ambivalence toward a type like Newman" on the one hand and a particular kind of technical problem on the other. Particular problems are thus raised by a narrator controlling the satire up to the point of the rejected revenge, with Newman's own self-image in control thereafter.

Two studies of *The Portrait* are both repetitive. Juliet McMaster's "The Portrait of Isabel Archer" (*AL* 45:50–66) is still another analysis stressing Isabel's limitations, "her morbid desire for suffering, her self-castigating morality, and her paralysing aetheticism." Joan Bobbitt's "Aggressive Innocence in *The Portrait of a Lady*" (*MSE* 4,i:31–37) recounts the variety of ways Isabel's "dismally consistent" action destroys others.

Two studies of *The Bostonians* are somewhat better, although both critical of the novel. Sonja Bašić's "Love and Politics in 'The Bostonians': A Note on Motivation" (*SRAZ* 33–36:293–303) sees the theme of sex and politics imperfectly joined in the novel, sees it in fact flawed by virtue of being at base "a struggle of love" rather than a "'struggle of politics," rather than the reverse as critics such as Irving Howe have maintained. And R. A. Morris, in "Classical Vision and the American City: Henry James's *The Bostonians*" (*NEQ* 46:543–57), sees the use of classical myth in the novel as James's attempt to encompass the city into an acceptable esthetic schemata. Unfortunately, maintains Morris, "his aesthetic and classical schemata" keeps breaking down "in the face of intractable realities of urban life"—apparently not accepting the purported break-down as an intention of the novel.

James's clear statement in the Preface notwithstanding, Sam B. Cirgus, in "The Other Maisie: Inner Death and Fatalism in *What Maisie Knew*" (*ArQ* 29:115–22), sees Maisie fatally trapped in the novel, caught as much as Sir Claude is caught in his fatal fascination for women. No escape, no life, is thus said to be possible. The "nothing" that her relationship with him leads to is only an intensification of the nothingness that all her other relations had led to. Carl Nelson's "James's Social Criticism: The Voice of the Ringmaster in *The Awkward Age*" (*ArQ* 29:151–68) is a more sensitive essay, maintaining that the moral vision of this novel resides in its picture of a decadent society in a decadent age, the esthetic method, in the pervasive irony that reveals the narrator's "inadequacy," one who damns himself "with participatory fervor." Especially good in this essay is the attention given to the way the words "everything" and "anything" are at "play" in the novel and in the ties that are revealed between the work as a whole and "The Art of Fiction."

Four studies of *The Ambassadors* are radically uneven. Robert Merrill's "What Strether *Sees*: The Ending of *The Ambassadors*" (*BRMMLA* 27:45–52) is a defense of Strether's action at the end of the novel as revelatory of one who now "sees" that his speech to Little Bilham of Book V was no less platitudinous than his even earlier view of Wollett, both being unequal to his final "new sense of life." Alan R. Shucard's "Diplomacy in Henry James's *The Ambassadors*" (*ArQ* 29:123–29) is another look at the diplomatic metaphors and images in the novel, revealing little that has not been revealed before except perhaps in the contention that James's attitude toward Hawthorne as an inexperienced diplomat (back in 1879) is remarkably similar to his attitude toward Strether. N. I. Bailey, in "Pragmatisim in *The Ambassadors*" (*DR* 53:143–48), sees Strether's actions in the novel everywhere paralleling the "pragmatic basis of conduct" except in its relatively pessimistic ending, that very exception, however, replicating "the course of American thought in the Twentieth Century from optimistic pragmatism to despairing existentialism." But it is William Veeder's "Strether and the Transcendence of Language" (*MP* 69[1971]:116–32), a now two-year-old essay, which is the most illuminating study of James's novel that I have seen in several years. Veeder's subject is "the stylistic drama" of the novel, ways in which Strether's language itself reveals his transformation from a kind of literalist to one with an awareness of language's inadequacies into finally his ability to make words "signify what they do not *say*," thereby being moved himself *and* moving the reader "to a fineness of emotion beyond any fineness in the words themselves."

Equally illuminating is John C. Rowe's expansive "The Symbolization of Milly Theale: Henry James's *The Wings of the Dove*" (*ELH* 40:131–64), an acute revelation of Milly's symbolic force far beyond that usually ascribed to her, how what she is and does discloses "the ambiguity of human relations," makes those who surround her aware of the ambiguity and mystery of consciousness itself," condemns them, in short "to circle about . . . [the] mysterious meaning now at the heart of their own being." Very good.

viii. Adaptations

A final word should be said here about three exciting film adaptations of works by Henry James, regardless of the dates of these annual volumes. For all good Jamesians, I am sure, will want to see at least the first four acts of Martin Lisemore's beautifully produced five-act version of *The Golden Bowl* and widely shown on Public Television's Masterpiece Theatre at various times since late 1972. Equally impressive is ABC-TV's two-part production of *The Turn of the Screw* starring Lynn Redgrave as the governess and first shown on its Wide World of Mystery Series in April of 1974. And, of course, what Jamesian would miss Peter Bogdanovich's production of *Daisy Miller* currently being shown in movie houses around the country, especially in view of his assertion that James had especially written the part of Daisy for *Cover Girl* starlet Cybill Shepherd!

Purdue University

8. Faulkner

James B. Meriwether

i. Bibliography, Editions, and Manuscripts

Long awaited, but a disappointment, was the publication of *Flags in the Dust*, the original, uncut version of Faulkner's third novel, *Sartoris*, in a text edited by Douglas Day from the typescript at the University of Virginia (New York, Random House). The brief editorial introduction is both inadequate and inaccurate; the text, as Thomas L. McHaney pointed out in an early review (*FCN* 2:7–8) has been heavily copy-edited in ways not noted in the introduction. With its inaccuracies and silent editorial changes, as McHaney points out, "Now *Flags in the Dust* is consistent in form with the great majority of Faulkner's other published works. It exists for the reading public in a corrupt text."

The annual Faulkner issue of *MissQ* (26:243–417), except for book reviews, is devoted to Faulkner's "manuscripts and typescripts, his unpublished and uncollected writings," as the editor, James B. Meriwether, notes in a Foreword. Five brief but highly significant, previously unpublished pieces by Faulkner are included. "And Now What's To Do" (pp. 399–402) is obviously autobiographical, dealing with his boyhood; unfinished, it apparently dates from the mid-1920s. What is presumably an earlier draft of the 1933 introduction to *The Sound and the Fury* (first published in 1972, *SoR* 8:705–10) is supplied, like "And Now What's To Do," from the "Rowanoak" papers found in a closet in Faulkner's house in 1970. This version is longer, more autobiographical, in many ways inferior; but it contains a number of comments by the author of *The Sound and the Fury* that shed light upon himself, if not upon his book. Less illuminating is "A Note on *A Fable*" (pp. 416–17), which was apparently written as dust-jacket copy for that novel, and was preserved, though not used, by Saxe Commins, Faulkner's editor. From the important group of early Faulkner papers recently acquired by the Berg Collection of the New York Public Library is taken "Nympholepsy" (pp. 403–09), an expansion and reworking of the 1922 sketch "The Hill." Michael Millgate, in "Faulkner on the Literature of the First World War" (pp. 387–93), publishes, also from the Berg Collection, the text of a one-page note by Faulkner, "Literature and War," which was apparently written early in 1925. Millgate's essay is a valuable analysis of the piece itself, and of Faulkner's use of World War I sources and of the significance of the war in Faulkner's writings generally.

Two long bibliographical pieces in the same issue of *MissQ* also have considerable textual importance. Keen Butterworth, in "A Census of Manuscripts and Typescripts of William Faulkner's Poetry" (pp. 333–59), lists all the known and available MSS. and TSS., including fragments, and provides, where possible, data concerning their dates and relationships with other versions, published and unpublished. Though Faulkner's poetry is minor, this is a major piece of research, and it points to the need for an edition of all the poems, with reliable text and apparatus. Eileen Gregory, in "Faulkner's Typescripts of *The Town*" (pp. 361–86) describes an almost complete (and previously ignored) early TS. draft of *The Town*, preceding the printer's setting copy. (Both are in the Faulkner papers at the University of Virginia.) The article, as the author notes, "undertakes to make available, by description and quotation, the most significant data from" a group of related TSS. for *The Town* and *The Mansion*, including passages either not present in or differing from the published text of *The Town*, drafts of a genealogy of the Snopes family, and a group of letters or drafts, previously unpublished but intended for publication, written in 1955 and dealing mostly with integration and racial prejudice in Mississippi.

In " 'Hong Li' and *Royal Street*: The New Orleans Sketches in Manuscript" (pp. 394–95), Noel Polk provides the text of a brief piece Faulkner added to a MS. fair copy he made in 1926 of the group of sketches, entitled "New Orleans," he had published in the *Double Dealer* in 1925. Also of bibliographical and textual significance are four items from this issue of *MissQ* listed elsewhere in the present essay: Noel Polk, "William Faulkner's *Marionettes*," and Thomas L. McHaney, "The Elmer Papers: Faulkner's Comic Portraits of the Artist" (section *v*); and Béatrice Lang, "An Unpublished Faulkner Story: 'The Big Shot,' " and Frank Cantrell, "An Unpublished Faulkner Short Story: 'Snow' " (section *ix*).

Gerald Langford, in "Insights into the Creative Process: The Faulkner Collection at the University of Texas" (*William Faulkner: Prevailing Verities and World Literature*, pp. 115–33),[1] includes a partial list of the MSS. and TSS. in this important collection. The comments on these papers—*e.g.*, those on the *Sanctuary* material—are not always reliable. Likewise to be used with caution is Max Putzel's "Evolution of Two Characters in Faulkner's Early and Unpublished Fiction" (*SLJ* 5:47–63); *e.g.*, the author's surmise that the unpublished story "With Caution and Dispatch" was abandoned by Faulkner when he wrote *Sartoris*, which ignores Faulkner's statement that he wrote it much later.

An important group of Faulkner letters from the *Scribner's* archive at Princeton are made available in James B. Meriwether, "Faulkner's Correspondence with *Scribner's Magazine*" (*Proof* 3: 253–82). The letters and annotations provide previously unavailable information concerning a number of Faulkner's stories during the period 1928–35.

ii. Biography

The postponement until 1974 of the publication of the official biography by Joseph Blotner leaves little of biographical importance in 1973. The biographical information appearing in the general critical items listed in section *iii* can be safely ignored. On the other hand, a certain amount of significant biographical data can be found in the pieces listed in section *i* by Thomas L. McHaney on the "Elmer" papers and by James B. Meriwether on the *Scribner's* correspondence, and the autobiographical content of Faulkner's "And Now What's To Do," also listed in section *i*, should be noted again here.

iii. Criticism: General

a. **Books.** Two general studies, quite different in their intended audience, have very little to contribute to their fields. Lewis Leary, in *William Faulkner of Yoknapatawpha County* (New York, Crow-

1. W. T. Zyla and W. M. Aycock, eds., *William Faulkner: Prevailing Verities and World Literature—Proceedings of the Comparative Literature Symposium*, Vol. 6 (Lubbock, Texas Tech. Press); hereafter cited as *Prevailing Verities*.

ell), is apparently attempting to provide an introduction to Faulkner for a wide audience, but the highly unreliable biographical chapter and the equally inaccurate accounts of the major novels and a few of the stories ignore most of what has been done by Faulkner scholars for the past 20 years, and the book as a whole simply emphasizes the need, now of some years' standing, for a brief, reliable, useful introductory guide to Faulkner. Aiming considerably higher, but likewise a failure through ignoring what has already been done in the field, is Joseph W. Reed, Jr.'s *Faulkner's Narrative* (New Haven, Yale Univ. Press). There are isolated insights of value in the chapters on Faulkner's aesthetic theories and narrative devices, and on the short stories; but the chapters on the novels are rendered virtually useless by ignorance of previous criticism and scholarship, by factual errors, and by narrow critical sympathies. Throughout, the book gives the impression of belonging to an earlier age of Faulkner criticism; *e.g.*, the statement "Edmund Wilson was right. *Intruder in the Dust* is an unsuccessful pamphlet," or the unenlightening comments on *The Wild Palms* and *Go Down Moses.*

Nor can the two general anthologies of Faulkner criticism published in 1973 be considered really useful. Linda Wagner's *William Faulkner: Four Decades of Criticism* (East Lansing: Mich. State Univ. Press), like its predecessors, *Two Decades* and *Three Decades,* includes little of the first-rate work done on Faulkner and all too much of the well-known and often-anthologized. Even feebler is Dean Morgan Schmitter's *William Faulkner: A Collection of Criticism* (New York, McGraw-Hill). (It is reviewed briefly by James B. Meriwether in *MissQ*, 26:471–72.) For years one of the chief problems of the Faulkner field has been the fact that so much good work has been done that has been almost entirely ignored. This gives every editor of an anthology of Faulkner criticism an unusually rich opportunity—but one which is all too often lost, as it was in these two cases.

***b.* Articles.** There are occasionally sensible or perceptive comments in Mary Sue Carlock's "Kaleidoscopic Views of Motion" (*Prevailing Verities*, pp. 95–113), which deals primarily with the three female figures Caddy, Addie, and Eula, but there is nothing here sufficiently new to make it worth reading. The same can be said of Alfred Kazin's "The Secret of the South: Faulkner to Percy" (*Bright Book of Life,* pp. 23–42); despite the promise of the title, this is little more than a rehash of Malcolm Cowley's introduction to the Viking *Portable Faulkner*. There is hardly more to James Dahl's "William Faulkner on Individualism" (*WGCR* 6:3–9) than a string of quotations from Faulkner; the vague commentary can be safely ignored, as can three inaccurate and journalistic general pieces on Faulkner and his hometown and works by Radu Lupan, "In Jefferson, Acasa la Faulkner" (*Luceafarul* [Romania], April 21, p. 1); Harold Martin, "Caravan to Faulkner Country . . . and Beyond" (*Southern Living* 8:117–18, 120, 122–25); and Robert Vare, "Oxford, Miss., Which William Faulkner Transcended, Is as He Left It" (New York *Times*, Jan. 14, sec. 20:3, 11).

iv. Criticism: Special Studies

***a.* Ideas, influences, intellectual background.** There have been a number of recent studies of Faulkner's influence and reception abroad. The most important of them is Edith Zindel's *William Faulkner in den deutschsprachigen Ländern Europas: Untersuchungen zur Aufnahme seiner Werke nach 1945* (Hamburg, Harmut Lüdke), which was published in 1972. Dealing with the period between 1945 and 1967, it provides a comprehensive study of the reception of his works in the German-speaking countries of Europe, with a full bibliography of translations and of criticism, including reviews. Carefully researched and organized, this is a very useful reference.

Five papers dealing with Faulkner's reception abroad were published in *Prevailing Verities*. Cleanth Brooks, in "The British Reception of Faulkner's Work" (pp. 41–55) surveys the predominantly hostile reaction to Faulkner by his British reviewers. His reception in France was quite different, as has been amply demonstrated, and little is added to what has already been said on the subject by Percy G. Adams's "Faulkner, French Literature, and 'Eternal Verities'" (pp. 7–24). Necla Aytiir in "Faulkner in Turkish" (pp. 25–39) lists translations into Turkish and comments on the problems of his translators. There is little to be learned about Faulkner from David H. Stewart's "Faulkner, Sholokhov, and Regional Dissent in Modern Literature" (pp. 135–50), but Glauco Cambon, in "My Faulkner: The Untranslatable Demon" (pp. 77–93) not only comments on his problems in translating *Absalom, Absalom!* into Italian, but also offers a good deal of information about other critics and translators of Faulkner in Italy.

In a 1971 essay first noted now, "Reasons and Characteristics of Faulkner's Influence on Modern Latin-American Fiction" (*ALitASH* 13[1971]:349–63), Katalin Kulin lists a number of South American writers who have been influenced by or show significant affinities with Faulkner. One of them, Gabriel Garcia Márquez, is the subject of an essay by Florence Delay and Jacqueline de Labriolle, "Márquez est-il le Faulkner Colombien?" (*RLC* 47:88–123), which compares the two writers at perhaps excessive length. And Alastair B. Duncan's "Claude Simon and William Faulkner" (*FMLS* 9:235–52) examines Faulkner's influence upon the French novelist.

In "Faulkner and the Cavalier Tradition: The French Bequest" (*AL* 45:580–89) Richard A. Milum usefully surveys part of Faulkner's use of French materials in his fiction, but omits too many important matters, like the French setting of *A Fable* and Faulkner's use of the Franco-German conflict in both world wars generally. Less useful, but providing a brief overview of the subject of Faulkner's Indians is Jean Rouberol's "Les Indiens dans l'Oeuvre de Faulkner" (*EA* 26: 54–58). Only the quotations from Civil War sources are useful in Matthew C. O'Brien's "William Faulkner and the Civil War in Oxford, Mississippi" (*JMH* 35:167–74), which ignores what has been done on the subject by scholars like Andrew Brown and overlooks the importance of the Civil War in Ripley and Tippah County as a source for Faulkner's fiction.

David Jarrett's "Eustacia Vye and Eula Varner, Olympians: The Worlds of Thomas Hardy and William Faulkner" (*Novel* 6:163–74) is too long for the material it contains, but comments usefully on similarities between these two characters and between *The Return of the Native* and *The Hamlet.* Also too long is Mick Gidley's "Elements of the Detective Story in William Faulkner's Fiction" (*JPC* 7:97–123), which catalogues a great number of techniques in Faulkner's fiction which can also be found in the detective story—and can also be found, as Gidley himself points out, in other novelists like Balzac, Dickens, and Conrad. He suggests, at length but unconvincingly, that S. S. Van Dine's character Philo Vance is a source for Gavin Stevens. More useful is Cleanth Brooks's suggestion, in "A Note on Faulkner's Early Attempts at the Short Story" (*SSF* 10:381–88) that

Faulkner knew and drew upon Irvin S. Cobb's character Judge Priest in his Gavin Stevens stories.

In an uneven essay that too often loses sight of the fact that Faulkner was more interested in rendering character than in presenting his own views, in his novels, Herman E. Spivey brings together a number of useful quotations from Faulkner and from his critics on the subject of innocence, the Edenic myth, and progress, in "Faulkner and the Adamic Myth: Faulkner's Moral Vision" (*MFS* 19:497–505). The topic is obviously an important one and calls for more attention, particularly in connection with Isaac McCaslin's views in *Go Down, Moses*—a work which Spivey mentions only briefly.

***b.* Language and style.** There is a new book, Edwin R. Hunter's *William Faulkner: Narrative Practice and Prose Style* (Washington, D.C., Windhover), but at best it says again what has been said before, and all too often offers errors and misreadings that could have been avoided by a better knowledge of Faulkner's work—or of what has been written about it. (But see below, under *As I Lay Dying*, for an example of the general contribution to the subject that a more sharply focused and carefully wrought study can make, even if confined to a single work.)

***c.* Race.** See under section *i* for the first publication, in the article by Eileen Gregory, of a group of Faulkner letters dating from 1955 which deal with racial prejudice in Mississippi.

v. Individual Works to 1929

Noel Polk's "William Faulkner's *Marionettes*" (*MissQ* 26:247–80) is the first extended study of this important but unpublished play, which Faulkner wrote in 1920 and made into little booklets, lettered, illustrated, and bound by hand. Three, perhaps four, copies are known to have survived, and Polk, basing his study on two at the University of Texas, provides us with one example of the small handful of important studies of Faulkner's apprentice work. Analyzing the literary sources of the work, Polk shows that *Marionettes* is, among other things, "a remarkable synthesis" of Faulkner's reading, and a far more sophisticated and ambitious accomplishment than has been previously noted. This essay promises to be a particularly influential one, for it sheds new light on images and techniques that appear throughout the early poetry and fiction, published and unpublished.

A similarly rich, carefully researched, and highly illuminating study of an early Faulkner work is Thomas L. McHaney's "The Elmer Papers: Faulkner's Comic Portraits of the Artist" (*MissQ* 26:281–311), which deals not only with the surviving portion of the unfinished novel "Elmer" which Faulkner wrote in 1925, but also provides the first study of the unpublished story "Portrait of Elmer," dating from a few years later, which Faulkner based upon it. (Both are in the Faulkner collection at the University of Virginia.) McHaney's careful research and fine critical reading of this material, and the way in which he relates it to Faulkner's life and to his other works, are models of literary scholarship in this field.

Soldiers' Pay is the subject of another exemplary essay, Michael Millgate's "Starting Out in the Twenties: Reflections on *Soldiers' Pay*" (*Mosaic* 7,i:1–14). Drawing upon the manuscript and typescript material newly available in the Berg Collection of the New York Public Library, and noting a number of previously unrecorded sources for the novel, including autobiographical, Millgate shows how *Soldiers' Pay*, with its "calculated rhythms, cultivated imagery, and static elegance," was nonetheless "an essential stage" in Faulkner's development as an artist.

Despite the publication of *Flags in the Dust* in 1973 (see section *i*), Faulkner's third novel fared none too well. Nothing new on the subject was added by James Gray Watson's " 'The Germ of My Apocrypha': *Sartoris* and the Search for Form" (*Mosaic* 7,i:15–33) or by Ronald G. Walker's "Death in the Sound of their Name: Character Motivation in Faulkner's *Sartoris*" (*SHR* 7:271–78). Nor does the attempt seem productive, in T. H. Adamowski's "Bayard Sartoris: Mourning and Melancholia" (*L&P* 23:149–58), to explain young Bayard's grief over his dead twin in terms of Freud's "Mourning and Melancholia" and Otto Fenichel's "Depression and Mania."

Already mentioned in section *i* is the publication of an important early draft of Faulkner's 1933 introduction to *The Sound and the Fury*. Calvin S. Brown, in "Dilsey: From Faulkner to Homer" (*Prevailing Verities*, pp. 57–75), offers a thoroughly sensible interpretation of this important character, pointing out the error of critics who have seen her primarily in terms of racial stereotypes, rather than as a servant; however, he appears to err himself in saying that Faulkner modeled her after the Faulkner family servant, Mammy Caroline Barr, who seems to have been different from Dilsey in almost every possible way.

Four other essays, however, add nothing useful to what has already been written—and generally more than once—about this novel: Charles D. Peavy's "'If I'd Just Had a Mother': Faulkner's Quentin Compson" (*L&P* 23:114–21); John L. Longley, Jr.'s "'Who Never Had a Sister': A Reading of *The Sound and the Fury*" (*Mosaic* 7,i:35–53); William V. Davis's "Quentin's Death Ritual: Further Christian Allusions in *The Sound and the Fury*" (*NMW* 6:27–32); and José M. Ruiz Ruiz's "El sentido de la vida y de la muerte en *The Sound and the Fury*, de W. Faulkner" (*FMod* 13:117–38).

vi. Individual Works, 1930–1939

A major event was the publication of André Bleikasten's exceptionally able and comprehensive study, *Faulkner's As I Lay Dying* (Bloomington, Indiana Univ. Press). Originally published in 1970 in France (Paris, Armand Colin) in a double volume with the Pitavy study of *Light in August*, it has been revised and expanded somewhat; and despite its somewhat pedestrian prose, which suffered in the translation from the French, it is at once the most complete and most useful study of *As I Lay Dying*. Separate chapters are devoted to genesis and sources, language and style, technique, characters, setting, themes, and critical reception; and the notes and annotated bibliography of secondary sources attest the thoroughness of the research that went into the volume. Other critics have dealt better or at greater length with various aspects of the novel—the bibliography here is an excellent guide to them. But nowhere else has so much information about *As I Lay Dying* been brought together and usefully presented; nowhere else have so many approaches been synthesized and worked into a coherent and persuasive view of this elusive novel. Modest, sound, and above all useful, it is to be hoped that *Faulkner's As I Lay Dying*, with its companion volume on *Light in August*, will provide a model for similar monographs on each of Faulkner's major books.

Smaller in scope but still of major importance is an essay by E. Pauline Degenfelder, "Yoknapatawphan Baroque: A Stylistic Analysis of *As I Lay Dying*" (*Style* 7:121–56). It would be difficult to overpraise this wide-ranging study, which deals brilliantly on the various styles within the novel and goes on to discuss with equal illumination such matters as characterization and point of view. Much of what is said here on such matters as the intrusion of Faulkner's own "voice" into the narrative (see pp. 131–32) is applicable to many other Faulkner works, and throughout, excellent use is made of Faulkner's own comments on stylistic matters.

After reading the work of Bleikasten and Degenfelder, it is more than ordinarily discouraging to encounter again the lightweight and the trivial: Joseph Gold's " 'Sin, Salvation and Bananas': *As I Lay Dying*" (*Mosaic* 7,i:55–73), and John B. Rosenman's "A Note on William Faulkner's *As I Lay Dying*" (*SAF* 1:104–05).

Of no particular importance, considering what else has been written on the subject, is Calvin S. Brown's "*Sanctuary*: From Confrontation to Peaceful Void" (*Mosaic* 7,i:75–95). But Pat M. Esslinger's "No Spinach in *Sanctuary*" (*MFS* 18:555–58), which purports to be an examination of comic strip influences upon the novel, merits at least passing notice as the silliest article on Faulkner in many years (Popeye is Popeye, so Temple is Olive Oyl; but Popeye is also "Daddy" Warbucks, so Temple is Li'l Orphan Annie).

It is a relief, after a few such examples of authorial and editorial irresponsibility, to turn to François Pitavy's *Faulkner's Light in August* (Bloomington, Indiana Univ. Press), which, like the Bleikasten study of *As I Lay Dying*, is revised, enlarged, and translated from its 1970 French version (Paris, Armand Colin). Like its companion volume, it is a model of critical and scholarly responsibility. If other critics have provided greater illumination upon one aspect or another of the novel, Pitavy has drawn upon them to present his own critical synthesis, and no other published study of *Light in August* is so comprehensive and useful. In organization and in method, his monograph is much like Bleikasten's; and like Bleikasten, Pitavy demonstrates a variety of sound approaches to Faulkner's fiction that should serve as models for other critics to follow in the study of other Faulkner novels.

Quite different from Pitavy's concise, well-organized, and coherent approach is a very long and highly uneven essay by R. G.

Collins, "*Light in August*: Faulkner's Stained Glass Triptych" (*Mosaic* 7,i:97–157), which suffers (as Pitavy's study never does) both from lack of knowledge of what has been done on *Light in August* and lack of knowledge of the Faulkner field generally. On the other hand, though it too fails to take into account what others have done on the subject, Franklin G. Burroughs, Jr.'s "God the Father and Motherless Children: *Light in August*" (*TCL* 19:189–202), is still a very interesting, and at times profound, general study of the important themes and characters of the novel.

In "When Did Joanna Burden Die?: A Note" (*SLJ* 6:43–46), Cleanth Brooks argues convincingly, from clues within the published text, that the date of her killing was August 6, 1932. In "Faulkner's Misogynous Novel: *Light in August*" (*BSUF* 14:11–15), Jackson W. Heimer argues unconvincingly, by ascribing the opinions of some of his characters to Faulkner, that the novel shows that Faulkner was a misogynist.

Duane MacMillan's "*Pylon*: From Short Stories to Major Work" (*Mosaic* 7,i:185–212) offers lengthy summaries of four stories ("Ad Astra," "All the Dead Pilots," "Honor," and "Death Drag") to show what they have in common with *Pylon*, but neither their similarities, nor the subsequent brief analysis of the novel itself, convey any real significance.

Cleanth Brooks, who has several times before made major contributions to our understanding of *Absalom, Absalom!*, returns to the subject in an important essay, "On *Absalom, Absalom!*" (*Mosaic* 7,i:159–83), in which he corrects some errors in the introduction to Gerald Langford's 1971 study of the manuscript and comments further on the character of Thomas Sutpen. Replying to several critics who have questioned the interpretation of Sutpen in his 1963 book on Faulkner, Brooks significantly expands that interpretation, and in the process shows Faulkner's treatment of that character to be even more rich and complex. Much less useful, because it repeatedly falls into the traps, which Brooks avoids, of considering the novel to be "about" the South, or "about" race, is John V. Hagopian's "*Absalom, Absalom!* and the Negro Question" (*MFS* 19:207–11), which begins well but ends poorly; his conclusion, that "The novel as a whole clearly repudiates Southern racism," is hardly helpful. More useful, though very brief and sketchy, is Hagopian's "The Biblical Background of Faulkner's *Absalom, Absalom!*" (*CEA* 36:

22–24), in which, after pointing our further parallels than have already been commented upon between Faulkner's story and that of David and his son Absalom, sensibly refuses to force his evidence too far.

Viola Sachs, in the chapter on *Absalom, Absalom!* in her *The Myth of America* (The Hague, Mouton) mentions, in her notes, a great many critics who have written on this novel, but her text shows few signs of familiarity with them, and despite an occasional insight, can be safely ignored. Two other general studies which likewise fail to take into account what has already been done and contribute little or nothing to the subject are Patricia Tobin's "The Time of Myth and History in *Absalom, Absalom!*" (*AL* 45:252–70) and Richard Gray's "The Meanings of History: William Faulkner's *Absalom, Absalom!*" (*DQR* 3:97–110). Nor is there anything to be learned about the novel from the analysis of its first sentence in John Stark's "The Implications for Stylistics of Strawson's 'On Referring,' with *Absalom, Absalom!* as an Example" (*Lang&S* 6:273–80). On the other hand, there are comments of real value to be found in Glauco Cambon's essay already cited (in section ***iv***), despite such occasional slips as confusing Faulkner's characters' ideas with those of their creator.

vii. Individual Works, 1940–1949

The only recent essay of any consequence upon *The Hamlet*, or the early Snopes material generally, is Edwin Moses's "Faulkner's *The Hamlet*: The Passionate Humanity of V. K. Ratliff" (*NDEJ* 8:98–109), which, though it contains too much plot summary, makes some good points about Ratliff and praises *The Hamlet* as a great comic novel, with rejuvenation its theme. Perhaps the extent to which Ratliff is rejuvenated, at the end of the book, is overstated, and certainly most critics have seen the ending as darker in tone, the irony more savage, than he does, but this is still an essay worth careful reading. A minor note on the occurrence of the same phrase in the novel and in a Faulkner poem is Richard A. Milum's "'The Horns of Dawn': Faulkner and a Metaphor" (*AN&Q* 11:134). A pleasant piece that tells us something about country stores but not about *The Hamlet* is Andrew Pfeiffer's "'No Wiser Spot on Earth': Community and the Country Store in Faulkner's *The Hamlet*" (*NMW* 6:45–52).

And to be avoided is Nancy Norris's "*The Hamlet, The Town,* and *The Mansion*: A Psychological Reading of the Snopes Trilogy" (*Mosaic* 7,i:213–35), which all too often twists and distorts the novels to fit a thesis; e.g., "the combination of letters" in the last name of Labove "suggests the separation of 'love' by 'Ab,' a man characterized earlier in *The Hamlet* as having been beaten at horse trading." Nor is Gerald J. Smith very persuasive, in "A Note on the Origin of Flem Snopes" (*NMW* 6:56–57), when he tries to show a connection between the Scopes trial of the 1920s and the name Snopes.

Little of consequence was done on *Go Down, Moses.* The most useful of the lot is Albert J. Devlin's " 'How Much It Takes to Compound a Man': A Neglected Scene in *Go Down, Moses*" (*MQ* 14:408–21), which shows the importance, in forming Isaac McCaslin's attitude towards sex and miscegenation, of the scene when, as a child, he witnesses his mothers reaction to his Uncle Hubert's mulatto mistress. The same writer records a few, but by no means all, of the chronological inconsistencies of the novel in "Faulkner's Chronology: Puzzles and Games" (*NMW* 6:98–101), which would have benefited from acquaintance with Rosemary Stephens's "Ike's Gun and too Many Novembers" (*MissQ* 23, [1970]:279–87). A sensible if unexciting reading of "Pantaloon in Black" which ignores practically everything written on it is Donald R. Noble's "Faulkner's 'Pantaloon in Black': An Aristotelian Reading" (*BSUF* 14:16–19). And there are occasional—but only occasional—insights of value in the chapter on "The Bear" in Viola Sachs's *The Myth of America* (The Hague, Mouton), which refers to more criticism than is actually used. And, in view of what has already been written, there are not even occasional insights to recommend T. H. Adamowski's "Isaac McCaslin and the Wilderness of the Imagination" (*CentR* 17:92–112); William B. Stone's "Ike McCaslin and the Grecian Urn" (*SSF* 10:93–94); and in two pieces by Haney H. Bell, Jr., "The Relative Maturity of Lucius Priest and Ike McCaslin" (*Aegis* 2:15–21) and "Sam Fathers and Ike McCaslin and the World in Which Ike Matures" (*Costerus* 7:1–12).

The only attention given *Intruder in the Dust* is E. Pauline Degenfelder's "The Film Adaptation of Faulkner's *Intruder in the Dust*" (*L/FQ* 1:138–48), which contains many inaccuracies and misreadings but also some interesting information about the film script and the shooting of the movie in Oxford.

For *Knight's Gambit*, the only contribution is Gidley's essay, noted already in section ***iv***.

viii. Individual Works, 1950–1962

Very little was done on Faulkner's post-Nobel Prize period. Two minor studies of *A Fable* are Robert W. Hutten's "A Major Revision in Faulkner's *A Fable*" (*AL* 45:297–99), which points out a change in speakers for a speech that appears in *Notes on a Horsethief* and in the novel, and Richard T. Dillon's "Some Sources for Faulkner's Version of the First Air War" (*AL* 44:629–37), a 1972 article which points to Eliott White Springs's *War Birds* and *Leave Me with a Smile*, and two stories by James Warner Bellah as sources for *A Fable* and other Faulkner works that deal with flying in World War I. Already mentioned in section ***i*** is Faulkner's previously unpublished note on *A Fable*, and Eileen Gregory's essay on the typescripts of *The Town* and *The Mansion*. A sympathetic general essay, Allen Shepherd's "Code and Comedy in *The Reivers*" (*LWU* 6:43–51), only occasionally offers something new, and Mildred K. Travis's "Echoes of *Pierre* in *The Reivers*" (*NConL* 3:11–13) fails to show that Faulkner was drawing here on Melville.

ix. The Stories

Two useful critical essays dealing with unpublished, but significant and largely neglected stories are Béatrice Lang, "An Unpublished Faulkner Story: 'The Big Shot'" (*MissQ* 26:312–24), and Frank Cantrell, "An Unpublished Faulkner Short Story: 'Snow'" (*MissQ* 26:325–30). Thomas L. McHaney's essay on the unfinished novel "Elmer," noted in section ***v***, also deals with the unpublished story "Portrait of Elmer." Noted in sections ***i*** and ***iv*** are Cleanth Brooks's essay on the early stories, and the Faulkner-*Scribner's* correspondence, which concerns both published and unpublished stories during the period 1928–1935. Although it must be used with caution, the chapter on the short fiction in Joseph W. Reed, Jr.'s *Faulkner's Narrative* (already noted in section *iii. a*) is worth consulting.

Other contributions to our knowledge of the short fiction have less to offer, and this continues to be the most neglected area of Faulkner studies. There are occasional critical comments of value in M. E. Bradford's "An Aesthetic Parable: Faulkner's 'Artist at Home'" (*GaR* 27:175–81). Two brief notes suggest, independently and unpersuasively, the Ransom poem "Emily Hardcastle, Spinster" as a source for "A Rose for Emily": Marion Barber, "The Two Emilys: A Ransom Suggestion to Faulkner?" (*NMW* 6:103–05), and Paul Levitt, "An Analogue for Faulkner's 'A Rose for Emily'" (*PLL* 9: 91–4). But there is even less to recommend in Howard Faulkner's "The Stricken World of 'Dry September'" (*SSF* 10:47–50) and in Sally Bethea's "Further Thoughts on Racial Implications in Faulkner's 'That Evening Sun'" (*NMW* 6:87–92). And to be ignored are Beverly Y. Langford's "History and Legend in William Faulkner's 'Red Leaves'" (*NMW* 6:19–24), Peter G. Beidler's "A Darwinian Source for Faulkner's Indians in 'Red Leaves'" (*SSF* 10:421–23), and Elmo Howell's "Faulkner's Enveloping Sense of History: A Note on 'Tomorrow'" (*NConL* 3:5–6).

University of South Carolina

9. Fitzgerald and Hemingway

Jackson R. Bryer

The fact that this year's survey is unusually long can be explained by two factors, one regrettable, the other a cause for mild rejoicing. The first is that it includes a large number of items from 1970–72 which were inadvertently overlooked previously. The second is that not only has the sheer volume of comment on Fitzgerald and Hemingway increased in recent years, but the number of worthwhile pieces has also. It is no longer possible to dismiss with a brief derogatory remark a good proportion of the year's work. Interesting new developments which one can find in this year's survey include the appearance of some excellent general essays on Fitzgerald and Hemingway and several new studies—notably Sheldon Grebstein's book on Hemingway—which deal closely with texts. A trend of previous years which, happily, continues is the valuable work on resources for the study of these two writers performed by Matthew J. Bruccoli and C. E. Frazer Clark, Jr., not only in the pages of the *FHA* but through book publications.

i. Bibliographical Work and Texts

Hemingway at Auction: 1930–1973 (Detroit, Gale), compiled by Matthew J. Bruccoli and C. E. Frazer Clark, Jr., is a volume of far more interest and value than a brief description of it would suggest. It reproduces pages from sixty auction sale and fifty-five dealers' catalogues containing books, letters, and manuscripts of Ernest Hemingway. Aside from much interesting information about printings of Hemingway's books (most of this is available in Hanneman's bibliography), it contains the most extensive detailed information we will ever have about Hemingway letters. This is because many of the catalogue listings not only describe the letters but also quote at length from them. Thus, this seemingly dull reference book is a mine of material for future scholars. It does far more than document the fluctuations of Hemingway's reputation (prices are listed); as Charles W. Mann notes in his Introduction, "As we will never read his collected letters, these pages will remain the only medium through which, however fragmentarily, we can still occasionally hear his voice."

Bruccoli has provided us with another invaluable resource for further scholarly research, *"The Great Gatsby": A Facsimile of the Manuscript* (Washington, Microcard Eds.). There is more here than simply the facsimile itself; Bruccoli's Introduction stands as the best detailed examination of the composition of *Gatsby*; and, taken as a whole, the volume provides all the raw materials necessary for the type of textual study of *Gatsby* which is so badly needed.

Encouraged by Bruccoli's pioneer work in this area, worthwhile shorter textual pieces on Fitzgerald continue to appear. Chief among this year's is James L. W. West, III's "Notes on the Text of F. Scott Fitzgerald's 'Early Success'" (*RALS* 3:73–99). West shows convincingly that the text of Fitzgerald's essay as published in the October 1937 issue of *American Cavalcade* is significantly different from the text which Fitzgerald originally wrote. Working from two typescripts of the essay, West shows how seriously cut the published version was and reconstructs it as its author intended it to be. This is a meticulous piece of scholarship, although one can well ask whether "Early Success" is significant enough to warrant it.

This last quibble obviously does not apply to John M. Howell and Charles A. Lawler's similarly exhaustive textual essay, "From Abercrombie & Fitch to *The First Forty-Nine Stories*: The Text of Ernest Hemingway's 'Francis Macomber'" (*Proof* 2[1972]:213–81). Howell and Lawler examine all the available texts of one of Hemingway's most famous and oft-studied stories: the ribbon copy used to set its original appearance in 1936 in *Cosmopolitan*; the Young and Mann inventory of the carbon copy of the typescript used to set the first book form publication in 1938 (in *The Fifth Column and the First Forty-Nine Stories*); the edited 1936 *Cosmopolitan* text; the 1938 Scribner's text; and the 1947 *Cosmopolitan* reprinting of the story. Besides providing a complete list of emendations and variants, the authors do an excellent job of showing how changes made by Hemingway and by the editors of *Cosmopolitan* affect any interpretation of the story.

The shorter textual studies are also equally divided between Fitzgerald and Hemingway. Lucy M. Buntain's "A Note on the Editions of *Tender is the Night*" (*SAF* 1:208–13) compares the two versions of the novel, concluding that neither "emerges as the one which is obviously superior." She suggests that Fitzgerald actually wanted to write two different novels, hence his indecision about the two texts. The original edition fulfills his plan "to expose the sham and superficiality of the expatriate life"; while the second implies his later intention to tell of the " 'Spoiled priest . . . losing his idealism, his talents, and turning to drink and dissipation.' " Thus, "the competing editions of *Tender* indicate Fitzgerald's painful indecision about what his novel should ultimately mean." Buntain's analysis seems more convincing than her interpretation of why it is so.

In "F. Scott Fitzgerald to Arnold Gingrich: A Composition Date for 'Dearly Beloved' " (*PBSA* 67:452–54), James L. W. West establishes January or February 1940 as the composition date of Fitzgerald's strange sketch about a black railroad club car steward based on a letter to *Esquire* editor Gingrich. The text of the letter is included.

The two Hemingway items are of more marginal interest. Both appear in the 1973 *FHA*. George Monteiro's "Hemingway's Pléiade Ballplayers" (pp. 299–301) supplies explanatory notes for two references to old-time baseball players in "The Three-Day Blow" and corrects several errors made by Roger Asselineau in identifying baseball players in his Pléiade edition of Hemingway's fiction. Michael Peich, in "Hemingway and *Kiki's Memoirs*" (pp. 315–16), describes a pirated and previously unrecorded edition of the book for which Hemingway wrote an Introduction.

The "Supplement" sections on Fitzgerald and Hemingway in *Sixteen Modern American Authors: A Survey of Research and Criticism*, edited by Jackson R. Bryer (Durham, N.C., Duke Univ. Press; New York, Norton [paper]), are among the longest in this revised and updated edition of bibliographical essays (published originally in 1969 as *Fifteen Modern American Authors*). Surveying Fitzgerald research during the past four years, Bryer notes that, in 1970–72 alone, "close to a dozen books entirely or largely concerned with Fitzgerald have been published," and that "significant advances" have been made in meeting many of the needs in Fitzgerald studies articulated in the 1969 version of his essay. These advances plus what Bryer calls "continuing redundancy and occasional outright foolishness" are described and evaluated in a 17-page supplement to his original piece. It takes Melvin J. Friedman 24 pages to update the late Frederick J. Hoffman's essay on Hemingway, remarking at the outset, "The indication is that we are in the midst of a serious reappraisal and stocktaking of the Hemingway reputation, with the personal myth being punctured and deflated at every turn while the work gets vigorous new readings." These two bibliographical essays, now current through early 1973, stand as reliable starting places for researchers who are understandably reluctant to plow through the ever-increasing volume of material in print on Fitzgerald and Hemingway.

Wayne E. Kvam's *Hemingway in Germany: The Fiction, the Legend, and the Critics* (Athens, Ohio Univ. Press) was undoubtedly conceived of as more than the annotated bibliography that it eventually became. Kvam intended, as he states in his Introduction, to "offer a more reliable explanation for Hemingway's popularity in Germany, add further insight into his more controversial writings, and provide a new vantage point from which to assess Hemingway's contribution to world literature." What emerges, however, after a valuable first chapter which sketches German attitudes towards American literature before 1933 is a series of summaries of German responses to Hemingway's works. While Kvam occasionally suggests reasons why German readers and critics were particularly taken with Hemingway, there is very little depth to his analyses. Typical is his assertion that "the favoritism for the German people that Hemingway has Cantrell express [in *Across the River and Into the Trees*], is likely to have influenced the German critical reaction," thus accounting for the novel's much more favorable reception in Germany than in America. Throughout, summaries of German reviews and articles are dutifully recorded, with little or no effort at weeding out redundancy or providing interpretation. Kvam could have accomplished just as much by putting together an annotated bibliography of German criticism of Hemingway, with a brief introductory essay. As with so much recent work on both Fitzgerald and Hemingway, this book represents the inflation of what is at best a fit subject for a long article into a full-length work.

In "F. Scott Fitzgerald's Book Sales: A Look at the Record" (*FHA*, pp. 165–73), Elaine P. Maimon provides valuable documentation on a much-abused topic: the status of Fitzgerald's books and sales during the last years of his life and for the period of what has come to be called the "Fitzgerald Revival." Maimon includes a chart which lists, by year, the number of single Fitzgerald titles in print from Scribner's, and the total sales. These figures, while they exclude editions of Fitzgerald's books published by other publishers, nonetheless provide some fascinating statistics. Fitzgerald did not die "out of print," as he himself thought and as various of his critics have contended; eight of his books were in print in 1940, but only 72 copies of them were sold during that year. In the period 1947–50, only one Fitzgerald title was in print (*Gatsby* and *The Last Tycoon* in one volume) and total sales for the four years were 1,657, with 866 during 1950. Thereafter, of course, sales rose steadily; until, in 1968, the last year on Maimon's chart, they totalled 448,420 on 16 titles.

Among the briefer enumerative materials we have the inevitable addenda and annual listings. William White contributes "Two More Hanneman Addenda" (*HN* 3:14–15); while Matthew J. Bruccoli supplies more entries for his Fitzgerald bibliography (1972), including items inadvertently omitted as well as those appearing since the date of the book's publication (*FHA*, pp. 339–46). All three of the enumerative listings in the 1973 *FHA* were prepared by Margaret M. Duggan. "Fitzgerald in Translation" (pp. 355–56) is a brief supplement to a much longer list in the 1972 *FHA*. "Fitzgerald Checklist" (pp. 349–54) and "Hemingway Checklist" (pp. 357–62) are extensive compilations of material by and about each author published in the last two or three years. While both lists exclude many items, they are extremely valuable in including such obscure types of material as reprintings of Fitzgerald and Hemingway pieces in anthologies, foreign studies, brief but often significant mentions of the two writers in books largely devoted to other subjects, and local newspaper items.

Overlooked in last year's survey was an important first publication of Hemingway material, the three-part (December 20, 1971, January 3, 1972, January 10, 1972) appearance in *Sports Illustrated* of a 55,000-word excerpt from a manuscript dealing with hunting in Africa, entitled "African Journal." Based on Hemingway's experiences in late 1953 as a volunteer ranger at the Masai Game Reserve at the foot of Mt. Kilimanjaro, the episodes selected (from a total manuscript of 850 pages) make for an exciting narrative and show their author at his best in describing his own experiences in a quasi-fictional style, much in the mode of *A Moveable Feast*. There are exciting pursuits of wild lions and leopards and interesting conversations with locals—natives and game wardens. As Charles W. Mann suggests in a review (*FHA* [1972], pp. 395–96), these excerpts imply that the full "Journal" deserves book publication.

The only previously unpublished Fitzgerald material of substance to appear in 1973 is contained in Matthew J. Bruccoli's edition of *F. Scott Fitzgerald's "Ledger"* (Washington, NCR Microcard Eds.). This little book, which Fitzgerald began probably in 1919 or 1920, contains five sections. The first is a "Record of Published Fiction—Novels, Plays, Stories"; the second is a record, by year, from 1919 to 1937, of "Money Earned by Writing Since Leaving Army." The listing is itemized so that one can see just how much Fitzgerald earned per story, novel, movie, and other writing as his career progressed. Part three is a list of "Published Miscelani [*sic*] for which I was paid" between 1919 and 1936. Part four lists "Zelda's Earnings" from 1922 to 1934; and part five, the most important section of the *Ledger*, contains Fitzgerald's "Outline Chart of my Life" from 1896 to 1935. All of this material has been utilized extensively by previous scholars; and much of it, especially the bibliographical information provided by Part One, is more readily accessible in other forms. But the autobiographical fifth section is valuable not so much for the events recorded, most of which have, again, been mentioned by biographers, as for its over-all tone and for the type of material which its compiler chose to include. Dominating every page of this diary are mentions of people met—often just a name jotted down—and places visited. If further evidence is needed that Fitzgerald was first and foremost an observer of persons and places, this is surely abundantly clear in the *Ledger*. But, as with Bruccoli's *Gatsby* facsimile noted above, the *Ledger* is basically valuable as a resource for further research of many sorts.

Two other Fitzgerald volumes essentially collect in book form previously uncollected fiction. *Bits of Paradise: 21 Uncollected Stories By F. Scott and Zelda Fitzgerald*, selected by Scottie Fitzgerald Smith and Matthew J. Bruccoli (London, Bodley Head), includes 11 previously uncollected stories by Scott, nine fictional sketches by Zelda, and one piece written by the two in collaboration. As Bruccoli notes in his Preface, of the 160 or so stories Scott published, only 96 have been collected; and those included here are the best of those remaining. Many of them show the effects of having been composed for a *Saturday Evening Post* audience: an exaggerated sentimentality, concern for love and money, and contrived happy endings. Perhaps more significantly, unlike Fitzgerald's best work, these are heavily plotted stories. Only one of them, "The Swimmers," contains anything like the emphasis on an ambience which is at the heart of his best work; and it is, not surprisingly, the most worthwhile of the collection.

Taken as a group, Fitzgerald's *The Basil and Josephine Stories*, edited by Jackson R. Bryer and John Kuehl (New York, Scribner's), probably succeed more consistently than the pieces in *Bits of Paradise*, just because they do suggest a time and place rather than simply a story. While the individual stories in this volume are sometimes weak (this is particularly true of the Josephine series), they do benefit greatly from being presented as two full series in juxtaposition. As Bryer and Kuehl point out in their Introduction, motifs and themes recur throughout the two series; and the Basil series at least can be viewed as a planned cohesive unit. And, unlike the stories in *Bits of Paradise* ("The Swimmers" is, again, the one exception), many of these pieces demonstrate Fitzgerald's dual ability to evoke a time and place while at the same time viewing them with a mixture of nostalgia and ironic humor. It is this kind of detachment amidst immersion, the basis of what Malcolm Cowley calls Fitzgerald's "double vision," which gives the Basil and Josephine stories their value.

In "F. Scott Fitzgerald's Contributions to *The American Credo*" (*PULC* 34[1972]:53–58), James L. W. West, III, identifies Fitzgerald's contributions to H. L. Mencken and George Jean Nathan's edition of *The American Credo* (1920) through the markings in Fitzgerald's personal copy of the book. Finally, in "Ways of Seeing Hemingway" (*FHA*, pp. 197–207), Matthew J. Bruccoli dispells the notion that Lillian Ross's famous *New Yorker* profile of Hemingway was a deliberate "hatchet job" which angered its subject. He prints the complete text of an article in which Ross describes the circumstances surrounding the writing of the piece and reproduces facsimiles of Hemingway's own set of proofs of the original profile, proofs which contain, in Hemingway's handwriting, only minor suggested revisions.

ii. Letters and Biography

Aside from the Fitzgerald letter to Arnold Gingrich noted above, the 1973 *FHA* presents the only other two items which legitimately fall into this classification. In "Recent Hemingway at Auction" (pp. 295–97), C. E. Frazer Clark, Jr., describes three groups of Hemingway letters recently sold at auction. "An Unrecorded Hemingway Public Letter" (pp. 227–29) is a facsimile of a letter written in 1939 on behalf of American veterans of the Spanish Civil War who were being refused re-entry to the United States.

There is the usual quota of biographical pieces on Fitzgerald and Hemingway this year. Most of these are in the form of brief personal reminiscences and several are more charming than informative. The two best biographical items, however, are carefully researched essays by Roger Asselineau and André Le Vot, respectively, on Hemingway and Fitzgerald in Paris (*FHA*, pp. 11–32; 49–68). These two articles are the core of the published proceedings of a conference on Fitzgerald and Hemingway in Paris, held at the Institut d'Études Américaines on June 23–24, 1972. The published record of these proceedings fill the first 89 pages of the 1973 *FHA* and include, besides the two excellent essays already noted, briefer reminiscences by Harold Loeb, Merrill Cody, Florence Gilliam, André Chamson, and Donald Ogden Stewart, an annotated literary map of the Montparnasse area of Paris, and the text of a roundtable discussion among the conference's participants.

Treating the other Fitzgerald biographical items chronologically, Herbert Gorman (*FHA*, pp. 113–18) provides three "Glimpses of F. Scott Fitzgerald," including his version of the celebrated encounter with James Joyce at a dinner in honor of Sylvia Beach. Margaret Culkin Banning remembers "Scott Fitzgerald in Tryon, North Carolina" (*FHA* pp. 151–54), in the late 1930s. Typical of most views of Fitzgerald during the last years of his life, Banning paints a fairly depressing portrait of "a pasty-faced man who didn't look healthy and wanted almost too desperately to sell what he wrote." In contrast, in "Sisyphus in Hollywood: Refocusing F. Scott Fitzgerald" (*FHA*, pp. 93–104), Frances Ring (Fitzgerald's Hollywood secretary) and R. L. Samsell attempt to debunk the mythic "image of F. Scott Fitzgerald in Hollywood as a physically faded, anti-social alcoholic, irresponsible, an all but defeated man." Utilizing personal recollections and statements of "percipient witnesses," Ring and Samsell do a good job of demonstrating that, although the continuing drain on his physical and financial resources took their toll, Fitzgerald was thought of with affection by those who knew him and "his perspective was positive. . . . he was always looking ahead, working up new dreams, firing up new hopes, planning one project after another." While the authors no doubt overdo their attempt to redress the balance about their subject, their essay is a convincing presentation of a minority viewpoint.

Two other Fitzgerald biographical pieces deal with his death and burial in Maryland. James V. Murfin's "The Fall of a Literary Light: The Last Days of F. Scott Fitzgerald" (*Maryland*, 4,i[1971]:20–23) briefly chronicles Fitzgerald's ties to Maryland and describes the circumstances of his burial there. In "The Myth of Fitzgerald's Proscription Disproved" (*FHA*, pp. 175–79), Joan M. Allen contends that none of Fitzgerald's books were ever proscribed by the Catholic Church and that he was refused Catholic burial solely because he was not a practicing member of the Church.

The four Hemingway biographical items divide into two of substantial length and two notes. Alexander Winston's "If He Hadn't Been a Genius He Would Have Been a Cad" (*ASLHM* 43[1972]: 25–40) is a chatty description of Hemingway from age 21 until 1927, when he married Pauline. Winston concludes his casually written article by pointing out the applicability of a Hemingway phrase to the author's own life: "A good man is hard to understand." Unfortunately, Leo Schneiderman, in "Hemingway: A Psychological Study" (*ConnR* 6,ii:34–49), does not heed this admonition. Schneiderman finds Hemingway all too easily understood and finds him a psychiatrist's dream, noting all sorts of aberrations and abnormalities. What he fails to do is to present convincing evidence for his conclusions, drawing most of them from the writings. Reading fiction as autobiography has always been a dangerous experiment and its pitfalls are nowhere more perfectly demonstrated than in this unconvincing essay.

Far less ambitious are William White's "Ernest Hemingway and Gene Tunney" (*HN* 3,ii:10) and John O'Brien's "I Am Sure I Saw Ernest Hemingway" (*FHA*, pp, 303–05). White retells an anecdote concerning a Hemingway-Tunney encounter during which the author challenged the boxer who was forced to throw him "a good little liver punch," which almost knocked Hemingway out. O'Brien remembers a brief encounter with Hemingway at Harry's New York Bar in Paris on June 2, 1927.

iii. Criticism

***a.* Collections.** Both new collections are among the first titles to appear in the McGraw-Hill Contemporary Studies in Literature series. Kenneth E. Eble's *F. Scott Fitzgerald: A Collection of Criticism* (New York, McGraw-Hill) has the expressed aim to "Focus upon recent critical articles, to avoid reprinting articles already available in other collections, and to refrain from using portions of books." Eble's selections range over Fitzgerald's entire career, with each novel receiving at least one essay. In his collection, *Ernest Hemingway: A Collection of Criticism* (New York, McGraw-Hill), Arthur Waldhorn takes a somewhat different approach. He selects only eight pieces (Eble reprints 12), each of which "takes an overview rather than fixes upon a single work" and thus we get a variety of approaches to Hemingway's total canon rather than close studies of individual novels. Both principles of selection are valid; and they may well be dictated by the directions of recent critical comment on Fitzgerald and Hemingway. We have very few good general essays on Fitzgerald; most of the best material has been in the form of critical studies of specific works. With Hemingway, this is not the case; hence a different process of selection is dictated.

***b.* Full-length studies.** The dearth of full-length critical work on Fitzgerald continues. None was published in 1973. The three full-length studies of Hemingway still display, to varying degrees, the recent tendency (already noted above with respect to Kvam's book) to push a simple thesis too hard and produce a study whose length far outweighs its intrinsic value.

This is perhaps most apparent in Lawrence R. Broer's *Hemingway's Spanish Tragedy* (University, Univ. of Ala. Press). Simply stated, Broer's thesis is a plausible and interesting one: "Whereas Hemingway's early heroes, those least affected by the author's Spanish enthusiasm, evince a sense of vulnerability and helplessness in the face of life's uncertainties, his later heroes—those conceived after the author's emotional and artistic commitment to what he came to view as the Spaniard's *particularismo*—are distinctly aggressive and bellicose in nature." The succeeding chapters labor rather tediously to prove this; and the ultimate effect is to make the reader wonder just how worthwhile the endeavor has been. To be sure, there are scattered insights throughout; but, as in so many studies of this sort, the amount of space and attention a work receives here is determined less by its intrinsic literary worth than by its value to the thesis being presented. Thus, Broer's chapter on *Death in the Afternoon* is the pivotal section of his study and that book is treated solely with respect to Hemingway's attitude towards bull-fighting. There is no doubt that Broer's approach is legitimate; one merely wonders whether a full book is necessary to present it.

Sheldon Norman Grebstein also takes a very definite and limited approach in *Hemingway's Craft* (Carbondale, So. Ill. Univ. Press); but his *modus operandi* seems more successful, probably because it is a more original one. Grebstein's concern is with "Hemingway's craftsmanship: those aspects of structure, language, and narrative technique which distinguish his writing from all other." Because this is obviously a very broad topic, Grebstein's book is necessarily diffuse and succeeds best as a series of essays on various aspects of Hemingway's technique. Some of this material appeared in periodical articles before incorporation into the book and has been commented on—largely affirmatively—in previous editions of *ALS*. Grebstein's studies of structural patterns in Hemingway's stories and novels—the recurrence of a "journey structure," a design based on movement from inside to outside or outside to inside, structure by means of formal divisions of a novel, and alternation and counterpoint patterns within pieces of fiction—are convincingly presented. Succeeding chapters examine such other areas of craftsmanship as Hemingway's narrative perspectives and his use of various kinds of narrator figures, the ways in which he uses dialogue, and the nature of humor in his works. Throughout, Grebstein deals very closely with the texts themselves; and his study is refreshingly free of cant about Hemingway's themes and life-style. Again, Grebstein occasionally goes too far in seeing patterns and structures; but, hopefully, the basic concerns of his book signal a future attention to Hemingway's writing as art rather than as autobiography or social history. A dividend in the book is an Appendix in which Grebstein does a brief but suggestive study of the manuscripts of *A Farewell to Arms* and *For Whom the Bell Tolls*. Grebstein's research definitely implies a need for further work in this area.

Samuel Shaw's *Ernest Hemingway* (New York, Frederick Ungar) in the Modern Literature Monographs series is neither as focused nor as ambitious as the Broer and Grebstein studies. But, if Shaw's brief book can be said to take a point of view, it is one which is opposed to Grebstein's. Shaw feels that "the critical emphasis on Hemingway as stylist does not do justice to him"; for his real contribution has been that of "bringing to fiction a new dimension, some new correspondence with the indefinable *reality* that creative literature strives to fathom." In his attempts to demonstrate this rather vague assertion, Shaw remains quite far from the texts of the fiction and tends to make statements rather than study the works in any sort of close reading. He very seldom quotes from the fiction; and his book is perhaps best for brief plot summaries of the novels and major stories.

c. General essays. The most encouraging development in Fitzgerald and Hemingway studies this year is a marked increase in the number of worthwhile general essays. We even have two good pieces on Fitzgerald and Hemingway. George Monteiro's "The Limits of Professionalism: A Sociological Approach to Faulkner, Fitzgerald and Hemingway" (*Criticism* 15:145–55) is much less forbidding than its title suggests. Monteiro uses Talcott Parsons's concept of "affective neutrality" in the role of the physician in society as a touchstone to a study of *Tender Is the Night* and three Hemingway short stories, with emphasis on "Indian Camp." Parsons's concept is defined as "the neutralization of the affections—that is, the deadening or the setting-aside of normal human emotions—for the purposes of enabling one's medical training and objectively learned technique to control one's behavior." It is the "subtle tension" which this produces—between "objective professional practice" and "human affections"—which Monteiro traces through the works. In each, he observes, "an individual fails, and in each case the failure is one of professional objectivity—a failure of affective neutrality." The section on "Indian Camp" is particularly interesting because Monteiro's focus is on Nick's father rather than, as in most commentary, on Nick.

Ruth Prigozy, in "A Matter of Measurement: The Tangled Relationship Between Fitzgerald and Hemingway" (*Commonweal* 95:29 Oct. [1971]:103–06,108–09), starts with the famous Hemingway-Morley Callaghan boxing match for which Fitzgerald acted as referee, seeing their respective personalities exemplified well in their behavior on that occasion. For Fitzgerald, Hemingway was "the embodiment for his dreams of personal heroism and physical superiority." Fitzgerald was, for Hemingway, an alter ego, "a repository for his very real insecurities and sexual worries." Thus, Prigozy points out, "each writer began to act out the other's conception of himself, thereby attesting to the power of what psychologists call the 'self-fulfilling prophecy.' "

All four of the general essays on Fitzgerald are original and provocative. The best is James W. Tuttleton's chapter, "F. Scott Fitzgerald: The Romantic Tragedian as Moral Fabulist," in his *The Novel of Manners in America* (Chapel Hill, Univ. of N.C. Press, 1972). Tuttleton's essay is the best to date on Fitzgerald as a social novelist of manners. He dwells briefly on *This Side of Paradise* (dealing with its portrait of "class attitudes toward sexual promiscuity giving way to generational attitudes") and at length on *The Great Gatsby*. The latter he sees as a novel of manners developing two interrelated themes: "Jay Gatsby's dream of recapturing a lost love in the inaccessible world of the fashionable rich . . . ; and the growth of Nick Carraway's moral sensibility." Out of these two themes comes a third—"a critique of the American dream of romantic wonder." Throughout, Tuttleton blends a systematic approach to the subject matter of the fiction with a sensitivity to the manner of its presentation.

Walter Wells does almost as good a job with another aspect of Fitzgerald's work in "The Hero and the Hack," the last chapter in his *Tycoons and Locusts: A Regional Look at Hollywood Fiction of the 1930s* (Carbondale, So. Ill. Univ. Press). Wells' focus is on *The Last Tycoon* and the Pat Hobby stories and, in them, he finds most of the elements he has traced through the Hollywood fiction discussed earlier in his book. These he then points out in Fitzgerald's work and they include "the loss or confusion of identity; the end of love and of innocence; the corruption of normal sexuality; human decay; the death of art, of values, and of dreams; the breakdown of language; an all-pervading sense of the waste of human energies" and "the persistent confusion between reality and illusion." As with Tuttleton's study, the great weakness of Wells's approach—its narrowness—is also its greatest strength. Because both Tuttleton and Wells view Fitzgerald from the vantage of critics who know a great deal about the one perspective they present, they are best able to present that perspective persuasively.

Carol Irish's "The Myth of Success in Fitzgerald's Boyhood" (*SAF* 1:176–87) rejects the theories that a sense of inferiority was at the root of Fitzgerald's early desires for financial success, social prestige, and athletic glory. Irish goes back to the St. Paul of Fitzgerald's boyhood and discovers that Fitzgerald was actually well-liked and respected by his peers and that "those barriers which did exist were usually constructed by Fitzgerald himself." These barriers were more personal than financial or social ones; and Fitzgerald's "intense pursuit of success" can be traced through the values he encountered at St. Paul Academy. Irish examines the author's earliest writings, in that school's magazine, *Now and Then*, concluding that Fitzgerald's ambitions and aspirations were far more typical and normal than heretofore acknowledged. This is a very revealing and convincing piece of scholarship.

Of equal interest but more tenuous is "The Evasion of Adult Love in Fitzgerald's Fiction," by Jan Hunt and John M. Suarez (*CentR* 17:152–69). Hunt and Suarez contend that Fitzgerald portrayed women as either "monsters of virtue" or "monsters of bitchery" because his heroes "actually need, however unconsciously, to perceive such images of women, even if they must distort reality in order to do so." The obvious next step, which the authors all too easily take, is to identify Fitzgerald with his heroes and to speculate that he may have used his fiction "as a vehicle for projecting his own need to avoid adult love." This last seems an unnecessary and unwarranted extension of what begins as a careful study of Fitzgerald's women characters.

There are 12 general essays on Hemingway this year. Coincidentally, one, John W. Presley's " 'Hawks Never Share': Women and Tragedy in Hemingway" (*HN* 3,i:3–10), deals with Hemingway's female characters. Presley sees them as "subtle threats, depleting the sexual and psychic reserves of the male." Most of what he points out seems obvious but it is a well-organized essay.

Robert C. Holder, Jr., looks at two Hemingway males in "Count Mippipopolous and Greffi" (*HN* 3,ii:3–6), noting that, at first glance, both "appear somehow to stand outside the stream of time and change that threatens to overwhelm the protagonist in each novel." In reality, however, both have sacrificed much of what Jake Barnes and Frederic Henry strive for: "The example they provide is that of the successful survivor who is not among the ranks of the very good, gentle or brave, but who, through a severely limited set of values or the ironic resignation of old age, comes to terms with a world that will triumph in the end."

"Ernest Hemingway: A Psychiatric View" by I. D. and M. Yalom (*Archives of General Psychiatry* 24[1971]:485–94) is a very readable attempt to fathom the reasons for Hemingway's suicide by considering "the major psychodynamic conflicts, apparent in his life style and fiction." An equally systematic and convincing essay is Steven R. Phillips's "Hemingway and the Bullfight: The Archetypes of Tragedy" (*ArQ* 29:37–56) which seeks to show that a tragic pattern can be found very early in Hemingway's career through his reactions to the tragedy of the bull and the bullfight. A somewhat clumsier attempt to find significance in Hemingway's writing on bullfighting is John R. Dunbar's "Hemingway's 'Moment of Truth'" (in Klaus Lanzinger, ed. *Americana-Austriaca: Beitrage zur Amerikakunde* [Vienna, W. Braumuller, 1970]). Dunbar focuses on *Death in the Afternoon* after briefly considering several of the novels; because "while giving us the same fundamental meaning as the novels, it records that meaning with more breadth and depth and brilliance. . . . it is only in this book that Hemingway lifts the meaning of this moment above the personal and limited, out of the realm of sport and into the realm of art."

As always, there are several essays which compare Hemingway with other writers. Kenneth G. Johnston's "Journeys in the Interior: Hemingway, Thoreau, and Mungo Park" (*ForumM* 10,ii[1972]:27–31) examines the sharp contrast between Thoreau's and Hemingway's allusive use of African explorer Mungo Park in order to point out the philosophical distance which separates the two authors. For Thoreau and Park, "the introspective journey was a quest for communion with the divine"; Hemingway saw Park as naive, viewed the explorer's faith as irrational; and the Hemingway hero found a "void at the center of his world." Johnston's conclusions hardly seem original enough to warrant the effort involved. Thomas L. McHaney's essay, "Anderson, Hemingway, and Faulkner's *The Wild Palms*"

(*PMLA* 87[1972]:465–74), on the other hand, is a highly skilled and original examination of the allusions to Hemingway and Anderson in Faulkner's novel. McHaney contends that this material "spells out clearly the basic differences between Faulkner and Hemingway regarding the nature of human and fictional reality and indicates agreement between Faulkner and Anderson."

Alfred Kazin is also, by implication, interested in the Hemingway-Faulkner contrast in the chapter on Hemingway, "A Dream of Order: Hemingway," in his *Bright Book of Life.* He views Hemingway as the "last great embodiment of the belief that experience can look entirely to literature for its ideal" and as the last American writer who believed "in a conscious perfectability through the right ordering of words." He sees him as eventually giving way to Faulkner whose technique "showed narrative not as a triumph *over* experience, but as the struggle of language to find support for the mind in its everlasting struggle with the past." Kazin's piece is brief and not very specific in its analyses; but the thesis which he presents is very convincing, although one should read his entire book in order to evaluate it justly.

Among the influence studies, Edwin S. Gleaves, in "Hemingway and Baroja: Studies in Spiritual Anarchism" (*REH* 5[1971]:363–75), suggests plausibly that "Baroja's influence may have been one of the most important of Hemingway's career" in that "Baroja chose the path of 'spiritual anarchism,' extreme individualism, which was at the time a practicable and convenient direction for the disillusioned young Hemingway to take, and one that he followed, in fact, until the Spanish Civil War." Commenting on Hemingway's influence on later writers, Sanford Pinsker, in "Rubbing America Against the Grain: Writing After Hemingway" (*Quadrant* 80[1972]:48–54), sees that influence as having declined in the last few years. In a very superficial piece, James T. Farrell suggests (*FHA*, pp. 215–25) that Hemingway's early work is his best and has very harsh words for *For Whom the Bell Tolls.* Finally, Erik Nakhdjavani, in "Of Strength and Vulnerability: An Interview with Philip Young" (*Dialogue* [Univ. of Pittsburgh at Bradford, Pa.] 1,iv.5–22), prints Young's comments, valuable as always, on Hemingway as a literary artist.

***d.* Essays on specific works: Fitzgerald.** The usual disproportionate amount of attention given to *The Great Gatsby* is even greater this year with 10 out of 15 essays devoted to that one novel. Significantly, only three of the 10, however, deal with the novel by itself. Chief among these is F. H. Langman's "Style and Shape in *The Great Gatsby*" (*SoRA* 6:48–67), which starts from the unique and admirable premise that we read *Gatsby* "for the sake of its distinctive voice, or voices, for the way in which it puts things, at least as much as for the significance of the episodes it recounts." Unfortunately, Langman's analysis of style is unsophisticated and disorganized; but, even so, his approach to the novel is so much the one that is needed that we can excuse a good deal of its clumsiness. Peter Gregg Slater's "Ethnicity in *The Great Gatsby*" (*TCL* 19:53–62) is more cogently argued. Slater's thesis, also quite a new one, is that "a heightened awareness of ethnic differences does constitute a significant element in the book." His focus is on Nick's "ethnocentric interpretation of the American dream," although he does stray at the end of the piece into the all too common speculation as to how much Nick's views are a projection of Fitzgerald's. Happily, Barry Gross does not take this course in "Back West: Time and Place in *The Great Gatsby*" (*WAL* 8:3–13). Gross deals with the opposition of East and West in the novel, pointing out that, if *Gatsby* were a nineteenth-century novel, then the West would be the geographical and psychological direction of the future, and the East, of the past. But as it is, "West is past, East future"; and this is how we should take Nick's remark that the novel has been the story of the West and Westerners who shared a common deficiency. Their deficiency is their inability to live in the future; what they seek is the past. Gross's reasoning is cogent and this is an excellent article.

Two essays deal with the Romantic heritage of *Gatsby*. In "The Romantic Ancestry of *The Great Gatsby*" (*FHA*, pp. 119–30), Robert E. Morsberger brings together virtually every Romantic writer in suggesting sources for the novel. Everyone from Scott through Dumas, Conan Doyle, London, Kingsley, and Sabatini to Dickens is discussed as a literary analog that might have influenced Fitzgerald. This is a poorly organized and obviously highly speculative essay. Because it is more narrowly focused, Leslie F. Chard, II's "Outward Forms and The Inner Life: Coleridge and Gatsby" (*FHA*, pp. 189–94) seems more legitimate in its contention of analogies between Coleridge's "Dejection: An Ode" and *Gatsby*. Chard sees Coleridge's poem as its author's "lament for the personal loss of 'My shaping spirit of Imagination,'" while Fitzgerald's novel is his expression of "a similar but greater tragedy: man's loss of 'something commensurate to his capacity for wonder.'" The basic difference is that "Coleridge's speaker is aware of the futility of continued striving, just as he is aware of the difference between valid and false ideals, whereas Gatsby and his world will continue to seek their false gods." In the course of the article, Chard draws interesting parallels between the basic situations of the two central figures—their desire for the unattainable ideal, the power of mind to transcend physical realities—but he does not utilize these parallels very successfully to illuminate Fitzgerald's novel.

Two of the other essays involve *Gatsby* with American traditions. Brian M. Barbour's "*The Great Gatsby* and the American Past" (*SoR* 9:288–99) is the year's best essay on *Gatsby*. Barbour relates the two opposing forces in the novel to two American dreams stemming from two American thinkers, Franklin and Emerson. The Franklinian dream "is one of self-validating materialism that is ignorant about the inner, positive meaning of the freedom it posits as its end, and is in fact complacently blind with respect to any positive moral values or genuinely spiritual sense of human life." The Buchanans embody this dream "in its least attractive form." The Emersonian self, in contrast to the Franklinian self, is not based on wealth but rather "on the moral ground of its own bedrock puritanism. Much of its power lies in its promise to free the ordinary self from the materialism, stagnancy, and moral complacency of the enacted Franklinian dream." Gatsby's is a version of the Emersonian dream, although he began in his youth with a Franklinian ideal which he later repudiated. Thus, Barbour notes, Fitzgerald's novel dramatizes the fundamental American conflict embodied in these two dreams, concluding that an Emersonian man cannot survive in a Franklinian world.

In "Romeo and Juliet in the New World: A Study in James, Wharton, and Fitzgerald 'Fay ce que vouldras'" (*Costerus* 8:109–76), John H. Randall looks at *Gatsby*, *Daisy Miller*, and *The House of Mirth* as American novels in which, as in Shakespeare's play, a tale of romantic love is "freighted" with "meanings that are, in the broad sense, political." By politics, Randall means "the organization and exercise of power within a particular group." He concludes, "The political meaning of these love stories suggests to me the tragi-comic tension in our nation between the aspirations of our founding fathers . . . and our social customs and modes of behavior, which all too often give those ideals the life." Randall's thesis is intriguing; but it often seems as if he is defining as political, forces which could just as easily be denoted as social pressures.

The remaining three *Gatsby* items are more specific and limited in their points about the novel. M. Gidley's "Notes on F. Scott Fitzgerald and the Passing of the Great Race" (*JAmS* 7:171–81) deals with the often-raised topic of Tom Buchanan's theories on race. Gidley traces them to Madison Grant's *The Passing of the Great Race* and Stoddard's *The Rising Tide of Color*, sources already cited in earlier research. Similarly redundant is Vincent Kohler's "Somewhere West of Laramie, On the Road to West Egg: Automobiles, Fillies, and the West in *The Great Gatsby*" (*JPC* 7:152–58; the essay is wrongly attributed to Robert A. Corrigan in the issue). Most of Kohler's remarks about the influence of the Jordan Company's automobile advertising on the characterization of Jordan Baker has already been covered by Laurence E. MacPhee (see *ALS 1972*, p. 143). Taylor Alderman's highly speculative "The Begetting of Gatsby" (*MFS* 19:563–65) finds sources for the name Jay Gatsby in the *OED* and in the work of William Dean Howells.

Of the two essays on *Tender Is the Night*, Scott Donaldson's " 'No, I Am Not Prince Charming': Fairy Tales in *Tender is the Night*" (*FHA*, pp. 105–12) is the best. Taking note of Fitzgerald's references to fairy tales in the novel, Donaldson claims that they "suggest the drastic consequences in failure of perception and in moral corruption of swallowing whole the sentimentalized view of the world implicit in this fiction." But Fitzgerald also is very careful "to separate his book from the sentimental, romantic fairy tale which, it is strongly implied, has been responsible for much of the moral irresponsibility he deplores." This is a highly original and provocative essay.

In "The Unconscious Dimension of *Tender Is the Night*" (*SNNTS* 5:314–23), George D. Murphy is guilty of the same mistake so frequently cited above in other essays—he uses Fitzgerald's fiction as a touchstone to his life. Here, the focus is on Dick Diver and his collapse, which Murphy sees as caused by his super-ego's failure "to come effectively to terms with the disruptive, libido-charged impulses of his id and ego." But then he views Diver's breakdown as a foreshadowing of Fitzgerald's own, concluding, "Fitzgerald proved as unable to portray explicitly this dysfunction in Dick's personality as he was unable to confront directly its symptoms in his own."

The one essay on *The Beautiful and the Damned,* Leonard A. Padis's "*The Beautiful and Damned*: Fitzgerald's Test of Youth" (*FHA*, pp. 141–47) is rather elementary in its conclusion that Fitzgerald's second novel represents his "first major attempt . . . to reconcile his romantic faith in the magic of youth with his morally ingrained suspicions that life wasn't 'the reckless business' for which he and his creatures had been taking it."

There are three essays on Fitzgerald short stories in the 1973 *FHA*, emphasizing once again that publication's awareness of just where research is needed. Lawrence D. Stewart's " 'Absolution' and *The Great Gatsby*" (pp. 181–87) presents the original notion that the short story and the novel "are basically irreconcilable." This is so because "the short story's alleged Gatsby-as-boy is a child who has no awareness of Father Schwartz's dilemma and who uses the priest's behavior as justification for developing quite different notions. It takes uncommon faith to believe that Rudolph could have evolved into the man who gave his name to Fitzgerald's most polished novel."

David Toor's "Guilt and Retribution in 'Babylon Revisited' " (pp. 155–64) also seeks to refute a previously stated view. Toor disputes the contentions of Roy R. Male and Seymour Gross that Charlie Wales is not troubled by ambivalence and that Charlie's ambivalence is not the result of "suspension between two worlds." Toor sees the world of the story as one not of "external retribution" but one in which payment for errors is self-punishment which leads to guilt and to "further degeneration of the mind—neurotic reinforcement of behavior that leads eventually to total insanity or a form of suicide."

Thomas E. Daniels, in "Pat Hobby: Anti-Hero" (pp. 131–39), contends that this series has not received the attention it deserves. He feels that the stories are much more than "warm-up exercises" for *The Last Tycoon*; for, in them, Fitzgerald created a character "quite different from what he had done in the past" and presented him objectively as a likeable and worthless rogue; and he also presented an excellent portrayal of Hollywood and the movie industry. Daniels's point is no doubt valid; but the grounds on which he urges it seem superficial.

***e.* Essays on specific works: Hemingway.** There are more than twice as many articles on *A Farewell to Arms* this year—seven—than on any other Hemingway novel. Happily, the majority of these are close readings of the novel itself. Arnold E. Davidson, in "The Dantean Perspective in Hemingway's *A Farewell to Arms*" (*JNT* 3:121–30), makes a distinction between the "protagonist actor and the protagonist narrator" and notes that Frederic Henry can both evaluate and feel. Davidson finds the prototype for this kind of narrative perspective in Dante's *Inferno*, where we observe "the man who is in Hell and the man who has been through it, who has learned, perfectly or imperfectly, the lessons that Hell should teach." Davidson is particularly effective in showing how this narrative perspective determines and controls the action of Hemingway's novel.

In another well-done piece, John Stubbs's "Love and Role Playing in *A Farewell to Arms*" (*FHA*, pp. 271–84), the emphasis is on the way Frederic and Catherine use their love as a defense "against the paralysis that awareness of human insignificance can produce." Stubbs sees their love as a form of role-playing which is ultimately not strong enough "to withstand the intrusion of life at its harshest." Again, however, as with Davidson's essay, Stubbs's work is most compelling when he explores how this pattern affects the strengths and weaknesses of the two characters. Somewhat further from the text are two weaker articles, David L. Carson's "Symbolism in *A Farewell to Arms*" (*ES* 53[1972]:518–22) and Phillips G. and Rosemary R. Davies's "'If You Did Not Go Forward': Process and Stasis in *A Farewell to Arms*" (*SNNTS* 2[1970]:305–11). Carson's focus is on the first chapter of the novel and its use of "symbolic suggestion" and associative symbols which enable Hemingway to strip his prose of the excessive verbiage characteristic of the "sandhill" school of naturalistic description. The point made in the Davies article, that *A Farewell to Arms* "is about process and about the necessary illusion that stasis is possible," rests on a somewhat closed approach to the novel and seems very close to the tack taken more exhaustively and convincingly by Chaman Nahal in his recent book on Hemingway (see *ALS 1972*, pp. 138–39).

Roger Sharrock's "Singles and Couples: Hemingway's 'A Farewell to Arms' and Updike's 'Couples'" (*Ariel* 4,iv:21–43) deals with Hemingway's men and women as "divided halves of a sole personality when they are apart" in contrast to Updike's men and women who "remain couples in their lovemaking whether the relationship is jealous, dissatisfied or tender." Turgidly written, Sharrock's distinction is neither clearly presented nor particularly useful. Also of dubious validity is Ronald Hartwell's suggestion, in "What Hemingway Learned From Ambrose Bierce" (*RS* 38[1970]:309–11), that Hemingway's memory of Bierce's "An Occurrence at Owl Creek Bridge" influenced his creation of the escape scene in *A Farewell to Arms.* Finally, Charles A. Norton's speculations on "The Alcoholic Content of *A Farewell to Arms*" (*FHA*, pp. 309–14) seem excessive in claiming that "attention to the alcoholic content of this work is important to a proper interpretation of its meaning in many of its finer points."

The best of the four essays on *For Whom the Bell Tolls* is Linda W. Wagner's "The Marinating of *For Whom the Bell Tolls*" (*JML* 2:533–46). Wagner demonstrates very convincingly how the novel underwent a long period of pre-writing in the form of Hemingway's newspaper columns, five short stories, a movie scenario, and *The Fifth Column.* Her conclusion, that "the eventual scope and balance of *For Whom the Bell Tolls* might well have been less successful had Hemingway not had the chance to pre-write in the shorter works," is amply supported through her careful use of examples. This is scholarship working with literary criticism in the best blending of the two forms.

Mary Allen takes a definite point of view in "Hail to Arms: A View of *For Whom the Bell Tolls*" (*FHA*, pp. 285–93). Allen rejects a symbolic reading of the novel that encourages a view of Robert Jordan as a moral hero. Allen complains, "Under the guise of Donne's brotherhood, Biblical thee's and thou's, a love affair, and talk of the evil of war, *For Whom the Bell Tolls* applauds a man for killing other men and for seeking his own death, all for a very remote cause. . . . The title from Donne becomes ironic. The test of a man is the same as elsewhere in Hemingway, that of individual courage, revealed through mortal combat, not through brotherly or romantic love." While Allen may be more argumentative here than is necessary, the point she is making is a good one and her essay is clearly developed.

Two essays in *HN* deal, respectively, with Jordan's death and laughter in the novel. In "The Education of Robert Jordan: Death With Dignity" (*HN* 1,ii[1971]:14–20), Donald J. Greiner contends that *For Whom the Bell Tolls* "has less to do with a revelation of Hemingway's politics at the time of the Spanish Civil War than it does with the questions of how one dies and of what circumstances are necessary to give one a death with dignity—death as a form of art." Based on more than his father's suicide, Jordan's decision to sacrifice himself is a result of his 70 hours with the guerillas who teach him that "each man's death is a private act because only he knows all of the particular circumstances." Cathy N. Davidson's "Laughter Without Comedy in *For Whom the Bell Tolls*" (*HN* 3,ii:6–9) examines three types of laughter in the novel: (1) a person who appears to be laughing with someone, but is really laughing at him; (2) a character who attempts to ease tension through a joke, an attempt which backfires; and (3) malicious cynical laughter. Davidson relates this humorless and hollow laughter to the themes of the novel.

The three essays on *The Old Man and the Sea* are all excellent. Linda W. Wagner's "The Poem of Santiago and Manolin" (*MFS* 19:517–29) sees the work as a "lyric novel" in which "all segments of the book—structure, imagery, word choice, characters, plot—create a single organic whole." She does a superb job of closely examining the language and structure of the novel, showing that Hemingway ended his career as he began it—as a poet. In "Ernest Hemingway, Mati Zalke and Spain: To the Symbolic Meaning of 'The Old Man and the Sea'" (*ALitASH* 13[1971]:315–24), Jozsef Kovacs makes the intriguing suggestion that "it was in this novel that the writer said his last word concerning the Spanish war." Kovacs maintains that Hemingway spoke about "the struggle of an old man against the sharks . . . in such a way that he really spoke about Spain, about the fight of people against the dark forces of humanity." This is a highly original and well-argued essay. Joseph M. Flora, in "Biblical Allusion in 'The Old Man and the Sea'" (*SSF* 10:143–47), finds an affinity between the repetition of the phrase "far out" in the novel and a story in Luke 5:4–11, in which Jesus suggests to the fishermen that they must "launch out" if they would catch fish. Thus, Hemingway's novel "illustrates the essence of Christian discipleship and does so in specifically biblical terms."

There is only one essay of any substance this year on *The Sun Also Rises*, Morton L. Ross's "Bill Gorton, the Preacher in *The Sun Also Rises*" (*MFS* 18[1972–73]:517–27). Ross sees Gorton as the voice of Hemingway's code in the novel, noting the number of imperative statements he makes. He then lists Gorton's five "commandments": (1) utilize a little; (2) never be daunted; (3) work for the good of all; (4) show irony and pity; and (5) do not question. A full and convincing discussion follows, in which Ross stresses that Gorton's code is not a moral code at all but one of manners. Robert Murray Davis, in "Irony and Pity Once More" (*FHA*, pp. 307–08), traces one of Gorton's "commandments" to Paul Eldridge's *Irony and Pity: A Book of Tales* (1926).

Of the two articles on *Across the River and Into the Trees*, the more sharply focused and better is Kenneth E. Bidle's "*Across the River and Into the Trees*: Rite de Passage à Mort" (*FHA*, pp. 259–70), Bidle examines Colonel Cantwell as "an old warrior who prepares for death in the same way as he lives—on the primitive instinctive level—by performing rituals that are timeless and universal." He traces the eight rituals (sacrifice, baptism under fire, holy orders, sacred dining, sexual union, confession and penance, extreme unction, and blood-letting) performed by the Colonel to complete his *rite de passage à mort*, "the ultimate ritual of human existence." Bidle's argument is systematically and convincingly presented. Robert Hipkiss, in "Ernest Hemingway's *The Things That I Know*" (*TCL* 19:275–82), deals in more general issues—the knowledge Cantwell gains about war, love, and truth—and his discussion degenerates into a series of platitudes.

Death in the Afternoon, which figures so prominently in Broer's book and Dunbar's essay (see above), is the subject of a highly conjectural essay by John Raeburn, "*Death in the Afternoon*, and the Legendary Hemingway" (*FHA*, pp. 243–57). Raeburn sees *Death in the Afternoon* as the piece of non-fiction most important to Hemingway's personal fame, because it is "the most nearly comprehensive formulation of his public personality." He demonstrates this by finding the work a composite of a number of sketches, each highlighting a distinctive aspect of Hemingway's personality and clustering around nine stances that Hemingway assumes in the book—"sportsman, paradigm of masculinity, destroyer of pretension, arbiter of taste, world-traveler, exemplar of the good life, insider, battle-scarred stoic, and heroic artist." This is a well-organized article, although of dubious validity.

In "A Degree of Alchemy: *A Moveable Feast* as Literary Autobiography" (*FHA*, pp. 231–42), Jill Rubenstein maintains that the book is "Hemingway's portrait of the artist as a young man, a retrospective account of the end of innocence and the confrontation of experience in the loneliness that is the only mode in which the artist may thrive." She suggests that, stylistically, Hemingway performs an act of alchemy in transforming the materials of autobiography into the materials of art through a "deliberate confusion of factual material and fictional technique." Aside from Carlos Baker's chapter in the revised edition of his critical book on Hemingway, this is the best piece in print on *A Moveable Feast*.

Turning to discussions of the short stories, two essays deal with several stories together. Working from letters to the editors of *Cosmopolitan* and typescripts, John M. Howell, in "Hemingway's 'Metaphysics' in Four Stories of the Thirties: A Look at the Manuscripts" (*ICarbS* 1,i:41–51), examines "After the Storm," "The Short Happy Life of Francis Macomber," and two other stories. Howell shows through a close attention to Hemingway's revisions in these pieces that the author was coming to the "growing emphasis on the theme of spiritual union which dominates *For Whom The Bell Tolls*." Again, this article weds scholarly research and literary criticism extremely effectively. Much less sophisticated is S. P. Jain's "Some Hemingway Stories: Perspectives and Responses" (*LHY* 12,i[1971]:53–64), in which "The Battler," "A Way You'll Never Be," and "A Natural History of the Dead" are linked through a concern with a common area of experience—"damnation of having to live as opposed to damnation of death in a universe where inescapable violence is the presiding metaphor."

Of the three essays on "The Short Happy Life," the only one worth taking seriously is James Nagel's "The Narrative Method of 'The Short Happy Life of Francis Macomber' " (*ES* 41:18–27). Nagel disputes Robert B. Holland's naming of Hemingway as narrator of the story, finding instead "a mixture of shifting third-person limited and omniscient statements which together provide five (counting the lion) perspectives from which the physical and psychological action is viewed." Using this awareness of narrative perspective, Nagel finds that "Macomber does indeed undergo substantial growth, that Wilson is hypocritical, that Margot fears the change in her husband but shoots him accidentally, and that the story ends ironically with Wilson's torment of her." R. F. Fleissner's ridiculous piece, "The Macomber Case: A Sherlockian Analysis" (*Baker Street Journal* 20[1970]:154–56, 169), is not even worth mention as a parody; and Theodore L. Gaillard, Jr.'s "The Critical Menagerie on 'The Short Happy Life of Francis Macomber'" (*EJ* 60[1971]:31–35) is a very simplistic study of Hemingway's use of animals in the story.

There is, of course, the annual essay on "The Confusing Dialogue in Hemingway's 'A Clean, Well-Lighted Place,'" this time by Scott MacDonald (*SAF* 1:93–101), who insists redundantly that "the alteration in the dialogue of 'A Clean, Well-Lighted Place' changes the meaning of the text significantly and, as a result, cannot help but create more confusion than it was meant to solve." Kelsie B. Harder displays a good deal more originality in "Hemingway's Religious Parody" (*NYFQ* 26[1970]:76–77) by suggesting that Hemingway parodied the Paternoster and the Ave Maria in the story. By "nullifying each religious symbol in the Paternoster and Ave Maria," Harder observes, "Hemingway allows the older waiter to comment sensitively and significantly on the desolation of human existence."

Four articles deal with Nick Adams stories. In "Hemingway's 'The Doctor and the Doctor's Wife'" (*ArQ* 29:19–25), Stephen D. Fox contends that the story pivots around the accusation made by Dick Bouton and is thus "a portrait of civilized half-truths" and presents Nick "at a certain stage of his development, when he is still involved in the complex dilemmas that surround him." It also implies the standards that Nick will return to and adopt overtly at a later stage in his life." Scott MacDonald, in "Implications of Narrative Perspective in Hemingway's 'Now I Lay Me'" (*SAF* 1:213–20), makes a distinction between the Nick who convalesces in Italy and the Nick who narrates the story, concluding that "Now I Lay Me" is "largely concerned with Nick 'now,' still suffering from the shock of being blown up and still fighting through a difficult night long after his physical convalescence has ended."

In a logical and well-documented essay, "To Be and Not to Be: Paradox and Pun in Hemingway's 'A Way You'll Never Be'" (*Style*

7:56–63), Paul Witherington claims that Nick is involved in a balancing act: "Nick's dilemma comes from his simultaneous attraction to position (rest, certainty, necessity, death) and pose (movement, confusion, possibility, life). At the beginning of the story these appear in hopeless opposition. At the end, they come together in true focus." Peter Thomas, in "A Lost Leader: Hemingway's 'The Light of the World'" (*HAB* 21[1970]:14–19), starts with Hemingway's intention to make this story the first one in *Winner Takes Nothing* and sees it as closely related to its biblical source, and as a piece framed by a journey from darkness to darkness.

The title of Marshall Myers's "A Tagemic Analysis of Hemingway's 'A Very Short Story'" (in Daniel G. Hays and Donald M. Lance, eds. *From Soundstream to Discourse: Papers From the 1971 Mid-America Linguistics Conference* [Columbia, Univ. of Mo.]) is self-explanatory. The study, although highly technical, succeeds in its intention "to provide the critic with raw data for drawing his conclusions about the author's artistry."

g. Dissertations. Reflecting the general increase in the volume of comment on these two writers, seven dissertations on Fitzgerald were recorded in 1973, while six dealt in part or wholly with Hemingway.

University of Maryland

This chapter could not have been completed without the research assistance of Joanne Giza and Roberta Robbins.

Part II

10. Literature to 1800

J. A. Leo Lemay

Two major books about early American literature appeared in 1973. Richard Slotkin's brilliant examination of frontier literature, *Regeneration Through Violence*, and Larzer Ziff's revisionistic synthesis *Puritanism in America*. To judge by the quantity of scholarship, Charles Brockden Brown has almost moved into the ranks of the other major colonial authors—Edward Taylor, Benjamin Franklin, and Jonathan Edwards. I have indicated the more prominent place that Brown now holds in our scholarship by devoting a new section (*vii*) to "Brown and his Contemporaries." As the Bicentennial of the American Revolution approaches, it seems ironic that more attention is being devoted to the Loyalists than to the Patriots—but such is the temper of the times. As usual, the scholarship on the New England colonists dominates our interest in the 17th century, and even by including most of the Southern 18th-century colonial writers in the section on the South (*iii*),I can not make it compare with the longest section below, that on the Puritans (*ii*).

Several valuable editions appeared in 1973. Roger Williams's *A Key into the Language of America*; Increase Mather's "Confutation of Solomon Stoddard's 'Observations Respecting the Lord's Supper,' 1680"; Franklin's writings for the year 1770 (vol. 17 of *The Papers of Benjamin Franklin*); the *Adams Family Correspondence* for 1778–1782; and *The Journal of Samuel Curwin.* Although too many inadequately researched articles (a continuing fault in Franklin scholarship) and hopelessly solipsistic essays (the besetting sin of Edwards scholarship) appeared during the year, there were also a number of significant contributions to our knowledge. I can single out David L. Parker's thoughtful piece on Ramus and the Puritans; T. G. Hahn's careful study of Urian Oakes's *Elegie*; Paul R. Lucas on the theology of Solomon Stoddard; David L. Minter on Mary Rowlandson; Edward J. Gallagher's sensitive examination of Franklin's "Way to

Wealth"; Lewis P. Simpson's highly original interpretation of the satiric mode of the early National wits; and a host of good things by Robert D. Arner.

i. Edward Taylor

Gene Russell's *A Concordance to the Poems of Edward Taylor* (Washington, D.C., Microcard Editions) is an expertly produced, useful tool, based upon Donald E. Stanford's standard text, *The Poems of Edward Taylor* (1960). Happily, entire lines are printed (except for the word *thy*), so that the contexts of the key words may be ascertained from the concordance itself. Russell lists on p. xiii the words not included ("a, an, am, are, and," etc.). The introduction continues Russell's defense (see *ALS 1971*, pp. 150–51) of Taylor's use of off-rhymes, but it is marred by Russell's senseless slurs on the poetic ability of Taylor's American contemporaries, Benjamin Tompson and Michael Wigglesworth. And Russell briefly discusses Taylor's probable pronunciation. Karl Keller's appreciative preface "The Words of Edward Taylor" in Russell's' *Concordance*, pp. xv–xix, sees Taylor as a precursor of the Yeats of "Sailing to Byzantium"—a poet who can "like his bird in its wicker cage (I,8) at least 'tweedle,' sing, turn himself into sound in the silence." Keller claims that Taylor's most frequent persona is "that of a writer writing about trying to write." Keller stresses Taylor's love for words and, through them, the poet's sense of God as the highest esthetic.

Taylor's use of Tobias Bentelm's *Electorale Saxonicum* in Meditations 2.109 and 2.113, as well as in 2.56, is one subject of Harrison T. Meserole's wide-ranging "Edward Taylor's Sources" (Weintraub and Young, eds., *Directions*, pp. 121–26), which calls for more investigation of the sources, pointing out that investigation of Taylor's interest in and use of folklore has just begun. Indeed, too often the deliberate folkoristic content of early American writing has been overlooked or ignored. No one has treated the proverbs and folk expressions in Wigglesworth's *Day of Doom* (which owes much of its power and memorability to these pervasive clichés) or the reflection of folk beliefs in any of the colonial writers (such a study of Cotton Mather would be very rewarding). But now Robert D. Arner's two articles, Meserole's words, and B. J. Whiting's essay (noticed below)—all suggest that this important aspect of early

American writing is beginning to receive attention. In "Proverbs in Edward Taylor's *God's Determinations*" (*SFQ* 37:1–13), Arner not only shrewdly comments on the proverbs Taylor uses (and on his proverbial expressions), he also analyzes the effects of Taylor's use of proverbs. I noticed that two of Taylor's proverbs cited by Arner are also found in Mather's *Magnalia* (see B. J. Whiting, below). Arner also skillfully examines the tripartite structure of Meditation 1.40, demonstrates its reliance upon an intricate verbal structure which shifts back and forth from sound to meaning (comparing Taylor's technique to that of the later prose of James Joyce), and points out the "complex interconnection of levels of meaning and associated thoughts" ("Folk Metaphors in Edward Taylor's 'Meditation,' 1.40," *SCN* 31:6–9). In tracing Taylor's rejection of the efficacy of the human intellect as the basis of conversion, Arner shows how Taylor relies upon a number of folk beliefs and folk expressions in violently yoking together his complex combinations of learning and homeliness.

Edward Taylor annotated a copy of Thomas Taylor's *Christ Revealed: Or the Old Testament Explained; A Treatise of the Types and Shadowes of our Saviour* (1635), and used Thomas Taylor's theories in the typological sequence of Meditations 2.1–29, particularly 2.26 and 2.27. Gordon E. Slethaug ("Edward Taylor's copy of Thomas Taylor's *Types*: A New Taylor Document," *EAL* 8:132–39) believes that "the general order of Thomas Taylor's *Types* and Edward Taylor's 'Second Series of Meditations' suggests an attempt at a poetic history of the Old Testament, relating persons and events in Jewish history to the role of Christ." Slethaug might also have told us how this Christological typology of Thomas Taylor and Edward Taylor differed from the order and interpretation of other typological commentaries on the Old Testament. Nor does Slethaug comment on the seemingly Ramistic characteristics of Edward Taylor's diagram of Adam's attributes. In another source study, Donald E. Stanford shows that Taylor echoed two poems by Cleveland in his "Verses made upon Pope Joan" ("Edward Taylor and the 'Hermophrodite' Poems of John Cleveland," *EAL* 8:59–61).

According to Jeff Hammond and Thomas M. Davis, Taylor reflects by his denial the common portrayal of Death as represented on gravestones, broadsides, and emblem books, for Taylor believed that the intervention of Christ makes Death a soothing "Down bed" for the saved ("Edward Taylor: A Note on Visual Imagery," *EAL* 8:126–31). At the same time, the authors contend that despite the Biblical authority for the common images associated with death, their appearance in Taylor's poetry reflects these visual representations, rather than the Bible. Taylor's interest in science, particularly as displayed in his poem on "The Great Bones of Claverack" is the subject of Lawrence L. Sluder's "God in the Background: Edward Taylor as Naturalist" (*EAL* 7:265–71). Sluder points out the humorous qualities of this poem, written "in a mocking, jocular style." Francis A. Simonetti believes that certain sounds are identified with Taylor's spinning wheel image and others with the weaving and dying process ("Prosody as a Unifying Element in 'Huswifery,'" *BSUF* 14,iv:30–31). And Sibyl C. Jacobson presents an overview of the imagery used in the Meditations, remarking on Taylor's wit, defending the ostensible inconsistency of the imagery, and categorizing the images according to the speaker-meditant's relationship with Christ ("Image Patterns in Edward Taylor: Prayer and Proof," *CP* 6,i:59–67).

ii. Puritanism

A dominant thesis of Larzer Ziff's *Puritanism in America: New Culture in a New World* (New York, Viking) is that the New England culture achieved a distinct identity by 1640, flourished during the following decades, but declined into provincialism in the years following King Philip's War (1675–76), the revoking of the old Massachusetts charter (1684), and the granting of the new charter (1691). "Culture by 1720 had become thoroughly provincial" (p. 296), claims Ziff. Too bad that Clifford K. Shipton did not live a few more months and review Ziff's book. What Ziff has done, essentially, is to re-embody the old "declension" thesis of New England culture in a modern and powerful version—a thesis that Shipton, in his essay "The New England Clergy of the 'Glacial Age,'" *PCSM* 32 (1933): 24–54, thought he had laid to eternal sleep. But I believe that Shipton would have found much to admire in Ziff's book. The observations upon the provinciality of Benjamin Colman (who is presented as the New England version of Isaac Watts) are valid—and entertaining. They also illustrate one of the book's faults, its use of sweeping generalizations. Ziff credits Colman's English friend, Elizabeth Rowe, with beginning the religious sentimental tradition so hilariously burlesqued in Mark Twain's "Ode to Stephen Dowling Bots, Dec'd" by Emmiline Grangerford. The tradition, however, existed before Elizabeth Rowe took it up, as the splendid burlesque by Jonathan Swift, *A Meditation upon a Broom Stick* (1710), demonstrates. Disregarding Powhatan, Ziff has Miantanimo "first" sound "the unavailing call for Indian union in the face of European ferocity" (p. 93). Disregarding Maryland, Ziff calls Rhode Island "the first tolerating state in the English-speaking world" (p. 104). But Ziff has numerous excellencies, including passages of splendidly clear exposition of complicated historical events (e.g., what lay at stake in the meetings of the Synods), sensitive portrayals of cultural values in conflict (e.g., the achieved brotherhood of Benjamin Church and Annawon, opposing leaders in King Philip's War), and instances of keen literary sensitivity (e.g., on New England's climate as metaphor). Most colonialists will be irritated by Ziff's statement that Edward Taylor's "modern fame derives in great part from the historical fact that nobody else in the America of his day produced verse of that quality" (p. 258), for he implies that if Taylor were an English poet, he would justly be ignored. But Taylor's contemporaries Thomas Traherne and Henry Vaughan—both far less complex and less interesting than Taylor—are duly celebrated for their poetic attainments. Ziff's book is not primarily a theological, literary, economic, political, institutional, social, imperial, intellectual, or historical study of American Puritanism—but it is all of these at once. Because it is so all-encompassing, it has weaknesses—but no one before Ziff has so successfully treated so many aspects of New England Puritanism as a unified whole.

Ursula Brumm's interpretive critical and bibliographical monograph, *Puritanismus und Literatur in Amerika* (Darmstadt, Wissenschaftliche Buchgesellschaft) is now the best single guide to both the scholarship and recent interpretations of American Puritanism, from 1620 to 1760. In addition to individual sections (and long bibliographical notes) dealing with the major and minor writers from William Bradford to Jonathan Edwards, Brumm treats puritan history, theology, and culture, and surveys the influence of Puritanism on later American literature. Less comprehensive and less detailed than Brumm is Emil Oberholzer's "Puritanism Revisited," in Alden T. Vaughan and George Athan Billias, eds., *Perspectives on Early American History: Essays in Honor of Richard B. Morris* (New

York, Harper & Row). Oberholzer's survey has special value in isolating a number of vexing questions in Puritan historiography. But Michael D. Hall's critico-bibliographical essay covered roughly the same ground as Oberholzer, and did it better: "Understanding the Puritans," in Herbert J. Bass, ed., *The State of American History* (Chicago, Quadrangle Books), pp. 330–49.

Although Hall played down both the importance of Ramistic logic in the Puritan mind and the value of a thorough understanding of Ramistic logic in analyzing American Puritan theology ("Understanding the Puritans," pp. 333–34), his opinion has now been superseded by David L. Parker's article "Petrus Ramus and the Puritans: The 'Logic' of Preparationist Conversion Doctrine," *EAL* 8:140–62. Only Leon Howard, in his brief chapters devoted to the 17th and 18th centuries in *Literature and the American Tradition* (New York, Doubleday, 1960), has matched Parker's perceptive view of the influence that the reasoning process has upon the writings (and the character) of a people. If Michael Kammen, in his provocative study *People of Paradox: An Inquiry Concerning the Origins of American Civilization* (New York, Knopf, [1972]) had enjoyed the advantage of reading Parker's essay in manuscript (or Howard's book in print), he might have been able to ground his generalizations about the paradoxes of American civilization in the basic ways of thinking (by dichotomization, schematization, contrast, and contrariety) of the earliest Americans. What Parker does is to prove that Thomas Hooker and Thomas Shepard were both Ramists (i.e., they both reasoned according to the system of Ramistic logic) and to show how this method of reasoning enabled these dominant American Puritan theologians to go beyond Calvin in analyzing the conversion process. They both argued for the individual's necessity of preparation for salvation and were able, by Ramistic logic, to anatomize the nature of the preparatory stages of conversion. Parker's article is thus a necessary supplement to the standard work by Norman Pettit on the Puritan doctrine of conversion, *The Heart Prepared: Grace and Conversion in Puritan Spiritual Life* (New Haven, Yale Univ. Press, [1966]).

J. Rodney Fulcher, in "Puritans and the Passions: The Faculty Psychology in American Puritanism," *JHBS* 9:123–39, surveys the background of faculty psychology in American Puritanism, tracing the tradition from Aristotle, Thomas Aquinas, Pierre de la Primaudaye, and, in the 17th century, Edward Reynolds, Descartes, and Hobbes, before turning to the American Puritans. He shows how Thomas Shepard places more emphasis on the role of the affections than either Thomas Hooker or the rationalist Samuel Willard, and suggests that it was Shepard's attention to the affections that made him especially useful to Jonathan Edwards in revising the psychology underlying the Puritan morphology of conversion. Unfortunately, Fulcher's overview was evidently written and accepted for publication before the appearance of Norman S. Fiering's more discriminating study, "Will and Intellect in the New England Mind" (see *ALS 1972*, p. 158), but Fulcher could have consulted William J. Scheick on Taylor's faculty psychology (see *ALS 1970*, p. 152).

Turning to individual studies on the earliest American Puritans, we encounter Robert Daly's essay on "William Bradford's Vision of History" (*AL* 44:557–69). Daly argues that Bradford, following John Foxe, uses Eusebian providential history rather than Augustinian stasis. He explains Bradford's selection of contents as a reflection of his Deuteronomic Formula (i.e., a sense of special destiny). But when, after 1632, the evidence that Bradford saw pointed to a failure of Plymouth Colony's special mission as an example to America and England, Bradford gradually changed the tone from one of confidence to lament, and came to regard the history as private, rather than public. The change, according to Daly, was demanded by Bradford's adherence to truth, seen through Eusebian historiography. Bradford's talented and pleasure-loving opponent, Thomas Morton, is the subject of a terse note by William J. Scheick ("Morton's *New English Canaan*," *Expl* 31: item 47), who believes that Thomas Morton compares his book to the Trojan horse, hoping that the book will cause the downfall of the Plymouth Puritans by its appeal to the King. And Keith L. Sprunger, in "The Dutch Career of Thomas Hooker" (*NEQ* 46:17–44) traces this founding Puritan's difficulties with the Rev. John Paget and the Dutch classis in Amsterdam, and notes Hooker's developing congregationalism under the influence of the Rev. John Forbes at Delft.

There are a number of welcome studies on the puritan American poets. Using the allegorical meanings as established in the Quaternions as a gloss for the hermeneutics of "Contemplations," Anne Hildebrand ("Anne Bradstreet's Quarternions and 'Contemplations,'" *EAL* 8:116–25) argues that "Contemplations" rejects nature and turns to God in images based upon classical and medieval traditions. Hildebrand's thesis seems valid enough, though I believe that the numerous Biblical echoes in "Contemplations" are more important to an understanding of this splendid spiritual autobiography than are the medieval schemes of the Quarternions. Edwin T. Bowden makes a case for combining the esthetic approach to a work of art with the historical and cultural in "Urian Oakes' Elegy: Colonial Literature and History" (*ForumH* 10,ii[1972]:2–8). Bowden comments on the metaphysical quality of Oakes's wit, identifies a few classical and Biblical allusions, remarks on the imagery, and claims that the "general movement" of the *Elegie on Thomas Shepard* warns Americans of the failure of the American puritan experiment. Bowden also finds that Oakes makes "a clear statement of the Puritan theory of simplicity and directness in verse, not just the Augustinian refusal of artificial heightening but a deliberate choice–in origin a rich mixture of the esthetic, the utilitarian and the theological–of the direct and the immediate in style, the parallel of the 'plain style' in prose." But, in an excellent essay with more attention to detail, T. G. Hahn ("Urian Oakes's *Elegie on Thomas Shepard* and Puritan Poetics," *AL* 45:163–81) traces various Renaissance elegaic topoi in Oakes's elegy, comments on his use of rhetorical figures and commonplaces, and notes in passing an echo of Edmund Spenser's *November Eclogue.* Hahn identifies numerous Biblical allusions before, in view of the pervasive classical and humanistic traditions in the elegy, questioning the validity of the usual generalizations concerning the puritan esthetic. I believe that Hahn proves his case with regard to Urian Oakes. But American Puritans did not subscribe to a monolithic puritan esthetic. And we should expect Oakes, who was New England's most famous classicist, to reflect classical and Renaissance learning–along with Biblical–in his poetry. Another (see *ALS 1972*, p. 162) of Oakes's Latin speeches has been painstakingly edited by the expert Leo M. Kaiser ("Tercentenary of an Oration: the 1672 Commencement Address of Urian Oakes," *HLB* 21:75–87). Oakes had returned from England the year before, and in the Commencement address of 1672 welcomed Leonard Hoar as the new president of Harvard. As usual, Kaiser splendidly annotates the numerous classical allusions.

Two notes concern the influence of major English poets on American puritan poets. Robert D. Arner finds that Nehemiah Walter echoes Milton in a 1688 (Arner uses the Old Style dating, 1687) blank-verse elegy ("Nehemiah Walter: Milton's Earliest American Disciple?" *EAL* 8:62–65). And Jessie A. Coffin ("Arcadia to America: Sir Philip Sidney and John Saffin," *AL* 45:100–04) shows that the 71 maxims in John Saffin's commonplace book are adapted from Sidney's *Arcadia.* In a study of "The Pastoral and the Primitive in Benjamin Tompson's 'Address to Lord Bellamont'" (*EAL* 8:111–16), Neil T. Eckstein suggests that the classical echoes in Tompson's 1699 occasional poem welcoming Lord Bellamont as Governor of Massachusetts reflect "a fairly accurate bell-weather of prevailing English taste," while criticizing Tompson's imagery for lacking "the studied polish of John Dryden." Eckstein seems to me to miss the point. Tompson is joking about the clash of Virgilian super-civilized pastoral traditions with the real primitivism of America. And when Tompson calls America an Eden rather than Arcadia (cf. p. 113), he is no more reflecting the "Bible Commonwealth" than are the writers of the Southern and Middle colonies when they use the same imagery. They all use the common traditions of promotion literature.

Two final pieces devoted to the poets are editions. Leo M. Kaiser ("Three Hymns Attributed to George Moxon," *EAL* 8:104–10) edits the hymns and suggests that the second one, dated "Novem. 1670," may be a Thanksgiving Day poem. And Diane Bornstein has edited Philip Walker's poem on King Philip's War, "probably written" just after Michael Pierce's defeat on March 26, 1676 ("'Captain Perse & his coragios Company': Philip Walker," *PAAS* 83:67–102). Bornstein points out that Walker echoes Benjamin Tompson's *New England's Crisis* (Boston, 1676) and possibly Tompson's *New Englands Tears* (London, 1676), as well as John Foxe's *Acts and Monuments* and the Bible. She emphasizes Walker's debt to the genre of the broadside ballad and discusses his phonetic spelling.

Harold Jantz's learned and engaging essay ("America's First Cosmopolitan," *PMHS* 84[1972]:3–25) calls attention to a hitherto-unknown Latin edition of the collected works of the American alchemist "Eirenaeus Philaletha Cosmopolita," *Anonymi Philalethae Opera omnia* (Modena, Italy, 1695). Jantz shows that one of the components ("Cabala, Speculum Artix, et Naturae, in Alchemia") of the volume was not by the Cosmopolite (Jantz's name for "Cosmopolita") but a Latin version of the German *Cabala, Spiegel der Kunst und Natur: in Alchyinia* (Augsburg, 1615). Jantz reaffirms the standard identification of "Eirenaeus Philoponos Philalethus" as George Starkey and argues that Starkey may also have been the Cosmopolite. In passing, Jantz comments on the European travels of John Winthrop II, and calls attention to a previously overlooked account of Winthrop by his contemporary, Johann Rist.

Roger Williams was well-served in 1973 by the appearance of an annotated critical edition of *A Key into the Language of America*, ed. by John J. Teunissen and Evelyn J. Hinz (Detroit: Wayne State Univ. Press). The long introduction includes a brief biographical sketch of Williams and an appreciation of *A Key's* literary quality, emphasizing Williams's use of the emblematic mode. The textual notes include substantive differences among all later editions, and the commentary valuably glosses allusions and obscure passages. Teunissen and Hinz have also treated "Roger Williams, St. Paul, and American Primitivism" (*CRevAS* 4:121–36), claiming that Williams viewed himself as a Pauline figure, that he thought of his attempts to convert the Indians in terms of Paul's attempt to convert the Gentiles, and that his primitivism in *A Key* reflects Paul's attitude toward the Gentiles.

Seymour Van Dyken's *Samuel Willard, 1640–1707: Preacher of Orthodoxy in an Era of Change* (Grand Rapids, Michigan, Eerdmans Publishing Co., [1972]) presents a valuable biography of Willard, whose elaborate *Compleat Body of Divinity* (Boston, 1726) is the summa theologica of American Puritanism. Van Dyken discusses Willard's position in various major controversies, but does not analyze Willard's greatest work, the *Compleat Body*. Although Willard's younger contemporaries are quoted in a brief appreciation of "Willard as Preacher" (pp. 40–44), Van Dyken does not himself examine Willard's effectiveness as a preacher or as a stylist. And I can not really believe that Willard was always so "moderate" and wise as Van Dyken presents him—nor that his occasional opponents, such as Increase Mather, were so "conservative."

Everett Emerson and Mason I. Lowance, Jr., point out that the existence of a previously unknown manuscript by Increase Mather ("Increase Mather's Confutation of Solomon Stoddard's 'Observations Respecting the Lord's Supper,' 1680," *PAAS* 83:29–65) testifies that the controversy over admission to the Lord's Supper crystalized at the Synod of 1679, rather than, as has been generally supposed, in the first decade of the 18th century. Emerson and Lowance edit the document from a transcription made by Cotton Mather, evidently after 1700. Since they published the manuscript, William L. Joyce reports finding Increase Mather's original (*PAAS* 83:343–44). The theology of Solomon Stoddard is carefully analysed by Paul R. Lucas ("'An Appeal to the Learned': The Mind of Solomon Stoddard," *WMQ* 30: 257–92). Lucas shows that Stoddard did not have widespread support. Even among other New England Presbyterians, Stoddard stood practically alone in his repudiation of Reformation ecclesiology, in his espousal of Old Testament discipline, and in his argument for institutionalized salvation through converting ordinances. Lucas finds the heart of Stoddard's early individualism in his concept of an Instituted Church; and he believes that Stoddard changed (or, at least, appeared to change) his opinion after 1712, when Stoddard portrayed the efficacious sermon as the means of conversion. Thus Stoddard adopted, in his last years, an evangelical position and looked on Paul and the Pauline epistles as his archetype and guide. Lucas, whose article supersedes Perry Miller's treatment as the best brief guide to Stoddard's theology, comments on the opposition of Edward Taylor and the Mathers.

Bartlett Jere Whiting gives a foretaste of his collection of the proverbs of early America in a listing of the "Proverbs in Cotton Mather's *Magnalia Christi Americana*" (*NM* 73 [1972]:477–84). Robert Brunkow says the obvious about Mather's "religious-oriented philosophy of history" in "An Analysis of Cotton Mather's Understanding of the Relationship of the Supernatural to Man as Seen in History" (*HMPEC* 42:319–29). And Pershing Vartanian adds nothing to what Clifford K. Shipton and Theodore Hornberger have already told us about "Cotton Mather and the Puritan Transition into the Enlightenment" (*EAL* 7:213–24).

Two articles comment on the Indian captivity. David L. Minter's appreciation of the achievement of Mary Rowlandson ("By Dens of Lions: Notes on Stylization in Early Puritan Captivity Narratives," *AL* 45:335–47) shows that her tract is both exemplary for others and an examination of her own experience for its evidence of her salvation. Although Minter does not mention the genre of the spiritual autobiography, what he has done is to show how the earliest puritan captivity narratives reflect the subject and technique of that dominant puritan literary genre. Like Kathryn Whitford (see *ALS 1972*, p. 183), Robert D. Arner surveys the story of Hannah Dustin (who murdered her sleeping Indian captors) as presented by Cotton Mather and later writers ("The Story of Hannah Dustin: Cotton Mather to Thoreau," *ATQ* 18:19–23).

iii. The South

Literature and Society in Early Virginia, 1608–1840 (Baton Rouge, La. State Univ. Press) gathers together a number of essays by Richard Beale Davis on George Sandys, William Fitzhugh, Arthur Blackamore, William Byrd, Samuel Davies, James Reid, Thomas Jefferson, William Munford, and Francis Walker Gilmer. Davis treats such general topics as letter-writers in 17th-century Virginia, witchcraft in the colonial South, the Shenandoah Valley as a subject of topographical writing, and the pre-Revolutionary culture of Virginia. His essay herein reprinted on "The Intellectual Golden Age in the Colonial Chesapeake Bay Country" (see *ALS 1970*, p. 159) provides much of the evidence used by David Curtis Skaggs, in "Thomas Cradock and the Chesapeake Golden Age" (*WMQ* 30:93–116). Skaggs describes the life and writings of Thomas Cradock, with brief notes on his numerous extant manuscript sermons, an interesting description of his satirical "Maryland Eclogues in Imitation of Vergil's," his hymns, and his poetic versions of the psalms. Skaggs quarrels with the aspersions cast on Southern colonial culture by Carl Bridenbaugh, Daniel Boorstin, and others, but speaks of "the imitative nature of Chesapeake literati." The fact is that the second-rate writers of early America were no more imitative than the second-rate writers of England. James Ralph in England had no more or less talent than James Ralph in America—he did have more opportunity to publish. The comparisons of Boorstin and Bridenbaugh, however, are to the New England colonies, not to England. And Skaggs, along with most authorities on Southern culture, would readily concede that New England, in the 17th century, had a more vital and active intellectual and theological tradition than the South. But the balance gradually became less lop-sided in the early 18th century.

Robert D. Arner attributes to John Smith, rather than the Rev. William Symonds, the passage in *The General History of Virginia* concerning cannibalism ("such a dish as powdered wife I never heard of") and then examines the subsequent black humor of cannibalism in American literature from George Alsop to Mark Twain

("John Smith, the 'Starving Time,' and the Genesis of Southern Humor: Variations on a Theme," *LaS* 12:383–90). And in "A Note on John Hammond's *Leah and Rachel*" (*SLJ* 6,i:77–80), Arner examines the implications for Hammond's promotion tract of the Biblical imagery of the title, pointing out that the story of Jacob in Genesis furnishes parallels to two subjects treated by Hammond, the indentured servant experience and the American Dream.

Knox Mellon, Jr., presents an excellent biographical sketch of Christian Gottlieb Priber (1697–1744?), a German who took an L.L.D. at Erfurt University in 1722, was forced to flee Western society because of his utopian beliefs, emigrated to South Carolina by the fall of 1735, and attempted to set up his utopia in Cherokee Territory ("Christian Priber's Cherokee 'Kingdom of Paradise,'" *GHQ* 57:319–31). Because Priber, by his shrewd advice to the Cherokees, became a threat to the imperial ambitions of the English and French, he was hunted by both nations, finally captured by the English, and evidently died in prison in Georgia. "Americanus," who wrote the first account of "Priber, A Jesuit Missionary" in the *London Magazine* for September, 1760 (and whose identity puzzles Mellon), was Edward Kimber, then editor of the *London Magazine*, and formerly a traveller in America. And the sermons preached before the Trustees of Georgia in London are surveyed as "full fledged, full bodied apologia for aspects of Trusteeship Policy" by Phinizy Spalding, who concludes with a bibliography of them ("Some Sermons Before the Trustees of Colonial Georgia," *GHQ* 57:332–46).

iv. Franklin and the American Enlightenment

The year 1770 was another incredibly busy one in the life of Franklin, as William B. Willcox, ed., *The Papers of Benjamin Franklin*, vol. 17 (New Haven: Yale Univ. Press) documents. The literary highlights include Franklin in a variety of tones—from the delightful mock-heroic of his burlesque of the newspaper reporting of the English court, "The Cravenstreet Gazette" (wherein Franklin portrays himself both as the flirtatious "Dr. Fatsides" and as the hopelessly unreformed Head of State), to the ruthless opponent of English policy in America (publishing such American propaganda in the colonial newspapers as "Every Englishman considers himself as King of America," p. 214). There is Franklin urging the Americans to continue their nonimportation agreements: "if we do not now persist in this Measure till it has had its full Effect, it can never again be used on any future Occasion with the least prospect of Success, and . . . if we do persist another year, we shall never afterwards have occasion to use it" (p. 113). And there is Franklin irascibly annotating his copies of British pamphlets on the colonies: "Infamous Lie! . . . False . . . An absolute Lie . . . A vile Lie . . . Ignorance! . . . Another infamous Lie! . . . you lying Villain!" (pp. 372–74). Regretably, the editors are no longer attempting to list contemporary publication and republication of Franklin's propaganda (though Verner Crane includes such information in his edition of *Franklin's Letters to the Press*, 1950), so that the *Papers* are an incomplete guide to the contemporaneous effect of Franklin's writings. And, even more regretably, the writings are sometimes reprinted from Crane's edition, even though the original publications are extant.

James A. Sappenfield's *A Sweet Instruction: Franklin's Journalism as a Literary Apprenticeship* (Carbondale: So. Ill. Univ. Press) devotes major attention to the Silence Dogood essays, the Busy Body essays, the *Poor Richard* almanacs, and the *Autobiography*. On all these, Sappenfield has insights, but the reader is generally disappointed: partially because (as Alfred Owen Aldridge has pointed out in *WMQ*, 31 [1974]:522–24) the scholarship is so thin. In an excellent article ("The Rhetorical Strategy of Franklin's 'Way to Wealth,'" *ECS* 6:475–85), Edward J. Gallagher analyzes the dramatic movement within Franklin's famous skit "The Way to Wealth." Gallagher believes that the opening and closing frame "is the most important part of the essay." He argues that when the crowd present at the sale approves the doctrine of Father Abraham's speech but immediately practices the contrary, the reader deems the people fools, thus making "a spontaneous judgment which commits him to the validity of the doctrine." Gallagher notes that the strategic shift in the last sentence has great force because it is, paradoxically, both unexpected and well prepared for.

In his usual graceful and shrewd prose, Lewis Leary ("Benjamin Franklin," in *Comic Imagination*, pp. 33–47) stresses Franklin's mastery of tones and personnae, his "tumultuous energy," and the revelations in the private letters, "which allow glimpses behind the familiar mask of doughty Ben Franklin to the intelligence and artistry that molded its features so well." Verner W. Crane first pointed out ("Dr.

Franklin's Plan for America," *MAQR* 64 [1958]:322–33) that Franklin "seems to have been the first to rationalize the westward movement into something like a frontier thesis," and quoted Franklin's 1752 view of the America of the future as "Settlements between the Atlantick and the Pacifick Oceans." Now James H. Hutson's "Benjamin Franklin and the West" (*WHQ* 4:425–34) surveys Franklin's many ties with the frontier: his theorizing on the influence of the frontier (especially his influential theory that the population of America doubled every 20 years because of the *lebensraum*); his successful attempts to win frontier lands, first for the British Empire in America and later for the fledgling United States; his attitudes toward the Indians (though Hutson does not sufficiently consider Franklin's audience and occasion before generalizing about Franklin's attitudes toward the Indians); and his own involvement in attempts to gain Western land. Another article that repeats what Verner Crane had already told us (in "Franklin and the Stamp Act," *PCSM* 32 [1937]:56–77) is Kirk Willis's "The Background of Benjamin Franklin's Imperial Apostasy, 1751–1766" (*PH* 40:123–36), which comments on the significance of Franklin's private marginalia, where one does not have to take into consideration Franklin's audience.

In an undocumented but convincing essay, Melvin H. Buxbaum ("Hume, Franklin and America: A Matter of Loyalties," *EnlE* 3 [1972]:93–105) claims that Franklin and Hume fell out in 1771, that Hume sided with Alexander Wedderburn, who excoriated Franklin in the House of Lords, and that Hume's attitude toward the colonies was based upon "his notions of what was best for English Establishmentarian interests." Max Hall engagingly recounts the story of his research for his *Benjamin Franklin and Polly Baker* (1960) in "An Amateur Detective on the Trail of B. Franklin, Hoaxer," *PMHS* 84 [1972]:26–43. Although marred by an inadequate knowledge of Franklin and of Franklin scholarship, John H. McLaughlin's "His Brother's Keeper: Franklin's Sibling Rivalry" (*SAB* 38,iv:62–69), which attributes Franklin's early drive for wealth and learning to his earliest disappointments and to his rivalry with his brother James, has considerable validity. I would go further, and blame too his early anti-clericalism on his disappointment at being denied an education (he recalls hearing his father's reasons for taking him out of school in the *Autobiography*) which in turn deprived him of the possibility of becoming a clergyman and doomed him (as it seemed to him at the time) to the role of a "Tallow Chandler." And Richard VanDerBeets ("Milton in Early America: The Example of Benjamin Franklin," *MiltonQ* 6, ii [1972]:33–36) gathers a number of Franklin's references and allusions to Milton, but he ignores both the *New England Courant* and the *Pennsylvania Gazette*, though Albert Matthews briefly commented on the former in his article, "Knowledge of Milton in Early New England," *Nation* 87 [1908]:624–25, 650.

A number of essays reflect American participation in Enlightenment ideas. William D. Andrews examines "The Literature of the 1727 New England Earthquake" (*EAL* 7:281–94) for the explanations of the causes of the earthquakes and the theological positions of the ministers who preached about them. He finds, contrary to the usual supposition, that the Boston ministry was more old-fashioned and traditional in its theological and social ideas than its rural counterpart. Andrews also has pointed out that the Rev. William Smith (best known as Provost of Franklin's Philadelphia Academy) used the *translatio* theme (i.e., the supposed westward movement of civilization) in a poem published in *Some Thoughts on Education* (1752). He calls attention to Smith's quandary, for the "rising glory of America" necessarily implies the decline of England; and Smith was an Anglophile. Some Americans earlier than Smith who used the theme (Cotton Mather and Richard Lewis come to mind) were, contrary to Andrews, bolder than Smith ("William Smith and the Rising Glory of America," *EAL* 8:33–43).

Robert G. Weyant ("Helvetius and Jefferson: Studies of Human Nature and Government in the Eighteenth Century," *JHBS* 9:29–41) briefly sketches two attitudes toward human nature in the 18th century: the first, that human nature was egocentric, is the position of Claude Adrien Helvetius (whose widow was the recipient of Franklin's proposition in the form of a bagatelle, "The Elysian Fields") and of Jeremy Bentham; the second, that human nature is sociocentric, is the thesis of the Third Earl of Shaftesbury, of the Scottish moralists, and of Jefferson. Weyant claims that the egocentric philosophy of human nature involves belief in the determination of individual behavior by environmental circumstances and thus supports a theory of strong central government which structures the environment of its citizens for their own benefit. On the other hand, the sociocentric philosophy of human nature implies that the citizen will naturally (because of his "moral sense") behave decently to his neighbor.

Thus a weak government best allows men to exercise their natural goodness. Robert M. Benton in "The John Winthrops and Developing Scientific Thought in New England" (*EAL* 7:272–80) ignores the best scholarship on the subject in his brief survey. Vern L. Bullough describes the pseudonymous *Aristotle's Masterpiece*, a popular sex manual of the 18th century ("An Early American Sex Manual, or, Aristotle Who?," *EAL* 7:236–46), and Joan Hoff Wilson ("Dancing Dogs of the Colonial Period: Women Scientists," *EAL* 7:225–35) comments on the "patrician sexism" of colonial America.

v. Edwards and the Great Awakening

Clyde A. Holbrook's *The Ethics of Jonathan Edwards: Morality and Aesthetics* (Ann Arbor, Univ. of Mich. Press) deals with Edwards's thoughts concerning natural morality (i.e., secondary virtue or morality without grace), practical morality (social problems), true virtue (i.e., morality with grace), and aesthetics. The technique employed by Holbrook is to frame a series of theological definitions and then to question Edwards's writings in light of these definitions. The trouble is, that although the definitions of theological objectivism (the all-importance of God), theological subjectivism (a focus on man—while not denying God), and theological utilitarianism (man's self-interest) seem to involve important distinctions, they are not the primary subjects of theology in Edwards's day. I find the book more concerned with a modern theological understanding of Edwards than with his relation to other puritan theologians or to Enlightenment ideas. Those interested in Jonathan Edwards's own ideas would be better advised to read Perry Miller, Edward H. Davidson, Alfred Owen Aldridge, or Roland A. Delattre. An article concerned with "Jonathan Edwards as a Literary Artist" (*Crit* 15:156–73) by John Griffith begins by rehearsing some of the contemporary approaches to Edwards, and argues that he should be considered primarily as a writer. To prove his case, Griffith examines the "Personal Narrative," saying that Edwards did not write it as a model for others but as ritual, "a literary act of worship more than an act of communication." His examination of *The Nature of True Virtue* argues that the "treatise becomes a logician's rendering of the mystical sense of life's radical oneness."

Two articles deal with Edwards and Newtonian science. In "Jonathan Edwards' Optics: Images and Metaphors in Some of his Major Works" (*EAL* 7:21–32), Ron Loewinsohn points out the general influence of Newton's *Optics* on Edwards before claiming that Edwards distinguishes between "the physical, mechanical aspect of reality" seen by sinners, and the "whole of light," spiritual as well as physical, seen by the saints. The article is marred by such undocumented (and false) generalizations as in "the Age of Reason men felt themselves estranged from nature." Richard Lewis's "A Journey from Patapsco to Annapolis" is one American exception that comes to mind in rebuttal to Loewinsohn's claim that "Not until Wordsworth's 'Evening Walk' (1787) do we get a landscape poem in which the poet is described as being *in* the world he presents, participating in and being directly affected by the world." Jean-Pierre Martin's essay, "Edwards' Epistemology and the New Science" (*EAL* 7:247–55) maintains (without refuting the relevant scholarship, or even citing it) that the new science had little effect on Edwards. He argues that Edwards's epistemology descends from the Ockhamist tradition through Calvin to Edwards, and concludes that "the greatness of Edwards may reside in his effort to solve the Kierkegaardian antinomy between the esthetic and theological degrees of consciousness, not by any new scientific method but by the harmonies of an inherited epistemology."

And two articles continued Perry Miller's thoughts on the relationship of Edwards to later American literature. Mason I. Lowance, Jr., is more concerned with the use of archetypal symbolism (especially the circle) in Edwards and later writers than with the influence of Edwards (or Puritanism or typology) on Emerson and Thoreau ("From Edwards to Emerson to Thoreau: A Revaluation," *ATQ* 18:3–12). And William H. Parker has written an undocumented, pretentious article on "Jonathan Edwards: Founder of the Counter-Tradition of Transcendental Thought in America" (*GaR* 27:543–49), which contains such nonsense as "Edwards is the voice who first warns of the weakening of the religious impulse in American society."

Happily, there are three good pieces on Edwards's contemporaries. In "An Anglican Critique of the Early Phase of the Great Awakening in New England: A Letter by Timothy Cutler" (*WMQ* 30:475–88), Douglas C. Stenerson prints, with an introduction and notes, Cutler's letter of May 28, 1739, on Edwards's *Faithful Narrative*, where Cutler gives a prejudiced evaluation of Edwards's efforts to initiate a revival. Basing his brief overview mainly upon the writings of Samuel Davies, Gilbert Tennent, and Ebenezer Pemberton, Glen T. Miller ("God's Light and Man's Enlightenment: Evangelical Theology of Colonial Presbyterianism," *JPH* 51:97–115) isolates four characteristics of the group of ministers with whom Edwards was identified by his contemporaries. These ministers generally (although Miller himself supplies examples where these positions are contradicted) reveal a consensus about the importance of (1) the light of nature and of rational experience; (2) the esthetic experience of religion; (3) morality, emphasizing self-denial and love; and (4) the centrality of the conversion experience, as well as its most important functions. Finally, in clear expository prose, Craig Gilborn relates the difficulties of the Calvinistic Samuel Davies and William Tennant in collecting funds for the infant Princeton from the liberal English dissenters ("The Reverend Samuel Davies in Great Britain," *WP* 8:45–62).

vi. The Revolutionary Period

Lyman H. Butterfield and Marc Friedlaender have splendidly edited the *Adams Family Correspondence* for April 1778 to September 1782 (vols. 3 and 4 of the "Family Correspondence" of *The Adams Papers*; Cambridge, Mass., Harvard Univ. Press). Abigail Adams is the hero in these volumes. Invariably interesting, she is the Anne Bradstreet of letter writers. Her concerns about her house and family are charming; her literary interests and knowledge are extensive; she complains about the role allotted women; and I even enjoy her foibles—both her identification with John Adams's pettinesses (especially when in the shade of Franklin) and her literary flirtations (how much duller the world would be without flirtation) with John Lovell. Of couse John Adams is fascinating, partially because he is so often fascinated, because he is always thinking, working, and trying, and because he was a major actor in the great events of his day. The literary scholar could wish that more of the quotations were identified—and that unidentified references and allusions might be cited as such in the otherwise excellent index. Adams's good friend, Benjamin Waterhouse, is the subject of a note ("Benjamin Waterhouse and Junius," *AN&Q* 11:131–32) by Francesco Cordasco on Waterhouse's *An Essay on Junius and his Letters* (1831). Cordasco maintains that the real significance of Waterhouse's *Essay*, which argued that William Pitt, First Earl of Chatham, was Junius, lies in its "search for the historical precedents which justified" the American Revolution. I might mention that *contra* Cordasco, Waterhouse was not a "liberal Jeffersonian": see the fine note on him by Butterfield and Friedlaender in the *Adams Family Correspondence*, 4:32–34.

The penman of the American Revolution, Thomas Paine, is the subject of two articles. In "The Moral Economics of Tom Paine" (*JHI* 34:367–80), William Christian says that Paine "alone of the reformers and radicals broke with the notion that government could only play a role in restraining the people, and advanced the suggestion that it could play a continuing role after the revolution." Winthrop D. Jordan's far-fetched and one-sided argument ("Familial Politics: Thomas Paine and the Killing of the King, 1776," *JAH* 60:294–308) claims that the "subliminal" appeal of *Common Sense* is to the latent psychological desire to kill the father. He ends on an ironic note by pointing out that "the sons of the Revolution soon lapsed into acclaiming their staunchest leader as the Father of His Country." Jordan ignores the fact that the Americans were, in part, responding to the British paranoia about America: to adopt Jordan's approach, one may say that the Americans were only responding to the British efforts to stifle the child before it grew too powerful for them.

Lewis P. Simpson's thoughtful essay, "The Satiric Mode: The Early National Wits" (*Comic Imagination*, pp. 49–61) opposes the deliberative mode of the Federalist Papers, the Constitution, and other documents of the genesis of the American Republic, to the "apocalyptic style" characteristic of the satire (and much other writing) of the day. He points out how much of the satiric poetry produced by Philip Freneau, John Trumbull, and Joel Barlow is in the apocalyptic mode, torn between the "millennial and doomsday attitudes toward American history." He asks why the American satirists lacked the sense of ironic humor of their great English models of the neoclassic period, and suggests that the answer lies in the equalitarian, democratic nature of American society. Hugh Henry Brackenridge, in *Modern Chivalry*, tried to answer the question, but finally failed to understand that the Republic of Letters was not synonymous with the Republic of America.

Satire is the subject of Lester B. Scherer's "A New Look at *Per-*

sonal Slavery Established" (*WMQ* 30:645–52). Scherer claims that this ostensible attack on Benjamin Rush's *Address Upon Slave-Keeping* really satirizes Richard Nisbet's pro-slavery *Slavery Not Forbidden by Scripture* (1773). Scherer compares it to a satire in the November 15, 1773, *Pennsylvania Packet*, and suggests that both it and the newspaper piece may be by Benjamin Rush. Robert D. Arner, "Daniel Coe to Thomas Shreeve: Primitivism in Satire" (*SLN* 10,ii:80–82), prints Coe's *Address to Mr. Thomas Shreeve* (1772) as an example of primitive satire, which "resembles nothing so much as a curse." The career of one of the great book and manuscript collectors of the Revolutionary period, who was appointed "Historiographer" by the Continental Congress, is surveyed by Paul G. Sifton ("A Disordered Life: The American Career of Pierre Eugène Du Simitière," *MSS* 25:235–53). And several letters by Bernard Romans, author of *A Concise Natural History of East and West Florida* (1775) to the English botanist, John Ellis, are printed by John D. Ware ("The Bernard Romans–John Ellis Letters, 1772–1774," *FHQ* 52,ii: 51–61).

Although Irwin Silber's *Songs of Independence* (Harrisburg, Stackpole Books) devotes a brief chapter to songs about America before the Revolutionary Period and another to songs following the Revolution (through 1812), it is essentially an anthology of Revolutionary songs. Silber evidently does not know the best previous work on American ballads of the colonial period, Charles H. Firth's *An American Garland* (Oxford, Blackwell, 1915), and he relies too heavily upon secondary sources (especially Frank Moore's *Songs and Ballads of the American Revolution*, 1855). But his book is now the best anthology available of early American songs. Silber, however, lacks a "feel" for the stylistic differences between late 18th- and mid-19th-century songs: to my judgment, the song "Mad Anthony Wayne," pp. 100–01, is clearly not contemporary with the American Revolution, and I would guess that it dates from the mid-19th century. An anthology of key political documents from the Old Dominion is Robert L. Scribner, ed., *Revolutionary Virginia 1763–1774. A Documentary Record* (Charlottesville: Univ. Press of Va.). It contains such pieces as Patrick Henry's Stamp Act Resolutions (the variant texts should have been gathered here and printed); Richard Bland's *An Inquiry Into the Rights of the British Colonies* (1766); selections from Thomson Mason's "British American" essays; and

Thomas Jefferson's *Summary View of the Rights of British America.* I wish that some attention were paid to the belletristic writings (particularly the poetry of Robert Bolling and Thomas Burke), but that was not the editor's purpose.

Catherine S. Crary's valuable loyalist anthology, *The Price of Loyalty: Tory Writings from the Revolutionary Era* (New York: McGraw-Hill), surveys the most dramatic events of the Revolution, emphasizing the plight of the Tories. The esthetic excellence of the writings was not a primary consideration in the selection; and from a literary point of view, there are too many snippets and oversights. The Loyalist poets are ignored. Nor is there any prose by Jonathan Boucher or John Randolph—two of the best Southern prose writers. But this scholarly, well-indexed, and fresh selection of Loyalist writings vividly presents the dilemmas of the American Loyalists. A major source of information on the ex-patriot loyalists, a valuable guide to England, and an entertaining diary is *The Journal of Samuel Curwen, Loyalist* (2 vols. Cambridge, Mass., Harvard Univ. Press), now well edited by Andrew Oliver. Curwen's American identity makes him resent slurs on the American patriots, even though he expected the English to defeat his old companions (p. 221). On the other hand, Curwen becomes upset when in the company of someone too "American" (p. 225). Curwen's letters are not printed in this edition, though extracts from them are given in the editor's notes, which unfortunately neglect—as is too usual—literary allusions.

Gordon E. Kershaw's "A Question of Orthodoxy: Religious Controversy in a Speculative Land Company" (*NEQ* 46:205–35) sheds light on the early career of the Anglican minister and Loyalist poet Jacob Bailey. George Athan Billias traces the changing attitudes toward the American Loyalists, from their contemporaries to the present ("The First Un-Americans: The Loyalists in American Historiography," in Vaughan and Billias, eds., *Perspectives* [see p. 183], pp. 282–324). And Robert M. Calhoon surveys our present knowledge of the Loyalists ("Loyalist Studies at the Advent of the Loyalist Papers Project," *NEQ* 46:284–93).

Less scholarship appeared on the patriots than on the loyalists. J. F. S. Smeall carefully determines the roles of Brackenridge and Freneau in their early collaborative poem before moving to a consideration of the differing interpretations of the same themes (primitivism, mythology, and the *translatio* idea) by the two poets ("The

Perspective Roles of Hugh Brackenridge and Philip Freneau in Composing *The Rising Glory of America*," *PBSA* 67:263–81). Two articles focus on Brackenridge's novel. Joseph H. Harkey's "The Don Quixote of the Frontier: Brackenridge's *Modern Chivalry*" (*EAL* 8:193–203) adjudicates the question of the influence of Cervantes upon Brackenridge, demonstrating that the influence is pervasive. And Wendy Martin's "The Rogue and the Rational Man: Hugh Henry Brackenridge's Study of a Con Man in *Modern Chivalry*" (*EAL* 8:179–92) examines a large variety of the objects of satire in *Modern Chivalry*, paying particular attention to the social backgrounds of the Jeffersonian era and to the socio-intellectual puritan heritage of Brackenridge. I wonder, however, if the characteristics of Captain Farrago should be so completely identified with Brackenridge?

William Bartram's fascinating and influential *Travels* is rarely studied, but Robert D. Arner's examination of the archetypal structure should encourage future readings ("Pastoral Patterns in William Bartram's *Travels*," *TSL* 18:133–45). Arner comments on the "three-part pastoral pattern" of the *Travels*, which begins "with the naturalist's withdrawal from society," focuses "upon an encounter with nature . . . intensely personal and fraught with ambiguities," and ends with his return to civilization. Arner finds that Bartram's response to nature is ambivalent throughout the book, but that it is more positive in parts one and two, and more negative in part three, when "the wilderness is both the cause and symbolic setting of man's degeneration into a bestial or semi-bestial condition in which the irrational dominates the rational." Vincent Freimark examines the character sketches in Timothy Dwight's travel journal ("Timothy Dwight's Brief Lives in *Travels in New England and New York*," *EAL* 8:44–58), questioning why Dwight deified some individuals and vilified others. He finds an explanation in the "pattern of paternalism dear to Dwight," claiming that "the father image pervades Dwight's generally hierarchical thought."

vii. Brown and His Contemporaries

Sydney J. Krause's "*Ormond*: Seduction in a New Key" (*AL* 44:570–84) surveys seduction in English novels before Charles Brockden Brown, notes that Brown is wittier than any previous writer treating seduction, and finds Brown unique in having Ormond argue that there is nothing inherently wrong with fornication (Benjamin Franklin, in "The Speech of Miss Polly Baker" and elsewhere, is an exception to Krause's reasonably-valid generalization). Carl Nelson also deals with Ormond, focusing on the role of the narrator, Sophia ("A Just Reading of Charles Brockden Brown's *Ormond*," *EAL* 8:163–78). Nelson believes that the novel essentially portrays a conflict between the moral sentimentalist Sophia and the practical realist Ormond. He claims that, although the sentimentalist wins the battle, Brown undercuts the point-of-view of his narrator by having her heretically subordinate God "to her own design." And Sophia's triumph in Constantia's killing of Ormond not only negates life-producing sexuality but also symbolically renounces the values of worldliness. Brown's novel, in Nelson's view, basically examines the schemes of justice available to man, and condemns the life-denying implications of moral sentimentality.

Carl Nelson also, in a general estimate of Brown, claims that Brown's intention in his novels is to portray the psychology of his characters ("Brown's Manichean Mock-Heroic: The Ironic Self in a Hyperbolic World," *WVUPP* 20:26–42). He attempts to prove Brown's special interest in the new science of psychotherapy, and finds that his characters are often studies in abnormal psychology. Their ruling passions range between the "enthusiastic rationalism" of the Illuminati, and the sentimentality and hyperbolic rhetoric of his feminine narrators. Nelson discusses Brown's "Adini Fragment," the Carwin fragment, *Wieland*, and *Ormond*, especially focusing on the self-righteous Sophia. Philip Russell Hughes explores *Edgar Huntley* as an example of Jungean myth psychology, with Edgar Huntley himself ambivalently fulfilling the role of hero ("Archetypal Patterns in *Edgar Huntley*," *SNNTS* 5:176–90). The mythopoetic explorations of the various characters are somewhat more convincing than one of the concluding generalizations: "Both the prose and the mythic elements indicate that Brown wrote *Edgar Huntley* as a 'trip' (psychedelic) out of the perceptual schemata of his rationalist age." R. B. Jenkins believes that Brown's attitude toward virtue as presented in *Wieland* may attack a traditional theological position ("Invulnerable Virtue in *Wieland* and *Comus*," *SAB*, 38,ii:72–75).

By contrasting the attitudes of Benjamin Rush and Brown toward the plague, William L. Hedges skillfully reveals—and makes his reader appreciate—the strengths and weaknesses of Rush as a writer and thinker ("Benjamin Rush, Charles Brockden Brown, and the American Plague Year," *EAL* 7:295–311). Hedges characterizes the "real theme" of *Arthur Mervyn* as "the perils of conscientiousness." The diary of Brown's constant companion and friend has been edited by James E. Cronin: *The Diary of Elihu Hubbard Smith, 1771–1798* (Philadelphia: American Philosophical Society). This younger Connecticut Wit was a student of Noah Webster, John Trumbull, Ezra Stiles, and Benjamin Rush. Smith's diary sheds incidental light on nearly every literary figure in New England and the Middle Colonies of his time.

A play by the first biographer of Brown is the subject of Norman Philbrick's "The Spy as Hero: An Examination of *André* by William Dunlap," *Studies in Theatre and Drama: Essays in Honor of Hubert C. Heffner* (The Hague: Mouton, [1972]). Philbrick analyzes the reasons why Dunlap's play failed, blaming the poor performance of Thomas Abthorpe Cooper, the elitism reflected in the play, and the choice of a spy for the role of a hero in the jingoistic period of 1798. Philbrick also discusses Dunlap's quarrel with a pseudonymous theater critic. Finally, Robert D. Arner shows that William Hill Brown attempted to make his novel illustrate the conflict between Richardsonian sentiment and Stearnean sensibility, but that the most important themes in the novel arise from his puritan inheritance ("Sentiment and Sensibility: The Role of Emotion and William Hill Brown's *The Power of Sympathy*," *SAF* 1:121–32). "Nature" in *The Power of Sympathy* is opposed to grace; the human condition is one of sin, constantly reenacting the fall of man (and echoing Milton's *Paradise Lost*); and the novel "deserves to be linked with Hawthorne's novels as a book that, in testifying to the power of sympathy, also testifies to the even greater power of blackness."

viii. General and Miscellaneous Studies

Richard Slotkin's *Regeneration Through Violence* is now the best literary and cultural study of the significance of the frontier in early American literature and culture. Henry Nash Smith in *Virgin Land* (1950) and Leo Marx in *The Machine in the Garden* (1964) both paid some attention to American literature of the 17th and 18th centuries as necessary backgrounds to their themes, but it is obvious to every colonialist that neither Smith nor Marx had much knowledge of or interest in the earlier period. Slotkin has both. His thesis is that "the first colonists saw in America an opportunity to regenerate their fortunes, their spirits, and the power of their church and nation; but the means to that regeneration ultimately became the means of violence, and the myth of regeneration through violence became the structuring metaphor of the American experience" (p. 5). Though one might expect a good deal of cant to follow this fashionable and "relevant" thesis, there is none. Slotkin's painstaking methodology, high intelligence, and hard work are evident in every paragraph of this long book. He has more significant observations to make about nearly every early American writer who treated the frontier (e.g., John Underhill, Mary Rowlandson, Benjamin Church, St. John de Crèvecoeur, and John Filson) than any previous scholar. Slotkin overstates the importance of the frontier literature in the total scheme of American literature; he makes the usual mistake of thinking that New England literature of the 17th century is equivalent to American literature of the 17th century; and his scholarship occasionally lags behind his criticism (e.g., his discussion of Lovewell's ballad does not mention the thorough essay by George Lyman Kittredge, "The Ballad of Lovewell's Fight," *Bibliographical Essays: A Tribute to Wilberforce Eames* [Cambridge, Mass.: Harvard Univ. Press, 1924], pp. 93–127, and his remarks on stanza sixteen [p. 183] would have been more telling if Slotkin had known that the text he cites is not the original, but a folk adaptation: see stanzas 27 and 29 as printed in Phillips Barry, "Songs of the Pigwacket Fight," *Bulletin of the Folk-Song Society of the Northeast*, 4 [1932]:4);—but, considering the great wealth of information, insight, and rigorous thought, these are minor quibbles. Slotkin's brilliant book is a major contribution to the study of American literature and culture.

Richard VanDerBeets's useful anthology *Held Captive by Indians: Selected Narratives, 1642–1836* (Knoxville: Univ. of Tenn. Press) contains the Jesuit captivity of Isaac Jogues (1642); the famous captivity of Mary Rowlandson (1676); John Gyles's exciting tale (1689); Elizabeth Hanson's (1724, written by the Friend, Samuel Bownas); Robert Eastburn's French and Indian War narrative (1756); a native American Black's, John Marrant (1770, written by William Aldridge); the pot-boiler Manheim anthology (1793); Charles Johnston's low-keyed narrative (1790); Mary Kinnan's sentimental story (1791); and Rachel Plummer's Texan captivity (1836).

VanDerBeets supplies an informative introduction, annotations (especially good for ethnographic details), four maps, and an index. His choices of copy-texts, however, are made without rhyme or reason, and the valuable prefatory materials from the various captivities are sometimes omitted. Thus the scholar may enjoy the convenience of reading this modern edition, but he should also read (and cite from) the originals. The attitudes and impressions of those Britons who traveled among the Southeastern Indians between 1660 and 1763 are described by J. Ralph Randolph, *British Travellers Among the Southern Indians 1660–1763* (Norman, Univ. of Okla. Press). Randolph devotes considerable space to John Lederer, John Lawson, Robert Beverley, Hugh Jones, William Byrd, and Henry Timberlake, but there is little of value to the student of American literature here, for the remarks rarely rise above a pedestrian description and classification of the notes about the Indians.

We all know some people whom we like despite themselves. I like Evelyn Page's *American Genesis: Pre-Colonial Writings in the North* (Boston: Gambit) despite itself. Page chronologically surveys the travel literature (in French, Spanish, and English) of America north of Mexico from Columbus to Samuel de Champlain, Captain John Smith, and Marc Lescarbot, before examining various themes, motifs, and strategies in the literature. The text is vague and without notes. The sparse chapter references at the end of the book list primary sources, but pay little attention to modern scholarship. Time and again while reading Page, I turned to Samuel Eliot Morison's *The European Discovery of America: The Northern Voyages* (New York: Oxford Univ. Press, [1971]) and to the *Dictionary of Canadian Biography* in order to satisfy my curiosity about a point she raised. Page sometimes condescends to her reader and sometimes to her authors. She concludes her discussion of Thomas Hariot by calling him "something of a bore" (p. 110)—but she notes how Hariot went beyond his predecessors, comments on his purposes in writing the book, and even alertly cites an implied syllogistic argument. I assume that the Jacques Le Moyne de Morgues drawing that she refers to (p. 90) as "recently surfaced, in a listing at auction" is the one of the "Young Pictish Woman" now in the collection of Paul Mellon, reproduced in the excellent (and inexpensive) edition of Thomas Hariot, *A Brief and True Report of the New-Found Land of Virginia: the Complete 1590 Theodore De Bry Edition*, ed. Paul Hulton (New

York: Dover, [1972]), p. xii; but Page, typically, does not tell us. Nevertheless, she (sometimes entertainingly and acutely) discusses the writings of the major explorers, and she often aroused my curiosity.

"Human Comedy in early America" by Louis B. Wright (*Comic Imagination*, pp. 17–31) repeats the old cliché that the colonists were serious people often guilty of "unconscious" humor (with examples from the unfunny Michael Wigglesworth and the self-consciously amused Samuel Sewall), but Wright does find deliberate humor in Captain John Smith, Thomas Morton, Nathaniel Ward, George Alsop, Ebenezer Cook, and especially William Byrd. Byrd is one of the sources dealt with by Pat Rogers, "An Early Colonial Historian: John Oldmixon and *The British Empire in America*" (*JAmS* 7,ii:113–23), who evaluates the sources of the second edition (1741) of Oldmixon's standard 18th century history of colonial America. Rogers says nothing about the sources for the section on Maryland, but when I read Oldmixon some years ago, I noticed that he echoed both Andrew White's *A Relation of Maryland* (1635) and George Alsop's *A Character of the Province of Maryland* (1666).

Richard Slotkin's "Narratives of Negro Crime in New England, 1675–1800" (*AQ* 25:3–31) describes the typical puritan execution sermons and crime narratives before examining those that deal with black criminals. In an Emersonian metaphor, Slotkin says that the typical narratives consist "of a series of concentric spheres—the family, the state and the cosmos—each of which is paternalistically organized." And rebellion against the father augurs future rebellion against society and against God. Slotkin believes that "The myth-scenario of social history" presented in the black crime narratives "is one in which society is embodied in the white woman—pure and perhaps virginal—who is violated and defiled by the black rapist of revolution and anarchy, while 'liberal' (i.e., permissive; morally and sexually loose) whites stand by and encourage, apologize for and protect the black ravisher." He adds that "The comprehensive network of associations in guilt makes the execution and its accompanying ritual and literature a ceremony of exorcism, in which the ritual murder of the black villain rids the state of a generalized Evil as well as the specific culprit."

Finally, I should mention the several articles about early American books and bibliography. The checklist of early American imprints has a further supplement (see *ALS 1972*, p. 182) in Roger P. Bristol's "American Bibliographical Notes" (*PAAS* 83:261–76). James Thomas Clancy has compiled "Native American References: A Cross-Indexed Bibliography of Seventeenth Century American Imprints Pertaining to American Indians" (*PAAS* 83:287–341). Edwin Wolf, 2nd, superbly lists 25 "Colonial American Playbills" (*PMHB* 97:99–106), correcting all the standard early American bibliographies, and casting doubt upon the authenticity of the "earliest" extant playbill. In "Loyalist Newspapers of the American Revolution 1763–1783: A Bibliography" (*PAAS* 83:217–40), Timothy M. Barnes includes brief listings of the Loyalist writings (and occasionally identifies the author) in the papers. A thorough, scholarly examination of the printing and importation of German books, together with a survey of the kinds of German books popular in early America (including astrological and erotic titles, as well as belles-lettres), has been compiled by Robert E. Cazden, "The Provision of German Books in America during the Eighteenth Century" (*Libri* 23:81–108). Cazden corrects two datings in Evans (n.39) and adds a 1798 German imprint to the standard bibliographies (n.62). Samuel J. Rogal has gathered together "A Checklist of Eighteenth-Century British Literature Published in Eighteenth Century America" (*CLJ* 10:231–57), which, like several of the above lists, would be more useful if standard bibliographical references (especially the Evans numbers) were given.

University of California, Los Angeles

11. Nineteenth-Century Fiction

M. Thomas Inge

Again, the quantity of published material about authors covered in this chapter declined, as it did last year. The high quality reached in 1972, however, has not been maintained, although a few scholars and critics produced some excellent books, especially Jon L. Wakelyn, Kevin Starr, Louis D. Rubin, Jr., George N. Bennett, and Fredson Bowers, to name a few. Presumably because of financial exigencies, little progress was made in the publication of CEAA volumes: one volume in the Stephen Crane edition appeared and none in the Cooper, Simms, and Howells editions. Plans have been announced for the continuation of all these editions in 1974. An amazing total of 66 dissertations were recorded, 27 of them on general themes and topics (with several duplications), eight on Cooper, five on Howells, four on Irving, three each on Bierce, Cable, Chopin, Crane, and John William DeForest, two on Norris, and one each on Simms, Paulding, Chesnutt, Garland, and Lafcadio Hearn.

i. General Topics

Intended to be a comprehensive survey of the development of short fiction and its authors, Arthur Voss's *The American Short Story* falls somewhere in its style and content between an undergradute study guide and headnotes for an anthology. The beginning reader might find it a useful summary of what we know, but there are few original insights. Most major and minor writers are touched upon, including from the 19th century Irving, Harte, Crane, and the regional writers. Eleven previously published essays from the 1950s and 1960s have been brought together by Kenneth S. Lynn in *Visions of America* (Westport, Conn., Greenwood Press), including his introductions to editions of *Uncle Tom's Cabin* and *The Octopus* and an essay on Howells incorporated in his biography (see *ALS 1971*, p. 179). Another reprint anthology is *According to Hoole: The Collected Essays and Tales of a Scholar-Librarian and Literary Maverick* (University, Univ. of Ala. Press) in which W. Stanley Hoole has included many of his pioneering essays on 19th century Southern writers such as Simms, Johnson Jones Hooper, Willis Brewer, Jeremiah Clemens, and John Gorman Barr. Arlin Turner has written a remarkably concise but informative guide to "Interpreting Nineteenth-Century American Literature" (*ASAIN* 11,iii:3–15).

The relationship between short fiction and the development of the American magazine, a topic needful of fuller study, is considered with authority and intelligence in several essays in the *Gohdes Festschrift*: "Local Color and the Rise of the American Magazine" by Kimball King, "Magazine Editors and the Stories of Thomas Nelson Page's Late Flowering" by Harriet R. Holman, "The *St. Nicholas* and the Serious Artist" by Elizabeth C. Saler and Edwin H. Cady, and "The Pre-eminent Magazine Genius: S. S. McClure" by editor Woodress. All are highly informative, as is Rayburn S. Moore's "The Magazine and the Short Story in the Ante-Bellum Period" (*SAB* 39,ii:44–51). John R. Crume has written a useful brief survey of "Children's Magazines, 1826–1857" (*JPC* 6:698–706), and *ALR* devoted its spring issue to late 19th-century children's literature with bibliographical essays and annotated checklists by R. Gordon Kelly, Fred Erisman, and Christa R. Kline. The serious study of literature for children as literature is a development which should be encouraged, and these research materials will prove helpful.

ii. Irving, Cooper, and Their Contemporaries

There was a sharp decrease in attention to Irving this year and only one essay of distinction. In "Irving Sets the Pattern: Notes on Professionalism and the Art of the Short Story" (*SSF* 10:327–41), Eugene Current-Garcia tests the thesis that the American short story began with Irving in 1819 and concludes, after a careful and sensible scrutiny of the evidence, that he did "indeed set the pattern for the artistic re-creation of common experience in short fictional form. . . ." There were two essays on an often-neglected work: Wayne R. Kime follows a pattern of careful explication to outline "The Completeness of Washington Irving's *A Tour on the Prairies*" (*WAL* 8:55–65) and Martha Dula provides a brief piece of literary history in "Audience

Response to *A Tour on the Prairies* in 1835" (*WAL* 8:67–74). The textual problems resulting from multiple authorship (Irving, James Kirke Paulding, and William Irving) are addressed by Martha Hartzog Stocker, "*Salmagundi*: Problems in Editing the So-called First Edition (1807–08)" (*PBSA* 67:141–58). In an equally meticulous piece of research, Kenneth W. Graham examines "The Influence of James Kirke Paulding's *Diverting History* on Washington Irving's Sketch 'John Bull'" (*PBSA* 67:310–22). Wayne R. Kime completed several pieces of useful detective work in "Washington Irving and 'The Extension of the Empire of Freedom': An Unrecorded Contribution to the *Evening Post*, May 14, 1804" (*BNYPL* 76[1972]:220–30); "The First Locomotive to Cross the Rocky Mountains: An Unidentified Sketch in the *Knickerbocker Magazine*, May 1839, by Washington Irving" (*BNYPL* 76 [1972]:242–50); and "Washington Irving and 'To a Mountain Daisy': An Anecdote of Robert Burns in America" (*SSL* 10:186–89).

The one full-length American book on Cooper (see also Chapter 19, *v*) is a volume in "The Critical Heritage Series" by George Dekker and John P. McWilliams, *Fenimore Cooper: The Critical Heritage* (London, Routledge & Kegan Paul), in which the editors have compiled critical documents to reflect Cooper's reception by American and European contemporaries from 1822 to 1898 and contributed a useful essay surveying the development. The selections are good, the pieces by Conrad, Melville, Simms, and Poe being of special interest, but the checklist of American reviews of Cooper's works is too selective to be of much utility. Cooper is among the numerous authors encompassed by Richard Slotkin's comprehensive and formidable study of the frontier, *Regeneration Through Violence*, where the Leatherstocking novels are analyzed for their depiction of the conflict between Christian and Indian mythology on the symbolic importance of the wilderness. Other writers discussed more briefly are Robert M. Bird, Simms, and the humorists of the Old Southwest. Nicolaus Mills's *American and English Fiction in the Nineteenth Century* (Bloomington, Ind. Univ. Press) includes a chapter on "Sir Walter Scott and Fenimore Cooper" which examines the similarities of *Rob Roy* and *The Prairie* as a part of his general challenge to the genre criticism fostered by Lionel Trilling and Richard Chase. Also disagreeing with a common critical assumption—that Cooper ignored the picaresque genre—A. Owen Aldridge finds that the little-known *Autobiography of a Pocket-Handkerchief* belongs to a sub-genre of the picaresque, the adventures of inert objects ("Fenimore Cooper and the Picaresque Tradition," *NCF* 27 [1972]:283–92). The essay, a model of scholarly exposition, actually tells us something new about Cooper. Two thematic studies are Jay S. Paul's "Home as Cherished: The Theme of Family in Fenimore Cooper" (*SNNTS* 5:39–51) and John Gerlach's "James Fenimore Cooper and the Kingdom of God" (*IllQ* 35:32–50). The first explores the theme of collective self-preservation and the second the idea of the presence of God in the community of man; both are competent and interesting.

The great surge of interest in Simms continues unabated, although it brought only one book this season. The book, however, is an excellent piece of historic scholarship, *The Politics of a Literary Man: William Gilmore Simms* by Jon L. Wakelyn (Westport, Conn., Greenwood Press). Many will disagree with Wakelyn's thesis, that Simms sacrificed his devotion to art and literary distinction to an ardent defense of the South, but he has supported his conclusions with a careful analysis of private and public documents and produced a first-rate study in intellectual history. The most valuable and useful essay to appear this year is Charles S. Watson's "William Gilmore Simms: An Essay in Bibliography" (*RALS* 3:3–26), a judicious survey of Simms criticism and scholarship from the 1830s to the present.

Watson has also written a very thorough explication of the thematic imagery in Simms's novel *The Yemassee*, "A New Approach to Simms: Imagery and Meaning in *The Yemassee*" (*MissQ* 26:155–63), which demonstrates the viability of this approach to his fiction and argues favorably for a better reputation as a craftsman. A slightly more specialized but complementary study, which deals at the same time with possible influences, is "Simms's Use of Milton and Wordsworth in *The Yemassee*: An Aspect of Symbolism in the Novel" by Thomas Hubert (*SCR* 6,i:58–65). In "William Gilmore Simms and the American Indian" (*SCR* 5,ii:57–64), Elmo Howell takes a general look at the fictional use of a minority group by a writer somewhat more objective than most in his attitudes. Two primary documents have been made available in well edited texts: "A New Letter of Simms to Richard Henry Wilde: On the Advancement of Sectional

Literature" (*AL* 44:667–70) by James E. Kibler, Jr., and "The Idylls of the Appalachian: An Unpublished Lecture" (*AJ* 1:2–11, 146–60) by Miriam J. Shillingsburg.

Three early 19th-century gothic novelists—Charles Brockden Brown, Richard Henry Dana, Sr., and Washington Allston—are given a comparative analysis by Donald A. Ringe in "Early American Gothic: Brown, Dana and Allston" (*ATQ* 19:3–8).

iii. Local Color, Humor, and Popular Fiction

Americans and the California Dream 1850–1915 by Kevin Starr (New York, Oxford Univ. Press), encyclopedic in its grasp of cultural minutia and expansive in its comprehension of the symbolic patterns of American history, is a most impressive effort to capture the social, psychological, and symbolic importance of the settlement of one state in the national imagination. In addition to memoirs, journals, letters, sermons, architectural plans, and news reports, Starr draws on the fiction of a host of writers, including Ambrose Bierce, Bret Harte, Jack London, Frank Norris, Bayard Taylor, and Mark Twain. Also impressive are the attractive and superbly edited works of two neglected local color writers. *Grace King of New Orleans: A Selection of Her Writings* (Baton Rouge, La. State Univ. Press) contains a broad selection of all types of writing by the Louisiana author, including her major fiction, and an excellent biographical introduction by the editor, Robert Bush. Rodman W. Paul has drawn on a hitherto unpublished manuscript for his edition of *A Victorian Gentlewoman in the Far West: The Reminiscences of Mary Hallock Foote* (San Marino, Calif., The Huntington Lib., 1972), nicely illustrated with period photographs and a selection of Mrs. Foote's fine illustrations. Hopefully those books will encourge some critical attention to the works and reputations of Miss King and Mrs. Foote, both minor but interesting writers.

Interest in Sarah Orne Jewett increased considerably this year. Michael W. Vella, "Sarah Orne Jewett: A Reading of *The Country of the Pointed Firs*" (*ESQ* 19:275–82), labors with some success to prove that in her best-known work the "pictorial style reinforces the novel's theme while it functions architectonically . . . ." John B. Humma's "The Art and Meaning of Sarah Orne Jewett's 'The Courting of Sister Wisby'" (*SSF* 10:85–91) is a good explication of a neglected though often anthologized story, and James Woodress's "Sarah Orne Jewett and Willa Cather: Anti-Realists" (*EST* 5:477–88) argues with sense and support that both authors should be classed as romantics rather than realists. Richard Cary, who has done more for Miss Jewett's reputation than anyone else, has assembled a comprehensive cross-section of criticism from 1885 to 1972, *Appreciation of Sarah Orne Jewett: 29 Interpretive Essays* (Waterville, Maine, Colby College Press). All of this material adds to Miss Jewett's growing stature.

The Kate Chopin renaissance appears pretty much over, although a few late entries have come in. Cynthia Griffin Wolff, "Thanatos and Eros: Kate Chopin's *The Awakening*" (*AQ* 25:449–71), argues with overwhelming thoroughness what should be an obvious matter—that aside from its anticipations of "the woman question" or the work of D. H. Lawrence, a major importance of *The Awakening* "derives from its ruthless fidelity to the disintegration of Edna's character." Taking a psychological stance on the same issue, Ruth Sullivan and Stewart Smith ("Narrative Stance in Kate Chopin's *The Awakening*," *SAF* 1:62–75) assert that "The author chose to use a complex narrative stance in which Edna is presented alternately as an unusual woman with significant problems admirably dealt with and as a narcissistic, thoughtless woman, almost wantonly self-destructive." "Per Seyersted: Kate Chopin. A Critical Biography" (*Edda* 71[1971]: 341–66) contains two disputations by Daniel Aaron and Sigmund Skard on Seyersted's doctoral dissertation published in 1969 (see *ALS 1969*, p. 171).

Dissatisfied with the traditional readings of George Washington Cable's first two novels *The Grandissimes* and *Dr. Sevier* for their social themes, Donald A. Ringe ("The 'Double Center': Character and Meaning in Cable's Early Novels," *SNNTS* 5:52–62) succeeds in finding a new critical approach by analyzing the author's use of a pair of heroes through whose interaction the meanings of the novels emerge. Ringe's essay is a good corrective to Elmo Howell's typical approach to Cable which disparages the artist in favor of the reformer ("George Washington Cable's Creoles: Art and Reform in *The Grandissimes*," *MissQ* 26:43–53). The point of "The Ethnic and Religious Prejudices of G. W. Cable" by J. John Perret (*LaS*

11[1972]:263–73) is that although a strong champion of the black man's cause in the 19th century, Cable nurtured the usual WASP prejudices against French-speaking Creoles and Acadians of the Catholic faith, but the argument demands more support than Perret provides.

One chapter of Paul C. Wermuth's study *Bayard Taylor* (TUSAS 228) considers Taylor's five volumes of fiction written in the 1860s, but Wermuth is hard-pressed to find anything positive to say about them except that they "are not so bad as the great bulk of fiction" of his day. "Bret Harte on Bayard Taylor: An Unpublished Tribute" by Luther S. Luedtke and Patrick D. Morrow uncovers and publishes in translation for the first time an obituary tribute to Taylor written by Harte in 1878 and published in German in the *Berliner Tageblatt* (*MarkhamR* 3:101–05). "Defiant Light: A Positive View of Mary Wilkins Freeman" by Susan Allen Toth (*NEQ* 46:82–93) is a pleasant appreciation of Miss Freeman's positive side, and John Q. Anderson performs his usual skilled detective work on a little-known writer in "Louisiana and Mississippi Lore in the Fiction of Sarah Anne Dorsey (1829–1879)" (*LaS* 11[1972]:230–39).

Ernest Cassara undertakes a difficult task in "The Rehabilitation of Uncle Tom: Significant Themes in Mrs. Stowe's Anti-slavery Novel" (*CLAJ* 17:230–40) and reaffirms the notion that Harriet Beecher Stowe's heart was in the right place: "She sought in her way to awaken Christian America to the barbarities of the slave system in the conviction that quickened consciences would lead to a new awakening." Although the subject easily requires a much fuller study, William L. Slout has provided a brief summary of "*Uncle Tom's Cabin* in American Film History" (*JPF* 2:137–51). In "Patterns of Violence and Non-Violence in Pro-Slavery and Anti-Slavery Fiction" (*CLAJ* 16:426–37), Marian E. Musgrave finds that many abolitionists held the same prejudiced and stereotypical views of blacks as did the slave holders. W. Edward Farrison examines the historical evidence for the alleged liaison between Thomas Jefferson and the slave Sally Hemings, which served as subject matter for William Wells Brown's novel *Clotel*, in "Clotel, Thomas Jefferson, and Sally Hemings" (*CLAJ* 16:147–74), but he can come to no certain conclusion. Nicholas Canady, Jr., has described "The Antislavery Novel Prior to 1852 and Hildreth's *The Slave* (1836)" (*CLAJ* 16:175–91); James H. DeVries discusses the second novel written by a black American,

The Garies and Their Friends by Frank J. Webb (1857), in "The Tradition of the Sentimental Novel in *The Garies and Their Friends*" (*CLAJ* 16:241–49); and Robert E. Fleming cites various types of "Humor in the Early Black Novel" (*CLAJ* 16:250–62).

Taken altogether, the 32 separate essays by 24 critics assembled by Louis D. Rubin, Jr., in *Comic Imagination* constitute the best book on American humor to appear since Walter Blair's standard critical anthology *Native American Humor* in 1937. Originating in a series of broadcasts prepared for the Voice of America, most of the essays are models of sound scholarship, sensible judgment, and graceful style. Nearly all major and minor writers and movements are discussed within a well-organized editorial format to which Rubin has added introductory and concluding commentaries. Drawing on anecdotes, cartoons, and humorous sketches published in the 19th century in such humorous periodicals as *The Spirit of the Times*, *Puck*, *Yankee Nations*, *Judge*, and *Life*, Rudolf Glanz has attempted a survey of *The Jew in Early American Wit and Graphic Humor* (New York, Ktav Publishing House). Though superficial in its commentary and stodgy in style (a competent editing was needed), as an anthology of examples of ethnic verbal and visual humor the book will be of use as a resource for further study. A good many writers are addressed or discussed in *Letters of George Ade* (West Lafayette, Ind., Purdue Univ. Studies), intelligently selected, annotated, and edited by Terence Tobin.

Before moving on to full chapters devoted to the confidence man as found in Harte, Twain, Hawthorne, Howells, James, and Melville, Susan Kuhlmann in *Knave, Fool, and Genius* locates his origin in the rugged, common-sensical backwoods hunter such as Daniel Boone and David Crockett, and analyzes his development in the works of A. B. Longstreet, John S. Robb, Johnson Jones Hooper, and J. G. Baldwin. Her assessment of Hooper's Simon Suggs is one of the most perceptive I have read—concise, intelligent, and informative, like the rest of the brief book. Three essays on individual humorists are "Seba Smith Embattled" by Cameron C. Nickels (*MHQ* 13:7–26), a biographical piece on two "duels" with words fought by the Maine humorist; "The Many Roles of Nasby" by Dennis E. Minor (*MarkhamR* 4:16–20), a general appreciation of the several facets of the character created by Ohio humorist David Ross Locke; and "The Lovingood Patriarchy" by Ormonde Plater (*AJ* 1:82–93), a survey of the uses of nudity and sexuality in five Sut Lovingood stories by Tennessee humorist George Washington Harris.

Science fiction editor and anthologist Sam Moskowitz has been engaged in scholarly efforts to recognize and revive interest in several forgotten popular 19th-century writers in the speculative fiction line. The earliest stories about faster-than-light travel, non-human but friendly aliens, or a time machine (seven years before Wells) were written in the 1870s and 1880s for the New York *Sun* by Edward Page Mitchell. Moskowitz has retrieved thirty of these amazingly advanced tales, as well as the biographical facts of Mitchell's career, for his edition of *The Crystal Man* (Garden City, N.Y., Doubleday). The facts of the career of another lost writer in the horror, fantasy, and science fiction fields are recounted in three essays by Moskowitz on William Hope Hodgson, a British contributor to popular American magazines, in the first three issues of the revived *Weird Tales* (47,i: 38–49; ii:62–73; iii:35–48). As editor of *Weird Tales*, Moskowitz is also reprinting stories by several 19th-century authors, such as Julian Hawthorne's daughter Hildegarde, Frank Norris, Muriel Campbell Dyar, Nathaniel T. Babcock, Albert Bigelow Paine, Cleveland Moffett, and Emma Frances Dawson, with brief biographical and appreciative headnotes. Kenneth M. Roemer's "1984 in 1894: Harben's *Land of the Changing Sun*" (*MissQ* 26:29–42) discusses a forgotten Utopian novel by William N. Harben which anticipates George Orwell's *1984* and Aldous Huxley's *Brave New World.*

Eight Dime Novels edited by E. F. Bleiler (New York, Dover) is an over-sized facsimile reprint of several popular novels, with a critical introduction: *The Bradys and the Girl Smuggler* by Francis W. Doughty (1900), *Frank James on the Trail* (1882), *Scylla, The Sea Robber* by Frederick Van Rensselaer Dey (1905), *Deadwood Dick, or The Prince of the Road* by Edward J. Wheeler (1877), *Adventures of Buffalo Bill* by Prentiss Ingraham (1881), *The Huge Hunter* by Edward S. Ellis (1882), *Frank Merriwell's Nobility* by William G. Patten (1899), and *Adrift in New York* by Horatio Alger, Jr. (1903). Anne Trensky has provided a perceptive survey of "The Bad Boy in Nineteenth-Century American Fiction" (*GaR* 27:503–17), and John Ditsky draws on a popular novel by Charles Carleton Coffin, *The Seat of Empire* (1870), in his pursuit of the meaning of the word "grit" before Charles Portis and John Wayne gave it new popularity: "True 'Grit' and 'True Grit'" (*Ariel*, 4, ii:18–31).

iv. Howells, Realism, and Post-Civil-War Fiction

George N. Bennett's new study *The Realism of William Dean Howells* (Nashville, Vanderbilt Univ. Press) has all the qualities of his earlier study *William Dean Howells: The Development of a Novelist* (1959)—calm reason, sound judgment, and clarity of style. Bennett examines the novels of the last part of his career, from 1889 to 1920, measuring them against Howells's own intentions as a "psychological novelist," whose fiction studies the conflicts between unconscious desire and conscious motive that shape people's character, and as a realist, whose most valuable function is to reveal character: "The fulcrum on which the realist balances his art is not an ethical proposition, not a judgement of society, neither a criticism of nor a plan for the correction of the economic system, but the study of individuals." Bennett argues against viewing the progress of Howells's career as a move toward "a growing social awareness culminating in the explicit economic criticism of the novels of the early nineties and lapsing thereafter into tepid repetition and critical timidity." The analyses of the twenty works of fiction by Bennett easily accomplishes his goal of demonstrating what he sees as a "coherent and continuous literary consciousness and practice." One can only come away from the book with increased respect for Howells the artist and successful practitioner of his own critical theories.

Few practicing critics have as extensive a knowledge of or as deep an appreciation for the intellectual life in American culture as Lewis P. Simpson. All of his essays are a pleasure to read, and this is especially true of "The Treason of William Dean Howells" in his collection *The Man of Letters in New England and the South* (Baton Rouge, La. State Univ. Press). The essay is a reading of Howells's reminiscences about American men of letters, *Literary Friends and Acquaintance* (1900), which Simpson feels has "a complex inner dimension of meaning . . . a suspicion—irrational but compelling—that in the very midst of success and power he had betrayed the ideal of literary life in America." It is a subtle and provocative piece of criticism and like Bennett's book adds another dimension to our understanding of the late Howells. The remaining critical essays tend to be very specialized. "The Houses of Fiction: Domestic Architecture in Howells and Edith Wharton" by Jan Cohn (*TSLL* 15:537–49) takes a revealing new approach by examining the uses of the house as setting and symbol in the works of the two authors, especially *The Rise of Silas Lapham* and *The House of Mirth*. John W. Crowley has provided a brief but debatable analysis of "The Oedipal Theme in Howells's *Fennel and Rue*" (*SNNTS* 5:104–09), while two other critics come up with interesting parallels in what might strike one at first as unpromising comparisons: John Graham, "Struggling Upward: *The Minister's Charge* and [Nathanael West's] *A Cool Million*" (*CRevAS* 4:184–96), and Sam B. Girgus, "Howells and [Herbert] Marcuse: A Forecast of the One-Dimensional Age" (*AQ* 25:108–18). Both these last two pieces serve to suggest the relevance of Howells's social vision to modern problems.

A quantity of primary material was brought into print this year. *W. D. Howells as Critic* (London and Boston, Routledge & Kegan Paul) is a comprehensive sampling of 54 critical essays written between 1860 and 1911, with detailed introductions and notes by one who knows the subject well, Edwin H. Cady. The entire fall issue of that invaluable journal, *ALR* (6:267–424), is devoted to Ulrich Halfman's excellent compilation of "Interviews with William Dean Howells," also available as a separate cloth-bound book. Other material includes: "In 'The Silken Arms of the Aristocracy': William Dean Howells' Lecture in Indianapolis, 1899" by Robert Rowlette (*IMH* 69:299–319), which draws on newspaper coverage of the event; "'A Gentle Foe'—A New W. D. Howells Letter" (of 1900 to Sir Arthur Quiller-Couch) edited by F. G. Atkinson (*N&Q* 20:260–61); "'Howells as His Head Makes Him': A Phrenologist's Report" from an 1899 newspaper (*AN&Q* 11:115–16) and "Tarkington in Defense of Howells and Realism: A Recovered Letter" also of 1899 (*BSUF* 14:64–65), both recovered by Robert Rowlette. In the area of bibliography, Vito J. Brenni's *William Dean Howells: A Bibliography* (Metuchen, N.J.: Scarecrow Press) is intended to update the earlier work by William M. Gibson and George Arms (see *ALS 1971*, p. 180) and Jacob Blanck (see *ALS 1963*, p. 113). The volume must be used with great caution, however, since it is neither accurate, consistent, complete, nor usable according to reviewer David Nordloh (*AL* 46:229–30).

Although J. P. Stern's *On Realism* (London and Boston, Routledge & Kegan Paul) is intended, according to the book jacket, to be an introductory guide for "both the student and general reader" and to "provide a clear description and critical evaluation of the term," neither will find it very useful unless already schooled in the work of Eric Auerbach and Ludwig Wittgenstein which provides the conceptual basis. Drawing entirely on European literature, not a single American realist is mentioned, strange to say, in this erudite example of philosophical criticism disguised as a student guide. Much more useful for the student or general reader is Jane Bernadete's critical anthology *American Realism* (New York, G. P. Putnam's Sons), containing 43 excerpts and essays by and about the realism and naturalism in the work of Whitman, Howells, Mark Twain, James, Garland, Norris, Dreiser, and Steinbeck.

What must be Ambrose Bierce's most frequently anthologized and adapted short story is the subject of an anthology edited by Gerald R. Barrett and Thomas L. Erskine, *From Fiction to Film: Ambrose Bierce's "An Occurrence at Owl Creek Bridge"* (Encino, Calif., Dickenson Publishing Co.). In addition to the text of the story, there are six pieces of criticism on the story, shot analyses of the two film versions of the story with selected stills, and five essays on the films. In "Can Ohio and the Midwest Claim Ambrose Bierce?" *OQ* 16: 84–88), David D. Anderson says "yes," if heredity and environment count for anything: "In temperament, in philosophy, in subject matter, he is most assuredly more related to the rural iconoclasm, the small-town freethinking tradition that gave a multitude of Midwesterners . . . to the world." One of Howells's theoretical allies is reassessed by Robert S. Fredrickson in "Hjalmar Hjorth Boyesen: Howells 'Out-Realisted' " (*MarkhamR* 3:93–97), basically a comparison of their theories of realism. Harold Frederic's best known novel is given a provocative psychological analysis by John W. Crowley, "The Nude and the Madonna in *The Damnation of Theron Ware*" (*AL* 45:379–89), and Jean Frantz Blackall details Frederic's use of a revised paragraph from a story in *Marsena* ("Harold Frederic: A Provocative Revision," *N&Q* 20:257–60). Two worthwhile critiques of Charles W. Chesnutt's most popular stories are "Chesnutt's 'The Sheriff's Children' as Parable" by Ronald Walcott (*NALF* 7:83–85) and "Chesnutt's 'The Goopered Grapevine' as Social Criticism" by Theodore R. Hovet (*NALF* 7:86–88).

v. Stephen Crane

Perhaps the single most important Crane item to appear this year, for scholarship anyway, is the facsimile edition of the manuscript of *The Red Badge of Courage*, edited and with an introduction and apparatus by Fredson Bowers (Washington, D.C., NCR/Microcard Editions, A Bruccoli Clark Book). Volume 1 of this boxed, limited edition contains an extensive essay on the composition, description, revision, and publication of the manuscript, and an apparatus providing all the evidence any scholar would wish to study the making of Crane's best-known piece of fiction. Volume 2 is a photographic facsimile of the complete manuscript, including all discarded leaves of antecedent drafts and false starts, reduced to four-fifths its actual size for convenience in use. *Stephen Crane: The Critical Heritage*, edited by Richard M. Weatherford (London and Boston, Routledge & Kegan Paul), reprints 138 contemporary reviews and notices of Crane's major books and eight critical essays of 1915–26 to provide a panorama of his reputation during his lifetime and the following decades. This is valuable primary material made conveniently available. Volume 8 of the University of Virginia Edition of the Works of Stephen Crane, devoted to *Tales, Sketches, and Reports* (Charlottesville, Univ. Press of Va.) appeared this year. Edwin H. Cady has provided a useful short historical introduction, and editor Fredson Bowers has appended to the more than 180 items (768 pages) an exhaustive history and analysis of the text and several textual appendices (415 pages). This massive volume brings us one step closer to the completion of this distinguished edition.

Leland Krauth's "Heroes and Heroics: Stephen Crane's Moral Imperative" (*SDR* 11,ii:86–93) suggests that Crane's conception of the heroic in *The Red Badge of Courage* is in conflict with the conventional notion of military heroism and this "unresolved tension accounts for the strained ambivalence with which Crane views his 'hero's' overall achievement." There were two critiques of the story "The Monster": Charles W. Mayer examines "Social Forms Vs. Human Brotherhood in Crane's *The Monster*" (*BSUF* 14:29–37) and Charles E. Modlin and John R. Byers, Jr., interpret "Stephen Crane's 'The Monster' as Christian Allegory" (*MarkhamR* 3:110–13). Crane's accurate rendering of "the realistic, less pleasant, aspects of childhood" is Ellen A. Brown's primary concern in "Stephen Crane's

Whilomville Stories: A Backward Glance" (*MarkhamR* 3:105–09), and George Monteiro annotates a single line of a poem in "Crane's *A Man Adrift on a Slim Spar*" (*Expl* 32:item 14). James Nagel takes fresh looks at three stories in "The Narrative Method of 'The Open Boat'" (*RLV* 39:409–17), "Structure and Theme in Crane's 'An Experiment in Misery'" (*SSF* 10:169–74), and "Stephen Crane's 'The Clan of No-Name'" (*KAL* 14:34–42). All eight of these formalist essays are at a minimum informative, and at best workmanlike, yet none point out any new paths in Crane criticism.

A few miscellaneous pieces and notes are worth mentioning. Jesse E. Crisler provides the historical background for one of Crane's collaborative dramatic efforts in "'Christmas Must Be Gay': Stephen Crane's *The Ghost*–A Play by Divers Hands" (*Proof* 3:69–120). "Abraham Cahan, Stephen Crane and the Romantic Tenement Tale of the Nineties" (*AmerS* 14:95–107) is a comparative analysis of two artists and their urban fiction, too close to reality for the comfort of their age, by David M. Fine. Stanley Wertheim surveys additional potential background reading for Crane in "*The Red Badge of Courage* and Personal Narratives of the Civil War" (*ALR* 6:61–65). James B. Stronks, "Garland's Priviate View of Crane in 1898 (With a Postscript)" (*ALR* 6:249–50) notes a brief mention in Hamlin Garland's diary, and Richard M. Weatherford, "Stephen Crane and O. Henry: A Correction" (*AL* 44:666) identifies the author of a parody of Crane, thought to be written by O. Henry, as Paul M. Paine.

vi. Naturalism and the Late Nineteenth Century

Those with an interest in Frank Norris and an interest in the translation of fiction into film will be fascinated by Herman G. Weinberg's reconstruction of Erich von Stroheim's classic adaptation of *McTeague* in *The Complete Greed* (New York, E. P. Dutton & Co.). Originally 9½ hours in length and intentionally faithful to the novel, *Greed* was cut to 2½ hours for distribution much to Stroheim's chagrin. A copy of the complete version has never been discovered, so Weinberg has combined 52 recovered production stills with 348 stills from the film and the complete text of the dialogue. The result is a most unusual visual and literary experience for readers who know the novel.

Most of the Norris material tends to be bibliographical items or minor notes. Joseph Katz completed two useful resource items. "The Shorter Publications of Frank Norris: A Checklist" (*Proof* 3:155–220), a thorough and comprehensive piece of scholarship, and "The Elusive Criticisms Syndicated by Frank Norris" (*Proof* 3:221–51), which locates and publishes several lost literary essays. Mukhtar Ali Isani has edited and introduced a review essay by "Jack London on Norris' *The Octopus*" (*ALR* 6:66–69); James Stronks published "A New Frank Norris Letter" (*BCCQN*, Spring:40–42) of marginal interest; and Joseph R. McElrath, Jr., made a correction in biographical data concerning "Norris' Return from Cuba" (*ALR* 6:251). D. B. Graham, "Studio Art in *The Octopus*" (*AL* 44:657–66), adumbrates several aspects of the San Francisco artistic milieu of the late 1890s, which Norris used in his novel. Despite its comprehensive title, "Women as Superfluous Characters in American Realism and Naturalism" by Jan Cohn (*SAF* 1:154–62) is a very brief survey of female stereotypes in novels by Norris, Dreiser, Henry B. Fuller, London, and Howells, among others. The essay cries for qualification and expansion.

The most welcome piece of Garland scholarship to appear in years is *Hamlin Garland and the Critics: An Annotated Bibliography* by Jackson R. Bryer, Eugene Harding, and Robert A. Rees (Troy, N.Y., Whitston Publishing Co.). Intelligently arranged, thoroughly annotated, and usefully indexed, over 1300 pieces of secondary comment are made readily accessible. "Hamlin Garland and Reform" by Lewis O. Saum (*SDR* 10,iv:36–62) is an informative and balanced reassessment of Garland's varied reform thought and its relation to the intellectual currents of his age. More specifically literary in its orientation is T. Jeff Evans's examination of "The Return Motif as a Function of Realism in *Main-Travelled Roads*" (*KanQ* 5,iv:33–40).

Several other late 19th-century writers received searching scrutinies this year. Edward Bellamy's spiritual and intellectual complexity is competently surveyed by Thomas A. Sancton, "Looking Inward: Edward Bellamy's Spiritual Crisis" (*AQ* 25:538–57), and "Bellamy, Morris, and the Image of the City in Victorian Social Criticism" by T. M. Parssinen (*MQ* 14:257–66) compares Bellamy with one of his strongest British critics, William Morris, specifically their attitudes towards the modern industrial city. "Making the Sublime Mechanical: Henry Blake Fuller's Chicago" by Guy Szuberla (*AmerS* 14:83–93) explains how novelist Fuller articulated his new idea of urban space and his vision of the ideal cityscape. John Pilkington's "Fuller, Garland, Taft, and the Art of the West" (*PLL* Supplement to vol. 8:39–56) documents substantially his view of *Under the Skylights* by Fuller as a *roman à clef* in which Hamlin Garland and Lorado Taft figure. Curtis Dahl profiles two novels by Nathan Chapman Kouns of Missouri in "A Radical Historical Novelist of the '80's" (*GaR* 27:49–55).

In addition to the previously mentioned articles, the two general issues of *ALR* offered a variety of materials on other 19th-century fiction writers: "Louisa May Alcott (1832–1888)," a review of criticism by Alma J. Payne (6:27–43); "Immigrant Ghetto Fiction, 1885–1918: An Annotated Bibliography" by David M. Fine (pp. 169–95); "Helen Hunt Jackson (1830–1885): A Critical Bibliography of Secondary Comment" by John R. Byers and Elizabeth S. Byers (pp. 197–241); "'Word-Murder': An Early Joseph Kirkland Essay Published Anonymously" (pp. 73–79), and "Two Additions to the Joseph Kirkland Canon" by Audrey J. Roberts (pp. 252–54); and three statements prepared on the topic of women in late 19th-century fiction for the 1973 MLA American Literary Realism Seminar with Joseph L. Carter on Garland, W. Gordon Milne on Harold Frederic, and Alma J. Payne on Louisa May Alcott. The usual period illustrations, advertisements, and portraits continue to make *ALR* as attractive as it is consistently useful.

Virginia Commonwealth University

12. Fiction: 1900 to the 1930s

Warren French

As we sink ever deeper into the sordid Seventies, the trend noted during the last several years towards noncommital biographies, unannotated bibliographies, and aimless appreciations of fictionists of those once castigated decades that are rapidly becoming the "good old days" accelerates. A dazzling exception to the prevailing tedium is *Nathanael West: The Cheaters and the Cheated*, edited by David Madden; but West is more closely akin to his successors than his contemporaries, and the essays in this imaginatively conceived symposium were collected four years before its publication, at a time when the intellectual and critical atmosphere was quite different from what it has become.

i. General Studies

No single recent book has been devoted to the fiction of the first four decades of this century, but several books about larger subjects have dealt extensively with some of this fiction. The writers have, however, either limited themselves to a discussion of a few outstanding novelists or to the fiction of a single decade.

The two major books dealing with novelists discussed in this chapter are Malcolm Cowley's *A Second Flowering: Works and Days of the Lost Generation* (New York, Viking), which despite its comprehensive subtitle and appended list of hundreds of writers active during the 1920s limits discussion to reminiscences of a small group of writers, including only John Dos Passos, Thornton Wilder, and Thomas Wolfe of those to be mentioned later in this essay, and Alfred Kazin's *Bright Book of Life*, which is primarily concerned with writing since World War II and considers only James Gould Cozzens, John O'Hara, and Katherine Anne Porter of those discussed in this chapter. Working from the premise that Hemingway is "the last great embodiment of the belief that experience can look entirely to literature for its ideal" (p. 3), Kazin—in one of his few generalizations—observes of Cozzens and O'Hara that "the very closeness, shrewdness, felt superiority of observation that gives American novelists of manners their intense interest" also has made them victims of changing fashions (p. 104).

Writing also primarily about post-World-War-II literature, Richard Lehan in the opening sections of *A Dangerous Crossing* discusses Jean Paul Sartre's debt to John Dos Passos's experimental techniques and Albert Camus's debt to James M. Cain's portrayal of the passive, misfit hero, as well as Richard Wright's complicated relationship to the development of existentialist thought.

Robert H. Elias devotes most of two chapters of *"Entangling Alliances with None": An Essay on the Individual in the American Twenties* (New York, Norton) to writers. One chapter will be summarized in the discussion of the writers of the Harlem Renaissance; in the other, Elias illustrates his general principle that "the major poets and novelists even when they are critical of their society, usually share principal assumptions responsible for what they reject" (p. 160). Pointing out that the hero of the 1920s was "the one individual . . . whose accomplishments appeared to have been unaided," as exemplified by Charles Lindbergh (p. 161), Elias outlines the way in which the major twenties' novels of Sinclair Lewis, John Dos Passos, F. Scott Fitzgerald, and Ernest Hemingway reject participation in society not as an ideal but as a reality. Able summaries of familiar points about the novels—evidently prepared for a more general audience than literature specialists—build toward the conclusion that "perhaps the most unqualified expression of reverence for the natural and against the social is E. E. Cummings's *The Enormous Room*, in which every vestige of the institutional world is reduced to an absurdity, and progress is measured by the narrator's appreciation of inarticulate spontaneity" (p. 184).

Richard H. Pells devotes the longest of eight sections of *Radical Visions and American Dreams: Culture and Social Thought in the Depression Years* (New York, Harper and Row) to "Documentaries, Fiction, and the Depression" (pp. 194–251), stressing the autobiographical quality of novels by Michael Gold, Edward Dahlberg, Jack Conroy, James T. Farrell, Nelson Algren, Henry Roth, Henry Miller, William Saroyan, Ernest Hemingway, John Steinbeck, and

Richard Wright in which "the central event was not so much a conversion to revolutionary politics as an assertion of personal identity" (p. 202–Elias also points out that in the 1920s Americans tended towards anarchism rather than radicalism). Generally discerning "an underlying conservatism," even in the radical writers of the 1930s, Pells also points out "in the efforts of writers as different as Daniel Fuchs and William Faulkner a common emphasis on acceptance rather than action, tolerance rather than anger, resignation rather than revolution" (p. 240). The one book that Pells finds "genuinely radical both in form and content" in the Depression period when most "social novels" ironically turned out to be "introspective, pessimistic, traditionalist, and apolitical" is James Agee's *Let Us Now Praise Famous Men*, which introduces innovations "as a way of trying to redefine the relationships between observer and observed, analysis and empathy, internal emotions and the external world" (pp. 246–47).

One group of novels from the depression years is examined in detail in Walter Wells's *Tycoons and Locusts: A Regional Look at Hollywood Fiction of the 1930s* (Carbondale, So. Ill. Univ. Press), which develops the thesis that careful scrutiny of novels by James M. Cain, Horace McCoy, John O'Hara, Nathanael West, F. Scott Fitzgerald and others "makes it clear there *is* an aesthetically significant Hollywood-Southland regionalism" characterized by "a single, overriding theme" of dissolution, developed through motifs of violence and deception and a narrative tone of irony and cynicism (pp. 10–12). Wells fails to observe that this description of a particular provincial fiction might be applied to many of the novels produced in the 1930s throughout the Western world. The literature of the depression also figures prominently in Jerre Mangione's *The Dream and the Deal: The Federal Writers' Project, 1935–1943* (Boston, Little Brown, 1972), a history of this landmark effort with which writers like Jack Conroy, Ralph Ellison, Nelson Algren, Vardis Fisher, and Richard Wright were at times associated.

Two articles briefly present important theses about the literary treatment of our two most often discussed ethnic minorities. Donald G. Baker's examination of "Black Images: The Afro-American in Popular Novels, 1900–1945" (*JPC* 7:327–46) discloses that from 1900 to 1921, "racist sentiments were particularly virulent, hostile, and demeaning towards Black Americans"; from 1922 to 1938 the image was still negative but less stridently hostile, while from 1939 to 1945, during World War II, the Afro-American practically disappeared from best sellers except Lillian Smith's *Strange Fruit.* Samuel I. Bellman's "Sleep, Pride, and Fantasy: Birth Traumas and Socio-Biologic Adaptation in the American-Jewish Novel" (*Costerus* 8:1–12) complains that critics have overemphasized the presentation in fiction of the *substance* of the immigrants' cross-cultural conflicts and stresses the importance of the "shadow side" of fiction like Montague Glass's Potash and Perlmutter stories and Henry Roth's and Daniel Fuchs's novels. This "shadow side," Bellman maintains, "has to do with *the way* in which the Jewish immigrant to America, or the descendant of immigrants, tries to transcend his present position."

A more sweeping subject related to our early 20th-century fiction is broached by John Ditsky's "Carried Away by Numbers: The Rhapsodic Mode in Modern Fiction" (*QQ* 79[1972]:79–84), which discusses the use of the "catalog" technique associated with Homer and Whitman by Henry Miller (*Black Spring*), John Dos Passos (*U.S.A.*), John Steinbeck (*The Grapes of Wrath*), Sinclair Lewis (*Arrowsmith*), and F. Scott Fitzgerald (*The Great Gatsby*). Ditsky argues that "from an isolated and contributing phenomenon involving the domination of matter over form," the style he labels "rhapsodic" has "finally merged with the general literary tendency of our time"—to be carried away by numbers.

The individual writers discussed in this chapter will be grouped as in the past seven reviews under six general headings, two of which will be subdivided to indicate the growing attention to black writers.

ii. Inheritors of the Genteel Tradition

Certainly the major event of the American literary year was the meticulously planned and bountifully supported International Seminar on "The Art of Willa Cather" at the University of Nebraska—Lincoln, October 25–28, bringing together distinguished speakers and commentators from all over the world to celebrate the centenary of Willa Cather's birth. Bernice Slote and Robert E. Knoll devised and managed a program that sponsors of similar future events may well study as a model.

The proceedings of this gathering will be discussed in a future volume after they are published. The centennial year itself, however, was distinguished by the publication of *Willa Cather: A Pictorial*

Memoir (Lincoln, Univ. of Nebr. Press), with a text by Bernice Slote and photographs especially taken for the celebration by Lucia Woods and collected from other sources, presenting in color and black-and-white scenes associated with Willa Cather's early years in Virginia and Nebraska and with the places that she later lived and wrote about in the East, the Southwest, and Canada.

Another elegant tribute to this great lady of letters is the September issue of the *CLQ*, which presents five long considerations of her work. Half the issue is devoted to one of her often neglected novels, *My Mortal Enemy* (1926). Harry B. Eichorn's "A Falling Out with Love: *My Mortal Enemy*" (10:121–38) is an impressive analysis of the novelist's use of references to Shakespeare (*King Lear*, *King John*, and *Richard III*) and Bellini's opera *Norma* to "bypass" the narrator Nellie Birdsong in order "to let the reader know more about Myra than Nellie can tell him" through suggesting Myra Henshawe's awareness of the relevance of the allusions to her own life and using "Shakespeare to suggest the life that Myra wishes she could have lived . . . Bellini to suggest the life that Nellie would have preferred for her." Theodore A. Adams argues less ambitiously in "Willa Cather's *My Mortal Enemy*: The Concise Presentation of Scene, Character, and Theme" (10:138–48) that this shortest of her novels and "most extreme example of tightly restricted form," despite a "superficially random air," "perhaps stands alone in its possession of a unity which is both simple and flawless." After calling attention to "an unfortunate trend in Cather criticism in which the novelist's fiction is confused with her life," John J. Murphy proceeds in "The Respectable Romantic and the Unwed Mother: Class Consciousness in *My Àntonia*" (10:149–56) to suggest that if anything "defeats the potential of Cather's West it is the emergence of classes and the materialistic struggle accompanying it." James R. Bash's "Willa Cather and the Anathema of Materialism" (10:157–68) pursues the theme of this "cultural and chronological primitivist's" detestation of the "ugly crest of materialism" that manifested itself in mechanization and standardization, misuse of the land, and devotion to money making. In "The Sculptor and the Spinster: Jewett's 'Influence' on Cather" (10:168–78), editor Richard Cary rounds off this collection of tributes to Willa Cather's unimpeachable individualism by analyzing changes that the writer made in two printings subsequent to the original appearance of her short story, "The Sculptor's Funeral," in an effort to show that she "signally" failed after meeting Sarah Orne Jewett "to infuse this fundamental story with finer perceptivities" that might have made it imitative.

James Woodress speculates in another study of the relationship between the writers, "Sarah Orne Jewett and Willa Cather" (*EST* 5:477–88) that Miss Jewett greatly but subtly influenced Miss Cather to abandon a Jamesean approach to writing and adopt a Wordsworthian one. Woodress argues also that these two writers often classified as realists should be recognized as romantics. He contributes also to the *Gohdes Festschrift*, "The Pre-eminent Magazine Genius: S. S. McClure" (pp. 171–92), which is valuable to the study of Willa Cather because of the details it provides of her editorial career with McClure's publications—the work that brought her first important recognition.

David and Mary-Ann Stouck, who last year collaborated on "Hagiographical Style in *Death Comes for the Archbishop*" (*ALS 1972*, p. 239), publish separate pieces on Willa Cather also. Mary-Ann Stouck's "Chaucer's Pilgrims and Cather's Priests" (*CLQ* 9 [1972]:531–37) points out parallels between Cather's later novels and *The Canterbury Tales* arising from both writers' regarding "their characters in the light of religious or moral conviction rather than from the viewpoint of psychological development with its stress upon cause and effect." David Stouck winds up a series of articles considering Willa Cather's entire career with "Willa Cather's Last Four Books" (*Novel* 7:41–53), in which he suggests that while she explored "archetypal dimensions of the human imagination" in earlier novels, her often-slighted last publications are "informed throughout by a profound regret that youth in its self-absorption is so often cruel and indifferent." Willa Cather was one of the few Americans, Stouck believes, who followed the circuitous artist's path that ultimately "returns its pilgrim to life."

Sister Lucy Schneider also continues a series extending over several years with three more articles on Willa Cather's "Land-Philosophy." Two concern the expression of this philosophy in late books (also considered in David Stouck's article)—"Of Land and Light: Willa Cather's *Lucy Gayheart*" (*KanQ* 5,iv:51–62) and "Willa Cather's 'The Best Years': The Essence of Her 'Land Philosophy'" (*MQ* 15:61–69). "Artistry and Instinct: Willa Cather's 'Land Philosophy'" (*CLAJ* 16:485–504), however, sums up the discussion that began in 1968 with a listing of the seven cardinal points of this philosophy that views the land as: "a symbol for essences," "good by nature" but sometimes seemingly evil in operations, a blending of "the elemental and the traditional," "a force actively operating on man," "the source of harvests," the source as well of "openness and breadth of vision," and finally a force fostering transcendence.

Curiously the approach of the centenary of Ellen Glasgow's birth in 1874 has not resulted in a renewed flurry of critical interest in her work; but Edith Wharton continues a subject of increasing interest as the society she epitomized becomes increasingly legendary. James Tuttleton refashions material from several earlier articles for his perceptive account in *The Novel of Manners in America* (1972) and also contributes a detailed analysis of Wharton studies in the manner of the entries in the newly published *Sixteen Modern American Authors*, "Edith Wharton: An Essay in Bibliography" (*RALS* 3:163–202).

David Clough scrutinizes some of Mrs. Wharton's less often discussed novels in "Edith Wharton's War Novels: A Reappraisal" (*TCL* 19:1–14), which charges the generally acknowledged failure of *The Marne* and *A Son at the Front* to the novelist's inability to adjust to change, with the result that "her best books are set in the past." When she did accept the finality of the change to a new post-war society, Clough continues, she was also able to give an edge of irony to novels like *The Age of Innocence*; but "her attempts to write about the war are too close to the change itself" to produce other than "a defiant yet hopeless stand against the course of history."

Other essays make specialized points of interest. Jan Cohn's "The Houses of Fiction: Domestic Architecture in Howells and Edith Wharton" (*TSLL* 15:537–50) presents Mrs. Wharton as less ambivalent than Howells toward the reward of material achievement with a great house, probably because her "aversion toward the new moneyed rising class" was less complex than his. Robert McIlvaine's "Edith Wharton's American Beauty Rose" (*JAmS* 7:183–85) suggests that Wharton's extensive use of rose imagery may have been suggested by John D. Rockefeller, Jr.'s striking statement in support of big business that the "American beauty rose can be produced in the splendor and fragrance which bring cheer to its beholder only by sacrificing the early buds which grow up around it." Donald Phelps's vaguely titled "Edith Wharton and the Invisible" (*Prose* 7:227–45) is a rambling appreciation of the novelist which makes the point that she renders characters that are not typical but archetypal, because of "that precisely appraised magnitude and weight, that perception of shopkeepers or farmers or salesmen as emanations of their circumstances."

The House of Mirth is linked with *Daisy Miller* and *The Great Gatsby* in John H. Randall's detailed "Romeo and Juliet in the New World: A Study in James, Wharton, and Fitzgerald, 'Fay ce que vouldras'" (*Costerus* 8:109–76) which reads all three as stories of the way in which "the protagonist insists on freedom in the form of unconventional, spontaneous behavior in search of love," which incurs strong antagonism, usually in the form of social snobbery, that ultimately destroys the protagonist. Wharton enthusiasts should also not miss the involved argument in Adeline R. Tintner's "James's Mock Epic: 'The Velvet Glove,' Edith Wharton, and Other Late Tales" (*MFS* 17 [1972]:483–99) that Henry James's short story "The Velvet Glove" is an elaborate literary joke on Edith Wharton, "who plays the dual role of Artemis and the Scribbling Princess."

One of the most surprising phenomena of the last few years has been the increasing interest in those writers beginning with Owen Wister who transported the attitudes of the genteel tradition westward as they began to lose their hold in the East. Richard W. Etulain's *Owen Wister* (WWS 7) is precisely the kind of account that we have needed recently of this "revived" author. Etulain has no illusions about Wister's importance as an artist and recognizes that his subject "is a more important figure for the literary and cultural historian than he is for the student of American belles lettres" (p. 46). Etulain provides a far more comprehensive account than we have had before of Wister's early Lin McLean stories; and, although he finds nothing really new to say about *The Virginian*, his discussion of the novel as evidence of Wister's "ambiguous response" to the West concludes with this statement that summarizes—as an introductory guide of this kind should—many recent comments about Wister's one major book: "The ending of *The Virginian* is Wister's testament of acceptance. Like many other men of the progressive era, Wister came to terms with industrialism and accepted the likelihood of its dominance. Though he would continue to long for wide-open spaces and for the symbolic old West, he turned to the machine as a key to the future of America" (p. 37).

The most ambitious treatment thus far of *The Virginian* is Sanford Marovitz's "Testament of a Patriot: The Virginian, The Tenderfoot, and Owen Wister" (*TSLL* 15:551–75), which provides a more thorough history than Etulain's book of the creation of the novel and its role in Wister's life. Marovitz also pays more attention than previous writers to the transformation of the tenderfoot narrator "from a laughable greenhorn to an experienced Western hunter," through the narrator's constant analysis of his own experience. But Marovitz presses his case too far when he claims a Jamesean consciousness for the narrator and argues that Wister succeeds in making the novel a testament to his faith not only in the West, but the United States as a unified nation by uniting in the narrator and the Virginian "the two halves of America . . . through their representatives." Marovitz writes not about the melodramatic tale that Wister—with limited technical skill and an ambivalent viewpoint fashioned—but about the better novel that could have been built around the material that Wister employs.

Only a brave or foolhardy person would undertake a new survey of Walter Van Tilburg Clark's fiction in the wake of Max Westbrook's noteworthy study (see *ALS 1970*, pp. 229–30); yet L. L. Lee's *Walter Van Tilburg Clark* (WWS 8) is a creditable account that wisely draws upon Westbrook's without imitating it or unwisely attacking it. Lee shows no evidence of a real insight into Westbrook's concept of "sacrality," but his introduction is a valuable stepping-stone for readers who may find Westbrook's book initially difficult. Lee's basic argument is that "Clark's vision *was* truly tragic" (p. 13), and this is indisputably sound preparation for his conclusion that in Clark's work the American dream "has turned bad, and perhaps one cannot make it good again" (p. 43). The reader must achieve this understanding before he can pass beyond it—as Westbrook does—to what a poet that Clark admired, Robinson Jeffers, called "the tower beyond tragedy."

One popular Western writer is the subject of a full-length study, Carlton Jackson's *Zane Grey* (TUSAS 218), a scrupulous and respectful book that provides a thorough record of Grey's career but makes no critical point about his work except the artistically irrelevant one that it is historically accurate. Another once popular "Western" writer (though not of "Westerns" in the usual sense) is re-examined in Joe L. Dubbert's "William Allen White's American Adam" (*WAL*

7:271–78), which argues that the Kansas newspaper editor's attempt to create in *In the Heart of a Fool* (1918) a major novel "based on the tension between the forces of spiritualism and materialism in America" was repudiated by an audience that was moving away from "thoughts of sacrifice and the moral enlistment of noble and high purposes"—a movement that many would interpret as sounding the death knell for the genteel tradition.

Not many critics are concerning themselves with later representatives of the fading tradition, although two bibliographical guides to writings about James Gould Cozzens have appeared: James R. Meriwether's *James Gould Cozzens: A Checklist* (Detroit, Gale) describes only Cozzens's own writings; Pierre Michel's *James Gould Cozzens: An Annotated Checklist* (Kent, Ohio, Kent State Univ. Press, 1971) also abstracts material from secondary sources including book reviews.

iii. The Redskins

When Philip Rahv applied the term "redskins" to the upstart challengers of the "paleface" defenders of the beleaguered genteel tradition, he could scarcely have imagined that reviews of criticism of American writing during the first decade of this century might come to concentrate largely on Jack London and Owen Wister as representatives of these groups, but the London revival continues to outstrip even the Wister revival.

One of its most curious evidences is A. W. Freeman's *A Search for Jack London* (Chicago, Adams Press), a brief work by a communications technician, who tells of an enthusiasm for London that began in 1938. Freeman's book is almost entirely limited, however, to accounts of books *about* London rather than London's fiction. Seeking through biographies to discover "who Jack London really was," Freeman reaches the conclusion that London was neither a great writer nor a great agent in producing social change, but a "Humanist," remembered for his feelings of brotherly love.

Also of slight value as literary criticism, but valuable as cultural history is Kevin Starr's analysis in *Americans and the California Dream, 1850–1915* (New York, Oxford Univ. Press) of some of London's infrequently discussed later works—*Burning Daylight* (1910), *The Valley of the Moon* (1913), and *The Little Lady of the Big*

House (1916)—as the novelist's effort to create a "last will and testament to California possibilities." Starr describes *Burning Daylight*—named for the principal character—as a back-to-the-soil novel, advocating "a not too startling version of the good life" out-of-doors, typical of many versions of turn-of-the-century California theorizing. Starr also discusses the recently little studied Gertrude Atherton, another California propagandist, and describes as a road to self-delusion her repeated concern with the interplay between biological heritage and local culture that she believed produced best results through a blending of traditional aristocratic and exotic strains. Further evidence of Jack London's California chauvinism is afforded by Mukhtar A. Isani's "Jack London on Norris' *The Octopus*" (*ALR* 6:66–69), which reprints a review from the short-lived *San Francisco Impressions* (1901), in which London glowingly describes Norris's promise as realized in "The Epic of the Wheat."

After two years of heavy activity sparked by the celebration of the Dreiser centennial, attention to the most conspicuous challenger of the genteel tradition has understandably abated. (See also Chapter 19,*v*.) Donald Pizer continues his studies, however, by returning in "A Summer at Maumee: Theodore Dreiser Writes Four Stories" in the *Gohdes Festschrift* (pp. 193–204) to some rarely examined short stories published before *Sister Carrie* in order to trace the relationship of themes and techniques employed in "When the Old Century Was New," "The Shining Slave Makers," "Nigger Jeff," and "Butcher Roagum's Door" to those in later novels. Pizer finds the early stories foreshadow Dreiser's preoccupations with the view that life is "essentially circular," the triangular pattern of authoritarian parents driving a child seeking excitement into the hands of a would-be seducer, and a "tendency toward the parody of sentimental or hackneyed narrative patterns" (p. 203).

Two critics study techniques Dreiser devised for manipulating readers. Mary E. Burgan's "*Sister Carrie* and the Pathos of Naturalism" (*Criticism* 15:336–49) is a useful companion piece to Warwick Wadlington's "Pathos and Dreiser" (*ALS 1971*, p. 216). Burgan describes the different kinds of pathos that Dreiser uses in his effort to make Carrie acceptable as a heroine and central figure to readers who might not approve of her behavior. Editor Hans-Joachim Lang contributes to his *Der Amerikanische Roman: Von den Anfängen bis zur Gegenwart* (Düsseldorf, August Bagel Verlag) "Dreiser, Jennie Gerhardt" (pp. 194–218), which points out that although from the viewpoint of literary realism, Jennie is the least convincing character in the novel named for her, Dreiser makes her appealing through flights of fancy that induce readers to share her feelings.

Two other critics go behind the scenes of the production of novels. Philip Gerber follows up last year's "Dreiser's Debt to *Jay Cooke*" (*ALS 1972*, p. 244) with "The Financier Himself: Dreiser and C. T. Yerkes" (*PMLA* 88:112–21), in which he traces parallels between the life of the fictional hero of the Frank Cowperwood trilogy and the Chicago financier who provided the principal model for him. Jack Salzman's "The Curious History of Dreiser's *The Bulwark*" (*Proof* 3:21–61) reproduces a salesman's "dummy" copy of *The Bulwark*, prepared in 1916, when the novel was announced for publication, and compares its contents with the parallel sections of the novel finally published in 1945. Salzman argues that the version that finally reached print is essentially the result of the editing of Donald B. Elder.

The *DN* in its fourth volume continues to bring together reviews, interviews, and biographical notes. Of particular interest is Ellen Moers's "A 'New' First Novel by Arthur Henry" (4,ii:7–9), which identifies a long forgotten *Nicholas Blood, Candidate* (1892) as the actual first published novel of this man who became a close friend of Dreiser's after they met in 1894. Moers speculates that Henry kept this early effort secret from Dreiser and other friends because "it is a smoothly-written piece of rabid anti-Negro propaganda."

Ronald Gottesman and C. Loring Silet have chronicled in *The Literary Manuscripts of Upton Sinclair* (Columbus, Ohio State Univ. Press, CALM 2) the five-hundred thousand manuscript leaves—about half letters—in the Lilly Library at Indiana University—Bloomington. Gottesman discusses in "Some Implications of *The Literary Manuscripts of Upton Sinclair*" (*Proof* 3:395–410) the possibility of at last producing a thorough and complete biography of the prolific polemicist by drawing upon this vast mass of documents.

Of those writers who cheerlessly chronicled the urbanization of the United States between the Civil War and World War I only Abraham Cahan, because of his contribution to the development of the Jewish-American novel, continues to receive steady attention. David M. Fine's "Abraham Cahan, Stephen Crane, and the Romantic Tenement Tale of the Nineties" (*AmerS* 14:95–107) compares Cahan's first novel, *Yekl, A Tale of the New York Ghetto* (1896) with Crane's *Maggie* and points out that, though Cahan "drew his materials directly from the life he knew at first-hand and Crane from life observed from the perspective of an outsider," the same ironic and detached point-of-view pervades both these books that "failed to win the immediate positive recognition they deserved" because they made readers uncomfortable by "refusing to conform to the sentimental and romantic assumptions of the popular tenement tale." Dan Vogel's "Cahan's *Rise of David Levinsky*: Archetype of American Jewish Fiction" (*Judaism* 22:278–87) claims that Cahan's best-known novel "formulated the first two archetypal characteristics of American-Jewish literature: the theme of the consequences of the collision of Old World Orthodoxy with New World materialistic emancipation, and the anti-hero as the central character of the drama."

iv. The Iconoclasts—The Revolt against the Village

Since the death of John Dos Passos, last survivor of the great "debunkers" of the myth of the American village as the seat of homely virtues, the now aging works of those gadflies whose reputations declined during the 1940s and 1950s have become the subject of affirmative reevaluations.

Sinclair Lewis receives the biggest boost from a thoughtful new book appraising his art, morality, and polemics and three articles extolling the scope of his achievement. James Lundquist's *Sinclair Lewis* (New York, Frederick Ungar) provides a well-balanced discussion of the way in which Lewis's turning one-by-one "to the topics that any student of American culture must first understand before he can understand anything—the small town, the businessman, the scientist, the preacher, the capitalist in search of culture, the latent fascism in American democracy, and race relations" makes him "a writer of lasting importance in understanding America" (p. 32). The editor of the *SLN* concludes his compact account with the provocative observation that "if there is a single word that may be used to describe and categorize Lewis's books," it is "garish," because "they embody a particular kind of contemporaneity that is effectively defined in the word 'pop' and its implication of obsession with the bizarre forms and life patterns that are part of the everyday world in the economy-of-abundance democracies of this century" (p. 128).

The other essays reinforce Lindquist's argument that Lewis "helped his readers to become part of the intellectual movement that now seems to be the most significant part of twentieth-century American history, the development of a national self-awareness" (p. 32). Martin Light's "The Quixotic Motifs of *Main Street*" (*ArQ* 29:221–34) concentrates on the single novel, arguing that regarding it as an expression of quixotism can uncover the source of its vitality and appeal "by placing it in a significant literary context." Light concludes that paradoxically because Carol Kennicott continues to see "as her aspirations demand" rather than resign herself to humdrum reality, "she is more honest and more deceived than anyone around her and thereby both more trapped and more alive."

James Lea's "Sinclair Lewis and the Implied America" (*ClioW* 3:21–34) and Glen A. Love's "New Pioneering on the Prairies: Nature, Progress, and the Individual in the Novels of Sinclair Lewis" (*AQ* 25:558–77) make similar large claims for seeing Lewis's work as a whole as creating an American mythology. Lea argues that Lewis not only depicted the contemporary world, but also created a past for the United States based on his own assumptions of a better world that had its potential thwarted by "the reckless tending of the national garden" portrayed in the major novels of the 1920s. Love searches for "patterns of affirmation" in the works of a novelist usually read as a "nay-sayer" and finds also that the Lewis hero endeavors "to assert not only his own individuality," but to commit himself also to the shaping of a new society. The novelist's best works, therefore, not only spell out an "appropriate role for new leaders of America," but preserve also "an important record of the impact of modern technology upon the tenaciously held Arcadian myths of middle America" (p. 577).

Maxwell Geismar also makes grand claims for a writer more neglected than Lewis in the largely biographical *Ring Lardner and the Portrait of Folly* (New York, Crowell, 1972), which presents Lardner's fiction as "a curious kind of inverted biography," debunking his own career and related to the work of Mark Twain and a whole line of American humorists who remind us that "the only way to endure the pain and tragedy of life . . . is through the divine gift of laughter" (p. 115).

A once very popular novelist and friend of Lewis's, who is now almost totally forgotten, is the subject of James Justus's "Joseph

Hergesheimer's Germany: A Radical Art of Surfaces" (*JAmS* 7:47–66), an examination of Hergesheimer's account of his travels in *Berlin* (1932). Justus points out that it is surprising to find in an account of Germany in 1931, "the nature of the Nazi threat is never actualized . . . even in the most sinister or bizarre episodes," but he attributes this absence to Hergesheimer's refashioning "the cities he visits into constructs of *his* space" and chooses "only those moments in their presentness that are required for his self-absorbing imagination to distil, ready-made, as artifice."

Like these studies of Lardner and Hergesheimer, two new books about John Dos Passos are almost entirely biographical: Melvin Landsberg's *Dos Passos' Path to "U.S.A.": A Political Biography, 1912–1936* (Boulder, Colorado Associated Univ. Press, 1972) deals almost entirely with the novelist's involvement in public affairs as a preparation for his writing, and Townsend Ludington's *The Fourteenth Chronicle: Letters and Diaries of John Dos Passos* (Boston, Gambit) incorporates these documents with a biographical narrative. Even Lois Hughson's "In Search of the True America: Dos Passos' Debt to Whitman in *U.S.A.*" (*MFS* 19:179–92) is largely biographical in its tracing of the way in which Dos Passos's effort to capture—like Whitman—"the soul of America" was aided by Stephen Crane's "fidelity to actual cadence and vocabulary" suggesting that this "soul" might be incarnated in his own work. Hughson finds, however, that "the vision of humanity that brought Whitman a triumphant satisfaction" permits Dos Passos only a triumphant hunger because he fundamentally believes "in the ultimate impassibility from history to myth, diversity to unity." Dos Passos's concept that triumph comes only through suffering is brought out also by Robert McIlvaine's "Dos Passos' *Three Soldiers*" (*Expl* 31: Item 50), which notes that John Andrews's sympathy for all life is the indirect cause of his suffering a wound that in turn leads to an increase in his integrity.

William Leigh Godshalk's "Cabell's *Cream of the Jest* and Recent American Fiction" (*SLJ* 5,ii:18–31) compensates for the lack of other studies of the novelist by the magnitude and debatability of its claim that "from one point of view, at least, Cabell is technically and thematically the forebear of the fiction of the 50's and 60's," because his character Kennaston, by standing "in a long line of twentieth-century protagonists who are mentally abnormal," looks forward to, among others, Kurt Vonnegut, Jr.'s Billy Pilgrim (in *Slaughterhouse-Five*), who also when he finds reality too much for him must create through the convention of fictional biography "another dimension in which to exist."

Christiane Johnson makes an almost equally large and subjective claim for another relatively little studied work in "Langage et point de vue dans la nouvelle de Sherwood Anderson: 'The Strength of God'" (*EA* 26:187–94). Johnson maintains that although the work uses a very limited vocabulary, each word is charged with all the significance that the protagonist, consciously or not, finds in himself and that these words contribute to his infatuation by serving as a defense mechanism to enable him to avoid seeing things more clearly. (Another study of Anderson is discussed in the next section along with other works about Jean Toomer.)

v. The Iconoclasts—The Rise of Black Consciousness

Accounts to supplement Nathan Irvin Huggins's *Harlem Renaissance* (*ALS 1971*, pp. 225–26) continue to appear, though no other writer has yet presented such a comprehensive overview. Noel Schraufnagel's *From Apology to Protest: The Black American Novel* (Deland, Fla., Everett/Edwards), which appears to have been completed before the publication of Huggins's book, devotes only eight of 200 pages to the period and dismisses Jean Toomer's recently much-discussed *Cane* as "a potpourri of stories, poetry, and drama that treats racial matters in a relatively objective manner while at the same time illustrating the problem of a black identity in a country dominated by white values" (p. 13). Like Huggins, Schraufnagel considers white novelist Carl Van Vechten's *Nigger Heaven* (1926) the book that inspired black writers like Claude McKay and Wallace Thurman. While this brief account is a useful summary of important authors and titles, the concluding judgments that "black novelists before 1940 did not reveal a great deal of technical skill" and that Richard Wright is the first important black to create "an art form out of the protest novel" are scarcely adequate in view of other recent analyses of Langston Hughes, Thurman, and Toomer.

A more provocative view is Robert H. Elias's in "*Entangling Alliances with None*" that the writers of the Harlem Renaissance "despite the new awareness of a group expression and communal effort . . . were in their self-centered individuality unable to perceive the need to challenge the narrow self-concern pervading the decade in economic, social, and political thinking" (p. 160). Related points that also need further consideration are Robert C. Hart's in "Black-White Literary Relations in the Harlem Renaissance" (*AL* 44:612–28) that the black writers had no association with really prestigious white writers of the period and that white patronage resulted in the distortion of black writing to meet white expectations, even though "white support did help some gifted black writers to write some worthwhile things." The extensive help that some of these black writers also received from a prominent official of the NAACP is described in Edward H. Waldron's "Walter White and the Harlem Renaissance: Letters from 1924 to 1927" (*CLAJ* 16:438–57). Also of unusual biographical interest is Phyliss Martin Lang's "Claude McKay: Evidences of a Magic Pilgrimage" (*CLAJ* 16:475–84), which describes interviews published in *Pravda* and *Izvestia* during McKay's trip to Russia between September, 1922, and June, 1923.

Jean Toomer continues to fascinate critics. Larry E. Thompson's "Jean Toomer as Modern Man" (*Renaissance 2* 1[1971]:7–10) is a general introduction that presents his life as a quest "for singularity in himself and mankind." The growing literature on *Cane* is augmented by Mary Jane Dickerson's "Sherwood Anderson and Jean Toomer: A Literary Relationship" (*SAF* 1:163–74), which calls attention to the similarities of Toomer's novel to *Winesburg, Ohio*, which also lacks "any conventional plot structure." Dickerson also finds Anderson's *Dark Laughter* (1925) a response to *Cane* in its treatment of "the conflict between man in nature and man's growing industrialization and urbanization." Since "the only common American experience seems to be the rural, land-oriented search for material and spiritual sustenance," Dickerson finds both novelists' work achieving a mythological dimension in reviving the origins of our heritage and revealing "the awesome dimensions of the quest of white people and black people who still possess a sense of their elemental sources in the land." Michael J. Krasny's "Design in Jean Toomer's *Balo*" (*NALF* 7:103–04) points out that this poorly-constructed, one-act sketch about black life in Georgia (written in 1924) also is concerned like *Cane* with "the forces which inhibit, pervert and destroy innate spirituality."

vi. The Expatriates

The approach of the centennial of Gertrude Stein's birth on February 3, 1974, has produced nothing like the preparations made for the Willa Cather centenary (not even a postage-stamp tribute), but the fourth and final issue of the short-lived *The Widening Circle* (Columbus, Ohio) offered a commemorative tribute devoted principally to short recollections of Miss Stein by editor William D. Baker, Donald Gallup, Donald Sutherland, Virgil Thomson, and others. Two critical articles illuminate her still perplexing works. Harry R. Garvin's "The Human Mind and *Tender Buttons*" (pp. 11–13) argues unconventionally that the reader of Stein's pieces "must discipline his human mind austerely and intensely" in the same way that the writer disciplined hers in composing and that "all critical interpretations of *Tender Buttons* . . . should be based at least initially on the critic's feelings in his own *consciousness* while actually reading each portrait." Allegra Stewart's "Flat Land as Explanation" (pp. 22, 31–33) explains Stein's belief that "a country, like an individual, has a 'bottom nature' " and argues that Stein's "emphasis upon the homelessness of the American" reflects "a profound grasp on her part of the nature of the American psyche, denuded of those inner images and old world modes of feeling still so alive in England and France."

Another intriguing explanation of a Stein work is Lawrence D. Stewart's "Gertrude Stein and the Vital Dead" (MDAC 1[1972]: 102–23), which discloses that Stein showed no interest in detective stories until 1933 when a curious death she learned of inspired the composition of *Blood on the Dining-Room Floor.* Although even Stein herself called this work "a detective story," Stewart finds it rather "an autobiographical meditation upon the mystery of Madame Pernollet's demise." A more general consideration of Stein's techniques, L. T. Fitz's "Gertrude Stein and Picasso: The Language of Surfaces" (*AL* 45:228–37), describes her style as sharing with the painter's: "(1) a cubist approach; (2) a style which concentrates on what is seen rather than what is remembered; and (3) a calligraphic or nonsymbolic concept of language." The relationship of Stein's style to Picasso's is also the subject of Reid Maynard's "Abstractionism in Gertrude Stein's *Three Lives* (*BSUF* 15,i:68–71), which concludes that her abstractionism is finally too didactic and that a purely stylistic substitute for a conventional plot is not enough.

Another writer's style that is still often found puzzling is considered in Edward Gunn's "Myth and Style in Djuna Barnes's *Nightwood*" (*MFS* 19:545–55), which provides detailed illustrations of the critic's theory that Barnes uses a vast range of continually recurrent and interrelated images to draw "a parallel between certain historically recognized myths and certain personal myths in much the same fashion as certain contemporary psychologists."

vii. The Cosmogonists—Porter, Steinbeck, West, Wilder, Wolfe

As we move along in the Seventies, interest increases in those five authors who with William Faulkner created the most ambitious and apocalyptic visions of man's situation in the dark days of the 1930s.

Katherine Anne Porter's vision continues to elude critics. John Edward Hardy's *Katherine Anne Porter* (New York, Frederick Ungar) provides—like many past articles and books—perceptive readings of individual stories, but no comprehensive assessment of her achievement. Hardy groups the short stories into those dealing with the family as a "hideous institution," "always supported in its evil work by other institutions" (p. 14), those presenting childless couples as leading "stifling lives," if anything "even more miserable" than those of the parents in her fiction (p. 46), and those generally considered "her finest work," in which "the central figures are people whose desperate preoccupation with themselves cuts them off from effective communication with all other human beings" (p. 62). He also joins M. M. Liberman in defending *Ship of Fools* against disappointed attackers, by arguing that it is not at all a conventional novel, but what he "would not attempt to define, but only cautiously to describe, as a tragic satire" (p. 112), foreshadowed among her own works by "The Leaning Tower" and "Hacienda." Hardy's caution, expressed in the last quotation, though understandable and commendable, fragments his work. In an opening biographical chapter, he quotes Miss Porter as explaining to a friend that when she nearly died of influenza in 1918, she had "what the Christians call the 'beatific vision' " and that "if you have had that, and survived it . . . you are no longer like other people" (p. 53). We await the critic who can explain her work in the light of this perception of herself.

Actually Joseph Weisenfarth makes a start in this direction in

"Negatives of Hope: A Reading of Katherine Anne Porter" (*Renascence* 25:85–94). He writes with a heated enthusiasm rarely found today in the decorous business of literary criticism about the way in which her stories may be comprehensively viewed as showing "man how and why he is spiritually blind and how and why he hates," yet as also showing "with as much intensity, if more rarely, how and why he can be reborn and live again." Here is one critic who should be encouraged to expand his work.

If Katherine Anne Porter still really awaits discovery, John Steinbeck has surely been discovered. Not even the works of the much-honored Willa Cather received during 1973 the critical attention accorded Steinbeck in six books and monographs, including Richard Astro's *John Steinbeck and Edward F. Ricketts: The Shaping of a Novelist* (Minneapolis, Univ. of Minn. Press), the most important contribution to Steinbeck studies since Joseph Fontenrose's *John Steinbeck: An Introduction and Interpretation* ten years ago. Starting from the sound premise that "earlier studies of Steinbeck's philosophy of life have been short-sighted and incomplete," Astro discusses in detail the long-vexing question of the influence on Steinbeck of Edward F. Ricketts, a marine biologist, who served as a model for principal characters in six of Steinbeck's novels, most notably *In Dubious Battle* and *Cannery Row.* Drawing on unpublished writings of Ricketts, Astro first points out the ambiguities created by the difference between Ricketts's concept of "non-teleological thinking" and the conventional philosophical concept of teleology. Ricketts, Astro believes, applies the term to "an open approach to life by the man who looks at events and accepts them as such without reservation or qualification, and in so doing perceives the whole picture by becoming an identifiable part of that picture" (p. 38). Astro then analyzes the two men's contributions to "The Log" from *Sea of Cortez* and the shifting influence of Ricketts's ideas on Steinbeck's fictions, pointing out disagreements between them and reaching the conclusion that "Steinbeck is at his best as a writer, not when he fictionalizes a given set of Ricketts' precepts about man and the world, or when he totally ignores Ricketts, but rather when he examines critically what he regards as the virtues and flaws in Ricketts' vision and integrates the marine biologist's way of seeing with his own commitment to human progress" (p. 229). An enjoyable accompaniment to Astro's book is Steve Crouch's *Steinbeck Country* (Palo

Alto, Calif., American West Publishing Co.), which illustrates many of the places associated with Steinbeck and Ricketts.

The indefatigably industrious Tetsumaro Hayashi, editor of the *StQ*, has edited also two reference guides that will serve for some years to come as the cornerstone of Steinbeck studies. *A New Steinbeck Bibliography, 1929–1971* (Metuchen, N.J., Scarecrow) supersedes Hayashi's *John Steinbeck: A Concise Bibliography (1930–1965)* (1967). The entries in the new book, limited to "primary and secondary sources written in English," are not only expanded, but also rearranged, numbered, and indexed for more convenient reference than in the first book. (Over eighteen hundred secondary sources are listed.)

Hayashi's *Steinbeck's Literary Dimension: A Guide to Comparative Studies* (Metuchen, N.J., Scarecrow) complements the bibliography with surveys of Steinbeck criticism by the editor and by Peter Lisca, although the main purpose of the volume is to bring together ten essays comparing Steinbeck with other novelists and one about his relationship to Adlai Stevenson. Nine of these essays have previously appeared in the *StQ* or elsewhere and have been earlier summarized in *ALS* (besides the essay on Stevenson, these include comparisons with Dickens, Faulkner, Hemingway, Kazantzakis, Daniel Mainwaring, John Milton, Robert Penn Warren, and Emile Zola). In one of the hitherto unpublished pieces, "The God in Darkness: Steinbeck and D. H. Lawrence" (pp. 67–82), Richard F. Peterson continues a subject explored earlier by Reloy Garcia (see *ALS 1972*, p. 255) and finds that only during a "brief but critical period of time" in the early 1930s when Steinbeck was working on *To a God Unknown* "Lawrence's fiction provided a model" for him. In the other new piece, "Steinbeck and Salinger: Messiah-Moulders for a Sick Society" (pp. 105–15), Warren French argues that, despite dissimilarities, *The Grapes of Wrath* and *The Catcher in the Rye* are alike in providing the kind of refurbishing that "the American literary idiom" perennially needs in order to break the hold of the dead hand of the past upon it and to bring it closer to "expressing the feelings of the discomforted elements in American society," through conjuring up afresh out of the "American myth of the perpetual frontier," "colloquial Messiahs."

The fifth new book about Steinbeck, Warren French's *A Filmguide to "The Grapes of Wrath"* (Bloomington, Ind. Univ. Press) might lie outside the scope of this survey, except that, although focused primarily on the film version of Steinbeck's novel, it contains much material comparing the novel with the film, including a detailed chart of similarities and differences between them (pp. 74–87). The principal point of the comparison is that "the final point of the movie is exactly the opposite of the novel's. It is an insistence that survival depends not upon changing and dynamically accommodating one's self to new challenges [as in the novel], but rather upon passively accepting one's lot and keeping plodding along" (p. 226).

Perhaps the late Lawrence Williams Jones's brief *John Steinbeck as Fabulist*, edited by Marston LaFrance (SMS 3) can scarcely be called a book, but it is one of the most important analyses to appear so far of the failure of Steinbeck's later fiction. Using terms derived from Sheldon Sacks's *Fiction and the Shape of Belief* (1964), Jones argues that Steinbeck, who was all his life hospitable to "the various conventions of parable," during the latter half of his career wrote not "novels" but "apologues." Jones concludes that Steinbeck had increasing difficulty with this rigorously exacting form because he could never develop "a compelling vision of evil to match his vision of good," so that his work lacked the balance needed to make it fully relevant to 20th-century man.

Much more has been written recently about Steinbeck, however, than these six books. Of some three dozen dissertations announced in 1973 dealing with writers discussed in this chapter (eight on Willa Cather alone), the one promising the most original and valuable approach to one of these fictionists is Clifford L. Lewis's "John Steinbeck: Architect of the Unconscious" (*DAI* 34:781A), a University of Texas dissertation based upon unpublished manuscripts and letters in the University's collection that argues that all of Steinbeck's writing has attempted to show the influence of the unconscious upon a person's life.

A start toward exploring this topic is made in one of the papers printed in the Spring 1973 issue of *UWR*—those delivered at the 1972 meeting of the John Steinbeck Society, which—with an introduction by John Ditsky—constitute the equivalent of yet another short book about Steinbeck. Robert DeMott's "Toward a Redefinition of *To a God Unknown*" (8,ii:34–53) provocatively rejects earlier critics' treatment of the novel as a "mystical" study of man's relationship to God and argues that "it does not move toward God, but toward man" and "attempts to demonstrate how the unconscious impinges upon and often crosses into the conscious realm of man," so that it is actually the unconscious that is "the unknown god within . . . upon which the cyclical continuance of man and nature depends."

Peter Lisca's "Keynote Address: New Perspectives in Steinbeck Studies" (8, ii:6–10) introduces this group of essays representing "current trends in the continuing re-evaluation of Steinbeck's critical importance" by calling attention to the "first scholarly importance" of the establishment of such still-missing standard sources as a full-length biography and critical editions of manuscripts and letters. Leo Gurko's "*Of Mice and Men*: Steinbeck as Manichean" (8, ii:11–23) argues that "underlying the novel and controlling it, is Steinbeck's vision of the universe as the scene of a decisive and unpredictable encounter of immense forces," in which the antagonists embody the principles of mind and body as they are considered to be at war in the Manichean heresy, which Gurko calls the most suspenseful of the great religions. Richard Astro's "Steinbeck and Ricketts: The Morphology of a Metaphysic" (8, ii:24–33) sums up the relationship treated at length in Astro's book that has already been discussed, stressing especially the influence on Steinbeck of Professor William Emerson Ritter's doctrine of "the organismal conception of life."

The *StQ* carried fewer critical articles in 1973 than in earlier years. One issue is dedicated to Joseph Fontenrose and prints tributes to his work along with some brief notes of "Advice to Graduate Students" from familiar Steinbeck critics. *The Red Pony* stories are individually analyzed, however, in a second special number (Winter, 1973) devoted to *The Long Valley*. Robert H. Benton's "Realism, Growth, and Contrast in 'The Gift'" (6:3–9) shows how in the first story of the cycle the eduction of young Jody Tiflin is guided by ranch-hand Billy Buck, "the natural man," rather than the boy's insensitive father. Richard F. Peterson's "The Grail Legend and Steinbeck's 'The Great Mountains'" (6:9–15) really deals with not just the second story but the whole cycle and concludes that in both this story and "The Leader of the People," Jody "transcends the naturalistic level of experience he encounters in 'The Gift' and 'The Promise' and gains insight into the value, purpose, and source of the human spirit through what he learns from old and seemingly useless men." Robert H. Woodward's "Steinbeck's 'The Promise'" (6:15–19) complements Benton's essay by again emphasizing Billy

Buck's role in Jody's education through the ranch-hand's showing the boy that even in the face of pain some men keep human promises "when natural promises are unfulfilled." Richard Astro's "Something that Happened: A Non-Teleological Approach to 'The Leader of the People'" (6:19–23) argues that this much discussed story "excites feeling and compassion only as means towards comprehension and never toward the establishment of precise value judgments."

In a kind of mournful epilogue to these close readings of *The Long Valley* stories, Robert K. Morsberger's "The Price of 'The Harness'" (*StQ* 6:24–26) points out why a recent television adaptation of the story, "well done though it was in its way . . . is not justified in claiming Steinbeck as its source." In a useful note, "IITYWYBAD" (*StQ* 6: 53–54), Kathleen Farr Elliott explains that the mysterious acronym in Chapter 15 of *The Grapes of Wrath* is made up of the first letters of the question, "If I tell you will you buy a drink?" In one biographical note, "Steinbeck and *Summer Time Ends*" (*StQ* 6:67–73), John Hargrave explains that his "gargantuan experimental novel" of 1935 might never have been published without Steinbeck's enthusiastic support; in another, "Genesis of the *Sea of Cortez*" (*StQ* 6:74–80), Joel W. Hedgpeth attributes the final writing of Steinbeck and Ricketts's collaborative effort to Steinbeck. Useful also is Hidekazu Hirose's "Japanese Steinbeck Criticism in 1971" (*StQ* 6:99–104), which summarizes nine articles, several dealing with the novelist's little studied first and last novels, *Cup of Gold* and *The Winter of Our Discontent*.

But *The Grapes of Wrath* is not overlooked. Continuing the discussion of one of the most controversial parts of the novel in "The Ending of *The Grapes of Wrath*: A Further Commentary" (*Agora* 2:41–50), John M. Ditsky theorizes that the final action marks not only Rose of Sharon's "personal attainment of maturity," but also "the completion of a sociological change—the development of a sort of Moynihan-syndrome of absent father and ruling mother—that has been seen coming throughout the novel." A. Carl Bredahl, Jr.'s "The Drinking Metaphor in *The Grapes of Wrath*" (*StQ* 6:95–98) argues somewhat tenuously that "the image of drinking and the novel's thematic concerns develop together, both emphasizing the need to move from the isolated *I* to the self-supporting *we*."

Horst Groene provides in "The Themes of Manliness and Human Dignity in Steinbeck's Initiation Story 'Flight'" (*NS* 22:278–84) a less depressing interpretation of the story than that of most critics. Groene finds that "Pepé regains his human dignity at the end of his flight and . . . dies a manly death according to the traditional paisano code of honor" and that "Nature honours his bravery with a symbolic burial." Likely to prove far more controversial is Charles E. May's theory announced in "Myth and Mystery in Steinbeck's 'The Snake' " (*Criticism* 15:322–35) that the story is "a reaction of the mythic world against the efforts of science to obliterate it." May sees the mysterious woman who visits a laboratory to buy a snake as emerging out of the depths of the sea and going back into them never to be seen again.

One of the most varied and imaginative critiques ever to be offered of a single novelist of this period is *Nathanael West: The Cheaters and The Cheated*, ed. David Madden (Deland, Fla., Everett/Edwards), which collects essays entered in a competition sponsored in 1969 by the publisher and the *Southern Review*. Of thirteen critical essays, only the contest winner, T. R. Steiner's "West's Lemuel and the American Dream" (see *ALS 1971*, p. 236) has appeared previously. (It is also the only essay to deal exclusively with *A Cool Million*.) The book contains also a biographical sketch by Gerald Locklin (pp. 1–15) and an annotated bibliography compiled by Helen Rushton Taylor (pp. 323–41). Most unusual, however, is the "confluence of voices" that Madden has devised to introduce each group of essays—a montage of quotations from West, his friends, writers who influenced him or have been influenced by him, and critics including the contributors. The resulting "dialogue" provides an overview of West's achievement that defies summary.

Only two essays are general studies; the rest discuss individual novels. James H. Bowden's "No Redactor, No Reward" (pp. 283–97) questions West's place in American literature by comparing his work with the Bible, especially Ecclesiastes, and concluding that "there is no Heavenly City offered as an alternative" in West's work "after the Abomination is burnt down," because "he isn't at all sure that we can expect one" (p. 297). Starting from the premise that Americans have always been confidence men, "peddlers of assurance" in the iconography of nations, Warwick Wadlington goes on in "Nathanael West and the Confidence Game" (pp. 299–322) to argue that West "saw that the modern failure of confidence is a national as well as an individual catastrophe" (p. 299).

Two long essays explore West's still puzzling first novel. Gerald Locklin's "*The Dream Life of Balso Snell*: Journey into the Microcosm" (pp. 23–56) proclaims the tale "one of the most complex books this side of Joyce," but finds its complexity a coherent, not chaotic "attack on the complete artificiality of consciousness" as manifested in "art, history, religion, philosophy, psychology, bourgeois axioms" (p. 40) that is ultimately "a rejection of life itself." John M. Brand's "A Word is a Word is a Word" (pp. 57–73) similarly sees the novel as West's first step toward a total negation of man that begins with his repudiation of his Jewish heritage.

Three critics discuss the novel that many consider West's best. Lawrence W. DiStahl's "Aggression in *Miss Lonelyhearts*: Nowhere to Throw the Stone" (pp. 83–101) finds the narrative beginning with the title character's activating "two apparently contradictory impulses"—a Christ-complex and the protective deadening of the senses—and ending with the character's becoming "placidly convinced of the unreality and ultimate oneness of things, and . . . therefore able to deceive with impunity and unable to distinguish love from danger" (p. 99). Marcus Smith's brief "The Crucial Departure: Irony and Point-of-View in *Miss Lonelyhearts*" (pp. 103–10) answers Wayne Booth's charges in *The Rhetoric of Fiction* that the novel is unintentionally ambiguous by arguing that its great appeal "is due precisely to the careful balance that West establishes and maintains between ironic and sympathetic norms" (p. 109). James W. Hickey's "Freudian Criticism and *Miss Lonelyhearts*" (pp. 111–50) is an involved effort to repudiate previous interpretations as superficial and to defend "the legitimate place of Freudian theory as a tool of literary criticism" by establishing through its use "some new, constructive insights about the main character and central issues" of the novel (p. 115).

Kingsley Widmer launches the discussion of West's last novel with "The Last Masquerade: *The Day of the Locust*" (pp. 179–93), keynoted by the distressing pronouncement that "West's insight was that the basic American repressed character was to merge with the Hollywood counterfeit of it—as it has in our puritanic decadence—providing the largest masquerade of civilization" (p. 192). In "From American Dream to Pavlovian Nightmare" (pp. 201–19), Robert I. Edenbaum finds a little more comfort in the novel by treating Tod Hackett, who is capable of growth and change, as the central character, whose painting and whose attempts to help another character "are the small stone he throws that reclaims him from apathy and despair" (p. 216). Donald Torchiana's "*The Day of the Locust* and The Painter's Eye" (p. 249–82), also treats Tod as the central character in a much more complex and upbeat amassing of evidence to demonstrate that West gave "his novel a solid depth of realism that most American fiction cannot command" by allowing Tod "to see through the eyes of Goya, Daumier, Magnasco, Rosa, Guardi, and Desiderio . . . the local chaos of Hollywood as a timeless image, a subject worthy of man's meditation, and a symptom crying for Biblical allusion and the utterance of prophetic art" (p. 252), a judgment that conflicts sharply with Walter Wells's chapter in *Tycoons and Locusts*, which describes the novel as an "intensely regional" work that indicts Hollywood brutally as "the corrupt residue of America's manifest destiny, a 'pleasure dome decreed' which became instead the graveyard of the Great American Dream" (p. 68).

The other two contributors to David Madden's symposium contrast *The Day of the Locust* to novels by two distinguished Jewish writers. Lavonne Mueller's "Malamud and West: Tyranny of the *Dream Dump*" (pp. 21–34) finds both West's novel and *The Natural* indictments of "the masses, and the mass media that feed on them, for so blatantly distorting what should remain as rather harmless, diversionary games" (p. 233). Max Apple's "History and Case History in *Red Cavalry* and *The Day of the Locust*" (pp. 235–47) finds that West and Isaac Babel "are not chroniclers of topical 'issues' to be disregarded when the appropriate government agency takes charge," but "literary formalists of impeccable stature who make out of human fragments and a surreal environment an ordered literary totality" (p. 247).

M. C. Kuner's *Thornton Wilder: The Bright and the Dark* (New York, Crowell, 1972) is part of a new series on 20th-century American writers. After weighing elements of affirmation and negation in Wilder's works about the past and the present and also those about "the oneness of history," Kuner reaches the conclusion that the stories are all affirmative, "bright." "We know that the dark is there," because Wilder has told us so, but "he removes all the drama and anguish from the picture and simply recounts them from a distance" (p. 214).

Hugh Holman's "Thomas Wolfe, *Scribner's Magazine*, and the

Blest Nouvelle" (*Gohdes Festschrift*, pp. 205–20) proves the most comprehensive of several new studies of the novelist. Holman maintains that despite the length of Wolfe's four major novels, the form most congenial to him was the short novel of 15,000 to 40,000 words and that Maxwell Perkins's insistence that *Look Homeward, Angel* should be followed by a "big book" was injurious to Wolfe's career (p. 207). An interesting footnote to Holman's argument is provided by Patrick Miehe's evidence in "The Outline of Thomas Wolfe's Last Book" (*HLB* 21:400–01) that a plan for organizing *The Web and the Rock* is not at all Wolfe's work, but editor Edward Aswell's.

Two distinguished Southern critics have appraised Wolfe's achievement. Ruel E. Foster concludes in "Thomas Wolfe's Mountain Gloom and Glory" (*AL* 44:638–47) that "Wolfe's mountain experience is central and integral" to his accomplishment and that "once he had left his mountain village he lost much of the certitude and clear vision that were part of his heritage." Louis D. Rubin, Jr., in "Thomas Wolfe Once Again" (*NCHR* 44:638–47) describes Wolfe's work as "the dramatized record of a talented and romantic young writer's encounter with the experience of being an artist in America" and expresses doubt that when Wolfe died he was moving away from romantic self-assertion as other critics have theorized. At odds with Rubin's position is A. Carl Bredahl, Jr.'s somewhat unfocused call in "*Look Homeward, Angel*: Individuation and Articulation" (*SLJ* 6,i:47–58) for the recognition of the existence of some kind of narrator who is distinct from both Thomas Wolfe and Eugene Gant.

viii. Richard Wright and Tough Guys of the Thirties

As this essay will demonstrate, criticism of depression-years' literature focusing upon the urban dispossessed is beginning to be displaced by polemical analyses of writers—mostly Southern inheritors of the Agrarian tradition, but also some Western primitivists—concerned with the lost prospects of a rural paradise. Richard Wright, however, continues to attract most attention. Michel Fabre's *The Unfinished Quest of Richard Wright*, trans. Isabel Barzun (New York, William Morrow), proves a far longer and better ordered study than Constance Webb's 1968 biography. The study is controlled and directed by the French critic's theory that Wright's literary and political activities cannot be separated but must be viewed as a whole constituting a prematurely curtailed quest for a definition of Man that makes Wright "a representative man" in the Emersonian sense. Fabre supplements his long study with a speculation in "Richard Wright's First Hundred Books" (*CLAJ* 16:459–74) seeking to identify those that the novelist probably read before 1940.

A narrower emphasis in Noel Schraufnagel's chapter on Wright in *From Apology to Protest* (pp. 21–32) is evident from its title, "Wright and the Protest Novel." Schraufnagel stresses that Wright's work differs from "the apologetic protest of its predecessors" in dealing neither with a protagonist of exceptional abilities or a tragic love affair, but rather with the way in which "the depravity of a life limited by racial policies eventually leads to an explosive situation" (p. 23).

Other critics propose new readings of much discussed works. James R. Giles's "Richard Wright's Successful Failure: A New Look at *Uncle Tom's Children*" (*Phylon* 34:256–66) traces through the short stories a shift from a concern with youth and adults who meet heroic but lonely deaths to Sue in "Bright and Morning Star," who dies "martyred to Communism, and thus triumphs over all the forces that have limited the characters in the first four stories." John R. May in *Toward a New Earth* (Notre Dame, Ind., Univ. of Notre Dame Press, 1972), overlooked in last year's summary, finds vestiges of Christian apocalypse in *Native Son*, since Bigger's release from the tensions imposed upon him by the white world "comes finally through acts of violence—private moments of apocalypse that are simultaneously acts of creation" (p. 165). Reinforcement for this frightening thesis (which could help explain Hitler's behavior) is supplied by Richard E. Baldwin's "The Creative Vision of *Native Son*" (*MR* 14:378–90), which argues that while the novel "concludes with an implicit threat of chaos and destruction," it also offers the possibility of a world in which men could live in contact with each other if they could realize the potential of love, community, order, and creativity. Gayle Gaskill's "The Effects of Black/White Imagery in Richard Wright's *Black Boy*" (*NALF* 7:46–48) brings the discussion of Wright back down to earth by arguing that, while Wright refuses to limit himself to "an artificial inversion of the old black-as-evil pattern," we can see in his account a perception of "power and knowledge in blackness, repression and impotence in whiteness."

Robert E. Fleming's "Overshadowed by Richard Wright: Three

Black Chicago Novelists" (*NALF* 7:75–79) calls attention to Waters E. Turpin's *O Canaan!* (1939), Alden Bland's *Behold A Cry* (1947), and Frank London Brown's *Trumbull Park* (1959), all of which—Fleming contends—provide insights into the problems of black life in a big city not found in the work of better known writers.

Finis Farr's *John O'Hara* (Boston, Little Brown) proves more conventional than Fabre's book on Wright and limits its discussion of novels and short stories almost entirely to plot summaries. In *Tycoons and Locusts*, Walter Wells finds *Hope of Heaven* (1938) one of O'Hara's failures because "style clashes with substance." Wells describes the novel as an "allegory wrought by an essentially unallegorical sensibility, by a writer with other talents and impulses demanding exercise in his work" (p. 39). He finds that the more "elemental conceptions" of Horace McCoy and James M. Cain succeed better in handling "Hollywood-Southland" material.

Wells also finds McCoy's *They Shoot Horses, Don't They?* better fiction than Cain's *The Postman Always Rings Twice*, because "McCoy's protagonist-narrator Robert Syverten possesses a tonal and intellectual consistency that [Cain's] Frank Chambers lacks" and McCoy's novel is also "infused with subtleties wholly lacking in *Postman*." Wells goes on to say that McCoy's novel deals particularly with the corruption of aesthetic values; whereas Cain's book "panders shamelessly to subliterary taste" (p. 34). Wells is also one of an increasing number to have his say about Raymond Chandler, whose *Farewell, My Lovely* "develops many of the same patterns of dissolution evident in other Southland novels" (p. 73).

Wells's condescending conclusion, however, that though Chandler's novel is "exceptionally good mystery fiction," it must be "judged within that genre" (p. 84) is beginning to be challenged. E. M. Beckman's "Raymond Chandler and An American Genre" (*MR* 14:149–73) argues, quite to the contrary, that Chandler's works are not conventional detective stories, but "novels which use elements of a particular fictional tradition [to] either amplify or destroy established constructions, not from malice but from a superior artistic imagination." Julian Symon's affectionate reminiscence, "The Case of Raymond Chandler" (*NYTM*, Dec. 23: 13, 22, 25, 27), also brands "unforgivable" Robert Altman's film version of *The Long Goodbye* for treating "flippantly something conceived with seriousness."

ix. Thirties Regionalism

But even "tough guy" fiction is not growing so rapidly in critical esteem as the once almost totally overlooked regional novels of the 1930s. Caroline Gordon is being apotheosized into a cult goddess (see also *ALS 1971*, pp. 242–43. A group of devotees in Texas offer *The Short Fiction of Caroline Gordon: A Critical Symposium*, edited by Thomas H. Landess (Dallas, Univ. of Dallas Press, 1972) as a tribute following the novelist's visit to their school. Six articles deal with varying numbers of the author's short stories. Louise Cowan leads off with "Aleck Maury: Epic Hero and Pilgrim" (pp. 7–31), which describes the most substantial group of stories as embodying the "epic vision" of one of those heroes who "endeavor to maintain manliness and courage in a communal and cosmic realm, obeying whatever divine imperatives are given them, following a code of honor in a society that is in perpetual disorder" (pp. 7–8). Robert S. Dupree's "Caroline Gordon's 'Constants' of Fiction" (pp. 33–51) takes Wayne Booth to task for taking Gordon to task in *The Rhetoric of Fiction* and argues that "she recognizes that neither sincerity, nor technical skill alone is adequate for great art; they must also be made indissolubly the same thing in order for fiction to possess conviction" (p. 34). Editor Thomas H. Landess's "Caroline Gordon's Ontological Stories" (pp. 53–73) discusses four early works that are "structurally and textually simpler than her later works and are understandable in terms of modes of conduct which have their roots in an ontology which is pre-Christian as well as Christian, European as well as Southern" (p. 56). Jane Gibson Brown's "Woman in Nature: A Study of Caroline Gordon's 'The Captive'" (pp. 75–84)—the only essay devoted to a single story—objects to critics' classifying "The Captive" as an "adventure story" or "Christian vision" and maintains that it is rather a narrative of the initiation of a white woman held prisoner by Indians into "the code of the wilderness," through which she ultimately achieves heroic stature and her own salvation. John R. Alvis's "The Idea of Nature and the Sexual Role in Caroline Gordon's Early Stories of Love" (pp. 85–111) points out a tension in four stories between two alternative perspectives on the order of the nature as—on one hand, "forest," "a generally beneficent source of moral and sexual principles" and, on the other, "a Dantesque 'dark wood' of human incapacity" (p. 109). Finally M. E. Bradford's "The

High Cost of 'Union': Caroline Gordon's Civil War Stories" (pp. 113–26) argues that the three stories show how the unilinear, simplistic approaches to human conditions that Americans used in the middle of the 19th century could lead only to the fragmenting of the situations depicted.

The six articles are marked by an evangelical enthusiasm quite in contrast to what W. J. Stuckey in *Caroline Gordon* (TUSAS 200, 1972) calls the novelist's characteristic "emotional detachment." The choice of a coolly judicious and scrupulous writer like Stuckey to provide an overview of this novelist's achievement restores a balance to the assessment of work often treated too reverently by its traditionalist admirers and too scathingly by its progressivist detractors. Stuckey agrees with other critics that Gordon is a "demanding writer" whose work requires "moral and esthetic responses that many readers are unable to make" (p. 12), but suspects that these qualities may be responsible for her being less popular and less often written about than might be expected, because modern audiences respond more readily to the anti-heroes that she spurns than to the heroic figures she creates. In his second chapter, Stuckey discusses "A Theory of Fiction," based on Aristotle and Dante, but influenced also by Henry James and Flaubert, that Caroline Gordon has developed, which demands a developed and resolved action "shaped consciously or unconsciously according to some principle of composition" (p. 19). Then in succeeding chapters, Stuckey applies this theory to involved analyses of the way her mind and imagination have worked in shaping her fiction. He concludes that her work is never imitative and clearly the product of a fully integrated sensibility, characterized by an emotional detachment that distinguishes her from other writers and makes her "our most unambiguous novelist"—the defender of a traditional morality.

This same morality has always greatly concerned Andrew Lytle, who is honored in *The Form Discovered*, ed. M. E. Bradford (Jackson, Univ. and College Press of Miss.), which reprints seven essays from the *MissQ* and a tribute by Allen Tate, along with Robert G. Benson's "Yankees of the Race: The Decline and Fall of Hernando de Soto" (pp. 84–96), which also appears elsewhere as "The Progress of Hernando de Soto in Andrew Lytle's *At the Moon's Inn*" (*GaR* 27:232–44). Benson describes Lytle's second novel as recording "the spiritual corruption of De Soto" as well as "the less dramatic but no less final" fleshly corruption of his lieutenant Tovar, who serves as the story's center of consciousness. Outside this collection, Frederick Y. Yu's "Andrew Lytle's *A Name for Evil*" (*MQR* 11:186–90) suggests the novel theory that the story analyzes the failure of the Agrarian movement, but fails to satisfy expectations it raises by never really explaining what "self-defeating" aspects of Agrarianism are dramatized.

Two articles by Samuel Irving Bellman in the same magazine suggest some unanticipated lines for future investigation by finding unexpected depths in the works of a writer usually dismissed as a charming but superficial regionalist. "Marjorie Kinnan Rawlings' Existential Nightmare, *The Yearling*" (*Costerus* 9:9–18) argues that although the existentialist philosophy is still too much in the process of formulation for us to speak of a specific corpus of its literature, *The Yearling* fits generally accepted definitions of this position, because throughout the novel we are "reminded that man is a lost soul, at the mercy of inscrutable, whimsical forces." "Writing Literature for Young People, Marjorie Kinnan Rawlings' 'Secret River' of Imagination" (*Costerus* 9:19–27) offers the history of the making of a short story, "The Secret River," as providing the important lesson that "the secret river of imagination is accessible and navigable" to anyone wishing to travel it badly enough to take the heavy risks involved.

Eastern and Western regionalists are not celebrated to anything like the extent that the Southern are. In part of a continuing series on a popular New England novelist, however, "Ben Ames Williams and the *Saturday Evening Post*" (*CLQ* 10:190–230), Richard Cary discusses the long association of the writer with the magazine and chronicles his contributions from 1917 to 1941. Wayne Chatterton's *Vardis Fisher: The Regional Works* (WWS 1, 1972) launches a new series of pamphlets devoted to Western writers with a respectful study of the neglected novelist's integrity that never really comes to grips with the question of why he has been neglected. Thomas J. Lyon's *Frank Waters* (TUSAS 225), a longer study of a related writer written from a similar viewpoint, provides a much more thoroughgoing and illuminating analysis of reasons why Waters is largely unknown to those outside Western literature specialists who might enjoy his work. Lyon finds Waters's position on most philosophical and historical questions an uncommon mixture of organic Amerindian and oriental thought with Western European rationalism. The novelist's greatest problem, Lyon argues, has therefore been "to find a mode that will carry both these diverse tendencies—the poetic, private intuition; the rationalized public instruction," so that his work is "both Oriental and Occidental" (p. 151).

For *ALS 1974* 20th-century fiction will be divided into three parts, and this essay will stop at about the end of what is now section six. The present writer then will turn his attention back to 19th-century American fiction.

Indiana University-Purdue University at Indianapolis

13. Fiction: The 1930s to the Present

James H. Justus

Except for a falling off in work on Mailer, last year's patterns of scholarship are still evident in 1973: continued interest in O'Connor, younger black writers, and the theory and practice of what is variously called *irrealism, disruptionist fiction*, and *surfiction*. Noticeable also is a resurgence of interest in the later Bellow and, because of her productivity of the past five years, the entire career of Welty. Although no one seems to be happy about it, the prevailing methodology is still that of the New Criticism—with explications, image studies, and theme-and-structure efforts dominating all other approaches. And more of the same can be expected: of the sixty dissertations reported in 1973, thematic studies outstrip all others. Individual authors most popular are O'Connor (with nine dissertations completed), McCullers (five), and Nabokov, Mailer, Barth, Bellow, and Malamud (three each). As in the recent past, nearly a third are studies of multiple authors and special topics—the search for identity (!), the writer as public figure, "garrison military" fiction, industrial labor novels, and the fictional portraits of Negroes, adolescents, suburbanites, and poor whites. Still needed are a criticism of larger perspectives and what Maurice Beebe calls "hard-core scholarship." Without wishing for Warren, Bellow, Mailer, or Barth to be ensnared by the pious and rigid orthodoxies with which the textual technocrats preside over our major 19th-century authors, we would all profit from studies of available manuscripts and other working papers, galley-proofs, and first editions of contemporary writers—as recent work by Victor A. Kramer on Agee and Frederick Asals on O'Connor indicates.

i. General Studies

***a.* Overviews and special topics.** The one comprehensive study of the year was disappointing. The scrupulous sensibility and commitment to fictional modes must always be remarked in anything Alfred Kazin does, but his *Bright Book of Life* is both quirky and evasive. His dislikes are clear: *The New Yorker* (that old horse); writers who are "too accomplished" for their own reputation; mere "virtuosi"; the new journalism; tension, paradox, irony, and other principles for reading literature; and all those writers "who went to Sewanee and had the social views of Donald Davidson, Allen Tate, Andrew Lytle, and Robert Penn Warren." Kazin's easy scorn for "unimpeachably well-executed novels" is easier to understand than his gauzy praise for novels which have "strength of feeling" or which depict "life as unhinderable human experience." Judgments curling from the elegant paragraphs (the dust jacket quotes eight) effectively fill the space where substantive criticism should be. If Kazin is still petulant about the solemnity of the old New Critics, he is also suspicious of recent novelist-critics who enjoy make-belief, illusion, artifice. He whips up a fine Laurentian fervor over William Maxwell's essay on "The Writer as Illusionist," and his odd rhetorical question—"Why should it be supposed that the creation of illusion is something wholly deliberate?"—reveals what the facile style usually manages to conceal: the simplistic belief that art is worthy only when it is merely life's looking-glass.

Ihab Hassan's new book, *Contemporary American Literature, 1945–1972: An Introduction* (New York, Frederick Ungar), appears to be designed more for undergraduates or foreigners than for the American scholar. It is compact, informative, and generally restrained in its judgments: its mood, admits Hassan, "is mainly presentational." After a general introduction which supplies social, historical, and cultural contexts, he devotes a segment to "Major Novelists" (Bellow and Mailer) and one to "Prominent Novelists" (Vonnegut, Barth, Hawkes, and others). "Without Conclusion" projects where contemporary fiction, which seeks "to affirm human existence in what may be termed a post-humanist future," may go with such figures as Richard Brautigan, Ronald Sukenick, Ishmael Reed, Rudolph Wurlitzer, and others. Hassan devotes sections to other genres and ends with a highly selective bibliography.

Nathan A. Scott, Jr., sees three figures standing at the "absolute center" of what is most deeply animating in contemporary American literature. *Three American Moralists: Mailer, Bellow, Trilling* (Notre Dame, Ind., Univ. of Notre Dame Press) is sophisticated pulpit oratory adjusted to literary audiences. Although all three are Stouthearts who demonstrate what it is like to reckon with "imperfect reality," Trilling seems to fit Scott's figural description best. *The Middle of the Journey* probes the "lesions of selfhood that can be laid open in the people of our age by the Idea," and the "centrist testimony" found in *The Liberal Imagination* most fully represents Trilling's continuing subject—"that complex reciprocity of pressure between literature and the Idea." Irving Howe's praise in "Reading Lionel Trilling" (*Commentary* 56, Aug.: 68–71) is more reserved because of Trilling's practice of personifying elements of consciousness into "such alien wraiths as Spirit and Will," and the "conservative inclinations that creep into his ethical persuasions."

With the decline in interest in the French existentialists, Richard Lehan's *A Dangerous Crossing* may be a work whose time has passed—indeed, it was begun in 1956. But Lehan makes a strong case for the continuing importance of Camus and Sartre, especially in the decade after World War II when they were reading American fiction; and, as he shows with Mailer, Bellow, and some who were unheard of when he first conceived this work, the counter-crossing of ideas, of conditions of mind, became a permanent part of our modern literature. A compact chapter on the Frenchmen traces a common drive, despite ideological differences, to "reconcile man with his uprooted surroundings, to formulate a philosophy of self, and to construct a purely secular ethic." Lehan maps the boundaries of a slippery term with point and grace.

In "The Current State of American Literature" (*SoR* 9:273–87), Cleanth Brooks discusses "the crisis in culture" as it affects modern writers generally. The dissolution of the community has brought about the smudging of the artist's proper function, but Brooks sees positive benefits still accruing to Southern writers and some of the Jewish and black writers. In a study of alienation, "The Breakdown in Communication in the Twentieth-Century Novel" (*SoQ* 12:1–14), Alice E. Lasater shows how this theme is always accompanied by technical approximations of the "breakdown," but a wobbly conclusion emphasizes variations more than similarities in such disparate novels as *Ulysses, Invisible Man, Room at the Top*, and *Herzog*. Neil P. Hurley's sketchy "Liberation Theology and New York City Fiction" (*Thought* 48:338–59) will be of little help to critics. It seeks to show the "personal appropriation of the great liberating events of the Bible" in novels from Edith Wharton to Edward Lewis Wallant.

After exploring the recent reaction against the emergence of Jewish writers in "The Progress of the American Jewish Novel" (*Response* 7,i:115–30), Alvin H. Rosenfeld suggests future directions which this writing might take. *Portnoy's Complaint* signals the end of one kind of Jewish novel, because parody is a form of subversion "possible only when a certain vein of creativity has all but run out and is being kept alive artificially." If the "immigrant trauma" as a source is losing its motivating energies, Rosenfeld thinks that Jewish Covenant theology is still able to stimulate meaningful fiction, citing *The Fixer*, in which Malamud turns from the Jew as metaphor for Everyman to the Jew of history. But Samuel I. Bellman, with some asperity, says the substance of Jewish fiction has been over-stressed. In "Sleep, Pride, and Fantasy: Birth Traumas and Socio-Biologic Adaptation in the American-Jewish Novel" (*Costerus* 8:1–12), Bellman declares an end of patience with running Sammy, cross-cultural conflict, and the confused immigrant and insists upon what he calls the "shadow side," deduced from studying the controlling metaphors in a series of arbitrarily chosen books.

Even more than the white gentile, says Stuart A. Lewis, the "Black represents the elemental America with which the Jew seeks to identify." "The Jewish Author Looks at the Black" (*ColQ* 21:317–30) explores images of the Negro in recent works by Malamud, Roth, Wallant, and Bellow. After declaring that "there really is no such thing" as "Jewish Humor" (*Comic Imagination*, pp. 329–38), Allen Guttmann admirably demonstrates that there is, concentrating mostly on the East European heritage of the *schlemiel* which shows up in such figures as Moses Herzog and Alexander Portnoy.

Tom Wolfe: The New Journalism (New York, Harper & Row) is an anthology of some of his pieces along with others favored by Wolfe and his collaborator, E. W. Johnson. In a long personal essay, Wolfe describes his efforts to rid himself of understatement, early battles with his own kind of "lumpenproles" by "men of letters," and his belief in "social realism." He cites four necessary devices which supply power to the meanest narrative: scene-by-scene construction, full recording of dialogue, third-person point of view, and "the recording of everyday gestures, habits, manners, customs, styles of furniture . . . and other symbolic details." If all this sounds familiar, Wolfe supplies an appendix of distinctions between his methods and those of lookalikes (from Defoe to Agee) in the history of literature.

All this will not impress Alfred Kazin, who sees Wolfe, a "dramatizer of celebrities in a pixie hah-hah style," as fiction's natural enemy. In "The Imagination of Fact: Capote to Mailer" (*Bright Book of Life*, pp. 209–41), Kazin remarks, "Journalists take themselves too seriously. First they describe facts, then they see 'trends,' and finally, they see themselves as a trend."

The gloomiest survey of post-war fiction to come along is Henri Peyre's "Is Literature Dead? Or Dying?" (*MQR* 12:297–313). Although the pressures of reality and the competitions of mass media add to their problems, Peyre puts the "poverty and the sterility of present-day literature" squarely on the writers themselves. They enjoy waylaying their readers to prevent them "from experiencing sympathy, love or admiration, scorn or hatred for their characters," choosing instead to "engage in private fights with language as the root of all deceptions and the tool of bourgeois privilege." Even the critics, he notes, are now proving that they can imitate the subtlety and arrogance of their subjects. Peyre doubts that a single novel by Warren, Bellow, or Styron will "survive"; he sees gifted but shallow talents in Updike, Roth, and Malamud; he is not convinced that the "representative novel of our age" can be one of those "stilted and self-conscious variations on a mythological theme"; and the newer generation, "fascinated but perhaps spoilt" by Borges and Kafka, is spiritually empty.

A similar stasis is evident to Kermit Vanderbilt, who traces the narrative evasions, abstract meditation, the ambiguous adjustments of the self and a corrupt society in "Writers of the Troubled Sixties" (*Nation* 17 Dec.:661–65). But in examining eight serious books that were also best-sellers of the decade, he sees an implicit hope behind the national soul-sickness: "the age-old route of penitence, meditation and reassessment."

Max F. Schulz's *Black Humor Fiction of the Sixties: A Pluralistic Definition of Man and His World* (Athens, Ohio Univ. Press) is long on black and short on humor, and the definition is so pluralistic that it becomes just as inclusive and overlapping as the older attempts which Schulz finds inadequate. That this humor is more ironic than comic casts doubts on the uniqueness of its contemporary practitioners. After an initial chapter on definition, Schulz devotes two chapters to Barth and Vonnegut; one chapter to Borges, Berger, Pynchon, and Coover; and another to the "conformist heroes" of Bruce Jay Friedman and Charles Wright. There is no comprehensive summary chapter, which might have pulled the disparate strands together, but in something called "Text References," Schulz appends plot summaries of 26 books.

Although he states that "definition, not explication" is his primary aim, the strength of Schulz's study lies in the interpretations of such works as *Lost in the Funhouse, God Bless You, Mr. Rosewater, Stern,* and *The Wig*, which are approached with vigor and sensitivity. And even though we get no precise definition of the crucial term, we get repeated instances of its major characteristics: the tendency to emphasize the profusion of choices in an absurdist universe, and the skepticism that man can ever be reconciled to a "nuclear-technological world intrinsically without confinement."

"The Mode of 'Black Humor'" (*Comic Imagination*, pp. 361–71) is a curiously diffuse essay by Brom Weber, who because he worries over the possible ethnic connotations of the term, is inclined to stretch the mode back to the Puritans, Poe, and Hawthorne. He sees its recent invigoration coming from French surrealists, but of all its practitioners (1955–65) only Walker Percy and Thomas Berger have survived "the morass of intellectual and moral void into which their brethren sank."

Stanley Trachtenberg tries out a new term in an important theoretical essay, "Counterhumor: Comedy in Contemporary American Fiction" (*GaR* 27:33–48). Unlike conventional comedy, which depends upon final escape from the unpleasant, the contemporary comic novel has as its substance suffering, pain, bewilderment, and the absence of cause and effect; in "the aimlessness of coincidence is the structure of design" in novels by Barth, Pynchon, and Hawkes. Reality thus becomes an "element that interferes with experience rather than a dimension in which it must be apprehended." The comic pose, the acceptance of the gap between reality and illusion, "has itself become the object of comic exposure." Unlike the absurdist hero, the counter-comedian slips, dodges, and ducks to avoid the final recognition that he shares in the "destructive responsibility" and even compels his own victimization "as a fulfillment of his freedom."

Christof Wegelin surveys "The Cosmopolitanism of Power in American Fiction" (in R. G. Popperwell, ed., *Expression, Communication, and Experience in Literature and Language*, Proceedings of the XII Congress of the International Federation for Modern Languages and Literature, Modern Humanities Research Assn., London, pp. 220–22), from the international marriage arrangement after the Civil War to the casual sexual alliances of American soldiers and European women since World War II. All war novels since 1945 are united in the fact that Americans and Europeans are no longer distinguished by national traits but only by their roles (conqueror and conquered, rich and poor, male and female). Wegelin sees the extensions of this shift in novels by Hawkes, and Vonnegut, all of which dramatize the extremities of power relationships.

Frank Gado has written a comprehensive and intelligent introduction to his collection of interviews with six writers who represent nearly half a century of American fiction, *First Person: Conversations on Writers & Writing* (Schenectady, N.Y., Union College Press). The writers are Glenway Wescott, John Dos Passos, Robert Penn Warren, John Updike, John Barth, and Robert Coover. All the interviews are valuable, but Coover's is especially so.

***b.* The new fiction: theories and modes.** Attention to the newest generation of fictionists has increased considerably, some of it generated by outright publicists but much of it thoughtful and measured. The first number of *Fiction International*, which celebrates "the transformations of sensibility, language, and formal and technical modes of the present and immediately upcoming periods," contains a series of brief critical and historical introductions to a handful of authors and two substantial interviews. John O'Brien conducts Ishmael Reed through a thicket of remarks about his own fiction but mostly listens to grousing over the lack of understanding shown it by New York intellectuals (pp. 61–70); and Jerome Klinkowitz elicits from Jerzy Kosinski some fascinating information about the "postscript" to *The Painted Bird* (which was not intended as part of the novel), his interest in photography, and his perception of language as man's connective link with both self and social reality (pp. 31–48).

Klinkowitz cites Kosinski and Donald Barthelme as examples of the newer forms in "Insatiable Art and the Great American Quotidian" (*ChiR* 25:172–77), and in a more substantial piece, "How Fiction Survives the Seventies" (*NAmR* 258:69–73), categorizes current new writers as "establishmentarians" (Bellow, Updike, Roth), "established innovators" (Barth, Pynchon, Vonnegut), and, for him the most interesting and vital, "disruptive fictionists" (Ronald Sukenick, Raymond Federman, and others). Klinkowitz analyzes this third group more thoroughly in "Literary Disruptions; or, What's Become of American Fiction?" (*PR* 40:433–44). Sukenick moves beyond "representational burdens" to embrace pure fiction, and Barthelme revitalizes the material of the world ("blanketing, trash, and *dreck*") by exploiting it in unlikely contexts. One of the disruptionists, Raymond Federman, writes his own brief, "Surfiction—A Position" (*PR* 40:427–32). His bumptious decision "to give fiction another chance" means replacing linear narrative with a fiction that will "unmask its own fictionality" and "expose the metaphor of its own fraudulence."

Arlen J. Hansen offers a cooler, more descriptive view, "The Celebration of Solipsism: A New Trend in American Fiction" (*MFS* 19:5–15). The new solipsism, a reaction to the deterministic denial of the power of man's creative imagination, can be seen in Vonnegut, Barthelme, Gass, Coover, and Brautigan, whose challenge is to "find a perspective that articulates the value and inescapability of subjectivism and yet avoids its delusions."

Perhaps the most important theoretical piece is "Scheherazade Runs Out of Plots, Goes on Talking; the King, Puzzled, Listens: An Essay on New Fiction" (*TriQ* 26:332–62), Philip Stevick's exploration of the radical shift in the concept of "what it means to tell." Disavowal of the empirical solidity of classic fiction has resulted in what Stevick sees as a perverse kind of time sense and spatial relationships, but he argues against Philip Roth's argument that the recent absurdity of ordinary life outstrips the novelist's ability to imagine. It cannot be demonstrated, says Stevick, "that there has been some kind of quantitative increase in lunacy and that this is the cause of the newness of new fiction." Though he suggests a few "axioms" toward an esthetic of new fiction, he rejects the kind of criticism which would use fiction as an exhibit in a historical design, with new fiction as the end of something or the beginning of something, "or an element in a cyclic movement." Gerald Graff, however, does just that in "The Myth of the Postmodernist Breakthrough" (*TriQ* 26:383–417). Recent fiction is a "logical culmination of the premises" of such earlier movements as romanticism and modernism; moreover, Graff feels the new sensibility is reactionary, and its products reinforce the effects of technocratic, bureaucratic society.

Richard Kostelanetz would agree with Stevick's observation that "public conceptualizing" has not yet caught up with the postmodernists. "The Rule of Ignorance & Philistinism" (*MQR* 12:27–41) attacks the "intellectual flaccidities" of conservative cultural commentators who are no longer interested in self-education. Much of the new art in general transcends the old formulations, but "stunted" critics at *Commentary, PR*, and the *NYRB* show no evidence that our "corpus of relevant knowledge has changed radically since 1920."

On the other hand, Nancy H. Packer would argue that indiscriminate praise has been accorded the new art, partly because of the mutual reinforcement of specialist critics interested in ingenuity and writers of ingenuity. In "Fiction's New Mode" (*SHR* 7:387–94) she lists three identifiable categories of the new fiction: the put-on (Barth at his best), aestheticism (Nabokov and his followers), and the celebration of the absurd (Genet). For all the new honesty about the process of writing ("the moving hand now seen"), what is missing is feeling. David C. Stineback's "On the Limits of Fiction" (*MQ* 14:339–48) argues that the novel's "greatest possibilities lie in its limitations: that there are things it cannot do and still be good." Joan Didion's fiction contains characters who are not "*worthy of being cared about* by its readers," whereas her brilliant journalism transcends its own sense of despair. Too many contemporary authors, he says, have been too concerned with directing the reader's attention away from an image of their experience toward the "inventive, ingenious mind of the author himself."

Because of an obsession with the medium itself, that ingenuity is questioned sharply in Thomas W. Molyneux's "Signs of the Times" (*ASch* 42:663–70) and Eric Larsen's "How Do You Write a Short Story in 1973" (*MinnR NRP* 4:132–37). Molyneux suggests that the excessive concern for language—metaphor, pun, parody—rather than human complexity blocks any possibility for a writer's growth: "It is the way of seeing that is finally important, not the way of speaking." Larsen sees no renaissance of the short story form as long as parody and satire are the dominant modes; the work of Barthelme and Gass is self-consciously coy—a "certain stultifying narcissistic motionlessness coated over with a luxury of words."

ii. Flannery O'Connor

Faced with the bewildering proliferation of critical glosses on a modest body of work, many of them rigidly executed partial portraits, J. O. Tate, Jr. spoke for many O'Connor readers when in a review (*FOB* 2:80–82) he recently asked, "Where is the critic who will demonstrate the verbal perfection of her best work . . . and who will show through the various analogues and models, the Catholic vision and Protestant energy, the sublimity and vulgarity, her profound unity?" The "perfection" may be an elusive and wrongheaded search, but surely some balanced view of O'Connor is worth continuing effort. Preston M. Browning, Jr., in "Flannery O'Connor and the Demonic" (*MFS* 19:29–41), similarly argues for more inclusive approaches than are possible with those which prove either a theological orthodoxy or a rebelliousness that turns O'Connor into a Georgia apostle of the *nouveau roman.* Browning observes that the very coincidence of mutually opposing truths gives the fiction its peculiar flavor and power; the down-home situations dramatize the dialectical relationship of the "holy and the demonic." The shock of evil, O'Connor's special insignia, suggests that her fiction is finally ontological.

Martha Stephens may not satisfy either Browning or Tate, but *The Question of Flannery O'Connor* (Baton Rouge, La. State Univ. Press) is as close as we are apt to get to seeing this author whole. She is the first critic to see profound differences between Teilhard's and O'Connor's moral vision: for the geologist-theologian, the created earth is "holy place"; for O'Connor, those who love the world can expect to be mocked. Stephens distinguishes between the technical cunning by which the author immerses us in the reality of her world and "the problem of assent." We have our ways in American criticism, she reminds us, of "evading doctrinal problems in the writers we admire," and one of the evasions in O'Connor's case is to see her as a comic writer. Stephens's first chapter is a model of its kind, explaining both the author's "seduction of the reader" and her "falsification of human experience as most of us know it."

Stephens's major effort goes into her evaluations of the two novels, partly because they articulate their creator's attraction to the grand story of Christian travail, the journey toward and achievement of holiness. The drama of the convergence of "religious and irreligious minds" is more fully realized at the end of *Wise Blood* than it is in any of the short stories, and the Powderhead segment of *The Violent Bear It Away* is fine art because of the author's good-tempered sympathy toward old Tarwater; after his death, the story moves "toward sanction and celebration of the old man's religious vision." Stephens alludes to many of the stories, especially those turning on the device of comic comeuppance about coddled children and complacent widows, but gives detailed readings of other kinds. She rightly points out that as a group, the 26 stories are closely knit and overlapping in situations, narrative strategies, themes, and details. *The Question of Flannery O'Connor* is a superb book, a model of unobtrusive scholarship and critical tact, detached enough to be unimpressed with the swollen reputation of its subject but sensitive enough to elucidate the achieved successes which are a major contribution to our literature.

Dorothy Walters's *Flannery O'Connor* (TUSAS 216) is a modest entry, though it evinces a more honest attempt to grapple with this author than some previous longer studies. Walters sees O'Connor's achievement as "Christian tragicomedy," with her single story the "age-old parable of Christian setting forth on his inexorable encounter with the various dragons of this world so that he may proceed toward the heavenly mount." Walters's illustrations of this single story tend to be mechanical: a chapter on "Stories of Grace and Revelation," one on "Studies in Black and White," still another on stories concerned with property. Some of her incidental observations are valuable: that "Good Country People" is a variation on the traditional frontier story of a double-dealing swap and duel of wits; that O'Connor's voice is usually that of the *eiron*; and that the intention "to serve a rigidly Christian view" is often countermanded by a demonic energy which suggests a belief more nihilistic than Christian.

"Evidences of the Prelapsarian in Flannery O'Connor's *Wise Blood*" (*XUS* 11,iii[1972]:1–12) do not abound, despite the reading offered by Martha A. Dula—they mostly concern the "hungry" hero searching for absolution in the world *east* of Eden. James L. Green ("Enoch Emery and His Biblical Namesakes in *Wise Blood*" [*SSF* 10:417–18]) finds that O'Connor uses both biblical Enochs in the characterization of the subplot: Enoch the son of Cain is straightforward; the parallel with Enoch the father of Methuselah is ironic.

In two essays, James C. McCullagh finds Hazel Motes suffering from oedipal flaws. In "Aspects of Jansenism in Flannery O'Connor's *Wise Blood*" (*StH* 3,i:12–16), he asserts that in the "underside" of theology, mostly the "Irish kind," the only sin is sexual. His more substantial essay, "Symbolism and the Religious Aesthetic: Flannery O'Connor's *Wise Blood*" (*FOB* 2:43–58), is too long in enunciating and confirming a thesis which is nevertheless convincing—that the tension of the novel exists because of the complex relationship between Motes's efforts to break away from his mother and his attempts to blaspheme his way to Christ. O'Connor's details—Motes's use of his mother's eyeglasses and his dream sequences—show that as long as Motes is haunted by his mother, he will be unable to "see."

Commenting on the last ten pages of *The Violent Bear It Away* in "Psychological Determinism and Freedom in Flannery O'Connor" (*Cithara* 12[1972]:26–33), Nancy B. Barcus argues that what seems to be a lack of psychological freedom governing the actions of the characters up to and including the drowning-baptism is finally resolved with the acknowledgement that evil is both internal and external: thus "real moral freedom" is involved.

"Flannery O'Connor's Early Fiction" (*SHR* 7:210–14) is Carter W. Martin's study of the author's Iowa thesis stories set against the chronologically arranged *Complete Stories* and the two published collections; O'Connor, Martin concludes, "improved as an artist in rough proportion to her movement toward a violent expression of her Christian themes." "Flannery O'Connor and the New Hermeneutic" (*FOB* 2:29–42) deals with the stories centering on the spoken word of revelation which announces conversion or condemnation. What John R. May identifies as a three-fold "hermeneutical sequence" are variations on traditional theological elements: "reality as manners *and* mystery, the description of a dramatic reality as composite of vision and judgment, and finally meaning or communication as revelation."

For Howard D. Pearce, however, in "Flannery O'Connor's Ineffable 'Recognitions'" (*Genre* 6:298–312), such moments of revelation are less theological than Aristotelian: O'Connor's "most fundamental thought" has correlatives to peripety and anagnorisis; but since her notion of the universe is both Christian and tragic, he proposes that we read her fiction as latter-day morality plays. Because Pearce is so intent on explicating the "not quite verbalized" recognitions, the potential generic distinctions fade away before they are made.

In "The Developing Art of Flannery O'Connor" (*ArQ* 29:266–76), Elmo Howell assures us that, because of her full acceptance of her "gentle background," in her later stories O'Connor was moving away from a nightmarish world to one "closer to the realities of home," the range of ordinary experience, "back to the homey and traditional as a source of sanity in a world given over to innovation." In what must be the minority report of the year, Howell believes the matrons of O'Connor's later stories "demand respect because of their solid middle-class virtues": if their spiritual vision is dim, they at least show "competence and moral propriety."

Howell thinks "Revelation" is one of the most successful later stories, partly because O'Connor is able to wed her religious interests with "her growing attachment to home." Samuel I. Bellman, however, using his key term like a latitudinarian in "The Apocalypse in Literature" (*Costerus* 7:13–25), finds the quiet often subliminal moment of insight to be the literary equivalent of theological apocalypse; but he calls "Revelation" an "exemplum designed to illustrate a point of doctrine." Joyce Carol Oates would seem to agree: she finds that this story in O'Connor's "greatest" book shows the author's belief that not only our virtues but also our rational faculties will be burned away. "The Visionary Art of Flannery O'Connor" (*SHR* 7:235–46) is directed toward the unity which Oates sees in the "collection of revelations" in *Everything That Rises Must Converge*, which points to "experiential truth that lies outside the sphere of the questing, speculative mind, but which is nevertheless available to all."

Forrest L. Ingram treats the first seven stories of this last volume as "O'Connor's Seven-Story Cycle (*FOB* 2:19–28); they appear not in the order of their previous publication but in a pattern which mutually reinforces juxtaposition, association and progression of themes, character types, motifs, situations, and symbols. The major structure is the "progressively revealed pattern, on all levels, of rising and converging" of individuals, classes, and generations.

Kenneth Scouten emphasizes O'Connor's "use" of the Oedipus story in the two novels and "A Good Man Is Hard to Find" in "The Mythological Dimensions of Five of Flannery O'Connor's Works" (*FOB* 2:59–72) and, less successfully, her use of a generalized classical world marked by goddesses, sacrificial figures, and archetypal fertility rites in "Good Country People" and "The Partridge Festival." Frederick Asals contends in "Hawthorne, Mary Ann, and 'The Lame Shall Enter First'" (*FOB* 2:3–18) that though this story owes something to *The Violent Bear It Away*, it owes "even more to elements dropped from that novel." The story coincides with O'Connor's introduction to *A Memoir of Mary Ann* and her association, according to Asals, of the little cancer patient with Hawthorne's "The Birthmark." The demonstration of the "transforming process" from Hawthorne to O'Connor has a certain airy thinness.

In meandering prose, William S. Doxey submits "A Dissenting Opinion of Flannery O'Connor's 'A Good Man Is Hard to Find'" (*SSF* 10:199–204) based on the shift in point of view halfway through the story from the grandmother to the Misfit.

iii. Norman Mailer

Nathan A. Scott, Jr., in "Norman Mailer—Our Whitman" (*Three American Moralists*, pp. 15–97), finds significant links between these two writers: their penchant for addressing "all the great public occasions" of their times, their innovations in language and style, the general slant of their careers, and their dedication to "the politics of salvation" through the recovery of "nature without check." Mailer's soteriology, argues Scott, is premised on the doctrine "of a sort of *via negativa*, the notion that a descent into hazard and darkness must precede any renewal of the heart or renovation of the commonweal." Scott's prose tends to be overripe, his organization is mechanically chronological, and his critical readings are astute without being very startling after a decade of sophisticated Mailer criticism.

Richard Lehan, in "The Outer Limits: Norman Mailer and Richard Wright" (*A Dangerous Crossing*, pp. 80–106), presents two aspects of Mailerian existentialism: the notions of "man as his own redeemer," which is murkily rendered, and "man in motion," which is persuasively well done. Lehan takes another look at *The Naked and the Dead*, minimizes both *Barbary Shore* and *The Deer Park*, and makes maximum use of *An American Dream* (which he reads as an allegorical embodiment of ideas about man as a pawn in a cosmic battle between God and the Devil).

In "The Earthly City of the Jews: Bellow to Singer," Alfred Kazin's single best chapter in *Bright Book of Life* (pp. 127–62), Mailer shows up as a Jewish overreacher who takes risks with his "adventurist fiction." Although he puts down *An American Dream* as a "snob document" which is unintentionally funny because of its posturings, Kazin admires Mailer's overall "sense of imbalance," derived from his tactic of welding together different orders of reality in order to reflect the tension between man's inner life and "the constant world of public threat."

Frederick Busch produces a good essay which begins with one story and moves out expertly to encompass Mailer's career from *The Deer Park* on. "The Whale as Shaggy Dog: Melville and 'The Man Who Studied Yoga'" (*MFS* 19:193–206) also is concerned with the troubling divisions: Sam Slovoda is a narrator who both includes and excludes the writer's personal problems, a part-artist who "renders dramatic his own fragmentation by creating his other self before the reader's eyes." This economical and perceptive essay takes seriously Mailer's claim that his long prologue to an unwritten work is "a descendant of Moby Dick" by examining a small but crucial event involving Ishmael and Pip.

Clive James takes a solemn look at "Mailer's 'Marilyn'" (*Commentary* 56 Oct.:44–49), linking this biography-in-novel-form with *The Deer Park*. As a lay psychologist, Mailer tries to make Marilyn Monroe's narcissism ours; more than in his previous books, he tries not always successfully "to give the mummery of what happens the majestic gravity of a created world."

iv. Saul Bellow and Bernard Malamud

Despite three comprehensive studies of Bellow by Peter Buitenhuis, Richard Lehan, and Nathan A. Scott, Jr., the later fiction is now receiving most of the attention.[1] In an admiring survey, "A Corre-

1. Nathan A. Scott, Jr.'s "Bellow's Vision of the 'Axial Lines'" (*Three American Moralists*, pp. 101–49) is a revised and updated version of the essay in *Adversity and Grace* (see *ALS 1968*, p. 214).

sponding Fabric: The Urban World of Saul Bellow" (*Costerus* 8:13–35), Buitenhuis stresses the diversity of styles, themes, and interests of a novelist who, unlike Hardy, Dickens, or Faulkner, cares little about creating an organic unity of place. But although each work defines a different problem, Buitenhuis finds a single thread: "the continual battle between free will and determinism," from the "Europeanized vision" of *The Victim* to the "capsule history of the West" registered in the consciousness of Artur Sammler.

Lehan, on the other hand, sees great consistency in the range of Bellow's corpus in "Into the Ruins: Saul Bellow and Walker Percy" (*A Dangerous Crossing*, pp. 107–45). All of his protagonists, intuiting the fact that to be human in all its rich complexity is to be one's own redeemer, find their humanity "somewhere between romantic affirmation and apocalyptic despair." Lehan is both persuasive and concise in his treatment of the mutual victims of *The Victim*, but what Augie March learns (that it is better "to live out one's own sense of the absurd than to die for the utopian vision") and Henderson realizes (that to change his state of mind is to change himself) comes closest of all the fiction to Lehan's existentialist reading.

Although Lehan believes that Sammler embodies the Bellovian hero at his best, Jennifer M. Bailey, in "The Qualified Affirmation of Saul Bellow's Recent Work" (*JAmS* 7:67–76), calls the latest novel "Bellow's most disappointing work," whose limitations are anticipated in *Herzog*. Both novels are unintentional parodies because Bellow is unable to balance "his protagonists' subjective reality with a convincing version of their social milieu." If Herzog is mythicized, Sammler is canonized; both are merely "fictional gurus." And while he admits that it is never difficult to find virtues in a work by Bellow, David Galloway ("*Mr. Sammler's Planet*: Bellow's Failure of Nerve" [*MFS* 19:17–28]) also finds only strain in the latest novel: "the narrative, the individual incidents, the carefully drawn characters do not directly support the burden of intellectual meaning Bellow wishes to ascribe to them." If the fiction itself is intellectually topheavy, Galloway finds the author in a distasteful "Sammleresque" position: "a contentment with the ways of the past, a dis-ease with the present, an avuncular superiority over unwashed radicalism."

In a more thoughtful essay which comes to similar conclusions, Robert Boyer finds that *Sammler* denies the possibility of a social reality that is not a direct reflection of a corrupted nature conceived largely in static, immutable terms. "Nature and Social Reality in Bellow's Sammler" (*CQ* 15:251–71) is an analysis of the implications of what Sammler calls "sexual niggerhood for everyone": the Negro, an emblem for values which have emasculated Western culture, is equated to a Darwinian nature that is ruthless, sordid, and attractive.

Two critics are more sympathetic to this novel. In "Imagining the Holocaust: *Mr. Sammler's Planet* and Others" (*Judaism* 22:288–300), Edward Alexander uses the concentration camp, from which Sammler has twice escaped his doom, as the chief locus of meaning for the novel because it is "the ultimate reality of twentieth-century life." Alexander concludes that Bellow succeeds imaginatively in appropriating his hero's "credentials" in order to link himself to those who survived as well as those who died in the holocaust. Stephen R. Maloney, in "Half-way to Byzantium: *Mr. Sammler's Planet* and the Modern Tradition" (*SCR* 6,i:31–40), concentrates on Bellow as "the contemporary heir to the great tradition" of Eliot, Orwell, and Yeats. Maloney sees definite links with author and protagonist, because both react negatively to rampant subjectivity and insatiability.

Despite Bellow's recent essay which castigated the barbarism of "pampered children" who gratify themselves in radical destructiveness, Allen Guttman, in "Saul Bellow's Mr. Sammler" (*ConL* 14:157–68), warns us that the "ironic distance between Bellow and Sammler disappears [only] when seen from a politicized perspective." Stressing the differences in background, experience, and general milieu, Guttmann insists that Sammler is not "a mouthpiece for the radical right."

In "Herzog, Order and Entropy" (*ES* 54:336–46), Norman Weinstein praises Bellow for being able to fuse a representation of chaos and despair with a Flaubertian sense of form. The five-day period in Herzog's self-analysis reveals an interlocking hierarchy of orders determined largely by modern science and technology in general and the law of entropy in particular; but despite their influence, Herzog retains his allegiance to "the law of the heart."

Lee J. Richmond argues in "The Maladroit, the Medico, and the Magician: Saul Bellow's *Seize the Day*" (*TCL* 19:15–25) that Tamkin is the thematic nexus of the novel. Though a fakir and charlatan, he is nevertheless a beneficent advisor who can heal the psychological wounds of Wilhelm, the "deluded inheritor of a bogus mythology of commerce," and be a surrogate father as well. Although in "The Earthly City of the Jews: Bellow to Singer" (*Bright Book of Life*, pp. 127–62), Alfred Kazin equates Bellow with the Jewish sage, whose favorite forms have always been short ("Bellow's best fictions are his shortest"), he finds inadequate such sage figures as Herzog and Sammler, whose "ideological moralism" and "dismissive jeremiads" are barriers to sympathy. He prefers not only the shorter forms but also their shorter protagonists, Leventhal and Wilhelm.

"Bellow's *Henderson* and the Limits of Freudian Criticism" (*Paunch* 36–37:39–46) is Michael Steig's rebuttal to an earlier essay by Judith Moss (see *ALS 1971*, p. 254). Just as Bellow himself is familiar with the theories and therapeutic methods of Wilhelm Reich, so his Henderson is rendered more understandable through a Reichian view of the relation between psyche and soma than with the Freudian concept of conversion hysteria. This subject is more thoroughly detailed in "Reichianism in 'Henderson the Rain King'" (*Criticism* 15:212–33) by Eusebio L. Rodrigues, who parallels the geography of Henderson's adventures with the stages of Reichian therapy: the illness is manifested in America, preliminary diagnosis occurs during his stay with the Arnewi tribe, and the cure comes when he goes to live with the Wariris. Since King Dahfu is the greatest Reichian in the novel, Bellow can poke fun at Reichianism as well as take it seriously.

The most substantial item to come from Sanford Pinsker's "Saul Bellow in the Classroom" (*CE* 34:975–82), an interview with students in 1972, is Bellow's statement that his being a "Jewish-American writer" is "sheer invention" by the media, including the scholarly kind.

"The American Schlemiel Abroad: Malamud's Italian Stories and the End of American Innocence" (*TCL* 19:77–88) is a richly contextual piece by Christof Wegelin, who traces the transformations of James's moral ambience through *Pictures of Fidelman.* Whereas James's American artist responds to the imperative of self-fulfillment, self-discovery for Fidelman is private rather than generic, and the matter of morality is not an issue.

In "The Promised End: Bernard Malamud's *The Tenants*" (*HC* 8,v[1971]:1–15), John Alexander Allen examines "symbiotic victimization" in several works in addition to *The Tenants.* David K. Kirby's "The Princess and the Frog: The Modern American Short Story as

Fairy Tale" (*MinnR NRP* 4:145–49) attempts to show how Malamud's "Angel Levine" (along with stories by Capote and Hortense Calisher) is involved with the problem of "the nature of modern fictional belief."

"The Magic Barrel" is the subject of two brief pieces by Richard Reynolds and Theodore C. Miller, the latter who links the story with *The Scarlet Letter* in "The Minister and the Whore: An Examination of Bernard Malamud's 'The Magic Barrel' " (*StH* 3,i:43–44); love is existential—"one must love even if all the evidence denies the emotion." Reynolds's " 'The Magic Barrel': Pinye Salzman's Kadish" (*SSF* 10:100–02) suggests that the matchmaker's final prayer is for effecting Stella's "resurrection," that through his art he can establish a prospect of happiness.

v. J. D. Salinger, Philip Roth, and I. B. Singer

In "Seymour's Suicide Again: A New Reading of J. D. Salinger's 'A Perfect Day for Bananafish' " (*SSF* 10:27–33), Gary Lane contends that the book of German poems alluded to by Muriel is Rilke's *Duino Elegies*, whose informing lamentations on man's insufficiency reflect precisely the problems bothering Seymour. William Bysshe Stein's "Salinger's 'Teddy': *Tat Tvam Asi* or That Thou Art" (*ArQ* 29:253–65) is a relentlessly Vedantic interpretation of this young detached spectator who "acts out his karmic destiny in the circus of phenomenal existence."

In "The Earthly City of the Jews: Bellow to Singer" (*Bright Book of Life*, pp. 127–62), Alfred Kazin comments that Philip Roth, who sees fiction as "a series of throwaway lines," is the first writer so obsessed with the Jewish family that he removes "all the mystery from the Jewish experience." Stanley Cooperman, in "Philip Roth: 'Old Jacob's Eye' with a Squint" (*TCL* 19:203–16), demonstrates what Kazin only suggests. Roth's attitude toward religion generally is that of a social realist, not that of a symbolist or moralist. Eliminating tragic emotion partly accounts for the essentially reductive quality of his work, but Cooperman finds *Letting Go* the best work because it successfully fuses universal human drama with "Jewishness."

Bernice W. Kliman's "Names in *Portnoy's Complaint*" (*Crit* 14, iii:16–24) is a self-explanatory argument for the importance of all kinds of evocative names—family, religious, cultural, historical, campy. Julie Braun characterizes Portnoy ("Don Juan as schlimazl") as a "White Anglo-Saxon Jew" and his chronicle as Roth's expression of the unique trials of being one ("Portnoy as Pure Confusion" [*CM* 13,ii:73–76]). "Reading Myself" (*PR* 40:404–17) is Roth's own solipsistic question-and-answer session about *The Great American Novel*, which he thinks is a departure from his other works because its comedy, directed at no specific targets, issues from his own genius to exist for its own inventive sake.

In a beautifully written, solid evaluation of what she calls the "Yiddish Poe," Grace Farrell Lee ("The Hidden God of Isaac Bashevis Singer" [*HC* 10,vi:1–15]) insists upon the importance of demonism in Singer's fiction; more than metaphors of psychological processes, demons invade the world "with power coextensive with the Creator of order" and recreate the cosmos in their own diabolical image.

Abraham Bezanker, uneasy with other critics' "placing" of Singer, uses Erik Erikson's "crises of identity" as a perspective to explain both Singer's diversity and his "integral quality." "I. B. Singer's Crises of Identity" (*Crit* 14,ii[1972]:70–88) is stronger in the thesis than in the proof, but Bezanker is persuasive in his discussion of the interrelationships of the individual and societal patterning in Singer's work; the crisis theory as an explanation of inherent tensions and often irresolute endings of the fiction should be examined further. Looking at Singer outside the usual ethnic contexts may be a healthy direction; certainly a common Singer theme—that human beings are driven by their emotional needs to behave in irrational but satisfying ways—is resonant of many non-Yiddish writers.

Sanford Pinsker's "Isaac Bashevis Singer and Joyce Carol Oates: Some Versions of Gothic" (*SoR* 9:895–908) is soft-core criticism; mostly it is an appreciation of these two writers' "power of the imagination," very little of which has anything to do with gothicism. For Oates it consists of "internalized" effects; for Singer, the assorted imps, devils, *dybbuks*, and other ghosts appear as "supernatural extensions of the general truth."

vi. John Barth and Thomas Pynchon

In an imaginative essay, "Cabell and Barth: Our Comic Athletes" (*Comic Imagination*, pp. 275–83), W. L. Godshalk links the Virginia writer's "resolute frivolity" and Barth's "cheerful nihilism" as similar ways to counter cosmic absurdity. Both use universal myths in their fiction; both are players of basically serious literary games; and both prescribe a "comic acceptance of reality followed by a stoical resignation."

In "John Barth's *The Floating Opera*: Death and the Craft of Fiction" (*TSLL* 14:711–30), Thomas LeClair concentrates on an "art for life's sake" strategy applicable not only to author and protagonist in this novel but also to its implications in the later work. The showboat is a carefully built structure "brought into existence and controlled" by Todd's double, Captain Adam, whose acts parallel the digressions in the novel. Todd's irresponsibility (the boats he works on) is a willful avoidance of "the integrity of fact," which he associates with death; his maneuvers also reveal Barth's own sympathy for creating alternatives to distasteful reality. *The Sot-Weed Factor* is the major text in "John Barth: The Artist of History" (*SLJ* 5,ii:32–46), in which Barbara C. Ewell discusses Burlingame's coping ways and Eben's discipleship in affirming the chaos even as he seeks to transcend it through "imposed" forms of identity and value.

Three critics focus on *Lost in the Funhouse*. In "John Barth's Artist in the Fun House" (*SSF* 10:373–80), Robert F. Kiernan argues for the conceptual and stylistic unity of the separate pieces in the volume; even the non-Ambrose stories complement the *Künstlerroman* structure. Despite its title, Beverly Gray Bienstock's "Lingering on the Autognostic Verge: John Barth's *Lost in the Funhouse*" (*MFS* 19:69–78) is a crisp and unpretentious study which shows how the metaphor in the title story broadens out to embrace the "tangle of history and men's minds." The whole matter of identity "tentatively resolves itself in the capricious immortality of the work of art," and if the reader joins these self-perpetuating equations, he too becomes immortal. Michael Hinden ("*Lost in the Funhouse*: Barth's Use of the Recent Past" [*TCL* 19:107–18]) concentrates on the dazzling number of modernist techniques used in this self-exhausting novel even as it mocks the forms and substance of modernist art.

Pynchon is William Harmon's most interesting example of "'Anti-Fiction' in American Humor" (*Comic Imagination*, pp. 373–84), which he calls a perennial "countervailing" impulse to story as the chief shaping principle, manifested in interest in plotless story and a mistrust of the all-knowing narrator. In his substantial essay, "Mass

Man and Modernism: Violence in Pynchon's *V.*" (*Crit* 14,ii[1972]: 5–17), Robert E. Golden sees this novel as Pynchon's vision of decadence; Stencil is his figure of artist for whom the processes of art, not the product, are paramount; and though the novel is a part of what it depicts, decadence is better than its alternative—death.

Though he finds too much mere smartness and too much rhetoric in *V.*, Alfred Kazin, in "The Absurd as a Contemporary Style: Ellison to Pynchon" (*Bright Book of Life*, pp. 245–81), praises *The Crying of Lot 49* for its compassion and imaginatively integrated narrative, qualities which he finds missing from most absurdist fiction. Except for some astonishing phrasing ("At the end of the frontier, American society has invaginated") and the skillful use of Norbert Wiener, Peter L. Abernethy's "Entropy in Pynchon's *The Cring* [sic] *of Lot 49*" (*Crit* 14,ii[1972]:18–33) is repetitive of earlier studies on the same topic by Charles B. Harris (*ALS 1972*, p. 297), Tony Tanner, and Anne Mangel (*ALS 1971*, pp. 257–58). In both substantive and mechanical ways, Abernethy's editors must share the blame for this article.

In "Pynchon's *The Crying of Lot 49*: The Novel as Subversive Experience" (*MFS* 19:79–87), Annette Kolodny and Daniel James Peters use Pynchon for their self-indulgent celebration of "alternative culture." Their personal anger over America's "maniacal desire for security in collective abstraction," more obvious than the freshness of their reading, suggests that the rage for relevance of the late 1960s is now showing up as shabby recipe criticism.

"A Dissent on Pynchon" (*Commentary* 56 Sept.:68–70) is self-explanatory; its author, David Thorburn, finds *Gravity's Rainbow* confused, tedious, and unpersuasive, and thinks that its ravenous reception speaks more about the literary culture than about the novel. Joseph Weixlmann has prepared the useful "Thomas Pynchon: A Bibliography" (*Crit* 14,ii[1972]:34–43), which incorporates previous bibliographies, editions, biographical pieces, essays, and dissertations.

vii. Kurt Vonnegut, Jr., Joseph Heller, and Ken Kesey

Vonnegut's critical coming of age is signaled by *The Vonnegut Statement*, a clutch of interpretations of varying quality, reminiscences, and a bibliography, edited by Jerome Klinkowitz and John Somer (New York, Delacorte Press/Seymour Lawrence). In addition to a survey of the novelist's career, "Kurt Vonnegut, Jr.: The Canary in a Cathouse" (pp. 7–17), and an essay on *Mother Night* and *Cat's Cradle* noted earlier (*ALS 1971*, p. 259), Klinkowitz contributes "Why They Read Vonnegut" (pp. 18–30), in which he examines the magazine pieces of the 1950s for links with the later fiction; and what he observes is repeated occasionally by other contributors: that the popular magazine stories were written from a consistent middle-class point of view. Klinkowitz collaborates with Asa B. Pieratt, Jr., and Stanley Schatt on "The Vonnegut Bibliography" (pp. 255–77), which includes foreign as well as domestic editions, dissertations, and previously published bibliographies (but omitting Betty L. Hudgens's *Checklist*—see *ALS 1972*, p. 303).

One of the most substantial contributions, John Somer's "Geodesic Vonnegut; or, If Buckminster Fuller Wrote Novels" (pp. 221–54), is virtually an introduction to Vonnegut, and a good one, seen from the principle of dynamic tension, which informs the fictive structures as well as the existential relationship between the author and his heroes. Along the way Somer provides perceptive contexts for reading this fiction: the spatial-form tradition, modern theories of physics, Robbe-Grillet's versions of schizophrenic protagonists.

Joe David Bellamy's "Kurt Vonnegut for President: The Making of an Academic Reputation" (pp. 71–89) explores some of the paradoxical reasons why a "swinging youth culture" finds Vonnegut such a guru: he is seen variously as "fatalistic moralist, cynical pacifist, holy atheist, anti-intellectual philosopher, apocalyptic futurist, and grim humorist." And like it or not, say Karen and Charles Wood, Vonnegut is a science fiction writer. In "The Vonnegut Effect: Science Fiction and Beyond" (pp. 133–57), they suspect that the author's dislike of the label arises not from his low opinion of the form but from "an understandable dislike of the general critical attitude toward science fiction."

James M. Mellard presents a McLuhanized Vonnegut based on a crucial seven-year period (1952–59) when the writer crossed "the aesthetic backwash between the pictorial old order and the oral-aural new." Mellard easily equates the Luddite theme of *Player Piano* ("the overthrow of the machine") and its technical aim, "the overthrow of the accepted literary conventions of . . . all the mechanical aspects of pictorialism associated with Henry James and the mimetic mode." *The Sirens of Titan*, though it absorbs diverse styles symptomatic of an electronic age, is also said to resemble Homer, *Beowulf*, and all kinds of folktales and ballads.

Vonnegut's works "form an apocalypse," says Glenn Meeter in "Vonnegut's Formal and Moral Otherworldliness: *Cat's Cradle* and *Slaughterhouse-Five*" (pp. 204–20). In passing, Meeter characterizes the "religion" of Vonnegut's work as "more completely Pauline than Paul's," and even the mediation of Northrop Frye fails to make this claim plausible. Jess Ritter's "Teaching Kurt Vonnegut on the Firing Line" (pp. 31–42) is an empty, self-congratulatory piece on how hip teachers should respond to both the author and his student fans. Tim Hildebrand's "One or Three Things I Know About Kurt Vonnegut's Imagination" (pp. 121–32) punishes the reader by extending those "things" to 36, all of them mod meditations on statements by Vonnegut and others. Robert Scholes includes both "A Talk with Kurt Vonnegut, Jr." (pp. 90–118) and a casual study of the author's undergraduate work on the *Cornell Daily Sun* in "Chasing a Lone Eagle: Vonnegut's College Writing" (pp. 45–54). "In Vonnegut's *Karass*" (pp. 55–70) is a reminiscence by Vonnegut's Indianapolis colleague, Dan Wakefield.

Jerome Klinkowitz also contributes "The Literary Career of Kurt Vonnegut, Jr." (*MFS* 19:57–67), a survey of the erratic publishing history and critical reception of the works through *Breakfast of Champions*. In "Vonnegut's Cradle: The Erosion of Comedy" (*MQR* 12:66–71), Stanley Trachtenberg argues that in *Cat's Cradle* the author makes a comic judgment of the "conventional movement from illusion to reality that comedy must make while resisting the darkly comic idea of lunacy as a narrative value."

Vonnegut's closeness to the Dresden raid accounts for the darker tone of his climactic novel, says Donald J. Greiner in "Vonnegut's *Slaughterhouse-Five* and the Fiction of Atrocity" (*Crit* 14,iii:38–51). The image of war, pervasive in the earlier works, is intensified in an anguished fictionalizing process, which includes the use of bland historical accounts and science fiction trappings as a buffer between the author and Billy Pilgrim. Joyce Nelson, in "*Slaughterhouse-Five*: Novel and Film" (*L/FQ* 1:149–53), has high praise for the film version of Vonnegut's novel, which, however, omits Kilgore Trout, the agent for Billy Pilgrim's transcendence over grief. Nelson's other contribution, "Vonnegut and 'Bugs in Amber'" (*JPC* 7:551–58), disputes those who see either messianic figures in the fiction or "brilliant defiance or noble self-sacrifice." William L. Godshalk's "Vonnegut and Shakespeare: Rosewater at Elsinore" (*Crit* 15,ii:37–48) is a fairly predictable explication of the novelist's techniques of using historical and cultural parallels in *Cat's Cradle* (*Moby-Dick*), *Happy Birthday, Wanda Jane* (*The Odyssey*), and *God Bless You, Mr. Rosewater* (*Hamlet*).

It would be a disservice to try to paraphrase Clinton S. Burhans's "Spindrift and the Sea: Structural Patterns and Unifying Elements in *Catch-22*" (*TCL* 19:239–50). Like his earlier analysis of *In Our Time* (inadequately noted in *ALS 1968*, p. 117), this closely reasoned essay considers not only plot and subplots but also motifs, thematic repetitions, and narrative links between chapters. In "'It Was All Yossarian's Fault': Power and Responsibility in *Catch-22*" (*TCL* 19:251–58), Stephen L. Sniderman's revisionist thesis is that in a fictional sense, Yossarian is the initiator of nearly every significant event in the novel, including most of the deaths. By making everything Yossarian's fault, Heller says that "the individual, not bureaucracy or the establishment, still holds the final trump."

In the introduction to his collection of previously published essays, *"One Flew Over the Cuckoo's Nest": Text and Criticism* (New York, Viking), John C. Pratt emphasizes the functional point of view of Bromden: it negates, he believes, Kesey's faith in such a force as the "Combine," and the Chief's restoration of fogless vision means that those "who believe in the Combine will repeatedly fail." In addition to the criticism, this anthology has a useful chronology, some hunks from Tom Wolfe's manic account of the Merry Pranksters, an early draft of the opening scene and some Kesey letters, Act III of Dale Wasserman's dramatic adaptation, and assorted clinical excerpts on "electric convulsive therapy" and "postlobotomy personalities."

Eliot M. Zashin admits that comparing this author to Plato and Rousseau "is a heavy burden to lay on Kesey," and most of his "Political Theorist and Demiurge: The Rise and Fall of Ken Kesey" (*CentR* 17:199–213) would be more convincing without the comparison. Drawing heavily on *The Electric Kool-Aid Acid Test*, Zashin writes of the "almost legendary" author who in trying to be both articulator of a political vision and a creator of new reality failed at both attempts. In "Christ in the Cuckoo's Nest; or, the Gospel According to Ken Kesey" (*Cithara* 12[1972]:52–58), Bruce E. Wallis sees Kesey's McMurphy as an analogous Christ, with the novel itself assuming the configurations of a gospel for "emulative and redemptive action."

Terence Martin's forceful and persuasive "*One Flew Over the Cuckoo's Nest* and the High Cost of Living" (*MFS* 19:43–55) discusses several of the related elements which unify the novel: the motif of female dominance, the literalization of metaphor, the stages of McMurphy's noise and silence, the emergence of sanative community to counter the leveling effects of Big Nurse. The Combine's power to control exists "in ratio to our unwillingness to forfeit manhood." Interdependence is the key: the hero moves from his solitary status through a "necessary, sacrificial" struggle to the role of iconographic victim whose legacy is manhood, friendship, love, community. Despite its title, Stephen L. Tanner's "Salvation Through Laughter: Ken Kesey and the Cuckoo's Nest" (*SWR* 58:125–37) is an examination of the novel's formal characteristics, especially organization and imagery. Tanner sees four cycles of action, each one beginning with an ascendant Big Nurse and ending with the ascendancy of McMurphy or what he represents.

viii. Vladimir Nabokov, John Hawkes, and Jerzy Kosinski

Imagination for Nabokov is "not just a form of memory, but a working back to our connection with nature," says Alfred Kazin in "A Personal Sense of Time: Nabokov and Other Exiles" (*Bright Book of Life*, pp. 285–317). Although the supremacy of fiction over reality is Nabokov's grand *donnée*, Kazin, uncomfortable with that, must narrow "reality" to "all constructed systems that seek to be absolutist versions of 'reality.' " He finally pictures Nabokov as a kind of émigré Lawrence, celebrating "the conclusive evidence of his own heart" and proclaiming "the indissolubility of life with fiction."

Susan Fromberg Schaeffer's distinguished essay, "*Bend Sinister* and the Novelist as Anthropomorphic Deity" (*CentR* 17:115–51), establishes the governing belief common to most of Nabokov's works: the conviction that "there is an ultimate artificer of human existence, and that one of the best tools for discovering the ultimate meaning of life and death is not philosophy but art." The artist-magician-god suggests his own divinity by using "divine spark" imagery and by pointing the reader's attention to the *process* of the finished work on which the artist "leaves his fingerprints."

K. A. Bruffee traces the subgenre of elegiac romance, the purpose of which is to release man from the grip of the past "by reordering his interior world," and applies it to a Nabokov work. "Form and Meaning in Nabokov's *Real Life of Sebastian Knight*: An Example of Elegiac Romance" (*MLQ* 34:180–90) argues that the hero is an abstraction which is drawn on memory and fantasy; though he fails to reach the goal of his quest, the narrator himself, representative of humanity, reaches his goal, which is not so much something to reach as it is "something to become."

Samuel Schuman admits that "Vladimir Nabokov's *Invitation to a Beheading* and Robert Heinlein's 'They' " (*TCL* 19:99–106) have no common literary source and no mutual influence. Yet both the novel and the science-fiction story are structured around an incompletely named hero "imprisoned for a crime of believing himself the only 'real' person in the world," both see the world as a stage set, and both conclude with the introduction of seemingly superhuman beings and the vindication of the protagonists' point of view.

James L. McDonald, in "John Ray, Jr., Critic and Artist: The Foreword to *Lolita*" (*SNNTS* 5:352–57), considers the author of the foreword not as an occasion for Nabokov's jokes but as a character performing his task "in an integral part of the novel." Posing as editor, Ray exercises "taste" and "compassion," and thus stands between the reader and the memoir. Fred Kaplan's "Victorian Modernists: Fowles and Nabokov" (*JNT* 3:108–20), a thin piece which promises considerably more than it delivers, discusses *The French Lieutenant's Woman* and *Ada* in light of their purposeful Victorian elements; in *Ada* they turn out to be a private past which is the key to "the nature of time and art." The Poe connection is confirmed again in a note by Thomas LeClair, "Poe's *Pym* and Nabokov's *Pale Fire*" (*NConL* 3,ii:2–3).

Andrew Field, the author of *Nabokov: His Life in Art* (see *ALS 1968*, pp. 208–09), has now compiled *Nabokov: A Bibliography* (New York, McGraw-Hill), which should be the standard bibliographic tool for years to come.

Frederick Busch's *Hawkes: A Guide to His Fictions* (Syracuse, Syracuse Univ. Press) is a first-rate critical assessment combining sympathy and detachment, breadth and depth. Busch is especially strong in perceiving and explicating prevalent image patterns (mostly animal) and characteristic textures (hallucinatory landscapes and characters whose mythic qualities loom larger than their social actuality). Busch brings a wide familiarity of modern literature to bear upon this important writer, and each of Hawkes's books gains from that familiarity. Though there is richness aplenty in all the chapters, the one on *Second Skin* is especially perspicuous.

Melvin J. Friedman's "John Hawkes and Flannery O'Connor: The French Background" (*BUJ* 21,iii:34–44), a tentative but useful piece, is stronger on Hawkes (and more convincing) than on O'Connor. These authors' connections with French symbolist poetry and the fiction of Robbe-Grillet, Beckett, and Sarraute, more often suggested than demonstrated, include their interest in "things" and surfaces and their use of the "picaresque attitude" and the "landscape of violence."

Lucy Frost believes that Hawkes's vision of contemporary America is shaped by "a fusing of static images with the temporal movement of narrative." In "The Drowning of American Adam: Hawkes' *The Beetle Leg*" (*Crit* 14,iii:63–74), she argues that the technique is a verbal equivalent of a landscape painting in its atemporal myth of the Fall.

"Parody in Hawkes' *The Lime Twig*" (*Crit* 15,ii:49–56) refers to both the "thriller" (and what Hawkes calls its "soporific plot") and the detective story; Lawrence K. Boutrous claims that Hawkes parodies these subgenres in order to create a new form projecting "an ambivalent world of destruction and hope." John M. Warner sees more serious literature lurking in the background in "The 'Internalized Quest Romance' in Hawkes' *The Lime Twig*" (*MFS* 19:89–95). Because of the allusions to Sidney, Spenser, Chaucer, Thackeray, James, and others, Warner reads the novel as a "metaphorical statement about art" which explores both the possibilities and the costs of internalized art, the romantic posture which attempts to free the self from worldly nature and to break through into a new, imaginative freedom.

In "The Unreliability of Innocence: John Hawkes' *Second Skin*" (*JNT* 3:32–39), Thomas LeClair describes the novelist's bold maneuver which allows him to hold the reader's reactions in tension between scorn for Skipper's hypocrisy and sympathy for an oedipally neurotic character who is the subject of so much dramatic irony.

The best summary to date of Kosinski's career is Gerald Weales's "Jerzy Kosinski: *The Painted Bird* and Other Disguises" (*HC* 9,iii [1972]:1–12), which illustrates the developing verbal mastery in the early nonfiction and its influence on the more accomplished novels. Samuel Coale locates Kosinski in a kind of stalemated area between those imaginations of the last century which sought to overcome or assimilate nature and those of the later naturalists who were overwhelmed by it. "The Quest for the Elusive Self: The Fiction of Jerzy Kosinski" (*Crit* 14,iii:25–37) shows, somewhat questionably, how the progressively deteriorating struggle for self-definition parallels the deterioration in the quality of the fiction; Coale considers the latest novel, *Being There*, as a philosophic fable in which human effort seems to have vanished.

Stanley Corngold pronounces Kosinski's consciousness to be "essentially Romantic" in the tradition of Proust, Valery, and Artaud—names appealed to by Kosinski himself. "Jerzy Kosinski's *The Painted Bird*: Language Lost and Regained" (*Mosaic* 6,iv:153–67) is itself almost poetic criticism with a clean, uncluttered thesis: that the loss of voice "names the loss of the power to interpret experience," and that the regaining of the voice signals the self unhurt and undefensive. In "The Radical Vision" (*MichA* 5:497–503), Paul Loukides argues that the "narrative vision" of *The Painted Bird* (along with *Catch-22* and *The Cannibal*) is skewed. The boy's evolution is accompanied by a voice which rejects myth after myth until it finally reaches the narrative voice of the novel—that of modern man.

ix. Robert Penn Warren, William Styron, Walker Percy, and James Agee

"Toward an Analysis of the Prose Style of Robert Penn Warren" (*SAF* 1:188–202) is a valuable, much-needed study by Allen Shepherd, who looks at diction, sentence length and structure, syntactical relationships, imagery, sound devices, clichés, and cinematic techniques. He finds in Warren's best work a creative tension between the Southerner's "sensuous apprehension of the word" and the academic's "detachment and ease with abstraction"; the later fiction, however, is plagued by nonfunctional rhetoric and characters obsessed with logomania.

David B. Olson builds his essay, "Jack Burden and the Ending of *All the King's Men*" (*MissQ* 26:165–76), on two arguable theses, one his own (that Warren's narrator is a character that readers dislike) and one advanced by earlier critics (that the last 12 pages of the novel are inconclusive). His argument nevertheless is that the ending is appropriate given Burden's character; it is the apex of a repetitive pattern "characterized by deep penetration and movement up to the verge of unequivocal consummation, and then a quick pulling back *before* consummation."

In "Styron's Meditation on Saviors" (*SWR* 58:338–48), William N. Nolte traces the intricate relationship between love, revolution, and power; the discontent that propels the revolutionary has a "subtle way of warping" his mind, transforming him into a savior, whose primary interest is "in discovering the self amidst the tensions of his mind and then relocating his self outside temporal affairs." Saviors are romantics, idealists, millennialists; Nat Turner becomes a prisoner of human solipsism, which places him in the "godlike position of creator and destroyer of both time and space."

Martin Luschei's *The Sovereign Wayfarer: Walker Percy's Diagnosis of the Malaise* (Baton Rouge, La. State Univ. Press, [1972]) contains a brief "intellectual biography," an account of the philosophical backgrounds of the fiction (mostly existential) and specific interpretations of the three novels, which though too long and leisurely are reasoned and clear. Luschei emphasizes not the author's detachment from the malaise he is describing but his necessary involvement in it, and he gives the most sensible account yet of the origins and use of such Percyisms as "repetition," "rotation," "everydayness," and "intersubjectivity." In the fiction the single story is that of a man whose hope lies in an active search for a way out of his closed-in state and whose journey must begin in the recognition of his exile and in "sharing the joys" of pilgrimage. Although Luschei believes that *Love in the Ruins* is the most ambitious probing of the malaise, Percy's great achievement may finally prove to be the translation of Kierkegaard into concrete American terms.

In "Novel's Ending and World's End: The Fiction of Walker Percy" (*HC* 10,v:1–11), Eugene Chesnick would agree with Luschei that Percy is not a dabbler in existentialism but a genuine philosophical explicator, having worked out for himself "a way of overleaping the ethical mode into the religious." His characters are interesting, however, not because of the resolution of intellectual dilemmas but because of their ironic sense.

Without any noticeable coherence, Walter Sullivan's "Southerners in the City: Flannery O'Connor and Walker Percy" fails to shed new light on either writer, and the segments on Percy are especially solemn in light of the collection for which this essay was written (*Comic Imagination*, pp. 339–48). Zoltán Abádi-Nagy, a professor of Kossuth University in Hungary, contributes "A Talk with Walker Percy" (*SLJ* 6,i:3–19), which is heavy on philosophical backgrounds. Percy confesses to being able to live with the description of him as a "philosophical Catholic existentialist."

A Way of Seeing: A Critical Study of James Agee (Amherst, Univ. of Mass. Press, [1972]) is an important book by Alfred T. Barson, who tactfully uses biographical details and the Agee papers at the University of Texas to buttress his thesis that Agee's first coronary in early 1951 marked the end of most of his first-rate work. (The composition of *A Death in the Family* he sets at 1947–49, not in the years closer to his death in 1955.) Barson believes the influence of Virgil and the writers of the Renaissance Catholic meditative tradition to be greater than that of Whitman, Jeffers, and American Quakerism; yet Agee's role as the passive artist waiting until reality affects him in such a way that his response can be both intelligible and spontaneous would seem to link him strongly to strategies made famous by Wordsworth and Keats.

Barson agrees with those critics who see Agee's agonizing between a respect for the moral significance of facts and the artist's cold-blooded manipulation of them; but the importance of his study lies in the freshly argued theses and incidental observations: that Agee attempted to create verbal analogies with music, that he was especially drawn to older poetic forms (the rondel and sestina), that he was profoundly influenced by I. A. Richards in 1931. Finally, Barson makes a convincing case for rejecting the notion that Agee's best work was with film in the early 1950s.

By 1945, Agee, burdened by the horrors of Hiroshima, had begun a satire of post-war America, which Victor A. Kramer describes in "Agee's Projected Screenplay for Chaplin: Scientists and Tramps" (*SHR* 7:357–63). The only part of this unfinished manuscript even nearly complete is an introductory speech which parodies American politics. Kramer suggests that this ambitious project was probably based on Agee's admiration for *Monsieur Verdoux* and his conversations with Chaplin.

x. Eudora Welty, Carson McCullers, and Truman Capote

Lewis P. Simpson has assembled one of the most impressive special issues of a journal to appear in some time: the Welty number of *MissQ* 25, which includes an appreciative personal piece by Charles East ("The Search for Eudora Welty," pp. 477–82), "A Eudora Welty Checklist" by Noel Polk (pp. 663–93), a reprint of William F. Buckley's *Firing Line* interview of 1972 ("The Southern Imagination: An Interview with Eudora Welty and Walker Percy," pp. 493–516), and "Some Notes on Time in Fiction" (pp. 483–92), in which Welty supplements her earlier statements on "place" in fiction.

Three essays discuss special aspects of Welty's general body of work. Thomas H. Landess, in "The Function of Taste in the Fiction of Eudora Welty" (pp. 543–57), tackles the issue of snobbery which some readers profess to see in her exposure of Southern tackiness. Breaches of taste and propriety, often *prima facie* evidence of vice, are the substance of Welty's inheritance from Austen and James, though in her work good taste and manners are not always essential proof of virtue. Nell Ann Pickett examines diction, rhythm, and grammar in "Colloquialism as a Style in the First-Person Narrator Fiction of Eudora Welty" (pp. 559–76). Reflecting various aspects of the Southern tradition, this style, most striking in "Why I Live at the P. O.," makes implicit distinctions "between those human values which are sustaining and those which are not." By "The Vision of Eudora Welty" (pp. 517–42), Ruth M. Vande Kieft means the imaginative wisdom of insight as well as literal vision. In this long but controlled essay, she is sensitive in articulating the creative tension between competing claims in Welty's fiction—action and stasis, clarity and blur, ordering sensibility and the haphazard—concluding that Welty has no singleness of vision, but "ambiguity, paradox, above all, mystery."

Thomas L. McHaney's "Eudora Welty and the Multitudinous Golden Apples" (pp. 589–624) is an exhaustive treatment of the author's use of myths and mythical allusions to structure *The Golden Apples.* Although heavy on plot summary, Charles C. Clark's "*The*

Robber Bridegroom: Realism and Fantasy on the Natchez Trace" (pp. 625–38) demonstrates that what seems to be an "amusing fictional amalgam of history, frontier humor, folklore, and fairy tale" is actually a statement on human ambivalence and duality.

Of those evaluating the later work, both Michael Kreyling and Carol A. Moore deal with *Losing Battles*. Stressing the larger, cosmic battle in his "Myth and History: The Foes of *Losing Battles*" (pp. 639–49), Kreyling sees mortality as the chief adversary. Moore describes how the close-knit family protects its members from experience by rejecting anything which threatens to expose their illusions in "The Insulation of Illusion and *Losing Battles*" (pp. 651–58). Analyzing Fay in "The Past Reexamined: *The Optimist's Daughter*" (pp. 577–87), Cleanth Brooks pictures an antagonist who, lacking the pieties that bind the generations, is rootless, amoral, self-aggrandizing; though this novel is no "tract for the times," it is a "document of our times." "Miss Eudora's Picture Book" (pp. 659–62) is a brief but illuminating statement on *One Time, One Place*, Welty's "family album" of snapshots taken during the Depression; it is, says M. E. Bradford, a tonic rebuke to those who try to force her work into connections "where they do not belong" and into the service of causes with which she is not directly concerned.

In addition to this special gathering, several other critical pieces are noteworthy. In "Eudora Welty's Comic Imagination" (*Comic Imagination*, pp. 319–28), Seymour L. Gross describes the inventiveness, variety, and virtuosity of the comic stories, which he sees as celebrative (in "the American transcendental comic tradition") rather than satirical, marked by "transformations of identities" and the "mischievous eruptions of nature and natural life." John F. Fleischauer, using *Losing Battles* as his chief example in "The Focus of Mystery: Eudora Welty's Prose Style" (*SLJ* 5,ii:64–79), superbly examines the often odd sentences, with their "uncertain progression," expletive and indefinite constructions, and organic similes. Her prose, which moves "by association and parallel structure, not by explicit logical progress," is marked by "gradual surges from indefiniteness to increasingly focused details charged with intensity," to culminations of feelings and impressions.

In "Conflict and Resolution in Welty's *Losing Battles*" (*Crit* 15,i:110–24), William E. McMillen concentrates on Gloria, who in surviving the contest between Julia and Granny, chooses the present and the future and succeeds in bringing her husband and daughter with her, without being "subdued and compromised by the shadows of the past." Antagonistic qualities coexist and even help one another in Welty's world, says Gordon E. Slethaug in "Initiation in Eudora Welty's *The Robber Bridegroom*" (*SHR* 7:77–87). Mike Fink and the goat survive as well as Rosamund and Jamie; initiation is a recognition of the complexity of life, the ability to experience evil, understand the self in relation to it, and "to accept the doubleness of nature, man, and God." "The Natchez Trace in Eudora Welty's 'A Still Moment'" (*SLJ* 6,i:59–69) is a fine combination of traditional scholarship and close critical reading by Victor H. Thompson, who sees a common bond in the white heron; its presence momentarily stills the egotism of Audubon (with his passion for recording everything), Dow (with his passion for saving souls), and Murrell (with his obsession with death).

In "Blacks as Primitives in Eudora Welty's Fiction" (*BSUF* 14, iii:20–28), John R. Cooley finds that black characters in five stories, except for "Powerhouse," are thin, unconvincing, hyperbolic, and eccentric because their creator allows the simplifying assumptions of primitivism to represent detailed portraits. "Eudora Welty and the Pulitzer Prize" (*SoR* 9:xx–xxiii) is Donald E. Stanford's editorial suggesting that the prize should have gone with more justice to one of two earlier works, *A Curtain of Green* or *Losing Battles*.

In "Carson McCullers, A Case of Convergence" (*BuR* 21,i:15–28), a sensible brief for the tactful use of psychology in literary interpretation, Irving H. Buchen finds that in McCullers's work a "minimum psychology" is matched by a minimum sense of history: her characters "are as cut off from the roots of their compulsion as much as her settings are severed from their connections with the past."

With admirable concision, John McNally analyzes "The Introspective Narrator in 'The Ballad of the Sad Cafe'" (*SAB* 38,iv:40–44), who shares his changing perceptions with the "listener-reader." The novella is an internal monologue of one whose "haunting recollections enable him to overcome his own *ennui* and to resist the atrophying pressures" of a familiar world. On the other hand, Joseph R. Millichap concentrates on genre in "Carson McCullers' Literary Ballad" (*GaR* 27:329–39) and finds that the ballad form absorbs the difficulties of mode, point of view, characterization, and structure. Its violence suggests the impulsiveness of archetypal human behavior; even the mill village exists in the "temporally imprecise world of human passion."

In "Gothic as Vortex: The Form of Horror in Capote, Faulkner, and Styron" (*MFS* 19:153–67), J. Douglas Perry, Jr., argues that structural devices as well as images and themes constitute gothic fiction. The concentricity, predetermined sequence, and character repetition of *Other Voices, Other Rooms* and *Set This House on Fire* indicate structural similarities to Melville, Poe, Monk Lewis, and Mary Shelley. The structural "hierarchy of horror" has sobering thematic implications: that the search for self-awareness is equivalent to "self-negation," that selfhood itself is an arbitrary but necessary construct of man's ignorance. This fascinating article is marred by its limits: only one work by each of the three writers is used.

Capote's natural forte, says Alfred Kazin in "The Imagination of Fact: Capote to Mailer" (*Bright Book of Life*, pp. 209–41), has always been the "selective creation of mood, tone, atmosphere"; and by yoking these skills to a central action, Capote created *In Cold Blood*, which is not only "a union of Art and Sympathy" but also a medium by which Capote could "instruct his countrymen on the depths of American disorder." Kazin feels that the fictional themes—corruption in the home, alienation, loneliness—recur with intensity in this nonfiction novel. "*In Cold Blood*: The Filmic Novel and the Problem of Adaptation" (*L/FQ* 1:132–37) is an imaginative structural study of the novel by Edward Murray, who finds aspects of the screenplay in its rapid pace, the fluidity of scene changes, the alternatives in point of view, and its "parallel editing." The actual film version, however, used these devices ineptly.

xi. Ralph Ellison, James Baldwin, and Other Black Writers

John O'Brien's *Interviews with Black Writers* (New York, Liveright) includes 13 previously unpublished ones—with Arna Bontemps, Cyrus Colter, Owen Dodson, Ralph Ellison, Ernest J. Gaines, Michael Harper, Robert Hayden, Clarence Major, Julian Mayfield, Ann Petry, Alice Walker, John Wideman, and Charles Wright; the volume also reprints interviews with William Demby, Ishmael Reed, John A. Williams, and Al Young. O'Brien supplies critical and biographical headnotes for each entry and in a perceptive introduction exposes what he regards as fallacies about black literature—that it is political and sociological, that it reflects the "black experience," and that black writers are a homogeneous school. O'Brien nevertheless advances his own thesis: "Whereas American literature is generally a record of man's inability to transcend the past (either historical or personal), black literature consistently reflects an individual's and a society's ability to escape the past and prepare for a future." Although he makes determinism an unduly strong element in the American tradition, his picture of the black man as "maker of his own myths" is convincing.[2]

David L. Carson's meaty interview, "Ralph Ellison: Twenty Years After" (*SAF* 1:1–23), records the novelist's statement that he had been unable to finish *The Education of Henry Adams*; but Stewart Rodnon attempts a comparison anyway in "Henry Adams and Ralph Ellison: Transcending Tragedy" (*StH* 3,ii:1–6). Both are said to deal "in depth with the human condition," to see life as a voyage which one must complete in order to "affirm one's humanity." Other source studies, some of them predictable, are more persuasive. Earl A. Cash, in "The Narrators in *Invisible Man* and *Notes from Underground*: Brothers in the Spirit" (*CLAJ* 16:505–07), examines Ellison's prologue and epilogue in light of part one of Dostoevsky's work. Leonard J. Deutsch's "Ralph Waldo Ellison and Ralph Waldo Emerson: A Shared Moral Vision" (*CLAJ* 16[1972]:159–78) proposes that the novelist's use of Emerson is not merely ironic or satiric. His protagonist, associated with Adam, Jonah, Judas, and finally Jesus, becomes an Emersonian idealist who affirms man's divinity. Oversimplifying Emerson unfortunately calls into question some of the parallels.

John Stark finds Homeric analogues, mostly ironic, in "*Invisible Man*: Ellison's Black Odyssey" (*NALF* 7:60–63); though Odysseus winds up at ease in Ithaca, the Ellison hero ends with "no allies or family, no happiness, and, above all, no real home." Barbara A. McDaniel suggests a literary debt with "John Steinbeck: Ralph Ellison's Invisible Source" (*PCP* 8:28–33), but the most convincing of all the recent source studies is Houston A. Baker, Jr.'s "A Forgotten Prototype: *The Autobiography of an Ex-Colored Man* and *Invisible Man*"

2. Two checklists should be noted. Supplementing Darwin T. Turner's *Afro-American Writers* (1970) is Carole Myers "A Selected Bibliography of Recent Afro-American Writers" (*CLAJ* 16:377–82); Robert A. Corrigan also contributes "Afro-American Fiction Since 1970" (*AmerS* 14,ii:85–90).

(*VQR* 49:433–49). The anonymous narrator of James Weldon Johnson's 1912 work "not only stresses his bifurcated vision, but also his intellectual genius," and although this artist-hero ends in a "static condition of self-recrimination," his role contains an influential dynamism which is incorporated into Ellison's hero.

In a two-part essay, William Walling first analyzes the "sense of displacement" in Ellison's novel ("Ralph Ellison's *Invisible Man*: 'It Goes a Long Way Back, Some Twenty Years'" [*Phylon* 34:4–16]), and then traces the radicals' disenchantment with the novelist between 1952 and 1968, when he was still committed to both American democracy and the primacy of art over politics ("'Art' and 'Protest': Ralph Ellison's *Invisible Man* Twenty Years After" [*Phylon* 34:120–34]). Walling admits that most adversary political readings of the novel are "culpably superficial."

Two brief pieces are studies of Ellison's early work. Leonard J. Deutsch's examination of "Ellison's Early Fiction" (*NALF* 7:53–59) supposedly proves that Ellison was never a radical, even in the late 1930s. Edward Guereschi, exploring Ellison's last short story before his novel appeared in "Anticipations of *Invisible Man*: Ralph Ellison's 'King of the Bingo Game'" (*NALF* 6[1972]:122–24), sees this 1944 story embodying familiar themes developed later (identity, self-delusion, betrayal) and even similar techniques (surrealism, symbolic vision).

James B. Lane's "Underground to Manhood: Ralph Ellison's *Invisible Man*" (*NALF* 7:64–72) is nothing more than a plot summary and an account of the novel's reception. Jacqueline Covo's "Ralph Ellison in France: Bibliographic Essays and Checklist of French Criticism, 1954–1971" (*CLAJ* 16:519–26) is a discursive discussion, together with some annotations.

"Black America and the Mask of Comedy" (*Comic Imagination*, pp. 349–60) is a solid historical and cultural essay by Richard K. Barksdale, who discusses the tradition of comic ridicule stemming from strategies of racial confrontation, seen notably in Charles Chesnutt but continued in both Ellison and Baldwin. According to Alfred Kazin's "The Imagination of Fact: Capote to Mailer" (*Bright Book of Life*, pp. 209–41), Baldwin's essays, not his fiction, are distinguished, primarily because in them we can see "his ability to turn every recital of his own life into the most urgent symbol of American crisis."

M. Thomas Inge's "James Baldwin's Blues" (*NConL* 2,iv[1972]: 8–11) is an explication of "Sonny's Blues," whose narrator, after failing his brother by not understanding him "and by extension his entire race," learns the responsibility of brotherly love only through recognition of alternative dilemmas and patterns for survival. In "The 'Uninhabitable Darkness' of Baldwin's *Another Country*: Image and Theme" (*NALF* 6[1972]:113–21), Barry Gross, studying the imagery of light and dark, concludes that all the characters except Cass give up their secrets to the light, an effort that must be undertaken for self-definition.

In "Racial Nightmares and the Search for Self: An Explication of LeRoi Jones' 'A Chase (Alighieri's Dream)'" (*NALF* 7:89–90), John O'Brien finds that this three-page story, prefiguring actions later in *Tales*, is a verbal montage of images of ghetto sights, sounds, and smells filtered through the consciousness of a sensitive young black. In "LeRoi Jones [Imamu Amiri Baraka] as Novelist: Theme and Structure in *The System of Dante's Hell*" (*NALF* 7:132–42), Lloyd W. Brown suggests that any future criticism of this novel must start with an analysis of Jones's style; he argues that irony, plot, and narrative point of view all embody distinct modes of perception.

John A. Williams continues to be the subject of solid criticism. Ronald Walcott, in "The Early Fiction of John A. Williams" (*CLAJ* 16[1972]:198–213), examines some of the autobiographical roots of the major work, as well as the evolution of his fictive world in *The Angry Ones* (1960), *Night Song* (1962), and his first important novel, *Sissie* (1963). Citing the "King Alfred" portion as his chief illustration in "The Nightmare Level of *The Man Who Cried I Am*" (*ConL* 14: 186–96), Robert E. Fleming speculates that the possibilities inherent in a grotesque underworld allow Williams a freedom impossible in the format of naturalistic protest common to many black writers.

In "The Resistance of John A. Williams: *The Man Who Cried I Am*" (*Crit* 15,iii:5–14), William M. Burke stresses the novelist's mixing of fact and fiction, almost as a *roman à clef*; he argues that the novel verifies one lesson wrung from the recent past—that in the battle against racial oppression, the black man has acquired a sense of human dignity earned by his response to oppression. In a masterful article which places the black versions of a perennial American figure in a context far broader than the 1960s, "An Examination of the Black Confidence Man in Two Black Novels: *The Man Who Cried I Am* and *dem*" (*AL* 44:596–611), Phyllis R. Klotman says that though his mask and peddled product may change, the salient characteristics of the type are permanent: "he is smooth-tongued, quick-witted and fleet of foot, a master of guile." Whereas the con man in William Melvin Kelley's *dem* springs from Ellison's Rinehart and the trickster of folklore, in Williams's black espionage agent, confidence is a metaphor of corruption, and the black spy ironically leads the black man "into ultimate darkness."

Despite its general title, Stanley Schatt's "You Must Go Home Again: Today's Afro-American Expatriate Writers" (*NALF* 7:80–82) is a casual look at the recent fiction of William Gardner Smith ("dean of expatriate writers") and William Melvin Kelley. In "The Vision of Man in the Novels of William Melvin Kelley" (*Crit* 15,iii:15–33), Donald M. Weyl sees an artistic decline from the earliest works because of a movement away from depiction of people to a soap-opera world (as in *dem*) with a reliance upon symbols and ideas.

Although Leela Kapai's "Dominant Themes and Techniques in Paule Marshall's Fiction" (*CLAJ* 16[1972]:49–59) is a general account of a writer who stresses traditional ties to an entire western heritage as well as innovations based on racial characteristics, its emphasis is on *Soul Clap Hand and Sing* (1961). In "Time Past and Time Present: The Search for Viable Links in *The Chosen Place, The Timeless People* by Paule Marshall" (*CLAJ* 16[1972]:60–71), Winifred L. Stoelting sees this author's "testament for survival of all people" implicit in both the action and the setting. Marshall's point is that capacity for destruction and man's survival instincts are part of the same cycle.

In "*The Autobiography of Malcolm X*: Beyond Didacticism" (*CLAJ* 16[1972]:179–87), David P. Demarest, Jr., suggests that white readers respond literarily rather than ideologically to this work because it evokes the tradition of spiritual autobiography in Christian literature. Jerome Klinkowitz and Karen Wood, in "The Making and Unmaking of *Knock on Any Door*" (*Proof* 3:121–37), is a gloomy recital of Willard Motley's 25-year struggle to get his novel published; his themes (racial assimilation, sexual adventure, human pity) were "reshaped to fit existing stereotypes," and the manuscript of the original "Leave Without Illusions" is so different from the published novel that collation is practically impossible. Klinkowitz also surveys a young black writer in "Reclaiming a (New) Black Experience: The Fiction of Clarence Major" (*OyezR* 8,i:86–89) and finds that his "modal techniques" are similar to those of the white *avant-garde*—imaginative fantasies cut loose from all visible moorings, counter-pointed narrative voices, and erratic narrative lines.

xii. Others

***a.* John Updike.** In "Professional Observers: Cozzens to Updike" (*Bright Book of Life*, pp. 97–124), Alfred Kazin dismisses Updike, Salinger, and Cheever as virtuoso writers too fond of that elegant "inch of ivory," the *New Yorker* columns. Updike's cerebral atmosphere allows his often memorable characters to struggle with nothing "except the reflections in their minds of a circumscribing reality that seems unalterable." In a modest but more useful piece, "John Updike: The Story as Lyrical Meditation" (*Thoth* 13,i[1972]:33–39), R. B. Larsen looks for the source of the author's verbal magic; he finds each story anchored to a central image or concept, often incremental, in the manner of the old-fashioned sketch.

Clinton S. Burhans, Jr., gives a thorough reading of Updike's most famous novels in "Things Falling Apart: Structure and Theme in *Rabbit, Run*" (*SNNTS* 5:336–51). Others have pointed out the prevalence of circles in this novel; Burhans suggests that this structural pattern shows that Rabbit is "less an absurd saint than a wasted victim," and that he and his society of malfunctioning institutions mirror each other. *Rabbit Redux*, "a sad story re-told," represents the "dogged compulsions" of Updike's social conscience to editorialize on the nice balance of the "mystery and banality" of self and place so obvious in *Rabbit, Run*—this is Eugene Lyons's fair treatment in "John Updike: The Beginning and the End" (*Crit* 14,ii[1972]: 44–59).

Using Karl Barth's *Dogmatics*, Edward P. Vargo interprets Updike's most ambitious novel as a "complete ritual," the narration "a patterned ceremony of word and action," in "The Necessity of Myth in Updike's *The Centaur*" (*PMLA* 88:452–60). With his liturgical bent, Peter hopes to find a pattern which will renew hope and meaning in his present life; he learns from his father's example that sensitivity to a sacral universe allows him to face such problems with time and death.

***b.* Jack Kerouac.** Ann Charters, the compiler of *A Bibliography of Works by Jack Kerouac* (1967), has now written *Kerouac: A Biography* (San Francisco, Straight Arrow). Though gracelessly written, this is an inevitably useful book not only for Kerouac but for the whole Beat movement. Charters draws on reminiscences, some from Kerouac during his final three years, but she has attempted to verify her facts by conventional scholarship. Despite the skill with which she sketches the transformation of a young football hero to eclectic celebrity, Kerouac as unlikely author still adheres to Charters's portrait. The relationship with Allen Ginsberg, Gary Snyder, William Burroughs, and others are more fully documented than they have ever been before, and the details of the compositional record of Kerouac's works are clarified. The biographer supplies photographs, chronology, an "Identity Key" for the transpositions of his friends into fictional characters, a "Bibliographical Chronology," and an astrological reading.

The modest revival of interest in Kerouac may lie in the prophetic fears about thought control and military power endemic to the San Francisco movement. John Tytell, in "The Beat Generation and the Continuing American Revolution" (*ASch* 42:308–17), lists the traits which made the Beats relevant to the 1960s: denial of artistic masks, belief in self-revelation and spontaneity, and trust in human potentials. If Tytell sees *On the Road* as characteristically American in its search for an unshaped life "free of preimposed patterns," a more sober judgment comes from Carole G. Vopat, who in "Jack Kerouac's *On the Road*: A Re-evaluation" (*MQ* 14:385–407), argues that the characters take to the road not to find life but to "leave it all behind." Sal Paradise's self-conscious posturings nullify his insistence on the life of instinct; his friends are not celebrating self but fleeing from identity. In "Future Hero in Paradise: Kerouac's *The Dharma Bums*" (*Crit* 14,iii:52–62), John E. Hart suggests that this novel is not merely a wandering hipster's search for true meaning but the "pilgrimage of organized spontaneity" by a hero whose antecedents include Odysseus, Don Quixote, Rasselas, and Nick Adams.

c. **Joyce Carol Oates.** In "The Artificial Demon: Joyce Carol Oates and the Dimensions of the Real" (*HC* 9,iv[1972]:1–12), Walter Sullivan finds that the technical élan of the stories fails Oates when she turns to longer fiction; the best of the novels (*A Garden of Earthly Delights* and *them*) also show that horror resides in the transformation of "the intimate and comfortable details of our lives." In "Joyce Carol Oates and an Old Master" (*Crit* 15,i:48–58), Rose Marie Burwell sees *A Garden* as a verbal Hieronymous Bosch and explores instances in which imagery and plot resemble the iconography of the famous painting to show that her realism is of the "metaphysical brand" that recognizes real evil in all human relations.

Carolyn Walker, in "Fear, Love, and Art in Oates' 'Plot' " (*Crit* 15,i:59–70), sees this story as a personal parody in which Oates undercuts her own hopes that art can make an ordered pattern out of an absurd world. In "Transformation of Self: An Interview with Joyce Carol Oates" (*OhR* 15,i:51–61), the author talks about the relationship between her fiction and poetry, her theory of art—the "externalization" of dream into structures—and her felt need "to chart the psychological processes" of those who suffer.

d. **Richard Brautigan.** In Terence Malley's *Richard Brautigan* (New York, Warner [1972]), the personality of the critic tends to overwhelm his subject in a book that sounds like literal transcriptions of classroom lectures, complete with false starts, retrenching, and loose confidences with the reader. This is nevertheless the best account of an imaginative but uneven writer. Malley makes the point that unlike other American autobiographical writers, Brautigan's experiences are not as important as his perceptions of them, the freshness of which stems from a "sense of distortion in his created world." Malley devotes space to poems and stories; but his major efforts are explications of *A Confederate General from Big Sur, The Abortion, In Watermelon Sugar*, and *Trout Fishing in America*—the latter an analysis of the failure of the old pastoral myth.

Neil Schmitz believes this novel even denies the form and language of the pastoral; in "Richard Brautigan and the Modern Pastoral" (*MFS* 19:109–25) he argues that *Trout Fishing* and *In Watermelon Sugar* are written not by a self-indulgent poet of the counter-culture but by an ironist critical of the myths of resurgent pastoralism.

***e.* James Dickey.** Donald J. Greiner's "The Harmony of Bestiality in James Dickey's *Deliverance*" (*SCR* 5,i[1972]:43–49) is an image study showing Dickey's aim in documenting the "menace and hostility in all men at all times" instead of contemporary urban America. Ed Gentry flounders out of his moral depth, but from the adventure comes self-awareness of the harmonious relationship of both his humanity and his bestiality. Peter G. Beidler is not as sanguine in his reading: " 'The Pride of Thine Heart Hath Deceived Thee': Narrative Distortion in Dickey's *Deliverance*" (*SCR* 5,i[1972]:29–40) is the first essay which argues logically and with considerable evidence that Dickey makes his protagonist kill not the rapist but an innocent hunter. To support his thesis Beidler cites factual details, corroborating verbal clues, the tendency of the plot to imitate movie adventures, and the epigraph from *Obadiah.*

In a packed little piece, "Dickey's *Deliverance*: The Owl and the Eye" (*Crit* 15,ii:95–101, C. Hines Edwards, Jr., believes the pattern of owl-and-eye images adds up to an "anti-romantic view of primitive man in nature," which teaches the survivors that killing in the course of things is part of the natural state. William Heyen's "A Conversation with James Dickey" (*SoR* 9:135–56) reveals some of the author's worst characteristics: his "aw-shucks" eroticism, his reverse snobbery, his arrogant purchase on the enticements of death, and his easy superiority to "mountain communities that are inbred to the point of imbecility and albinoism."

***f.* Miscellaneous.** Frederick Busch's "But This Is What It Is to Live in Hell: William Gass's 'In the Heart of the Heart of the Country' " (*MFS* 19:97–108) is an admiring analysis of Gass's sensitivity to the natural cycle, which produces "brilliant poetry of rot." In his breathlessly elliptical "3 Fingers/Figures of/for Gass" (*MinnR NRP* 4:138–44), Peter Schneeman professes to find important connections between *Walden* and "In the Heart of the Heart of the Country," both of which are "meditations on place."

Patricia Kane's "The Sun Burned on the Snow: Gass's 'The Pedersen Kid' " (*Crit* 14,ii[1972]:89–96) is a straightforward gloss on a story which manages to refresh the old tale of maturing adolescence. In Carole S. McCauley's "Fiction Needn't Say Things—It Should *Make* Them Out of Words: An Interview with William H. Gass"

(*Falcon* 5[1972]:35–45), Gass declares relevance in art "meaningless" and professes a liking for Sir Thomas Browne, Gertrude Stein, James Joyce, Henry James, and himself.

In "A Persuasive Account: Working It Out with Ronald Sukenick" (*NAmR* 258 Summer:48–52), Jerome Klinkowitz argues that unlike many novelists of Barth's generation, who suffer from "insipid reality," Sukenick makes his fiction do what it should: make "reality seem less unreal." Douglass Bolling discovers "two worthy experiments" in "Rudolph Wurlitzer's *Nog* and *Flats*" (*Crit* 14,iii:5–15), both of which reveal updated Bartlebys as solipsistic spokesmen.

Lynne Waldeland's "The Deep Sleep: The Fifties in the Novels of Wright Morris" in Joseph L. Mammola, ed., *Silhouettes on the Shade: Images from the 50s Reexamined* (Muncie, Ind., Ball State Univ.), pp. 25–43, although a superficial survey of the seven novels published between 1951 and 1960, is nevertheless useful in showing how fiction comments on history. The details of brand names, slang, and topical news serve to render Morris's work plausible and, cumulatively, indicate larger contemporary woes in American life—lack of authenticity, superficiality.

"Wallace Stegner: Trial by Existence" (*SoR* 9:796–827) is an impressive appreciation by Robert Canzoneri, who comments on a body of fiction resolutely unfaddish. Canzoneri is fine in his treatment of *Wolf Willow*, a book that eludes generic classification. During the course of Charles Israel's "Interview: George Garrett" (*SCR* 6,i:43–48), the author names Morris as his choice of "greatest living producing novelist," speaks without rancor about the South's uninterest in its contemporary writers, and articulates gracefully his belief that the great modernists "*started* something" with the novel as a form rather than finishing it off.

Martha Scott Trimble has produced the first substantial study of *N. Scott Momaday* (WWS 9), a no-nonsense monograph that is both biographical and critical. Trimble discusses the fiction, the lyrics, the autobiography, and the column which Momaday has written for the Santa Fe *New Mexican* since 1972. By contrast, Marion Willard Hylton's "On a Trail of Polen: Momaday's *House Made of Dawn*" (*Crit* 14,ii[1972]:60–69) is criticism as evocation; presumably because this novel is "difficult to analyze," what we get is a lyric paraphrase suggesting the Indian sense of time.

In "Notes on Nature in the Fiction of Reynolds Price" (*Crit* 15, ii:83–94), Allen Shepherd surveys most of the fiction and finds little in it that is naturalistic, agrarian, or pastoral. In another piece, " 'The Legitimate Heir' Making It New, or Fairly So" (*StH* 3,i:37–39), Shepherd emphasizes Price's continuity in the line of Southern writers of the past and his difficulty in carving out an individual place in that tradition.

Fred Erisman explores the significance of the milieu of *To Kill a Mockingbird* in "The Romantic Regionalism of Harper Lee" (*AlaR* 24:122–36); the stagnating and decadent town needs "functional romanticism," and Atticus Finch embodies the principles by which the town may be revitalized. Sanford Pinsker contributes both "A Conversation with David Madden" (*Crit* 15,ii:5–14) and an essay, "The Mixed Cords [sic] of David Madden's *Cassandra Singing*" (*Crit* 15,ii:15–26), which despite its rehashing of the plot, suggests some Lawrentian parallels in this impressive 1969 novel.

Stephen Goodwin conducts "An Interview with Peter Taylor" (*Shenandoah* 24,ii:3–20), who comments on other Southern writers, his compositional habits, and his future plans as a playwright. R. H. W. Dillard salutes a powerful and underrated writer of "experimental" Southern Gothic in "Letter from a Distant Lover: The Novels of Fred Chappell" (*HC* 10,ii:1–15). "The Blue Remembered Hills of Lauderdale County, Tennessee: Some Part of My History as a Writer" (*GaR* 27:340–55) is a charming semi-memoir by the short story writer, Robert Drake.

M. E. Bradford writes on two little-known Texas authors. "Arden Up the Brazos: John Graves and the Uses of Pastoral" (*SoR* 8[1972]: 949–55) is on *Goodbye to a River*, a "hard pastoral" because the movement is from settled society to a green world and back again. Its theme is the importance and difficulty of individualism. "Making Time Run: The Rich Harvest of George Sessions Perry" (*SwAL* 1[1972]:129–36) is devoted largely to *Hold Autumn in Your Hand*, which Bradford sees in part as Perry's answer to *The Grapes of Wrath*: an "agrarian exemplum" which argues that man is most thoroughly himself "when aligned with (and immersed in) the unbreakable calendar of being."

"The Popular Western: Essays Toward a Definition" (a special supplement of *JPC* 7,iii), edited by Richard W. Etulain and Michael

T. Marsden, is devoted mostly to western authors before 1930. Relevant here are Fred Erisman's "Growing Up with the American West: Fiction of Jack Schaefer" (pp. 710–16), Etulain's "The Historical Development of the Western" (pp. 717–26), and Dan D. Walker's "Notes Toward a Literary Criticism of the Western" (pp. 728–41).

Indiana University

14. Poetry: 1900 to the 1930s

Richard Crowder

i. General

It will be good news to many readers that T. S. Eliot is entering our chapter now for the first time. Beginning next year, (i.e., *ALS 1974*), Pound and Eliot will be treated in a separate chapter.

These two poets lead the list this year as topics for dissertations—seven on Pound, six on Eliot, and one on both. Frost is the subject of three, Jeffers of two. One study is of more or less sectional interest: "May Ward: Poet of the Prairie and Its People" (Kansas State). Other singles include Mark Van Doren, Cummings, and H.D. Robinson, Moody, Stickney, and Lodge are considered along with Stedman and Aldrich in a turn-of-the-century study (Brandeis).

Expl (Vols. 31–32) is not so generous with our poets as in recent years. There are only seven items in all: one on Cummings, two on Frost, and four on Hart Crane.

Two books of interest are Walter Sutton's *American Free Verse: The Modern Revolution in Poetry* (New York, New Directions) and Edwin S. Fussell's *Lucifer in Harness: American Meter, Metaphor, and Diction* (Princeton, Princeton Univ. Press). Sutton's book is a historical survey from Emerson and Whitman to Galway Kinnell. His references to Eliot, Pound, and Cummings will be discussed below. Fussell, in defending his theory of American poetry, dwells on Whitman, Pound, Eliot, Crane, Stevens, and Williams, with allusions here and there to Ransom, Robinson, and Frost. His starting point is that these poets are unwillingly linked with English traditions in literature and language, yet have managed to create a distinctly American flavor in their work. A third book is devoted not so much to the poetry as to the political stance of Pound and Eliot and will be considered in the sections discussing them. It is William M. Chace's *The*

Political Identities of Ezra Pound & T. S. Eliot (Stanford, Stanford Univ. Press), based on the premise that both poets were revolted by liberal democracy and expressed an unparalleled elitism.

ii. Pound

Sutton develops his ideas about Pound in two full chapters as well as scattered references throughout the book. He stresses Pound's insistence on innovation. After a survey of the early poems and an analysis of *Mauberley* (which he concludes is finally lacking in coherence), he turns to the *Cantos.* Here he defends the absence of continuity as probably growing from Pound's interest in the Chinese ideogram, but he sees, nevertheless, a unity in the search for enlightenment throughout this "modern epic." Like earlier critics he nominates the *Pisan Cantos* (rather than *Rock-Drill* or *Thrones*) as the climactic level of Pound's achievement, for here the poet has dropped his mask and is speaking movingly of his own "deprivations and . . . rewards."

Fussell says Pound's metric may be eclectic, but his basic theory "is pure American pragmatism" in revolt against the British heritage. The author points out that the principal 20th-century American poems are built around "a constituting metaphor," usually found in the title. In reading the *Cantos,* for example, relating to Dante is most helpful: the descent into hell, the succeeding salvation, and the falling away. Fussell finds a vigor of language in Pound which is a noticeable departure from English tradition.

Chace thinks Pound's political identity becomes confused with the issue of the Bollingen Prize, but in a hundred pages he examines the poet's admiration for Mussolini and his despair at the defeat of totalitarianism. Pound, "alone with a lucid vision of civilization purged of usury," wanted to speak to the world, but was always turning back to his own struggle (hence his "elitism").

Max Nänny's *Ezra Pound: Poetics for an Electric Age* (Bern and Munich, Franke Verlag) exploits the thesis that Pound employed the "image" and the ideogram as the only means available to him for investigating an environment more and more controlled by electric media. The immediacy and directness of these devices correspond in many ways to the chiefly oral quality of 20th-century communication, which necessitates absolute compression as well as omission of connecting words and phrases. The result is that Pound's poetry inevitably makes an increased demand for cooperation and creative activity by the reader.

Two interesting items have come to light in the Beinecke Library at Yale. Both articles are by William Carlos Williams. The first, "A Study of Pound's Present Position" (*MR* 14:118–23), written January 21–23, 1947, is an approving estimate of Pound's poetry from 1915 to 1925. When he started studying Chinese poetry, says Williams, he went astray. Further, he suggests that Pound's interest in usury and finance was a hindrance. Williams, however, acknowledges his personal debt to Pound for the "idea" of a present-day meter. The other article was written on January 13, 1950: "The Later Pound" (*MR* 14:124–29). The "fabric of the language" is the source of greatness in the later *Cantos*. Pound was searching for a present-day subtlety, for speed and flexibility. His absorption in finance and politics had served the purpose of showing him that the modern failure of a time sense (in the full Greek meaning of the phrase) had brought on destruction. On the other hand, in the writing of a good poem there was virtue, and the honest reading of a good poem provided the pattern for men to become better in business and in statesmanship.

Aiming at a popular readership, Alfred Kazin published "The Writer as Political Crazy" (*Playboy* 20 [June]:107–08, 136, 206–09). Pound's case is an example of "what madness, obscenity, and, above all, self-destruction total intemperance on the subject of politics can visit on an extraordinary writer." Though his poetry will always remain important, intellectual violence took its toll in both Pound's writing and his total life. Kazin stresses the music of Pound's verse. He compares the *Cantos* to "an old Saratoga trunk stuffed" full of everything imaginable, but "by sheer hypnotic incantation, he [made] his unbelievable contraption move." What disturbs Kazin is that, when Pound's political views took over, his style became "cheap, downright stupid."

Raising again the question of Pound's sanity, Jonathan Yoder sees Pound as constantly frustrated by the powers of usury (Helen/Circe/Eleanor). In "Pound as Odysseus, the Prisoner Psychotic" (*Rendezvous* 8:1–11), Yoder points out that again and again the poet's journey through today's society (hell) is presented as incarceration. For Pound, psychotic or not, in a profoundly irrational world the individual's only salvation was in creating a hero of himself. (He could not see that the Robber Barons had done just that.) His world needed a Hitler. Yoder concludes that, indeed, Pound was a victim of hallucinatory psychosis, unable to distinguish between dream and reality. But, asks Yoder, what is reality exactly?

Anthony Tatlow studies the compatibility in the methods of Pound and Bertolt Brecht in "Stalking the Dragon: Pound, Waley, and Brecht" (*CL* 25:193–211). Brecht, translating into German Arthur Waley's academic and literal translations of Chinese poetry, made the poems lively. His method and personality bring his work closer to the Pound of *Cathay* than to Waley. Pound's poems are made by three methods: the visual (Imagist), the speech and gesture, and the approximation to the original. Sometimes all three help shape a single poem.

D. S. Carne-Ross, in "The Music of a Lost Dynasty: Pound in the Classroom" (*BUJ* 21:25–41), transcribes a classroom discussion of lines from *Canto* 81. He and his class succeed in making a seemingly muddled passage finally lucid. Two things are accomplished here: an example of a searching teaching method and actual clarification of the lines for the reader. They are worth one's time.

John Kwan-Terry says that Pound's ideas about rhythm, melody, and pitch were more precise than in the practice of even most musicians, though the poet acknowledged that, whereas music can be merely an arrangement of tones, poetry must have meaning first of all. Finding great flexibility in cadence and the "lengthened foot," Pound nevertheless was always aware of meter even in his least consistent and unified passages. He emphasized the importance of rhyme in marking rhythms. The article is entitled "The Prosodic Theories of Ezra Pound" (*PLL* 9:48–64).

John Scotus Erigena, the ninth-century Irish philosopher, proved useful to Pound from the 1930s onward, as Peter Makin shows in "Ezra Pound and Scotus Erigena" (*CLS* 10:60–81). Erigena saw the universe as the manifestation of God, a concept Pound found congenial with his own sense of relationship between human and divine beings in a continuous but graded order of values.

Paideuma 2 is full of articles, information, and reprints of reference materials related to Pound, including "Notes and Queries," "Letters to the Editor," and "The Explicator." Barry S. Alpert edits a selection from letters of Pound to John Price, Pound's American agent for *The*

Exile. In "Ezra Pound, John Price, and *The Exile*" (pp. 427–48) Alpert maintains that Price never received the credit he deserved even though Pound had discovered some worthy American writers through Price's agency. Hugh Kenner, "D. P. Remembered" (pp. 485–93), recollects that Mrs. Pound remained very much "Kensington" all her days, in spite of the changing times. He records his conversations with her at Rapallo, March 22–25, 1965.

Pound's opera, *Le Testament de Villon*, is the subject of several articles. The section begins with a reprint of George Antheil's "Why a Poet Quit the Muses" from the *Chicago Tribune*, September 14, 1924 (*Paideuma* 2:3–6), in which the composer states that Pound's music is unintellectual, though brilliantly intelligent. This is followed (pp. 7–9) by Charles Shere's news item "Eastbay Artists Score Record Triumph" from the *Oakland Tribune*, September 17, 1972. He expresses the opinion that Pound's music led to "the revolutionary method" of his last *Cantos*. Robert Hughes traces the history of the composition of the opera and provides a synopsis of the plot by scenes. In "Ezra Pound's Opera: *Le Testament de Villon*" (pp. 11–16) he finds the use prophetic of "non-symmetrical rhythm, non-pitched instruments and pointillism," the form relying on the Villon poem and on increased density of intervals and complexity of rhythm. Larry Lyall continues the discussion in "Pound/Villon: *Le Testament de François Villon*" (pp. 17–22) by showing that the text brought together various elements of the medieval temperament that fascinated Pound. Lyall analyzes the Villon fragments Pound uses to show his vision of evil and his celebration of life as it is.

R. Murray Schafer's "The Developing Theories of Absolute Rhythm and Great Bass" (pp. 23–35) gathers up many of the poet's statements through the years about these two topics. Among other things, Schafer finds Antheil's influence on Pound to have been considerable. He defends Pound's ambiguities by saying that there can be no definition or discussion of rhythm without loopholes, even though the statements have a basic unity. "Absolute rhythm governs the proportions of the elements of masterpieces; Great Bass links the elements into an individual whole." That is, even with its imperfections, the whole of a masterpiece is coherent.

"K. R. H. and the Young E. P." by Carroll F. Terrell (pp. 49–51) tells the story of Pound's management in Venice and London of the concerts of Katherine Ruth Heyman, pianist, when he was broke and hungry. Though he later gave up the work, his friendship with her continued. This story is followed by Faubion Bowers's "Memoir within Memoirs" (pp. 53–66), which traces the pianist's career first by following her memoirs and then by relying on his own memory. He reveals that the friendship with Pound began as early as 1904.

Terrell makes several other contributions to *Paideuma* 2, chiefly through editing and reprinting esoteric documents referred to in the *Cantos*, "The Sacred Edict of K'ang-Hsi" (pp. 69–112) and "The Eparch's Book" (pp. 223–311), prepared by the Emperor Leo of Constantinople. Following "A Commentary on Grosseteste with an English version of *De Luce*" (pp. 449–62), Terrell gives the English version (pp. 455–62) and then Richard Grosseteste's Latin version (pp. 463–70). These various documents no doubt will be invaluable to some Pound specialists.

Georg M. Gugelberger looks to Pound's translation of Guido Cavalcanti (a friend of Dante) as a strong influence. In "Secularization of 'Love' to a Poetic Metaphor: Cavalcanti, Center of Pound's Medievalism" (pp. 159–73), Gugelberger emphasizes that Pound was not a love poet but found in the Italian writer an attractive concentration, a merging of love, poetry, and form. As for Dante's influence itself, James J. Wilhelm's "Two Heavens of Light and Love: Paradise to Dante and to Pound" (pp. 175–91) points out that the Italian's paradise was cosmological, in contrast with Pound's, which was mainly urban. Pound becomes Dante-Confucius in the late *Cantos*, where love is the necessary ingredient, where "social joy and grace abounding" supply the context. Wilhelm maintains that the years in St. Elizabeth's were salvaged by the image of Dante. In another article, Wilhelm discerns the influence of Anselm, medieval Archbishop of Canterbury. "In Praise of Anselm: An Approach to *Canto* 105" makes clear Anselm's rationality in the midst of love. The tension in this *Canto* rises between order and brute force. In spite of betrayal Anselm had a vision which led him through love to knowledge (the Pound ideal).

"Casting His Gods Back into the *Nous*: Two Neoplatonists and the *Cantos* of Ezra Pound" by Sharon Mayer Libera (pp. 355–77) shows that the poet was attracted to certain Neoplatonic ideas because they explain the necessarily heightened emotions of the creative artist. Intellectual Light (*Nous*) is related to Pound's pleasure in myth. In both Iamblichus (a second-century Syrian philosopher in

Alexandria) and Plethon (Georgius Gemistus, a 15th-century Byzantine philosopher) Pound found confirmation for his feeling that forms are only fleeting thoughts of the whole of things.

Leslie Palmer in "Matthew Arnold and Ezra Pound's *ABC of Reading*" (pp. 194–98) points out the similarities between Arnold and Pound. Though disagreeing in some matters of historical criticism, they were in considerable unanimity on specific authors. Pound was, however, his own man and took new directions in distinguishing between culture and anarchy. Frederick K. Sanders—"The 'French Theme' of *Canto* 70: An Examination of Ezra Pound's Use of Historical Sources" (pp. 379–90)—demonstrates Pound's skill in transforming materials about John Adams and France into strong poetry. Earle Davis argues, in "Ezra Pound: New Emphasis on Economics" (pp. 473–78), that there is value in the examination of Pound's idealistic theories by pointing out that political theory has taken Plato's *Republic* into account, impractical though it was.

On an earlier poem, Jo Brantley Berryman, in studying " 'Medallion': Pound's Poem" (pp. 391–98), refutes critics who ascribe this last part of *Mauberley* to the Mauberley persona himself and contends that it, along with "Envoi," is Pound speaking, forcing music into speech and weaving together "images drawn from our heritage of the graphic and plastic arts."

Articles appeared in still other journals, chiefly reminiscent in nature. When Victor Llona died in 1953, he left with Ernest Kroll the manuscript of his partially completed memoirs. Kroll has edited the chapter recreating the Paris of the 1920s—"With Ezra Pound before Rapallo" (*CimR* 2:7–17). Numerous anecdotes support the familiar portrait of the poet as generous, hard-working, though egocentric. Robert E. Knoll, in search of information about Robert McAlmon, spent an afternoon with Pound, recorded in "Ezra Pound at St. Elizabeth's" (*PrS* 47:1–13). Several callers came in during the course of the visit. Pound expressed his opinion about McAlmon, William Carlos Williams, Bryher Ellerman, Jews in general, and the Constitution. Knoll claims that Pound remained "a red-blooded American" all his life. On another afternoon Donald Pearce—"A Wreath for Ezra Pound: 1885–1972" (*Shenandoah* 24:3–14)—called on Pound in the presence of Dorothy Pound. Pound advised Pearce on the best Greek plays to teach in college, and the talk turned to Ford Madox Ford, little magazines, and other literary topics. Guy Davenport, in "Ezra

Pound 1885–1972" (*Arion* 1:188–96), reminisces about Pound in St. Elizabeth's and Venice and concludes that "we cannot diminish . . . the pervasive intelligence which drove him to both his tragedy and his greatness." Edward Foote also visited Pound at Olga Rudge's Venice residence during the poet's last days. "A Note on Ezra Pound" (*Prose* 7:71–78) records no evidence of the poet's fabled austerity and anger. The thread of the conversation was an attempt at identity of Cousin Agnes Foote as a link between the two men. Olga did most of the talking.

In a review article, "Ezra Pound" (*ConL* 14:240–46), Hugh Witemeyer puts Pound at the center of the modern period; it is from him that the other poets "can be studied most coherently." In another review article, "The Pound Errata" (*Encounter* 40[June]:66–68), Hugh G. Porteus outlines what he thinks still needs to be done for the period: an account of the long critical feuds among Pound, Eliot, Joyce, and Wyndham Lewis, as well as their private squabbles, but also their stout mutual defense when insulted by outsiders.

TLS (16 Mar.:292) carries an anonymous review article, "Fragments of Cracker," which proclaims Pound a "compulsive journalist" who did not know nearly as much as he thought he did and was plainly a "traitor" admired by the left-wing American literary establishment. In a letter to the editor (*TLS* 13 Apr.:420–21) D. S. Carne-Ross takes exception to the reviewer's phrase "the drivel of the later *Cantos*" as abusive, not critical. Other brief comments on Pound can be found in the following issues: 16 Mar.:292; 13 Apr.:420–21; and 20 Apr.:446.

Two bibliographical items from *Paideuma* 2 should be listed here: Robert Corrigan's "Ezra Pound Criticism, 1904–1917: Additions and Corrections" (pp. 115–24); and Donald Gallup's "Corrections and Additions to the Pound Bibliography (Part 2)" (pp. 315–24).

Now revised and enlarged, *An Examination of Ezra Pound: A Collection of Essays*, Peter Russell, editor, has been reissued by New Directions, New York.

iii. Eliot

In *The Political Identities* of Pound and Eliot (see above), William M. Chace says that Eliot's political views become confused with his religion. He thinks Eliot was condemning the age by escaping into the Church. Like Pound, he had difficulty addressing a wide readership because of his battles within himself. Edwin S. Fussell's *Lucifer in Harness* (see above) demonstrates in Part III, "What the Thunder Said," that Eliot remained loyal to American speech patterns. Walter Sutton, in *American Free Verse* (see above), refers to Eliot as the traditionalist who led the way to the conservatism of the generation of the late 1930s and the 1940s.

David Ward offers a lucid, restrained analysis of each of Eliot's poems and plays, using adroitly the scholarship of recent years. He explores the influence of F. H. Bradley's philosophy (the subject of Eliot's Ph.D. thesis) and of early 20th-century anthropologists at Cambridge. Eliot probably owed a great deal to Gilbert Murray for his sense of tradition rather than mere self-expression. Ward points out Eliot's inclination to see oppositions: tradition and individual talent; Augustine and Buddha; human and supernatural. Hence his title, *T. S. Eliot: Between Two Worlds: A Reading of T. S. Eliot's Poetry and Plays* (London and Boston, Routledge & Kegan Paul). Ward makes thorough use of relevant Bible passages and follows Eliot's growth toward and in Anglicanism with solid understanding. He is especially incisive on *The Waste Land*, mining the riches of Valerie Eliot's facsimile edition of the original drafts and Pound's annotations.

Another book that relies on the Bradley influence is Anne C. Bolgan's *What the Thunder Really Said: A Retrospective Essay on the Making of "The Waste Land"* (Toronto, McGill-Queens). An outgrowth of her 1960 Toronto dissertation, the book defends the idea that *The Waste Land* is "a failure only in Bradley's sense of the word—relative, that is, to the attainment of the Absolute." Bolgan expresses the wish that there were more noble "failures" like it. She arrives at this comment in her final chapter, where, using matter from an earlier essay, she investigates "The Love Song of J. Alfred Prufrock," *The Waste Land*, *Ash Wednesday*, and *Four Quartets* as "four quadrants in search of Bradley's circle of the Absolute." George Whiteside's "T. S. Eliot's Doctoral Studies" (*AN&Q* 9:83–87) is a descriptive cataloguing of the courses Eliot took at Harvard between 1911 and 1914 along with comments on some of his professors.

Eliot in His Time: Essays on the Occasion of the Fiftieth Anniversary of "The Waste Land," A. Walton Litz, ed. (Princeton, Princeton Univ. Press), contains eight articles the titles of which indicate something of the scope of the book: "*The Waste Land* Fifty Years After," by A. Walton Litz (pp. 3–22); "The Urban Apocalypse," by Hugh Kenner (pp. 23–49); "The First *Waste Land*," by Richard Ellmann (pp. 51–66); "The Waste Land: Paris, 1922," by Helen Gardner (pp. 67–94); "New Modes of Characterization in *The Waste Land*," by Robert Langbaum (pp. 95–128); "Precipitating Eliot," by Robert M. Adams (pp. 129–53); "Fear in the Way: The Design of Eliot's Drama," by Michael Goldman (pp. 155–80); and "Anglican Eliot," by Donald Davie (pp. 181–96). Of these Ellman's and Davie's and parts of Litz's essays had appeared elsewhere earlier.

Litz examines Bradley, Henry James, Conrad, Pound, Joyce, and Sir James Frazer as writers who appealed to Eliot. Kenner recreates from the facsimile the chronological steps in the making of *The Waste Land*. He thinks Dryden's *Annus Mirabilis* was important to Eliot. Ellman pieces together fragments of Eliot's biography to help clarify the circumstances and materials of the composition. Gardner speculates on the timing of Pound's assistance and suggests that Eliot had invented a structure that would allow him to compose when inspired and to cement the fragments together later. Langbaum relates "Preludes" and "Rhapsody on a Windy Night" to Bradley's view of "the opaque and discontinuous" self and so to the characterizations in *The Waste Land*. Adams believes that Eliot departed from Bradley's metaphysics of isolation beginning about 1922, but always retained certain reservations. Goldman demonstrates that the "ghosts" at the opening of Eliot's plays are gradually replaced by the "'horror, boredom, and glory" of other ghosts. Davie sees a great unevenness in *Four Quartets* because of tremendous tensions—private and public, musical and pedestrian, suggestive and "unsparingly explicit."

Ronald Schuchard, in "Eliot and Hulme in 1916: Toward a Revaluation of Eliot's Critical and Spiritual Development" (*PMLA* 88: 1083–94), finds Eliot close to Hulme as early as 1914. By 1916 he had already taken his stand as a "classicist" with Hulme's concept of Original Sin as the foundation of his thought. The Eliot chronology needs to be readjusted and his work reexamined between 1916 and 1928.

Marion Montgomery was the most prolific Eliot scholar during the year with a book devoted in great part to Eliot and three substantial articles. *The Reflective Journey Toward Order* (Athens, Univ. of Ga. Press) traces a line of descent from Wordsworth to Eliot (and

Pound and others). He claims that Eliot eventually discovered elements of romanticism in himself and decides that, in spite of Wordsworth's embarrassing failures, he must be acknowledged as the inescapable predecessor of Eliot (and even of Pound). In "Through a Glass Darkly: Eliot and the Romantic Critics" (*SWR* 58:327–35) Montgomery defends Eliot's change of attitude toward Wordsworth as a result of Eliot's discovery of the "counter-romantic" in the elder poet. John Henry Newman's *Dream of Gerontius*, though similar in view, is inferior to "Gerontion." Eliot contrasts Baudelaire (pursuing a state of blessedness) with Arnold (trying to save Christian emotions "without the belief"). Pater attempts an escape from romanticism through *ars gratia artis*. Then Pater's student, Hopkins, moves on to a reconciliation of past, present, and future, a state Eliot is trying to attain in *The Waste Land*. "Eliot's Hyacinth Girl and the *Times Literary Supplement*" (*Renascence* 25:67–73) answers a reviewer's comment that "hatred and fear of sex" were at the bottom of *The Waste Land*, in which desire beyond physical passion is unfulfilled. Montgomery declares that it is spiritual deprivation that the despair in the poem has grown out of. "Eliot and the Meta-poetic" (*InR* 9:29–36) reflects Eliot's shift from reason toward feeling, emotion, spirituality—even beyond poetry. From the fragments of "What the Thunder Said" the poet is beginning to set his house in order.

William M. Chace, in "'Make It Not So New'—*The Waste Land* Manuscript" *SoR* 9:476–80), points out that Pound hardly touched Part V, which makes tentative spiritual affirmation. Chace speculates this was because of Pound's view of the Church as corrupt. Further, what Eliot lost in omitting many "voices" at Pound's suggestion he regained in the "dramatic orchestration" of the plays.

An argument over the origin of *The Waste Land* breaks out between George Whiteside and Philip Waldron. Whiteside starts it all with "T. S. Eliot: The Psychobiographical Approach" (*SoRA* 6:3–27), in which he sets out a series of biographical facts supplemented by conjecture to show among other traits Eliot's fear of sex and his schizoid tendencies. Waldron says (pp. 138–47) Whiteside's reading is based on too much theoretical speculation. The two are still spatting on pages 253–56.

Another controversy develops between Craig Raine and P. Malekin with a contribution from Jayanta Padmanabha. Raine's "*The Waste Land* as a Buddhist Poem" (*TLS*, 4 May:503–05) sees the central theme as reincarnation, hence Buddhist. Padmanabha (18 May:556) and Malekin (25 May:587) take the non-Buddhist view. There are parting shots between Raine (15 June:692) and Malekin (29 June:749). The series is rather amusing.

Undaunted or unknowing, G. Schmidt, in "An Echo of Buddhism in T. S. Eliot's 'Little Gidding'" (*N&Q* 20:330), cites Henry Clark Warren's "chapter on . . . karma" in *Buddhism in Translations.* George M. Spengler's "Eliot's 'Red Rock' and Norris's *McTeague*" suggests that Eliot had read Norris's novel when he was young.

Rebeccah Kinnamon speculates that Eliot's 1927 translation of Jacques Maritain's essay "Poetry and Religion" might have been a source for *Ash Wednesday*, for Maritain insists that the survival of today's poetry depends on the admission of the poet that he needs more than his own abilities to attain the Absolute. Her essay is "Eliot's 'Ash Wednesday' and Maritain's Ideal for Poetry" (*GaR* 27:156–65). Another "influence" essay is Richard Abel's "The Influence of St.-John Perse on T. S. Eliot" (*ConL* 14:213–39). Abel analyzes particularly "Journey of the Magi," but finds traces of influence in other poems and the plays, not only in borrowing but in technical experimentation. The influence of an Eliot ancestor is suggested by the word "Daunsinge" ("East Coker"), says Linda Bradley Salaman in "A Gloss on 'Daunsinge': Sir Thomas Elyot and T. S. Eliot's *Four Quartets*" (*ELH* 40:584–605). Not very strong, Elyot's influence is still present, though it is in the direction of "human piety, labor, and wisdom, not . . . sacred vision." Eliot-Elyot (Dante-Virgil), however, share "the imagery of fire, . . . modest self-recognition, veneration for the past" and the importance of giving "high meaning" to love.

Edith Pankow—"The 'Eternal Design' of *Murder in the Cathedral*" (*PLL* 9:35–47)—says that Eliot's work will last because it observes the classic conventions, including the tragic flaw, the downfall, and the justification, when God rescues Thomas from man's fragmented state into ultimate union. Robert Langbaum proposes that Eliot tries in his last three plays to find the solution to the Christian paradox that one must lose himself to find himself. His characters reach self-understanding by understanding others. Langbaum's essay is "The Mysteries of Identity as a Theme in T. S. Eliot's Plays" (*VQR* 49:560–80).

C. A. Patrides, in "The Renascence of the Renaissance: T. S.

Eliot and the Pattern of Time (*MQR* 12:172–96), discovers in Eliot an urgency for recognizing past, present, and future as three "presents" in coexistence in the human mind, reflecting the "timeless moments" in the mind of God. (This parallels Montgomery's discovery about Eliot's affinity with Hopkins, above.) "T.S. Eliot as Thinker" (*JML* 3:134–42) by M. L. Raina is a review article containing interesting comments. Raina shows that Eliot has divided loyalties. For example, while denouncing totalitarian creeds, he calls for an authoritarian social order with Christians in the lead. Raina finds that Eliot's ideas are derived from writers of the late 19th and early 20th centuries, in other words, are not original. His best poetry, though, is deeply and personally felt, and in his plays, for all his aristocratic employment of myth and liturgy, he tries to touch the profound feelings of his audience. The values of Eliot's literary criticism lie in his occasional insight into writers he admires, his appreciation of the *avant garde*, his wide-ranging interest in form and craft, and his unerring taste. Raina feels that it is unavoidable to acknowledge that his ideas, inadequate though they be, have after all produced his poetry, about himself, but also about the age.

Eileen Kennedy describes her pilgrimage to the church where Eliot's ashes repose. In "Poet's Corner: Eliot's East Coker" (*CEA* 35:30–32) she tells how she and her companion virtually stumbled onto St. Michael's, East Coker, Somerset. She connects lines from the *Quartet* with the appearance of the landscape and the church.

Mildred Martin's *A Half-Century of Eliot Criticism: An Annotated Bibliography of Books and Articles in English, 1916–1965* (London, Kaye and Ward) lists 2,692 items (articles, reviews, books, and pamphlets), a well-arranged and very useful book with a carefully compiled index. *Renascence* (25:183–89) has reprinted for readers who might have missed it in volume 2 H. Marshall McLuhan's "Mr. Eliot's Historical Decorum."

iv. Frost

Elaine Barry divides her book, *Robert Frost on Writing* (New Brunswick, N.J., Rutgers Univ. Press), into two main parts: an essay on "Frost as a Literary Critic" and the larger section of "Texts" —Frost's writings of all kinds that contain his comments on the craft of poetry. Barry's essay itself is in three chapters. "The Scope of

Frost's Criticism" admits that the poet was hardly a conscientious and formal critic. "Frost as a Critical Theorist" underscores his emphasis on the importance of tone as an extension of the formal meaning of a word, though there is more to the problem than that: *form* is all-essential. And irony and humor he sees as necessary to the defense of one's belief in the eternal verities. "Frost as a Practical Critic" divides the poet's critical thinking into three overlapping chronological periods: (1) early concern with techniques, (2) linking of poetry and life philosophically, and (3) epistemology. The author discusses Frost's comments on the work of his contemporaries and a few earlier poets. Mostly, however, his practical criticism is too scattered and casual, sometimes even too careless, to be of great value, though at its best his wit and sophistication come through and he is seen to possess "a solid knowledge of the great tradition of English poetry." After the "Texts" the book concludes with notes and a bibliography. An index would have been useful.

Francis Lee Utley, in "Robert Frost's Virgilian Monster" (*ELN* 10:221–23) corrects Lawrance Thompson's reading of some "playful lines" Frost sent to his friend Carl Burell in 1902 or 1903 and decides that they are based on a private joke with Burell which the reader cannot possibly understand. Two other items of biographical material are Lloyd N. Dendinger's "Robert Frost in Birmingham" (*BSUF* 14:47–52) and Stearns Morse's "Lament for a Maker: Reminiscences of Robert Frost" (*SoR* 9:53–68). Dendinger's contribution is the transcription of a taped recording of Richebourg Gaillard McWilliams's account of two visits of the poet to Birmingham-Southern College. During his first visit (1956) he lectured to more than 1100 enthusiastic people on a rainy night, making fun of college professors that "interpreted" his poems. The next day he talked with a centenarian ex-slave before television cameras. His second visit (1957) is mentioned only briefly. Morse reflects on forty years of relationship with Frost through the Dartmouth connection, though the two men did not actually meet till Frost was sixty. Morse questions whether Robert or Elinor suffered more in their marriage relationship. He remarks that religion, but not theology, was of deep interest to the poet. He also observed that Frost (for what it is worth) had an Anglo-Saxon aversion to walking arm in arm with another man.

That Frost's concept of freedom is the foundation of his idea of the individual's relationship with society (family, state) is the thesis of Peter J. Stanlis's "Robert Frost: The Individual and Society" (*InR* 8:211–34). The *raison d'etre* of society is the full development of the individual. There must be no nihilism or anarchy, however, but, on the other hand, a planned state is unthinkable.

"Robert Frost: Dark Romantic" (*ArQ* 29:235–45) by Carl M. Linder relates Frost to Emerson and Melville in the tradition of "the terror of discovering the truth, uncertainty, and sense of loss." Ronald L. Lycette's "The Vortex Points of Robert Frost" (*BSUF* 14:54–59) reminds readers that Frost's phrase "vortex rings" applies to intense focus on experiences and material things, without which life would be empty, chaotic, lonely, and fearful. Lycette cites several poems in which the persona undergoes terrifying emptiness through limited vision or brief clarity through expansion (e.g., "Desert Places" and "West Running Brook"). He cites other poems to illustrate the vortex of love and the necessity of "perception and understanding" to escape the empty spaces (e.g., "The Silken Tent," on the one hand, and "Home Burial," on the other).

Two articles are concerned with Frost's interest in sound and voice. Tom Vander Ven's "Robert Frost's Dramatic Principle of 'Oversound'" (*AL* 45:238–51) emphasizes the poet's urgency to create precise voices in the reader's ear, but he was not simply a recorder of other people's speech, for he was at the same time expressing himself and hence the feelings of all mankind. The result was hovering tones incommunicable in print—"oversound." Frank Lentricchia, in "Robert Frost: The Aesthetics of Voice and the Theory of Poetry" (*Criticism* 15:28–42), proposes that for Frost a poem provided in permanent form what comes to us only rarely in daily conversation. He seemed to be striving for "an organic sound, not an organic meaning." This position, says Lentricchia, leads us away from the New Critics in the direction of the new Romantic critics, in search of examples of the poet's subjective self.

Laurence Perrine—"'Two Tramps in Mud Time' and the Critics" (*AL* 44:671–76)—contradicts the opinion of many readers. He finds the speaker in this poem about to yield to the lumberjacks. He ends, says Perrine, by talking, not about chopping wood, much as he loves it, but about writing poetry (his true vocation-avocation). Edward Jayne, too, departs from the usual critical view of a famous poem. His "Up Against the 'Mending Wall': The Psychoanalysis of a Poem by Frost" (*CE* 34:934–52) makes the claim that "Mending Wall" is not the innocent poem it is generally presumed to be. Jayne finds sexual imagery in the rocks (loaves), cows, gaps, yelping dogs, the pun in "two can pass abreast," apple trees eating pine cones, etc. (He sees masturbation in the boy's activity in "Birches.") For Jayne there is more than a suggestion of sodomy in telling the phallic stones to "Stay where you are until our backs are turned." Another look at "Mending Wall" comes from George Monteiro in "Robert Frost's Linked Analogies" (*NEQ* 46:463–68). He reads "The Tuft of Flowers" together with "Mending Wall" and finds "statement" (men work together) and "counterstatement" (even so, they work alone, when communication is impossible). Richard Foster's "Leaves Compared with Flowers: A Reading in Robert Frost's Poems" (*NEQ* 46: 403–23) also links several poems together to make them "richer or different or sometimes better." He couples "Leaves Compared with Flowers" with "Putting in the Seed" as its dark companion. Frost is not only grief-stricken at the death of leaves in autumn but also horrified at the apparent callousness of a creator that kills them off over and over again.

David R. Clark writes two studies of "Directive." "Robert Frost: 'The Thatch' and 'Directive'" (*Costerus* 7:47–79) shows that the two poems are complementary. "The Thatch" gives vivid expression to the wound which love and later death can inflict, a wound somewhat healed by time in "Directive." Clark concludes that desolation, a terrifying threat in "The Thatch," is accepted as the norm in "Directive." His "An Excursus upon the Criticism of Robert Frost's 'Directive'" (*Costerus* 8:37–56) is a chronological review of what the critics have said about this poem. (In twenty pages there are ninety-four "Notes.") Clark says that nearly all the critics seem to agree that Frost is affirming poetry as a momentary stay; but he himself thinks that the stay is permanent, not necessarily specified in Christian terms, but back at the "source," however that is to be defined.

Haskell House (New York) has reissued Gorham B. Munson's *Robert Frost: A Study in Sensibility and Good Sense* (1927).

v. New England

Malcolm Cowley, in "Cummings' One Man Alone" (*YR* 62:332–54), maintains that, more frequently than a casual reader would expect,

E. E. Cummings voiced the opinions of his generation, inventively and freshly, and made full use of the themes that engrossed the writers of the 1920s. Cowley spells out Cummings's favorite technical devices: calligram, cryptogram, the negative ("unthing"), and transformation of parts of speech. He thinks Cummings shifted from an early "recklessness and brio" to a "conservative Christian anarchism" in his later poems.

Walter Sutton, in *American Free Verse*, devotes a chapter to Cummings, who writes with "an elite of beautiful souls" in view. In his best satire he lashes out at society uniquely and with distinction, but his eccentricities are often not worth the effort of untangling. Not always are his ideas strong and, in fact, tend toward monotony. Helen Vendler, who always has interesting things to say, also finds Cummings tiring after a while. In a review article—"Poetry: Ammons, Berryman, Cummings" (*YR* 62:412–19)—she says there is too much bubbling, too much Apriling. His poems tend to droop in the middle between often memorable openings and closings. His mischievous delight in disintegration (cf. the grasshopper poem) and his inexhaustibly ingenious penchant for game-playing are a cover for a paucity of ideas. He is too certain that he knows what is good and what is bad; his affirmations are defiantly (and in the long run monotonously) utopian. Whereas in his early poems he could look at both sides (e.g., lust and exalted love), as he grew older, sentimentality became more and more characteristic. Also finding fault with Cummings is John Fandel—"E. E. Cummings: hee hee cunning's fonetty kinglish" (*Commonweal* 99:264–66). Fandel too thinks that solving the puzzles is not worth the effort. The chief exception as he sees it is the poem of the falling leaf and loneliness, in which the visual event is weighty with meaning. At the center of Cummings's eccentricity is the lower-case *i*, ironically emphatic because it opposes the customary capital. Fandel concedes that the poet's basic ideas can be profound, even a challenge to philosophers. (This apparently opposes Vendler's view.) He was obviously a sterling character. It is his playfulness and oddities that get in the way.

On the other hand, Irene R. Fairly finds his syntactic deviation a device for structural cohesion. The poem "a like a" is characterized by deletions and dislocations that actually bring "syntactic, semantic, and visual levels into a consistent whole." In "Syntactic Deviations and Cohesion" (*Lang&S* 6:216–29) she analyzes several other poems, noting that syntactic deviation is sometimes combined with parallelism, long "a recognized element of verse." Deviations are not new to poetry, but Cummings is nonetheless an original. William Heyen's "In Consideration of Cummings" (*SHR* 7:131–42) argues that the poet is trying through hyperbole to give emotion a fair deal in a culture where logic and reason are in the driver's seat. It is not just to say that his total credo is present in every poem. In fact, Cummings's own voice in his poems is at best elusive. Heyen opines that Cummings is in the end transcendental, is not concerned with any foolish consistency, glorifies intuition, maintains the optimistic posture, and basically desires to lead his readers to happiness and freedom. Orm Överland says in "E. E. Cummings' 'my father moved through dooms of love': A Measure of Achievment" (*ES* 54:141–47) that the poem succeeds not because of its theme of filial admiration (which could easily move into sentimentality) but because Cummings expresses possibly better than in any other poem "his humanistic and individualistic ideals, his belief in the potential divinity of man which underlies his disgust with manunkind." In spite of "intensely private" emotions, the language becomes universal through the poet's idiosyncratic speech pattern. (There seems to be none of Fandel and Vendler's impatience in Överland.)

James F. Smith, Jr., analyzes the protagonist's black companion in *The Enormous Room* in "A Stereotyped Archetype: E. E. Cummings' Jean Le Negre" (*SAF* 1:24–34). Cummings is never condescending toward Jean, in spite of picturing him as a comic out of a Negro minstrel, for the black represents individual triumph over the impersonal system, a "noble savage" against the corruption and futility of modern society.

Only two E. A. Robinson items have come to light, a falling away after the flurry at the time of his centennial. N. E. Dunn's "Riddling Leaves: Robinson's 'Luke Havergal' " (*CLQ* 10:17–25) points out in considerable detail parallels between the Robinson poem and the experience of Aeneas in Book VI of the *Aeneid* as he leaves Carthage and sees Dido's funeral pyre ablaze. The poet's symbolism (dead leaves, the wind, the West) suggests the rejecting of the old faiths of the 19th century. The voice "out of the grave" is the poet's own intelligence facing the fact of death. Dunn finds here the affirmation of contemplation as the only way to truth. The other Robinson article is by Carlos Baker: "Robinson's Stoical Romanticism: 1890–1897"

(*NEQ* 46:3–16). Baker makes use of letters (including several as yet unpublished, now at Princeton) to show the poet, through an overweening interest in death, ruin, and similar topics, to have been moved by the dark side of romanticism. And yet he believed in a sort of immortality, not delineated but nevertheless positive. In other words, through the gloom there shone frequent shafts of hope as in the poems of Keats and Wordsworth, which he was reading with a feeling of fellowship and sympathy.

Jay B. Hubbell makes a case for one of the less frequently read New England poets in "A Major American Poet: John Hall Wheelock" (*SAQ* 72:295–310). Hubbell quotes from a great many poems of Wheelock's to illustrate his skillful versatility and his lyric, reflective, and descriptive powers. He takes pleasure in Wheelock's love poems and in his humor and finds an admirable sense of the tragic and an appreciation of "the unity of all life."

On the basis of Trumbull Stickney's two books (1902 and 1905) A. H. Griffing—"The Achievement of Trumbull Stickney" (*NEQ* 46: 106–12)—assesses the poet's talent. He finds the influence of Browning and of Greek literature especially strong. He notes some sentimentality ("personal grief"), but lists several sonnets as being particularly successful in universalizing the poet's own emotion. R. W. Flint praises Stickney as fine, robust, and versatile. In a review article, "Yankees Bemused" (*Parnassus* 2:35–48), he remarks that Stickney had exceptional talent aided and abetted by an impeccable education. Paradox pervades his verse: disembodied vigor or energetic spirituality, "the tenuous and diffident made as tangible as roast beef." To get at the tormented emotions in Stickney, the reader must recognize "that American repression had usually been a vice of necessity rather than inclination." Flint also reviews the collected poems of Phelps Putnam, who, he thinks, was overpraised by his friends F. O. Matthiessen and Edmund Wilson. "Behind the cozy languour is a tone of planting defiant little flags in a well-clipped college yard." Indeed, he had been sexually very active as a Yale undergraduate, but in his poems his celebration of passion is tempered with contempt. His early work is his best, colored by "an innocent bravura." He later became mired down in characterless iambics. A third New Englander whom Flint considers is John Wheelwright, a marked contrast to Putnam. "His true coherence is a certain quiet, dry, oblique, swooping and hovering lyrical warmth and downrightness." He was thoroughly moved and influenced by Sacco and Vanzetti and by the Depression. Flint sees Wheelwright, the Harvard product, as both "the hanging judge and . . . the Hasty Pudding clown."

A chapter out of Amy Lowell's life is recorded by Claire Healey in "Amy Lowell Visits London" (*NEQ* 46:439–53). Lowell arrived in the British capital in 1914, stayed at the Berkeley, gave a dinner for the Vorticists at the Dieu-donne (restaurant), herself at one end of the table, Pound at the other, and made contacts with Ford Maddox Ford, Richard Aldington, and other writers. The article describes in detail her correspondence and activities as the central figure in the Imagist controversy—especially her difference with Ford. With Pound she apparently enjoyed a reconciliation about the time he left for Italy. Folcroft (Penn.) Library Editions has reprinted Clement Wood's *Amy Lowell* (1926).

vi. The Midwest, the Far West, and the South

William Alexander turns to a poet rarely given serious treatment. His article is "The Limited American, the Great Loneliness, and the Singing Fire: Carl Sandburg's 'Chicago Poems'" (*AL* 45:67–83). Alexander finds in "Limited" and the little group of poems that follow it a theme common to American writers in the first third of the century: the limitations of existence, of material progress, and of the perspective of the common American man. Alexander sees the entire book as having definite organization: from "Chicago" Sandburg moves into poems about the separation of Americans from "vital contact with their universe." He attempts to induce his readers to draw on "spiritual resources." He hopes to inspire "the coming men" to defy with joy both death and the industrial monopolies. The poet as journalist with the *Chicago Daily News* is the subject of James C. Y. Chu's "Carl Sandburg: His Association with Henry Justin Smith" (*JQ* 50:43–47, 133). Smith, city editor of the newspaper, recollected that Sandburg was "leisurely, genial, enigmatic." (For a discussion of proverbs in Sandburg, see chapter 17, section ***viii.***)

Sterling and Jeffers are the representatives from the Pacific Coast. Sterling is shown to have been indifferent to money, a typical rural bohemian of the Carmel of 1912, in Dalton Gross's "George Sterling's Life at Carmel: Sterling's Letters to Witter Bynner" (*Mark-*

hamR 4:12–16). Once a poet of promise, Sterling was to be remembered chiefly by literary conservatives.

Jeffers is another case altogether. Robert J. Brophy's *Robinson Jeffers: Myth, Ritual, and Symbol in His Narrative Poems* (Cleveland, Press of Case Western Reserve Univ.) is a profound and scholarly book, but very readable withal. Brophy brings to Jeffers's poems a sensibility intensively formed by religious perspectives. He shows how the myth-ritual approach illuminates the poet's glorification of tragedy by analyzing closely five of the long narratives. The headings of his study of "Tamar" suggest the method: "Introduction: Lee's Fall from the Cliff"; "Complication: Fall and Enlightenment"; "Crisis: Descent to the Dead and Rebirth"; "Catastrophe: Tamar's Assumption of Power"; "Denouement: Resolution by Fire." Brophy assumes that "the core of Jeffers' themes is predictably the same in all his poems." He proceeds then to analyze "Roan Stallion" and three other long poems in the same way. A close reading of "Apology for Bad Dreams" produces a summing up of Jeffers's thought and art. There are other helpful sections of this book, including a map of Jeffers Country, an extensive bibliography, and a soundly structured index.

Brophy works harder on Jeffers than does any other scholar in the country. He is the assiduous editor of the *RJN*, four issues of which appeared in 1973–34, 35, 36, 37. Besides descriptions of relevant holdings at Berkeley, Yale, and the Brooklyn Public Library, there are biographical contributions from Ward Richie, W. W. Lyman, H. Arthur Klein, Donnan Jeffers, and William Everson. Brophy himself contributes two essays on ritual. Two other essays may be listed: Susan Shaw's "Elements of Eastern Philosophy in Jeffers" (36:8–11) and Gary Garland's "Mann and Jeffers: Myth Definition and Subsequent Technique" (37:7–11). The titles of three essays published elsewhere indicate their treatment of the subject: Brian McGinty, "The View from Hawk's Tower: Poet Robinson Jeffers and the Rugged Coast That Shaped Him" (*AW* 10,vi:4–9); B. W. Griffith, "Robinson Jeffers' 'The Bloody Sire' and Stephen Crane's 'War Is Kind'" (*NConL* 3:14–15); William Everson, "Archetype West," *Regional Perspectives: An Examination of America's Literary Heritage,* John Gordon Burke, editor (Chicago, American Library Association). Folcroft (Penn.) Library Editions has reprinted Louis

Adamic's *Robinson Jeffers, a Portrait* (1929) and Melba B. Bennett's *Robinson Jeffers and the Sea* (1936).

Aiken, Ransom, and Davidson represent the South. Arthur Waterman maintains that "Consciousness is Aiken's answer to one of the central problems in modern life, namely the discrepancy, even the breakdown, between man and the world. . . ." His essay is entitled "The Evolution of Consciousness: Conrad Aiken's Novels and 'Ushant' " (*Crit* 15,ii:67–81). *Ushant* is the ultimate in consciousness in this sense. Calvin S. Brown sees *Ushant* "as honest as is humanly possible" in "The Achievement of Conrad Aiken" (*GaR* 27:477–88). Aiken's fiction uses the quotidian events chiefly as settings for interior action. But it was poetry that was Aiken's chief occupation. He experimented with a great variety of techniques and subjects, though he was often dominated by the memory of his parents. His basic themes are the common man, the physical world, and the conceptual world. The author asserts that Aiken's best poetry deserves much more attention than it has received. In a review article, "A Chronology of Awareness: A Poet's Vision" (*SR* 81:172–84), Frederick K. Sanders says, on the other hand, that he believes in time *Ushant* will be thought of as the pinnacle of Aiken's achievement. He compares it to *The Prelude*. Its theme is mutability in the strong sense, change as indispensable for sustaining life. Much of Aiken's best poetry, he feels, deals with the impossibility of returning "to the time before knowledge."

One of John Crowe Ransom's stoutest apologists, Robert Buffington—"Ransom's Poetic: 'Only God, My Dear' " (*MQR* 12:353–60)—indicates that the reader must ask what the poem knows. For Ransom the poem "knows" the objects of daily experience as well as their "qualitative infinitude." The poem must also "know itself" so that readers will be unable to attain the poem outside itself; yet a poem cannot simply "be"; readers will find pleasure in the poem as poem but, being human, they will also relate it to the everyday. Thomas Daniel Young details Ransom's biography from 1912, while he was still at Oxford, through the school year 1913–14, when he taught at Hotchkiss, to June and his return to Nashville. Young supplies new facts about this two-year period in "A Slow Fire" (*SR* 81:667–90). He shows through quotations from letters to his father the beginnings of Ransom's later critical position.

Davidson's "The Last Charge" and Tate's "Ode to the Confederate Dead" seem to prophesy the direction each writer would take in his career. This is the view David A. Hallman holds in "Donald Davidson, Allen Tate, and All Those Falling Leaves" (*GaR* 27:55–59). Tate became less and less committed to the cause of the South; in him the agrarian image was more poetic and intellectual than emotionally felt. On the other hand, Davidson remained totally loyal to the South, though, granted, with some despair; he became something of a loner in resisting modern trends.

vii. New York and Points South

Fussell (*Lucifer in Harness*) traces "The Genesis of Hart Crane's 'The Bridge'" through the poet's correspondence and decides that Crane failed to perfect his poem because he was not constant to the metaphor of his title. Furthermore, in the matter of language, in spite of "his yearnings to be a New Whitman, he is in fact a recycled Emerson-Dickinson." His diction was not at one with what was actually occurring in American poetry. (Incidentally, Fussell has produced a lively and readable book.)

Edward Brunner finds irresistible unity in Crane's *magnum opus*: the lines are so full of implications that any one line will draw the reader into the entire book. Brunner's opinions are stated in "'Your Hands Within My Hands Are Deeds': Poems of Love in 'The Bridge'" (*IowaR* 4:105–26). "To Brooklyn Bridge," more than mere introduction, brings to the poet "a way of acting" as poet in his future work. "The Harbor Dawn" captures the birth not only of love but of the poet himself as he realizes the significance of love. Brunner close-reads "Three Songs" and discovers the day dreams, the lust, and the nostalgia which it is the poet's task to go beyond through love. Helge Normann Nilsen, in "Hart Crane's 'Atlantis': An Analysis" (*DQR* 3:145–58), examines the bridge myth in both the early and the final drafts of "Atlantis." A methodical explication leads to the conclusion that Crane viewed history as a mass of events from which the poet creates his ideal. The poet's myth is linked with history, however, not in picturing a regulating force that shapes events but in providing a tentative image of unity which may then flourish in men's minds.

An invaluable descriptive catalogue of the books Crane owned has been published by Kenneth A. Lohf as *The Library of Hart Crane* (Columbia, Univ. of S.C. Press). The marginalia are especially revealing. Bookplates and dates of acquisition help to establish the volumes with respect to the chronology of the owner's life and times. Robert DeMott has revised Hilton and Elaine Landry's *A Concordance to the Poems of Hart Crane* (Metuchin, N.J., Scarecrow Press).

Covering more ground than simply New York's Harlem, Jean Wagner's *Black Poets of the United States: From Paul Laurence Dunbar to Langston Hughes*, Kenneth Douglas, trans. (Urbana, Univ. of Ill. Press), first published in France in 1963, is now offered in English. It is an exhaustive study (580 pages) of the compelling effect of slavery on the black mind and spirit as well as the structures of religious expression. It paints the background of the growth of the black lyric to 1900: Dunbar and his contemporaries and the influence of the minstrel concept, the black in popular song and in the writings of the Southern whites. Then Wagner turns his attention to the Negro Renaissance: Claude McKay, Jean Toomer, Countee Cullen, James Weldon Johnson, Sterling Brown, and others. Keneth Kinnamon has brought Wagner's bibliography up to date.

Langston Hughes, Black Genius: A Critical Evaluation, Therman O'Daniel, ed. (New York, William Morrow) is an anthology of critical essays discussing the black author's plays, fiction, and other writings, including his ten books of poetry. These articles give him place not just among his black peers but in the mainstream of American literature. Hughes's verse does not attract a great deal of critical attention these days. More interest is shown in his character Jesse B. Semple (Simple). James Presley, for example, in "The Birth of Jesse B. Semple" (*SWR* 58:219–25), describes a chance meeting of Hughes with a man and his girl in a Harlem bar in 1942. Hughes's first story, "Conversation at Midnight," appeared on February 13, 1943, and referred to his acquaintance of that evening as "My Simple-Minded Friend." The memory of the man was given flesh in the author's imagination until by the end of the year Jesse B. Semple was "maturing" and was the subject of countless newspaper columns and of five books. Phyllis R. Klotman maintains that Semple is not romantic, is no protester, no militant, has no charisma. The tales about him were popular because of his author's technique. Using the Afro-American oral form of the skit, Hughes wrote with apparent artlessness and simplicity in theme and character. Through the "common-man" appeal, the tales could reach every reader, not only black but white. Klotman hears the frequent sound of the blues: family, loneliness, left-lonesome, broke-and-hungry, and desperate going-to-the-river blues. Her article is "Jesse B. Semple and the Narrative Art of Langston Hughes," (*JNT* 3:66–75).

Phyllis M. Lang, in "Claude McKay: Evidence of a Magic Pilgrimage" (*CLAJ* 16:475–84), discusses the widespread acceptance of McKay by the Russian people in 1922–1923. It was "magical" because it brought him recognition, if only for a brief time. In the United States he was disappointed at being eternally rejected. Mark Helbling says McKay's anguish and defiance sprang from his horror at American racism. In "Claude McKay: Art and Politics" (*NALF* 7:49–52), Helbling says, however, that McKay's first responsibility was to his own creative genius with the result that any fusion of art and politics emerged from his own "existential act of creative expression."

Purdue University

15. Poetry: The 1930s to the Present

Linda Welshimer Wagner

i. General

In 1973, scholarship of contemporary poets increased both in quantity and quality. Of the poets covered by this essay, 40 dissertations appeared, nine on Wallace Stevens, seven on William Carlos Williams, five each on Robert Lowell and Theodore Roethke, two each on Randall Jarrell and James Merwin, and single dissertations on Gary Snyder, Marianne Moore, women poets collectively, Chicano poets, Black poets, those writing political protest poems, those comprising the Imagist school, and several other combination categories.

Many important studies of influence patterns were published, continuing the tendency noted in 1972 of critics to make judgments on the contemporary scene, instead of merely watching the activity with either awe or bewilderment. While most of these essays find the present directions in contemporary poetry valuable, M. L. Rosenthal bewails "the basic triviality of vision" that attempts, in various ways, to "demean the high artistic aims and genuine historical relevance of great poetry." He cites as exceptions to this leveling of aspiration the writing of Galway Kinnell, Amiri Baraka, Ramon Guthrie, Ted Hughes, and, as prototype, Ezra Pound. They each aspire to a meaningful "ordering" of their depictions of life, an ordering which presupposes their personal belief in some kind of system ("Some Thoughts on American Poetry Today," *Salmagundi* 22–3:57–70).

The basic impulse of modern American poetry is the subject of Walter Sutton's book, *American Free Verse*. Sutton traces the free verse movement to Romanticism, through Whitman, Dickinson and Crane, to Pound, Cummings, Moore and Williams. His last chapters are devoted to what he sees as "the conservative counterrevolution," the work of such poets as Ransom, Brooks, Tate, Eberhart, Jarrell, Lowell, Nemerov, Roethke, Schwartz, Shapiro, and Wilbur; which direction turns toward Eliot and away from the "radical experimentalism" of Williams and Pound. This interest in the ironic and sometimes metaphysical (but always formal) poem was undermined in turn by poets born in the 1920s and 1930s. These are the disciples of organic form, direct ancestors of Whitman (although perhaps not philosophically), Pound, and Williams.

Despite its title, *American Free Verse* is not simply a formalist history of poetics. Sutton's touchstone throughout the book seems to be the scope of the poet's attempts. Pound, Eliot, and Williams are thus like Whitman because they too were fascinated by the epic, by poetry that included social concerns. The conservative "middle" poets retreated, in a sense, into conventional poetic subjects as well as prescribed forms. Sutton finds the contemporary poetry of Thomas Merton, Denise Levertov, Charles Olson, Galway Kinnell, Allen Ginsberg, Kenneth Koch, and others satisfying because these poets are, once again, involved in assessing the realities of life, political as well as aesthetic.

Denise Levertov writes with the same insistence in her collected essays, *The Poet in the World* (Norfolk, Conn., New Directions). Levertov is one of the foremost aestheticians of modern poetics (her thorough statements on organic form, "rhyme," and structure comprise more than half of the book), but she also demands the poet's awareness of his artistic responsibility in today's world. This collection of thirty essays also includes her comments on poets Paul Goodman, Robert Creeley, Robert Duncan, H. D., Pound, and Williams.

Paul A. Lacey stresses many of Levertov's theories in *The Inner War, Forms and Themes in Recent American Poetry* (Philadelphia, Fortress Press, 1972). By studying the poetry of Levertov, Anne Sexton, William Everson, James Wright and Robert Bly, he concludes, "that poets use forms as ways to explore the problems of their time—existential problems, problems of faith and action—but that their themes and discoveries are fresh only because they grow out of the exploration of form and technique" (p. 1). Lacey has correlated material from a wide range of sources and seems justified in concluding that many contemporary poets do work from definite spiritual premises. This is a corrective view, reasonably well substantiated, to the more prevalent characterization that contemporary poetry is despairing. For Lacey, these particular poets have found their way past despair, often through the art which gives them some means of discovering truth.

Somewhat less convincingly, Harry J. Cargas attempts the same kind of combination study in *Daniel Berrigan and Contemporary Protest Poetry* (New Haven, Conn., College and University Press, 1972). Devoting chapters to six poets—Eberhart, Shapiro, Lowell, Ginsberg, Jones (Baraka), and Berrigan, Cargas tries to group the anti-war poems of World War II with the more recent social protest and anti-war poetry. His failure to convince lies in his inadequate support; we are given too few of the poets' views, either in their work or other prose; and too little reference to other secondary material, particularly for the more recent writers.

So we have the pervasive justification for organic form (since it surrounds us, we must deal with it), in recent years seen as a means of fuller self-knowledge, an aid to the "voyage of self-discovery" that Levertov cites. William Pratt returns to the original movement in a brief essay, "Imagism: A Retrospect Sixty Years Later" (*Words* 1:60–66), concluding that contemporary writing has never moved past this concern for the image, and is still finding new ways to work with it. John T. Irwin, in "The Crisis of Regular Forms" (*SR* 81:158–71) discusses both sides of the controversy, but bases his opinion of the books reviewed on whether or not they work as poems, not on whether or not they were written in free forms. Thus he can admire Charles Edward Eaton's formal poetry (while disliking several other books of conventionally shaped poems) as well as the organic form poems of David Wagoner and Theodore Weiss.

While the formalist controversy is still with us (and now 60 years since the Imagist principles first appeared in the 1913 *Poetry*), other essays have been pointing out different kinds of directions. Paul Zweig discusses "The New Surrealism" (*Salmagundi* 22–23:269–84) and contends that surrealism is so dominant that no one notices it any longer. "It has become part of the way our language works." Seeing Ginsberg and Frank O'Hara as the first poets to use the techniques of "dream imagery, free association and the language of insanity," in the late fifties, Zweig thinks that today's poets accept the stylized conventions and are willing, and eager, to depart from them. American surrealism has little in common with André Breton's doctrines; American poets are more interested in enriching the basic image-oriented poetics than they are in automatic writing. And at its best, Zweig sees the various devices of surrealism as other ways of reaching the deeper states of consciousness that may prove most fertile to poetry.

In this context, Galway Kinnell ("To the Roots: An Interview with Galway Kinnell," ibid., 206–21) makes the distinction between French surrealism (which is Zweig's focus) and Spanish, the latter made available in this country through the essays and translations of Robert Bly. Kinnell sees the Spanish influence of Pablo Neruda as more "useful." "French surrealism draws from the thinking part of the brain whereas the Spanish . . . wrote poems that flower from deep within them. What surrealism had given them was the license to let come out all those strange inner images" (p. 214). As Mark Cramer writes in "Neruda and Vallejo in Contemporary United States Poetry" (*RomN* 14:455–59), both poets have been influential among recent poets but particularly Neruda. Cramer lists as reasons: (1) Neruda's images are so subjective that they lead into the unknown; (2) his "irrational combination of plastic images" achieves "cumulative power"; (3) he is not afraid to deal with real life, even to protest against that life.

Kenneth Rexroth speaks to the Japanese influence in several of his essays from *The Elastic Retort* (New York, Seabury Press). While he considers Japanese Noh drama the country's most important gift, he points out that in poetry, "superpositioning," the technique of placing image beside image with no formal transition, is most important. Rexroth describes the real influence of both *waka* and *haiku* as "radical dissociation and recombination as in a cubist painting," the rearrangement leading to the fresh perception which, in turn, leads to "man at his most fulfilled" especially in the poems of Gary Snyder, Cid Corman, and Philip Whalen.

Charles Altieri describes one of the widest currents in American poetics, "From Symbolist Thought to Immanence: The Ground of Postmodern American Poetics" (*Boundary 2* 1:605–41). As Altieri sees contemporary poetics, and the culture surrounding it, mere technical innovation is unsatisfying, as is myth, or a limiting reliance on ethical system. What is valuable, according to Altieri, is the coalescence of the private and public view, now available to the contemporary writer.

He begins by making some accurate generalizations about modern poetics: (1) that the personal, direct, local, and anti-formal are more prevalent than the formalist and paradoxical; (2) that participation is more important than interpretation; (3) that poetry readings have led poets to an oral, communal style; and (4) that the strain of religious—or at least "sacramental"—poetry continues to grow. It is this bent toward "immanence" that Altieri finds most interesting on the contemporary scene. He selects Denise Levertov's expression (and realization) of the horror of modern living as found in *Relearning the Alphabet* a "magnificent experiment" in deriving "from domestic experience the germ of a simple public morality." Altieri covers many poets, not only contemporaries, in his wide-ranging essay, which should be read to be its most convincing.

Marjorie Perloff approaches the whole problem of influences from a practical perspective as she reviews thirty books of recent poetry ("Poetry Chronicle: 1970–71," *ConL* 14:97–131). She sees the poetry of the seventies falling into three currents: (1) in the minority, the Robert Lowell "autobiographical elegaic mode"; (2) the New York School, chiefly Frank O'Hara, whose adaptation of Williams's maxim Perloff phrases " 'No ideas until the poet names them and makes them his own' "; and (3) the Rimbaud group, "the oracular, visionary, intensely lyric mode" of Kinnell, Ammons, Wright; Neruda and Vallejo; and the Hungarian poet Ferenc Juhász. Of the three general groups, Perloff seems to admire most the third (although she has many good comments to make about O'Hara, but fewer about his followers). It is the risks, the attempts to reach basic human issues and yet let the poem work in its own personal way that make the work of Wright, Ammons, and Kinnell so impressive. As she says of the last, "Kinnell is one of the best poets writing today; because his risks are so great, his very lapses seem preferable to the limited successes of many other poets" (p. 125).

Karl Malkoff, in the very valuable *Crowell's Handbook of Contemporary American Poetry* (New York, Thomas Y. Crowell), includes these three categories and adds sections on "Beat poetry," "the New Black poetry," and "the Formal poets." He also discusses the history of contemporary poetry and summarizes developments in poetry "From Imagism to Projectivism," ending with what are for Malkoff the seminal poems in modern poetics, the *Cantos*, *Paterson*, and *Maximus*. Following this 42-page introduction, the book consists of an alphabetized listing of descriptions—most running at least two or three pages—of poets, schools, and movements. Each entry includes a bibliography of both primary and secondary materials. Nearly every poet listed in this chapter appears in the book, and most of Malkoff's judgments seem accurate (the handbook is meant to include those poets whose first books appeared only after World War II).

In contrast to these views of contemporary poetry as both thematically satisfying and technically exciting, Ray P. Basler complains about the vulgarity of much recent writing ("The Taste of It: Observations on Current Erotic Poetry," *Mosaic* 6:93–105). Basler's comparisons between erotic passages of modern poems with those from the Renaissance and the past 50 to 100 years are significant, and probably well-taken. His larger question is one of aesthetics, the place of waste (and the revulsion-attraction syndrome) in our art and in our culture, the limits of the "freedom in art" all modern artists have championed. And while Basler, too, opts for freedom, he joins with Karl Shapiro in his 1970 lament: "The down hill speed of American poetry in the last decade has been breath-taking for those who watch the sport. Poetry plunged out of the classics, out of the modern masters, out of all standards, and plopped into the playpen. There we are entertained with the feudal-buccal carnival of the Naughties and the Uglies . . ." (*LJ* 95:634).

Just as Basler feels that contemporary erotic poetry is reacting at least partly against "accepted standards of language and taste," so Edwin Fussell in *Lucifer in Harness* sees much of American poetry as the reaction against the accepted standards of both "the English language and the English literary tradition." By tracing the development of a truly "American" poetics in the areas of meter, metaphor, and diction, Fussell has made sometimes accurate correlations among poets from Poe to Williams. He is right in seeing many of the changes which have occurred in the past two centuries as at least partly the result of the American antagonism for English culture, "standards," but—since there is very little new information in the book—that point hardly warrants a full-length study. When precise, as he is on two pages in chapter six (the discussion of metrics), Fussell is helpful; but since the book lacks any reference to established criticism (of which there is much that supports his thesis), any reference system for the extensive quotations from the poets themselves, a bibliography, or an index, it is hardly useful in the highest sense.

His most interesting points are that American poetry has progressed by a series of explosions (two at least, created by Whitman and, in 1912–13, Pound) with poetry between gradually becoming more conservative (his view of Stevens starts here, that Stevens wrote "bad" poetry: "The gaudiness of the diction cannot forever conceal the fact that Stevens is saying virtually nothing . . . . Except on a few truly noble occasions, Stevens failed to keep faith with the American vernacular and in the long run the ongoing American vernacular will reduce him to the status of a minor poet," p. 165). Because in Fussell's view, "The line from Whitman to Pound is the radical tradition of American poetry," and because the radical tradition is the viable one (even though we are not told why), Fussell spends most of his time on the writing of Whitman, Pound, and Williams, whose *Paterson* he finds the best use of the "constituting metaphor" which is the most characteristic quality of American poetry.

If Fussell's book might be considered an example of critical "new journalism," several other surveys illustrate various critical approaches rather than writing styles. Norman H. Holland continues his work of psychoanalytic criticism directed toward readers of literature, rather than characters within the literature, in *Poems in Persons* (New York, W. W. Norton). The study is of interest here because much of it deals with the poetry and life of Hilda Doolittle.

Holland's view of H. D. is that her early Imagist poems can be read subjectively, that "No one, in English, has more subtly or more relentlessly sought to body forth a self in the heiroglyphs of myth, dream, and image than she" (p. 8), and that she is probably, after Dickinson, "America's greatest woman poet." Yet his interest lies chiefly in H. D.'s 1944 *Tribute to Freud*, the study of her relationship with Freud during 1933 and 1934. Holland sees in H. D.'s fascination with creating myths, using myth as her means of satisfying inner needs and outer demands, an evolution from early childhood alienation. He views the creative pattern as part of the writer's personal life-style, not an escape or sublimation from that life-style.

Structuralist criticism regarding poetics generally is summarized well by the essays included in *Approaches to Poetics*. Contributors to this volume of English Institute essays include Hugh M. Davidson, Frank Kermode, Richard Ohmann, Stanley E. Fish, Tzvetan Todorov, and Victor Erlich. The latter's essay, "Roman Jakobson: Grammar of Poetry and Poetry of Grammar," points up the central problems of any formal critical approach to poetry, but does acknowledge the difficulties of working with "the most highly organized and most teleological mode of discourse," the poem. Given the many facets of interpretation, the contributors to this volume agree that some critical tools are better than none, and that the most accurate reading of any work probably occurs when criticism, to quote Charles Rosen, is "a continuous movement between the whole text and the interior forms."

In *The Anxiety of Influence* Harold Bloom presents one view of what he has been calling "antithetical criticism." Seeing the development of poetics as the purposeful misreading of any predecessor by the currently powerful poets, Bloom posits some ideas about the effects of tradition: "The strong poet—like the Hegelian great man—is both hero of poetic history and victim of it. This victimization has increased as history proceeds because the anxiety of influence is strongest where poetry is most lyrical, most subjective, and stemming directly from the personality" (p. 62).

Using Freud's view of anxiety, Bloom creates a six-level pattern to describe the strategies poets have used in working out their resentments to their artistic heritage. Considering that Bloom's stated purpose is to bring some clarity to the problem of creating accurate critical views, he might better have chosen more accessible terms; as it is, we have *clinamen*, *tessera*, *kenosis*, *daemonization*, *askesis*, and *apophrades* to work with.

Since most of the book is theoretical, Bloom has little specific commentary on particular authors. Most of his examples come from the classic English poets, but in his conclusion he does turn to Roethke, Stevens, and Ashbery, some of the most interesting modern poets, at least in terms of Bloom's thesis.

A succinct discussion of the differences between modern poetry and prose is found in Howard Moss's Introduction to *The Poet's Story* (New York, Macmillan), short stories by twenty-three modern poets (Berryman, Kizer, Logan, Millay, O'Hara, Plath, Sexton, Wilbur, and others).

The Living Underground: An Anthology of Contemporary American Poetry, ed. Hugh Fox (New York, Whitsun Pub. Co.) includes an interesting biography section, 400 pages of poems, and an introduction in which Fox defines the poetic "underground": "a kind of neo-transcendentalistic estheticism that considers art . . . necessary"; its quest is to find "the reality behind 'processed' reality," partly through "reactivation of the senses" and the "total pre-occupation / with the / present" (i–ii).

The British view of modern American poetry finds its spokesman in Ian Hamilton. In *A Poetry Chronicle* (New York, Barnes and Noble), selected essays and reviews from the past decade, Hamilton sees the promise of American art to lie with Lowell, Berryman, Plath and the poets he categorizes as "more than technicians" (the Black Mountain poets, by default). Hamilton's irascibility is directed at any poet remotely connected with William Carlos Williams, the American idiom, or Robert Bly's "deep image." The collection includes survey essays and separate studies of Lowell, Berryman, Williams, and Eliot, in addition to those of British poets.

A. J. M. Smith's selected essays, *Towards a View of Canadian Letters* (Vancouver, Univ. of British Columbia Press), includes material published from 1928 to 1971. Smith writes on E. J. Pratt, Earle Birney, Margaret Avison, the Fredericton Poets, and others; he also includes many studies of Canadian literature and poetry at various periods in its history.

ii. Wallace Stevens

Although no book-length study of Stevens's poetry was published in 1973, several books were announced for 1974, dissertations numbered a new high of nine, and essays were plentiful. (Few critics appeared to be sharing Edwin Fussell's opinion that Stevens is a minor poet.)

J. M. Edelstein compiled *Wallace Stevens: A Descriptive Bibliography* (Pittsburgh, Pa., Univ. of Pittsburgh Press), which runs to 429 pages and is extremely competent.

Jay M. Semel offers a new explanation for the change in Stevens's poetics which occurred in the early forties ("Pennsylvania Dutch Country: Stevens' World as Meditation," *ConL* 14:310–19). Because Stevens was experiencing "grave family problems" in these years, Semel believes he went back into his own origins (hence, the interest in the Dutch culture, with its combination of pride, fortitude, and mysticism) and gradually arrived at his later "meditative" tone. Semel points out that Stevens wrote over 400 letters in attempting to trace the family lineage, and that family and place names appear increasingly in his poems, not—as Semel notes—a "retreat into the past, but a search for a source" (p. 315). That Stevens was successful, at least partly, seems evident from his poise within the later poems.

Frank Doggett locates several other reasons for Stevens's changes between the early poems and the later, especially his personal habits of writing (more a matter of preliminary meditation than extensive revision, in the later poems), his changed concepts of the ideal nature of poetry, and his own tendency to think inductively ("The Transition from *Harmonium*: Factors in the Development of Stevens' Later Poetry," *PMLA* 88:122–31).

Northrop Frye, in "Wallace Stevens and the Variation Form," suggests that many of Stevens's poems are structured like a musical composition, "in which theme is presented in a sequence of analogous but differing settings" (p. 395). He then extends this structural observation to Stevens's philosophy of life, saying that there are different levels of reality. Using Stevens's essay "A Collect of Philosophy," Frye ends by comparing and contrasting Stevens's attitudes with those of Eliot (*Literary Theory and Structure*, pp. 395–414).

Edward Butscher continues Frye's analogy with music, but speaks much more specifically about Stevens's uses of musical form and analogy ("Wallace Stevens' Neglected Fugue: 'Variations on a Summer Day,'" *TCL* 19:153–64). In his close reading of the poem, Butscher attempts to convince readers that it is one of Stevens's great poems because it has a suitable vehicle for his "obsession with a transcendental aesthetic." Structured like a fugue, the poem also contains vivid images, relaxed phrasing, and imaginative metaphors.

Richard P. Adams also makes use of "A Collect of Philosophy" in which Stevens quoted from Schopenhauer ("Wallace Stevens and Schopenhauer's *The World as Will and Idea*," *TSE* 20[1972]:135–68). Adams, in this major essay, relates Schopenhauer's ideas specifically to Stevens's poems, "Not Ideas about the Thing but the Thing Itself," "The Snow Man," "Tea at the Palaz of Hoon," "The Man with the Blue Guitar," "Of Bright & Blue Birds & the Gala Sun," "Mrs. Alfred Uruguay," "Asides on the Oboe," "Notes toward a Supreme Fiction," and "An Ordinary Evening in New Haven." Seeing much of Stevens's writing as an exploration of reality and the imagination, or what Schopenhauer called *will* and *idea*, appears to be a useful perspective for reading many of Stevens's most troublesome poems. (Previously unnoticed in *ALS* is Adams's helpful essay " 'The Comedian as the Letter C': A Somewhat Literal Reading," *TSE* 18 [1970]:95–114.)

Harold Bloom discusses Stevens's "masterpiece," *The Auroras of Autumn*, in "Death and the Native Strain in American Poetry" (*SocR* 39[1972]:449–62), using it and "The Owl in the Sarcophagus" to contrast British and American views of death, as expressed by Yeats and his Romantic ancestors. Of Yeats's poems, Bloom chooses "Cuchulain Comforted," identifying the English view of death as a social phenomenon; the American view has no such communal integrity. (The same concepts appear in part in "The Native Strain: American Orphism," in *Literary Theory and Structure*, pp. 285–304.

James E. Mulqueen discusses "Man and Cosmic Man in the Poetry of Wallace Stevens" (*SDR* 11,ii:16–27). He sees Stevens's view of poem and Cosmic poem (the central focus, toward which all single poems point) as analogous to the traditional view of man and his Cosmic counterpart. He reads "Chocorua To Its Neighbor," "A Rabbit As King of the Ghosts," "The Man with the Blue Guitar," "Asides on the Oboe," "Examination of the Hero in a Time of War," and others.

Bram Dijkstra's essay, "Wallace Stevens and William Carlos Williams: Poetry, Painting, and the Function of Reality" (*Encounters: Essays on Literature and the Visual Arts*, ed. John Dixon Hunt, London, Studio Vista [1971], pp. 156–71) stresses the importance of the 1913 Armory Show in both men's poetry. Dijkstra cites evidences within Stevens's poems of the influence of paintings by Duchamp, Delaunay, Matisse, Gaugin, Cézanne, Wouters, Rodriguez, and others; but more important, he advances his belief that graphic art came to *be* Stevens's reality, that he chose to "see" the world through its representation in paintings: "Stevens' progressive dissociation from the world of immediate sensory experience, and his willing recourse to the works of painters for his materials . . . taught him to see the natural world in terms of the schemata . . . of the painters he studied" (p. 165). Dijkstra sees the result of this aesthetic method in that Stevens's poetry "is all colour and music and form, and yet those elements rarely come together to form a sense of real experience."

Williams's choice of painters, much different from Stevens's, evinces his drive to understand and live in the real. He admired Demuth, Sheeler, Arthur Dove, Hartley, Steiglitz, and John Marin because they affirmed what he already knew to be his interest, finding the art that lay—however buried—in the real American landscape.

Dijkstra concludes by placing Stevens's attitudes toward art in "a dangerous American tendency to demand man's submission to a 'better world' of idealist metaphysics . . . in which theory and practice have no relationship and reality too often becomes merely a tool to be manipulated as the mind sees fit" (p. 171).

iii. William Carlos Williams

Many dissertations, several books scheduled for 1974 publication, numerous explicative essays—but only one major contribution to the Williams canon appeared in 1973, Jerome Mazzaro's *William Carlos Williams: The Later Poems* (Ithaca, N.Y., Cornell Univ. Press). Mazzaro's emphasis falls on *Paterson*, "Asphodel, That Greeny Flower" and the other poems of the fifties and sixties; he regards these works as the height of Williams's achievement. Mazzaro, however, does not see these later poems as representing a change in Williams's aesthetic; rather he relates the late poems to Williams's work during the twenties (stressing the theme of Kora/Persephone, for example). What is new in this study is Mazzaro's description of Williams's interest in Alfred North Whitehead and Charles Steinmetz; Carl Jung; and—to a lesser extent—Paul Cézanne, Stuart Davis, the cubists, and other painters. Mazzaro presents Williams as a voracious aesthetician, eager for all kinds of knowledge that might enrich his original imagist poetics, a man who used what was interesting to himself and his colleagues in all kinds of experimentation. The later poems were a culmination of that tendency.

Jackson R. Bryer's *Sixteen Modern American Authors* (Durham, N.C., Duke Univ. Press) now includes Linda Wagner's bibliographic essay on Williams, in addition to essays on the writers previously included in his *Fifteen Modern American Authors* (see *ALS 1971*, p. 306).

MR devoted a large part of their Winter issue to "A Garland for William Carlos Williams" (14:65–148). Edited by Paul L. Mariani, the section included photos and drawings of the poet and "Williams' Black Novel," Mariani's description of the way Williams came to collaborate with Fred Miller, editor of *Blast*, to write *Man Orchid* (the novel he wrote during the mid-forties, repr. pp. 77–117). Also included are two of Williams's essays on Ezra Pound, "A Study of Ezra Pound's Present Position" [January 21–23, 1947], pp. 118–23, and "The Later Pound" [January 13, 1950], pp. 124–29. To conclude, Emily Wallace has edited John W. Gerber's 1950 interview with Williams, pp. 132–48. All these materials were previously unpublished.

Mike Doyle's "William Carlos Williams: The White Clarity of Imagination" is a useful survey of the five works included in *Imaginations* (*WCR* 7,i[1972]:51–53). As Doyle points out, "Tension created by opposition between 'the thing itself' and 'the authentic spirit of change' is the central working principle of the improvisations, whose function is 'the shifting of category' . . . the disjointing process." He correctly connects this view of art with Henri Bergson by way of T. E. Hulme and Pound, and as Doyle concludes, these five works are important to any understanding of Williams because they prove convincingly that his allegiance may have been to 'the thing,' but that "this allegiance was held in the context of questing for 'the white of a clarity beyond the facts.'"

Several essays relate Williams to the younger poets who so much admired him. Marta Sienicka discusses his relationship with Olson, Duncan, Creeley, and Ginsberg in "William Carlos Williams and Some Younger Poets," *SAP* 4[1972]:183–93. See also Anthony Suter's "Basil Bunting et deux poètes américains: Louis Zukofsky et William Carlos Williams," *Caliban* 8[1972]:151–57.

Criticism still continues about *Paterson*, despite the many book-length studies of the poem. Robert Edward Brown's "Walking and the Imagination: William Carlos Williams' *Paterson* II," (*MPS* 4:175–92) relates Williams's use of the walking motif to a tradition at least as old as the Romantics: "walking is ownership" (p. 176). Williams moves, in Book II, between walking through actual space and imaginative; part of the tension of the poem results from that juxtaposition. Diane Ward Ashton accurately traces "The Virgin-Whore Motif in William Carlos Williams' *Paterson*" (*MPS* 4:193–209), and Charles Doyle contributes "A Reading of 'Paterson III,'" *MPS* 1[1970]:140–53. Gerald T. Gordon explicates "William Carlos Williams' 'Preface' to *Paterson*," *ContP* 1,ii:44–51. George A. Tice's collection of photographs (*Paterson*, Rutgers Univ. Press, 1972) includes many interesting photos of Garret Mountain, the Passaic Falls, the statue of Alexander Hamilton, and the town itself.

Paul L. Mariani opts for Williams's "Asphodel" as a masterful lyric poem in "The Satyr's Defense: Williams' 'Asphodel'" (*ConL* 14:1–18); Neil E. Baldwin discusses Williams's aesthetic in relation to Larbaud's ("Discovering Common Ground: A Note on William Carlos Williams and Valerie Larbaud," *AL* 45:292–97); Alexander Hutchison summarizes Williams's affinity to and admiration for the painters he cites in one of his late poems ("The Resourceful Mind: William Carlos Williams and 'Tribute to the Painters,'" *UWR* 8,i [1972]:81–89).

iv. Creeley, Olson, Ginsberg, Kerouac, Zukofsky, and Layton

Much new material on the writing of Robert Creeley and Charles Olson appeared this year. Mary Novik's *Robert Creeley: An Inventory, 1945–1970* (Kent, Ohio, Kent State Univ. Press) contains 210 pages of both primary and secondary materials. Primary listings are complete, and include books, periodical contributions, audio-visual and unpublished material; secondary items are selected. The book includes a foreword by Creeley.

Donald Allen has published ten interviews with the poet as *Contexts of Poetry: Interviews 1961–1971* (Bolinas, Calif., Four Seasons Foundation). Interviews are by Lewis MacAdams, Michael André, Charles Tomlinson, Linda Wagner, David Ossman, and others. Originally appearing in a variety of places, some of the interviews are here lengthened or otherwise changed; in all, they give valuable insight into the artistic milieu of the past 15 years as well as into Creeley's aesthetics. (See M. L. Rosenthal's "Problems of Robert Creeley," [*Parnassus* 2,i:205–14] for a discussion of this book and Creeley's *A Day Book.*)

Another part of Creeley's poetics was published as *Sparrow 6* (Los Angeles, Black Sparrow Press). Titled "The Creative," the essay draws on the work of many of the artists Creeley has long admired—Pound, Williams, Duncan, Zukofsky, and also Henry Corbin, Jackson Pollock, Wittgenstein, Siegfried Giedion and Jung. "One wants to keep on growing," Creeley concludes. The pamphlet closes with a recent poem, "For My Mother: Genevieve Jules Creeley."

Athanor 4, a Creeley issue, contains poems by Creeley, drawings by Bobbie Creeley, a chronology of the poet's life by Mary Novik, two new interviews with the poet, and letters between Olson and Creeley. Jerome Mazzaro ("Robert Creeley, the Domestic Muse, and Post-Modernism," pp. 16–88) sees the later writing as becoming more and more "domestic," and traces such an impulse from the earliest poems and statements on. Mazzaro feels that Creeley is most a part of the current poetic scene because of his insistence that each poet be true to his own idiom, his particular voice and his way of knowing as well. More allied with Kierkegaard's aesthetic than with ethical choices, Creeley's essentially private voice creates its own hesitancy as a part of his poem-as-process aesthetic.

Douglas Calhoun points out in his review of *A Day Book* and *Listen* (pp. 82–83) that Creeley has been increasingly involved with artists like Arthur Okamura, Robert Indiana, and Marisol, who work in collage or assemblage. Calhoun sees the recent writing as experimental, a means of putting old concepts and words into fresh relationships; a related effect is motion and, as Calhoun notes in comparing Creeley with Kerouac, "to keep in motion one has to be constantly and actively in the present."

"On Creeley's Third Change" is Fielding Dawson's brief analysis of the poet's later style (pp. 57–58), one of "total humility," the ego having nearly disappeared in the haste to understand "past associations and an almost infantile fascination with words." Also of interest is Warren Tallman's essay "Sunny Side Up" (pp. 64–66) and Cid Corman's review of *St. Martin's* (pp. 78–80).

Peter Elfed Lewis describes Creeley as the possessor of a fine sense of language, "an impressionist of feelings, a poet of emotional nuance," with "a touch of Mauberley about him" (p. 43, "Robert Creeley and Gary Snyder: A British Assessment," *Stand* 13[1972]: 42–47). He concludes, after discussion of Snyder as an idiom poet, that both Creeley and Snyder "are gifted but undeniably minor poets."

George F. Butterick has transcribed and edited Olson's *Poetry and Truth, The Beloit Lectures and Poems* (Bolinas, Calif., Four Seasons Foundation, 1971). Working from three lectures Olson presented in March of 1968, Butterick has constructed a helpful monograph. The lectures proceed from the first "cosmology," "The Dogmatic Nature of Experience," to the two statements of Olson's

"Belief." He opens the first lecture by reading a new poem which clearly marks his line of descent from Whitehead and other pragmatic philosophers:

> an actual earth of value to
> construct one, from rhythm to
> image, and image is knowing, and
> knowing, Confucius says, brings one
> to the goal: nothing is possible without
> doing it . . . .

During the course of these lectures, Olson discusses his admiration for Norse myth, Melville, mathematics, music, Kabir, Charles Pierce, and Gerhard Dorn. Butterick has added notes for Olson's references.

The 371-page Olson issue of *Boundary 2* (2, i–ii) includes two short essays by Olson ("Notes for the Proposition: Man is Prospective" and "Definitions by Undoings," pp. 1–12), 26 essays and reminiscences by such critics as Albert Cook, Charles Altieri, L. S. Dembo, and Matthew Corrigan, also the editor of this double issue. Only five of these essays are reprinted. Many of the essays are excellent; all of them are valuable, since most criticism on Olson at the present time is barely beyond the simple "enthusiasm" stage. Of the most interesting work, Don Byrd's "The Possibility of Measure in Olson's *Maximus*" adds terminology to appreciation (pp. 39–54); Robert von Hallberg makes important distinctions between Olson's use of what might appear to be Whitehead's concepts ("Olson, Whitehead, and the Objectivists," pp. 85–111); and Charles Altieri relates Olson's innovative poetics to the Romantic tradition. Altieri sees Olson as breaking with Romantic thought in two significant areas: Olson uses science as the source of his organicism, rather than pantheism; he also extends the Coleridgean idea that there is a poetic logic distinct from discursive logic. By combining science with poetics, Olson attempts to bridge the radical separations characteristic of modern thought.

Among the studies of particular poems are Robert Bertholf's ("The Distances," pp. 229–49), Guy Davenport's ("The Kingfishers," pp. 250–62), Maxine Aspel's ("The Praises," pp. 263–68) and essays on *Maximus* by Frank Davey, Daniel G. Hise, John Scoggan, Cory Greenspan, and L. S. Dembo.

Some critics today are telescoping the Beat writers into the Black Mountain group, although no valid reason for making such combination exists (the plethora of "new" groups probably exerts the pressure). Sympathetic though the writers of each group were toward the poems of the other clique, the Beats remain much more romantic, the Black Mountain poets, classicist, in their concern for craft. Sons of Bill though they all claimed to be (so too is Bly's "deep image" group), that similarity is hardly the basis for classification.

Gerard J. Dullea in "Ginsberg and Corso: Image and Imagination" (*Thoth* 11,ii[1971]:17–27) stresses the romantic character of the Beat movement (as being "completely anti-Establishment and completely pro-Self, . . . reveling in self-expression"). He finds most appealing the Romantics' "emphasis on emotions and their vision of a unified world." Dullea then compares the two poets, finding Corso the more conventional in that he seems to use his experiences *in* poems (albeit surrealistically) rather than using experiences *as* poems (Ginsberg's tactic). This essay is, however, not the definitive comment on Beat poetry.

Ann Charters's biography, *Kerouac*, may be the definitive biography of a contemporary poet (San Francisco, Straight Arrow Books). Written with an evident admiration for and thorough knowledge of Kerouac's writing, Charters includes critical comment with life story, enhancing and explaining the latter. For Kerouac more than many writers, his work was his life; information about the literature is thus crucial.

Charters divides the biography into three parts. The first, 1922–51, presents Kerouac as the would-be French Canuck writer, his years at Columbia, and friendships with Lucien Carr, William Burroughs, Allen Ginsberg, Neal Cassady, and Michael McClure (the photographs are ample). Part Two, 1951–57, traces the fulfillment of his life, as his writing begins to be published and, as a result of *On the Road*, *The Subterraneans*, and *The Dharma Bums* (1957 and 1958), the Beat culture was born. In Part Three, 1957–69, Charters describes Kerouac's gradual withdrawal from his friends, the culture he named, and his work, to Lowell, Massachusetts, living with his invalid mother and wife Stella. Charters includes several chronologies, an identity key to the characters in the novels, and full notes.

Two essays on Louis Zukofsky appeared in *MPS* 3, vi, Samuel

Charters's "Essay Beginning 'All'" (pp. 241–50) and Thomas A. Duddy's "The Measure of Louis Zukofsky" (pp. 250–56). The latter gives some precision to its terms, in finding in *A* a consistent concern "with aurality and measure." Different from Pound and Williams, Zukofsky is, Duddy thinks, because of his classical disposition, more interested in strict measure: *A* is to be twenty-four books, and each one of the books so far published has its own purposeful design. For Duddy, Zukofsky's approach mediates "between the large American voice . . . and the intimate lyric voice" (p. 256).

Mike Doyle's "The Occasions of Irving Layton" (*CanL* 54[1972]: 70–83) is a major survey of the Canadian poet most closely related to the post-Williams group. Doyle admits that Layton's early work suffered from a wealth of sometimes disjointed images, but for the later poems Doyle claims that Layton "manages a range of traditional forms impressively, sometimes magnificently" (p. 70). Doyle questions Layton's life-view, however, sensing in it dichotomies and limitations that are, to this point in his career, unexplained. A close reading of many poems follows.

v. Plath, Lowell, Berryman

The two books on Sylvia Plath published this year indicate again the high level of interest in her life and work—unfortunately perhaps in that order. Nancy Hunter Steiner's reminiscence of Plath's last year at Smith is little more than that, a chapter in the young poet's life (*A Closer Look at Ariel: A Memory of Sylvia Plath*, New York, Harper's Magazine Press). George Stade's long introduction (pp. 3–30) does summarize the familiar critical attitudes. Laurie Levy, one of the other *Mademoiselle* college editors the summer of 1953, presents a corrective view of Plath as a normally ambitious, bright coed of the fifties ("Outside the Bell Jar," *OhR* 14:67–73).

Eileen Aird's *Sylvia Plath* is a close critical study of Plath's major writing, one chapter devoted to each published book, a concluding chapter on imagery, and a bibliography which is largely British (New York, Barnes and Noble). While many of Ms. Aird's insights are good, her continuous reliance on information provided by Plath's estranged husband, Ted Hughes, is bothersome, particularly when his glosses contradict the intrinsic evidence of the poems. When she uses Plath's own aesthetics, however, Aird does provide some good approaches to the last poems (seeing "Daddy" and similar poems as what Plath called "light verse" because of the flip, choppy movement, off-rhymes, and impersonal tone).

Joyce Carol Oates attempts to place Plath in terms of her cultural significance, to see "the pathological aspects of our era which make a death of the spirit inevitable—for that era and for all who believe in its assumptions." According to Oates, that dismal era is over and consequently can be evaluated ("The Death Throes of Romanticism: The Poems of Sylvia Plath," *SoR* 9:501–22). Oates feels that Plath's own "moral assumptions"—evident in the poems—condemned her to her death; she summarizes these attitudes as a willingness to be beaten by unworthy forces, no community with the natural universe, and an inability to recognize even intellect, much less the Other or mysticism.

While attempts to place Plath's poetry in the wider context may be important, much textual work remains to be done. Marjorie G. Perloff's "On the Road to *Ariel*: The 'Transitional' Poetry of Sylvia Plath" (*IowaR* 4, 2:94–110) corrects the sometimes fallacious dating of many of the "middle" poems. Perloff makes the point that Ted Hughes's editing of *Crossing the Water* and *Winter Trees* (both 1971) is inaccurate and even misleading. Perloff discusses "Parliament Hill Fields" and "Little Fugue" as "transitional" poems, and contends from that discussion that this mode, rather than being different, is "simply the mode of *Ariel* in its early, tentative, often prolix form" (p. 102). Perloff concludes that since so many of the best poems in these two volumes really are *Ariel* poems, or early versions of them, Plath's range may be seen now to be surprisingly—and even disappointingly—small. She points out that imagery is almost interchangeable from related poems, and that different themes are rare.

Margaret D. Uroff's "Sylvia Plath on Motherhood" (*MQ* 15:70–90) is an important essay to correct the critical view of Plath as a death-ridden poet. As Uroff points out, Plath wrote many poems about mothering (and used it as an image of all making); but critics have ignored these poems. Because so much bad poetry exists on that subject, Uroff feels that Plath saw tackling the subject as "quite new and exciting." In her analysis of "The Disquieting Muses," "Point

Shirley," "The Manor Garden," "You're," "Heavy Women," "Mourning Song," "Magi," the candle poems, "Child," and "Brasilia," Uroff opens new ground for correlation.

Another important series of poems is the subject of Rose Kamel's essay " 'A Self to Recover': Sylvia Plath's Bee Cycle Poems," (*MPS* 4:304–18). Kamel relates the facts of bee keeping to Plath's insistent but varied use of the metaphor, stressing "the mercurial shifts of behavior" in bees, as well as the multiple roles the females play. Her close reading of the half dozen bee poems is helpful.

Robin R. Davis discusses imagery as connecting force throughout *Ariel* in "The Honey Machine: Imagery Patterns in *Ariel*," *NLauR* 1, ii:23–31, with special attention to the colors red, black, and white; and William Meissner reads "Tulips" ("The Opening of the Flower: The Revelation of Suffering in Sylvia Plath's 'Tulips,' " (*ContP* 1,i:13–18).

Robert Phillips's *The Confessional Poets* (Carbondale, Ill., So. Ill. Univ. Press) includes his Jungian analysis (*ALS 1972*, p. 347) of Plath's poems and novel. Phillips's study includes other chapters on Robert Lowell, whose 1959 *Life Studies* helped to create "confessional poetry," W. D. Snodgrass, Anne Sexton, John Berryman, and Theodore Roethke. To define this kind of poetry, Phillips mentions no restrictions on subject matter, often highly subjective; "balanced narrative poems with unbalanced or afflicted protagonists," asking instead of answering questions, and using common diction, as well as irony and understatement (p. 7). Phillips sees these poets —and this poetry—important because, in 1973, poetry is closer to Whitman than it was a generation before: "Openness of language leads to openness of emotion."

Of the poets he considers, Phillips sees Lowell, Snodgrass, and Roethke as the most successful, and discusses their major poems in detail. In Anne Sexton's poems, he notes a growing use of fictional situations, as if the strictly autobiographical mode were too restricting (a point which might well be made about every confessional/lyric poet read; how is the reader to know whether a poem is autobiographical—and should he even care?) Phillips's displeasure falls on Berryman and, less obviously, Plath: not for the *Dream Songs* but for *Love & Fame* in which Berryman has dropped his personae and writes genuinely confessional poetry. Phillips seems offended by these poems, not so much because of their artistry or lack of it, but because of Berryman's "total lack of commitment to higher values" (p. 99). Working with confessional poets does have its dangers.

Phillips sees Lowell as a poet brought to voice by the more autobiographical mode of *Life Studies*, and finds his excellences continuing in *Notebooks* (which he compares with *Leaves of Grass*) and the later collections.

This view of Lowell's most recent writing is not the norm, however. Donald Hall, in his *APR* column (2, vi:46) considers the last books as only "self-exploiting," the last decade, "a disaster." Adrienne Rich (ibid., 2,v:42–43) writes that "brilliant language, powerful images, are not enough . . . they can become unbelievably boring in the service of an encapsulated ego." Similarly, Marjorie Perloff sees in *The Dolphin* that Lowell's "famed confessional mode . . . reaches its point of no return" ("The Blank Now," *NewRep*, July 7/14:24–26) and Donald Davie complains that "*The Dolphin* pushes intimacy to a new extreme" ("Robert Lowell," *Parnassus* 2:49–57).

Most of the essays published on Lowell in 1973 tended to be retrospective rather than to focus on current books. John C. Hirsh points to the ambivalence in Lowell's attitude toward Colonel Robert Shaw, and Boston, in "The Imagery of Dedication in Robert Lowell's 'For the Union Dead,'" (*JAmS* 6[1972]:201–05). Steven Axelrod traces the changing response to Shaw in poems from Lowell's relative praise in "Memorial Positum, Robert Gould Shaw" (1863) through Moody's "Ode in Time of Hesitation" (1900) and Berryman's "Boston Common" (1942) to end with the much bleaker Lowell poem ("Colonel Shaw in American Poetry: 'For the Union Dead' and Its Precursors," *AQ* 24[1972]:523–37). Richard J. Fein's study of *Life Studies* relates it closely to the milieu of the late fifties, and Lowell's feeling of responsibility for those years ("Family and History in *Life Studies*," *NEQ* 46:272–78). Fein also hypothesizes that part of Lowell's strength as poet stems from "his rejection of the aggressive military figure and his fascination for such a personage"; he sees Lowell figuratively replacing his father with Shaw and Major Mordecai Meyers.

Jerome Mazzaro, in a long and complete essay, discusses the sources for many poems in *Imitations*, and also conjectures on the reasons Lowell was drawn to these free translations ("Imitations," *APR* 2,v:35–41. See also Mazzaro's essays on Lowell in *CompD* 7, "The Classicism of Robert Lowell's 'Phaedra'," pp. 87–106 and "Prometheus Bound: Robert Lowell and Aeschylus," pp. 278–90; see also "Robert Lowell's 'Benito Cereno'" in *MPS* 4,ii:129–58). Mazzaro's view is that not only Lowell's choices but also his changes in the original poems bring most of the imitations "in line with Lowell's own poetry." Therefore, Mazzaro suggests that in reading *Imitations*, the reader consider it as a unified book of Lowell's poetry, rather than comparing each poem with its original. As a unified collection, it remains a central book.

The most important contribution to Lowell criticism this year is Marjorie G. Perloff's book, *The Poetic Art of Robert Lowell* (Ithaca, N.Y., Cornell Univ. Press). Focused on the formal aspects of Lowell's poems, the book is a careful, well-substantiated study of his lyric poetry. Beginning with his characteristic imagery, which Perloff finds much the same throughout all his writing, she moves to *Imitations*. Using Lowell's "Nostalgia," a version from Rimbaud, Perloff finds that the poem is not successful (tone and image pattern is unsteady, and perspective shifts needlessly), and she also decides that the other poems in *Imitations* are too erratic to constitute a new mode of translation. She continues, attempting in chapter three to place Lowell's *Life Studies* as either a romantic or a realistic collection. Of this book—his best in her view, she writes, "I would posit that it is his superb manipulation of the realistic convention, rather than the titillating confessional content, that is responsible for the so-called breakthrough of *Life Studies* and that distinguishes Lowell's confessional poetry from the work of his less accomplished disciples" (p. 86).

Her analysis of these poems in terms of a "metonymic mode" is innovative and convincing, as is her chapter on Lowell's syntactic structures. The study closes with two chapters of wider focus, one following Lowell's Winslow elegies, the other comparing a Lowell poem with related work by Plath and Snodgrass. From this comparison Perloff concludes, "Lowell's direct influence, now at its height, will begin to decline in the later seventies. Nevertheless, Lowell surely remains our outstanding poet of midcentury . . ." (p. 183–84).

Ernest C. Stefanik's "Bibliography: John Berryman Criticism" (*WCR* 8,ii:45–52) is the first listing of secondary criticism available, and fills an important need.

Several useful essays on Berryman's poems appeared this year. John Bayley's "John Berryman: A Question of Imperial Sway" (*Sal-*

magundi 22–23:84–102) finds the *Dream Songs* and *Love & Fame* as important as Lowell's poems, because they present "a new verse and a new self in it" (p. 84). Rather than being "confessional," Berryman's poems work through a technique so brilliant, so right, that they remain "art," no matter how patently autobiographical they may be. "To make a poetic 'I' as free and even more free, as naturalistic and even more so, than a prose ego, and yet quite quite different: that is the secret of the American new poetry which appears to reach its apogee in Lowell and Berryman" (pp. 86–87). Bayley compares Berryman as well with Yeats, Auden, and Dylan Thomas, and relates all his poems to this thesis, concluding that in poetry, rather than in fiction, lies the hope for American letters.

Jo R. Porterfield in "The Melding of a Man: Berryman, Henry, and the Ornery Mr. Bones" (*SWR* 58:30–46) thinks that the poet's greatest achievement is "an ability to picture metaphorically man's place in the world" (p. 30). Porterfield continues, impressionistically, to discuss the three personae of the poems, using the poet's 1972 suicide as pivotal, and concluding that life is both "cage" and "parapet," and that man maintains his difficult balance between them.

In "The 'Tough Songs' of John Berryman," (*SoRA* 6:257–68) James Tulip locates Berryman as an intensely American poet, both in terms of his themes and his aesthetic movement between "rational" and "passionate." Tulip makes good if brief correlations with the Anne Bradstreet poems and with Stephen Crane's Henry Fleming.

Among the many "appreciations" are Edward Butscher's "John Berryman: In Memorial Perspective," *GaR* 27:518–25; William Meredith's "In Loving Memory of the Late Author of the *Dream Songs*," *VQR* 49:70–78; and Saul Bellow's "John Berryman," Preface to Berryman's *Recovery* (New York, Farrar, Straus and Giroux), ix–xiv.

vi. Jacobsen, Rich, Sexton, Wakoski, Atwood, Levertov, Bishop, Sarton, and others

Josephine Jacobsen remarks in *From Anne to Marianne: Some Women in American Poetry* (Washington, D.C., Library of Congress), pp. 13–28, that poetry written in colonial America, by women, was what one might expect from "a body of literate, highly privileged slaves." "In general, life is seen as something to be endured; emotion as something foredoomed; death as a release, even for the young" (p.

16). Bleak as life—and women's opportunity for creative effort—was, women did still persist, although with little success.

Jacobsen sees Emily Dickinson and Marianne Moore as atypical women poets because they *did* break the stereotypical view and write from within their own natures (even in Moore's case, when her subjects are not "personal," her attention to those subjects is most certainly intimate). Regarding more contemporary women's poems, Jacobsen states, "The liberation by art precedes the liberation by circumstance" (p. 21). She finds the future to hold only promise, to be, in fact, "an incoming tide of good poetry by American women."

Robert Boyers's "On Adrienne Rich: Intelligence and Will" (*Salmagundi* 22–23:132–49) sees Rich fighting that timeless battle, to free herself from all the conceptions of feminine poet—consequently he finds her sixth book, *The Will To Change*, central. Boyers admires her "dignity and casual elevation . . . . Imagination here is in the service of intelligence." Seeing *Necessities of Life* as the best of Rich's books, Boyers discusses each, and does qualify his enthusiasm with an attitude too familar from male critics, when he finds in Rich's recent work "a quality of impatience and of rashness that is a little disappointing," especially since it lessens the "quality" of the poetry.

In contrast, Grace Schulman (*APR* 2,v:11) finds Rich's seventh book, *Diving Into the Wreck* "a new definition of self." Recognizing too that metamorphosis has been an integral part of Rich's poetics, Schulman finds this latest change—a purification through fire, reminiscent of the phoenix image—most effective. "In the strongest poems of Adrienne Rich, the saving humanity incorporates traits of both sexes and allows for vacillation between them." Androgyny provides, for Rich, the means to reach "a broader vision of human wholeness."

Helen Vendler is less enthusiastic about Rich's most recent work, considering it "dispatches from the battlefield." She has confidence, however, that this interim work will develop into "a more complete poetry" ("Ghostlier Demarcations, Keener Sounds," *Parnassus* 2:5–30).

As Rich writes in "When We Dead Awaken: Writing as Re-Vision" *CE* 34:18–30, the re-vision of women's identity—sexual, social, and artistic—requires a radical new critique of literature. The "energy of creation" and "the energy of relation" must coalesce; women must benefit from these tense times, and supply themselves with a feminine myth-making tradition. See also Rich's columns in *APR* 2,i:16–17 and 2,v:42–43.

In addition to the chapters on Anne Sexton's writing included in Paul Lacey's *The Inner War* (see p. 330) and Robert Phillips's *The Confessional Poets* (see p. 348), Sexton herself contributes "A Column: The Freak Show" to *APR* 2,iii:38–40. Some of her remarks about the difficulty of giving "performances" of intimate art objects add support to the critical views of her artistic use of personal material. In "The Sacrament of Confession" (*The Inner War*, pp. 8–31), Lacey recognizes not only Sexton's concern with "saying" personally meaningful things but her "continual preoccupation with both thematic and technical means for giving significant shape to her poetry" (p. 12). Lacey's essay is a well-substantiated corrective to the critics who discuss only theme whenever they face a supposedly confessional poet.

Muriel Rukeyser praises Sexton's *The Book of Folly* in "Glitter and Wounds, Several Wildnesses," *Parnassus* 2,i:215–22; see also Ira Shore's "Anne Sexton's 'For My Lover . . . ,' Feminism in the Classroom," *CE* 34:1082–93.

Joyce Carol Oates has written six columns for *APR* in 1973, one of them dealing with Diane Wakoski's work ("A Cluster of Feelings: Wakoski & Levine," 2,iii:55). Oates admires Wakoski because her "voice" is recognizable, her poems "lyrically dramatic," not afraid to risk "imprudence and outrage." Rosellen Brown shares this view of Wakoski as a "larger-than-life" figure (confessional poetry made to create personae rather than just to bare) in "Plenitude and Dearth" (*Parnassus* 1,ii:42–59). She feels that her appeal—at least in her recent writing—may be somewhat limited because under its surface—"cool, syntactically innocent, damn hard sometimes"—"beats a heart as sentimental as old gold" (p. 53). More bothersome to Brown is the fact that much of Wakoski's poetry is bogged down in undistinguished prose-like phrases. While she admires the richness of style and quantity, Brown would like to prune to *le mot juste.*

Wakoski's regular columns in *APR*, "The Craft of Carpenters, Plumbers, & Mechanics," share the same distinction as her poems, and place her, with Denise Levertov, as one of the important essayists for contemporary poetry (see especially *APR* 2,iii:15–16; 2,v:55–56 and 2,vi:20, 29). In "A Tribute to Anaïs Nin," (2,iii:46–47), Wakoski places Nin's *Diaries* in the context of the 20th century *modus operandi,* "form is an extension of content," and sees her continuing work on the diaries as very influential in many new tendencies within conventional literary *genres.* Perhaps more important, Wakoski sees Nin as "a symbol in her diaries of the life of total commitment and involvement with human beings" (p. 46).

Marge Piercy's "Margaret Atwood: Beyond Victimhood" (*APR* 2,vi:41–44) grants many of the same qualities to this young Canadian writer. Versatile in that she writes fiction, poetry, and criticism, Atwood yet has the difficulty (which Piercy thinks she shares with many other women writers just now) of creating believable and valid solutions for her life view: Atwood writes effectively of the problems her female protagonists face, but her solutions for their post-realization stages are less satisfying than Piercy would conceive.

Paul Lacey's chapter on Denise Levertov ("A Poetry of Exploration," in *The Inner War*) stresses her poetics as a revelation of her philosophic seriousness, her "sense of holiness." A close reading of poems from the earliest collections of poetry (in which the Hassidic influence was strong) as well as recent, substantiates this view. Carol A. Kyle's essay "Every Step an Arrival: 'Six Variations' and the Musical Structure of Denise Levertov's Poetry" (*CentR* 17:281–96) relates this early sequence poem to a suite, and then follows the analogy to discuss imagery of "step" and "dance" within other of the poems. Ralph Mills defends Levertov's later writing, especially *Footprints* ("In the Fields of Imagination," *Parnassus* 1,ii:211–24) as being unmarred by her earlier political interests. "Levertov is a poet of flexibility, depth and imaginative growth. She has become one of those figures around whom a large part of our sense of what has occurred in American poetry in the past fifteen or so years revolves" (p. 219). Part of Levertov's anima comes from her relation to nature, and Mills sees Maxine Kumin's strengths in her recent *Up Country* as being her "capacity for seeing," her relation to and use of nature. She is a skillful poet, who knows her poetics—and her subjects—well.

In "Days and Distances: The Cartographic Imagination of Elizabeth Bishop," (*Salmagundi* 22–23:294–305), Jan B. Gordon sees the heart of Bishop's poetry as conflict, a move between perception and the unknowable, of self-knowledge and mystery. Gordon locates an interesting image pattern used to illustrate these themes, that of cartography, and especially of geographical extremities—straits, peninsulas, promontories, icebergs, capes—and water. Evocative as these images of alienation might be, Gordon seems to feel that Bishop's approach to poetry mirrors her tactic in choosing imagery, that it is somewhat programmatic, "technical," and therefore less satisfying than other, contemporary lyric poetics.

Agnes Sibley's *May Sarton* (TUSAS 213, 1972) is a thorough critique of both Sarton's novels and poems. Considering Sarton primarily a poet, Sibley employs her own poetics to explicate her writing and her stylistics. Sibley concludes that Sarton is an important modern writer because of her affirmative stance ("Her belief is in man and in cultural continuity with the past, in order and beauty, in all that characterizes the great humanistic tradition," p. 149). The book includes a chronology and selected bibliography.

vii. Theodore Roethke

Straw for the Fire, from the Notebooks of Theodore Roethke, 1943–63, arranged and selected by David Wagoner (New York, Doubleday, 1972) is a rich collection of unpublished poems and poem fragments, as well as lecture notes, essays, and prose entries from the "277 notebooks and 8,306 loose sheets" which Wagoner used to make this compilation. Wagoner has titled many of the selections, usually from phrases within them; he has pieced together several versions of an image or idea, even when many years—and many notebooks—separate them; he has, in short, been called on to know these notebooks intimately, and he has done his work well, giving even these random selections a touch that Roethke would have approved.

Theodore Roethke, A Bibliography by James Richard McLeod (Kent, Ohio, Kent State Univ. Press) offers a complete listing of primary, secondary, unpublished, and miscellaneous items. Complete with chronology, this is a thorough presentation.

A Concordance to the Poems of Theodore Roethke, ed. Gary Lane and programmed by Roland Dedekind (Metuchen, N.J., The Scarecrow Press, 1972) lists each significant word, the lines in which it appears, and their location in Roethke's *Collected Poems*. The book concludes with a word-frequency table.

Among the most convincing essays this year are Richard A. Blessing's "Theodore Roethke: A Celebration" (*TSE* 20[1972]:169–80) in which Blessing focuses on the actual arrangement of words in a poem as the index to Roethke's genius. In free forms, Roethke uses many verbs, lists of actions, sound played against sound, and associative leaps in imagery; in conventional forms, in which he is especially adept, repetition and shifts in rhyme and line length are highly successful. Blessing thinks Roethke's elegies among his best work.

The same critic deals with Roethke's 12-poem sequence as an erratic mixture of dark moods and light ("Theodore Roethke's Sometimes Metaphysical Notion," *TSLL* 14[1972]:731–49). Discussing each of the poems in *Sequence, Sometimes Metaphysical* in detail, Blessing finds that the sequence format accurately permits Roethke to present "the dynamic flow of experience," a mixture of somber periods and happy, never a simple progression from one to the other.

George Wolff's "Syntactical and Imagistic Distortion in Roethke's Greenhouse Poems" (*Lang&S* 6:281–88) presents these distortions from the 1946 poems as another instance of Roethke's control of poetic elements within his best work. Brendan Galvin's "Theodore Roethke's Proverbs" (*CP* 5,i[1972]:35–47) explains Roethke's process of moving from notebook to poem, with special attention to his fascination with proverb or maxim. Galvin sees Roethke ennobling his personae through his upward progression in proverbs throughout the poetry.

viii. Nemerov, Hoffman, Merwin, Wilbur, Gregory, Ignatow, Ciardi, and others

Julia A. Bartholomay's *The Shield of Perseus, the Vision and Imagination of Howard Nemerov* (Gainesville, Fla., Univ. of Fla. Press, 1972) is the first book-length study of Nemerov. Bartholomay establishes categories for Nemerov's poems, sometimes basing her observations on Peter Meinke's earlier pamphlet *Howard Nemerov*; she approaches the body of work reasonably, and her conclusions appear to be sound. She makes much use of Nemerov's own commentary about the poem and its process and, in conclusion, sees Nemerov as expressing "a faith based on affirmation through doubt" (p. 147). His mastery of the relatively long philosophical poem (and riddle and rune), rather than the brief lyric, follows from this attitude.

James M. Kiehl speaks also of Nemerov's power to lead readers "to the wonderful, unaccounted for" ("On Howard Nemerov," *Salmagundi* 22–23:234–57). He is particularly interested in Nemerov's use of dream sequences, of scientific concepts and imagery, his use of the language of satire and irony, and his abilities with puns, riddles, and word play. Robert Stock's "The Epistemological Vision of Howard Nemerov" (*Parnassus* 2:156–63) presents the late work as the most satisfying.

In "Poetry and Meaning," (*Salmagundi* 22–23:42–56) Nemerov shows his ability once again to discuss the clichés of criticism with wit and perception. His point here is that contemporary poems are sometimes divorced from language well used ("the pleasure of saying something over for its own sweet sake, and because it sounds just right," p. 48) and from the traditional province of poems ("the power of poetry to be somewhat more like a mind than a thought"). He abhors, too, the posture of the literary mind—"dry, angry, smart, jeering, cynical . . . a smart shallowness and verbal facility" appears, unfortunately, in both criticism and poetry. Nemerov calls for an end to such posturing, and a return to the real conventions of poetry.

Michael Lowe has compiled *Daniel Hoffman, A Comprehensive Bibliography* (Norwood, Pa., Norwood Editions) which includes an interview with Hoffman, the complete range of primary items, and secondary essays and reviews of his criticism as well as his poetry.

Carol Kyle writes on W. S. Merwin's optimistic view of life, using *The Lice* as the most powerful illustration of her thesis ("Riddle for the New Year: Affirmation in W. S. Merwin," *MPS* 4,iii:288–303). After an intensive reading of the poems in *The Lice*, Kyle observes that "Surrealism in Merwin's poetry is much more than a technique; it is a large, affirmative vision, optimistic in the connections among all things" (p. 296). Merwin's pervasive use of the needle-and-thread image is one means of suggesting that the apparent fragments of modern life can be re-ordered. Jarold Ramsey ("The Continuities of W. S. Merwin: 'What Has Escaped Us We Bring with Us,'" *MR* 14:569–90) finds more similarities than differences in the 20 years of Merwin's poetry, similarities accruing chiefly from imagery of "bells, mirrors, gloves, stones, doorways; birds, whales"; and "behind them all, inexhaustible in its numenousness, the sea" (p. 569). In this context of on-going concern and attitudes, Ramsey places *The Lice*, seeing it too in relation to Robinson Jeffers, to protest poetry, and to conventional poetic techniques. His highest praise, however, goes to Merwin's 1970 *The Carrier of Ladders*. Anthony Libby ("Fire and Light, Four Poets to the End and Beyond," *IowaR* 4,ii:111–26) sees

Merwin as the most inherently pessimistic of the best poets writing today (Bly, Hughes, Dickey) yet perhaps also the most able to come to terms with the realities that force us to find myth as recourse. John Bayley's "How to be Intimate Without Being Personal" (*Parnassus* 2,i:115–22) praises Merwin's 1973 books, *Asian Figures* and *Writings to an Unfinished Accompaniment.* In 1972, *MPS* included two essays on Merwin, John Vogelsang's "Toward the Great Language: W. S. Merwin," pp. 97–118, and Jan B. Gordon's "The Dwelling of Disappearance: W. S. Merwin's *The Lice,*" pp. 119–38.

Another special issue of *MPS* (4,i) focused on Horace Gregory. Including essays by David H. Zucker, Linda Wagner, Daniel Stern, Arthur Gregor, Victor A. Kramer, M. L. Rosenthal, William V. Davis, Robert Phillips, and others, the issue assessed the progression from Gregory's early "Objectivist" poems, the thirties work, to the later poems. His use of American themes, his relation to the Pound-Williams idiom, his use of nightmare images, and other critical observations are made.

Several essays survey the fruitful career of David Ignatow. Jerome Mazzaro in "Circumscriptions: The Poetry of David Ignatow" (*Salmagundi* 22–23:164–86) considers Ignatow—for all the fact that his poems remain short, "small songs"—"something approaching a major voice" (p. 164). Mazzaro stresses Ignatow's reliance on open-endedness, on montage, and on the real employment of silences. Harvey Swados, writing in *APR* 2,iii:35–36 ("David Ignatow: The Meshuganeh Lower"), emphasizes Ignatow's themes from actual life—money, love, death—and their place in his poetics.

Ralph Mills edited *The Notebooks of David Ignatow* (Chicago, The Swallow Press), 375 pages of excerpts from nearly 40 years of notebooks. This quantity gives us a convincing picture of the life of a comparatively unsuccessful writer—until the past decade. As Alfred Kazin summarized in "The Esthetic of Humility" (*APR* 3,ii:14–15), "The ideas are commonplace, the writing is threadbare . . . yet this is a life itself" (p. 15).

John Ciardi has collected over 100 of his *Saturday Review* "Manner of Speaking" columns into a book of that title (New Brunswick, N.J., Rutgers Univ. Press, 1972). Many of the essays have to do with the writing (and reading) of poetry; none is strictly "literary criticism" but most are urbane, witty observations in the familiar essay tradition. "An Interview with John Ciardi" appears in *FQ* 4,ii–iii:69–84.

William Heyen's "On Richard Wilbur (*SoR* 9:617–34) is a well-balanced attempt to describe the qualities of Wilbur's poetry that keep us reading it, regardless of trends. Heyen points to Wilbur's genuine voice, his naturalness; his consistent moral view, which is stable but never saccarine or easy (Heyen compares him with Frost in this respect); his humor; and, most important of all, his passion—"of a whole spirit's agonizing for something that will suffice, and of that spirit's joy in finding that in its world there is something that sometimes will" (p. 634).

Russian poet Joseph Brodsky also praises Wilbur for his craft and his humanity ("On Richard Wilbur," *APR* 2,i:52). See also D. R. Sharma, "Richard Wilbur: An Analysis of His Vision" (*PURBA* 4, ii:43–50).

ix. Warren, Tate, Jarrell

Louise Cowan, in *The Southern Critics* (Dallas, Tex., Univ. of Dallas Press, 1972), discusses the work of Tate, Davidson, Warren, Brooks, Lytle, and Ransom, primarily from the perspective of their criticism. Since this is a monograph, each discussion is brief, but Cowan does emphasize Donald Davidson's role as equal to that of Ransom and Tate in establishing the Southern critical school. Interested in the oral tradition of poetry, Davidson pressed for some relation with folk art, for the need of regional ties for any writer, and for the lyric voice (as opposed to the modernist ironic speech). Were it not for Davidson, new criticism might have been less reasonable than it ultimately became. (Cowan hastens to add that the Southern critics used various critical approaches, whatever was appropriate to the subject being presented: "their discipline was poetry, . . . their outlook was classical and Christian; their concern was the welfare of human culture, to the extent that it could be furthered through literature" [p. 75].)

From the J. Howard Woolmar Company (Andes, N.Y.) comes *A Catalogue of the Fugitive Poets* (1972) with Louis D. Rubin's essay "Fugitives as Agrarians: The Impulse Behind *I'll Take My Stand*" (pp. 9–26). Differentiating somewhat between the two groups,

Rubin nevertheless stresses the sense of community (nonindustrialized community) as integral to their ethics as writers and as people (as illustrated by Tate's "Ode to the Confederate Dead" and other poems by Warren, Davidson, Tate, and Ransom). The catalogue includes books and periodicals through 1929, and selected more recent items.

Austin Warren's "Homage to Allen Tate" (*SoR* 9:753–77) is interesting for its survey of recent criticism on Tate's work, and for its biographical information.

George Nitchie reminisces about Randall Jarrell in the same issue ("Randall Jarrell: A Stand-in's View," pp. 883–94) but the most pertinent essay on Jarrell's writing this year is Robert Weisberg's "Randall Jarrell: The Integrity of His Poetry" (*CentR* 17:237–55). Weisberg sees a divided Jarrell—a genial almost childlike man set against the darker poet, obsessed with the lost-innocence theme—whose dichotomies are resolved only in his best poems. Among these Weisberg discusses "The Death of the Ball-Turret Gunner," "The Grown Up," "A Well-to-do-Invalid," "The One Who Was Different," "The Lost World," "A Hunt in the Black Forest," "The House in the Wood," and "Thinking of the Lost World" (most of these from the last book, *The Lost World*, Jarrell's best and most controlled collection, in Weisberg's view).

x. Minority Poets

Stephen Henderson's introduction to *Understanding the New Black Poetry* (New York, William Morrow) clarifies several basic concepts. Henderson, as editor of the collection, insists that modern black poetry stems from two traditions, the written and the oral (music, folk, jazz) which sometimes converge. He discusses prevalent themes, what he terms "saturation" ("communication of blackness"), and linguistic structures, pointing out that in the latter section the black diction differs from white in virtuoso naming and enumerating, wordplay, jazz-like rhythmic effects, hyperbolic and metaphysical imagery, and understatement.

John O'Brien, in his introduction to *Interviews with Black Writers* (New York, Liveright), stresses the impact of the oral tradition and also the force of black novels, especially those of McKay, Toomer, Wright, and Ellison. Among the 17 interviews included are informative ones with Robert Hayden, Ishmael Reed, Alice Walker, John Williams, Charles Wright, Al Young, and Clarence Major (see the latter's column in *APR* 2,vi:17 on the impact of *Invisible Man* as poem, the fading line between today's best prose and poetry).

Geneva Smitherman does the most cogent job of identifying characteristics of black idiom in "The Power of the Rap: The Black Idiom and the New Black Poetry" (*TCL* 19:259–74). She views the modern "Black Art Revival" as different from the Harlem Renaissance in that today's writers see themselves first as blacks, then as writers; and because of that identity, refrain from any elitist position in art. Citing Franz Fanon on the psychological importance of a specialized idiom, Smitherman describes the language peculiarities of Black speech (slang, the use of *be* and its forms, phonological spelling) but points out that these are minor matters unless they also appear in Black *styles* of speech. Some of these she identifies as

(1) The Dozens—caustic, humorous insults, often about mothers.

(2) The Toast—narrative, rhymed tales, often about sexual prowess.

(3) Call-Response—speaker and audience in rhythmic alternation.

(4) Signification—ritualized insult.

(5) Rhyme, sound, and rhythm integral to Black speech.

A related essay is Bernard W. Bell's "Contemporary Afro-American Poetry as Folk Art" (*BlackW* 22,v:17–26, 74–87). Using such poets as Don Lee, Ted Joans, Bob Kaufman, Al Young, Sonia Sanchez, and others, Bell concludes that much modern Black poetry shows a reaffirmation of Black folk values, "a celebration of the Black masses and musicians as heroes," and "a validation of the poetic qualities of Black speech and music."

Roy P. Basler considers Melvin B. Tolson the writer most likely to represent modern American culture ("The Heart of Blackness—M. B. Tolson's Poetry," *New Letters* 39:63–76). Discussing Tolson's poetry from his 1944 *Rendezvous with America*, Basler commends the unfinished *Harlem Gallery* (1965). "Tolson has written of American life as it is and will be . . . and it is not 'negritude,' although he has plenty of that, but 'humanitude' that enabled him to accomplish the feat" (p. 75).

Theodore R. Hudson's *From Leroi Jones to Amiri Baraka, the Literary Works* (Durham, N.C., Duke Univ. Press) is the first full-length study of a writer whose work is attracting much critical attention. Hudson has done a relatively thorough study. The book includes discussions of Jones's life, philosophy, and aesthetic views, and then proceeds to the writing, arranged by genre rather than chronology. Writing from *Home*, essays from 1960 to 1965, to *Raise Race Rays Raze* is discussed first, followed by chapters on the fiction ("essentially autobiographical"), poetry (Jones's primary interest, at least until recently), and drama (his most innovative contributions to literature). In his conclusion, Hudson contends that Jones's changes in aesthetic (in poetry, from lyrical to statement-oriented; in drama, from avant garde to pageant) stem from his increasing involvement in Black nationalism; that his Romanticism places him in an enduring literary tradition; and that whether or not his present writing insures his standing as a major writer, he has been the most important black writer of the sixties. Hudson includes a thorough bibliography.

Mary Ellen Brooks also summarizes the stages in Baraka's development ("The Pro-Imperialist Career of LeRoi Jones," *L&I* 11 [1972]:37–48), as does William C. Fischer in a major survey of Jones's development. He places the young poet, early, as much influenced by Williams (for his insistence on speaking in one's own voice) and by the Beats (for their "cultural ambience"). Fischer sees the process of Jones's own writing as a means to his "racial re-orientation" ("The Pre-Revolutionary Writings of Imamu Amiri Baraka," *MR* 14:259–305). John Baker asks some difficult questions in his "LeRoi Jones, Secessionist, and Ambiguous Collecting," *YULG* 46[1972]:159–66, when he describes the dilemma of acquiring work by people whose impact may be primarily "sociological": "Can a 'literature' written in the vernacular of a special culture . . . endure as art?"

In "Transformations," Julius Lester discusses the latest books of Sam Cornish, Al Young, and Machael S. Harper (*Parnassus* 1,ii:126–32), preferring the language excitement of Harper to the simple directness of the others, and noting that only Cornish "writes consciously as a black" in his choice of subjects.

Robert P. Sedlack's "Mari Evans: Consciousness and Craft" (*CLAJ* 15[1972]:465–76) catalogues the poetic devices Evans uses in her book *I Am a Black Woman*. Eugene E. Miller's "Some Black Thoughts on Don L. Lee's *Think Black!*" (*CE* 34:1094–1102) surveys Lee's attitudes and stylistics.

Interest in the poetry of Gwendolyn Brooks continues high. Annette O. Shands discusses Brooks's *Report from Part One* in *BlackW* 22,v:51–52, 70–71. A special issue of *CLAJ* (17:1–32) contains these essays: "Gwendolyn Brooks: The 'Unconditioned' Poet," by Marva R. Furman, pp. 1–10; "Aestheticism Versus Political Militancy in Gwendolyn Brooks's 'The Chicago Picasso' and 'The Wall,'" by William H. Hansell, pp. 11–15; "Racial Themes in the Poetry of Gwendolyn Brooks," by Clenora F. Hudson, pp. 16–20; and "Gwendolyn Brooks: A Bibliography," by Jon N. Loff, pp. 21–32.

Joel Hancock describes "The Emergence of Chicano Poetry: A Survey of Sources, Themes, and Techniques" (*ArQ* 29:57–73). He sees Chicano literature as maturing, occupying a central position in the movement toward ethnic identity. Much poetry has been written, often on nationalistic themes with special interest in history (Tenochtitlán and contemporary Mexico) and ancestors. Pervasive too is the theme of social injustice in the United States and possible action against that injustice.

Hancock mentions the work of Octavio I. Romano-V. (his epic "Mosaico Mexicano") and Alurista, a leading anthologist who writes in a mixture of Spanish and English (as do many Chicano writers).

xi. Ashbery, Ammons, O'Hara

John Gruen writes in *The Party's Over Now, Reminiscences of the Fifties—New York's Artists, Writers, Musicians, and Their Friends* (New York, Viking, 1972), "John Ashbery has been our most elusive friend. Today John, along with Kenneth Koch and the late Frank O'Hara, has become a major poet" (p. 155). Naturally, Gruen does not write critically about these poets, but his memoir contains interesting material—and many personal interviews—about these writers and their relationships with painters and musicians during the formative fifties and the developmental sixties (chapters 12 and 13, pp. 141–71, are central). Of some relevance also is Dore Ashton's *The New York School, A Cultural Reckoning* (New York, Viking).

Harold Bloom discounts Ashbery's association with this "New York School" (although the fact that Ashbery and O'Hara were part of the city's art and literary circles from the early fifties on seems incontestable) because he finds Ashbery a "unique figure." Bloom would associate Ashbery—if at all—with only A. R. Ammons ("John Ashbery: The Charity of the Hard Moments," *Salmagundi* 22–23:

103–31). "Ashbery goes back through Stevens to Whitman" (p. 103). Bloom discounts Ashbery's second book, *The Tennis Court Oath*, entirely (although do not those poems, too, in their complete reliance on montaged fragments, echo Whitman?); he chooses only the poems on which his own elaborate post-Romantic critical view will work, preferring *The Double Dream of Spring* (1970) and *Three Poems* (1972). Perhaps it is part of the critical dilemma that Bloom sees Ashbery's work in terms of Shelley and Emerson rather than Marisol.

Hyatt H. Waggoner surveys "The Poetry of A. R. Ammons: Some Notes and Reflections" (*Salmagundi* 22–23:285–93) with particular attention to his nature poetry. Waggoner sees Ammons as "a visionary poet in the Neoplatonic tradition," with many ties to Emerson. Robert Morgan discusses poems from Ammons's 1955 *Ommateum*, finding his basic themes—the failure of the search for unity and identity, and the role of language in that search—already present ("The Compound Vision of A. R. Ammons' Early Poems," *Epoch* 22: 343–63).

Reviews of some substance include Richard Howard, "Auguries of Experience: *The Collected Poems 1951–71* of A. R. Ammons," *Boundary 2* 1,iii:712–15 and "Poetry: Ammons, Berryman, Cummings," *YR* 62:412–25, in which Helen Vendler admires Ammons's new sparcity of modifiers, people, things; she concludes that he writes a poetry that works because it completely abjures the romantic. William Meredith, in "I Will Tell You About It Because It Is Interesting" (*Parnassus* 2,i:175–84) compares Ammons with Frost in character, intelligence, and his "fascination with dialectics" and finds him "like Roethke in his use of nature and nature imagery."

Charles Altieri finds "The Significance of Frank O'Hara" to lie in his belief that the present is "a landscape without depth," that its surface presentation makes the artist's condemnation evident (and thus, O'Hara becomes "pop" poet, content to arrange objects and images of the present) (*IowaR* 4,i:90–104). He sees O'Hara opposing Bly and Olson who believe that the self has only to find, to locate, the source: for O'Hara, Altieri believes, the self must be creative even without knowing his ground, his roots. With references to Jacques Derrida, Altieri creates O'Hara's value system as affirmative skepticism (at times sheer exuberance) and humility; and these attitudes have been influential for the other New York poets.

xii. Bly, Wright, Logan, Dickey, Kinnell

"Intellectual and relentlessly emotional," Joyce Carol Oates characterizes Robert Bly's *Sleepers Joining Hands* ("When They All Are Sleeping," *MPS* 4:341–44), and perhaps that description is apt for Bly's steady (and growing) impact on contemporary poetry. Oates compares Bly's essays (in Part II of the collection) to those of Erich Neumann, tracing his philosophy to Carl Jung and anthropologist Johann Bachofen, and seeing him—through his own work and his editing of *The Seventies*—as "unique at the present time" (p. 344).

Anthony Libby's "Fire and Light, Four Poets to the End and Beyond," (*IowaR* 4,ii:111–26) reads Bly, Hughes, Merwin, and Dickey as apocalyptic, similar in interesting ways in theme, technique ("highly visceral surrealism") and philosophy. Libby sees Bly's view of the present as apocalyptic in Darwinian terms rather than Christian. Bly's faith in mysticism as a means of awakening man is evident in his *Seventies* essays and in those poems that use imagery of primal, earth mother, and light.

Paul A. Lacey's chapter on Bly in *The Inner War* gives a good survey of both his writing and his critical career. Viewing the poem as a moral act, representative of man's deepest knowledge, Bly has consistently urged people to see the harmonies between inner and outer, emotional and intellectual, human and natural worlds. Because Lacey's chapter stops before the last books, he does not find resolution to the angst that permeates *The Teeth-Mother* and *Light Around the Body*. The promise of that resolution, however, is inherent.

Bly's essays have been available recently as columns in each issue of *APR* (as well as throughout *The Seventies* and in *Field* 10:31–36). One of the most important of these columns is "Developing the Underneath," *APR* 2,vi:44–45, in which Bly explains his poetics in relation to Jungian thought and then discusses the poems of Louis Simpson, Allen Ginsberg, James Tate, Galway Kinnell, Denise Levertov, Ai, and others.

Several essays on James Wright also attempt to describe the reason for his influence on contemporary poetry. James Seay's "A World Immeasurably Alive and Good: A Look at James Wright's *Collected Poems* (*GaR* 27:71–81) traces much of Wright's later work to his admiration for Neruda, Vallejo, Guillén, and Georg

Trakl, particularly in regard to their visionary quality and sense of spontaneity. The change that led to Wright's 1963 *The Branch Shall Not Break* was, Seay believes, "a radically altered concept of what a poem should reveal about experience" (p. 72). Seay sees Wright's themes as remaining fairly constant—loneliness, empathy for social outcasts, identity with the natural world, and—most recently—with a beloved (his discussion is similar to that of Lacey in *The Inner War*).

Charles Molesworth ("James Wright and the Dissolving Self," *Salmagundi* 22–23:222–33) discusses Wright's relationship to the Romantics. Molesworth characterizes Wright's central myth as being "that the poet must lose himself in things, for only there will he find his tongue, the only agency of his true survival" (p. 229). Wright's own essay on Richard Hugo echoes some of these observations ("Hugo: Secrets of the Inner Landscape," *APR* 2,iii:13).

Charles Altieri's long essay "Poetry as Resurrection: John Logan's Structures of Metaphysical Solace" (*MPS* 3:193–224) traces the poet's development from the explicitly Catholic poetry of *Cycle for Mother Cabrini* to the still-affirmative but socially aware, undoctrinaire recent poems. "Poetry is a secular form of religion," Logan writes. Altieri surveys key poems from each of Logan's collections in proving that the poet has found, within his admittedly secular context, a means to his formerly religious satisfaction.

William H. Chaplin follows the same patterns, pointing out that Logan escapes being "confessional" because of his focus on orthodoxy in many areas ("Identity and Spirit in the Recent Poetry of John Logan," *APR* 2,iii:19–24; see also Richard Howard's "The Anonymous Lover," *APR* 2,v:7–8).

Norman Silverstein sees James Dickey as a thoroughly Southern writer, conventional in his poetics and in his life (where he is just as obviously masculine) ("James Dickey's Muscular Eschatology," *Salmagundi* 22–23:258–68). He sees Dickey as a later Fugitive, yet also acknowledges that the poet's "country surrealism" is far from the classical restraint of Ransom and Tate. Telling more about Silverstein than about Dickey, the essay concludes—somewhat unexpectedly—that "the preferred medium for his verbal talents will be the novel."

Anthony Libby, conversely, sees Dickey as close to Bly and Merwin ("Fire and Light," *IowaR* 4,ii:111–26), "a poet of ultimate violence and of transformation, of human movement into animal consciousness" (p. 121). Because Dickey has tended to move away from the mythic, his later poems stress not man's communion with the natural world so much as his survival in it (and, repeatedly, Dickey's laurels go to the "fittest").

In "A Conversation with James Dickey" by William Heyen (*SoR* 9:135–56) Dickey makes clear his admiration for poets Randall Jarrell and Galway Kinnell, and says—among many interesting comments—"the true creative act is to conceive, first, a thing, and then to find your way through the process of the administration of formal technique to making that strange vision live" (p. 138). See also the Dickey interview in *Craft So Hard To Learn*, ed. George Garrett (New York, William Morrow, 1972).

Ed Ochester reviews Kinnell's *The Book of Nightmares* as "spiritual autobiography," a mixture of private and larger, social concerns, all written with "the authenticity of agony" ("The Shape of the Fire," *MPS* 3,v:230–37). In the poem, structurally, "the interdependence of love and death" is shown, successfully, over and over.

Charles Molesworth sees Kinnell's recent work as establishing a completely new attitude in modern poetry ("The Rank Flavor of Blood: Galway Kinnell and American Poetry in the 1960's," *WHR* 27:225–39). Molesworth differentiates between irony and empathy, as prevailing modes in American poetry; *irony* results from points of tension, from "opposing vectors," whereas *empathy*, artistic compassion, is "a systemic consciousness, an awareness of the field on which and through which the forces of experience act" (pp. 231–32). That Kinnell has progressed—in the major poems of *Body Rags* ("The Poem," "The Porcupine," and "The Bear") and *The Book of Nightmares*—"beyond the suspension of irony toward the immersion of empathy" seems to Molesworth indicative of "a new post-modern aesthetic in contemporary American poetry" (p. 232).

Kinnell's own essay, "Whitman's Indicative Words" traces Whitman's influence on Lawrence and Neruda and, in the United States, after a century of delay, Ginsberg. Kinnell locates Whitman's influence in the "mystic music" of his long line, and—most important—the spiritual and energetic vision there contained (*APR* 2,ii:9–12).

It seems clear in 1973—from the kind of criticism being written, and from the writers being considered critically—that the primary interest for the student and reader of poetry today lies in more than an imagist approach to the concrete details of this world. As Anne

Halley concludes after reviewing nearly one hundred books of current poetry, "for a good many poets now writing, the ambiguity of meaning shimmering above objectively perceived, real experience is no longer interesting" ("Struggling in Poetry," *MR* 14:847–64; p. 858).

Michigan State University

16. Drama

Walter J. Meserve

i. Histories, Indexes, Research Guides, Dissertations

The most ambitious book published this year on American drama and theatre is Garff B. Wilson's *Three Hundred Years of American Drama and Theatre: From Ye Bare and Ye Cubb to Hair* (Englewood Cliffs, N.J., Prentice-Hall). It is a well-illustrated volume in which the author surveys the development of drama, theatre, radio, and television in America. For the beginning student this history provides an adequate introduction and a popular appeal through Wilson's artfully reconstructed "evenings at the theatre" for selected years in American history. For the serious student and scholar of American drama and theatre the book is disappointing and without real value. There is almost no evidence of research beyond the standard and readily available works, while the scope of the undertaking is impossibly large. A clear analysis of the contribution of playwrights, actors, and theatre managers would have helped considerably, but this assessment is lacking. Sketchy, cursory, uncritical, discursive in style, this history does not approach the kind of scholarship which the subject demands.

Slowly the history of American theatres is being brought into perspective. William C. Young's work in this area is distinctive—*Documents of American Theater History, Vol. 1: Famous American Playhouses, 1716–1899; Vol. 2: Famous American Playhouses, 1900–1971* (Chicago, American Lib. Assoc.). The documents, which describe nearly 120 theatres in volume one and nearly 80 in volume two, include diaries, letters, newspaper articles and reviews, playbills, and architectural drawings. A valuable reference work, the volumes also provide material on the historical importance of the theatres. Mary C. Henderson's *The City & the Theatre: New York Playhouses from Bowling Green to Times Square* (Clifton, N.J., James T. White &

Co.) presents a history of New York's playhouses followed by a good number of pictures of these theatres with accompanying descriptions.

The recent volumes from the Chicoral Library have a value for large libraries but are too expensive at $49.50 per volume for the interested reader. The three pertinent volumes are edited by Marietta Chicorel–*Chicorel Theatre Index to Plays in Anthologies, Periodicals, Discs and Tapes*, Vol. 1 (New York, Chicorel Lib. Pubs., 1970), Vol. 2 (1971), Vol. 3 (1972). Material is listed by author, play, anthology, and editor's name; it is also presented by nation and historical period. The indexes are called comprehensive, but they are, if so, only with reference to the Western world. The *Dramatic Criticism Index* (Detroit, Gale Research, 1972), edited by Paul F. Breed and Florence M. Sniderman, is advertised as a bibliography of commentaries of playwrights from Ibsen to the Avant-Garde, but it is very limited and selective, valuable for the more obvious works on major individuals. Another selective approach to modern drama is James F. Bonin's *Prize-Winning American Drama: A Bibliographical & Descriptive Guide* (Metuchen, N.J., Scarecrow). A more valuable bibliography is James M. Salem's *A Guide to Critical Reviews: Part I: American Drama, 1909–1969* (Metuchen, N.J., Scarecrow). This is Salem's second edition of this guide which now includes 290 dramatists and references to more than 1700 plays. It includes, of course, no scholarly journals but is a handy reference for American and Canadian periodicals and the *New York Times.* The comment that this edition includes playwrights from the 18th and 19th centuries, however, is misleading. It does list a number of playwrights, but only one play from these centuries was recorded as being produced during the 1909–69 period. Another guide that one might not have noted is Heather McCallum's *Research Collections in Canadian Libraries* (Ottawa, Nat. Lib. of Canada), which is available from Ottawa for $1.20. It includes functional paragraph inventories of federal, provincial, university, public library, museum, special, and private collections. Its emphasis is obviously on Canada, but there is much that is relevant to research in American drama and theatre.

For those completing dissertations this year O'Neill clearly had the greatest appeal. Four candidates built their theories around his symbolism, expressionism, failed comedies, and relationship of the sexes. There were two dissertations on Arthur Miller, two on Tennessee Williams, one each on Edward Albee and William Dunlap. As usual, there were a number of dissertations on aspects of American theatre.

ii. From the Beginning to 1915

This year, compared with previous years, there were few items dealing with pre-O'Neill drama and theatre. Two of these items, however, were book-length studies. The first was David F. Havens's *The Columbian Muse of Comedy* (Carbondale, So. Ill. Univ. Press). The subtitle describes the book as concerned with "the development of a native tradition in early American social comedy, 1787–1845," but this is misleading. There is no concern for development of an American comedy. About a third of the book deals with Tyler's *The Contrast*; another third discusses Dunlap's *The Father*, Barker's *Tears and Smiles*, and Bird's *City Looking Glass*; the final third is divided between a discussion of nine minor comedies and Ritchie's *Fashion.* There is an introduction describing the literary atmosphere but no concluding commentary. The analysis, particularly of the minor plays, is valuable for the student of American drama, but the lack of a focus in the volume weakens its over-all importance.

A few essays considered scattered plays and playwrights of the 19th century. In "Boker's *Francesca da Rimini*: The Brothers' Tragedy" (*ETJ* 25:410–19) Jules Zanger provides a strong and well-written argument to suggest that the play belongs, not to Francesca, but to Paolo and Lanciotto. Boker, he explains, brought a new conception to the central characters through his emphasis on character over plot and discovery and revelation over the traditional ironies of the inevitable. It is a good thesis, one important to anyone reading the play. In an essay dealing more generally with the drama of the mid-19th century, "An Earnest Purpose: American Drama at Mid-19th Century" (*Players* 48:60–64), Walter J. Meserve attempts to show the lasting impact of this drama by commenting on the continuing reputations of *Fashion, Francesca da Rimini, Uncle Tom's Cabin,* and *The Octoroon.* Albert E. Johnson added to a previous interest in Dion Boucicault—"Real Sunlight in the Garden: Dion Boucicault as a Stage Director" (*ThR* 12[1972]:119–25)—with a well-defined analysis of Boucicault's early career, 1838–40, as an actor: "Dion

Boucicault Learns to Act" (*Players* 48:78–85). Johnson has now written a number of carefully researched essays on Boucicault. For those interested in Booth, L. Terry Ogyel provides "The Edwin Booth Promptbook Collection at the Players: A Descriptive Catalog" (*TS* 14,i:72–111). Another of the growing number of fine young scholars is Alice M. Robinson, whose dissertation on select concepts in early American drama showed outstanding research and excellent critical perception. Her essay on "James A. Herne and his 'Theatre Libre' in Boston" (*Players* 48:202–09) discusses the problems of producing *Margaret Fleming* and relates them to current interest in an independent theatre in Boston, which Hamlin Garland shared with Herne.

Estranging Dawn: The Life and Works of William Vaughn Moody (Carbondale, So. Ill. Univ. Press) by Maurice F. Brown follows Moody's life almost week by week in an attempt to explain his contributions to two distinct literary genres. Generally, Brown evaluates Moody's poetry better than he does his drama, but he does show in a convincing fashion that Moody's prose plays deserve the attention of the drama historian. In all of the plays Brown explores Moody's sources of inspiration, his moods, and his problems in composition; and he presents detailed plot commentary. Brown sees *The Fire-Bringer* as the best poetic drama then written in America, a conclusion that all critics would not accept. Although Brown does a good job with *The Great Divide*, details of the differences between this play and the earlier play, *The Sabine Women*, would have increased the value of his discussion. His commentary on *The Faith Healer* is excellent, as he equates its theme—flesh vs. spirit—with Moody's own life and artistic struggles.

iii. Drama from the Modern Period

Among the book-length studies that deal with the modern period of American drama, *Century of Innovation: A History of European and American Theatre and Drama Since 1870* (Englewood Cliffs, N.J., Prentice-Hall) by Oscar G. Brockett and Robert B. Findlay attempts the greatest scope. Although the beginning date is 1870, the material on American drama and theatre before World War I is limited to about four pages. Generally speaking, American drama and theatre prior to 1945 are not allowed much space or attention. Instead, the strength of the history for the student of American drama and theatre lies in the authors' ability to analyze and assess America's development in these arts that came from stimuli in Europe. Throughout the emphasis is on theatre rather than on drama as literature. Another volume which includes analyses of American and European drama is Robert B. Heilman's *The Iceman, the Arsonist, and the Troubled Agent* (Seattle, Univ. of Wash. Press). During the past 25 years Heilman has written at length on theoretical approaches to dramatic form. His attempt in this volume is to divide drama into two forms: tragedy and melodrama. For American drama he uses the plays of O'Neill, Miller, and Williams to try to understand these forms, to discover the tragic accent. His approach is penetrating and stimulating although not always convincing, but his is the kind of search that one finds encouraging.

Lewis W. Falb's *American Drama in Paris, 1945–1970* (Chapel Hill, Univ. of N.C. Press) reveals the reaction of the French to American plays through excerpted reviews and general assessment by the author. Emphasis is placed on O'Neill, Miller, Williams, Albee, the Old Guard (those whose careers by World War II drew the attention of France to American drama), musical comedies, and the overflow of "success and failure." Falb provides a chronological listing, a bibliography, and among his conclusions the observation that "naturalism" was the form among American plays that the French most enjoyed. Seymour Reiter's *World Theatre: The Structure and Meaning of Drama* (New York, Horizon Press) makes very little use of American plays. *Our Town* is noted briefly in the chapter on Sanskrit drama, and *The Hairy Ape* is mentioned in the chapter on "Submerged Structure." The author's approach is sufficiently esoteric and scattered that the reader finds little perceptive thought. Mardi Valgemae's "Expressionism in the American Theatre" (in Ulrich Weisstein, ed., *Expressionism as an International Literary Phenomenon* [Paris, Didier], pp. 193–203), is a sketchy resumé of his *Accelerated Grimace: Expressionism in the American Drama of the 1920's* with little more than play titles added for the years since 1930.

One book which will irritate the serious student of American drama and theatre while pleasing the casual reader is Philip C. Lewis's *Trouping* (New York, Harper & Row). Its subtitle is "How the show came to town," and it carries such chapter headings as "Moist Eyes and Wet Pants." A slick, fast-moving, irresponsible volume, *Trouping* provides a rambling, quite disconnected, and distorted narrative of the theatre by one whose own part in it—"Personal, In Conformation"—forms the conclusion. The irritating part is the mixture of fact and fiction, which creates a sometimes fascinating but frequently misleading picture of the subject. The organization of the material is as wild as the assumptions which the author makes. Essentially, he writes an interesting story, but one should never mistake it for history.

In a footnote to books dealing with the modern period the commemorative issue of *The Carolina Play-Book* (Chapel Hill, Univ. of N.C. Press) should be mentioned. John W. Parker edited this issue which includes a number of essays relating to the Carolina Dramatic Association whose 50th anniversary the issue celebrated. Most significant for the wider audience, however, is Hubert Heffner's essay on "The Growth of Academic Theatre in the United States" (pp. 1–11), which describes the development of academic theatre before World War II most effectively and emphasizes the necessary interrelationship of drama and theatre. Relative to that Carolina dynasty is an essay entitled "A True American Artist: Paul Green" (*Players* 48:210–15) by John Clifford. He emphasizes the belief in the ideals of America which Green narrates in his symphonic dramas and concludes that those are not merely pageants but histories of America which tell the story of a people in conflict.

***a.* Eugene O'Neill.** Arthur and Barbara Gelb published a second edition of their *O'Neill* (New York, Harper & Row). New material is added in an Epilogue which provides an account of Carlotta O'Neill's final years. The second volume of Lewis Sheaffer's work on O'Neill, *O'Neill, Son and Artist* (Boston, Little, Brown and Co.) provides the same dedication to research and careful interpretation of information that distinguished his earlier book. Using a variety of letters, documents, and interviews, Sheaffer presents an individual portrait, scholarly yet most humanly devised, of O'Neill from 1920 until his death. Interestingly written, the book presents an excellent view of O'Neill's attitudes, his day to day problems, his love/hate struggles—a portrait of the dedicated artist. In an essay entitled "Dionysus and Despair: The Influence of Nietzsche upon O'Neill's Drama" (*ETJ* 25:436–42) Maurice M. LaBelle looks at a particular influence upon O'Neill's work. Although the study is not sufficiently detailed to be ultimately convincing, LaBelle provides a clear view of the Apollonian-Dionysian dichotomy and sees the apex of the conflict in *Desire Under the Elms*. Thereafter O'Neill's pessimism deepens. Michael Hinden maintains that Nietzsche's interest in a fundamental unity underlying all phenomena fascinated O'Neill. In *The Great God Brown* Hinden finds O'Neill's most elaborate exploitation of Neitzsche's ideas—"*The Birth of Tragedy* and *The Great God Brown*" (*MD* 16:129–40). Frank R. Cunningham looks at this play from a distinctly different point of view in "*The Great God Brown* and O'Neill's Romantic Vision" (*BSUF* 14:69–78). But in contrast with the well-written and carefully organized Hinden essay Cunningham's romantic appreciation is filled with jargon and offers no really new ideas.

One of the best essays written on any aspect of American drama this year is Arthur H. Nethercot's "The Psychoanalyzing of Eugene O'Neill: P.P.S." (*MD* 16:35–48). Although the point made—identifying a particular book that O'Neill read—is minor, the process of scholarly research that Nethercot explains is solid and exemplary. The essay might well be required reading for all students enrolled in "Introduction to Graduate Studies." Albert Rothenberg and Eugene D. Shapiro are more centrally concerned with psychoanalysis in "The Defense of Psychoanalysis in Literature: *Long Day's Journey into Night* and *A View from the Bridge*" (*CompD* 7:51–67). In this essay they contrast the simple tension in *View from the Bridge* with the slow but complex defensive sequence in *Long Day's Journey*. Attacking O'Neill from another point of view, "The Women of O'Neill: Sex Role Stereotypes" (*BSUF* 14:3–8), Lois S. Josephs complains that O'Neill never reached beyond traditional sex roles after *Beyond the Horizon*, never created an American Nora. There were two well-written essays on *The Iceman Cometh*: Winifred L. Frazer's "O'Neill's Iceman—Not Ice Man" (*AL* 44:677–78), and Nancy Reinhardt's "Floral Patterns in *The Iceman Cometh*" (*MD* 16:119–28). The Reinhardt essay shows how the visual and aural "purposeful patterning" help one to better understand the play.

***b.* Hellman, Anderson, MacLeish.** Just as the 19th-century dramatists were slighted by this year's scholars, the dramatists whose careers emerged between the two world wars received little critical attention. Lorena Ross Holmin published her dissertation, *The Dramatic Works of Lillian Hellman* (Uppsala, Almqvist & Wiksell), which provides a play-by-play assessment of structure and character. James Eatman considers Hellman's *Little Foxes* as an historical drama showing the past, present, and future but submerges his analysis in such a morass of jargon that his thesis loses its effect. Philip M. Armato tries to clarify Hellman's meaning in "'Good and Evil' in Lillian Hellman's *The Children's Hour*" (*ETJ* 25:443–47). After equating *good* with *mercy* and *evil* with *cruelty* and haphazardly relating the action to *The Merchant of Venice*, Armato concludes with some force that Karen's final compassionate acceptance of Mrs. Tilford's atonement stops the cycle of evil and is, therefore, the ultimate good.

Two articles appeared on Maxwell Anderson, one on Archibald MacLeish. In "Maxwell Anderson: Poetry and Morality in the American Drama" (*ETJ* 25:15–33) Esther Jackson sees Anderson as influenced by Whitman and influencing Tennessee Williams in his creation of a native stage language emphasizing poetic qualities. John Bush Jones suggests in "Shakespeare as Myth and the Structure of *Winterset*" (*ETJ* 25:34–45) that Anderson's interest in "mythic views of drama" may explain his varied use of Shakespeare in *Winterset.* When Jones's conclusion attempts to tie in all emotional and intellectual responses to the drama, however, his argument loses its effect. *Archibald MacLeish, A Checklist* (Kent, Ohio, Kent State Univ. Press) is the work of Edward J. Mullaly and includes 58 books and pamphlets plus 176 items by selected critics.

c. Arthur Miller. Frank Bergmann's "Arthur Miller" (pp. 450–70, in *Amerikanische Literatur der Gegenwart*, Martin Christadler, ed., Stuttgart, Alfred Kröner Verlag) evaluates and defends Miller's artistry and presents a detailed analysis of *Incident at Vichy* as a play about man's celebration of life over death. Joel Shatzky tries to explain the narrowness of the American dream in a series of five motifs which he sees reflected in *Death of a Salesman.* His essay, however, "The 'Reactive Image' and Miller's *Death of a Salesman*" (*Players* 48:104–10) tends to reduce American drama to a most simplistic view in emphasizing its patterned limitations, which he sees represented in Miller's play. Helen McMahon, "Arthur Miller's Common Man: The Problem of the Realistic and the Mythic" (*D&T* 10[1972]:

128–33), finds three basic myths in Miller's plays—the American Dream, the dream of the common man, the Judeo-Christian myth—but concludes that his presentation of a heroic common man distinguishes him from others writing on this theme. Each essay, interestingly enough, suggests a comparison of Miller's concepts with universal themes.

d. **Tennessee Williams.** Approaches to the study of Williams were more varied. Two dealt with the problem of the artist in society. Using the plays in Williams's late collection, *Dragon Country*, Albert E. Kalson views his preoccupation with the interrelationship of life and art—"Tennessee Williams Enters *Dragon Country*" (*MD* 16:61–67). Kalson's point that Williams has been disillusioned with the artist as a life-force is well stated, while his conclusion that Williams may never rediscover his art is perhaps the sad inevitability. In "Submitting Self to Flame: The Artist's Quest in Tennessee Williams, 1935–1954" (*ETJ* 25:199–206) Robert Skloot pictures the artist-as-victim struggling to create beauty and searching for peace and purity. But he does not see this struggle and search in later works by Williams.

From an actor's point of view Thomas L. King provides some insight into Williams's first great stage success. In "Irony and Distance in *The Glass Menagerie*" (*ETJ* 25:207–14) he explains how Tom's soliloquies suggest the humor, the irony, and the form of the play. The play is Tom's, and the change in tone which his soliloquies clearly indicate establish the play's movement and climax. Gerald Berkowitz looks desperately for a clue or device by which he may distinguish and yet relate each Williams play. His answer in "The 'Other World' of *The Glass Menagerie*" (*Players* 48:150–53) is a "definite locus" which distinguishes a particular play's setting from the rest of the universe. In *Menagerie* it is the Wingfield apartment, but neither for this play nor for others in the Williams canon is his argument very believable. In something of a footnote to another Williams play, John J. Mood—"The Structure of *A Streetcar Named Desire*" (*BSUF* 14:9–10)—examines Blanche's first speech as a statement of her past (Desire) and the action of the play (Elysian Fields). A final note on Williams should list "Tennessee Williams: Twenty-five Years of Criticism" (*BB* 30:21–39) by Delma E. Presley.

iv. The Contemporary Scene

From one point of view Catherine Hughes's *Plays, Politics, and Polemics* (New York, Drama Book Specialists) sums up a fair amount of contemporary American drama, but her emphasis is on plot rather than analysis and critical evaluation. Part One asks the question "American Hurrah?" and deals with such plays as *The Crucible* and *Indians.* In Part Two she discusses the politics of war in *Pueblo* and *Bombed in New Haven* among other plays. The conclusion stresses the approach presented in *The Deputy* and *The Investigation.* Another writer, Esther Jackson, examines "American Theatre in the Sixties: The Drama of International Crisis" (*Players* 48:236–49) and sees the problem of language, "a production grammar" as most significant. In Jackson's opinion the Living Theatre, building upon the basis of surrealism, has shaped the syntax which interests man in his theatre and thereby enabled playwrights to create their experiences in a popular theatrical language.

One of the journalistic critics whose ideas command attention is John Lahr. In *Astonish Me, Adventures in Contemporary Theatre* (New York, The Viking Press) one of his essays reveals some shrewd insight into the contemporary scene. In describing the plays of "Neil Simon and Woody Allen: Images of Impotence" (pp. 120–36) as written with moral confusion, without wit or irony, his attack is strong, but his evidence is also compelling. This "impotence on stage," produced by the "castrati of capitalism," is, for him, the "theatre of the silent majority." Among other playwrights whom he discusses in *Astonish Me* are "Jules Feiffer and Sam Shepard: Spectacles in Disintegration" (pp. 102–19). The plays assessed here are *The White House Murder Case,* a satire on the manner in which those in authority constantly numb the average man, and *Operation Sidewinder,* a dramatized search into history as it reveals events in contemporary life. Two other academic essays on contemporary playwrights might be noted. John Bush Jones's concern for the "effect of mythicizing" history in "Impersonation and Authenticity: The Theatre of Metaphor in Kopit's *Indians*" (*QJS* 59:443–51) might have helped clarify an issue surrounding theatre as history had he written in a clear, effective prose style. "Robert Lowell's *Benito Cereno*" (*MD* 15:411–26) became the focal point of Mark W. Estrin's thesis that drama may show the future through the past. Although the comparison between Lowell's play and Melville's story seems irrelevant to his interpretation, Estrin explores the racial conflict in the play as it reveals social and political argument applicable to the present decades.

a. **Edward Albee.** In the ebb and flow of that ocean of criticism, which seems more often than not simply to inundate the reading public rather than to raise it to heights of understanding, Albee's work rode a crest this year. To Philip C. Kolin's "A Supplementary Edward Albee Checklist (*Serif* 10,i:28–39) add *Edward Albee at Home and Abroad: A Bibliography* (New York, AMS Press), a reasonable collection of reviews, articles, and miscellaneous materials with Albee's published works, compiled by Richard E. Amacher and Margaret Rule. *Abroad,* however, refers only to the Western world. Other articles on Albee this year ranged from " 'Santayanian Finess' in Albee's *Tiny Alice*" (*NConL* 3,v:12–13) by James E. White to "St. George and the Snapdragons: The Influence of Unamuno on *Who's Afraid of Virginia Woolf?*" (*ArQ* 29:5–13) by Duane R. Carr. A number of critics chose particular themes. In "The Process of Dying in the Plays of Edward Albee" (*ETJ* 25:80–85) Melvin Vos describes the lack of love which leads to death and shows the awareness in *All Over* that dying has become a process of self-knowledge. In another study of "Reality and Illusion: Continuity of a Theme in Albee" (*ETJ* 25:71–79) Lawrence Kingsley argues that *Zoo Story* is a prologue to a search for reality which Albee finally discovers in *Delicate Balance.* "Coming of Age in New Carthage: Albee's Grown-up Children" (*ETJ* 25:53–65) by Charlene M. Taylor studies the use of language, games, and clusters of images to suggest the movement of Albee's characters into an adult world. Brian Robinson repeats the judgment of others in "De *Qui a peur de Virginia Woolf* à *Delicate Balance*: Le Talent d'Edward Albee sur le declin" (*RUO* 43:270–76).

Zoo Story and *Virginia Woolf* were subjected to various points of view. Jerry's dog story and Tobias's cat story were used by Carol A. Sykes in "Albee's Beast Fables: *The Zoo Story* and *A Delicate Balance*" (*ETJ* 25:448–55) to show Albee's growing pessimism and changing attitude toward humanity. In a brief note, Mary M. Milan argued in "Albee's *The Zoo Story,* Alienated Man, and the Nature of Love" (*MD* 16:55–59) that Jerry's inability to love prompts a violence which dramatizes the "tragedy" of a society incapable of communication. Robert S. Wallace presents a tenuous thesis in "*The Zoo Story*: Albee's Attack on Fiction" (*MD* 16:49–54). The play, he argues, is an exposé of the use of fiction as a substitute for life.

In a poorly realized essay on "*Who's Afraid of Virginia Woolf?* and the Patterns of History" (*ETJ* 25:46–52) Orley I. Holtan suggests that the play is an allegory for the American historical experience and that George's marriage and career may be considered as analogues of American history. Yet there seems to be no point to these observations. In a different view of the play—"Albee's *Who's Afraid of Virginia Woolf?*: A Long Night's Journey into Day" (*ETJ* 25:66–70)—Thomas P. Adler emphasizes Nick and Honey and sees their salvation through the suffering of George and Martha. James E. White travels a worn road in "Albee's *Tiny Alice*: An Exploration of Paradox" (*LWU* 6:247–58) while Anthony Hopkins—"Conventional Albee: *Box* and *Chairman Mao*" (*MD* 16:141–47)—discusses in a rather hodge-podge fashion certain aspects of the play, which are characteristic of Albee's writing.

***b.* Black Drama.** LeRoi Jones's popularity seems to grow each year as a focal point for the study of Black drama in America, although in many essays on Black drama and theatre the emphasis is being placed upon the developing concept rather than the individual practitioner. Theodore R. Hudson emphasizes change and development in *From LeRoi Jones to Amiri Baraka: The Literary Works* (Durham, N.C., Duke Univ. Press). Essays tended to assess the attitudes or contributions of the artist rather than particular plays: John McClusky, "In the Mecca (Imamu Amiri Baraka)" (*SBL* 4,iii:25–30); Lou Anne Pearson, "Leroi Jones and a Black Aesthetic" (*Paunch* 35[1972]:33–66); Esther M. Jackson, "LeRoi Jones (Imamu Amiri Baraka): Form and the Progression of Consciousness" (*CLAJ* 17:33–56); Richard Lederer, "The Language of Leroi Jones' *The Slave*" (*SBL* 4,i:14–16); C. Lynn Munro, "LeRoi Jones: A Man in Transition" (*CLAJ* 17:57–78).

Black Images in the American Theatre (Brooklyn, Pageant Poseidon) by Leonard C. Archer presents an historical review of Black Americans on stage, screen, radio, and television. *Black World's* Annual Theatre Issue (22,vi) is another valuable source. The 1973 issue contains an interview with Lonne Elder III, reports of Black Theatre in cities across the country, and a play by Don Evans,

Sugar Mouth Sam Don't Dance No More. A report on the New Black Theatre–Shelley Steele's "'White Port and Lemon Juice': Notes on Ritual in the New Black Theatre" (*BlackW* 22,viii:4–13,78–84)–discusses those established patterns which have meaning for the individual audience. An explanation of the purpose of ritual drama appears in an essay by Carlton W. Molette III, "Afro-American Ritual Drama" (*BlackW* 22,vi:4–12).

c. A Final Comment. Each year the number of essays on the subject of American drama grows until evaluators of necessity must become more and more selective. The number of plays written and produced each year in America also grows. In "The New Play in America, 1972" (*Players* 48:160–72) Donald Fowle reports 1138 premieres of American plays, a rise of 12 percent over the previous year. Growth in quantity is, of course, healthy, but it is the quality which must be more and more carefully assessed.

Indiana University

17. Folklore

John T. Flanagan

Previous reviews of the year's work in folklore have been comprehensive enough to include material folklore or folk life. But the enormous amount of research now being done in this area plus the obvious desirability of limiting this survey to verbal aspects of folklore have made it necessary to eliminate such coverage. Those who accept William Bascom's definition of folklore as verbal art, a contention discussed below, may well agree with this decision. Others will hopefully find a bibliography of material on folk life elsewhere.

Research in folklore continues to proliferate, even to the extent of an emphasis on the history of folkloristics. Joseph C. Hickerson's "A Tentative Beginning Toward a Bibliography on the History of American Folkloristics and the American Folklore Society" (*JFI* 10:109–11) lists 39 items relating to the development of folklore studies and courses in the United States between 1895 and 1971. John Horden and James B. Misenheimer, Jr., contributed almost a hundred items dealing with myth, legend, and folklore to the *Annual Bibliography of English Language and Literature for 1971* (London, Modern Humanities Research Association, 46:107–11), a substantial number of which are American. James H. Penrod and Warren I. Titus compiled a selective list of some 40 items relating to folklore in the *AQ* (25:274–76). Harold C. Conklin published his *Folk Classification: A Topically Arranged Bibliography of Contemporary and Background References Through 1971* (New Haven, Yale Dept. of Anthropology [1972]) an extensive list of some 5,000 entries but with only marginal appeal to the folklorist. Volume XI of *AFS*, edited by Richard E. Buehler and a corps of assistants, contains 1,098 items, garnered often from obscure or esoteric publications. The coverage is somewhat unsystematic, and since the arrangement is alphabetical by the periodicals cited the prospective user must invariably begin with the index of authors and titles.

Several volumes demand notice although they have only limited utility for the folklorist. David E. Pownall edited *Articles on Twentieth Century Literature: An Annotated Bibliography, 1954–1970* (New York, Kraus-Thomson). The folklore material here is widely scattered. Norma O. Ireland's *Index to Fairy Tales, 1949–1972, Including Folklore, Legends and Myths in Collections* (Westwood, Mass., Faxon) is a helpful finding list. Elsie B. Ziegler's *Folklore: An Annotated Bibliography and Index to Single Editions* (Westwood, Mass., Faxon) is apparently intended for secondary schools and aimed at readers who want bland popularizations of original folktales. Many of the most famous Grimm tales are not even mentioned.

Three compilations of material preserved in archives could well prove useful. Judith Tierney edited *A Description of the George Korson Folklore Archives* (Wilkes-Barre, Pa., King's College Press), an inventory of material about Pennsylvania coal mining donated to King's College by the indefatigable collector of mining lore and subsequently added to by his widow. Alice N. Loranth in "The European Ethnic Folklore Resources of the White Collection" (*JOFS* n.s. [1972]1:25–37) describes the John G. White collection in the Cleveland Public Library now numbering some 36,000 volumes. Florence Ireland's "The Northeast Archives of Folklore and Oral History" takes up an entire issue of *NEF* (13:3–85) and depicts the collection initiated and continued by Edward D. Ives. Tape recordings, transcripts, and manuscripts are itemized.

An index to one of the most important folklore publications also appeared in 1973. James T. Bratcher's *Analytical Index to Publications of the Texas Folklore Society* (Dallas, So. Methodist Univ. Press). This 322-page volume includes brief synopses of some 2,000 tales (some of them indeed factual and historical) and an extensive index given over to personal and place names, diseases, songs, proverbs, ethnic material, all found in the annual volumes of the Texas Folklore Society. The editor's work is meticulous.

Doug Rutherford contributed an unusual item to the *Seattle Folklore Society Journal* (5,ii:14–24): "A Partially Annotated Bibliography and Discography of the Bluegrass Music of Bill Monroe and his Blue Grass Boys, and Lester Flatt and Earl Scruggs and the Foggy Mountain Boys." He comments on various magazine articles and also identifies the instruments and musicians for commercial recordings.

The *1971 MLA International Bibliography*, edited by Harrison T.

Meserole with many assistants, includes about 1,940 folklore items arranged under such topical headings as Prose Narratives, Folk Poetry, Folk Customs, Beliefs and Symbolism, and Material Culture. Subdivisions are further arranged geographically and alphabetically by author. The coverage is catholic if not exhaustive and the range of periodicals from which items are taken is impressive. Unfortunately since the 1971 list appeared only in 1973 much of the material is hardly current. There are no annotations.

Once again Merle E. Simmons's "Folklore Bibliography for 1972" (*SFQ* 37:153–313) is the most useful single compilation available to students of American folklore. The current list preserves the basic ten-part division of the material included. Within each section the arrangement is alphabetical by author, there is an extensive list of contributors and biographical articles, and the annotation is careful and often full. The extensive corpus of Spanish and Latin-American material reveals the editor's Hispanic bias but one can only be grateful for such a thorough examination of current material. Subsequent issues of this indispensable bibliography will appear in the *JFI*.

i. History and Theory

Folklorists are perennially concerned about the definition of the term folklore and the need to justify in scientific language the discipline with which they are concerned. Several articles confirm their uneasiness about these matters.

In 1965 William Bascom delivered an address entitled "Folklore, Verbal Art, and Culture" to the American Folklore Society at Denver, which was not published until eight years later (*JAF* 86:374–81). Bascom defined folklore from the viewpoint of the traditional anthropologist as verbal art (thus including myth, legend, proverb, riddle, tale, texts of ballads and songs) but did not intend his definition to cover material folk traditions. His definition has been challenged and also supported. Bascom continues to believe it is valid. In another article, "Folklore and the Africanist" (*JAF* 86:253–59) Bascom returns to his anthropological conception of folklore, argues with some of his critics, and contends that the motif and tale type numbers so religiously applied by some folklorists are not in themselves sacrosanct and might even be futile if they reveal nothing more about the texts themselves.

Richard M. Dorson in "Is Folklore a Discipline?" (*Folklore* 84: 177–205) analyzes the history of folklore scholarship for an English audience and emphasizes that folklore needs a power basis and intellectual leadership to flourish. Research institutes, museums, folklore societies, and above all universities which grant degrees and encourage scholarship are essential; but there must also be dedicated and able scholars like the 19th-century Englishmen whom Dorson termed the great team of folklorists. He uses his experiences at Indiana University to support his logical but combative essay. Dan Ben-Amos in "A History of Folklore Studies—Why Do We Need It?" (*JFI* 10:113–24) touches on some of the same ground but alludes to the low status of folklore among other disciplines and comments that middle and upper class people who devote themselves to their social inferiors might be guilty of intellectual slumming. Ben-Amos believes that folklore today is a craft, not a science; it lacks theories and ideas. A possible answer to Ben-Amos is provided by Kenneth Laine Ketner in "The Role of Hypotheses in Folkloristics" (*JAF* 86:114–30); he suggests that the true folklore scholar must begin with a hypothesis to be confirmed or refuted before he collects any data at all. Ketner questions the value of conventional archives and then launches yet another definition: "Folkloristics is the scientific study of certain universally distributed kinds or modes of human interaction processes." The application of social science technical jargon to folklore in this article is not always successful.

Two articles by D. K. Wilgus deal primarily with folksongs and their analysis. In "The Future of American Folksong Scholarship" (*SFQ* 37:315–29) Wilgus combines a review of bibliographical material with a plea for closer study of the text, the tune, the singer, the performance, and the cultural milieu. He then uses as an example the ballad about the death of an automobile racer at Daytona Beach in 1928. Clever detective work has established this ballad to be the creation of Rev. Andrew Jenkins but probably its role in oral tradition is due to its rerecording by Vernon Dalhart. In " 'The Text is the Thing' " (*JAF* 86:241–52) Wilgus discusses two aspects of folksong scholarship, the text and the thing; he then reiterates his argument that the student must consider language and form as well as texture and context. His example this time is "The Little Grave in Georgia" recorded in 1927. The song not only has similarities to the better known ballad "Little Mary Phagan" but owes something to an Irish tradition going back to County Meath and County Cavan. Commercial recordings, Wilgus contends, can be considered valid field texts for folksong study.

Patrick Mullen in another theoretical article, "Modern Legend and Rumor Theory" (*JFI* [1972]9:95–109), attempts to distinguish between legend and rumor. Both have plausibility and spring from reality and both depend on a carefully established setting. Mullen's distinction is rather nebulous. Two articles by Kay Cothran in *KFQ* develop obvious points. "Participation in Tradition" (18:7–13) offers the title concept as superior to having folklore or being folk. "Agon, Ecology, and Folkloristics in Context" (18:159–79) again raises the question of folklore as a discipline and insists that young folklorists must either produce more specialists or teach people of all sorts the importance and value of folklore. But they apparently cannot do both.

W. F. H. Nicolaisen in "Folklore and Geography: Towards An Atlas of American Folk Culture" (*NYFQ* 29:3–20) advances a tenable argument in support of the recently initiated American Folklore Atlas. He points out that folklore items often have a strong connection with locality, that climate, temperature, and site often affect tradition. Hence folk culture maps can be a valuable guide for study. W. K. McNeil in "The Eastern Kentucky Mountaineer: An External and Internal View of History" (*MSF* 1:35–53) contends that historians must know the external facts about an area but that these are not always sufficient. The average citizen's views about bootlegging, farming, entertainment, education, and industrial practices are important too. An historian like John Gunther might misrepresent eastern Kentucky mountaineers but a writer like John Fox, Jr., surely sentimentalized his material. McNeil uses interviews, mining ballads, murder tales to provide a more reliable picture of life in the Kentucky mountain area.

In "Unintentional Substitution in Folklore Transmission: A Devolutionary Instance" (*NYFQ* 29:242–53) William M. Clements explains how he used a ghost story in the classroom to prove that repeated reproduction and serial reproduction of a narrative often result in obvious inconsistencies.

An interesting panel discussion at Indiana University dealt with the problems of folklore archivists in making their material available. Ellen J. Stekert chaired the panel, a number of professional folklore archivists contributed, and the results appear in *FForum* (6:197–210).

The June–August number of *JFI* deals with the contributions of various distinguished folklorists to the field. Brief biographical data are supplied, titles are mentioned, and some estimate of the importance of the work is given. Regna Darnell in "American Anthropology and the Development of Folklore Scholarship, 1890–1920" (10:23–39) pays particular attention to Franz Boas. Esther K. Birdsall in "Some Notes on the Role of George Lyman Kittredge in American Folklore Studies" (10:57–66) observes that Kittredge's influence on folklorists was out of proportion to the actual folklore work he published. Actually he was best known professionally as a Shakespearian. R. Gerald Alvey in "Phillips Barry and Anglo-American Folksong Scholarship" (10:67–95) calls attention to Barry's versatility, private resources, and dedication to the Folk-Song Society of the Northeast; his best work appeared in its bulletin. Michael J. Bell in "William Wells Newell and the Foundation of American Folklore Scholarship" (10:7–21) stresses Newell's early editorship of the *JAF* and his interests in folklore theory and collecting. Timothy H. H. Thoresen in "Folkloristics in A. L. Kroeber's Early Theory of Culture" (10:41–55) synopsizes some of the California anthropologist's early folklore articles and gives an exposition of his later theories.

An interesting article by Wayne Viitanen, "Folklore and Fakelore of an Earthquake" (*KFR* 19:99–111), deals with the famous New Madrid earthquake of 1811–12. Careful reading of newspaper accounts and travellers' diaries suggests that some genuine folklore is associated with the catastrophe: weather disturbances, high temperature, singular animal behavior, even odd displays of religiosity. But some of the most familiar tales, such as the formation of Reelfoot Lake, are linked with sentimental Indian stories and phony aboriginal dialogue. Here two kinds of lore are inextricably mixed.

Several articles deal with folklore and the teaching profession. William R. Ferris in "American Folklore" (*YAM* 36:10–17) has some thoughtful things to say about the subject in general and in addition comments on courses he himself taught at Yale. Field work and films reenforced library work and stimulated student interest. The August issue of the *JOFS* (n.s. 2:1–42) deals with teaching folklore in Ohio schools. Different viewpoints are expressed since Kathy Rensch teaches in an elementary school, Angus Gillespie in a private school, and Bruce V. Roach in a state-supported junior college. Gillespie's article points out that children in better secondary schools seem unreceptive to folklore since they are unsympathetic to labor unionists, hippies, and beatniks, and even the fellow teachers are somewhat supercilious.

ii. Ballads

Interest in ballads continues whether they be English and Scottish songs with a New World history or songs with an American provenience. Critical discussion ranges from theory and structure to the genesis of individual native ballads.

Eleanor R. Long in "Ballad Singing, Ballad Makers, and Ballad Etiology" (*WF* 32:225–36) deals with the similarity or even identity of various ballads and suggests that a careful study of narrator-types might shed light on a basic problem. She offers four categories of folk artists whom she labels perseverating, confabulating, rationalizing, and integrative. The distinctions she draws seem valid, but the article often adds jargon to a rather muddy field.

The language of the ballads is the subject of two thoughtful essays. W. F. H. Nicolaisen in "Place-Names in Traditional Ballads" (*Folklore* 84:299–312) observes that specific place names appear in ballads because of historical events, because singers wish to confirm authenticity or impart remote atmosphere, or because the balladist substitutes actual names for names he fails to recognize. Nicolaisen finds place names used as structural devices, in incremental repetition, and in refrains. In "A Reconsideration of the Commonplace Phrase and Commonplace Theme in the Child Ballads" (*SFQ* 37:385–408) Kenneth A. Thigpen, Jr., calls attention to the role of commonplaces in familiar stories and cites as evidence the ballads collected by William Motherwell in 1825 from four ladies in a Scotch hamlet. Thigpen contends that the clichés he discusses seem personal rather than communal and may well reflect terms peculiar to their community. Other commonplaces such as a request for news or angry words are obviously more general.

J. Kieran Kealy in "The Americanization of Horn" (*SFQ* 37:355–84) discusses the well known "Hind Horn," Child 17, which has over a dozen American variants. He comments that all versions seem to agree on four points: the anonymity of the hero, the imprecise reasons for his departure, the gift of a love token, and a final recognition or reconciliation scene. In "Scott's 'Jock of Hazeldean': the Recreation of a Traditional Ballad" (*JAF* 86:152–60) Charles G. Zug, III, studies the composition of "Jock of Hazeldean" which was admittedly rewritten by Sir Walter Scott about 1816. Scott may well have remembered "Katherine Janfarie" and "Lochinvar" but more importantly he revealed his own temperament, experience, and literary preferences in thus treating traditional materials. Incidentally Scott reduced the length of the original song in his final version.

Several brief articles deal with individual ballads. Alton C. Morris in " 'The Rolling Stone': the Way of a Song" (*SFQ* 37:331–54) traces the history of a ballad dating back to a 1695 dialogue by Henry Purcell. The framework of the narrative was shifted to the American West from London and the transformed work appeared in an American popular song album published in 1802. Subsequent texts were retrieved by H. M. Belden and Vance Randolph. The moral of the old ditty is clear enough: a rolling stone gathers no moss. In " 'The Last Longhorn': a Poetic Denouement of an Era" (*SFQ* 37:115–22) Lawrence Clayton shows how a ballad collected by John A. Lomax in 1916 describes specific aspects of the cattle trade. Two other cowboy songs are the subject of investigation by Austin E. Fife. In " 'The Trail to Mexico' " (*MSF* 1:85–102) Fife made an exhaustive study of one of the most popular western ballads, which began as a parody of an old nautical song and is probably most familiar in the synthetic text of John A. Lomax. Fife examined 118 texts from books, periodicals, sheet music, commercial recordings, and unpublished manuscripts, but he found no single text that could claim authority or even completeness. In "The Strawberry Roan and His Progeny" (*JEMFQ* [1972]8:149–65) Fife prints some dozen variants of Curley Fletcher's classic western ballad about a bronco that proved to be more than a match for its riders; the texts include sequels, imitations, and parodies, plus one version in Pennsylvania Dutch. Fife provides no music and little comment but an extensive bibliography of printed versions and phonograph records.

Lynwod Montell in " 'My Mother Slew Me; My Father Ate Me' " (*KFR* 19:42–44) gives a version of the traditional story from a Negro in Monroe County, Kentucky. A local Mississippi ballad is used by John O. Park in " 'The Kosciusko Bootlegger's Gripe': A Ballad as History and Argumentation" (*MSF* 1:27–32) to show how a well known song can preserve regional history. Park observes that although the song was probably the work of a Negro bootlegger it is neither a protest piece nor a specifically racial work. W. Amos Abrams in "Pure Coincidence—If Not, Why Not?" (*NCarFJ* 21:177–80) describes his luck in finding a text of "Sweet Sally," an American version of Child #295, "The Brown Girl." Professor Abrams is also the author of "Della Adams Bostic: Sweet Singer of Old Songs" (*NCarFJ* 21:132–46), an account of Mrs. Gordon L. Bostic of Mooresboro, N.C., who provided an old family text of ballads which included versions of "The House Carpenter," "Lord Lovel," and "Sweet Sally." Some of this material subsequently appeared in the *Frank C. Brown Collection of North Carolina Folklore.*

A single American ballad is the subject of Anne B. Cohen's study, *Poor Pearl, Poor Girl* (Austin and London, Univ. of Texas Press). On February 1, 1896, the headless corpse of Pearl Bryan was found near Fort Thomas, Kentucky. Shortly afterward a ballad was composed about the murder and had wide distribution. Cohen analyzes some 135 texts of the ballad, derived from field work or ballad archives, and distinguishes six basic types of the song. Both contents and language reveal signs of formulaic composition: set verbal sequences, conventionalized characters, scenes, and even plot. This elaborate study of the Pearl Bryan ballad concentrates on the formulaic elements.

iii. Folk Song

Specialists in folk song continue to collect and evaluate but show an increasing interest in studying the singers themselves, their training and their milieu. Thus Herschel Gower in "Wanted: the Singer's Autobiography and Critical Reflections" (*TFSB* 39:1–7) pleads for information beyond mere vital statistics. Collectors of folk songs, in his opinion, would do well to investigate the social and economic level of the singers. Thus we know too little about Mrs. Margaret Hogg, who once sang for Walter Scott; in contrast, John and Alan Lomax provided helpful information about both Leadbelly and Jelly Roll Morton. In a somewhat more general article, "Folk Song and Culture: Charles Seeger and Alan Lomax" (*NYFQ* 29:206–17), William R. Ferris gives a resumé of comments on folk song made by Seeger and especially by Lomax. Various styles of singing are described:

solo, choral, singing in unison. Ferris approves Lomax's contention that singing style represents geographical, economic, and social conditions, an ethnographic approach which is important in evaluating folk music.

Individual singers in various parts of the country have attracted attention. Thus Inez Cardozo-Freeman in "Arnulfo Castillo, Mexican Folk Poet in Ohio" (*JOFS* [1972], n.s., 1:2–28) describes a *bracero* from Guanajuato, Mexico, who came to Ohio and continues to write and sing *corridos* there. In his songs he celebrates his birthplace and ancestry but also chooses such a theme as the assassination of John F. Kennedy. Timothy Lloyd in "Sam Bowles; the Traditional Country Musician in Rural and Urban Contexts" (*JOFS* [1972], n.s., 1:37–49) studies a Negro folk musician from Kentucky, now resident in Ohio, who lived in an Appalachian rather than a black environment and learned to sing and play by imitation of mountain groups. At first merely a local performer, Bowles has become a familiar figure on college campuses and concert stages in the greater Washington area. Two brothers from West Virginia are the subject of James J. McDonald's "Principal Influences on the Music of the Lilly Brothers of Clear Creek, West Virginia" (*JAF* 86:331–44). Mitchell and Everett Lilly grew up and still reside in a small community near Beckley in Raleigh County. After singing in local schools and churches, they moved on to radio, did some recording, and for a number of years performed at a Boston resort dedicated to hillbilly music. Largely self-taught, they shaped their music after hearing the programs of the Monroe brothers, the Blue Sky Boys, and the Carter family. The Lilly brothers belong to the mountain style string-band tradition which now survives as bluegrass. Appendices to McDonald's article describe their instruments and list their songs. A Tennessee singer is described by Charles K. Wolfe in "Jack Jackson: Portrait of An Early Country Singer" (*JEMFQ* 9:139–45). Jackson early performed for the Nashville radio and made records; he gave up professional singing in 1934. Wolfe describes him as both a guitarist and a vocalist and provides a discography.

In " 'Miller Boy,' One of the First and Last of the Play-Party Games" (*NCarFJ* 21:171–76) John Q. Anderson gives the music and text of a popular singing game that was familiar in Wheeler County, Oklahoma, in the 1930's. Extensive notes suggest other variants of this piece.

John M. Hellmann, Jr., finds that the influence of American blues music has infiltrated abroad and has affected the singing style of the Rolling Stones. In "'I'm A Monkey': the Influence of the Black American Blues Argot on the Rolling Stones" (*JAF* 86:367–73) Hellman observes that the young British middle class group was attracted to the blues songs of American Negroes because of the heavy rhythms, the frank and coarse language, and the revolt against alienation and repression. The Rolling Stones adopted the vivid and almost uniformly sexual imagery of the blues singers and freely employed obscenities familiar to an ethnic audience. But they used the new argot in highly sophisticated ways.

In a 1972 magazine article, "Selections from the Hell-Bound Train" (*MSF* 1:55–68), Glenn Ohrlin described briefly a forthcoming book and sampled some of his songs and headnotes. *The Hell-Bound Train* (Urbana, Univ. of Ill. Press), with a biographical preface by Archie Green and a lengthy biblio-discography by Harlan Daniel, gives a hundred songs from Ohrlin's repertory with accounts of their genesis and his introduction to them. Ohrlin, a rancher-singer now living in Arkansas, sings ballads, laments, cowboy ditties, most of which reflect range life and are thick with allusions to cattle and rodeos. The songs included are often Ohrlin's own variants of familiar titles ("Dakota Land" or "The Strawberry Roan," for example). The headnotes often give extensive data about authors and titles, such as McClintock's "Hallelujah, I'm a Bum" or O'Malley's "Cowboy's Life." Ohrlin's book, handsomely produced, is a valuable addition to collections of American folk songs.

Charles W. Joyner in "The Repertory of Nancy Jones As a Mirror of Culture in Scotland County" (*NCarFJ* 21:89–97) discusses the songs of a southern North Carolina woman. A performer on both piano and autoharp, she derived her material from other singers as well as from radio and hymnbooks. Joyner describes her singing style and points out that her preference runs to short, lyrical, and often didactic pieces, few of which have been collected. Nancy Jones's temperament seems to conflict with her songs; despite her own liveliness and sunny disposition she often sings of the hardships and frustrations which are indigenous to southern folk culture. Joyner also edited in 1971 a collection not previously noted here: *Folk Song in South Carolina* (Columbia, Univ. of S.C. Press). The book includes a thoughtful essay on the importance of folk music and three short chapters on ballads, religious songs, and seculars. Joyner remarks that South Carolina's musical heritage is a fusion of British and African traditions. Most of his examples come from printed sources.

The relationship between popular music and folk song is explored by Anne and Norm Cohen in "Tune Evolution As An Indicator of Traditional Musical Norms" (*JAF* 86:37–47). They consider fourteen popular songs for which the original sheet music is available but which remain current in folk tradition and then examine the changes that have occurred in tunes and language. The discussion is illuminating but not always easy to follow for a reader untrained in music.

One interesting reprint should be cited here. In 1855 John Gordon McCurry of Hart County, Georgia, published *The Social Harp*, some 222 songs, many of which McCurry himself composed. These are chiefly white spirituals. Daniel W. Patterson and John F. Gorst edited a facsimile reprinting of the collection (Athens, Univ. of Ga. Press), to which Patterson contributed an excellent introduction which sheds considerable light on 19th-century rural singing practices.

iv. Folk Tales and Legends

The prose tale represents an area which folklorists continue to mine profitably. Although all sections of the country yield material, rural regions still seem richer than urban ones.

In "Mountain Legend in Eastern Kentucky" (*KFR* 19:58–78) Diana Bianchi gives autobiographical data derived from Hobe Grilles, a retired coal miner. Grilles was a gossip and storyteller of local repute. William Hugh Jansen provides folklore motifs and numbers, needlessly heavy annotation for somewhat thin material. Jack Welsh in "The Bell Witch" (*KFR* 19:112–16) reviews a famous witch tale of 19th-century Tennessee and tries to supply additional evidence. But he adds nothing of significance and indeed finds that most of the authorities involved show surprising agreement. In "The Devil's Goin' To Get You" (*NCarFJ* 21:189–94) Bruce Bastin records four devil tales from Orange County, North Carolina, derived from rural Negroes. Familiar themes found here are the appearance of the Devil, the wild hunt, and the suspicions of blues musicians held by many blacks.

A farmer who moved from Tennessee to Kentucky in 1905 and later returned to his original state is the subject of Kenneth W. Clarke's monograph, *Uncle Bud Long: the Birth of a Kentucky Folk Legend* (Lexington, Univ. Press of Ky.). Long lived a marginal existence and became famous for his thrift and primitive way of life. Many stories circulated about him. Clarke writes gracefully about Long's milieu in Warren County and describes effectively the topography and the people. But the tales are summarized and the reader misses Long's own language.

Two articles deal with an Indiana folk figure, Benjamin Kuhn of Hartsville and Anderson, a semiliterate farmer who told many tales about himself and his father-in-law. Donald Allport Bird and James R. Dow in "Benjamin Kuhn: Life and Narratives of a Hoosier Farmer" (*IF* [1972]5:143–263) provide "an in-depth analysis of a narrator's relationship to his material" which depends on both interviews and documents. Their study presents biographical data, narratives, and evaluative commentary. Kuhn's repertory includes memorats, local legends, animal tales, beliefs, and religious anecdotes (even visions), as well as much agricultural data. In another article with a clumsy title, "'Ah,' He Says, 'I've Heard of You.' 'Oh,' I Said, 'No Doubt!' Status Seeking Through Story Telling" (*NYFQ* 29:83–96), Dow identifies Kuhn as clever and quick-witted, a cross between an American Gothic and a Tyl Eulenspiegel. Kuhn's tales are again placed in the previously mentioned categories.

In "Drugged and Seduced: A Contemporary Legend" (*NYFQ* 29:131–58), Andrea Greenberg gives the basic story of a freshman coed who is molested at a fraternity party after being rendered unconscious by drugs or drink. This is a migratory legend which has been reported throughout the country but usually without specific proof. Most freshman and sophomore girls seem to have heard the tale. Another equally familiar story is "The Surpriser Surprised: A Modern Legend" (*FForum* 6:1–24), which William Hugh Jansen first heard about 1935 and which today exists in countless variants although it is apparently not recorded in the usual type indexes. Jansen comments that the crux of the story is the final meeting of a young couple, after a long engagement, in various stages of disarray, only to be surprised by the friends or family. The girl is so shocked that she becomes insane.

In "Folklore from the *Frontier Index*, Wyoming Territory, 1867–68" (*KF* 18:15–44) James R. Dow reports miscellaneous folklore from a Wyoming territorial newspaper, which was published along the right of way of the Union Pacific Railroad. The collection includes humorous items, ethnic slurs, and several tall tales.

Elaine K. Miller collected some 160 narratives from Mexicans resident in California in 1966–67, most of them dealing with life in the Mexican states of Jalisco, Puebla, Durango, and Zacatecas. She published 82 of these items in *Mexican Folk Narrative from the Los Angeles Area* (Austin and London, Univ. of Texas Press) and used two basic categories: legendary narratives (religious, witchcraft, buried treasure) and traditional tales (animal, magic, romantic stories). The material is given in Spanish with brief English summaries.

The entire April issue of the recently renamed *NCarFJ* consists of student-collected folklore from North Carolina and includes articles on hog-killing, jump rope rhymes, children's games, and superstitions. Glenda Poston's "Tall Tales from Perquimans County" (21: 40–47) is a medley of hunting yarns and fabulous adventures. The tales are told in the local vernacular which is well suited to the material.

The staff-written *Foxfire 2* book edited by Eliot Wigginton (Garden City, Anchor Press/Doubleday) resembles its highly successful predecessor, the *Foxfire* book of 1972. It is again a miscellany which focuses more on folk life than on verbal folklore. But one chapter, "Boogers, Witches, and Haints" (pp. 324–61), collects ghost stories, superstitions, and "booger tales" from a variety of informants. Student interviewers found that many of these narratives were told largely for entertainment, while the "ghosts" reported in the tales were often illusions, atmospheric phenomena, or even tricks. The tales, however, confirm that Appalachian experiences survive in oral tradition. Certainly one should never look back at a ghost, while a rooster crowing at midnight is a sure omen of misfortune.

Wayland D. Hand's article "Legends in Place-Name Study" (*IN* 4:37–50) is a fascinating account of the role that legends play in geographical nomenclature. Many place names derive from individual persons, history, and topographical features, but often legends are also involved. Hand chooses examples from the western states to show how specific events figure in place names and how, on the other hand, certain names belie their origin.

One of the most attractive volumes of 1973, although the curious illustrations and eccentric shifts of type somehow suggest the Christmas coffee table as its eventual destination, is Richard M. Dorson's *America In Legend: Folklore from the Colonial Period to the Present* (New York, Pantheon Books). Dorson groups his material around three symbolic or typical figures: Religious Man, Democratic Man, and Economic Man. To this discussion he appends a section on the contemporary drug culture. Folk heroes like Davy Crockett, Mike Fink, Sam Patch, and Yankee Jonathan get substantial attention, whereas the Negro and the Indian are ignored. Roughly one-third of the book is devoted to occupational lore dealing with miners, cowboys, lumberjacks, oil drillers, and railroaders. Dorson provides helpful historical backgrounds and careful documentation for his material.

v. Folk Speech

Students of folk speech cast a wide net to pursue their interests. In "*Cracker* and *Hoosier*" (*Names* 21:161–67) Raven I. McDavid, Jr., and Virginia McDavid discuss two widely known terms which are often used pejoratively. Both names still connote the loutish or the comic but have become somewhat more neutral in the course of time. Audrey R. Duckert in "'Place Nicknames" (*Names* 21:153–60) suggests various kinds of geographical nicknames which can be affectionate, derogatory, or simply convenient. Among the more common origins are shortenings by syncope or initials, deprecation, promotional coinages, compass points, and ethnic or economic labels. Familiar examples include Frisco, Philly, Sin Village or Fun City, North End, Gold Coast, and Shanty Town. In "The Place-Names of Chester Township, Wabash County, Indiana" (*IN* 4:4–30) Rowan K. Daggett examines the place names of a small part of one middlewestern state and explains the origins of the names of schools and buildings as well as geographical nomenclature. Curiously enough only one name, Wabash itself, seems to be genuinely Indian. In another study of Hoosier toponymy, "Southern Indiana Place-Name Legends as Reflections of Folk History" (*IN* 4:51–61), Dennis R.

Preston contends that the place names of the state reveal more folk history than most people realize. He groups his material in six categories (the Indian past, the pioneer past, the violent past, the Civil War past, the French past, and the religious past) and offers examples to confirm his argument that place names preserve a popular image of a region's history. An extensive study of a more remote region is James W. Phillips's directory entitled *Alaska-Yukon Place Names* (Seattle and London, Univ. of Wash. Press), which gives origins and a pronunciation guide.

Miscellaneous information about Italian-American speech and dialect is contained in Lydia Q. Pietripaoli's "The Italians Came Up Watertown Way" (*NYFQ* 29:58–79), otherwise a mishmash of local history, social customs, and superstitions. The conventional speech of children, notably as it is revealed in games, is the subject of "Tradition and Change in American Playground Language" (*JAF* 86:131–41) by Mary Knapp and Herbert Knapp. The authors discovered a surprising uniformity throughout the country although their rather slim evidence, gained chiefly from Monroe County, Indiana, and the Canal Zone, reenforced by data from questionnaires, casts some doubt on the validity of their conclusions. They found that "Kings X," "Cooties," and "Jinks" were widely familiar terms on the playgrounds.

Occupational speech is always interesting if rather special. Robert J. Schwendinger in "The Language of the Sea: Relationships Between the Language of Herman Melville and Sea Shanties of the 19th Century" (*SFQ* 37:53–73) reexamines a familiar subject but claims that the nautical diction of Melville's novels is closely parallel to the actual language of sea chanteys. Extensive quotation of songs like "Blow the Man Down" and "The Banks of Newfoundland" proves the point. Steven A. Schulman collected some 27 commonly used lumberjack expressions in "Logging Terms from the Upper Cumberland River" (*TFSB* 39:35–36). In a rather unusual study entitled "Folklore and Women: A Social Interactional Analysis of the Folklore of a Texas Madam" (*JAF* 86:211–24) Robbie Davis Johnson recounts his experience in interviewing a Miss Hilda, proprietress of a famous brothel in a central Texas town. Although he says little of the superstitions and beliefs of the inmates, he contends that Miss Hilda controls both the girls and their patrons by verbal means. Thus her folklore, her anecdotes, seem deliberately contrived to enforce her rules, while both the girls and the patrons often seem unaware that they are being manipulated. In sharp contrast John H. McDowell's "Performance and the Folkloric Text: A Rhetorical Approach to 'The Christ of the Bible'" (*FForum* 6:139–48) examines the folk sermon of a Negro preacher and its impact on the congregation. A typical sermon would include talk, chanting, and singing, all designed to secure the preacher's union with his audience. Response from the congregation is essential. McDowell believes that in analyzing a folk sermon one must carefully study pronominal usage as well as proverbs, taunts, and insults.

Two articles deal with somewhat more abstract aspects of folk speech. James E. Spears in "The Metaphor in American Folk Speech" (*NYFQ* 29:50–57) concentrates on familiar comparisons in folk speech ("as cool as a cucumber," "as yellow as gold," "as dumb as an ox") and concludes that such expressions are not only surprisingly common but often humorous and poetic. George W. Boswell for an article entitled "The Operation of Popular Etymology in Folksong Diction" (*TFSB* 39:37–58) utilized a Middle Tennessee collection of some 859 ballads and songs for the purpose of studying their syntax and pronunciation. Boswell points out that the grammar of these songs is generally faulty. Tenses and agreement are frequently careless and folk etymology accounts for curious confusions or substitutions (*walls* for *wars*, *sextant* for *sexton*). Neologisms and archaisms are also common.

An historical article by Jared Harper and Charles Hudson, "Irish Traveler Cant in its Social Setting" (*SFQ* 37:101–14), examines the argot of itinerant Irish workers (not gypsies) who emigrated to the United States during the potato famine and made their living as tinkers, umbrella menders, and mule and horse traders, especially in the South. Commonly termed Cant, their speech derives from a Gaelic dialect or patois called Shelta, which apparently originated from a desire to mystify onlookers or to communicate secretly within the group. This cant still exists but it is declining and is generally known only by males.

vi. Folk Heroes

New American folk heroes are constantly being promoted, while the credentials of older figures are submitted to reexamination. Folk heroes are indifferently desperadoes, tricksters, or military leaders. Thus Rosemary M. Laughlin in "Attention, American Folklore: Doc Craft Comes Marching In" (*SAF* 1:220–27) makes a case for a dining car waiter. The hero of a short story by James Alan McPherson ("A Solo Song: for Doc"), Doc Craft has obvious analogues with such occupational heroes as John Henry, Casey Jones, and Joe Magarac. He is unable to ascend very high on the economic ladder but within limits he succeeds by wit and skill.

In "Thomas Sharp Spencer, Man of Legend" (*THQ* [1972]31: 240–55) Walter T. Durham presents a historical sketch of a frontiersman and Indian fighter who died in Tennessee in 1794. His biography is somewhat shadowy but his enormous strength, great size, and backwoods derringdo have survived in legend. Larry D. Ball in "Black Ketchum; the Birth of a Folk Hero" (*MSF* 1:19–25) deals with Thomas E. Ketchum, a New Mexico outlaw during the 1896–99 period known as Black Jack. After acting as train robber and paid assassin Ketchum was executed by decapitation in 1901. Ball attributes to him not only the usual personal attractiveness and occasional generosity but a moral code which forbade tobacco and liquor. Ketchum's exploits did not survive in oral tradition but the lore about him apparently continues to grow.

A somewhat ironic tone characterizes Bruce A. Rosenberg's careful article, "Custer: the Legend of the Martyred Hero in America" (*JFI* [1972]9:110–32). Rosenberg traces accurately the facts of Custer's life and considers all viewpoints about his death. To him Custer is probably the most popular hero of the American people, the chief figure in a legend influenced neither by tradition nor by history but both spontaneous and natural. An interesting complement is provided by Harrison Lane in "Brush, Palette and the Battle of the Little Big Horn" (*Montana* 23:66–80), in which the author reproduces some sixteen paintings of the Custer massacre, all of them of course without documentary support and all showing the imagination of the artist. Custer is variously portrayed as on foot or on horseback, in dress uniform or in western costume, brandishing sabre or pistol. In all cases he is romanticized or heroized. Lane concludes that the Custer legend is present and indestructible.

The hero as trickster or confidence man is the point of Phyllis R. Klotman's "An Examination of the Black Confidence Man in Two Black Novels: *The Man Who Cried I Am* and *dem*" (*AL* 44:596–

611). After a brief survey of the confidence man in American fiction and plot summaries Klotman shows that William Melvin Kelley's *dem* sketches a black folklore trickster against a Harlem background. Kelley's hero finds black support for his trickery aimed at the whites. But John A. Williams's *The Man Who Cried I Am* introduces a black espionage agent who dupes or betrays his own group. It is suggested that one of Williams's characters, Mississippi-born and a disaffected Communist, may be based on Richard Wright.

In *Knave, Fool, and Genius* (Chapel Hill, Univ. of N.C. Press) Susan Kuhlmann presents a study of confidence men in 19th-century American fiction. Her examples are arranged to some extent geographically: the East and Southeast have Davy Crockett, Simon Suggs, and Ned Brace; the West Jack Hamlin, Col. Sellers, and the Duke and the King; the other world Westervelt and Joseph Dylks; the Old World two figures from Henry James not normally labeled in this way, Serena Merle and Kate Croy. Finally, almost alone, there is Melville's Confidence Man. To accommodate all these examples Kuhlmann wrenches her definition of confidence man a bit, but her discussion is interesting and often acute.

vii. Cures, Beliefs, and Superstitions

Folk medicine continues to fascinate collectors of folklore, while students of popular beliefs and superstitions persistently till very fertile ground.

In "Herbs of the Southern Highlands and Their Medicinal Uses" (*KFR* 19:36–41) Gladys Mullins lists 22 plants common to Pike County, Kentucky, and gives brief accounts of their therapeutic value. She includes catnip, poke, sassafras, jimpson weed, and balm of gilead. Carole E. Hill in "Black Healing Practices in the Rural South" (*JPC* 6:849–53) studies Negro healing practices and reports on interviews with both herb doctors and their clients. Potions, oils, and Biblical charms are employed while the power to heal is transmitted from one sex to another. Bleeding, toothaches, fungus diseases, and warts are all ailments which healers can apparently cure. Similar evidence appears in Paul K. Vestal, Jr.'s "Herb Workers in Scotland and Robeson Counties" (*NCarFJ* 21:166–70), a survey of rural therapy in North Carolina. Whiskey is a prime ingredient of many of the herb concoctions, but Vestal lists some 25 panaceas with instructions how to use them. In Addie Suggs Hilliard's "A Lick o' Lemon" (*KFR* 19:79–86) the history and folklore of the lemon are reviewed. Folk traditions, individual informants, and even old cookbooks served as sources. Medicinally the lemon has proved useful in a variety of ways: to soothe if not always to cure colds, coughs, even diphtheria. The lemon is traditionally a panacea for rheumatism, and nine swallows of lemon juice are a sovereign remedy for hiccoughs.

Clarence Meyer's volume *American Folk Medicine* (New York, Crowell) is a more extensive survey of folk remedies, though the prefatory notice warns readers that it is not intended in any way as an endorsement for the therapy it describes. After an interesting essay on early American practitioners of the art of healing Meyer devotes some 250 pages to common conditions treated in American folk practice and ends with a bibliography and both the common and botanical names of useful plants. Some of the remedies listed are signed but mostly they are anonymous.

A special form of folk medicine is the use of drugs or plants to inhibit or increase sexual potency. In "Aphrodisiacs, Charms, and Philtres" (*WF* 32:153–63) Eleanor R. Long reports on the potions and charms utilized over the centuries to stimulate sexuality. Aphrodisiacs such as mandrake or ginseng were commonly employed as well as hippomanes (thorn apple) and cantharides. Potions often included human hair or excretions. Although Long used the UCLA archive of folklore she cites little American material. In "Saltpeter: A Folkloric Adjustment" (*WF* 32:164–79) George W. Rice and David F. Jacobs consider the common belief that saltpetre is put into the food of soldiers, students, or summer campers to serve as an anaphrodisiac. They state categorically that saltpetre or potassium nitrate has no value whatsoever as an antisexual agent, and they try to account for widely spread rumors about it by examining certain social groups. A very small number of informants casts some doubt on their conclusions. Medical beliefs of a different kind are the subject of Lois A. Monteiro's "Nursing-Lore" (*NYFQ* 29:97–110). The author, a registered nurse herself, considers a hospital as an urban folk community and treats death beliefs, death euphemisms, and tales about operations or hospital care which are common to both nurses and physicians.

Beliefs of another kind stimulated various articles. Hugh Agee in "Ghost Lore from Sevier County, Tennessee" (*TFSB* 39:8–9) reports accounts of mysterious footsteps and lights as well as spectral cars from one informant. Louis Winkler and Carol Winkler in "A Reappraisal of the Vampire" (*NYFQ* 29:194–205) survey world beliefs about the vampire and contend that he is a far more formidable figure than either demon or witch. Brom Stokes's *Dracula* is of course cited. In "My Travels With Medicine Man John Lame Deer" (*Smithsonian* 4, ii:30–37) Richard Erdoes describes a Sioux shaman and his beliefs. According to the Indian, a medicine man can be a healer, a conjurer, or even a sacred clown (*heyoka*). Erdoes offers vivid details about the Sioux sun dance. A voodoo performer named Mother D. from Tucson is the subject of Loudell F. Snow's " 'I Was Born Just Exactly With the Gift' " (*JAF* 86:272–81). Mother D. includes Negroes, Indians, and Mexican-Americans among her clientele and claims some competence in curing arthritis, tumors, and asthma; but it appears that her chief service is the alleviation of mental or nervous troubles. To do this she simply exercises her "gift." Her office has both religious and voodooistic trappings, and probably she understands poverty and fear better than medically trained professionals who are generally bluff and unsympathetic. She attributes her success to a legacy from her grandmother.

The April, 1973, issue of *JOFS* (n.s., 2:2–37) includes three articles by Beverly Hawkins, Linda Miller, and Hope Smith, all students in a folklore class at Ohio State University and all reporting on some aspect of black urban culture. Included are proverbs, tales, taunts, the dozens, and Negro behavior at a weekend party. Guests at the party are labeled as Stuck-ups, Skilled Dancers, Wall Flowers, Pretty Folks, and Mr. and Miss Popularity.

viii. Literary Use of Folklore

Folklorists who continue to scrutinize American poetry and fiction often detect folklore in unusual places. Both major and minor writers have employed folklore more frequently for various purposes than the ordinary reader realizes.

Two articles reveal the use of proverbs by poets who in other ways are worlds apart. Robert D. Arner in "Proverbs in Edward Taylor's *Gods Determinations*" (*SFQ* 37:1–13) contends that the Puritan poet introduced imps, devils, and witchcraft into his verse as well as a surprising number of proverbs, some of them of clearly domestic origin. Some examples cited are "out of the frying pan into the fire," "nick of time," "soon ripe, soon rot," and "a beggar on horseback can ride well." Wolfgang Mieder in "Proverbs in Carl Sandburg's Poem *The People, Yes*" (*SFQ* 37:15–36) finds some 322 different proverbs cited in Sandburg's work, proof of the poet's desire to use American folk speech without pretension or literary quality. Mieder lists the proverbs alphabetically by key words and includes references to four standard dictionaries of proverbs. "Man" and "money" are two of the more common key words.

No one will be surprised to learn that Washington Irving, Herman Melville, and William Faulkner used folklore in their work, but occasionally writers choose a new angle of approach. In "Washington Irving and New England Witchlore" (*NYFQ* 29:304–13) James W. Clark, Jr., reexamines "The Devil and Tom Walker" and "The Legend of Sleepy Hollow" as well as the *Knickerbocker History of New York* to pinpoint Irving's use of what he terms witchlore. Clark contends that Irving's main source was Cotton Mather's *Magnalia.* Horace Beck in "Melville As a Folklife Recorder in *Moby-Dick*" (*KF* 18:75–88) compares Melville's language and materials with his own recent experiences among whalemen operating out of the island of Bequia in the West Indies in 1971. Beck concludes that whaling practices in *Moby-Dick* conform to current practices in the Caribbean and that Melville's great novel is both history and documentation. In "Folklore References in Faulkner's *The Hamlet* and *As I Lay Dying*" (*JOFS* [1972] n.s., 1:1–10) Robert C. Ferguson touches on folklore motifs, carefully given index numbers, in two of Faulkner's novels and points out that the writer employed such material for characterization, situation, and thematic development. Ferguson seems unaware that other critics have preceded him.

The trickster figure continues to attract attention. Wendy Martin in "The Rogue and the Rational Man: Hugh Henry Brackenridge's Study of a Con Man in *Modern Chivalry*" (*EAL* 8:179–92) feels that Teague O'Regan is both trickster and con man; indeed *Modern Chivalry* is probably the first American novel in which such a figure appears. Teague strives to be a clergyman, philosopher, politician, and scholar but his disguises are promptly penetrated. In portraying Teague's protean roles Brackenridge probably intended to show the ease with which a con man in a democracy can take advantage of public confidence. William H. Wiggins, Jr., in "The Trickster as Literary Hero: Cecil Brown's *The Life and Loves of Mr. Jiveass Nigger*" (*NYFQ* 29:269–86), examines a much later novel. The hero of Brown's book, George Washington, is a black trickster figure who in the critic's words becomes a racial metaphor for the Afro-American community. The setting of this novel is largely Copenhagen from which the hero eventually departs to return to "Charlie" country.

Two essays in George E. Kent's *Blackness and the Adventure of Western Culture* (Chicago, Third World Press [1972]) deal with folklore in the work of Negro authors. "Langston Hughes and Afro-American Folk and Cultural Tradition" (pp. 53–75) studies Hughes's use of folklore in verse, drama, and fiction and provides copious examples. Specifically Hughes employed blues, folk aphorisms, tall tales, slave narratives, fragments of spirituals, and folk sermons. But Kent feels that Hughes was uneven and probably lacked the big vision essential for major work. In "Ralph Ellison and Afro-American Folk and Cultural Tradition" (pp. 152–63) Kent deals chiefly with *The Invisible Man*, in which "the whole gamut of Ellison's descriptions of the functions of folklore find their place." Kent emphasizes that Ellison never uses folklore for its own sake but more than most writers grapples "with the power, the cryptic messages, and the complexity of folk tradition."

Ellison's novel also figures in Philip E. Sullivan's "Buh Rabbit: Going Through the Changes" (*SBL* 4:28–32), which contends that Harris's original briar patch figure has undergone some surprising transformations but still exists (Old Gray Goose, Stagolee, Mr. Jiveass Nigger, and Sweet Sweetback). Buh Rabbit today lives in the ghetto, the prison, perhaps in exile; he is still curious, gregarious, self-aware, and tough. In other words, the resisting black has retained his personality.

Lawrence Clayton's "Hamlin Garland's Negative Use of Folk Elements" (*FForum* 6:107–08) admits that Garland used folklore in many of his books and in different forms—folk speech, songs, and games. But he insists that Garland's people were depleted rather than fulfilled by living close to the earth and eventually chose to leave the farms. Hence Garland introduced folklore as a means of condemning rustic ways of life. Richard F. Peterson in "The Grail Legend and Steinbeck's 'The Great Mountains'" (*StQ* 6:9–15) speculates about the meaning of two important symbols in a Steinbeck tale and wrenches his argument to find analogies with the Grail legend. In "Mrs. Almira Todd, Herbalist-Conjurer" (*CLQ* [1972] 9:617–31) Sylvia Gray Noyes describes Sarah Orne Jewett's character in *Country of the Pointed Firs* and points out her familiarity with such herbs as camomile, mullein, elecampane, pennyroyal, and bloodroot. Mrs. Todd was seldom paid and did not compete with doctors, but many country people found her herbal therapy efficacious. In "Carson McCullers' Literary Ballad" (*GaR* 27:329–39) Joseph R. Millichap claims that the short novel, *Ballad of the Sad Cafe* (1943) is virtually a literary ballad and can be best interpreted in that way. Despite the absence of song and folk art the McCullers work exists in the traditional world of the ballad. The argument is tenable, if strained. In "Robert Penn Warren: The Ballad of Billie Potts" (*Fabula* 14:71–90) Adam John Bisanz examines a true literary ballad and finds it an example of tradition-based material. The article, written in German, bears the subtitle: "Ein amerikanisches 'Memorabile' auf dem Hintergrund europäischer Überlieferung." Ruth Moose in a slight note called "Superstition in Doris Betts's New Novel" (*NCarFJ* 21:61–62) finds that *The River to Pickle Beach* (1972) is rich in folklore and superstition.

Several more general items need citation here. Kay L. Cothran in "Magazine Travel Accounts of Piney Woods Folklife" (*TFSB* 39:80–86) examines late 19th-century magazine articles dealing with backwoods life in Georgia and the Carolinas. She admits that their writers often provided ample data about diet, clothing, speech, and manners but deplores the air of superiority constantly shown. Moreover, climate and temperature often caused the crackers to appear more lazy, dirty, and shiftless than they actually were. Merrill Maguire Skaggs in *The Folk of Southern Fiction* (Athens, Univ. of Ga. Press [1972]) studies the plain people or the yeomanry of southern local color stories. Skaggs is especially concerned with the social milieu of her characters but she pays little attention to the common material of folklore and of course excludes the Negro. She finds that the most important social institutions were the courtroom and the church. Charles J. Klein and Jack Bernet in "From String Stories to Satellites: Portrayal of the Native Alaskan in Literature and Folklore" (*BRMMLA* 27:167–73) present a cursory survey of the Alaskan Eskimos and Indians as they appear in fiction by such authors as Jack London, James Oliver Curwood, Rex Beach, and Robert W. Service. The article also gives data about contemporary native Alaskans and includes an interesting account of the character Raven, ubiquitous in Alaskan tales. Raven, both creator and destroyer, is at times vicious or virtuous; he survives wherever native folklore is preserved.

The most thorough study of an American writer's use of folklore published during 1973 is certainly Ronald L. Baker's *Folklore in the Writings of Rowland E. Robinson* (Bowling Green, Ohio, Bowling Green Univ. Popular Press). Robinson, a minor regionalist who made Vermont his bailiwick, used his knowledge of rural speech and folkways to present interesting characterizations and readable tales. His creation of Uncle Lisha and his shop where the cobbler's friends, Yankees and French Canadians alike, congregate is memorable. Baker establishes Robinson's use of local dialect, superstitions, tall tales, and folk beliefs to reflect a milieu in a way which a writer inattentive to local traditions would have found impossible. The book, originally an Indiana University dissertation in folklore, is admirable.

ix. Minor Forms of Folklore

Minor forms of folklore such as riddles and jokes stimulated some attention, although no definitive work devoted to them appeared during 1973.

Waln K. Brown in "Cognitive Ambiguity and the 'Pretended Obscene Riddle'" (*KF* 18:89–101) deals with riddles as a means of transmitting obscene or sexual allusions. The pretended riddle is both clever and designedly ambiguous. Indeed it often depends on a pun for its comic effect. For example, "What's indecent? When it's long, hard, and deep, then it's indecent." In "An Ethnic Joke from the Mid-South" (*MSF* 1:103–05) Kelly H. Sellers tells the story of a half-literate Negro who applies for a job from his white employer. Given a mathematical test which is obviously beyond his capabilities he luckily answers a basic question correctly and presumably is hired. In "Some Migratory Anecdotes in American Folk Humor" (*MQ* [1972]25:447–57) John Q. Anderson shows how four basic stories flourished in various parts of the country and were narrated by such authors as James Hall, Joseph Baldwin, John Bernard, Joseph M. Field, and J. Frank Dobie. The four types include the hat-in-the-mud tale, the tale about limited sleeping quarters and undressing in public, the swallowing an oyster raw tale, and the tale about the unlimited hospitality inflicted by planters on their infrequent guests.

In contrast Dan Ben-Amos ventures on a more ambitious study in his article "The 'Myth' of Jewish Humor" (*WF* 32:112–31). Ben-Amos cites the familiar contention of Sigmund Freud in 1905 that Jewish jokes are unique in being directed against themselves, in other words self-criticism. Later writers (even Philip Roth in *Portnoy's Complaint*) have repeated this theme of self-deprecation. But Ben-Amos disputes the validity of the theory; to him, "National humor is an idea; self-ridicule is a behavioral pattern." Moreover, actual joke texts recently collected do not confirm the argument. There is no social identification between the ridiculer and the ridiculed and, even more to the point, the narrator is not the butt of the story. Particularly pertinent are the familiar clever rabbi stories in which the narrator is actually a trickster and certainly not an ethnic or tribal victim. Ben-Amos's argument is extremely plausible although it could benefit by additional evidence.

Norine Dresser in "Telephone Pranks" (*NYFQ* 29:121–30) gives examples from Los Angeles schoolchildren of impish or exasperating telephone calls which elicit admiration from the juvenile listeners. The callers, shielded by anonymity, can offer phony prizes, annoy tradespeople, or make sexual jokes (asking, for example, for an orgy-sized bed). There is obviously no fear of retaliation.

In "Little Orphan Annie and Lévi-Strauss, the Myth and the Method" (*JAF* 86:345–57) Ellen Rhoads analyzes Harold Gray's familiar comic strip, "Little Orphan Annie," using especially four isolated episodes printed in 1935–45. To her the comic strip is a form of folklore, and if in Lévi-Strauss's argument the purpose of myth is to mediate life's contradictions, then comics like "Little Orphan Annie" can serve the same purpose. The analogy seems a bit tenuous.

Alvin Schwartz collected two volumes of verbal trickery clearly intended for a juvenile audience: *A Twister of Twists, a Tangler of Tongues* (Philadelphia, Lippincott [1972]), and *Tomfoolery: Trickery and Foolery With Words* (Philadelphia, Lippincott). Both volumes, illustrated by Glen Rounds, use folklore books and journals as their chief sources.

In "Arabic Gestures" Robert A. Barakat uses evidence collected mostly in the Middle East to define and illustrate gestures (*JPC* 6:749–93). Much of this material previously appeared (*KFQ* [1969] 14:105–21). Although the gestures are most commonly found in the Arab world many of them have universal meaning. Barakat classifies them as autistic or personal, culture-induced (such as sitting, walking, eating), technical (limited to work or professional groups), and semiotic or folk (substitutes for speech and arbitrary in meaning).

x. Anthologies

A number of anthologies of folk material have appeared recently, miscellaneous compilations which vary considerably in value and which represent substantially different points of view.

North Carolina Mountain Folklore and Miscellany (Murfreesboro, N.C., Johnson [1972]) by Horton Cooper is a potpourri of riddles, rhymes, superstitions, proverbs, tales, and magic formulas, collected throughout a lifetime by an octogenarian mountaineer. Dim illustrations represent some aspects of mountain life. *A Treasury of Georgia Folklore* by Ronald G. Killian and Charles T. Waller (Atlanta, Cherokee Pub. Co. [1972]) presents material gathered from 1936–40 by workers for the Federal Writers Project. The random tales, beliefs, songs, and bits of folk wisdom are seldom identified and have little scholarly value. The editors properly call much of their data "folklore notes." Tristram P. Coffin edited *The Book of Christmas Folklore* (New York, Seabury Press), an anthology of Christmas rites, customs, and tales obviously intended for the holiday trade. There are numerous allusions to and substantial quotations from such writers as Irving, Dickens, O. Henry, Hardy, and Tennyson. Space is given to familiar Christmas ballads, Thomas Nast's sketch of Santa Claus, the "Second Shepherd's Play," Virginia O'Hanlon's *New York Sun* letter, and Rudolph the red-nosed reindeer. Coffin also edited jointly with Hennig Cohen a much more substantial volume, *Folklore from the Working Folk of America* (Garden City, Anchor Press/Doubleday). The book represents the occupational lore of the United States: cowboys, miners, lumberjacks, sheepherders, farmers, soldiers, fishermen, even professional sports heroes. Among the dozen legendary figures given special treatment are Paul Revere, Johnny Appleseed, Joe Hill, Casey Jones, Daniel Boone, and the Rev. Peter Vinegar. Material for the book was culled from professional folklore journals and various archives or personal collections. Much of it is necessarily familiar, but the collection is a useful development of a single theme.

One of the most handsome books published during the year is Horace Beck's *Folklore and the Sea* (Middletown, Conn., Wesleyan

Univ. Press), the work of a nautical *aficionado* who drew on archives, museums, and libraries besides extensive personal experience for his material. Beck presents a rich variety of marine lore: songs, superstitions, customs, history, anecdotes, and the lingo of the forecastle. But there are surprisingly few allusions to the literature of the sea (Melville or Conrad, for example), and the focus of the volume seems to be more coastal than pelagic. Nevertheless, one can read here about the Flying Dutchman, Davy Jones's locker, the Loch Ness monster, and Captain Kidd; and one can learn about tattooing, ships' names, and scrimshaw.

The *Encyclopedia of Black Folklore and Humor* which Henry D. Spalding edited (Middle Village, N.Y., Jonathan David [1972]) is more ambitious than useful. Despite its 589-page bulk and its extensive coverage, it is carelessly compiled with faulty or missing annotations and an unreliable bibliography. Capsule biographies of such important black figures as W. C. Handy, Billie Holiday, and G. W. Carver are provided but Ralph Bunche is omitted. The introduction by J. Mason Brewer, a leading Negro folklorist, stresses that the Negro is a person and not a type.

A very different kind of book and one of the most valuable compilations to appear in 1973 is Alan Dundes's *Mother Wit from the Laughing Barrel* (Englewood Cliffs, Prentice-Hall). Dundes has selected material about Negro folklore, interpretations rather than the texts themselves. White contributors include H. L. Mencken, Alan Lomax, Stanley Hyman, Richard M. Dorson, and Howard W. Odum; Negro contributors number Zora Neal Hurston, Ralph Ellison, Eldridge Cleaver, and Charles W. Chesnutt. The categories range from folk speech and belief to folk narrative, music, and humor. It seems particularly appropriate for N. N. Puckett to discuss Negro lore and for Langston Hughes to assess Negro humor. Dundes supplies headnotes and ample bibliographical references with his customary thoroughness.

xi. Obituaries

Obituaries of several prominent folklorists appeared during the year. Often they are personal tributes by colleagues or fellow workers but they usually include a valuable summary of the scholar's achievements. Fred F. Knobloch's notice of Arthur Kyle Davis, Jr. (1897–

1972), stresses Davis's work in collecting and editing ballads found in Virginia (*SFQ* 37:127–29). Richard M. Dorson's account of Edwin C. Kirkland (1902–72) emphasizes Kirkland's service as editor of the *SFQ* and his collecting of material from the subcontinent of India (*SFQ* 37:123–25). Hector H. Lee in his obituary of Archer Taylor (1890–1973) recognizes Taylor's distinguished work as a proverb specialist (*WF* 32:262–64). Another tribute to Taylor, the work of six different writers, appears in the *FForum* (6:no pagination)

A tribute of a different kind recalls the work of Mody C. Boatright, the Texas folklorist who died in 1970. Ernest B. Speck edited and Harry Ransom wrote an introduction to *Mody Boatright, Folklorist* (Austin and London, Univ. of Texas Press). The 198-page volume is an anthology of Boatright's essays published from 1927 to 1970, divided into four areas: the cowboy, the frontier, the oil industry, and folklore and the folklorist in contemporary society.

Keith S. Chambers in "The Indefatigable Elsie Clews Parsons" (*WF* 32:180–98) provides brief biographical data about Mrs. Parsons and evaluates her work as anthropologist and folklorist. From about 1916 onward her publications were folklore-centered, she served as associate editor of the *JAF* for 25 years, and she made innumerable field trips to the Caribbean, Mexico, and the American Southwest in quest of tales and legends. Chambers remarks that Mrs. Parsons was primarily a collector, not a theorist, but calls attention to her multifarious activities and to her personal and financial encouragement of contemporary folklore scholars.

University of Illinois

18. Themes, Topics, and Criticism

Michael J. Hoffman

All my predecessors have lamented that the materials relevant to this section of *ALS* are massive and intractable. They were right. To be genuinely comprehensive the reviewer would have to present a simple list of publications without commentary. The choice I have made is to be selective and personal, trusting my own insights as to the major directions taken in both literary theory and in the overall interpretations of American literature during 1973. I shall limit the field to books and exclude articles, since major theoretical statements appear primarily in volumes and not in periodicals. When an essay is sufficiently interesting it is usually reprinted or made part of a larger work, and it is at that time that its influence is felt.

I shall further confine myself to two major areas of interest: (1) Important statements about the range of American literature that go beyond the scope of any one of the *ALS* chapters. Included for treatment here will be several major anthologies of American literature that appeared during 1973. I shall examine them with an eye to both their pedagogical usefulness and how they document changing critical taste. (2) The major trends in contemporary theory. The whole enterprise of American critical theory, and thus literary scholarship generally, is undergoing its most important change since the New Criticism. Behind this change lies the interest of American critics in phenomenological criticism and Structuralism. Not only have a number of American authors adopted the methods of Georges Poulet and Roland Barthes and of the diverse schools they represent, but a great many European critics hitherto known to us only by name are now being translated. The appearance of some of these books in English is tantamount to original publication for most of us. Because these methods are still relatively novel within American universities and because many of us have until now resisted these "new" ways of looking at literature, I shall spend the first portion of this essay examining works of phenomenological and structuralist literary theory published in 1973.

i. Literary Criticism and Theory

An excellent entrée into the "new" criticism of Europe is *European Literary Theory and Practice: From Existential Phenomenology to Structuralism*, ed. Vernon W. Gras (New York, Delta), an inexpensive paperback collection of prominent essays about Phenomenology and Structuralism. The anthology is divided into two sections, one of "Theory" and the other of "Practice," each containing three to six essays using one of the two critical approaches. The slant of the essays is heavily philosophical, ranging in Phenomenology from Martin Heidegger and Jean Paul Sartre to Maurice Merleau-Ponty and Paul Ricoeur. The best of the philosophical essays is Merleau-Ponty's "What is Phenomenology?" the introduction to his well-known book *The Phenomenology of Perception*. In the essay Merleau-Ponty discusses the psychological foundations of the "phenomenological reduction." "The real has to be described," he says (p. 73), "not constructed or formed," and he goes on to talk about critical perception as an act of describing the reality inherent in a particular linguistic act or work of literature. Since perception is "lived reality," the critic's task is to "live" the reality of the created work. This "reality," however, does not lie simply in its words, for as Gras says in his excellent Introduction, language is never sufficient to encompass a situation through which a writer has lived. A writer is therefore constantly involved in decentering and recentering the language as he found it, in order somehow to imply " 'the excess of what [he has] lived over what has been said.' For a literary critic, it is mandatory that he understand this gesture by taking up the author's style and living through the excess of the author's experience over what has been said already. In this way he comes to understand the author's original project and shares in his world" (p. 7).

All the phenomenological critics here agree that the act of interpretation is more an act of empathy than one of analysis, more an exploration of the "structures" of the mind behind the work (a mind implied by and expressed in the work) than of an artifact already produced. A literary work is itself an act, the creator's expression of his own mind through the inadequate medium of language. In addition, the work expresses all of the author's life we need to know, and so even though we often have what looks superficially like intentionalist criticism, the phenomenologist does not demand evidence external to the text.

The structuralist activity—which must be distinguished from Phenomenology—looks beyond the individual author to a set of Platonic structures that exist beyond individual artists and works and are common to all experience. The specific literary work expresses these basic structures, which range from the linguistic to the mythic. The essays in this section of Gras's volume are much less philosophical than those of the Phenomenology section, because Structuralism derives primarily from linguistics and anthropology. Claude Lévi-Strauss's "The Science of the Concrete" and Roland Barthes's "The Structuralist Activity" are particularly helpful to the uninitiated reader, although the best demonstration of the structuralist activity comes later in the anthology in Lévi-Strauss's "The Structural Study of Myth," which includes his famous discussion of the Oedipus myth. This is a brilliant piece of work, fairly accessible on a careful reading. What the skeptical American reader misses, however, in all of these essays, is an interest in the textures and tones of language.

Gras's anthology contains, in addition, pieces by Poulet, Gaston Bachelard, Ludwig Binswanger, and the English anthropologist Edmund Leach. Almost all the essays are worth reading more than once. They have been chosen with care, and Gras's introduction, while sometimes murky, is on the whole very helpful.

A more representative and comprehensive collection (800 pages worth) is Gregory Poletta's *Issues in Contemporary Literary Criticism* (Boston, Little, Brown), which represents the field of criticism since 1955 (a few essays appearing here were written earlier, but not many). It is the best book of its kind I know of, although for courses in Modern Literary Theory one would want to supplement it with earlier material from about 1920 on. Poletta includes a number of the same writers as Gras, such as Barthes, Poulet, Lévi-Strauss, and Bachelard. But he ranges throughout American criticism as well, including those critics influenced by the "new" criticism, such as

Hillis Miller and Geoffrey Hartman, as well as others. Hartman's two essays, "Beyond Formalism" and "Toward Literary History" are, in fact, among the most impressive in the volume.

The book is organized not by schools of criticism, but by the following: "The Place and Performance of Criticism," "The Writer's Intention," "The Literary Performance," "The Reader's Response," and "Literature's Relation to the World." Poletta's long introductions to each section are models of clarity which define the issues and separate the various critical positions with consummate skill. The book ought to be read by anyone unfamiliar with its contents.

A number of full-length phenomenological and structuralist works of criticism were published during 1973, some in translation and some by American critics. One of the most impressive was a translation of *The Logic of Literature* (*Die Logik der Dichtung*) by Käte Hamburger (Bloomington, Indiana Univ. Press). This phenomenologically oriented treatment purports to apply to literary texts the linguistic "logic" of statement found in ordinary language. Hamburger begins with Roman Ingarden's suggestion that "an object in literature has only a purely intentional existence" (p. 19), and exists only through the agency of an intending consciousness. It is the nature of this intending consciousness that creates language systems and recreates the objects that language is made to represent. Hamburger is primarily interested in the nature of language and not in the nature of the intending consciousness, and this differentiates her immediately from a French "critic of consciousness" like Poulet. Not that she pays *no* attention to the intending consciousness, but she sees the speaker primarily in relationship to the statements he makes about "reality." Since all language is constituted by statements about reality made by various kinds of speakers, Hamburger has then to make a case for the special quality of literary language. She justifies her activity by suggesting that, "as Hegel has stated, the *continuous comparison of creative with non-creative language* is the methodological means requisite to extracting the structure of literature (as a collective phenomenon)" (p. 23). Hamburger makes nice distinctions between the various ways historical statement becomes fictional and how different kinds of intending voices create statements whose referential contents constitute their fictionality. Because the German use of the concept of fiction is broader than ours and includes all kinds of belletristic statements rather than just the storytelling aspects of narrative, her critical instrument has a useful flexibility.

The problem, however, is that she is too literal in applying the concept of the "statement-subject," or speaker. As American criticism has made us aware, the narrative voice and that of the author are rarely the same. The narrator is always a persona, and the relationship between the writer and the statement has therefore many levels. The words of the novel are always at least a statement within a statement, and in Conrad or Faulkner they are more complex than that. Certainly the case Hamburger makes for the voice of the lyric poem being the genuine voice of the author is debatable. Still this is a stimulating book, and its discussion of the various levels of fictional representation is one of the most interesting I have read.

Before I go on, I should like to mention four books I received from the Northwestern University Press too late for inclusion in this review. They are Roman Ingarden's *The Literary Work of Art* and *The Cognition of the Literary Work of Art*, Mikel Dufrenne's *The Phenomenology of Aesthetic Experience*, and Hugo Friedrich's *The Structure of Modern Poetry*, all of them appearing in Northwestern's series, *Studies in Phenomenology and Existential Philosophy*. I shall discuss them in *ALS 1974*. It is gratifying to see Roman Ingarden's works in English, and equally disappointing to hear that the Northwestern University Press is going under. I hope some other house will continue this worthy series.

American critics have been aware of phenomenological criticism for a while now, certainly since Georges Poulet taught at Johns Hopkins and enlisted Hillis Miller as his disciple. Now, however, a new generation of critics, readers of Miller as well as Poulet and Bachelard, Merleau-Ponty and Sartre, trained in the United States in the last decade, are producing works of a new kind of phenomenological criticism, less academic, certainly—even perhaps, to resurrect an old Sartrean term, *engagé*. Such a critic is John Vernon, whose first book, *The Garden and the Map: Schizophrenia in Twentieth-Century Literature and Culture* (Urbana, Univ. of Ill. Press), is one of the year's most lively and committed works of criticism. Vernon, who is also a poet, cites as his authorities such figures as Norman Brown, Merleau-Ponty, Herbert Marcuse, R. D. Laing, and Rollo May, and if these people are not your cup of tea, then you might find the book as infuriating as did a splenetic reviewer in *TLS*. For Vernon modern culture is schizophrenic, and he sees the most important 20th-century writers as attempting to go beyond this cultural disease (map culture) to search for a wholeness (the garden) that can only be called aboriginal. The basic intentionality Vernon discovers behind the work of such seemingly diverse writers as Joseph Conrad, William Burroughs, and Theodore Roethke is the movement toward a kind of Wordsworthian garden where man lives in an undissociatedly total sensibility.

Vernon inveighs apocalyptically against the structures of Western logic and rationality. Like Laing he finds madness where the rationalist finds sense, and he sees in the so-called madness of a schizophrenic like Roethke (I use the term clinically) a kind of genuine reasonableness, because in Roethke's poetry there is a mergence of body with time and space. Like Norman Brown in *Love's Body*, Vernon opposes all separations, be they mind-body, inner-outer, poet-world. This is a disturbing but plausibly argued book, committed to an apocalyptic vision but founded still in a "rational" discourse that enables it to be understood by the uncommitted.

Another work by a young scholar-critic is Cary Nelson's *The Incarnate Word: Literature as Verbal Space* (Urbana, Univ. of Ill. Press). Less overtly philosophical and as oriented toward spatial metaphors as Vernon's was to temporal, this book is also written in a poetic, visionary tone. We feel the influence of Poulet and Bachelard throughout, particularly of their concerns with basic responses to space and with the creator's consciousness: "I view verbal form as an author's projection of a self-protective and self-generative space that transcends or escapes historical time. The writer's need to create is gradually transferred to the reader, both sharing a desire to enact the work. Thus an author's 'vision' extends for us as a text that generates a self-sufficient world when we read it. . . . Each essay is a perceptual dialectic in which author and critic move toward simultaneity. Verbal space is the locus of an interaction between the reader and the text" (p. 4). Nelson's interesting readings range from an opening chapter on the medieval poem *Pearl* to one on "Radical Space in Burroughs." Each chapter is headed by a photograph, painting, or photo-montage intended to symbolize the space implied in the reading that follows. The final chapter, "Fields: the body as a text," is written in spaced-apart, short paragraphs full of cryptic statements or quotations that move alogically toward a point of view, in much the same manner as Brown's *Love's Body.* Clearly Vernon and Nelson share culture heroes as well as perspectives. Clearly also, they each grant the act of criticism the autonomy we have heretofore allowed only to the poet.

David Halliburton's *Edgar Allan Poe: A Phenomenological View* (Princeton, N.J., Princeton Univ. Press) claims to be "the first general interpretation of an American author from a phenomenological point of view" (p. 21), and perhaps it is. I can think only of Paul Brodtkorb's book on Melville, which is a study of just *Moby-Dick.* Halliburton's work is disappointing, however, because it has too many obligatory, thesis-proving readings and because it needed more ruthless editing. At half the length it would have twice the substance. The Introduction is an adequate summary of phenomenological method, but little more. Halliburton's chief critical device is to identify with the narrative consciousness in Poe's poems and tales. This could have had interesting results, given the strange nature of most of Poe's narrators, but Halliburton does not maintain his point of view very well. As a result, he either stresses obvious kinds of structures, such as the grammatical and punctuational patterns of the poems, or he gives conventional readings that seem not to depend on his critical instrument. His many overly long quotations show a lack of critical digestion. We still await the first good full-length phenomenological study of an American author.

The structuralist movement was represented in 1973 by a number of works. A recent collection of papers from the English Institute, *Approaches to Poetics*, is an excellent introduction to some of the structuralist inquiry currently being conducted. All the essays but two are by American contributors, the exceptions being those by Frank Kermode and Tzvetan Todorov—the latter a leading French critic. There is an essay on Roman Jakobson, by Victor Erlich, one by Hugh Davidson on Roland Barthes, and another by Frank Kermode in which he uses Barthes and Structuralism to set a context for recent fiction, as exemplified by Thomas Pynchon's *The Crying of Lot 49* and Anthony Burgess's *MF*. An essay by Richard Ohmann presents a theory of literature based on John Austin's theory of speech acts, but like most attempts to use linguistics to illuminate literary texts it is unsatisfying. The best piece in the book is by Stanley Fish, its modish title, "What Is Stylistics and Why Are They Saying Such

Terrible Things About It?" notwithstanding. Fish scathingly reviews the inadequacies for literary criticism of most linguistic theory; he suggests that we must first reconceive the reader as an active, meaning-giving participant in the literary activity. The final essay by Tzvetan Todorov asks for a science of literary criticism, but he asks it in terms that seem old hat, particularly since Frye's *Anatomy of Criticism*, another structuralist work, made the same demand with more grace and erudition almost two decades ago.

Still, Todorov is anything but a negligible critic, a fact made clear by his excellent book, *The Fantastic: A Structural Approach to a Literary Genre*, which has just had a timely translation and American publication (Cleveland, Case Western Reserve Univ. Press). Todorov's book is one of the best generic studies I have read. His methodology is thoroughly structuralist: "First, we must be aware that it [the literary text] manifests properties that it shares with all literary texts, or with texts belonging to one of the sub-groups of literature (which we call, precisely, genres). . . . Second, we must understand that a text is not only the product of a pre-existing combinatorial system . . . ; it is also a transformation of that system" (p. 3). In defining the fantastic as a genre Todorov uses primarily structural, nonsemantic qualities that have to do with activities taking place within the narrative, such as the interactions of characters, the voice of the narrator, and the various kinds of plot. In locating individual members of the genre, however, Todorov makes recourse to semantic categories—to the meanings found in the work, which he calls its "themes." He devotes the latter half of the book to describing these themes, using a kind of binary system (the computerized, structuralist version of the dialectic) to set up the pattern of contrasts within which works define themselves. Such categories raise as many problems as they solve. While generic description is certainly an important part of literary discourse—indispensable in fact—we would be foolish not to see the ways in which it is highly problematic.

Another interesting, though problematic work is Eric S. Rabkin's *Narrative Suspense*, which has the catchy subtitle "*When Slim Turned Sideways . . .*" (Ann Arbor, Univ. of Mich. Press). Rabkin uses a kind of phenomenological reduction to isolate his field of discourse and then a structuralist analysis to define it. For Rabkin the crucial experience for the reader of any narrative is the question "And then?" He suggests that we all share a subliminal awareness of such categories as metaphor and irony, context, fictional "reality," and various kinds of suspense. He also suggests that there are four narrative levels (one immediately wonders why not three or five?). Various specific passages, according to Rabkin, operate either procontextually, anti-contextually or neutrally. He then sets up a grid with the contextual categories listed across the top, and down the side he uses a series of categories of reader response that he has carefully developed (I would list them, but they make little sense outside the context of the book). Grids using binary oppositions are quite common to structuralist thinking. They do isolate categories and make clear the generic distinctions we tend to accept either as conventions or in-tuitions. Why, however, Rabkin's categories have more validity than any others and why they cannot be increased to infinity by the use of subtle distinctions remains a question the structuralists have not satisfactorily answered.

It is difficult, however, to be ambivalent about Harold Bloom's *The Anxiety of Influence*. I can think of no recent work that will arouse more admiration or cause greater consternation. One cannot locate Bloom in any school; he is genuinely eclectic. For him criti-cism is not just an exercise of the intellect; it is a consecrated act of the same importance that his culture-heroes Blake and Yeats attach to poetry. Bloom even begins and ends his book with a poem.

His theory states that the history of poetry is characterized by the influence earlier poets have on later ones, particularly those whom the present poet sees as his immediate ancestors, his fathers. The re-lationship to the "father" is characterized by anxiety, and because of this anxiety the present poet inevitably misunderstands the earlier one, a misunderstanding Bloom calls "misprision." "The history of fruitful poetic influence," he says, "which is to say the main tradition of Western poetry since the Renaissance, is a history of anxiety and self-saving caricature, of distortion, of perverse, wilful revisionism without which modern poetry as such could not exist" (p. 30). Bloom sees all history as the progress from generation to generation, from one revolt against the father to another. He defines six different types of "misprision" (giving them Greek names) and develops examples of each one of these types in a separate chapter.

How one would possibly transmit such a theory in the classroom I could not begin to say, but in its outlines the theory makes good sense. It is when we get down to specific poetic relationships that the difficulties obviously begin. And the problem still remains as to what constitutes influence in the first place. No matter how sophisticated the critic is in applying Bloom's categories, even if he stays wholly within the texts of related poems, he has ultimately to be involved in mind-reading or reductionism. One thinks uncomfortably of John Livingston Lowes; but Bloom is too sophisticated to take that road to Xanadu. Even so, there are many more influences on the poet than other poets, many traditions of which he is a part. Bloom may have a father fixation himself, but that does not mean that all his poets have as strong a one as he. Poets also have mothers, wives, children, and dogs. They read newspapers and get upset about politics and religion. Both Frye and Bloom are wrong to suggest that the notion of a "literary tradition" is anything more than a limited critical construct. But, though serious, my disagreement with Bloom is genuinely respectful. One cannot simply dismiss his ideas.

Other books by individual critics include *The Uncollected Essays and Reviews of Yvor Winters* (Chicago, Swallow). The pieces collected here go back to 1922 and include a lot of Winters's apprentice work from the 1920s and 1930s. One long essay with an enormous title does prefigure what Winters was soon to write: "The Extension and Reintegration of the Human Spirit Through the Poetry Mainly French and American Since Poe and Baudelaire." But, frankly, this collection is of interest primarily to readers who already have a commitment to Winters's work. It is still a lot better to read the books collected in *In Defense of Reason.* The Introduction by editor Francis Murphy is too concerned with apologizing for Winters's notorious quirkiness. Why bother? Winters needs no apologies; what he does need is a careful critical reassessment, but this introduction does not do the job.

Another collection, by a critic quite unlike Winters, is Arthur Moore's *Contestable Concepts of Literary Theory* (Baton Rouge, La. State Univ. Press). This collection of essays covers a great many literary topics, all of them concerned in some way with theoretical problems, including, in particular, "Formalist Criticism and Literary Form," "The Case for Poetic Obscurity," and "The Theoretical Liabilities of Literary Criticism." Moore has many qualities we associate with good criticism; he is skeptical, urbane, and erudite; he is ironical, thoroughly rational, and sensibly relativistic. What I finally miss here is an overall theoretical framework, a critical instrument I can take away to use in my own work. While the system-builder is constantly prey to dogmatism and inflexibility, he does have a rationalizing principle other than his own sensibility and intelligence. I am left by a critic like Moore with a sense that I have simply read a number of interesting essays by a clever man.

The remaining works of criticism are collections of essays organized around a central theme or subject, three of which are *Festschriften.* One of them, compiled in honor of W. K. Wimsatt, is *Literary Theory and Structure*, an excellent collection containing pieces by a number of important American critics, many of whom were Wimsatt's students at Yale, and many others his colleagues. I cannot review all the interesting essays here, even some by such distinguished critics as René Wellek, Hugh Kenner, Northrop Frye, and Cleanth Brooks. The book is divided into two sections, one on "theory" and the other on "structure," by which is meant more practical criticism, but the most interesting pieces appear in the theoretical section. There are, for example, essays by Frederick Pottle explaining Ferdinand de Saussure's categories of the synchronic and the diachronic, Marie Boroff discussing the expressive power of poetic language, Thomas McFarland using a theory of the various kinds of poetic content to oppose the formalist tenets that form, content, and language are indivisible. Alvin Kernan's "Aggression and Satire: Art Considered as a Form of Biological Adaptation" uses Kenneth Burke, Norman Holland, and Morse Peckham to show the ways human beings use art to adapt to cultural and biological demands, and Martin Price develops a generic theory of "The Fictional Contract." The most interesting essay in the second section is "The Native Strain: American Orphism," in which Harold Bloom follows the American Orphic tradition from Emerson through Whitman and Emily Dickinson to Wallace Stevens and up to the present in John Ashberry. This piece is cut from the same cloth as *The Anxiety of Influence.*

Another *Festschrift*, this one for I. A. Richards, is less successful. Edited by Reuben Brower, Helen Vendler, and John Hollander, *I. A. Richards: Essays in His Honor* (New York, Oxford Univ. Press) is primarily a retrospective look at Richards and his considerable influence on literary studies. Unfortunately, most of the essays are too valedictory in tone. Some of the few serious pieces are rewarding, however. Cleanth Brooks is informative on "I. A. Richards and the

Concept of Tension," and Helen Vendler has useful insights about Richards and Roman Jakobson and their respective theories of language. There is a short, suggestive essay by Kathleen Coburn that compares Richards to Coleridge. The most intellectually distinguished piece is Geoffrey Hartman's attempt to define Richards's theory of the relation of poetry and psychology. In an essay entitled "The Dream of Communication," Hartman uses the term "psychoesthetics" to describe Richards's characteristic critical activity.

The third *Festschrift*, compiled in honor of Henry Sams, is *Directions in Literary Criticism: Contemporary Approaches to Literature* (University Park, Penn. State Univ. Press). Edited by Stanley Weintraub and Philip Young, all 24 essays are in either literary criticism or literary theory. The trouble is that there does not seem to be any rationale behind the collection. Everyone here did his own thing, and the result is a motley, with some good pieces, some trivial, but little satisfaction to be gotten from the whole. Frank Brady's "Fact and Factuality in Literature" is worth looking at, and a piece by Kenneth Burke, "An Eye-Poem for the Ear," complete with glosses written by himself, is fun. But by and large, reading this book is a struggle, primarily because of its extreme heterogeneity.

Many figures associated with the Wimsatt *Festschrift* appear in *Romanticism: Vistas, Instances, Continuities* (Ithaca, N.Y., Cornell Univ. Press), edited by David Thorburn and Geoffrey Hartman. This is a competently put-together collection whose cumulative effect is disappointing. When compared with *Romanticism and Consciousness*, edited a few years ago by Harold Bloom, this one seems thin. The only distinguished essay here was, ironically, written by Bloom about Emerson. The trouble with this collection is that it is too genial, too agreeable. Romanticism has been one of the most controversial problems in recent literary history. An essay by Morse Peckham or Earl Wasserman, both of whom would have disapproved of almost everything here, would have made for a more intellectually rewarding experience than this dull concensus.

Two more collections deserve mention. Both are volumes of *The Yearbook of Comparative Criticism*, edited annually by Joseph Strekla, which brings together critical essays from all over the world written around a central topic. The two volumes published in 1973 are *The Personality of the Critic* and *Literary Criticism and Sociology*

(University Park, Penn. State Univ. Press). The former is more successful. One essay by John Fizer is an excellent introduction to the criticism of Roman Ingarden whose works, as I have mentioned, are now being translated into English. Two essays written from polar critical positions also make for lively reading. "Absolutism and Judgment," by Paul Ramsey, restates the Yvor Winters argument against "relativism" with the same gusto, ill temper, and logic-chopping rigidity. One wonders why Ramsey is so emotional about the matter until one realizes that the stakes are not literary but theological. Of course, I betray my own prejudices when I say that I admire greatly Murray Krieger's essay, "The Critic as Person and Persona," in which he makes the case for the ultimate inability of the critical act ever to be anything *but* a personal encounter between the critic and the text. Criticism, for Krieger, arises from the tension that develops between the system-building persona and the deeper self of the critic that experiences the world personally.

Strelka's second anthology is less interesting, perhaps because of the less developed state of literary sociology as a discipline. *Literary Criticism and Sociology* shows how badly the field needs to establish a good theoretical base. Too much of the writing is full of special pleading, which betrays an uneasiness about an unestablished field. Even the essays by Harry Levin and René Wellek seem simply occasional. With the possible exception of pieces by Maxwell Goldberg and Hans Rudnick, there is nothing close to the quality of Q. D. Leavis's old study of the reading public or of the work being done in England by Malcolm Bradbury, Raymond Williams, and Matthew Hoggart, or, for that matter, in this country by Leo Lowenthal.

As an addendum to this section I should like to discuss two works by prominent representatives of English studies, both concerned with the role of the "humanities" in education. The books clearly arose out of the recent turmoil that forced us to redefine the "relevance" of our enterprise. Both volumes are interesting, humane, and finally tepid, revealing some basic limitations in our thought about the "humanities."

O. B. Hardison, Jr., director of the Folger Shakespeare Library, has sounded a clarion in the title of his book, *Toward Freedom and Dignity: The Humanities and the Idea of Humanity* (Baltimore, Johns Hopkins Univ. Press), with its obvious allusion to behaviorist B. F.

Skinner's *Beyond Freedom and Dignity*. It is easy for an English professor to nod in assent to almost everything Hardison says, but that is just the problem: it is too easy. Hardison never defines what he means by the humanities. He just assumes we all know, and he says little about the social sciences, either to define them or to differentiate them from what goes on in the humanities. Hardison suggests that "vocational education . . . trains servants of a system—any system—not responsible citizens" (p. 93). While this is true, it is wrong to think that a nonvocational education in the "humanities" has the inside track on moral responsibility. The perpetrators of Watergate were predominantly lawyers, not computer programmers. And what about Martin Heidegger and the Nazis? Hardison suggests that Humanism is the best preparation for the future leaders of our technological society. He therefore calls for a complete educational reform on humanistic lines. Not that he necessarily is wrong. It is just that we have heard all this before.

One might have expected a more radical treatment of the same subject from Eugene Goodheart, both from his work on D. H. Lawrence and the title of his book, *Culture and the Radical Conscience* (Boston, Harvard Univ. Press), but the results are disappointing. Goodheart is not an avowed humanist-elitist but rather a left-liberal social critic. He rejects the intellectual vapidity of the "counter culture" that grew up in the last decade, and while I am more sympathetic than he to Marcuse, Brown and Laing, I am very happy to see someone with the right credentials debunking Theodore Roszak, whose recent book *Where the Wasteland Ends* strikes me as radical kitsch. Goodheart's university would be less committed than Hardison's to an Oxbridge humanism, but it would not be so structurally different. What Goodheart wants is a committed, enlightened, "disinterestedness" in humanistic studies. He carefully avoids words like "detachment" and "objectivity" and cites Michael Polanyi's *Personal Knowledge* as a credo.

The problem with both these books is that they are visionary and reformist without having the energies of genuine prophecy. Both authors are sincerely concerned, but they finally propose just another version of what we already have. This is hardly what anyone could call change.

ii. New Anthologies

A few new anthologies published during 1973 go beyond the editorial hackwork of many paper-wasting books to make genuine statements about the traditions in our literary study.

The most important of those collections was edited by Cleanth Brooks, R. W. B. Lewis, and Robert Penn Warren: *American Literature: The Makers and the Making* (New York, St. Martin's Press). This anthology attempts a major statement about American literary traditions, and its preface, "Letter to the Reader," is quite explicit about the methods and motivations behind the text. The editors, all of them well known, agree that literary art is a dialectic between its forms and "undefinable reality." They have included what they call "Primary" and "Secondary" kinds of literature, the former because it is undeniably "good" and the latter because it helps to explain more major achievements or to expose interesting partial failures.

The method is interesting, with both assets and virtues. What the editors do is employ more apparatus than I have ever seen in an anthology. They use long introductory essays to create a context and write what amounts to a literary history. Their essays introducing major authors are as long as the average periodical article and include biographical as well as critical assessments. Some of these essays are good enough to be anthologized in their own right, such as the ones on Emerson and Melville. Even with individual works there is a short introductory essay. What all this adds up to is a running dialogue with all the authors and their works. I have never seen an anthology so completely in the control of the editors, and these are, of course, three of our finest critics. All this is to the good. So too is the range of the selections, particularly because they represent certain traditions not normally given such important status, such as the following categories of minor writers in the 19th century: nature, political, humor, and "literary" historians (Parkman, Prescott, etc.). There is also a generous helping of folk songs and Indian oratory and poetry.

I find some of the selections less than good, however. The work from the Puritans is too conventional—no new names or fresh works. There is too little representation of the 18th-century political pamphleteers, particularly in light of the amount of 19th-century political writing included later. And there are no Loyalist writers. In the selections from Emerson there is too much excerpting. Why not have the complete texts of *Nature*, "Self-Reliance," "Thoreau," and "Historical Notes of Life and Letters in New England"? None of them are that long. Better to have left out one or two than to have cut them all up.

The second volume begins with Emily Dickinson and goes from there to give excellent representation to the late century intellectual movements. The collection is good on modern poetry, as one might expect, and has a fine selection of Afro-American writers. But the selections from Henry James do not give an adequate sampling of all his stages. There is a long selection from Gertrude Stein, the longest in any anthology so far, and a lot of essayistic discussion of her work. But the bibliography at the end does not include either the present writer's book (1966), Allegra Stewart's (1967), or Richard Bridgman's (1970), the last the most important book ever on Stein. One wonders if the scholarship elsewhere is as careless. All these books were in print long before this collection was assembled, and so one wonders just who made up the bibliographies. A work-study student, perhaps?

Even with its faults, however, this is a stimulating and sophisticated anthology, too much the latter, I am afraid, to be useful in introductory courses. This is really a book for upper-division or graduate students. It is an attempt of a particular generation of critics to sum up their version of a tradition (with modish concessions to "nature" and "Indians" and "Blacks"). In that sense it is a very useful document. But I am afraid that it will be of most use to professors in boning up for their lectures.

Two other important collections were published around the turn of the year. Although they both bear 1974 copyrights I shall make an exception and talk about them comparatively during this volume of *ALS*, since it is rare that three major anthologies appear so closely together.

A large two-volume text called *American Literature* has been published by Macmillan, under the general editorship of George McMichael, with advisory editors, Richard P. Adams, Frederick Crews, J. C. Levenson, Leo Marx, and David E. Smith. The first volume is entitled *Colonial Through Romantic*, and the second *Realism to the Present*. This conventional anthology has a minimum of apparatus and is designed for introductory courses. The short essays on the various periods are good for beginners. A number of full-length works are included here in the first volume, such as Franklin's *Autobiography, The Scarlet Letter, Walden,* and *Song of Myself.* The volume ends with a long selection from Whitman.

Volume II begins with exactly the same selections from Whitman that conclude the first one. This is an excellent idea, for the instructor can now teach Whitman in either half of his survey course. There is a long, excellent selection from Emily Dickinson and a very good representative one from Henry James. The full-length works in this volume include *Huckleberry Finn, Daisy Miller, The Red Badge of Courage,* and *The Hairy Ape,* and the selection of recent literature is very good. This anthology has an attractive format, a minimum of footnotes, clear type, and single columns (in contrast to the double columns of Brooks, Lewis and Warren). It even has a pretty good instructor's manual. The lack of highly developed categories leaves the instructor free to organize the course in his own way.

What I find lacking, however, is a serious critical point of view. The editorial work is a bit too transparent. Certainly this is a welcome contrast to a volume that leaves the instructor no room, but one misses a consummate critical sensibility. This is a good beginning text, but not much more.

Also appearing recently was the fourth edition of Bradley, Beatty, and Long's *The American Tradition in Literature,* now published by Grosset and Dunlap but still distributed by Norton, and newly re-edited by George Perkins. Some important changes have been made here. There is more Colonial as well as more Afro-American and Indian literature. Deleted is *The Scarlet Letter* from Volume One and *Huckleberry Finn* from Volume Two. Added to the Emerson section is "Fate," from *The Conduct of Life.* Perkins has used CEAA texts wherever possible, as in Emerson's *Nature,* "The American Scholar," and the "Divinity School Address," and in Crane's *Maggie.* The beefed-up section of modern poetry is now perhaps the best of any of the three anthologies. This collection has also anticipated McMichael's solution to the problem of Whitman, and has in fact gone him one better. Whitman appears at the end of the first volume and at the beginning of the second volume, only not in the same selections. Volume One emphasizes the early poetry, including the "1855 Preface" and *Song of Myself* (although in the "deathbed" version). "When Lilacs Last in the Dooryard Bloom'd" appears in both volumes, but the second volume also has a large bulk of poetry beginning with some of the "Sea Drift" poems, as well as a selection from *Democratic Vistas* and *Specimen Days*. All in all, this use of Whitman in both volumes makes a great deal of sense, although I should have preferred the 1855 version of *Song of Myself* in Volume One.

Perkins has retained the old categories of organization, which means the usual conventional labels. The introductions have been brought up to date, but the critical attitudes are those of the *LHUS*. Still, while the critical posture here is not so sophisticated as in Brooks, Lewis, and Warren, the level of scholarship is higher, and the format is single columned and more easily readable. The footnoting is the best of the three collections. Frankly, this is still the book I would choose for a beginning survey in American literature, although I shall undoubtedly make more personal use of Brooks, Lewis and Warren.

The other anthologies are less ambitious attempts to cover smaller traditions. Theodore L. Gross has edited *The Literature of American Jews* (New York, The Free Press), which contains a short foreword by Elie Wiesel. This excellent collection is organized simply and chronologically, its first section beginning in the 19th century with writers like Isaac Mayer Wise and Emma Lazarus. The second part, "Between the Wars," contains selections by such writers as Ludwig Lewisohn, Henry Roth, Michael Gold, and Clifford Odets. The third section, "After the War—A Creative Awakening," contains selections from the great flowering of American Jewish writers, including Paul Goodman, Herbert Gold, Philip Roth, Norman Mailer, and Isaac Bashevis Singer. There are poets like Karl Shapiro, Delmore Schwartz, and Allen Ginsberg and essayists like Leslie Fiedler, Lionel Trilling, and Isaac Rosenfeld. The collection would have been enhanced further by more contemporary writers, such as Ronald Sukenick, Stanley Elkin, and Leonard Michaels, but the editor might have been hampered by a limitation on space. The book seems clearly designed for a trade as well as a text market. For the most part the editor has tried to avoid excerpting from longer works and gives complete texts of stories and essays.

For really contemporary fiction, however, one should turn to Jack Hicks's *Cutting Edges: Young American Fiction for the '70s* (New York, Holt, Rinehart, and Winston). This is the best anthology of recent fiction on the market. Most of the writers are genuinely young, although there is the exception of someone as young in spirit as Kurt Vonnegut. Some of the young writers are well known already —Donald Barthelme, Richard Brautigan, and Ken Kesey—but many have not even had books published yet. Hicks, a former editor of *The Carolina Quarterly*, has obviously combed the literary quarterlies and made some discoveries. Minority writers are carefully represented: Black writers by such figures as Ernest Gaines and Cecil Brown, Chicano writers by Thomas Sanchez, and Chinese-American writers by Frank Chin. While Hicks's attempt to be ethnically comprehensive and modish in terms of new fictional styles leads him to some rather uneven selections, this is nonetheless as representative an overview of contemporary fiction as one could want. The Introduction is an excellent essay on the contemporary fictional consciousness, written almost from the inside. The book contains a useful appendix with capsule statements about each of the authors.

The final anthology is John Conron's *The American Landscape: A Critical Anthology of Prose and Poetry* (New York, Oxford University Press). With the rise of general interest in ecology and the natural landscape this is a welcome addition for those who are planning courses in these subjects. The writings collected here are both journalistic (in the broadest sense) and belletristic. Conron begins with a section called "Twentieth-Century Landscapes of Ruin," which charts the current disillusionment with the treatment of our natural resources. He then goes back to the beginnings of interest in the American landscape, starting with a reference to "Vineland" in a Medieval Latin text and proceeding to Columbus and the Renaissance explorers. Then there is a section of writers about the American Dream, 1620–1800, including William Bradford and Hector St. John de Crèvecoeur. From there Conron goes to selections from Enlightenment naturalists and writers on the sublime. Most of the anthology consists of writings from the golden age of American nature writing, the 19th century, with lots of material on the West. There are obvious selections from Mark Twain and Edwin Muir. My only criticism is that the selections are too short. One's appetite is merely whetted, and I think anyone teaching a course in the subject ought to supplement this anthology with a few full-length works, whether they be *Walden* or something by John Wesley Powell. The 20th-century selections are entitled "Twentieth-Century Symbolic

Landscapes" and include Hemingway's "Big Two-Hearted River" (both parts) and poems by Frost, Williams, and Stevens. The apparatus is good, helpful without being obtrusive. One might have liked even a bit more from the editor here. The format of the book is handsome, the texts are readable, and there is a long section of excellent illustrations.

iii. Overviews of American Literature

A number of 1973 books developed interesting theories of American literature and culture, some of which may have an impact on our thinking about our literary heritage.

The most impressive was Richard Slotkin's study of the frontier, *Regeneration through Violence*, winner of the Beveridge Award of the American Historical Association. As many reviewers have already suggested, this is now the most important book on the frontier experience, superseding the work of Henry Nash Smith, Leo Marx, and Edwin Fussell in theoretical sophistication and comprehensiveness. The book is not just a rehash of the Turner thesis, but its construct about mythic experience draws on such advanced theoreticians as Joseph Campbell, Mircia Eliade, and Claude Lévi-Strauss. Slotkin claims the first colonists saw that America presented unique regenerative possibilities for their fortunes, "but the means to that regeneration ultimately became the means of violence, and the myth of regeneration through violence became the structuring metaphor of the American experience" (p. 5). He traces the above myth from the first explorations to the eve of the Civil War, showing how the European vision and the colonial experience produced the peculiarly American concepts of violence that still plague us today.

The Indians who were the scapegoats for this violence emerge as key actors in the narrative, as does Daniel Boone, who became the major mythic figure of the early western settlements because of the treatment given him in John Filson's *Kentucke* (1784). Slotkin is clearly as influenced by D. H. Lawrence's vision of America as by the more academic writers on myth. Although originally a Ph.D. thesis, this is nonetheless a fully formed book—perhaps, in fact, a bit too full. The book is not only too long, but Slotkin's style is densely packed, and as a result the book is tiring. It is also shamefully overpriced ($25.00).

Another excellent book, important to all students of American literature, is historian Stow Persons's *The Decline of American Gentility* (New York, Columbia Univ. Press). Persons's claim is that the gentleman as an important social type had pretty much disappeared from American culture by the First World War. Although our conception of the gentleman was based on the British stereotype, Persons suggests that the model of the gentleman declined everywhere around the same time. It is his purpose to explore this phenomenon in an American context. His theory basically states that the decline of the gentleman corresponded to the rise of the "Mass." With the rise of a mass public the number as well as the concept of the gentleman began to diminish. Persons's models for literary gentlemen are, among others, Henry Adams and Fenimore Cooper. To those interested in the literary tradition represented by Cooper's Littlepage novels, William Dean Howells, and Henry James, as well as the Genteel tradition that survived until this century, this book is the best treatment we have of the subject. Especially recommended is a chapter called "The Heritage of de Tocqueville"; but all the chapters are good. The book shows extremely well how, in its decline, the genteel tradition looked everywhere for scapegoats, finding them in Immigration, money, the *nouveau riche*, the Jews, and the Blacks, and finally in mass society or the "mob." *The Decline of American Gentility* should be required reading for anyone who teaches American literature of that period.

Another book relevant to American literature is Cecil Tate's *The Search for a Method in American Studies* (Minneapolis, Univ. of Minn. Press). Tate's theory is that the concept of holism which has until now motivated the major books in American Studies must be replaced by a new sociological model developed more on structuralist lines. Since most of us have always accepted the concepts of discrete cultural entities and of culture as an organism, this book sounds promising, especially since it proposes a sophisticated model as replacement. The problem with the book, however, aside from its timidly solid academic dullness, is that it is out of date. Tate's strategy is to consider four major books in "American Studies," three of which are standard works for American literature as well: Roy Harvey Pearce's *The Continuity of American Poetry*, Henry Nash Smith's *Virgin Land*, John Ward's *Andrew Jackson, Symbol for an Age*, and R. W. B. Lewis's *The American Adam*. The most recent one of these works was published more than a decade ago. Why Tate chose to deal with such older works and not more recent ones I can only conjecture. Surely the conception for the book must have occurred a long time back, which is why the juxtaposition between Tate's holistic examples and his choice of Structuralism as a substitute is never more than a forced marriage. American Studies needs better theory than this.

Theoretical thinness also mars Sam Bluefarb's *The Escape Motif in the American Novel: Mark Twain to Richard Wright* (Columbus, Ohio State Univ. Press). All of us have commented at some point or other about the prevalence of flight in so many American novels. We have talked about restlessness and the longing to escape the restraints of civilization. Bluefarb organizes his work around these motifs and the change in attitudes toward flight throughout our literary history, claiming that his is the first book to treat this matter exclusively. The problem, however, is that this book is the thinnest kind of thematic study. Bluefarb's introductory chapter simply develops the outlines of a theory, almost wholly derivative of the Turner thesis, and he then writes a series of exemplary essays. This could have been an effective technique if Bluefarb had wanted to make a more theoretical statement about American culture and literature. If thematic studies are not tied to some larger theory, they are worth little more than the statements they make about individual works. Bluefarb's readings are competent, but his thesis teaches us almost nothing we didn't already know.

Another thematic study, better than Bluefarb's but sharing some of its faults, is Susan Kuhlman's study of the confidence man, *Knave, Fool, and Genius.* This major strain in American literature is again one we all point out to our students. Kuhlman traces it throughout James, Twain, Melville, Howells, and others, but this is not an important enough theme to carry with it a series of essays not tied to a larger theory of American culture. Again, I find such connections lacking. The readings of the novels are, by and large, very good. Kuhlman makes some interesting suggestions in her short conclusion about the difficulty of using the confidence man in contemporary fiction because of the uncomfortable encroachments of "reality." She gives as her example Clifford Irving, the "biographer" of Howard Hughes. The book was written before Watergate, but the relevance of Kuhlman's insights to that sorry business is only too apparent. This is a good minor work, but one regrets that it is not the important book it might have been.

An even more disappointing work, more ambitious but less well developed than Kuhlman's, is *Endless Experiments: Essays on the Heroic Experience in American Romanticism* (Columbus, Ohio State Univ. Press) by Todd Lieber. Lieber attempts to define the central experience of American Romanticism as the "heroic" attempts of authors to experiment endlessly with new artistic forms and attitudes. There are possibilities here, but Lieber shows an almost minimal acquaintance with what has been written on the general subject of Romanticism. He makes the common mistake of talking about "Romanticism" as if it were simply one thing. If, as Lieber says, the Romantic defines himself by his heroic seeking, why does he not mention Nietzsche, from whom the whole concept received its most vivid characterization? The only authority on Romanticism to whom Lieber refers is Arthur Lovejoy, whose essay on "The Discrimination of Romanticisms" appeared 50 years ago. Lieber begins with Emerson, treats Whitman and Melville and Poe's *Arthur Gordon Pym*, then leaps into the 20th century to Wallace Stevens and Williams's *Paterson*. Lieber's choice of authors seems sensible, although one could have suggested a few he has left out. Finally, however, this is just a thinly worked out treatment of an interesting conception, another insufficiently ripened Ph.D. thesis.

Another treatment of Romanticism is Michael J. Hoffman's *The Subversive Vision*. Hoffman adapts Morse Peckham's theory of Romanticism, as it is expressed in a series of essays and in *Beyond the Tragic Vision*. He applies Peckham's categories and his theory of the stages of Romanticism to American literature, differing with him on some points. A theoretical introduction introduces the reader to the theory and stresses a perspective on Romanticism that avoids definition and focuses on it as a developmental process. The rest of the book is organized around a series of essays that exemplify the various stages: Negative Romanticism, Analogism, Transcendentalism, Realism as a Philosophy, Realism as a Method, and Naturalism. Peckham's final stage, Stylism, according to Hoffman, does not appear in American literature until the beginning of this century. All the works Hoffman treats are well known, ranging from Poe's "House of Usher" through *The Scarlet Letter*, *Moby-Dick*, *Adventures of*

Huckleberry Finn, and concluding with *Sister Carrie.* There are ten critical readings in all, which attempt to link what was going on in American literature with corresponding movements and attitudes throughout the 19th century.

Another re-definition of 19th-century American literature is Nicolaus Mills's *American and English Fiction in the Nineteenth Century: An Antigenre Critique and Comparison* (Bloomington, Ind. Univ. Press). This interesting book attempts to refute the thesis about the American novel, originating with Lionel Trilling and made most specific by Richard Chase, that we must "classify American fiction as romantic and English fiction as novelistic" (p. 3). In the process Mills also takes on Joel Porte and Marius Bewley. He argues against the misuse of categories like the novel and the romance, but he gets involved in logic-chopping. Also, when he begins his own analyses he misuses some of his own categories. Admittedly, we all may have overstated the case by insisting that the characteristic American work of long fiction is a romance (what F. R. Leavis would call "a sport") and that "novelistic" American novelists are atypical. But in his zeal to prove that American and British novelists were really doing the same things, Mills is overly eager to find the similarities and to ignore the differences. He argues well against overblown theories of American uniqueness, and I find myself in general agreement with those of his assumptions. But his method of approaching specific works shows the lack of both a sophisticated theory of fiction and a viable theory of American culture. A pity, because Mills is a good arguer for much of his case, and his general point needs to be made more often. There are many things that the fiction of both the United States and Britain have in common during the period. But it does no good to insist that they have few differences. Mills often seems to choose similar works only to prove that they are similar. Even with these faults, however, this is still one of the interesting American literary studies of the year.

A new book by Edwin Fussell, *Lucifer in Harness*, is just as interesting as and even more questionable in its assumptions than Mills's. Fussell, best known for his book on the frontier, is a poet, and this is the credo of a committed craftsman making partisan remarks about the tradition within which he works—an ironic illustration of Bloom's thesis in *The Anxiety of Influence.* Fussell, in contrast to Mills, believes that there are definitely national traditions in the arts.

He sees two major traditions in American poetry, one represented by Whitman and the other by Pound. But although the thesis is a familiar one, the rationale is not, drawing as it does from a working poet's conceptions of meter, metaphor, and diction. Fussell's concept of the "constitutive metaphor" in Whitman is thought-provoking, and his idea that American poetic diction means a single word rather than a vocabulary sounds good until one begins to think of all the exceptions. Fussell is partisan to what he calls the tradition of the vernacular. Even his choice of Pound as representing the tradition of more concentrated craftsmanship shows Fussell's interest in someone who felt himself torn between the calls of the two supposed strains in American poetry. But when Fussell states of Wallace Stevens that he "failed to keep faith with the American vernacular" (p. 165) he is simply being silly (the phrase sounds just as ridiculous in context). The hidden agenda here seems to be a notion of democratic partisanship turned into a critical politics. In addition, Fussell's academic bravado style polarizes the reader. It is his choice, but I do not think he ultimately gets away with it.

A recently published translation of Claude-Edmonde Magny's *The Age of the American Novel* (New York, Ungar, 1972), first published in France in 1948, is a welcome addition to speculative thinking about American literature. Although some of the speculations in this book are dated, Mme Magny's theories of the relationship of film and American fiction are not. Magny shows how both the novel and the film reflect the emerging modern consciousness of the individual as an isolated member of a noncommunal crowd. She suggests that we are all like solitary movie-goers, and she proceeds to demonstrate how novelists like Hemingway and Dos Passos and Faulkner use cinema techniques in their work. Because of her commitment to her thesis, Mme Magny tends to overvalue novelists who use obviously cinematic techniques in their work, such as Dos Passos with his Camera Eye. But while her personal tastes in writers now seem strange to us, what remains is a challenging theory of American culture and fiction. The theoretical sections are closely reasoned and more convincing than the practical criticism.

Arthur Voss's *The American Short Story* is more valuable as a reference work than as literary history. This is an old-fashioned survey, touches all the bases, mentions all the relevant authors (and a number of obscure ones), gives a smidgeon of biography, some plot summary, career summary, and the important titles, and a sense of a critical concensus about the individual authors. There is very little, however, by way of historical background. Why the short story developed into such an important American form and why the story developed out of the tale, for instance, are problems that Voss does not really explore. This literary history has neither a theory of literature nor a theory of history behind it.

Afro-American literature was represented by a few interesting works during 1973, the best of which was a book by Stephen Henderson, *Understanding the New Black Poetry: Black Speech & Black Music as Poetic References* (New York, William Morrow). It deals with the problem of "soul" in Black poetry extremely well, avoiding a lot of academic pretentiousness as well as cheap sociology. The only pretentious note is a minor one of Black militancy, which seems *de rigeur* for any Black writer who wishes to be taken seriously in the Black community. But this tone is mitigated as the book progresses. Henderson defines his initial thesis by listing the five ways in which he says Black poetry can be defined (p. 7). He then lists three critical categories for discussing a "Black" poem—theme, structure, and saturation, by which he means primarily the poet's saturation in the "Black experience." Henderson is a bit too fond of these broad cultural generalizations. Still, he is excellent on the subject of how Black speech and Black music find their way into the fabric of Black poetry. His introductory essay is almost 100 pages long, which is why I am discussing it here rather than in the review of anthologies. The selection of poets and poems is also good, and I recommend this as one of the best books through which a white reader can gain a sympathetic understanding of the music in Black poetry.

For a comprehensive overview of Afro-American poetry from about 1890 to 1940, one can now read a translation of Jean Wagner's *Black Poets of the United States: From Paul Laurence Dunbar to Langston Hughes* (Champagne-Urbana, Univ. of Ill. Press). This was first published as a French doctoral thesis in 1962 and it has all the qualities of research associated with the French doctorate. It is extremely thorough in its coverage and it is the only full-length scholarly study of the field. The central thrust of the book is to link the racial and religious themes in the poetry. Wagner reads his poets with an eye to the metaphysical patterns that emerge from their verse. He is excellent on historical backgrounds and his sociological sense of

Black America is exceptionally good for one not a native. He covers such poets as Paul Laurence Dunbar, Claude McKay, Jean Toomer, Countee Cullen, James Weldon Johnson, Langston Hughes, and Sterling Brown, and gives a more than adequate sense of their careers and the major ideas in their poetry. The book has the limitation of being a little stodgy and dated. To get a sense of the spirit of the poetry one should still read Henderson.

The Hero and the Blues, by Albert Murray (Columbia, Univ. of Mo. Press), is a disappointment. It has a great deal to say about the hero but little about the blues. What Murray has to say about the literary hero is derivative of old myth critics, such as Gilbert Murray. His idea of artistic commitment derives from Thomas Mann. This is a literate, pleasant book, but Murray says little we haven't heard before, and the book's title is a misnomer. To talk occasionally about Duke Ellington is not to give a theory of the blues or to explain the cultural experience from which it derives, nor does it tell us what the blues have to do with the "hero."

The remaining works are collections of essays, one of which is particularly valuable. Louis D. Rubin, Jr.'s *The Comic Imagination* has about as many good essays as one could expect to find among 32 papers. All the essays in this volume were originally delivered as radio addresses over the Voice of America, and while some of them clearly show the effects of that format, most of the pieces here are high in quality. The contributors include many distinguished names in American literary studies. Since most of the essays will be discussed somewhere else in *ALS*, I shall just talk about a few of them. Rubin's Introduction, "The Great American Joke," explores quite perceptively the violence as well as the fun in American humor. Brom Weber's "The Misspellers" studies the dialect humorists of the middle and late 19th century. This excellent piece makes one hunger for a full-length book on the subject. Gerald Weales's essay on *The New Yorker*, "Not for the Old Lady in Dubuque," is hilarious and Allen Guttmann's piece on "Jewish Humor" is pretty good, although the funniest parts of it are the quotations—which may be, after all, as it should be. Constance Rourke's famous book is now more than four decades old, and the Walter Blair and Brom Weber anthologies appeared long ago. We need some fresh full-length treatments of this important topic.

The *Gohdes Festschrift* is an uneven collection, as are most festschrifts, but it is better than many others in that it is organized around a central topic, periodical publishing, which constitutes a subject in need of further work. Some of the essays are excellent. Charles Anderson's study of "Thoreau and *The Dial*" explores Thoreau's apprentice years through the surprising quantity of work he published in *The Dial.* Harriet R. Holman writes interestingly on Thomas Nelson Page and his dealings with turn-of-the-century editors late in his career. One of the better essays is by editor Woodress on the fantastic career of S. S. McClure and the reasons for the success of his famous magazine. C. Hugh Holman contributes an excellent piece on Thomas Wolfe and the way in which he claims Wolfe was detoured from his natural talent (that of the novella, of which he published a number in periodicals) by Maxwell Perkins, who forced him into the unnatural form of the novel.

The final collection is *Regional Perspectives: An Examination of America's Literary Heritage* (Chicago, American Library Assoc.), edited by John Gordon Burke. This is a set of long essays on American literary regionalism, written by creative writers who are natives of the various American regions. The essays are personal in tone and uneven, but for the most part their points of view are fresh. Particularly recommended are the pieces by Hayden Carruth on New England and William Everson on the West as an "archetype." This is a handsomely produced book with a very good bibliography.

To sum up briefly, I should say that 1973 saw its largest bulk of stimulating work in literary theory, particularly in books stemming from phenomenological and structuralist criticism. There were a number of more or less interesting attempts at major statements in American literature, but the only book that is sure to make a genuine difference in how we read our literature is Richard Slotkin's *Regeneration by Violence.* It may be that the interest in the "new" French critical methods will now stimulate fresh views of American literature. Let us hope so. The average work I read on American literature this year was competent but dreary. Certainly Slotkin's book was stimulated by European myth criticism as much as by American, and the vitalities of Bloom and Vernon and Nelson will hopefully bear fruit in the years to come, if not by their own work then by the work of others who, like them, have drawn from a fresh well.

University of California, Davis

19. Foreign Contributions

i. French Contributions

Jean Rivière

Six significant volumes make up the major contributions of French scholars to American literary studies for the year 1973. They cover a wide range of subjects and authors and use very different critical approaches. They may be considered a good vintage though not a bumper crop.

Professor Robert Rougé's book, *L'inquiétude religieuse dans le roman américain moderne* (Publications de l'université de Haute-Bretagne 4; Paris, Librairie C. Klincksieck), originally a dissertation defended in 1972, deals with "religious anxiety" and not religion as such. Most of the authors Rougé considers never had any precise religious affiliation, so that he tries to show not so much their faith or unbelief as their position in a world where God is dead. Professor Rougé considers paradoxically that in the godless world of today, men have never been nearer to God: religious anxiety means therefore the exploration of fundamental questions on man's life and his own relationship to the universe and human values. After an introduction on the renewal of interest in religious problems in the United States and a first part devoted to a thorough analysis of the conflicts in the American psyche between Puritanism, voluntarism, and empiricism, he goes on to study Nathanael West, Fitzgerald, Hemingway, Dreiser, Sherwood Anderson, Waldo Frank, Henry Miller, Steinbeck, Robert Penn Warren, and Faulkner. In his conclusion, he tries to establish a "theological dimension" in modern American fiction.

Professor Michel Terrier's book, *Individu et société dans le roman américain de 1900 à 1940: essai de poetique sociale* (*Etudes Anglaises* 52; Paris, Didier), also a 1972 doctoral dissertation, constitutes a new approach to the study of American realistic fiction. His main thesis is that all American realistic novelists were torn apart between a deep individualism and an attempt at redeeming a society they considered as quite opposed to their own human and artistic ideals. His book is very stimulating and proceeds, in the author's own words, from "a passionate reading of American novelists, in search of an ideal American community always escaping their grasp in the nightmare of today's real society." The different authors (or rather books, since Professor Terrier does not intend to give any thorough study of a particular writer) are analyzed under different headings after an introduction to American society and individualism. "Individu et histoire" contains studies of *The Jungle* and *Sister Carrie*; "société et mythe américain" of *The Great Gatsby*, "The Bear," *Babbitt* and *Miss Lonelyhearts*; "forme romanesque et société américaine," of *An American Tragedy*, *Studs Lonigan*, *The Octopus*, *Martin Eden*, *The Grapes of Wrath* and *Native Son*; "roman américain et révolution esthétique du 20ème siècle," of *Winesburg, Ohio*, *For Whom the Bell Tolls*, *You Can't Go Home Again*, *Tropic of Capricorn* and *Absalom, Absalom!* In a brilliant conclusion, the author explains how the individual and his psychological and moral consciousness are intimately intertwined with the real world, so that the American novelist's artistic creation can never be separated from the environment where he lived. Self and society are two inextricable paradigms of his art.

Roger Asselineau's introduction to *The Narrative of Arthur Gordon Pym* (*Les aventures d'Arthur Gordon Pym*, trans. Charles Baudelaire, collection bilingue; Paris, Aubier Montaign), consists of a complete analysis of the work's genesis and sources and a stimulating discussion of the different interpretations of Poe's story. He rightly recognizes all the positive elements in Marie Bonaparte's interpretation, particularly the broken link between Poe and his mother, and makes fun of Jean Ricardou's "nouveau roman" analysis of *Pym* as a sort of abstraction in black (the ink) and white (the paper). Pym's travels become less and less realistic and assume a metaphysical dimension in their depiction of the absurdity of human life. The most glaring mistakes in Baudelaire's translation are corrected in notes, but the question remains open: didn't Baudelaire's rendering do more for Poe's reputation in France . . . than Poe in the original?

Jean Harzic's book, *Faulkner: présence littéraire* (Paris, Bruxelles, Montréal, Bordas), provides both the student and the lay reader with a clear analysis of Faulkner as a man and as an artist. As a man, the novelist is linked with his times (double chronology: on one side, that of historical and literary events, on the other, that of Faulkner's life and works) and a few important questions are asked: is he a farmer or an intellectual, a Southerner or an outsider, a humorist or a tragic writer? His work (with special emphasis on *The Sound and the Fury*, *Light in August*, *Absalom, Absalom!*, *Requiem for a Nun* and *A Fable*) is viewed as the transmutation of historical time into psychological time. His art is analyzed both as that of a painter of men, manners, and settings and as that of a literary wizard using words as a musician does his chords and a sculptor his stone.

Du fantastique à la science-fiction américaine (*Etudes Anglaises* 50; Paris, Didier) is a book publication of the papers delivered before the 4th conference of the French Association of American Studies. Nine pieces in all allow the reader to follow the genesis of science fiction, get a clear view of its problems and main themes and especially the imaginary and realistic elements making up the new genre, the only attempt at a close, if somewhat morganatic, marriage between science and literature (too often of the pulp type). Yet science fiction is hailed by all contributors as an original feature of American literary and cinematographic art. Introduced by Roger Asselineau, it contains essays by Maurice Lévy, Annie Le Rebeller, Gérard Cordesse, Jean-Pierre Vernier, Jacques Goimard, Denise Fauconnier, Michel Thiéry, Leon E. Stover and Georges-Albert Astre.

Number 6 of *RANAM* also treats of the "fantastique" with three important articles on American literature: an analysis of W. G. Simms's *Paddy McGann, or the Demon of the Stump*, by Simone Vauthier, a study by André Bleikasten and Jean Deubergue of Ambrose Bierce's "The Death of Halpin Frayser," a view of John Hawkes as a reconstructed Kafka by André Le Vot. Apart from the general theme, the issue of the review closes with a study by Bleikasten of Caddy's and Quentin's relations in *The Sound and the Fury*.

Université Paris IX (Dauphine)

ii. German Contributions

Hans Galinsky

The arrangement of this selective survey will be both systematic and historical. Before I draw a detailed picture of German contributions, I wish to note the following general characteristics: (1) an impressive size, which, however, is due to the increased number of periodical articles rather than substantial monographs, (2) a growing use of English, and this not only in articles contributed to American periodicals but also in monographs published in German-speaking parts of Europe, (3) a predominance of literary history over literary criticism and theory, (4) primary stress laid on 20th-century authors and themes, with the secondary stress falling on the "American Renaissance," (5) a place for the novel and the short story in the foreground, with poetry in the middle, and drama in the back, (6) as to methods, a continuing prevalence of intrinsic study and comparative approach, yet a gradual rise of sociological and ideological interpretation as well as of linguistic analysis applied to literary texts, (7) a gratifying ascendancy of younger scholars, mainly among article-contributors, and an enduring predominance of academics, junior and senior, over contributors from outside of the halls of Academe.

***a.* Literary History.** Articles and monographs that open up a wider historical vista by covering more than one literary period are few in number. Concentration on a single period or even a single author is the mark of the overwhelming majority of publications.

Among those eight contributions of wider range, naturally mostly monographs, one meets studies in the developments of subgenres such as hymnody. Uniting musicology and theology with literary history, Ada Kadelbach, "Die Hymnodie der Mennoniten in Nordamerika (1742–1860)" (Mainz diss.), follows the transplantation, preservation and adaptation of the German hymn tradition in the United States and Canada. Other subgenres like the success story, the crime story and the western are investigated by Horst Kruse in his introduction to *From Rags to Riches: Erfolgsmythos und Erfolgsrezepte in der amerikanischen Gesellschaft* (Munich, Goldmann); Paul G. Buchloh and Jens P. Becker, *Der Detektivroman: Studien zur Geschichte und Form der englischen und amerikanischen Detek-*

tivliteratur (Darmstadt, Wissenschaftliche Buchgesellschaft); and Karl-Heinz Göller, "Fiktion und Wirklichkeit im Wildwest-Roman" (*LWU* 6:211–33). Topics of marked contemporary interest such as the search for identity and Black literature have also stimulated historical inquiry into more than one period. Arno Heller, *Odyssee zum Selbst* (Innsbrucker Beiträge zur Kulturwissenschaft, Sonderheft 32) exemplifies the former theme, starting out with Twain's *Huck Finn* and ending up with Flannery O'Connor's *The Violent Bear it Away*, while Monika Plessner's *Onkel Tom verbrennt seine Hütte* (Frankfurt, Insel) illustrates the latter topic. The material Plessner used ranges from ante-bellum prose to *Soledad: The Prison Letters of George Jackson*. Closely allied to the search for identity, the theme of initiation has invited comparison of its treatment in two different periods. As with Heller, Twain's *Huck Finn* and Salinger's *Catcher* show up as by now classical candidates for reinterpretation in Peter Freese's "*Adventures of Huckleberry Finn* und *The Catcher in the Rye*: Zur exemplarischen Deutung der Romananfänge" (*NS* 22: 658–68). The broadest historical panorama unfolds in a multinational reception study. *Nordamerikanische Literatur im deutschen Sprachraum seit 1945*, ed. by Horst Frenz and Hans-Joachim Lang (München, Winkler), from a post-1945 vantage point, observes German-speaking Europe's reception of American letters from Franklin to the present. This penetrating study presents the common efforts of two American comparatists, Frenz and Bernhard Fleischmann, and six European scholars, Jean-Paul Mauranges, a Franco-Swiss, Harro Heinz Kühnelt, an Austrian, and four Germans, Lang, Rudolf Haas, Klaus Lubbers and Martin Christadler. In its handiest shape, annalistic and combined with British literary history, American literature from 1890 to 1972 is made palatable to German readers in Wolfgang Karrer's and Eberhard Kreuzer's *Daten der englischen und amerikanischen Literatur von 1890 bis zur Gegenwart* (Munich, Deutscher Taschenbuch Verlag). An account of both literatures is rendered by decades, some 500 works are briefly described, bibliographies and an author-subject index are appended.

Of the studies selected for this survey more than 30 publications by perhaps 60 individual writers or participants in collective undertakings concentrate on a single period and/or a single author. The treatment of colonial literature in two monographs reflects the period's enduring hold on scholars familiar with the corresponding phenomenon of Baroque in German letters. Ursula Brumm's concise state of research report, *Puritanismus und Literatur in Amerika* (Darmstadt, Wissenschaftliche Buchgesellschaft), has for companion Astrid Schmitt-von Mühlenfels's *Die 'Funeral Elegy' Neuenglands* (Beihefte zum *JA*, no. 37), a thorough inquiry into a once prominent genre. In spite of present-day German philosophers', political scientists' and sociologists' rediscovery of the Enlightenment, German Americanists, in 1973, did not produce any special studies in its American species. Only its British reflex is explored by Hans Galinsky in two famous historical novels of the 19th century, "William Makepeace Thackeray, *The History of Henry Esmond, Esq.*, and *The Virginians*," a contribution to *Der englische Roman im 19. Jahrhundert*, ed. Paul Goetsch et al. (Berlin, Schmidt), pp. 124–49. Of early 19th-century authors Irving is the only one to attract continuous interest. Helmbrecht Breinig's Freiburg dissertation, *Irvings Kurzprosa: Kunst und Kunstproblematik im erzählerischen und essayistischen Werk*, Angelsächsische Sprache und Literatur, no. 6 (Frankfurt/M., Lang), centers on art and the problem of art in Irving's shorter prose pieces.

It is the "American Renaissance" that forms the first peak of German scholarly activity in 1973. Hawthorne figures as "the man of the year." Alfred Weber, *Die Entwicklung der Rahmenerzählungen Nathaniel Hawthornes: "The Story Teller" und andere frühe Werke (1825–1835)* (Berlin, Schmidt) throws light on a hitherto neglected aspect of Hawthorne's early narrative technique. Hans Hunfeld's Kiel dissertation, "Erinnerungsproblematik in den Neuenglandromanen Nathaniel Hawthornes" examines a problem basic to both the historical and the psychological novel. Dieter Schulz's article, "Imagination and Self-Imprisonment: The Ending of 'Roger Malvin's Burial'" (*SSF* 10:183–86), by way of its publication in an American journal, makes a most direct contribution to American literary scholarship. In the popular paperback series of Reclam, Brigitte Scheer-Schäzler has produced a critical edition of *The Scarlet Letter in German*, and added a succinct postscript to a novel lately popularized by German TV. Translating, editing and interpreting also combine in German Poe studies. Kuno Schuhmann's edition of Poe's *Werke* (Olten and Freiburg, Walter) has progressed to its third volume, which includes reviews and letters. Herwig Friedl, "Die Funktion der Perspektive in den Landschaftsskizzen E. A. Poes"

(*Archiv* 210:86–93) investigates a formal element, originally pictorial, in Poe's landscape sketches. Melville is discussed only once this year. Hartmut Krüger's Kiel dissertation, "Melville's Ahab und das Problem des Bösen," tries to solve the problem of the author's much-discussed attitude toward evil with the help of Melville's complete works and a critical use of Melville scholarship.

Research in the later 19th century reveals a rare concern with Howells. Ulrich Halfmann edited "Interviews with William Dean Howells" (*ALR* 6:Fall; also pub. as separate book by Univ. of Texas Press). The "international theme" gains a new dimension in Siegfried Neuweiler's Tübingen dissertation, "Das 'internationale Thema' in Reiseberichten und Essays." From its usual domain in the novel and the short story it is followed into its less well-known strongholds such as the late 19th-century travel reports and the essays printed in magazines between 1865 and 1900.

In striking contrast to this under-representation of the 1870s, 1880s and 1890s, the 20th century, both its pre-1945 and its post-1945 section, is given an extremely fair hearing. In the earlier part front seats are still occupied by Pound, Eliot, Faulkner and Hemingway. Reinhold Schiffer in "Der zweimal verwandelte Dionysos. Zur Mythenrezeption bei Ovid and Pound" (*Arcadia* 8:235–47) approaches Pound's adaptation of the Dionysos myth from a comparative viewpoint. Gerd Schmidt in "An Echo of Buddhism in T. S. Eliot's 'Little Gidding'" (*N&Q* 20:330) also hears ancestral voices, though not from the West but the East. The translation aspect of Faulkner's reception in Germany is competently studied in Eberhard Boecker's *William Faulkner's Later Novels in German* (Tübingen, Niemeyer). The enduring fascination for Germans of *Light in August* and the growing impact of linguistics on literary analysis are testified to by Wolfgang Schlepper's "Knowledge and Experience in Faulkner's *Light in August*" (*JA* 18:182–94). Faulknerian Man's "awareness of the past" is explored by a semantic-syntactic analysis of Faulkner's use of "to remember," "to know" and "to believe." More traditional tools of literary investigation are handled by Bernd Günter, "William Faulkners 'Dry September'" (*NS* 22:607–16). Linguistic methods are applied to Hemingway as well. Hans Galinsky, "Beobachtungen zum Wortschatz von Hemingways 'The Snows of Kilimanjaro'" (*Festschrift Herbert Koziol*, ed. Gero Bauer et al., Wien, Braumüller, pp. 87–104) compares trends of development in the vocabulary of American fiction (1935–50) to those in common speech. A less familiar guest in academic circles, Chandler, is welcomed by Jens P. Becker in "Murder Considered as One of the Fine Arts: Raymond Chandler's Erzählung 'I'll Be Waiting'" (*LWU* 6:31–42). Both the pre-war and the post-war periods are covered in Wilhelm Füger's *Das englische Prosagedicht: Grundlagen, Vorgeschichte, Hauptphasen*, Anglistische Forschungen, no. 102 (Heidelberg, Winter). Although it concentrates on the English prose poem, it includes the growth of the genre in 20th-century America.

The post-1945 period receives still closer consideration than its predecessor. *Amerikanische Literatur der Gegenwart in Einzeldarstellungen* (Stuttgart, Kröner), a survey of 18 novelists and short-story writers, five dramatists and seven poets, resulted from the joint efforts of 26 contributors, one French, the others German, under the editorship of Martin Christadler. McCullers and Capote, Salinger, Bellow, Malamud and Roth, Baldwin and Ellison, Donleavy and Nabokov, Kerouac and Burroughs, Mary McCarthy in the company of Mailer and Flannery O'Connor, with Barth, Heller and Vonnegut bringing up the rear, have been selected as representatives of post-modern fiction. Among the dramatists are such obvious musts as Williams, Miller and Albee. The inclusion of Inge and LeRoi Jones introduces facets of the American theater less frequently treated by German scholars. The exclusion of the musical remains regrettable. As for the poets, concentration on Lowell, Olson and Creeley, on Ginsberg and Ferlinghetti, Sexton and Plath strikes the reader as decidedly less post-modern than the choice made in the field of fiction. One of Christadler's contributors, Mrs. Scheer-Schäzler, also has selected Barth, Burroughs and Roth for her articles included in *Lexikon der Weltliteratur*, ed. Gero von Wilpert (Stuttgart, Kröner), but she has added to these authors some figures less well-known in Germany like Hawkes, Kosinski, and Pynchon. Vonnegut recurs in Leo Truchlar's "Fiktion und Realität in Kurt Vonneguts *Slaughterhouse-Five*" (*Sprachkunst* 4:114–23). Continuing regard for Saul Bellow motivates Peter Bischoff's Münster dissertation "Entfremdung und Suche in Saul Bellows Romanen." It applies such stock concepts as "alienation" and "quest" to Bellow's epic world. Hubert Selby serves as a means to a methodological end in Günther Deimer's Frankfurt dissertation, "Ein Verfahren zur Beschreibung argumentativer Dialogabläufe." "Another Day Another Dollar" in *Last Exit to Brook-*

lyn furnishes the material for yet another application of linguistic models to literary analysis. This interest in the oral rather than the strictly "literary" qualities reasserts itself in a rare study in contemporary American oratory, a Frankfurt dissertation by Jochen Schild on "Sprache und Herrschaft: Studien zur Theorie politischer Rhetorik und ihrer zeitgenössischen Praxis in den USA." Unreflected in *Amerikanische Literatur der Gegenwart*, the trend toward a political theater is given special consideration in Dieter Herms's "Mime Troupe, El Teatro, Bread and Puppet—Ansätze zu einem politischen Volkstheater in den USA" (*MuK* 19:342–62). With articles on Beat Poetry and Plath, however, one does return to ground covered by Christadler's survey. Hans Combecher's " 'In back of the real': ein Stück Beat Poetry" (*NS* 22:74–76) deals with a subgenre of modern American poetry familiar to hosts of German youngsters whereas Leo Truchlar's "Die Lyrikerin Sylvia Plath: Eine Skizze" (*Moderne Sprachen* 17:39–44) might well be the first introduction of this fine woman poet to readers of an Austrian teachers' journal.

***b.* Literary criticism and theory.** The number of works that, as a matter of course, include American developments in the wider framework of general literary criticism and theory has lately shown a gratifying increase. In 1973 the trend continued with Suzanne and Silvio Vietta's *Literaturtheorie* (Munich, Bayerischer Schulbuchverlag). For exclusive discussion American trends in both fields come up in three monographs, one dissertation and four articles. Small as their total number may be, they do include some of the finest work of the year. In chronological order of subject Wolfgang Binder's Erlangen dissertation "Das skandinavische, deutschsprachige und russische Drama in der Beurteilung durch die nordamerikanische Kritik 1890–1914" should be mentioned first. Variety and validity of literary criteria reveal themselves in this cross-cultural encounter. Pound's poetics furnishes the subject of a Swiss Habilitationsschrift by Max Nänny. With his study in *Ezra Pound: Poetics for an Electric Age* (Bern, Francke) he, as it were, consolidates a Swiss preemption in the Pound territory which began with the late Christoph de Nagy's *The Poetry of Ezra Pound: The Pre-Imagist Stage* (1960). Eliot was the subject of another major work, Armin P. Frank's *Die Sehnsucht nach dem unteilbaren Sein: Motive und Motivationen in der Literaturkritik T. S. Eliots* (Munich, Fink), which is the first German attempt to treat Eliot's criticism in toto. A philosophical and literary movement which Eliot outgrew is treated in a Münster dissertation by Bernd Lüking, "Geschichte und Theorie des amerikanischen New Humanism." More recent tendencies of American literary criticism inasmuch as they shape the reception of black literature are traced by Manfred Pütz in "'Black Literature' in der neueren Kritik" (*NS* 22:159–68). Literary theory of Marxist and Neo-Marxist provenience comes to the fore in Dieter Herms's *Agitprop USA: Zur Theorie und Strategie des politisch-emanzipatorischen Theaters in Amerika seit 1960* (Kronberg, Skripten Verlag). Anyone interested in the relationship of American literature and American studies will attach particular significance to Winfried Fluck's article "Das ästhetische Vorverständnis der 'American Studies'" (*JA* 18:110–29) and to a companion article by Olaf Hansen, "American Studies: Zur Theorie und Geschichte der Disziplin" (*JA* 18:130–72). This predictable upsurge of theoretical and critical activity, not infrequently blending with socio-economic issues, has revivified a debate that usually generates more heat than light. However, it prevents German Americanistics from growing stale and, to wind up with a quotation from T. S. Eliot, forces a good many of its teachers and writers "to think violently in order to discover the grounds of [their] disagreement."

Johannes Gutenberg Universität, Mainz

iii. Italian Contributions

Rolando Anzilotti

Two books on Afro-American writers appeared in Italy in 1973. Giuseppina Cortese's *Letteratura e coscienza nera: Gli scrittori afro-americani del Novecento* (Milano, Mursia) sympathetically examines Negro literature as part of the drama of man's liberation, concentrating on works of fiction writers like Hughes, Wright, Ellison, Baldwin, who are seen as united by the same motif: the search for a self-definition. Piero Boitani's *Prosatori negri americani del Novecento* (Roma, Edizioni di Storia e Letteratura) reflects more the attitude of the detached scholar and historian. The author, starting from the first appearance of American Negro prose, discusses the two aspects of it, the ideological-political and the literary one, including fiction, autobiography, the essay. Openly intended for the Italian reader, the book gives a well informed and perceptive critical view of Negro prose from Du Bois and Jean Toomer to Malcolm X.

T. S. Eliot's poetry was the subject both of Prospero Trigona's *Saggio su "The Waste Land"* (Napoli, Guida), which is an accurate analysis of the poem based on sound scholarship, and of Alessandro Serpieri's *T. S. Eliot: Le strutture profonde* (Bologna, Il Mulino), a much more ambitious work made up of some intelligent and stimulating essays which are connected by the author's own method of investigation. Serpieri mediates between a structural reading of Eliot's poetry and a study of the transformational systems on which the evolution of such poetry is based. The essay by Giordano De Biasio, "Saggio di lettura di due 'Frammenti' della Ur-Waste Land di T. S. Eliot" (*AFF* 1:331–46) offers a structural analysis of two short passages from those parts of *The Waste Land* that the poet discarded. The theatre of T. S. Eliot received attention by Maria Carmela Coco Davani, whose *Il teatro di T. S. Eliot: Da Sweeney Agonistes a The Cocktail Party* (Palermo, Flaccovio), can be considered as a useful introduction to its topic.

American modern poets still retained a large interest. Salvatore Simone's *E. L. Masters—1915* (Bari, Tip. Adriatica) is the first full-length study to appear on this popular poet in Italy. Though uneven, it has a good chapter on the sources from the Greek Anthology. *Giovani poeti americani* (Torino, Einaudi), an anthology introduced and translated by Gianni Menarini, stands as a competent, agile presentation of recent American poetry. It includes 51 poems (Italian text facing the English) written by 12 poets born between 1934 and 1944, from John L'Hereux to Lewis MacAdams. Agostino Lombardo gives a discerning appraisal of a group of New York poets in his "La scuola di New York" (*Almanacco dello Specchio* 2:190–93), which serves as an introduction to the Italian translations of poems by Frank O'Hara, Kenneth Koch, John Ashbery, done by P. Cacciaguerra and S. Sabbadini. Robert Lowell's poetic vision up to *Notebook 1967–68* is examined by Bianca Tarozzi in "Sogno e incubo americano (o di Robert Lowell)" (*Per la critica* 3:43–51). Tarozzi maintains that the unity of vision of the poet "arrives at a synthesis—the only possible one—of the self and of what is beside the self: general and specific insanity." Rolando Anzilotti's introduction to a translation of Lowell's *Prometheus Bound* (*Approdo* 62:69–72) points out the theatrical limitations of the play and stresses the close relations between the play and his poetry.

There were two articles on Pound: "Ezra Pound: il miglior fabbro" (*Paragone* 90:88–97) by Carlo Izzo, who, as a friend and translator of the poet, offers some interesting, personal recollections of their association, and "Ezra Pound lettore di Dante" (*NA* 517:243–50) by Tommaso Pisanti. The former includes a perceptive critical evaluation of Pound's poetry (the *Cantos* are "the author's quest for his own self by means of defining, through time and places, all the historical and cultural forms that conditioned him. . . . His productive and generous action in favor of writers and artists of all sorts was never bent on propagandizing his nebulous ideology but was always of a strictly literary order.") The latter is a concise but sound description of Pound's study of Dante, which shows on one side the contribution that Pound brought to Dante criticism, on the other the influence that Dante had both on Pound's poetics (and this is the best part of the article) and on his poetry.

The poetry of Emanuele Carnevali, a forgotten Italo-American poet who was well thought of in the circle of Harriet Monroe, is briefly but sharply analysed by Guido Fink in his note, "Le bugie colorate di Carnevali" (*Paragone* 290:86–88). This note, which is placed as an afterword to five poems by Carnevali translated into Italian, shows the "Italianness" of the poet's language and of treatment of his themes, and traces his inspiration to contemporary Italian poets as well as to Whitman and Sandburg.

Claudia Corradini Ruggiero in "Henry James as a Critic: Some Early French Influences" (*RLMC* 26:285–306) gives a useful and accurate analysis of the "specific effect of certain French influences and the early developments of Henry James as a critic." Though the field already has been investigated by other scholars, the author expands and deepens some aspects, as when she demonstrates that James received no influence from Ferdinand Brunetière as regards Baudelaire, since both James and Brunetière were indebted to Edmond Scherer.

Claudio Gorlier in his periodical reviews of American Literature, (*Approdo* 61:133–35) seizes the occasion of the appearance of the Italian translation of *The Damnation of Theron Ware* to point out Frederic's remarkable ability to focus the typical traits of the American province; he finds that, though built with a realistic frame, the novel succeeds in giving "the sense of American reality inasmuch as it renounces using realistic methods." In the following review (*Approdo* 62:136–39), Gorlier deals with the fiction of Jerzy Kosinski, whose first three novels have been translated into Italian. Kosinski's career, his bare, elementary prose, his representation of American metropolitan reality with its violence and horror and satire are aptly described and qualified.

In "Note su William Styron" (*AUL* 26:285–306), as well as in "Philip Roth e l'ebraismo americano (*Antologia Vieusseux* 32:35–49), Marxist-oriented Antonio Donno sees both writers as deeply aware of contemporary America's crisis and conflicts, and revolting, although in a dim and self-deluded way, against man's plight in an alienating society.

A very sound historical book bordering on sociology and folklore, which may be of interest to literary historians, is Anna Maria Martellone's *Una Little Italy nell'Atene d'America: La comunità italiana di Boston dal 1880 al 1920* (Napoli, Guida). The fruits of a long and careful research done on all the materials available, this volume presents the story of the Italians of Boston's North End. The author did not choose to take any particular stand or to generalize. She admirably sticks to her point, which is to trace the story of a community of immigrants within the story of a particular town of the United States. "It is a story neither bright nor black, a little gloomy, very Bostonian in its near composure," she concludes at the end of her detailed, well documented, and well written work.

Francesco Binni's ample introduction to the Italian translation of Nathanael West's *The Dream Life of Balso Snell* and *A Cool Million: La Vita in sogno di Balso Snell*, trans. A. Goldoni (Bari, De Donato) underlines the surprisingly modern treatment of language in West's early fiction, pointing out the novelist's demystifying role as regards the myths of American capitalism and mass media.

Two anthologies of translations on topics of possible relevance to literary study, are C. L. R. James, H. Baron, H. Gutman, *Da Schiavo a proletario* (Torino, Musolini), edited and introduced by B. Cartosio, and *I figli dei fiori: I testi letterari degli hippies* (Torino, E.R.I.), edited by Antonio Filippetti (*Università di Pisa*).

University of Pisa

[*Editor's note*: Professor Anzilotti did not include the latest issue of *Studi americani*, Vol. 17, which although dated 1971 actually appeared in 1973. This important journal carried the following articles: Sandro Melani, "L'epifania della morte in Emily Dickinson"; Gabriella La Regina, "*Rappaccini's Daughter*: The Gothic as a catalyst for Hawthorne's imagination"; Giovanna Mochi Gioli, "*The Turn of the Screw* nelle sue opposizioni strutturali"; Pietro Spinucci, "La poesia di Stephen Crane"; Fausto Fiumi, "Virgilio e il classicismo di T. S. Eliot"; Lucio Trevisan, "Il Canto 74 e il metodo poundiano"; Nadia Fusini, "Il diamante grande come l'America"; Bonalda Stringher, "James Agee"; Rachele Valensise, "Tre scrittrici del Sud: Flannery O'Connor, Caroline Gordon, Carson McCullers"; Elèna Mortara Di Veroli, "Dal Vecchio al Nuovo Mondo: Isaac Bashevis Singer"; Adriana Musumarra, "Il 'carnival' cosmico di Ray Bradbury"; Sergio Perosa, "Incontri americani"; Carmen Enrica De Silva, "Folktales afro-americani"; "La letteratura afro-americana in Italia," ed. by Stefania Piccinato.]

iv. Japanese Contributions

Akiko Miyake

[*Editor's note*: Instead of summarizing a large amount of American literary scholarship published in Japan in 1973, Professor Miyake has elected to review only what she considers the most significant work on American literature published in Japanese in that year.]

Utopia to America Bungaku [*Utopia and American Literature*] by Masajiro Hamada (Tokyo, Kenkyusha) is the culmination of ten years' research by one of Japan's senior Americanists. It is an ambitious study which is carried out with competence and is a thoroughly interesting book. Professor Hamada sees America as the place where, since the Age of the Reformation, people emigrated in search of spiritual regeneration. He extends his study back into the 17th century to include the religious colonies in the category of experimental societies and calls all these dreams, religious and secular, by the name of "Utopian Visions."

Professor Hamada portrays these "Visions" mainly through 19th-century American literature. He finds three major waves uplifting the hope for establishing ideal societies in America. The first began in the colonial period and extended until the end of the 19th century in two different visions: the Kingdom of God on earth and the agrarian paradise. The second wave came in the 1840s when, according to Emerson, everybody had one or two Utopias in his pocket. The third and last vogue of Utopianism appeared in the last decade of the century when Edward Bellamy's *Looking Backward* evoked more than 60 books imitating, criticizing, or refuting him.

Extensive and sure as Hamada's knowledge of American literature is, there is some limitation imposed by his methodology, which is to use literary works like Hawthorne's *The Scarlet Letter* and Longfellow's "The New England Tragedies" to generalize on the Puritans and the Quakers. He also uses Santayana's *The Last Puritan* and Dreiser's *The Bulwark* in a similar manner.

Hamada has great sympathy for the Mormons, whose exodus Vardis Fisher depicts in *Children of God.* He recalls the legend told to Jim Burden in Willa Cather's *My Ántonia* of the first Mormon settlers sprinkling sunflower seeds along the trail for the succeeding settlers to follow. This story becomes a metaphor of the American quest for the earthly paradise that began with Columbus's own westward voyage following the sun.

The arrangement of the material is very suggestive. Bryant, Crèvecoeur, Rölvaag, and Cather are linked together to illustrate the egalitarian rural life. Garland and Norris supply the documentation of the struggle to realize the agrarian paradise with speculating capital. There is a chapter on Utopian colonies like Brook Farm and Fruitlands and a chapter on "Imagination and Fantasy," in which the author treats work such as Poe's "The Domain of Arnheim," Melville's *Typee*, and Cooper's *The Crater.*

Hamada has read widely in American literature and has produced an engaging book. Some of his conclusions: American Utopianism remains within the framework of Christian morality; it rejects original sin and exalts man's innate goodness; it is predominantly romantic.

Kobe College

v. Scandinavian Contributions

Rolf Lundén

During 1973 Scandinavian scholars devoted themselves to the most varied facets of American literature. They contributed to the understanding of American fiction, poetry, and drama from Cooper to Flannery O'Connor, taking equal interest in thematic and stylistic aspects. But in this heterogeneity there seem to be two contemporary concepts which have received closer study than others: dialectics and alienation.

***a.* Prose.** One of the most substantial contributions during the year was Orm Överland's *The Making and Meaning of an American Classic: James Fenimore Cooper's "The Prairie"* (Oslo, Universitetsforlaget), which scrutinizes *The Prairie* with a thoroughness that rivals Cooper's own. Överland draws an accurate picture of the historical, biographical, and cultural context out of which Cooper's novel grew. He analyzes Cooper's use of sources and his artistic method, making the author stand forth, contrary to what has been believed, as a comparatively conscientious craftsman for an age that considered novel-writing no serious business. As to the meaning of the work, Överland sees Cooper's ambivalent attitude toward individual freedom and civilization as at least partially synthesized in that individual integrity must be sought within the social structure. Cooper lets the Bush family, being representatives of anarchic expansion, return to civilization and lets Middleton's expedition one year later stand for the order that must characterize progress. Although Överland's book reveals little of the literary context, for instance *The Prairie's* relationship to *The Pioneers*, it gives a penetrating look into Cooper's workshop and a perceptive interpretation of an American classic.

Two articles on Hawthorne appeared in 1973. Arne Axelsson argued in "Isolation and Interdependence as Structure in Hawthorne's Four Major Romances" (*SN* 45:392–402) that the concepts of his title have been unduly neglected, and that they may be seen as something of a key to the reading of Hawthorne. Axelsson sees the characters as representing different types of isolation, and in three of the major romances there is a general development from isolation to interdependence. In *The Blithedale Romance* the trend is reversed. This theme seems to influence the structure of the romances, particularly *The Marble Faun*, where each of the four characters, one after the other, undergoes a similar development from an isolated state, through a temporary union with his or her intended partner, through temporary separation, to final reunion.

Helge Normann Nilsen was also concerned with social relations in "Hawthorne's 'My Kinsman, Major Molineux'" (*Americana Norvegica* 4:123–36). He holds that Robin submits to social pressures and threats in the form of the stocks, the prison, the picture of his kinsman tarred and feathered, and finally chooses to adapt himself to an emerging social structure which Hawthorne depicts as unattractive yet overpowering. "Robin's progress is not one of psychic maturation in depth, but that of an adaptation that amounts to exchanging one form of dependence for another."

Georg Roppen's long and convincing article, "Melville's Sea, Shoreless, Indefinite as God" (*Americana Norvegica* 4:137–81) deals with both isolation and antithesis. Roppen reacts against the one-sided interpretations of *Moby-Dick* which see Ahab as Melville's main spokesman, neglecting the development of Ishmael. Both Ahab and Ishmael suffer from isolation, but their quests lead them to different goals. Ahab's fear that the whole world is a horrible void is confirmed; he moves toward *nihil*. Ishmael travels from suicidal isolation to a rediscovery of a world of meaning, a journey toward *plenitude*. And this polarity between the two protagonists is, according to Roppen, a more accurate representation of Melville's message.

"'Secret Mines and Dubious Side': The World of *Billy Budd*" (*Americana Norvegica* 4:183–92) by Otto Reinert is also devoted to antithetic attitudes in Melville. Reinert holds that *Billy Budd* is a testament neither of "acceptance" nor of "rejection." The dialectic elements in the story, England-France, law-mercy, angel-devil, etc., point to the fact that Melville's interest lies in the "deadly space between" these antitheses. Melville professes that everything in this world is ambiguous, an idea which Reinert finds supported by the undecided tone of the narrator.

Rolf Lundén has made antithesis the central concept of a whole book. *The Inevitable Equation: The Antithetic Pattern of Theodore Dreiser's Thought and Art* (Uppsala, Studia Anglistica Upsaliensia, Vol. 16) discusses an overall pattern of thought in the writings of Dreiser that may help us understand both his art and his personal development. Dreiser tended to see the world and man's life as a set of contrasts; antithesis was to him one of the basic principles of the universe. The book consists of two main parts. The first discusses Dreiser's ideas as expressed in his published and unpublished nonfiction, devoting much space to the unpublished "Notes on Life." The second and larger part explores the antithetic pattern of Dreiser's novels. The study of Dreiser's art is Lundén's main objective and the discussion of "Notes on Life" and other nonfiction is to be regarded as the necessary groundwork.

Another dissertation from the University of Uppsala treats a topic widely different from Dreiser's dialectic pattern. In *The Underside of the Weave: Some Stylistic Devices Used by Vladimir Nabokov* (Uppsala, Studia Anglistica Upsaliensia, Vol. 11), Jessie Thomas Lokrantz analyzes four threads in the Nabokovian tapestry: the intrusive voice, puns, proper names, and patterns of sound. She limits her discussion to the novels originally written in English: *The Real Life of Sebastian Knight, Bend Sinister, Lolita, Pnin, Pale Fire,* and *Ada.* Lokrantz argues that these devices make up the "foregrounding" technique of Nabokov, the "gamesmanship" and playfulness of his style. Her readings and interpretations are often revealing, laying bare the intricate pattern of Nabokov's style. However, the volume is rather slender; it is lacking in intellectual background.

The author to receive most recent notice from Scandinavian scholars is Flannery O'Connor. Susan Hill Oppegard gives a Christian appraisal of O'Connor's works in "Flannery O'Connor and the Backwoods Prophet" (*Americana Norvegica* 4:305–25). Oppegard states that there is one theme that recurs in each of O'Connor's stories: "man has been redeemed by the sacrifice of Christ and has thereby the treasures of life at his feet, only he seldom realizes it." Convincingly she compares the author's "Backwoods" prophets to those of the Old Testament, displaying a striking similarity between the two. The essence of the message preached by O'Connor's prophets is, according to Oppegard, "the Lord's merciless mercy," i.e. that His mercy, as epitomized in Jesus, can only be felt when man's pride is broken.

***b.* Poetry.** Much less interest has been given poetry and drama during the year. After a rather long-winded run-down of the narrators in "The Speaker Personae in E. A. Robinson's Early Dramatic

Poetry" (*Americana Norvegica* 4:193–210), Ulf Lie comes to the conclusion that to Robinson things and actions are not interesting in themselves but in how they are perceived, how they affect individuals. Robinson's early dramatic poetry is "a poetry of attitudes, of characters' attitudes to themselves, to things, actions, and to other human beings."

The concept of antithesis is basic to Erik Kielland-Lund's "Robert Frost: Poetry as Dialectics" (*Americana Norvegica* 4:237–68). This perceptive article argues that what has been considered Frost's lack of commitment to one philosophical system rather reflects a sophisticated understanding of "the epistemological paradox that although man may confront a transcendent order of reality, he can never conceptualize his understanding of it in any definite way." By being aware of the life-long argument in Frost's poetry between an empirical and a transcendent vision of reality, we may arrive at a better appreciation of his achievement as a philosophical poet. Kielland-Lund explores the various aspects of this dialectic pattern, showing that the conflicting visions seldom appear in the same poem, but that whole poems are balanced against each other.

c. Drama. Even in drama antithesis seems to be an attractive topic. Inger Aarseth devotes her article on O'Neill's *Mourning Becomes Electra*, "A Drama of Life and Death Impulses" (*Americana Norvegica* 4:291–304), to the dialectic of the drama, characterized in O'Neill's words by "life and death impulses." She analyzes such conflicting religious-mythical elements as Puritanism vs. Paganism, the human world vs. nature, the Mannon house vs. the moon, showing that these external opposites reflect the war that takes place within the characters themselves.

Finally, one may mention *The Dramatic Works of Lillian Hellman* (Uppsala, Studia Anglistica Upsaliensia, Vol. 10), in which Lorena Ross Holmin presents close readings of eight plays, focusing on Hellman's use of dramatic devices. Holmin convinces through fresh insights that Hellman is a better craftsman than has been believed. In spite of its rather limited scope, this is the kind of book that may benefit play directors who are about to produce Hellman.

University of Uppsala, Sweden

Index